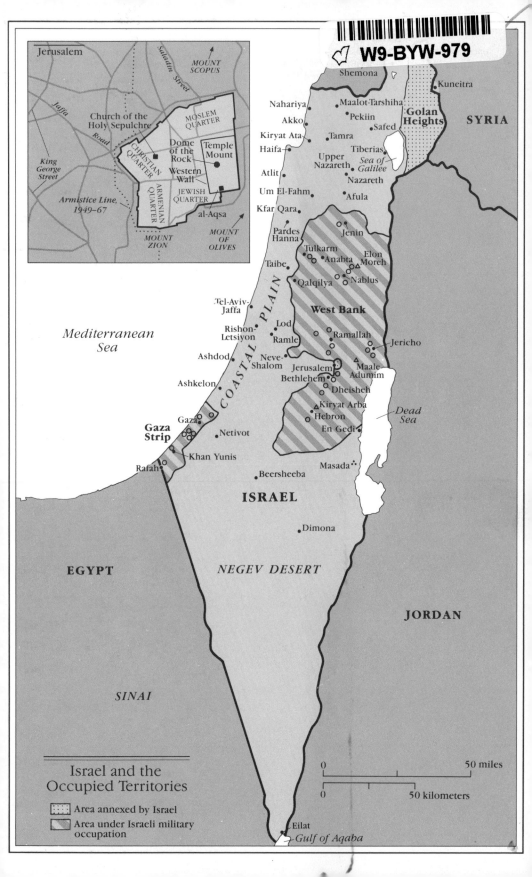

W9-BYW-979

Jerusalem (inset map)

MOUNT SCOPUS

Saladin Street

Jaffa

Church of the Holy Sepulchre

MOSLEM QUARTER

Dome of the Rock

Temple Mount

CHRISTIAN QUARTER

Western Wall

King George Street

ARMENIAN QUARTER

JEWISH QUARTER

Armistice Line, 1949–67

al-Aqsa

MOUNT ZION

MOUNT OF OLIVES

Shemona

Kuneitra

Nahariya

Maalot-Tarshiha

Golan Heights

SYRIA

Akko

Pekiin

Safed

Kiryat Ata

Tamra

Haifa

Tiberias

Upper Nazareth

Sea of Galilee

Atlit

Nazareth

Um El-Fahm

Afula

Kfar Qara

Jenin

Pardes Hanna

Tulkarm

Anabta

Elon Moreh

Taibe

Qalqilya

Nablus

Tel-Aviv-Jaffa

West Bank

Rishon-Letsiyon

Lod

Ramle

Ramallah

Jericho

Ashdod

Neve Shalom

Maale Adumim

Jerusalem

Bethlehem

Ashkelon

Dheisheh

Kiryat Arba

Gaza

Hebron

En Gedi

Dead Sea

Gaza Strip

Netivot

Khan Yunis

Rafah

Masada

Beersheeba

ISRAEL

Dimona

EGYPT

NEGEV DESERT

JORDAN

SINAI

Mediterranean Sea

COASTAL PLAIN

Israel and the Occupied Territories

Area annexed by Israel

Area under Israeli military occupation

0   50 miles

0   50 kilometers

Eilat

Gulf of Aqaba

ALSO BY THE AUTHOR

Russia: Broken Idols, Solemn Dreams

ARAB AND JEW

ARAB
and
JEW

Wounded Spirits in a Promised Land

DAVID K. SHIPLER

𝕿imes
BOOKS

Grateful acknowledgment is made to the following for permission to reprint previously published material:

ACTAC (Theatrical & Cinematic) Ltd.: Excerpts from *The Patriot* by Hanoch Levin. Reprinted by permission of the author and ACTAC (Theatrical & Cinematic) Ltd.

Haaretz Daily Newspaper: Excerpt by Zvi Bar-El from Haaretz Daily Newspaper and letter to the editor by Shlomo Ariel from Haaretz Daily Newspaper, December 1, 1983. Reprinted by permission of Haaretz Daily Newspaper, 21 Salman Schocken Street, P.O.B. 233, Tel Aviv.

The Institute for the Translation of Hebrew Literature: Excerpts from *The Vengeance of the Fathers* by Yitzhak Shami, English translation by Richard Flantz from *Great Hebrew Short Novels*, edited by Alan Lelchuk and Gershon Shakad. Translation copyright © 1983 by The Institute for the Translation of Hebrew Literature. Reprinted by permission of The Institute for the Translation of Hebrew Literature.

The Van Leer Jerusalem Institute: Excerpts from "Testimony of an Educator from Haifa" by Han Abu-Hana and "Diary" by Anton Shammas from *Every Sixth Israeli: Relations Between the Jewish Majority and the Arab Minority in Israel*, edited by Alouph Hareven. Copyright © 1983 by The Van Leer Jerusalem Foundation, Jerusalem. Reprinted by permission of The Van Leer Jerusalem Institute.

Raja Shehadeh: Excerpts from *The Third Way: A Journal of Life in the West Bank* by Raja Shehadeh. Copyright © 1982 by Raja Shehadeh. Reprinted by permission of the author.

Keter Publishing House Jerusalem Ltd.: Excerpts from *Arab Attitudes to Israel* by Yehoshafat Harkabi. Copyright © 1972 by Keter Publishing House Jerusalem Ltd. Reprinted by permission of the publisher.

Random House, Inc.: Excerpts from *Begin: The Haunted Prophet* by Eric Silver. Copyright © 1985 by Eric Silver. Reprinted by permission of Random House, Inc.

Library of Congress Cataloging-in-Publication Data

Shipler, David K., 1942–
Arab and Jew.
Includes index.
1. Jewish-Arab relations—1948–   . 2. Israel— Ethnic relations.
3. West Bank—Ethnic relations. 4. Gaza Strip—Ethnic relations.
5. National characteristics, Arab. 6. National characteristics, Israeli. I. Title.
DS119.7.S476 1986   956.94'05   86-5882
ISBN 0-8129-1273-X

Book design by Guenet Abraham

Manufactured in the United States of America

9 8 7 6 5 4 3 2

First Edition

For
Jonathan, Laura, and Michael

Go, set a watchman, let him
declare what he seeth.
—Isaiah 21:6

The spirit of a man will sustain
his infirmity; but a wounded spirit
who can bear?
—Proverbs 18:14

CONTENTS

CONTENTS

FOREWORD

I AM NEITHER ARAB NOR JEW. BY CULTURE AND CREED, I SHOULD suffer neither pain nor passion over the causes and battles that entangle the two peoples. And yet as I stand outside, looking in at the exchange of wound for wound, I cannot help caring. Whatever style of detachment the reporter in me achieves, it does not weigh deeply against the caring.

This is the burden of Jerusalem. During my five years there, writing for *The New York Times*, I gathered both affection and distaste for those mounting the struggle, sympathy for the personal lives that were wrenched by the conflict, revulsion over the zealous intolerance that fueled the strife. At times a rush of anger would propel me to the conviction that, in their mutual hatreds, both sides deserved each other. And then at other moments I was enveloped by a sense that both sides were right. As strongly as I wanted to leave the depressing struggle behind, I could not. Nothing in my sorrow and outrage was enough to overcome the hold that the Middle East had come to exert on me.

These shifting feelings were dictated not by any political ambivalence on my part, for what gripped me was not so much the politics as the human dimension of the Arab-Israeli confrontation. And within that human dimension, the question of how Arabs and Jews saw each other began to emerge as the central issue in my concerns, the target of my search for understanding. This book is the result of that search.

My effort here is not to find the right answers but to ask the right questions. Framed properly, and in the spirit of fair-mindedness that I hope I have achieved, the questions can illuminate and reveal and deepen knowledge. Thus, I offer no solutions to the conflict, I have no prescriptions for peace, I make no predictions for the future; there have been enough of those. I try here to convey the most intimate reality of thoughts and feelings, to get inside the emotions of the Arabs and Jews who face each other now, more than a generation after the founding of the tiny Jewish state on the rim of the vast Arab world.

This is not a book about the diplomatic, political, or military dimensions of the Arab-Israeli conflict. Nor is it a chronicle of Israel's domestic evolution. Those elements are presented only insofar as they shed light on the subject at hand. Rather, the purpose here is to examine the attitudes, images, and stereotypes that Arabs and Jews have of one another, the roots of their aversions, and the complex interactions between them in the small territory where they live together under Israeli rule: the strip of land between the Jordan River and the Mediterranean Sea. This area—which includes Israel, the West Bank, the Gaza Strip, and the annexed portions of Jerusalem and the Golan Heights—is the focus of the dispute, the most crucial place of confrontation.

It also happens to be where I spent most of my time while based in Jerusalem. Although I made occasional trips to Jordan, Egypt, and Lebanon, my energies were concentrated on digging into Israel and the occupied territories, where Jews and Arabs now have considerable experience with each other at close range. The Arabs who receive the most attention in this work are the Arabs of Israel, East Jerusalem, and the West Bank, who loom as more vital in representing and shaping the course of Arab-Jewish relationships than do the Arabs of the Gaza Strip and the Druse of the Golan Heights.

In all these zones and territories—defined and intersected by the fading boundaries and new frontiers that have been generated by war after war— Arabs who are neither Druse nor semi-nomadic Bedouins have come to be called "Palestinians," and I accept the convention as a useful term, without intending it to have a political connotation. I use "Palestinians," sometimes interchangeably with "Arabs," to mean those Arabs who now live or whose families once lived in the area known under the British Mandate as Palestine.

The resulting portrait allows the larger Arab world to recede into the background except where it provides the clear context for the development of Arab prejudice against Jews. Jordanian textbooks are examined, for example, because they are used surreptitiously—in illegal, unexpurgated editions—in West Bank schools. Saudi, Syrian, and Egyptian newspapers, broadcasts, and other commentaries are cited where they contain themes indicative of significant Arab attitudes. These expressions cannot be read or heard from the Arabs who live under Israeli control because those residents are not free to write and say publicly all that may come to mind against Israel or the Jews. Arabs subject to Israeli authority seem comfortable with political statements but wary of anti-Jewish remarks, which they understand may carry them into danger. Nor are they free—either in Arab countries or in the occupied territories—to go very far in the other direction, toward conciliation with Israel or tolerance toward Jews. Some who have done so in Gaza and the West Bank have been assassinated by radical Arabs. Therefore, I owe a debt of gratitude to those Arabs— some named, some who must remain anonymous—who have helped me move past the defenses, bluster, embellishments, lies, and caution into the more genuine realm of Arab viewpoints.

There is no such difficulty of access to the attitudes of Israeli Jews. They are the most open and candid of any people I have met anywhere in the world. They emerge here essentially on their own terms, without much need for reference to the Jewish Diaspora from which many of them originated, and from which many carry their views of Arabs. In all its great diversity, the Diaspora could itself be a subject of study in this regard, but it lies well beyond the scope of this work.

Unless otherwise specified, therefore, I use the term "Jews" to mean Israeli Jews, not Jews generally and not Jews who live outside Israel. In no way do I mean to imply that Israeli Jews are representative of Jews generally, or that their views are necessarily shared by Jews elsewhere. The word "Israelis," so often taken to mean Israeli Jews, is just too ambiguous here because so many Israeli citizens are Arabs. An "Israeli" can be a Jew or an Arab. Consequently, I have preferred the greater precision of the word "Jews" and have tried to avoid the term "Israelis" except where referring to Israeli officials or authorities, or where the meaning is otherwise clear.

I am grateful to countless Israeli Jews for their patient insights into their own society, which has developed from a series of scattered settlements into an established state and a regional power. In the minds of many of its distant advocates it may still exist as a web of perfect dreams, but in reality it has grown into a land of multiple internal problems and frailties. It has become more than an idea; it has become a real country with real inhabitants who display many of the real strengths and failures of people everywhere. The reality can be bitter, for as Israel moves into the final phase of the twentieth century, it is finding that its struggle for survival has been carried inside its own borders, inside the minds of its people. The problem has expanded from the issue of whether Israel will exist to what kind of Israel it will be. No longer is it merely whether the Palestinians exist as a people, but what kind of a people they are. This suggests the subtler questions that must now be asked.

The partisan will not find satisfaction in this book; at least I hope not. I hope to bother him, to nag him into facing unpleasantness. If he is tempted to stop when he first meets a difficult fact, I would only urge him to read on.

Every person in this book is real. There are no composite characters, a device that I oppose as antithetical to the integrity of a work such as this. Occasionally, at the individual's request, I have had to withhold personal details and names, and in a few cases I have assigned fictional names, which have been placed in quotation marks on first reference. A few chapters incorporate some bits and fragments and scattered passages drawn from my articles for *The New York Times* and *The New York Times Magazine*. The title of Chapter 2 is borrowed from John Milton, of course, and that of Chapter 3 from Hannah Arendt, who witnessed the banality of evil in Adolf Eichmann.

The time to do the actual writing of this book was kindly provided by A. M. Rosenthal, who granted me a year's leave of absence from the *Times*, for which I am most grateful. I spent the year as a guest scholar at the Brookings Institution at the invitation of John Steinbruner, who, with his colleagues, provided me with a perfect blend of serious calm and intellectual stimulation. For much of my basic approach to group identity and stereotyping, I owe an enormous debt to Harold Isaacs, whose own writings on the subject, especially *Scratches on Our Minds* and *Idols of the Tribe*, stand as landmarks in the search for understanding in this field.

Most of the interpreting and translating from Hebrew for this book was done by Carey Goldberg with remarkable skill and energy. Susan London did valuable research toward the end of my stay in Jerusalem and kept me abreast of developments after my departure. The translations of Arabic textbooks were done by Laura Blum. David Hamod interpreted from Arabic during some of the interviews, introduced me to several key Palestinians, and checked some of the translations and transliterations. My debts to others who helped educate me in the ways of Israel and the Middle East would fill many pages, but a few people were so special in my life there that they must be mentioned. I am most grateful to Allyn Fisher, Michael Widlanski, Julie Somech, Michael Elkins, Micha Bar-Am, Moshe Brilliant, Clinton Bailey, Meron Benvenisti, Rabbi David Hartman, and Jamil Hamad. Each played a different role, some close to the themes of this book, some in easing the way, others in shaping impressions into ideas. Julie Fallowfield and Jonathan Segal contributed the essential encouragement and enthusiasm.

The manuscript was read, commented upon, and criticized by Debby Shipler, Harold Isaacs, Thomas Friedman, David Harman, David Hamod, Meron Benvenisti, Anthony Austin, and William Quandt. I accepted many of their suggestions and ignored others, and so I bear sole responsibility for the result.

As generous and helpful as all these friends were in contributing to this effort, the most steadfast support, both in Israel and afterwards, has come from Debby, my wife. She and our children, Jonathan, Laura, and Michael, enriched the experience and maintained our small island of love and sanity in the surrounding sea of bitterness.

D.K.S.
January 1986

ARAB AND JEW

INTRODUCTION

> If the Lord delight in us, then he
> will bring us into this land, and
> give it us; a land which floweth
> with milk and honey.
> —Numbers 14:8

JERUSALEM IS A FESTIVAL AND A LAMENTATION. ITS SONG IS A SIGH across the ages, a delicate, robust, mournful psalm at the great junction of spiritual cultures. Here among the constant ruins and rebuilding of civilizations lies the coexistence of diversity and intolerance.

In Jerusalem, the moment of harmony comes at dawn. The first light sings a pastel tune on ancient stone. As the sun rises from behind the desert mountains across the Jordan and the Dead Sea, the rays touch the curve of the Mount of Olives, then illuminate the creations of man. The sunlight kindles the brilliant gold of the Dome of the Rock, built by Muslims around the massive stone from which the faithful believe Muhammad departed on his night journey to heaven. Then the adjacent al-Aqsa mosque is lit, followed by the newest blocks of towering stone yeshivas in the Jewish Quarter of the Old City, reconstructed by the Israelis as testimony to the revival of the Jewish state and to the holiness of Jerusalem to the Jews. The light catches the dome and eclectic superstructure of the Church of the Holy Sepulchre, built over the centuries by Christian denominations on the site determined by the mother of Constantine, Queen Helena, to have been the place of the crucifixion, the burial, and the resurrection of Jesus.

The new sun casts a rose glow on the sawtoothed top of the wall that encloses the Old City. Practically every ruler of Jerusalem has added to the city wall, changing its configuration, building on the levels of earlier epochs. And as the sun climbs, the illumination descends along the courses of stone, working its way back through time, lighting first the repairs made by the Israelis, as the city's latest conquerors, to the uppermost ramparts erected by the Turkish sultans of the Ottoman Empire, then teasing color out of the layers placed by the Byzantines, the Crusaders, King Herod, and finally, at the southeast corner, blocks that may have been laid during the time of Nehemiah, following the exile of the Jews in Babylon.

Within the walls, light slowly penetrates the narrow alleys and secluded courtyards where small communities of Jews, Muslims, Armenians, Greek Orthodox, Roman Catholics, and other ethnic and religious groups reside with intense devotion to their traditions and their faiths. Below al-Aqsa and the Dome of the Rock, the freshening day softens the shadow thrown by the massive blocks of Herodian stone that make up the revered Wailing Wall or Western Wall, which is the western retaining wall of the Temple Mount, or Mount Moriah, the plateau on which the Muslim shrines now stand, where the Temple of Solomon once stood, and where no Jewish place of worship has existed since the Second Temple was burned by the Romans in A.D. 70.

In most cities of the world, the first to wake are the servants and workers and merchants—the bus drivers, the garbagemen, the cooks, the calloused men and women who bear their produce to early-morning market. But in Jerusalem it is the pious who greet the dawn—the Muslims, Jews, and Christians who sacrifice sleep for prayer. Their calls and chants in the eerie half light of the Old City mingle in an overlapping minor key like separate strains of the same plaintive melody. At the wall,

Hasidic rabbis daven, their sidecurls swinging as they pray, *"Shma Yisrael* [Hear, O Israel]. *Adonai Eloheinu* [The Lord our God]. *Adonai Ehad* [The Lord is one]."* Deep inside the ornate sepulchre a few hundred yards away, the air is still laden with the heavy incense of an Armenian service just completed. Under the church's schedule of worship, which has remained unchanged since the Crusades, three Franciscan monks follow the Armenians, taking their places at the tiny altar and singing mass: "Christ has died. Christ is risen. Christ will come again." And reverberating among the arches and domes and cobbled courtyards comes the thin wail of the muezzin's call to prayer from loudspeakers on al-Aqsa: *"Allahu akbar* [God is most great]! *La ilaha illa Allah* [There is no god but God]. *Al-salat khayr min al-naum* [Prayer is better than sleep]!"* Like the Dead Sea, saturated with rich and poisonous salts and minerals, this small quarter of Jerusalem holds a concentration of congested traditions and convictions of beauty and rage.

Shadows move among the narrow, twisting alleyways. Orthodox Jews in broad-brimmed black hats, long black coats, black trousers, full beards, walk quietly to and from the wall, passing Arabs who wear white kef-fiyahs, the kerchiefs draped gracefully over their heads and held by circular thongs. The eyes of the Jews and of the Arabs slide past each other. Perhaps one gives a slight, silent nod to the other as they pass in the final moments of the night.

When the sun is high, and the flush of day is upon the city, the harmony of light becomes a dissonance of movement. Children scamper, shouting, using sticks to roll the rims of bicycle wheels along the cobblestones. Donkeys saddled with sacks of cement plod through the alleys. Arab merchants emerge, shouting morning greetings, throwing up the corrugated metal doors of their shops with an echoing clatter. They put out their cheap jewelry and their sheepskin rugs, their weavings and their brasswork, their trays of baklava and halva, their sacks of chick-peas and cardamom. The alleys begin to fill with the smells of leather and coffee and sweets, and of the bitter herbs that grow in the Judean Hills.

In my final weeks in Jerusalem, I walked as much as I could through the narrow alleys of the Old City to cling to the clashing sensations of time and history and belief. It was Ramadan, the Muslim month of fasting. Transistor radios, tuned to Radio Damascus, blared calls to prayer and commentaries on the Koran. I sat with my camera outside Damascus Gate, where curved stone steps rise like bleachers that put the throngs onstage as they flow in and out beneath the arch that opens a breach in the northern wall. In the gathering quiet of a Friday afternoon, when the preparations for the Jewish Sabbath overlap with the Muslim holy day, cross-currents of Jews and Arabs intersect through Damascus Gate, each person wearing his uniform, his badge of identity: Arab men in glistening white or checked keffiyahs, religious Muslim women, their heads bound tightly with shawls; Orthodox Jewish women covering their heads in the same tradition; Hasidic Jews wearing the black of the European shtetl, Orthodox Jews in plain yarmulkes as an expression of pious modernity. Israeli soldiers in loose-fitting olive-drab fatigues stroll laconically in pairs, Uzi submachine guns or M-16 automatic rifles slung casually on webbed straps across their shoulders; they are more alert than they seem. Young Arab students in jeans, Arab businessmen in dark suits and ties, Jews in shirts opened halfway down their chests, Franciscan monks in soft brown habits, Greek Orthodox priests in black cassocks, Scandinavian and American tourists—all raise a babble of languages as they move in and out through the gate. The Arabs and the Jews walk among one another, but they seem not to see each other. An Arab boy leads a lamb on a rope. Another boy prods a donkey along with a stick until they pass through the gate and disappear into the darkness of the twisting alleys inside.

I sat on the stone steps with my camera as often as I had time before I left. This was the finest theater in Jerusalem, and I didn't want to let go. All the characters in the drama of conflict were portrayed here in the swirling throngs, and I needed somehow to see them again with a fresh eye, to watch them through a telephoto lens and focus on their faces, one by one, instant after instant, and then to put the camera aside for a while and soak up the sensations of sight and sound that had become part of me, but which were now about to drift out of my daily life.

A bizarre calm, an odd absence of tension, enveloped the mingling of Arabs and Jews beneath Damascus Gate, as if each side moved comfortably within its category of self-containment. That this could be the case, that Jerusalem could be a tranquil island of workaday coexistence and also the spiritual heart of the competing Jewish-Arab claims to this land, testified to the ancient ambivalence of the city.

The name of Jerusalem in Hebrew is Yerushalayim—"City of Peace." In Arabic it is al-Quds, "The Holy." Since its first appearance in manuscripts as a Canaanite city-state in the Bronze Age nearly 4,000 years ago—and all through a succession of conquerors and rulers from King David and King Solomon and the Kings of Judah through the Babylonians, Macedonians, Egyptians, Seleucids, Greeks, Jewish Hasmoneans, Romans, Byzantines, Persians, Umayyads, Abbasids, Fatimids, Ayyubids, Crusaders, Mameluks, Ottoman Turks, British, Jordanians, and now again the Jews—Jerusalem has known no line between warfare and religion. It is a center of conflicting absolutes, of certainty, of righteousness. Its lofty refinement of intellect and theology has given enlightenment to its violence, mixing the wisdom of the ages into eternal bloodshed.

Jerusalem is located on a ridge of rolling hills that have historically divided two fundamentals of human society—the desert and the farm, the nomadic encampment and the sedentary village, the land of milk and the land of honey. On the east, the land runs down into the stark, dry Judean Desert and its milk-producing herds of goats tended by semi-nomadic tribesmen. On the west, the hills descend onto the coastal plain along the Mediterranean, with the sweet orchards and lush fields of the settled villagers. The land of milk and honey is thus two lands, merging and grinding at one another, shaping the nature of Jerusalem, which stands between the fertile and the arid, the rooted and the wanderer. And Jerusalem in turn has zealously nurtured both the worldly and the parochial, the scholar and the bigot. The thick walls surrounding the Old City keep nothing out and nothing in, but bear witness to the flow of faiths and hatreds through the great gates.

The lands of milk and honey no longer divide peoples with quite the clarity of ancient times. Since centuries before the idea of Zionism brought Jews to Palestine, Arabs have terraced the slopes and farmed the land in the valleys and on the seaward side of the Judean Hills, their villages often growing into small cities and spawning an urban population that has included writers, doctors, teachers, lawyers, and tradesmen. Jews since the 1967 war have gone eastward into the parched desert of the Jordan Valley to establish farms and fields with the modern tools of drip irrigation and plastic sheeting. Many Bedouins have stopped moving their goat-hair tents with the seasons, and live somewhat permanently in ramshackle shelters of plywood and corrugated tin among the desert hills outside the city. For the most part, the distinction that some scholars make between the ancient, roaming tribes of desert Arabs and the ancient, sedentary Jews has disappeared. In its place, a passion for the land—as divinely given, as a mystical force, as a symbol of peoplehood and nationality, as a place of origin and security—now governs the conflict and fuels the violence between the two peoples.

Spiritually and geographically, Jerusalem lies at the heart of the small area that forms the focus of this book—the sliver of territory reaching some fifty to eighty miles from the Jordan Rift* on the east to the Mediterranean on the west, and 256 miles from Lebanon in the north to Egyptian Sinai in the south. Scarcely more than a smudge on a map of the Middle East, this is the land most burdened and enriched by ancient history, most scarred and coveted by the Jews and Arabs who now face each other in combat, in distaste, in regard, in accommodation, in strange affinity. They and their perceptions of each other are the subject here, for the 3.5 million Jews and 2 million Arabs who live in Israel, the West Bank, the Gaza Strip, and the Golan Heights stand at the point of contact between the military, ethnic, and religious forces of the region.

Both peoples are victims. Each has suffered at the hands of outsiders, and each has been wounded by the other.

The Jews have come from scattered regions of a great Diaspora where they have rarely been able to enjoy unbridled pride and flourishing contentment in their Jewishness. At best, even in the most open societies where they have lived as a minority and have excelled in the dominant culture, Jews have been made to feel at least slightly alien when they have observed their holidays, followed their traditions, practiced their religion, and embraced their Jewishness. At worst, they have been subordinated, despised, vilified, imprisoned, and slaughtered. Throughout their history, they have been haunted by a corrosive sense of illegitimacy that transcends individual spasms of brutality, of which the exterminations of the Holocaust are the most recent and most monstrous example. And they have stood and fallen alone. Nobody has rescued them except

---

* The north-south fault marked by the Sea of Galilee, the Jordan River, the Dead Sea, and the valley of the Arava that runs to the Gulf of Aqaba.

incidentally, as the Allies liberated many from the concentration camps after defeating Hitler's Germany. World War II was not fought to save the Jews.

The hardships of the Palestinian Arabs in modern history bear no resemblance in scope or depth to those of the Jews. Subjected to Turkish brutality under the Ottoman Empire, British rule under the Mandate created by the League of Nations, political arrest by the Jordanian monarchy, and tough controls under Israel, the Arabs from this crucial slice of Palestine have suffered powerlessness and deprivation of liberty but never genocide. Their sense of distinctiveness as a Palestinian people has come not from an ancient source but largely in reaction to the creation and growth of Israel on part of the land where they lived. Their Palestinian awakening, even with its pre-state origins, was heightened by the upheavals of Israel's birth in 1948 and the refusal of the Arab governments to accept the presence of the tiny Jewish state on the edge of Arab territory. It gained further impetus when Israel captured East Jerusalem, the West Bank, and the Gaza Strip—along with the Sinai and Golan Heights—during the Six-Day War of 1967. The struggles generated a new subculture of Arabs divorced from their own land. In contemporary, personal terms, then, many Palestinian Arabs have been the victims of expulsion, displacement, and war. They have found themselves scattered and rejected in the Arab world at large, excluded from full participation in the Arab countries where many have settled, and confined to squalid refugee camps, often by the venal politics of their own leaders.

The feeling of aloneness is heavy on both sides. The wounds rub raw. An encounter between two victims, as one Israeli Jew observed, is "like fire and kerosene," a chemistry made especially volatile by the fact that both Arabs and Jews are minorities and majorities at once, their positions and roles intersecting and overlapping as the scope of the landscape shifts. The Jews historically have been a minority wherever they have gone, and they are a tiny minority in the vast Middle East. The Palestinians are part of the Arab majority in the region, but they are also a minority subgroup in the Arab world. In the territory under examination here, the Jews have finally become a majority, and have embraced the role with such alacrity that their official jargon refers to the Arabs under their control as "the minorities," as indeed they are within those boundaries.

.   .   .

9

History in the Middle East has a marvelous elasticity. It is easily stretched, twisted, compressed in the hands of its custodians, squeezed to fit into any thesis of righteous cause or pious grief. But it also has a way of springing back into an inconvenient form, a shape made of hard reminders. Certain features of the past remain as immutable as the ancient stones in Jerusalem—the Western Wall of huge Herodian blocks, the outcropping of bedrock from which Muhammad is said to have ascended to heaven, the stone core of Calvary now encased in ornate grillwork and marble in the Church of the Holy Sepulchre. The stones are cool to the touch, to the lips, to the Jewish, Muslim, and Christian fingers that tremble as they reach out in faith. The people are imprisoned by history.

To draw the boldest outlines of the past is to make Israel's basic case. To sketch the present is to see the Arabs' plight.

According to Genesis, this was the land that God gave to Abraham and his seed, and some of the Jews of modern Israel have articulated their biblical claim by returning to the Old Testament names of the places they now control: the West Bank Arab city of Nablus they call "Shechem"; the nearby Jewish settlement they call "Elon Moreh"; the West Bank they prefer to see rendered as "Judea and Samaria." Those Jews who rely on the biblical deed to the land take their history from the ancient period of 4,000 years or so ago, skipping easily over the centuries of Muslim rule that followed; those Arabs who regard history as their ally tend to begin with the Muslim conquests in the seventh century A.D., blithely ignoring the Jewish kingdoms that existed here 2,000 years before Muhammad made his appearance.

Jewish history has been molded by yearning. The promise of a sweet land drew the ancient Israelites in their exodus from Egypt and in their wandering through Sinai. Their attachment to Jerusalem, where they dwelled under King David and built their first Temple under King Solomon, then remained a source of abiding faith after they were crushed, enslaved, and exiled into Babylon in 587 B.C. There they sang and dreamed of returning to the holy city. And from there they did return to build and restore. Under Herod they erected their Second Temple, which survived until the Romans destroyed it by fire in A.D. 70 on a day still mourned by Jews who keep the firm traditions. They made memory a part of ritual, holding their devotion to Jerusalem as the city changed hands again and again in blood, as Muslim conquerors were ejected by the Crusaders in 1099 and then in turn drove out the Crusaders in 1187. The Muslims—through the Ottoman Turks—held Jerusalem until the end of World War I, when the British took over and set the stage for the reestablishment of a Jewish nation.

The Crusaders murdered, enslaved, or ousted the Jews of Jerusalem, but Jews began to return to the city under the Muslims, and during most of the intervening centuries between ancient and modern Israel, Arabs and Jews lived intermingled or in their own neighborhoods of Jerusalem, Hebron, Tiberius, Safed, and other towns. The Jews, most of them extremely religious, were wedded to the places by piety, not nationalism. Not until Zionism evolved as a movement in the nineteenth century—largely in reaction to pogroms in Russia—did significant numbers of European Jews begin to migrate to Ottoman-controlled Palestine. By 1845, Jews formed the largest single community in Jerusalem, the vanguard of an influx that gathered momentum after Great Britain endorsed the creation of a Jewish homeland through the Balfour Declaration of 1917. The migration gained urgency as Hitler came to power, promulgated anti-Jewish laws in Germany in the 1930s, then rounded up Jews in Germany and in the expanding sphere of German-occupied countries, restricted them to ghettos, shot them, deported them to concentration camps, and exterminated an estimated 6 million of them in the cause of racial purity. Out of this Holocaust grew the international compassion for the purpose of a new Israel as a sanctuary for the Jews.

Local Arab resistance to the Zionist enterprise began well before the formal creation of the Jewish state. As more and more Jews came to Palestine, a communal war commenced. Conducted from Arab towns and villages against nearby Jewish settlements, it fragmented the early Arab-Jewish relationships into a strange mosaic of clashes and coexistence. By the mid-1930s, Arabs in Palestine had endorsed the principle of "armed struggle" and in 1936–39 conducted the "Arab revolt," a futile series of riots and killings aimed at breaking the bonds of the British Mandate to block the coming of Israel.

Decimated by the catastrophe in Europe, weakened by war, the Jews who came to perch on the edge of the vast Arab region of the Middle East were idealistic pioneers, but they felt vulnerable enough not to exaggerate their capacity to demand, control, and govern. They pushed the British to make good on the promise of the Balfour Declaration—and some used terrorism as a weapon—but their mainstream was also ready for compromise. The Jewish Agency, as the precursor of the Israeli government, expressed its willingness to settle for only half of the land. It was prepared to accept a division of British-ruled Palestine west of the Jordan into two states—one Jewish, the other Arab. (The present Kingdom of Jordan, to the east, had been established on a large tract of Mandatory Palestine that Britain designated as an emirate in 1921.) The Jewish Agency's partition plan of 1946, followed by the United Nations plan of 1947 internationalizing Jerusalem and drawing boundaries between a Jewish and an Arab state, was less generous to the Jews than the final armistice lines that followed the 1948 war. If one looks today at the map of that Jewish Agency plan, it is a striking lesson in the fickle nature of compromise, recalcitrance, and history. Had the Arabs accepted partition, Israel would have ended up with considerably less territory than it gained through their rejection. But when the Arabs refused to tolerate a Jewish state in their midst, opposed the U.N. plan, continued the communal war against Jewish settlements, and then invaded as soon as Israel declared its independence in 1948, they provided the Jews with the most severe motive in battle: survival. When the fighting was done, the Israelis had won half of Jerusalem, parts of the Galilee, and areas of the Negev Desert that they had been willing, on paper, to relinquish.

The patterns of the wars that followed in 1956, 1967, 1973, and 1982 gave license to hatred and ground to extremists on both sides. Israel's capture of the West Bank after Jordan entered the 1967 fighting, and the subsequent unwillingness of the Arabs to negotiate peace for territory, allowed zealous Israeli Jews to settle and secure a hold on the West Bank, where about 750,000 Palestinian Arabs reside, making compromise more difficult and prolonging the hardships of the Palestinians who remained under Israeli military occupation in an atmosphere of violent lawlessness. Only in 1979 did Egypt find the key to winning back territory bloodlessly by signing a peace treaty with Israel in exchange for the Sinai. But gradually through these years, some moderate elements among both the Palestinians and the larger Arab world seemed to be approaching a pragmatic reconciliation with the fact of Israel's existence. A formal peace existed with Egypt, a de facto peace with Jordan, a tense standoff with Syria. Inside Israel and its occupied territories, the shadings of Arab-Jewish attitudes and interactions retained a somber complexity.

. . .

This is the broad sketch of history against which the mutual perceptions of Arabs and Jews have emerged. The resulting stereotypes and images possess a durability beyond the rapid events in which they have been nurtured. They do not change as quickly as the political alignments in Israel and the Arab world. They are not as fluid as the forces of battle. And they are less susceptible to peace treaties than might be wished, for now they have been insinuated like indelible stains into the respective cultures, literatures, and languages.

The relationships between Arabs and Jews are examined here in three dimensions: First, the broad forces that contribute to aversion, namely the engines of war, nationalism, terrorism, and religious absolutism. These form the milieu of the Middle East, the environment of tension and yearning in which hatred is mobilized, in which minds are scarred. Second, the catalogue of images, each of the other, some held in parallel, some unique to the Arab-Jewish relationship, some reminiscent of stereotypes between other groups in other societies. Third, the complexities of interaction, from cultural and religious affinity to the idealistic efforts of a few Jews and Arabs to reach across the gap of ignorance.

In none of these dimensions do Arabs and Jews confront each other as two monoliths, for each side is multifaceted, itself torn by tensions along ethnic, class, and religious lines. The Jews have gathered in Israel from the Western cultures of the United States and Europe, from the Islamic countries of the Middle East, from India and Argentina and the Soviet Union, from among the impoverished black villages of Ethiopia and the white affluence of South Africa. Culturally they range along the entire far-flung spectrum of human civilization, finding only their Jewishness in common. Politically they are angrily diverse, from slavishly pro-Soviet communists to liberal democrats to militant right-wing authoritarians. Religiously they endure a mutual hostility of a high pitch, for they include the extreme Orthodox who reject Zionism, the modern Orthodox who embrace it with zeal, the nonreligious who resent the imperious efforts of the fundamentalists to impose religious strictures on the secular majority. The more and less religiously observant do battle against one another in the political arena. Regional differences also create variations in attitude, with many Jews in Haifa, for example, living nearer to Arabs and having easier relations with them than do many Jews of the Tel Aviv area, who can reside in a wholly Jewish environment.

The Arab population is diverse as well. Among the Arabs who live between the Jordan and the Mediterranean, the boundaries of belonging— and friction—are defined by clan, village, region, religion, and the larger concepts of peoplehood: Palestinian and Arab. The tensions among them lie along the layers of identity. The extended family, for example, remains a powerful determinant of status and influence in a village, and revengeful blood feuds are still occasionally fought between clans. The village itself is an important focus of loyalty. Families and the descendants of those who fled from one town to another nearby during the war of 1948 say they are still known as "refugees," a label, used by other Arabs native to their place of sanctuary, that assigns to them the unending status of outsiders.

Conflicts run along the lines of armistice, politics, and religion. Arabs inside Israel are often considered suspect by Arabs outside; those who endorse compromise with the Jews are often detested by those who support a steadfast Palestinian nationalism. Muslims and Christians often express a mutual distaste that prevents them from cooperating even in village political affairs. Sedentary Arabs have little contact with semi-nomadic Bedouins, and the small Druse minority exists in cultural, religious, and geographical separation from the larger sweep of the Arab population. To the north of Israel, in Lebanon, these religious and ethnic divisions have erupted into a long civil war with Palestinians and Lebanese Druse, Christians, and Muslims slaughtering each other as they pull back into their enclaves of distinctiveness and separateness.

The labels of nationality are determined in part by where the Arabs live between the Jordan and the Mediterranean. Those who reside inside Israel proper—that is, within the pre-1967 boundaries of the Jewish state—are citizens of Israel with the rights to vote in local and national elections, to equal protection under the law, to the judicial system's due process, and the like. The vast majority of them are sedentary and are commonly known as "Israeli Arabs." Only a fraction are semi-nomadic Bedouins. All the Bedouins and more than three quarters of the sedentary Arabs are Muslim; the rest are Christian Arabs and Druse, the Druse practicing a religion whose secret tenets have roots in Islam and Christianity.

Those who live in East Jerusalem, the Arab half of the city captured by Israel during the Six-Day War, have for the most part retained their Jordanian citizenship, having declined the offer of Israeli citizenship after East Jerusalem was annexed to Israel in 1967. But even non-Israelis are allowed to vote in the Jerusalem municipal elections held every five years, and a growing minority of them are doing so.

The Arabs on the West Bank are almost all Jordanian citizens, although many, as Palestinians, are hostile to the Hashemite regime of King Hussein, who is of Hijazi origin; since the West Bank residents have lived under Israeli military occupation since 1967, they have not been offered, nor have they sought, Israeli citizenship, and they are subject to a system of military decrees and military courts resembling martial law. Most of the West Bank Arabs are Muslim, with a minority of Christians among them. Those in the occupied Gaza Strip are stateless, having been formerly occupied by Egypt, which never granted them Egyptian citizenship. The Druse on the Golan Heights, which Israel captured from Syria in 1967 and annexed in 1981, have also generally refused to accept Israeli citizenship, fearing retribution against their relatives in Syria or against their villages should Syria return to power in the Golan.

Every one of these categories of Arabs has a different relationship with the Israeli Jews, politically, legally, and attitudinally. The Druse inside Israel are generally accommodating, the Druse on the Golan Heights antagonistic. Israeli Arabs—those living inside Israel proper and enjoying Israeli citizenship—come to the relationship on a theoretically equal legal footing, whereas those living under military law on the West Bank and the Gaza Strip understandably display more antipathy and resistance to Israeli rule. Add to these variations the array of Israeli relationships with neighboring Arab countries—the peace and open border with Egypt, the quiet and selectively open border with Jordan, the confrontation and closed border with Syria, the alliances and hostilities with different Lebanese factions—and you have an Arab-Jewish interaction of enormous complexity.

Whatever happens in war or diplomacy, whatever territory is won or lost, whatever accommodations or compromises are finally made, the future guarantees that Arabs and Jews will remain close neighbors in this weary land, entangled in each other's fears. They will not escape from one another. They will not find peace in treaties, or in victories. They will find it, if at all, by looking into each other's eyes.

The time has passed when Jews and Arabs could face each other in simple conflict. They live together now in rich variety. There is no single Arab-Jewish relationship; there are many, and they require an elusive tolerance that must somehow run against the forces of war, nationalism, terrorism, and religious certainty.

PART ONE

Aversion

ONE

War:
Earth of Brass

But if ye will not hearken unto me,
and will not do all these commandments . . .
I will break the pride of your power;
and I will make your heaven as iron,
and your earth as brass.
—Leviticus 26:14, 19

SPRING IS A FLEETING SEASON IN ISRAEL. FRESH FROM THE WINTER rains, hills and pastures are cloaked in a lushness that passes quickly. Wild flowers burst into a riot of color, then vanish, and the desert, momentarily brushed with a tint of green from wisps of new grass, lies burnished again by a relentless sun. The sky takes on its summer tone of cloudless, pastel blue. Not a drop of rain will fall again until November.

In the spring, Israel marks a double holiday divided by a dramatic shift in moods, two days in a row fixed in the Hebrew calendar to observe the sorrow of war and the joy of rebirth. First comes the Day of Remembrance to honor the country's fallen soldiers, a solemn, moving, mournful time. Then, at sundown, the sadness is cast aside and the streets come alive in a festive air as Independence Day begins; the Israelis who have spent the daylight hours in cemeteries form circles in the streets and dance into the night. The main thoroughfares become great promenades for strolling couples and clusters of teenagers; parking lots are floodlit and bathed in music; across makeshift counters, grilled Middle Eastern delicacies and games of chance are offered. And the next morning many go into the brief abundance of spring for picnics and songs and story-telling with their old army friends from the 1948 War of Independence, the 1956 Sinai Campaign, the Six-Day War of 1967, the War of Attrition with Egypt in 1969–71, the Yom Kippur War of 1973, or the Lebanon War of 1982.

Six wars and nearly 15,000 Israeli deaths have scarred the landscape of this ancient land. The gravestones on Mount Herzl, the military cemetery at the edge of Jerusalem, are marching down the terraced hillside, cutting into the forest that was planted by Jewish pioneers as a gesture of reclaiming faith and return.

This hillside is where the journey into Arab-Jewish attitudes must begin, for war is the soil that nourishes those tangled weeds of hatred. All that happens in men's minds here happens on the ground of war— all the toughness, all the gentleness, all the fear, all the longing, all the shrinking back in anger, and all the reaching out in hope. War has hardened and softened, embittered and mellowed. Even during peaceful intervals its presence can be felt, scratching at the soul of Jerusalem.

For both Jews and Arabs, war has produced its own sorrow and glorification. The Jews have confronted it mostly through combat, mourning their dead, nursing their wounded, extolling their heroes, praying for peace and victory. The process of war has become a business with budgets and economists and scientists; it brings serious pleasure to some and provides an outlet for cruelty. Battle has its thrills as well as its regrets. But somehow war has not generated the lust in Israeli Jews that it has among some other peoples at other times. When it comes, it does not arrive with the clamor of stirring oratory or the jingoistic exhortations to conquer all. It comes instead with a quiet strain of melancholy.

War has not been precisely the same experience for the Arabs. In those countries that have sent their armies against Israel again and again, the battle has not consumed the entire nation as it has for the Jews: Each Arab country has been large enough to absorb defeat. But the dead have included many more civilians than in Israel; Arab industry has been wrecked more thoroughly by a skillful Israeli air force, etching deeply in Arab minds the image of Israel as a rabid juggernaut bent on grinding up and taking over Arab lands. In addition, the battle has been given religious connotation through the Islamic concept of *jihad*, or holy war against the infidel. And as Israeli peace activists lament, the Arab side has lacked a parallel peace movement. War, it seems, is integral to the conduct of human affairs. To speak or to act against it requires the courage of an Anwar Sadat, who then pays the price of his life, or the subtlety of a King Hussein, who survives as long as he takes only half steps.

For many of the Palestinian Arabs who live, or once lived, between the Jordan and the Mediterranean, war has meant something else: displacement from their home villages. That has been their central experience of war; except for those who have been struck directly by Israeli planes or naval vessels while in refugee camps in Lebanon, for example, they have not been touched by actual combat. War has come to them not as a clap of thunder, suddenly destroying, but as a corrosive cause that eats within. Their sorrow and glorification follow a different formula—a sorrow in defeat and a glorification in resistance. A young lad from a West Bank refugee camp who goes off to join the guerrillas of the Palestine Liberation Organization stirs mixed feelings among his family and friends—a dread of loss to his parents in many cases, a heroic portrait among his peers.

The enormous impact of war on Arab and Jewish perceptions of each other and of their own positions in the conflict was documented by a study of eleven-year-old children in Israel and the West Bank.[1] Although both groups of youngsters expressed intense patriotism and loyalty to their own sides, the Palestinian Arabs saw their struggle in an idealistic, romantic light, whereas the Israeli Jews gave war a pragmatic connotation. Nearly all the Arab children—94 percent—said that war was good if you defeated your enemy; the Jewish youngsters were divided, with 53 percent agreeing that war was justified by victory. Among a sample of American youngsters used as a control group, only 35 percent saw virtue in war.

More accord between the Arab and Jewish children was revealed on other points, however. A large majority within both groups believed that war was always necessary (81 percent of the Arabs, 71 percent of the Jews, and 54 percent of the Americans). High levels of anxiety were found among both the Arab and Jewish children, with the Jews fearing terrorist attacks, that "father will be called up for reserve duty," and that "father won't return home." The West Bank Arabs expressed the worry that their fathers would be arrested or their houses demolished by Israeli authorities, a standard technique used against the families of those branded as terrorists.

At eleven o'clock on the morning of the Day of Remembrance, sirens sound to honor the dead, and all of Israel comes heavily to a halt. Downtown in West Jerusalem, cars pull over, their drivers and passengers climb out and stand at attention, pedestrians stop in their tracks, storekeepers pause behind their counters, and the man who sells newspapers at the corner of King George and Ben Yehuda Streets interrupts his lilting call, falling silent while the sirens wail. In classrooms, children stand at their desks. In offices and factories, in fields and hospitals, Israelis are joined for two minutes in suspended reflection and homage, a rare moment of concord in a common grief.

On Mount Herzl, thousands of mourners move slowly through the cemetery gates in a broad river of sadness, their faces sculptures of suffering. They carry wreaths, bouquets, or small clusters of wild flowers they have picked along the way. They or their fathers have come to this place from Poland and Yemen, Morocco and Greece, Argentina and Belgium, India and the United States—scholars with soft hands, farmers with hard hands, wealthy and poor, men who pray and men who don't, mothers and fathers and brothers and sons and sisters and wives and friends of those who lie in the graves. All of Israel is here, every piece of the mosaic. There is an old, weathered man who saw the earliest days before the state. There is a delicate girl in army uniform sitting on an old gravestone, touching it with her hand, weeping without tears for a father she scarcely knew. There are small children who abandon their frolicking amid the heaviness, not knowing exactly why.

When the sirens sound, the flow of mourners shuffles to a stop, and the people stand in dignity and sorrow, held in their private thoughts, their flowers by their sides, as the sirens' solemn note holds high, then slides and wails down and dies. And the people move forward again, dividing as they go along the pathway into the sections of the cemetery devoted to their respective wars. A salute is fired, a bugle sounds, an army rabbi moves from grave to grave to chant the melancholy prayer for the dead. A weeping mother stretches face down on the long tombstone of her son; she clutches at it and cries some mangled words as if grabbing and calling to him to come back. The father stands stooped, then bends to put a hand on her shoulder.

In the newest section, the graves and the grief are as fresh as the turned earth. The mourners cluster among the gravemarkers, and at the far end, two cleanly dug rectangular holes stand open, waiting for the victims of the Lebanon war. Elsewhere, in the sections for the older battles, the survivors' agony is less raw, more subdued, scarred by time. There, at the grave of Yaacov Walzer, who was saved from the Nazis in Belgium at the age of two and killed in the fighting for Jerusalem at the age of twenty-seven, a small group of middle-aged adults stand, composed. Yaacov's brother Aryeh and sister Nellie Kremer raised him practically as parents after their mother and father disappeared from their home in Belgium into the Auschwitz concentration camp. The three children were taken in at great risk by a Christian family, which hid them for two years.

"He was two years old, and I was twelve," his brother says. "He was a boy who didn't understand anything, who didn't understand why, when Nazi troops came to search, he couldn't make any noise, couldn't say anything. I had to push a cloth into his mouth because he wanted to laugh, and I kept it there until he started to turn blue, then just at the last moment I took it out. From then on he knew. In 1948 we came to Israel. He went to Hebrew University, prepared for a doctorate in physics. He was a brilliant student. He had work published in an American physics journal. It's difficult to explain. We remained three children, three orphans. But we brought him up as a little child. He was our pride. We did everything to make it possible for him to continue his studies. I saw in him what I'd like to be, but I couldn't because of the circumstances. So my sister and I did everything possible so he could be somebody. He was so near to the goal. And in the Six-Day War he fell in Jerusalem. You can see here the destiny of a Jewish child who was saved by Gentile people who risked their lives to save Jewish children. Afterwards he came to his homeland, Israel, and here he fell in the liberation of Jerusalem." The liberation of Jerusalem, the conquest of Jerusalem.

The mourners stand among the graves, talking softly, filling cups and jars with water for the fresh flowers. Rivka Fass sits weakly on the stone of her son's tomb, stroking it, kissing it. Another Yaacov, he died in

Sinai in 1967. Now hard-won Sinai is given back to Egypt, "We are all afraid of war," says Yaacov's sister Hanni Zalmona. "We had these awful experiences. We don't have any sentiments for Sinai. We have sentiments for peace. He died for peace." A man approaches, Yaacov's best friend. He shakes hands with the father, silently, the way men do when they are at the edge of tears. He goes to the mother and embraces her. No words are spoken.

The impact of war looks simple from a distance. It should twist emotions into straightforward anger, weld hatred into the bones, seal off understanding. Not always so. At close view, war nurtures a somber complexity. An honest man who goes into battle confronts himself. His doubts gnaw; he broods on his fears; his pleasures enjoy a revived freshness. Sometimes he reaches out and touches.

Where Syrian and Israeli troops faced each other across a narrow ravine in Lebanon's Bekaa valley a year after the hard battles of the Lebanon war, they occasionally called and waved and sang to each other. Once, when the Israelis were lounging around without helmets or flak jackets, a state of relaxation contrary to regulations, the Syrians, who held slightly higher ground and could see well behind the Israeli position, started jumping and waving and yelling to get the Israelis' attention. The Syrians shouted in Arabic to Arabic-speaking Israeli soldiers that a high-ranking Israeli officer was driving up in a jeep. Well warned, the Israelis scrambled for their equipment and got into complete battle dress by the time their superior arrived.

In Sinai after peace was signed between Egypt and Israel, soldiers from the two sides visited each other routinely at an isolated checkpoint, greeted each other warmly, threw parties for each other in their tents, and simply became human beings in the vastness of the wilderness. The Israelis took water to the Egyptians, whose army was inefficient about supplies; the Egyptians, grateful but nervous about getting into trouble for having such friendly relations, asked that their names not be mentioned or their faces shown when we photographed them with Israeli troops.

Near the Strait of Tiran in Sinai the morning of January 27, 1982, a sturdy, muscular man in khaki shorts, a white T-shirt, and sandals drove his dusty white Saab through a twisting desert track that wound among old mine fields marked by tumbled barbed-wire fences. He pulled up to the wreck of a Mustang P-51, a propeller plane that had crashed three wars ago and had been made into a monument of sorts by encircling it with low posts. The plane still had a yellow stripe on the wing; the blue Star of David had faded to white, and the number "73" was still faintly visible after the years of bleaching sun and blowing sand. The man, his wife, and their three children got out of the car and looked at the wreck. From another direction, a tour bus full of Israeli girls lumbered up. Their teacher, a young man, had them gather around while he told the story of this lonely ruin in the desert.

It was during the Sinai Campaign of '56, the teacher explained to his students, and the plane had come to attack an Egyptian unit. As it flew low from out of the sun, to strafe with its six machine guns, it was hit, and crash-landed. The Israeli pilot, Jonathan Etkes, survived, was captured by the Egyptians, and was then released at the end of the war. As the teacher spoke and the girls listened, the man in the khaki shorts stood listening also, his arms crossed. He had a thick neck, and his thinning hair was cropped razor short.

When the teacher had nearly finished, the man stepped forward, climbed onto a wing of the plane, and said, "Excuse me. I'm Jonathan Etkes." His timing was masterful, and he loomed above them like some heroic apparition. "Oh!" the teacher shouted, and shook his hand. The girls gasped. A student who had stayed drowsily in the bus heard the commotion and called to her classmates, asking what was going on. "It's the pilot!" they screeched. And the pilot, Jonathan Etkes, told his story, correcting only a few details of the teacher's version. "They had thirty-seven-millimeter radar guns, Russian guns," he said, and went on to explain that the Egyptians had shot down a jet aircraft, a Mystère 41. "Benny Peled was the pilot; he later became commander of the air force. I started to see all the ack-ack, the puff. As long as you see it, it's good," he laughed. "The one that hits you, you don't see," and he laughed again as he continued his account. "Benny Peled, he fell, and in order that he wouldn't be captured, I remained to do some strafing, and he ran to the mountains. The sun was south, and we came from the south strafing." He made his hand go like a plane, diving, soaring, turning. "I went to sea, pulled up, and came from the south again. I suddenly saw shooting on the left side. They got me here, see?" He pointed to the scar on his leg. He looked down into the array of fresh faces upturned in rapture. "I wanted to run, but my legs didn't want to run, so I was running in my imagination, lying here. I lost consciousness. At five o'clock they took me." When he had finished, the girls crowded around him for a while, then were herded back into their bus, which rumbled off into the silence of the desert.

The day that Etkes visited his crash site had heavy meaning for him. It was on that date, twenty-five years before, that he had been released in a prisoner exchange, and the anniversary had become his private holiday. After Israel regained Sinai in the 1967 war and he could simply drive down from his home in Tel Aviv, he had brought his family to the crash site every January 27. This was the last time; Sinai was going back to Egyptian control three months hence in what he felt would be a bitter peace. After Sadat's 1977 visit to Jerusalem, Etkes was honored, as a former prisoner of war, by being selected as one of three Israeli pilots to fly the first El Al plane to Cairo, carrying a party of officials to prepare for a return visit by Menachem Begin. But Etkes was gloomy about the future. "To be honest, I have very, very bad feelings," he told me as we stood in the sun. "How many times can the enemy fool you? I really hope that this peace remains, though personally I'm pessimistic."

His little girl, Tal, climbed into the cockpit while his wife, Mira, snapped pictures. Etkes strolled quietly around the aircraft tapping the wings and poking the ailerons. The dry desert is kind to machinery, and the ruins of warfare last well after the names of those who perished have been forgotten.

The Egyptians had tortured him as a prisoner. "They were very rough, but I was lucky to be in Egypt rather than Syria," he said. "They burned me with cigarettes." He pointed to a white spot on his cheek. "All my lips were burned, my nose, eyebrows, and ears. This was the easy part. They put surgical clamps on my tongue and started to turn them as you would open a sardine can, until you can't breathe anymore." They used syringes to give him shots all over his body, of what he did not know. They cut away dead flesh from his wounded leg without using anesthetic. "My head was as big as a watermelon. Electric shocks. I was completely naked. They put water on me to have good connections."

The interrogators wanted to know about a planeload of high-ranking Egyptian officers that Israeli fighters had shot down just before the war; the Egyptians were worried that the officers had been taken prisoner. But "they were so full of hate," Etkes recalled, "all they wanted was to see me suffer, and they didn't pay attention to the information. They deserve some credit for the amount of hatred and the amount of satisfaction they drew from the torture." His eyes burned intensely beneath his bushy eyebrows. Then suddenly he guffawed as he remembered the positive side. After his release, a false rumor circulated that the Egyptians had castrated him, he said. A lot of Israeli women wanted to find out firsthand whether it was true.

The experience of Etkes hardened his politics and his perception of Arabs' attitudes. "The heart of the conflict is the lack of acceptance of Jews here by Arabs," he declared. "This is the heart of the problem, not the Palestinians. I want to live. In order to live, I have to be the one to decide what's good for me. If you push me back to the wall too far, I won't be responsible for what I do." He had an old claim here: his children were the eighth generation on his mother's side to live in Palestine, he noted. "When Napoleon was defeated in Moscow, they were in Hebron already," he said of his wife's ancestors. "So my friend Arafat can't tell me that this isn't my home."

When Jonathan Etkes had finished talking, I had a few words with his son, Dori, a pleasant lad of sixteen. "It's my father's story," he said. "I've heard the story many times. I don't feel much, to tell you the truth. I'm going into the army in a few years, and maybe then I'll start to understand."

War has various lessons in its curriculum, and each student draws individually from the scholarship of combat. If the enemies are separated, distant, they can easily be dehumanized in each other's eyes, and the course of organized, governmental violence is not a difficult one for a society to incorporate into its values. But for Arabs and Jews whose homes lie between the Jordan River and the Mediterranean, the relationships are not so simple. They have lived together locked in each other's grip, enduring a prolonged state of twilight warfare that has alternated between armed battle and de facto peace. Jews and Arabs are expected to kill each other one year, then reside nonviolently beside each other the next, then again pick up arms when the time comes. Moreover, in war, Jews must kill some Arabs and tolerate others, somehow distinguishing between warriors and neighbors.

"Humanistic education is always complicated and difficult," said El-hanan Naeh, a talmudic scholar from Hebrew University, "because to educate people to be more humanistic is to tell them to live with ambiguity and to like ambiguity—not only to live with it as an accident but to understand human nature as ambiguous. It's very difficult, and it's especially difficult in an age of tension, especially in war. In every society, murder is the worst crime. It's not easy to teach people that you shouldn't murder; you shouldn't murder every day, every day, every day, and then at 10:30 there's a war, and you should murder. Anyone who won't shoot is punished. You shouldn't shoot anyone, then the bell rings and you try to shoot everyone, then after a week the bell rings again and you shouldn't do it."

Long personal histories make war integral to the way Jews and Arabs think about these matters. Many Arabs in Jerusalem can trace their ancestry back generations, into the dim mists of early Muslim rule. One Muslim family, for example, remains the custodian today of the keys to the Church of the Holy Sepulchre, having first been charged with this duty by Caliph Omar in the seventh century.

Like Jonathan Etkes, Elhanan Naeh counted the Jews of nineteenth-century Hebron among his forebears. Those on his father's side came in the 1830s and '40s from Russia to Hebron, and to the Galilean towns of Tiberius and Safed; those on his mother's side journeyed from Galicia, now in Poland, to live in Tiberius, Safed, and Jerusalem. "The Turks exiled them to Egypt, as Russians, during the First World War," Naeh said. They returned to Palestine after the war, in 1920.

Although Naeh's ancestry gave him a sense of context and wisdom, the long view can also reinforce dogmatism. For some, war never ends; Arabs never become individuals. The battleground is all around them, in their yards and streets and playgrounds. The Arab stonemasons, students, bus drivers, and doctors who live in the next town or the next neighborhood remain soldiers in an enemy force. So it is for Alexander Finkelshtein, a short, bulky communications worker of fifty-five with a bushy moustache, powerful arms, and a penchant for giving lengthy historical lectures to bolster his fierce prescription for Jewish purity. He also was born in Israel—when it was still Palestine, under the British Mandate—and in 1948 he fought for the independence of the fledgling Jewish state against the invading Arab armies. He walks with a limp from that war, whose combat is so fresh in his memory that he can look out from his town of Upper Nazareth, a community of white concrete apartment houses built on a high plateau, and reconstruct the battles in the hills and valleys of the Galilee, where he served as a commando with the Palmach, the strike force of the Haganah, the pre-state Jewish defense organization.

In 1980, Finkelshtein formed a group of Jewish residents to combat what he called "Arab penetration" of Upper Nazareth—namely, the arrival of Arab families, citizens of Israel, who were exercising their legal right to rent and buy apartments in the largely Jewish city. Finkelshtein called his group Migenim al Nazeret Illit, Hebrew for "Defenders of Upper Nazareth," and for short used the acronym Mena, which means "prevention." Those he gathered around him despised Arabs, politically, culturally, and, in a sense, racially. They blocked apartment doors as Arab families tried to move in. They threatened Arabs with violence if they did not move out. They urged their fellow Jews to refuse to rent or sell to Arabs. And as Finkelshtein took me on a tour of Upper Nazareth and what he called "lower Nazareth"—the Arab city of Nazareth, in ancient days the home of Jesus—it became clear that he saw the infiltration of Arab families essentially in military terms, that he applied a military analysis to social issues. "Here is the road to Tiberius," he announced as we stood on a high point and he gestured out into the valleys. "All those villages along the road are Arab. We want to show you how we are surrounded by Arab villages. Upper Nazareth was founded in '57 on a line of confrontation during the War of Independence. It was an area where Arab pirates operated. Gangs gathered here and attempted to conquer the Valley of Jezreel. The war was run with strong and cruel force.

"The Arab area is getting stronger numerically," he continued in angry apprehension. "They get health insurance. They spread propaganda poison against Israel. Their confidence is growing. We were very tolerant for a very long period of years. But today we've reached a national catastrophe, after we realized the Arabs were getting money from Saudi Arabia and Arafat with the intention of appropriating houses, getting back what was taken from them in the time of the war. Galilee was taken by the blood of our sons." Constructing a new building, in Finkelshtein's view, was something akin to a unit's taking a strategic hill or an important pass. "Here," he said, pointing to a piece of vacant land near Nazareth, "they applied to build a mosque on eighty dunams [twenty acres], a school and a mosque. We will go to the High Court to try to stop them." He was especially offended at the richness and neatness of some of the Arabs' villas on the outskirts of Nazareth, spacious houses in traditional Arab style. "Look at these houses, all for one family," he said with contempt and, perhaps, envy, for he lived in a small, messy apartment.

At the end of the day, on the way down from Upper Nazareth, the gentle hills of Galilee were deepened by the late light of afternoon. Where I saw beauty, Finkelshtein saw threat. Both were illusions mixed with truth, blended into caricatures of the complex reality.

War imposes its own values, its standards of honor. For Shimon Avidan, who also had a long view, these principles remained as unyielding as bedrock. He had come from Germany in 1934 after Hitler gained power, and he looked exactly like the founding father that he was, an old man with white hair, a clear eye, and sharp moral pain. My wife, Debby, and I went to see him after Israel invaded Lebanon in 1982, after Israel's army swept up the Lebanese coast through towns and refugee camps where armaments were mixed with civilians, after Israel besieged and bombed and shelled congested West Beirut, after Israel sent Lebanese Christian Phalangists into Palestinian refugee camps, where they massacred at least 700 to 800 men, women, and children. Avidan was suffering as he watched his country, his army, depart from the standards he felt he had upheld as the commander in 1948 of Israel's southern brigade.

We drove to his kibbutz, Ein Hashofet, nestled in tranquil, forested hills in Galilee. He spoke about his feelings. "No war is ethical," he said. "You are preparing people to behave in an unethical way, to kill somebody else. You are trying to do it in the most effective way. And the question is the aims of the war: Are they acceptable? Are they moral? Are they serving your nation?" The PLO in southern Lebanon, though no match for the Israeli army, was a legitimate target, he thought, but the wider war executed by Israel eroded morality. "For the first time, the state of Israel pushed aside the basic belief that when you fight you have to be absolutely sure you're fighting for a just cause. War is always a bestial thing that has to be avoided as long as is morally possible. You should come out of it as a human being, as a man who did the right thing, for the right aim, [who can say,] 'We are fighting for a just cause. We are morally right.' "

As he watched the fighting in Lebanon unfold, he said, "I felt myself like a split personality. I was running with the soldiers and cleaning up the area, and I felt myself standing with the civilian population, without water, without shelter. I had my flashbacks. And please understand me: I know the difference between what was done to Jews and to Palestinians. But there are two pictures in my mind, one of Palestinian children advancing with their hands up. You have seen the picture of the children in the Warsaw Ghetto. Another, of an Arab woman in shell shock, holding the hand of a soldier. The Israeli soldier gave her water. She wouldn't let go of his hand. Take this soldier. He will never return the same man he was. And this Arab man. He could be my father. And I can't look at him like my enemy. You will enter a vicious circle, blood for blood, and at the end you cannot remember where was the beginning. And you are not more just than the other side. We now look like every other nation."

These were hard words for an old warrior to say about his country. Warfare had turned its attack inward. And so, when Debby and I asked Shimon Avidan about '48, he brightened. Lebanon was entirely devoid of the clean righteousness he felt about that first war. He pulled out his scrapbooks of photographs, remarkable shots of the desert platoons, of Beersheba as a few shacks, of Eilat as a camp. "You have to remember that the War of Independence happened at a time when nearly everybody here had lost part of his family. Losing the war meant to lose the last hope. That brought the feeling in everybody that he alone had to take on the task. We felt very strongly that to take a life was a terrible thing. We wanted to do everything to defeat the fighting forces, but that nobody else should suffer. In Ashkelon, the Egyptians had a strong garrison. We attacked. There was a group of [Arab] textile workers there. They came to my command post and asked to stay on. I decided so it should be. I ordered no looting. I'm sorry that the next day when we entered the town, they retreated together with the Egyptians. In every war such things happen.

"We were absolutely barefoot," he continued as he flipped the pages and showed us the snapshots. "But to be barefoot does not handicap you if you are proud of it. We had no artillery. But they had fortified points. So what we had to do was to find the right man to take dynamite." In one picture, a cannon of sorts stood on wooden wheels—good for nothing much except making a loud noise, Avidan recalled with a chuckle. Then he caught himself in his nostalgia. "I don't think today I have to be sorry that we are no longer poor," he said. "I am very proud that we have all this supply. But it is good to remember who I am and where I come from—a small nation."

When we had looked through the albums and he had put them away, Debby and I bid our farewell and thanks. And as we drove out of the hills of Galilee, Debby observed that no Israeli who had fought in Lebanon was ever going to have the experience, years from now, of pulling out photograph albums of that war and recalling that fight with the nobility and pride of Shimon Avidan and his War of Independence.

Nostalgia, a romance with the past, contains an element of falsehood. For Israeli Jews, too close to their formative past to face it squarely, the years in which the state was built exist suspended from reality as expressions of the dream. Those who now decry anti-Arab bigotry, religious zealotry, Jewish terrorism, and the affinity for violence often fall into the passionate misconception that these are wholly new ingredients to the Jewish state, that the humane moralism of the initial venture was once pristine and has been lost, that something precious has been stolen from the lofty enterprise. Through my years there, I came to feel that there was something too stark in this neat juxtaposition. Shifts took place, to be sure, as Israel became a real country with real people and real defects, when the dream confronted reality. But the changes came in shades of grey, not blacks and whites, and more continuity ran through the Jews' violence against Arabs than most Jews were willing to admit. Indeed, a synthetic Israeli history has grown up, accepted widely in classrooms and living rooms, about the departure of Arabs from Israel during the 1948 war.

The official myth, widely believed by Israeli Jews, has it that the 700,000 Arabs who fled their farms and villages and cities, most of them then barred by Israel from returning, did so only for two reasons: They left willingly, not wishing to live in a Jewish state, and they were ordered out by the commanders of the Arab Legion, who anticipated a decisive military campaign that would return the Arab residents over the ruins of a defeated Israel. In short, the Jews had no responsibility whatever for the flight of the Arabs. The truth of this is only partial. As Palestinian Arabs recall, and as Israeli documents show, Arab residents of the new state of Israel ran for a mixture of reasons. Some were simply running from the fighting, as in any war. Others have told me that they heard the Arab Legion's broadcasts telling them to leave and took heed, although some pro-Arab authors have contended that checks of available records show no such broadcasts having been made. Some who were wealthy enough to afford a trip to Beirut or Amman went for what they believed would be only a few weeks, and they were so confident that they did not even take all their valuables along. But others were deliberately and forcibly expelled by the Jews. And others fled because they were convinced that if the Jews got into their villages, they would massacre men, women, and children as they had done in the Arab village of Deir Yassin in April 1948, one month before Israel became a state.

As a society, Israel is not ready to accept the fact that some of its finest heroes expelled Arabs, for to do so would be an acknowledgment, not only of dark impulses in that noble undertaking but also of some legitimate Arab claim to property or compensation. In history textbooks, in classroom instruction, in much of the public discussion of the 1948 war, a blank curtain is drawn over the expulsion, and allegations are dismissed as Arab propaganda. "What we learned in school," said Susan London, a recent Hebrew University graduate, "was that they ran away even though the Jews were very nice to them, and the mean Arabs didn't help them."

When Yitzhak Rabin, former prime minister, defense minister, and commander of the Harel Brigade in 1948, wrote his memoirs in 1979, a political-censorship committee prohibited him from publishing a section on his involvement in the expulsion of Arabs from the towns of Lod and Ramle, near Tel Aviv. The committee, as Rabin explained to me, comprised five Cabinet members headed by the justice minister; all former government employees had to submit manuscripts both to the military censor and to that political panel, which struck the following text from Rabin's book:

> While the fighting was still in progress, we had to grapple with a troublesome problem for whose solution we could not draw upon any previous experience: the fate of the civilian population of Lod and Ramle, numbering some 50,000. Not even Ben-Gurion could offer any solution, and during the discussions at operational headquarters, he remained silent, as was his habit in such situations. Clearly, we could not leave Lod's hostile and armed populace in our

rear, where it could endanger the supply route to Yiftach [another brigade] that was advancing eastward.

We walked outside, Ben-Gurion accompanying us. [Yigal] Allon repeated his question: "What is to be done with the population?" B.G. waved his hand in a gesture which said: "Drive them out!" Allon and I held a consultation. I agreed that it was essential to drive the inhabitants out. We took them on foot toward the Bet Horon road, assuming that the Legion would be obliged to look after them, thereby shouldering logistic difficulties which would burden its fighting capacity, making things easier for us.

"Driving out" is a term with a harsh ring. Psychologically, this was one of the most difficult actions we undertook. The population of Lod did not leave willingly. There was no way of avoiding the use of force and warning shots in order to make the inhabitants march the ten to fifteen miles to the point where they met up with the Legion.

The inhabitants of Ramle watched, and learned the lesson: Their leaders agreed to be evacuated voluntarily, on condition that the evacuation was carried out by vehicles. Buses took them to Latrun, and from there they were evacuated by the Legion.

Great suffering was inflicted upon the men taking part in the eviction action. Soldiers of the Yiftach Brigade included youth movement graduates, who had been inculcated with values such as international fraternity and humaneness. The eviction action went beyond the concepts they were used to. There were some fellows who refused to take part in the expulsion action. Prolonged propaganda activities were required after the action to remove the bitterness of these youth movement groups, and explain why we were obliged to undertake such a harsh and cruel action.[2]

Many elderly people and small children, without sufficient water, died in the overpowering heat during the forced march.[3] Although this went unmentioned by Rabin, in other respects his account resembled those by some non-Israeli historians, and he told me that he was puzzled by the Cabinet committee's decision to censor it. Yet Israelis as a whole are so determined to block out this unsavory element of their history that Rabin's revelation had little impact. After it was published in *The New York Times*, the muffled reports on it that were carried by Israeli news organizations engendered almost no reaction or debate. The state-owned Israeli radio tried to obfuscate and confuse the picture by finding people to claim that there was such chaos that nobody really knew what was going on. One of the radio station's interviewees was an Arab who turned out to have been about five years old at the time. Yigal Allon, probably to protect his (and his country's) reputation, denied the Rabin version vehemently without having read it. In any event, he said, "If a war had not been imposed on us, all this suffering could have been avoided."

The expulsions left their marks on the Arabs. George Habash, who was studying in Beirut when his family was driven from Lod, later became head of one of the PLO's most radical factions, the Popular Front for the Liberation of Palestine. A schoolmate of his, a woman now living in the crumbling coastal city of Jaffa, lost a child. As fighting began, she and her baby daughter had been taken from Jaffa to her home village of Lod by her husband, a shopkeeper who made the miscalculation that they would be safer there. When Arab inhabitants were expelled from the town in the summer heat, they did not have enough food and water; the little girl, then a year old, died during the long walk to the area of Bir Zeit, on the West Bank. The mother managed to return to Jaffa a year and a half later through the auspices of the Red Cross and the Israeli government, but she holds her bitterness toward the Jews and has refused to study Hebrew. In the intricacies of contrast, her son, born in 1950, has developed close friendships with Jews, works as a civil engineer for the city of Tel Aviv, and fondly recalls Sabbaths as a boy, when he was paid half a pound for lighting the candles in the synagogue across the street.

After the Rabin memoirs on Lod and Ramle, further evidence of expulsions came to light as Israeli Foreign Ministry documents from the period began to be declassified. Benny Morris, a reporter from *The Jerusalem Post*, sifted through large volumes of information and collected data on the Israeli efforts to clear Arabs from the northern Negev, particularly the Faluja pocket, where Jewish troops fired into the air to frighten the 2,400 Arab inhabitants and whispered threats of attack and revenge. At the time, this occasioned considerable debate within the new Israeli government and provoked protests from the United Nations representative, Ralph Bunche. But virtually all the Arabs there left for the Hebron region, where they and their descendants now live on what is called the West Bank.[4]

Morris found other material in official Israeli archives that documented expulsions from many parts of the country. These occurred in several cycles, he said. One involved villages in the coastal plain from which most Arabs had fled in February and March 1948. On April 3, the Haganah, as the precursor of the Israeli army, ordered the 994 residents of Khirbet Azzun to leave their village. On April 10, the 620 Arab residents of Ad Dumeira, the 910 Bedouins from Arab an-Nufeiat, and the 340 Bedouins of Arab al-Foqara were expelled from their settlements. On April 15, some 650 Arabs from Miska and an uncounted number from Khirbet as-Sarkas were ordered out. Another cycle in May and early June involved Arab villages near the southern front. Najd and Sumsum, with populations of 600 and 1,200 respectively, were ordered evacuated by the Haganah on May 12. Zarnuga and Kaukaba, with populations of 2,600 and 1,870, were emptied by the Givati Brigade on May 27, the documents show. Arab Rubin's 1,550 residents were expelled on June 1, and Yibna, with a population of 5,920, was emptied June 4. The 800 Arabs from the village of Huj were expelled on May 28, although the village had been regarded by officials as "pro-Jewish." Its *mukhtar*, or head man, had been assassinated in January 1948, on a visit to Gaza, because of his pro-Jewish sympathies.

Morris found evidence of a few expulsions in the Galilee, most notably at Tsaffuriya. Arab villagers who remained were evicted from a strip about six to ten miles wide along the Lebanese border, although most of them, including those from the Christian villages of Ikrit and Biram, were pushed into Israel rather than Lebanon. During October and November of 1948, several expulsions followed massacres. At Ilaboun, in eastern Galilee, a force of Golani troops killed villagers and then ousted the survivors, although they were later allowed back. In the south, a massacre at Dueima by the 89th Battalion, 8th Brigade, was followed by the expulsion of the remaining residents. They were never allowed to return.[5]

All this would come as a great surprise to most Israelis, for although it is only a partial list of what Morris has discovered, it represents a side of history that has been largely suppressed. One high-school textbook gave a fleeting glance at the issue, saying, "The Israelis claim that the Arabs left their homes under the advice of their leaders, who told them to go in order that they not hinder the invading military movements into the country, and promised them that they would soon return behind the victorious Arab armies. The Arabs claim that they were driven out by the Israelis. Both claims are correct; both claims are also incorrect." But no details on expulsions were provided.

The Deir Yassin massacre, more openly discussed in Israel, has been researched extensively by historians with various perspectives. Since the killing was done by radical Jewish undergrounds and not by the mainstream Labor Zionists, the Israeli academic and political establishment has felt less need to suppress the basic story, although detailed evidence remains beyond public access. Through more than three decades of internal Israeli political conflict, Laborites and other centrist and leftist Israelis often cited the massacre as testimony against the character of Menachem Begin, who was leader of the Irgun when his group and the Lehi—known as the "Stern Gang," after its founder, Avraham Stern—crept into the village at dawn on April 9, 1948. Begin was at home in Tel Aviv, not on the scene, and his biographer Eric Silver concludes that he probably did not plan a massacre beforehand or realize fully the dimensions of the one that had taken place when he issued his euphoric message to his troops:

"Accept my congratulations on this splendid act of conquest. Convey my regards to all the commanders and soldiers. We shake your hands. We are all proud of the excellent leadership and the fighting spirit in this great attack. We stand to attention in memory of the slain. We lovingly shake the hands of the wounded. Tell the soldiers: you have made history in Israel with your attack and your conquest. Continue thus until victory. As in Deir Yassin, so everywhere, we will attack and smite the enemy. God, God, Thou hast chosen us for conquest."[6]

Silver's meticulous research, producing one of the most fair-minded accounts that has been done, concludes that Deir Yassin, a village in the hills on the outskirts of Jerusalem, was of no immediate military threat to the Jews. Although its hilltop position would have made it dangerous in the hands of an Arab enemy, its residents were considered passive; its leaders had agreed with those of an adjacent Jewish neighborhood, Givat Shaul, that each side would prevent its own people from attacking the other. The Haganah, the main-line, Labor-dominated Jewish defense organization, saw an eventual need for military control over the town but no reason for offensive action; Silver postulates that a peaceful understanding similar to those reached with other Arab villages was possible. The Irgun and Lehi, however, laid plans for an attack, received reluctant

Haganah acquiescence, and went in with about 120 men. As the leader, Benzion Cohen, later said of the participants, "The majority was for liquidation of all the men in the village and any other force that opposed us, whether it be old people, women or children."

Emotions were running high after a 1,500-man force of the Arab Legion had massacred Jewish residents of Gush Etzion, a cluster of kibbutzim south of Jerusalem, following a five-month siege. Bodies were mutilated and some surviving Jewish soldiers raped and tortured by the Arabs. Aviva Hazaz, whose first husband was part of a patrol sent in an effort to break through to the encircled settlers, recalled the tragedy with fresh pain thirty-five years later. The force tried and failed and returned, and was then sent out again the following night. Every one of them was killed. "I lost not only my husband but all my friends in one day," she said. "I was the last to say good-bye to them."

The Jewish fighters who planned the attack on Deir Yassin also had a larger purpose, apparently. A Jerusalem woman and her son, who gave some of the men coffee in the pre-dawn hours before their mission, still recall the guerrillas' talking excitedly about the prospect of terrifying Arabs far beyond the village of Deir Yassin so that they would run away. Perhaps this helps explain why the Jewish guerrillas did not bury the Arabs they had killed, but left the bodies to be seen, and why they paraded surviving prisoners, blindfolded and with hands bound, in the backs of trucks through the streets of Jerusalem, a scene still remembered with a shudder by Jews who saw it. News of the assault sent a bolt of panic through Arab communities, where Deir Yassin quickly became a name of infamy and a source of terrible fear that served its goal of provoking flight by those who thought the Jews would do the same in every Arab village.

Despite Begin's insistence throughout his life that Deir Yassin was a battle and not a massacre, it was both, and the research has now been extensive enough to remove most doubt about what happened. Silver confirms the finding by other authors that a loudspeaker truck, with which the Arab villagers were to be warned to surrender, got stuck in a ditch too far from the village for its message to be heard. And the villagers, who had posted watchmen, fought when the Jews approached. Each family had at least one gun; five Jews were killed and thirty-five wounded. So beleaguered were the Irgun and Lehi men at one point that the Haganah, even with its doubts about the wisdom of the attack, sent a platoon with a two-inch mortar and a machine gun to provide brief help. When the Jewish fighters later made their way into the village, they burst into houses and shot whole families, including several old men who had dressed in women's clothes in a vain attempt to acquire immunity. A group of at least eighty Arab prisoners were also killed. The final Arab death toll is put variously at 116 to 240 or 250. A witness, Meir Pa'il, a Haganah intelligence officer who had heard about the upcoming assault and decided on his own to watch it, told Silver:

"It was a massacre in hot blood, it was not pre-planned. It was an outburst from below with no one to control it. Groups of men went from house to house looting and shooting, shooting and looting. You could hear the cries from within the houses of Arab women, Arab elders, Arab kids. I tried to find the commanders, but I did not succeed. I tried to shout and to hold them, but they took no notice. Their eyes were glazed. It was as if they were drugged, mentally poisoned, in ecstasy."

Pa'il took gruesome pictures and wrote a report to his superiors, beginning it with the first lines of a Hebrew poem composed by Chaim Nachman Bialik following the 1903 pogrom in Kishinev, in which 49 Jews were killed and 500 injured by a Russian mob:

Arise and go to the city of the killing and you will come to the courtyards,
and with your eyes you will see and with your hands you will feel on the fences
and on the trees and on the stones and on the plaster
the congealed blood and the battered brains of the slain.

Significantly, the mainstream in Israel also conspired to cover up the most vivid evidence, although the Haganah was disturbed and the massacre later served Labor as an ugly episode with which to stain Begin. Pa'il's report and photographs have never been released from official secrecy. A newsreel cameraman who filmed the latter part of the assault boasted about his scoop to another newsman who worked for Haganah intelligence, Silver writes. The agent then "drove to Lydda airport and switched the film before it could be flown to London. Movietone News received 400 feet of Jerusalem cloud formations."

Furthermore, textbooks do not tell Jewish children the truth. A book used in ninth grade and published in 1981, *The History of the People of Israel*, puts a twist on the Deir Yassin incident: "The men of Lehi and Etzel [the Irgun] went out to conquer this village through which convoys to Jerusalem were attacked. They called over a loudspeaker to all the residents to evacuate the village." Then Begin's description from *The Revolt* is quoted as the final word, asserting, "A considerable portion of the Arab population listened to the warning and were saved. Others didn't leave their stone houses. . . . It was necessary to conquer house after house. In order to quiet the enemy the attackers used many hand grenades. The civilian population which didn't heed the early warnings suffered heavy losses." The textbook's passage then concludes: "Arab propaganda has given heavy publication to the incident."

In his memoir, *The Revolt*, Begin offers a revealing remark. Referring to the "propaganda," he writes: "Out of evil, however, good came. This Arab propaganda spread a legend of terror amongst Arabs and Arab troops, who were seized with panic at the mention of Irgun soldiers. The legend was worth half a dozen battalions to the forces of Israel. . . . In the result it helped us. Panic overwhelmed the Arabs of Eretz Israel. Kolonia village . . . was evacuated overnight. . . . Beit-Isla was also evacuated."[7]

The remaining stone houses of Deir Yassin have now been fenced into a compound that serves as an Israeli mental institution. Nearby are acres of earth and stone and concrete mixed into swirls of rubble. Jews call it Givat Shaul, the name of the surrounding Jerusalem neighborhood. Arabs still call it Deir Yassin. An Arab merchant, giving directions for picking up a television set to a Jew who speaks both Hebrew and Arabic, told him first in Hebrew to go to Givat Shaul. Then, after they had switched to Arabic, the merchant told him to go to Deir Yassin. The issue is one of language, vocabulary, memory.

Jamil Ahmed went to Deir Yassin, a pilgrimage to his own house, made with his wife and sons and daughters right after the 1967 war put the refugee camp to which he had fled in Jericho under Israeli control. He was about fifty years old at the time, having lived twenty of his best years in exile from his land, a land he remembers fondly as bountiful with grapes and olives. I met him at his simple house, one of the few left in the ruins of a refugee camp outside Jericho, and we sat outside on a crude patio among lemon and orange trees and grapevines as he had tea served and told his story.

He lived at the edge of Deir Yassin. The Jews came early in the morning, shooting. "My cousin Youssif was killed, my brother Aisa. I saw many friends killed. They would enter the houses and throw bombs. I saw prisoners who were butchered—they machine-gunned them, seven or eight of them. They took them, as prisoners, raised their hands, and took them to the end of the road at the edge of the village near my house and sprayed them with gunfire. A blind man was also shot like that. A child, seven years old, was also killed that way. Many women were killed. Other women were taken prisoner and put into trucks. I was in my house, carrying a gun, defending the village. It was an old rifle from World War I, British." He laughed at the futility of defense with such a weapon.

At noon, he snuck out of his house and went to the nearby village of Ein Kerem. From there he spent seven years moving from place to place, village to village, "looking for work, working odd jobs," as he put it. "I had nothing really except the clothes I had on," he said. In 1955 he and his family settled in the camp near Jericho. When the 1967 war came and the Israeli army pushed eastward, he, his wife, and their children fled east across the Jordan River to escape what they feared, wrongly, would be another massacre by Jews. "People in the camp were saying that the Israelis were killing people. We were afraid the same thing would happen as in 1948." But he could not find work or housing in Jordan, and after a week he and his family snuck back across the Jordan River into the West Bank. He needed to visit Deir Yassin again.

His visit to his home touched him so deeply that only flowery embellishment seemed appropriate in the telling. His family approached the gate of the mental hospital, he recalled, and a guard stopped them. The women and girls remained outside, but he and his sons were insistent enough to push their way in. They found his house being used as an administration building, and they visited the grave of his uncle. And in a gesture of return and possession, in a moment of pride and defiance, they drank water from his old cistern. "When I went to see my lands and my house, I actually fainted from the pain and suffering," said Ahmed, now a frail old man with an unshaven grey stubble on his gaunt and craggy cheeks. "It is like my whole heart and all my life was all lost in that moment when I went and saw." He trembled. "I will continue to remember my house, and I will pass it on to my sons."

He looked at his son, Ziad, who said, "I have been told this often, and I will pass it on to my children."

And how did he feel about Jews after all these years? At the question, vigor seemed to flow briefly into the old man's veins. "If somebody takes this glass of tea from you, how will you feel?" he asked angrily. "They have taken all our property and lands. It will be in our hearts and minds that the Jews have taken our land. I hate them. Before that, we had very good relations with the Jews. We used to visit each other until the foreign Jews came." He named a Yemenite Jew who had been a friend. Ahmed had looked for him after the '67 war but was told that he had died. "It never goes from my mind. Even during sleep I think about Deir Yassin. I have these moments of anger and nightmares. What my father built and my grandfather—all of this is dear to me. The Jews are like the Nazis," he declared. "They hate the Arabs, like the Nazis hated the Jews. They hate us, and I don't know why." He suddenly seemed sapped of strength again. "A Jew is killed, they take revenge on all the Palestinians who are around. Now they are putting these bombs in mosques. Why do you think they're putting bombs in mosques? Because again they want us to get out. They don't want any Arabs here." Would he flee again? "Not even if they kill us. Where would we go? Hussein doesn't want us. There is no place for us to go."

From his garden, Jamil Ahmed looked out over a sweeping landscape of empty, crumbling mud shells of houses in the abandoned camp near Jericho, once the homes of refugees like him, who had fled again during the '67 war and had not returned. Together, the buildings made up an eerie ghost town in the desert, resembling the ancient ruins that archaeologists painstakingly excavate to sift and scrutinize the riches and tragedies of earlier civilizations.

Since Deir Yassin, other names have been carved into the Arabs' monument of grief and hatred, and into the Israelis' legacy of guilt; they include Kfar Kassem, Qibya, Sabra and Shatila, and some of them are tainted with the theme of Deir Yassin, Lod, and Ramle—the theme of expulsion, the theme of terrorism, the use of civilian suffering against the military and political aims of the enemy. Many West Bank Palestinians have a special view of this historical continuity, one that ascribes more conspiratorial calculation than probably exists. They saw in the Jewish terrorism of the late 1970s and early 1980s a grand plan to create a psychological climate of such fear among the Arabs that they would flee from the West Bank in panic upon any outbreak of war or other substantial disorder. This view of Israeli motives always seemed too logical and explicit to be wholly accurate in a turbulent, diverse, and politically raucous society such as Israel's; it seemed partly a projection of Arab motives in conducting their own terrorism against Jews. And yet the accusation struck a true note somewhere in the overtones of Israeli attitudes, somewhere in the arpeggio of violence that ran through the years following 1948.

Kfar Kassem is not widely discussed in Israel any longer, although it remains in the ledgers of history as the most cold-blooded massacre conducted directly by agents of the Jewish state. It came against the background of repeated terrorist attacks on Israeli civilians by Arab fedayeen who were infiltrating mostly through Sinai from Egypt and, to a lesser extent, from Jordan. On October 29, 1956, the eve of Israel's Sinai Campaign, the army ordered all Israeli-Arab villages near the Jordanian border placed under a wartime curfew that was to run from 5 P.M. to 6 A.M. the next day. Any Arab on the streets would be shot. No arrests were to be made.

But the order was given to Israeli border police units only at 3:30 P.M., without time to communicate it to the Arabs affected, many of whom were at jobs or in their fields. Some of the Israeli border policemen who were to implement the curfew raised the obvious questions in a briefing with Colonel Yissachar Shadmi, according to testimony at their trial before a military tribunal. "What shall I do with a person who returns home after the curfew is imposed and does not know about it?" Major Shmuel Malinki recalled asking the colonel.

"I don't want any soft-heartedness, and I don't want any arrests made," Colonel Shadmi was quoted as replying.

"Bearing this in mind, what shall I do?"

"May Allah have mercy on their souls."

Colonel Shadmi denied ever having said such a thing; he was not prosecuted, was later promoted to brigadier general, and in 1982 was an honored guest at President Yitzhak Navon's reception for soldiers wounded in the invasion of Lebanon. *The Jerusalem Post* then described him reverently as "a near-legendary figure in the army" without any reference to the Kfar Kassem massacre.

Having his orders, Major Malinki proceeded to brief his subordinate officers who were to command troops in eight villages, telling them, in the court's words, "to shoot to kill at all curfew-breakers without any discrimination and without mercy." When one of his lieutenants asked what should be done about women, children, and other villagers returning late from work, Malinki stressed that "there was to be no sentiment and no favorable discrimination," the court found. In seven of the villages, no massacre took place, because Malinki's subordinates softened his instructions. One unit commander, figuring it was useless to argue with the major, moved the curfew from 5:00 to 5:30 P.M. in his four villages, ordered stragglers escorted home, and forbade any of his men to open fire without the explicit order of an officer. In three other villages, local officers changed the orders to suit the situations.

In Kfar Kassem, border troops took up position at various points. Four men at the northern end of the village saw three or four women filling jugs from a water barrel at 5:10 P.M. "I did not want to shoot them, because I felt that they were unaware of the curfew," said Private Shalom Porado. So he shouted and waved and called to them to go home. They ran to their houses. At 5:20, two men and a teenage boy approached the troops. When they were about twenty-five yards away, Porado again shouted and waved. When they spun around and ran away, he fired a warning burst from his submachine gun. When they did not stop, he ordered his men to shoot them, and all three were killed.

Villagers were coming home from the fields in the backs of trucks and on bicycles. The troops shot group after group of them. "I did not open fire until 5:20," said Lance Corporal Shalom Ofer, a twenty-seven-year-old deputy squad leader. "Then about fifteen villagers, riding bicycles, approached. I stopped them and told them to dismount. They began to run away. I opened fire with my rifle, and the other two men in my section opened fire with their weapons. We killed them.

"A truck with villagers came. I wanted to escort them to the village, but they began to run away. We shot them.

"Another truck came with seven or eight persons. The same thing happened.

"A truck came with four persons. The same thing happened.

"A wagon with five villagers came. The same thing happened."

The troops fired into one truck carrying fourteen women and four men. Villagers were hauled out of trucks, lined up, and shot. Ofer ordered that women and children be shot repeatedly until none remained alive. In all, forty-seven Arabs, all Israeli citizens, were killed during the early hours of the curfew at Kfar Kassem.[8]

The official reaction was somewhat ambivalent. The military censor, Walter Bar-On, issued a blanket ban on any reporting of the massacre, with the result that nothing was known to the broad Israeli public until six weeks later, when David Ben-Gurion announced to the Knesset the findings of a secret inquiry commission. Bar-On conceded in 1984 that the censorship of the news had "no security justification," and that, especially after the Sinai fighting had ended, the ban constituted nothing more than "suppression of a very embarrassing story."[9]

Eleven border policemen were charged. They tried to defend themselves by citing their superiors' commands, an especially distasteful argument for Israeli Jews with a memory of the Nazis' pleadings at Nuremberg that they were merely following orders. Out of that history had come a basic principle of the Israeli military and police: Obeying an illegal order is illegal and does not constitute a defense. And thus, the remark of one of the accused, Lance Corporal Gavriel Uliel, seemed an eerie echo: "I shot because I was ordered to; if I received an order to shoot my own family I would obey."

Eight of the accused were convicted. Major Malinki was given a prison sentence of seventeen years, Lieutenant Gavriel Dehan and Lance Corporal Ofer fifteen years, and the others somewhat lesser terms. But Ben-Gurion later urged substantial reductions in their sentences; the president, the military appeals board, and the chief of staff cut the terms so that Malinki and Dehan served three and a half years, and Ofer three. Nobody spent more than three and a half years in jail.

If there was any official calculation that killing civilians in Kfar Kassem would somehow serve a larger military or political purpose, it remained well out of view. Although the massacre occurred in the context of terrorism, war, and hatred, it appeared to be the result of a military action gone awry, of men without the mettle to reject orders they knew were wrong. That was not quite the case in other incidents, when civilians were often deliberate targets in an effort to spread fear or apply leverage on governments. During the War of Attrition with Egypt in 1969, for example, as Egyptian forces launched repeated attacks on Israeli positions in Sinai, Israel bombarded Egyptian villages along the Suez Canal, forcing the evacuation of 750,000 civilians, destroying 55,000 homes, and killing and wounding an untold number. It was a pressure tactic on the Egyptian authorities.

Qibya, a Jordanian border town, was the target of a 1953 reprisal raid by the Israeli army's Unit 101, commanded by a young colonel named Ariel Sharon. Replying to an attack on Israelis by Arab terrorists who had stolen across the border, Sharon's commandos, famous for ruthlessness, blew up forty-five houses, killing sixty-nine Arab villagers. Sharon said he had no idea that the houses were occupied, but the attack fit into the successful pattern of holding Arab civilians and governments responsible for the use of their territory by terrorists, and of punishing them severely for complicity. The practice brought Israel relatively quiet borders with Jordan, Syria, and Egypt, which eventually saw their interests served by closely patrolling their sides of the frontiers.

Thirty years later, Sharon, as defense minister, and other high officials were held "indirectly responsible" by a state investigatory commission for the massacre of Palestinians by Lebanese Christian Phalangists who were aligned with and supplied by Israel, and whom Sharon had sent into the Beirut refugee camps of Sabra and Shatila in September 1982. There, the Phalangists had shot and stabbed men, women, and children numbering at least 700 to 800, according to Israeli military intelligence. Arabs had killed Arabs, but only the Jews chewed over their own guilt; Israel investigated thoroughly while Lebanese authorities conducted a whitewash, even falsifying the statistics on the dead to minimize the numbers of women and children, thus making it appear to have been a battle rather than a massacre. The Lebanese contended that only 8 women and 12 children were among 470 dead. Begin's office tried to plant the false figures in the American press, and Sharon repeated them in a speech to an Israel Bonds dinner in New York. The numbers were accepted with alacrity by the Jewish Press, a Brooklyn-based tabloid, which published a huge headline: "Lebanon Attorney General Reveals The Truth: 'Massacre' was a P.L.O. Battle." They even appeared on the editorial page of The Wall Street Journal as if they were unquestioned facts. Nevertheless, the pretense that the atrocity had not taken place was swallowed by the truth, for the Red Cross had counted and recorded many of the bodies, and reporters entering the camps immediately afterwards had seen whole families lying dead around their dinner tables and in their beds, young men with their hands bound, old people, many children.

Israel had been motivated primarily by a drive to protect its borders, this time by installing in Beirut a strong and friendly government headed by the Phalangist leader Bashir Gemayel. For years, the Palestinian refugee camps had been the headquarters of the PLO's state within a state, extending from Beirut into southern Lebanon, well within artillery and rocket range of Israel's northern towns and kibbutzim. During their invasion of Lebanon and the ouster of the PLO from Beirut in the summer of 1982, some Israeli officials had expressed the hope that they would see a tough, authoritarian Phalange-led government disperse the Palestinians and break up the camps to preclude the slums' becoming, once again, PLO bases of political and military influence in Lebanon and hotbeds of terrorism directed against Israel. The degree to which Israeli policy-makers felt themselves capable of preventing this from happening corresponded to their growing and mistaken pride in themselves as sophisticated and streetwise players in the rough games of Arab rivalries, vengeance, and politics. Among some in the prime minister's office, the Foreign Ministry, the Defense Ministry, and the Mossad, it became fashionable to speak in wise tones of Israel's coming of age, of its integration into the Middle East, of its ability to fight like Arabs when needed and still maintain humane values as Jews. But the simplistic Israeli stereotypes of Arabs as primitive and tribal did not serve the policy-makers in Jerusalem very well, and the willingness of some officials to differentiate between the Jews' right to humane democracy and the Arabs' need for violent autocracy led Israel quickly into a confrontation with its own morality.

Yuval Ne'eman, the head of the right-wing Tehiya Party, unwittingly demonstrated the depths to which Israeli thinking was dragged by the quagmire of factional and religious warfare in Lebanon when he made a remark calculated as a criticism of naiveté in his government: "Bashir Gemayel impressed me very much as the modern condottiere who, with methods reminding you of the Sforzas and the Borgias in Italy in the fifteenth century, might have, by killing some of his adversaries and poisoning the rest and doing other actions of that type, he might have remade the Lebanon, and there would have been a new Lebanon, perhaps. With his assassination, I think—and I was sure from that moment on—there was no more hope for Lebanon to reconstitute itself. I'm sorry to say that this was not realized and that the Begin Government held on to the original view." It was realized, actually, perhaps not by Begin, who never quite grasped the roughness of the play in Lebanon, but certainly by Sharon and others who were putting all their chips on Bashir Gemayel's ruthlessness.

When Gemayel was assassinated in September 1982, just days before he was to take office as president of Lebanon, Israel saw its scheme jeopardized, moved its troops quickly into West Beirut, and dispatched into the Palestinian camps a Phalangist militia with a long history of revenge against Muslims. In the Israeli habit of denigrating Arabs as violent and uncivilized, the prospects of using Arab friends against Arab enemies must have conjured up clear images of, to say the least, a dirty fight against the Palestinians. Consequently, the three members of the investigating commission* responded with incredulity when Begin, Sharon, and other high officials protested that they had never imagined that the Phalangists, even in the heat of fury over the assassination of their leader, would commit such atrocities. "In the circumstances that prevailed after Bashir's assassination," the commissioners wrote in their final report, "no prophetic powers were required to know that concrete danger of acts of slaughter existed when the Phalangists were moved into the camps. . . . The sense of such a danger should have been in the consciousness of every knowledgeable person who was close to this subject. . . . From the Defense Minister himself we know that this consideration did not concern him in the least."

The practice of using Arabs against Arabs has long attracted Israeli officials who believe that Arabs are willing to be more brutal than Jews. Israeli Druse are often given tough jobs as border policemen facing demonstrators on the West Bank; they often engender more hatred from Palestinian Arabs than Jews do. I once told a West Bank mayor about seeing border policemen, outside Bir Zeit University during demonstrations, carrying long nightsticks with iron spikes tied to them so that when blows were landed, the sharp edges of the heads of the spikes would cut into the flesh. The mayor jumped to the conclusion that the policemen with such vicious homemade weapons were Druse. He dreaded contact with the Druse, he said. At least with Jewish soldiers, he explained, you can sometimes have a conversation, one human being to another.

Soon after I arrived in Israel, the *Times* stringer Moshe Brilliant invited me to meet some politicians at his apartment in Tel Aviv. Crowded into the room were men of fame, and as Moshe went the rounds of introductions, he came to a thin, sharp-eyed gentleman in the corner. "This is

---

* Yitzhak Kahan, chief justice of Israel's Supreme Court; Aharon Barak, a Supreme Court judge and former attorney general; and reserve general Yona Efrat.

Haim Landau, minister of transportation," said Moshe. "Before '48 he designed bridges by day and blew them up by night."

"Well," Landau said modestly, "only one of the bridges that I blew up had actually been designed by me." He had been in Begin's guerrilla underground before independence.

Virtually everyone in Israel has known war. Many have seen combat, and almost all know the experience of waiting for word from a loved one in battle. Every Cabinet in the country's brief history has contained men who were once warriors, men who have killed. And this brings a continuity of calloused wisdom to the mood of Israel, a hardness to the dreams.

To deny war is to deny reality, to embrace a supremely sane insanity. When Israeli soldiers during the 1982 Lebanon invasion began to suffer combat fatigue—the mental stress that often leads to withdrawal from the reality of battle—psychiatrists and other trained professionals moved in to render aid. The worst cases were evacuated to special bases set up for treatment. One man of thirty-five collapsed after seeing comrades blown apart by artillery shells, and he sat and stared in silence at a single spot at his feet. He refused to touch a rifle. Another spent twenty-four hours crying, yelling, rolling on the floor and crawling around, trying to piece together what he imagined were the parts of a friend's dismembered body. Some became blind, deaf, paralyzed. "Shell shock," "battle fatigue"; now, in the growing trend toward euphemism, it is called "combat reaction." And the treatment was given at a place with the manly, matter-of-fact name Combat Fitness Retraining Unit. The patients were never called "patients," and they were told that before they left they would overcome their gun phobia and be shooting on the rifle range. They laughed derisively at the idea, for almost none of them—in their temporary, so-called craziness—ever wanted to touch a weapon again. So the army exposed them gently and slowly to guns, first letting them look at gun parts on a table, then putting a bolt or a trigger assembly in their pockets to be carried around for a day or so. Gradually, the soldiers would return to reality. They would touch the parts of the gun; they would touch the gun; they would shoot the gun. And with few exceptions, they were cured; they were brought back from their demented state in which guns were repulsive objects to be shunned. They were ready to move back into the stable, sensible, sane world in which guns are embraced as the tools of a necessary trade.

In the wasteland of warfare are buried little nuggets of fondness for years long gone, when Arab and Jew lived more as neighbors than as enemies. These memories of the days before 1948 are cupped in the ruins of suffering, guarded gently, given a gloss that lends them a beauty they probably do not deserve. They surface now and then, especially in conversation with Arabs who need to remember the time before the Jewish state as a time of abundant happiness. Thus did Jamil Ahmed, survivor of Deir Yassin, speak with nostalgia, saying, "Before that, we had very good relations with the Jews. We used to visit each other until the foreign Jews came." He meant that Jews whose ancestry could be traced back for generations in Palestine were somehow of this land, unlike the alien interlopers who arrived later from Europe, North America, and Arab countries. Thus did the Arabs of Kfar Kassem, one year after the massacre, agree with the Jews to hold a *sulha*, a traditional Arab ceremony and meal to unite the families of murderer and murdered and resolve the outstanding grievance. About 400 attended in the Arab village, where the army's catering service provided an Arab-style meal. The chief rabbi of the nearby Jewish town of Petah Tikvah sent a message of goodwill. The village sheikh quoted a Muslim precept that "none fall, even by a killer's hand, until their allotted span has been completed." And an eighty-seven-year-old founder of Petah Tikvah, presiding over the ceremony, pleaded for the restoration of the good feeling that had existed for decades, noting that he had represented the Jews at many *sulhas* for murders in which Jews had been victims.[10]

Jews such as Dov Yermiya, born in Palestine before the Jewish state, also remember the decent relations that emerged out of conflict. He fought the Arabs, then befriended them. There were troubles in '21–'22, he said, in '29, and from '36 to '38. "When I settled in a kibbutz in the Galilee, we were fired upon by the Arabs who didn't want us there, in '38. But as soon as the troubles ceased, or stopped for a while, I managed to make good friends with the Arabs, and this friendship—not only did I enjoy it, it proved strong in the times of war that came afterwards. So my experience is that not only is it necessary, it's also possible."

Acts of terrorism and war, then, become the benchmarks of the Middle East, more definite than the fleeting seasons or the regularity of the calendars in measuring the distances between times of hatred, times of accord. They divide memory as precisely as the ticking of a clock.

Before 1948, before the first Arab-Jewish war, Jamil Hamad, now a journalist in the West Bank Arab village of Bethlehem, lived in a small town in Palestine called Rafat, near the Jewish town of Beit Shemesh. Rafat no longer exists; it was demolished in the 1948 war, when he and his family fled to the West Bank. But the memories exist strongly, and they are good ones. "To me, to all members of my family, the Jews were friendly," Jamil recalled. "We had very friendly relations. I never felt the mistrust. We played football. We would take them to our fields, give them presents—grapes, melons, eggs. They used to stay at our house. We used to stay at their houses." As a boy, he sometimes spent Friday nights with a Jewish friend in the next village. "I remember Shabbat evening," he said. "I loved to see them lighting the candles, praying in a language which I didn't understand. It was something I didn't have as a Muslim. I used to go back to my mother and father and ask, 'Why don't we have that?' To this very day I have a weakness for candles. I buy them frequently. When I have guests for dinner, I put a candle on the table and light it."

TWO

Nationalisms:
Paradise Lost

It is the poets whom the erring follow:
Seest thou not how they rove
distraught in every valley?
—Koran, Sura XXVI,
The Poets, Verses 224–225

THE SLIGHT, BAREFOOT BOY HAD NO PAST AND NO FUTURE. TWELVE
years earlier he had been born in the Jabaliya refugee camp, a crowded
slum of dirt paths and cinderblock houses on a squalid slice of desert
coastline, the Gaza Strip. There he was spending his childhood; there he
was likely to grow into adulthood, father his own children, and watch
them play along the same dusty pathways where he now invented games
and made toys from bottles and stones. There, to Jabaliya, his parents
and grandparents had fled in 1948 with other Palestinian Arabs from
Israel. But when he wandered one day into the raw concrete room of a
crudely built recreation center in the camp and someone asked him where

he was from, he did not say Jabaliya. He did not name the place of his birth, the place of his childhood, the place of his empty future. He pronounced another name, "Barbarit," and he spoke it with such disarming ease and clarity, his wide brown eyes so open and tender, that he made it sound real. Barbarit was his grandparents' village, up the coast in Israel, ten miles and four wars away. It was the place from which they had fled; it had been obliterated in the war of 1948, twenty years before the barefoot lad was born. Today it exists only in the memory—in a fantasy, really—and its orange groves are more voluptuous, its houses more luxurious, its life vastly sweeter than anything has ever been in reality. This is the Palestinian dream, a past and a future that imprison barefoot boys in rotting slums.

The politics of Palestinianism may feed on hypocrisy and cynical sloganeering, as much zealotry does, but the power of memory is authentic. And in the Palestinian memory, 1948 is the great divide, the parting of the fates of those who left and those who stayed. It marks the genesis of anger and regret, hatred and longing.

I encountered the strength of this in the war-torn summer of 1982, after the Israelis had ripped through Palestinian refugee camps along the Lebanese coast. The Israeli army tried to keep reporters out of the camps, but with the help of a sympathetic Israeli officer, I managed to enter Rashadiye, a camp on the beach south of the Lebanese city of Tyre. The fighting had been tough, and Palestinian boys of thirteen, fourteen, and fifteen had fired rocket grenades and wielded Kalashnikov rifles as the Israelis had attacked. After the battles, the Israelis had blown up shelters used also as bunkers, demolishing houses along with them, and had then sent bulldozers to cut swaths through the congested concrete homes. The slum was left half in ruins. Shreds of clothing and fragments of furniture lay twisted among the pulverized chunks of cement.

One of the residents picking through the remains was an old woman, Mariam Shaami. She was bent like a gnarled stick. Her eyes held a profound sadness, and she struggled on the edge of tears as she told me about the fighting, about the destruction, about her son, Hassan, lying dead somewhere beneath the ruins of her house, there; she pointed a bony finger. "I am completely broken," she said, mopping her eyes with a yellow tissue. "I lost my son, and my husband is sixty-four years old. There is nobody to look after us." She seemed ready to collapse into grief. But she did not do so—not until I asked her where she had come from originally, before '48. Then she sobbed and named a village in northern Israel called Bassa, and when I asked how life had been there, she wept in convulsive floods of sorrow at the memories of the beautiful house of her father and grandfather, the fields and olive groves of her childhood, the almond and fruit trees, the bananas and oranges. Although she had just endured fresh wounds, nothing opened the pain like the old ones; nothing released the ages of suffering like recollections of the tranquil contentment of her home in Palestine. She could hardly talk. She pointed to the ruins of her house. "I still have papers to land in Palestine," she gasped, "one hundred dunams," twenty-five acres. Now the papers were buried under the rubble.

Did she now wish that her family had stayed in 1948 to live in Israel? Oh, of course, yes, she said. And whom did she blame for all this hardship? Not the Jews, she said, and not her own Palestinian people, but the Arabs, by which she meant the larger Arab world, the Arab leaders, who had told her people to leave and had never helped enough to regain the land. "The blood of my son is equal to all the Arab governments," she declared bitterly.

I left her standing among the ruins. And at the end of the day, as we drove back down from Lebanon, through northern Israel, the Israeli officer gestured toward some old, broken walls of stone, half hidden in a field of unruly grass. That had been Bassa, he said, the old woman's village.

The longing for return is as integral to the Palestinian nationalism that has evolved since 1948 as it was, and is, to the Jewish Zionism that has moved thinkers and activists from the nineteenth century onward. Many Palestinian Arabs can see the futility of their dream now, recognizing that many of the old stone villages are gone for good from the terraced hills and citrus groves, knowing that an Arab Palestine cannot be created in the face of the powerful fact of a Jewish state. Many of those who think logically begin to divide their hopes into parts, to separate their desire for a return to what is now Israel from their aspiration for a more attainable Palestinian state that could be established, say, on the West Bank—not instead of Israel but next to it.

Nevertheless, the dream remains, even for those who know it is a dream, and it stirs more significant emotion than do the political nuances and intricate shifts of ambiguous position-taking by the professional Palestinian revolutionaries. A Jewish woman once went with an Arab to the ruins of his parents' village in Galilee; the residents had left in 1948 with promises from the Israelis that in three weeks they would be allowed to return. There was nothing there, and the young Arab man had not been born until years after the village had been abandoned. But as he took his Jewish friend through the ruins, he could point to this pile of stones and name the owner of the house, and to that broken wall and say who once resided there. "He wasn't even born," she said, amazed, "but he knows who lived where." Another Arab, from Haifa, made it a hobby to search for old, destroyed villages; only wells remained. And cactus always seems to grow there, planted—Arabs are convinced—by the Jews to thwart those who would explore and find and return.

Most Arabs who talk approvingly about a Palestinian state on the West Bank and Gaza Strip, living in coexistence with Israel, are natives of the West Bank or Gaza, not refugees from 1948. Or they are Israeli Arabs who never fled but remained through the '48 fighting and became Israeli citizens. They give up nothing by speaking of a state of such limited proportions, for they are already home and have no demolished villages to yearn for. By contrast, those who left in 1948, and especially those who still live in the slums that are called refugee camps, exist in an environment of intense indoctrination and political zeal whose obsession— the return—does not give way easily in a confrontation with pragmatism.

Moreover, the phenomenon of the refugee camp—of which there are sixty-one scattered throughout the West Bank, Gaza Strip, Jordan, Syria, and Lebanon—has become so central to the Palestinians' sense of duty and identity that the political leaders of Dheisheh, a militant Palestinian camp on the West Bank, reacted with alarm and protest to an Israeli suggestion in 1984 that its residents be dispersed into new, modern housing that would be built for them. Israel didn't have the money to follow through, but these Palestinians were ready to resist the charity and fight to maintain their visible suffering. "We feel that the camps are the mirrors of the Palestinian case," explained Hassan al-Jawad, a young man who grew up in Dheisheh. "Without the camps, I can say fully that the Palestinian case will not have a clear face."

Since Palestinian boys and girls in the camps are trained in their nationalism and schooled in its militant rhetoric, the intellectual atmosphere in which they are raised hardly resembles that of an open society. They grow up knowing what they are expected to think and to say, and they are conditioned to express a commitment without thought. Indeed, the camps are maintained by Palestinians themselves as monuments to their refugee status; the most militant among them fear that moving out and integrating into the surrounding Arab cities and farms would defeat their angry dream as completely as removing a thorn quiets pain. In effect, the world's major nations contribute to the cause by financially supporting the United Nations Relief and Works Agency, which administers the camps, runs their schools, and distributes food to those with refugee status. Most of the agency's local employees, whether teachers, doctors, or bureaucrats, are Palestinian nationalists, and outside Israeli jurisdiction the schools have often become explicit vehicles of political and military fervor. Examples were found in southern Lebanon after the Israeli invasion of 1982; near Sidon, Israeli officers showed reporters an UNRWA school where boys' rooms were papered with anti-Israel propaganda posters, their closets filled with combat uniforms, and their dormitory basements stocked with weapons and crates of ammunition.

Israeli authorities ruling the Gaza Strip and the West Bank prevent blatant militarization of the refugee camps, of course, but political indoctrination continues nonetheless, and young children inside the camps are more highly politicized than those outside. "Life in the camp is different from the city or the village," said Hassan al-Jawad. Hassan was thirty-one, wore a checked cabbie's cap, looked like Peter Lorre, and ran the youth center in Dheisheh.* "We teach our children. Everywhere you go there is something political you can touch. In the camps, every day you can see the soldiers; you can see the people go to prison from the camps and return after three years. In the camps, you can see people who have lost everything—land, houses, everything. I have a girl, three. She knows about Habash; she knows about Arafat."

In Dheisheh, as in Jabaliya, Palestinian children know the names of their parents' former villages in Israel and have pretty pictures of them in their minds. A ten-year-old, Issam, said that he was from Zakariya, whose site he has never visited, although he could do so easily. I asked him what he imagined it was like. "It's beautiful," he said. And what made it beautiful? "The kind of trees."

---

* In early 1986, Israeli authorities deported Hassan al-Jawad from the West Bank to Jordan.

. . .

The emotions are reinforced in the classroom. A Jordanian elementary-school reading textbook, used both in Jordan and surreptitiously in the West Bank, contains a passage called "Palestine."

"Palestine is my home and the path of my triumph. My homeland will remain the passion of my heart and the yearning melody on my lips. Strange faces are in my stolen land. They are selling my crops and occupying my home. I know my path and my people will return to my grandfather's home, to my warm cradle. Palestine is my home and the path of my triumph."

Another textbook includes poetry written in a traditional style of high-flown melodrama. By Abd al-Karim al-Karmi:

Palestine

Beloved Palestine, how will I live
Far from your plains and hillocks?
The bloodstained mountains summon me
In the horizon traces of tint linger
The crying seashores summon me
Time still echoes with sobbing
The bereft streams summon me
They depart without being strangers
Your orphaned cities summon me
Your villages with domes summon me

Friends ask, "When will we meet again?"
Are we to return after the absence?
Tomorrow we will return while the generations are listening
To each resounding step
We will return with the roar of the storms
With the resounding thunder and flame
With bleeding banners
Over the glitter of the lance's spearhead
And we, the revolutionaries, throughout the land
We will be welded together in the blaze of the neck yokes
So that the thousands of victims will return
Victims of iniquity, open every door!

Another writer popular with young West Bank Palestinians is Ghassan Kanafani, who was born in Acre, Palestine (now Akko, Israel), and worked as the spokesman for George Habash's Popular Front for the Liberation of Palestine before he was killed when his booby-trapped car exploded in 1972. His novels and short stories are filled with fervent, melodramatic yearnings to return and accounts of the hardship facing those exiled in the Palestinian diaspora. *Letter from Gaza* is a stirring call to Palestinian patriotism ending with a plea to return to Gaza. *Men in the Sun*, the title story in a collection of vignettes and short stories, tells the tragedy of three homeless Palestinians who, seeking good jobs, arrange to be smuggled for a fee from Jordan through the Iraqi desert to Kuwait. They ride in a tanker truck, and at each checkpoint, they climb into the empty tank to hide. Under the desert sun, the tank grows fearfully hot. At the second border crossing the driver is delayed, and the men in the tank die. He leaves their bodies on a garbage dump in the desert.

Although membership in the PLO is illegal on the West Bank, radical factions of the organization operate politically in Dheisheh, where the chemistry of Palestinian zealotry and Israeli occupation produces a vicious hostility. At one point, reacting to stone-throwing by camp youths, the Israeli army built cinderblock and concrete walls across all the roads leading from the camp to the main highway, sealing direct exits and forcing the 5,000 residents to take circuitous routes in and out of the slum. They smile angrily as they call their camp their "ghetto," relishing the opportunity to turn the language of Jewish suffering against the Jews. They enjoy symbols of their nationalism, such as the wall of a bedroom painted in the black, red, green, and white of the prohibited Palestinian flag. They wear sweatshirts with portraits of Che Guevara in the Palestinian colors. On the back of one boy's shirt were the numerals 12-11. I asked what they meant. "That," the boy answered, "was the date of the founding of the front of Habash."

It may be tempting to see Palestinian nationalism as artificial, a contrived argument mouthed by manipulated youths and adults who are either afraid to speak differently or simply know no other line of political attitude than that provided by one of the groups under the umbrella of the PLO. Many Israeli Jews tend to this view, feeling that Palestinians have no legitimate nationalism, no real peoplehood, no case. Policymakers have long acted on the assumption that if the PLO were eliminated, the "silenced majority" on the West Bank, for example, would be content to live peacefully under Israeli domination, foresaking the avowed aspirations for statehood. This has led Israel into substantial miscalculations, including its invasion of Lebanon, which was supposed to destroy the PLO and thereby induce a compliant abandonment of nationalism by West Bank residents. The Palestinians' national desires have proved more deeply rooted than the Israeli political establishment has been willing to recognize.

So alive and blinding is the dream that it has distorted elementary history for at least one Palestinian girl, an Arab teenager whose family had stayed in Israel in 1948. During a workshop for a mixed group of Arab and Jewish high-school students, the girl expressed the conviction that there had once been a Palestinian state, before it was destroyed by Zionism. She was mixing up Palestine as it had existed under the British Mandate, before modern Israel was born, with "Palestine" as a political aspiration, where it meant a future state to be run by Palestinians. None of the other Arab youngsters corrected her when she made the assertion, and when the Jewish students tried to set her straight, she did not believe them until they later produced an encyclopedia to prove their point. Then she was shocked. The misinformation would have been less surprising in a well-indoctrinated resident of a refugee camp in Syria. But this girl, living in Israel, had been educated in an Israeli school system for Arabs, a system carefully scrubbed clean of all suggestions of Palestinianism; she had absorbed her ideas not in the classroom but in the streets.

Palestine, like Zion, has become an idyllic place of return, a force of national hope blessed with perfection. Some Arabs who fled in 1948 are immersed in complex attachments and dreams that fasten variously on what is now Israel proper and on the land to which they fled—the West Bank—which they also regard as inherently Palestinian. These overlapping affections are described by Raja Shehadeh, a reflective lawyer in the West Bank town of Ramallah, who recalls, in his passionately written book *The Third Way*, a day in which his adulthood confronted his childhood, his adulthood of commitment to the West Bank, where he grew up, and his childhood spent looking at the hills and lights of Jaffa, inside Israel, from which his parents came.

> I walked out into the hills—away from the streets littered with the remains of burning tires, the children running from soldiers, the shop doors welded shut by the army—I walked out into the world

of my childhood. I stood on the westernmost point of the Ramallah hills and heard again the voices of the grown-ups, like a recurring chant: "We are here in Ramallah only for a while. We are camping here until the day we return to our lovely land. Soon our *gurba* [exile] will end." And they would stand with me where I stood today, and point out to the sea on the west and say: "Our land is there, where the plains are green and the orchards abundant." And this is how I grew up—thinking of our house as a campsite in hard, dry land. I would spend hours in the rocky hills with thistles around, looking out toward the blue, hazy, soft spot where the sea nestled. And I saved my love for that magic land, and at night Jaffa's lights filled my dreams. It did not matter that other lands were accessible. It was there that I wanted to be—here in rocky Ramallah I was only camping.

As I sat on a stone today looking west, I felt it all, vividly. And I tried to remember when it was that I realized I loved this rocky land, when I began to treat it as mine. I suddenly remembered seeing—very early on, when the occupation began—a group of Jewish schoolchildren near Ayn Kinya. A sign on a bus nearby said that the tour was organized by the American Zionist Youth Movement. Four older boys, about my age, guarded the pupils with submachine guns. I remember the hate, the hurt anger that I felt when I heard the instructor telling the boys that the olive trees they saw were the offspring of those planted by their patriarch Abraham, and that the terraces were built by the ancient Jews, who after years of wandering in the wilderness settled in the Promised Land. And then the instructor said in a harsh, nasal English that I can hear now: "See how badly this land is treated. It cries for you—for its true beloved sons to tend it back to life. You will make it bloom again."

And I remember now how I looked about at the land he was pointing at, at the hills I had quietly loved while my more romantic dreams were fastened on Jaffa; and thought: you treacherous hills, lying there so modest and silent. Soft and treacherous hills, you are a harlot, slyly seducing these boys. And I remember how, from then on, I grew increasingly jealous, possessive and angry at the same time. I finally began thinking of this land as seducing us all into war—calling us into its lap to fall bleeding—a vampire that will suck our blood as we fight for it. You, who were only a temporary camp for us—now we will die for you—you have pulled these boys here as Jaffa pulled them—again we shall die for our land.[11]

In person, Raja Shehadeh is understated, a small, bony man with intense merriment in his dark eyes and quiet precision to his conversation. When I sat with him in his law office on Main Street in Ramallah—the room musty, redolent of old books—he spoke of the uncomfortable confrontation of his fantasy about Palestine with the reality, about the imagination that was nurtured before the 1967 war as he looked from his home ground on the West Bank out across the Jordanian border into Israel. "I grew up with Palestine, the Promised Land, where everything was all right and would be all right, the lights could be seen in the evening, and so on," he said. "I think it's a very unhealthy thing, by the way. You can put anything on that [image] which you cannot reach." And then the 1967 war came, and suddenly Israel, in possession of the West Bank, was accessible to Raja Shehadeh and other West Bank Palestinians who had been brought up on the dream. He quickly discovered that the dream did not exist. "I had to make the bridge, which wasn't easy, between living with this paradise lost and then suddenly going back to it."

Israeli Arabs do not always find it easy to make clear judgments on whether it was better to run or to stay in 1948. Longtime residents of Jaffa, which has now been incorporated into Tel Aviv, still refer to new Jewish neighborhoods of high-rises by the names of the Arab families whose citrus groves used to be on those spots. It is a vocabulary of nostalgia and defiance. Bishara Bisharat, a physician whose parents left a small village in the Galilee and stayed in the Israeli city of Nazareth, pondered my question about whether he would rather that they had fled to Lebanon, as others from their village did. "I don't know—maybe it would have been worse, maybe better," he said. "When they came to Nazareth, they were refugees. I remember, we were eight years in one room, all my family, four children, three boys and one girl, with my father and mother and grandmother. In the same room. One room. And it was not a strong room. It had a thatched roof. There was a kitchen and a bathroom in the same room. Until I was about seven or eight. Father became a simple worker. He started with nothing. Sometimes I say I am lucky that we stayed here, sometimes not so much. Sometimes we look just at the economic situation, and it's not bad. Sometimes we look to freedom, and also in this it's not easy to think if it's better in Israel or to be in Lebanon now. The situation of the Palestinians is difficult all over the world—also here. But we're lucky that we stayed in our land."

The ambivalence, tinged with guilt, is reflected in other comments by Israeli Arabs who sometimes seem to feel that they must apologize for having failed to leave. "I had a café," explained an Arab man in Jaffa. "I sold coffee and tea. My father was blind, my mother was old. Where could I go? I think most of those who left thought they were going for a week. They left all their things in the house—money, jewels, gold. They heard about the pogroms they did in villages. The Jews made propaganda."

Pogroms. Ghettos. It is striking how thoroughly Palestinians have absorbed the language of the Holocaust, not merely as a propaganda technique but also as a badge of emulation, a sign of symmetry, a measure of how much they have learned from Zionism in fashioning their own Palestinian nationalism. Sometimes "Zionism" even creeps into their vocabulary in describing their own movement, despite the word's having become a term of the gravest opprobrium, one with the most sinister connotations when applied to Jews. "We have a Zionist dream in the future," said Hassan al-Jawad, of the Dheisheh camp; he was referring to the dream of Palestinian statehood.

Jamil Hamad, the Palestinian journalist from Bethlehem, saw the parallels. "The Palestinians bought the Holocaust symphony from the Jews to play their own way," he said, "so there is a Palestinian symphony around the West Bank and all over the Arab world: We suffered too much, we have been killed, we have been bombed, etc."

Two Palestinians from Gaza, speaking to a Jewish audience at Hebrew University, used these techniques in a way that intrigued Irene Eber, a Jewish professor there. "I was struck by their attempt to fit their recent Palestinian history into some kind of context that would make sense to Jews," she observed. "One of the things they said was this: that everybody on the West Bank, everybody in Gaza has a member of the family in Lebanon, in one of the Palestinian camps. Everybody in the West Bank and in Gaza has lost someone in that struggle in Lebanon. Everybody—and I'm filling this in—has a martyr. And everybody can make that kind of claim, that we have paid with our blood, we have made the blood sacrifice. We are paying with our blood, we are making this sacrifice, and therefore we cannot stop our struggle, because already too much blood has been spent. Now, I would say that the Jewish audience completely lost this; they just didn't hear it. It passed them. They didn't react to it. They didn't see it. And to me it was so clear. They all have someone who has died for the cause, and what is the cause? For a Palestinian state, and therefore there must be a Palestinian state. We cannot stop."

The Israeli writer Amos Oz conveys his sense of symmetry on a visit to the Arabic newspaper *Al-Fajr* in East Jerusalem. "The atmosphere in the editorial offices is similar, perhaps, to that in the office of a Hebrew-language journal or a Yiddish newspaper in Eastern Europe before the Fall: poverty and enthusiasm, lofty rhetoric and irritating prosaic hardships, poetry and politics."[12]

The Palestinians are demanding Jewish recognition of their suffering, the acknowledgment that they too have endured losses and hardship. And so they exaggerate that hardship, inflating it into a parallel with the Jewish suffering at the hands of the Nazis; the argument promotes only indignation from the majority of Jews. In the background stands the Arabs' culture of honor and face, a flowing style of ritual courtesy that few Western Jews in Israel are equipped to understand, let alone acquiesce in. Many Jewish military and police officials who grasp the extreme value the Arabs place on honor see it as a point of vulnerability and turn it against the Arabs by adopting the weapon of humiliation. Neither side really looks into the other's eyes.

The dynamics of suffering and honor figured in an analysis by Albert Aghazarian, an Armenian who lives in the Old City of Jerusalem and who regards himself, by culture and affinity, as both an Armenian and a Palestinian. He teaches and does public-relations work at the Palestinians' Bir Zeit University on the West Bank, and he endorses wholeheartedly the Palestinian nationalism that surrounds him.

"This is very simply like a house that was on fire and somebody's skin was burning," Albert said. "So he [the Jew] jumped out of the window to avoid the fire. He falls on the neck of somebody else [the Arab]. He breaks his neck. The one who lost his neck is complaining, and when he complains he receives the first punch. 'Can't you see that fire? Can't you see my skin?' he says.

" 'But my neck is really hurting.' When he keeps saying 'My neck,' then he gets the blow, he breaks his arm, and when he breaks his arm, he tells him, 'Why the hell do you do that? What wrong do I do to you?' And he breaks his other arm. He goes on breaking bone after bone while saying 'My skin' and 'The fire' and 'Look at the bruises and the scar I have.' This man [who jumped] is either deciding not to see that man, to break him in the dark, or to wish he would disappear and become invisible. The first thing you have to recognize is the legitimacy of the suffering of that man. Once you do that, the main issues will be resolved."

Albert may have been much too optimistic in believing that the conflict could be resolved by recognizing the Palestinians' suffering, but he put his finger on an element of the evolving parallels between the Palestinian and Jewish nationalisms. From his personal background he added the Armenian experience—the massacres at the hands of the Turks between 1915 and 1923—and saw similarities among all three. "Basically you have a people living on their land," he explained. "You uproot these people; maybe they are forced in a dislocated way to live in urban setups. Due to their circumstances they have to have some elements of excellence. You recognize that they are dynamic—good artists, doctors, lawyers, bankers, what have you. But they do not have any national or political rights. They have to be dispersed all over the place. They have constantly to challenge to what degree they want to assimilate or not, you see."

Indeed, Palestinians have used the Jewish experience in shaping their own response to their rejection and dispersal, and well-educated Palestinians living under Israeli control speak often of an unconscious Jewish-Palestinian interaction. In some measure, Palestinians also behave according to universal patterns among minorities in many cultures—and the Palestinians are a minority in two contexts, both as a small group among Arabs in the Middle East and as a less numerous and weaker group among the Jews who rule west of the Jordan River.

Like Jews in the Diaspora, Palestinians have stressed education as a way up for their children. "They feel the same way as the Jews," said Sammy Smooha, a sociologist at Haifa University. "Education is the most important thing. What do you want your son to be? They give you exactly the same answers as the Jews. They want him to be university educated, in the top occupations. They don't want their children to be farmers, to be workers. I call this the Israelization of the Arabs. They are deeply immersed in Israeli values and society. This is also a special quality of Palestinian society: You have to have movable property, and education is that."

Several Palestinian universities have been established and expanded on the West Bank since the Israeli occupation began in 1967, and many Palestinian families have pushed their children into higher learning either on the West Bank or abroad—in the Soviet Union, the United States, England, and Arab countries—for college degrees in medicine, engineering, and other practical fields. As one result, a surplus of Palestinian physicians has developed on the West Bank, many of whose residents have gone looking for jobs elsewhere, contributing to a large and scattered Palestinian diaspora. When I once asked how many people there were in a certain West Bank village, the *mukhtar*, or village leader, said, "Three thousand inside, three thousand outside." Most of those outside lived in New Jersey and Chicago. Many have gone to work on lucrative jobs in the Persian Gulf region. There and elsewhere in the Arab world, Palestinians tend to see themselves as more cultured, intelligent, and educated than non-Palestinian Arabs, who in turn apply to Palestinians stereotypes that are often echoes of the age-old bigotry against Jews as cleverly ambitious, arrogant, and suspiciously smart with money.

I asked Ibrahim Kareen, an East Jerusalem Palestinian who ran a pro-PLO news service, whether he saw Palestinian-Jewish parallels. "Yes," he answered. "Both of us are arrogant. We think of ourselves as distinguished in the Arab world. They think of themselves as distinguished in the world as a whole. It is true. We make fun of ourselves, Palestinians; we say every two Palestinians need three chairs. All of us are leaders. So you talk with the people in the café, they'll give you the best analysis of the situation, political analysis. Very hardworking, productive. Modestly speaking, the Gulf areas—Saudi Arabia, Kuwait—are indebted to the Palestinians. We have built their countries. We have built Jordan." The arguments resemble the Israelis' wisecracks that every Jew thinks he's a prime minister, that if you have three Jews you'll have five opinions. The Palestinians have acquired a duplicate, Jewish notion of themselves as highly politicized, hardworking, creative, and alone.

In many families, the Palestinian devotion to education has become enshrined only in the last generation. Ibrahim's father, a stonecutter who barely finished elementary school, "was a top student," Ibrahim said. "But my grandfather took him out of school and bought him a donkey so he could earn money." When he grew up and had children of his own, however, he pushed them into education. "My father forced my two elder brothers to finish school," said Ibrahim, who then became the first in his family to go to college.

He saw other Jewish-Palestinian parallels as well, between the Israeli army and the PLO, for example, which he distinguished sharply from the standing Arab armies. In Israel, "when there is a call for reserve duty, everyone goes," he said admiringly, "in contrast with Arab countries, where everyone will run away. In Arab countries, it is not fair. If you have a good relationship [with an official], your son is not drafted. Here, things are different: Everyone goes. I think to some extent the PLO forces might be similar to the Israelis in the sense that they enlist; there is order when needed and disorder when it is not needed. And everyone is an officer. There are discussions."

These tensions between Palestinians and other Arabs are scarcely noticed in the Israeli ideology of nationalism, which tends to lump Palestinians into the larger Arab world, arguing that some of the twenty-two Arab countries could absorb them and thus solve the "Palestinian problem." The former chief of staff of the army, Lieutenant General Raphael ("Raful") Eitan, was fond of telling Arabs to go elsewhere if they had complaints, a tactic he once used during an address to a mixed group of Arab and Jewish students at Ben-Gurion University in Beersheba. It was a turbulent crowd, divided into two camps, with most Jews supporting Raful, and all the Arabs, plus a smattering of Jews, opposing him. One of the Arabs in the audience was Azziz Awad, a young, slim, good-looking Israeli citizen who was devoting long hours of his own time trying to promote understanding by helping to conduct meetings and workshops between Arab and Jewish high-school students. He believed in coexistence. Raful obviously did not, and his coarse rantings ignited fury among the Arabs.

"What's the future of the Arabs on the West Bank?" someone yelled. Raful was silent for a long moment, as if framing an answer. So Azziz shouted from the back of the hall, "Another Sabra and Shatila!"

"Where are you from?" Raful asked in the style of an interrogator.

"Nazareth," answered Azziz. The general lived four miles down the road from Nazareth.

"Your place is not here," said Raful. "Your place is in Saudi Arabia."

A Jewish soldier then spoke up, saying to the retired general, "I'm ashamed that you're in the Israeli army."

The exchange made headlines in the Israeli press, and I asked Raful about it when I visited him at his moshav, or farming village, of Tel Adashim. He was working out behind his house, hammering big nails sloppily into a broken board. Wearing blue work clothes with a piece of rope as a belt, he growled at me as I approached, shook my hand roughly, and kept hammering as we talked, stopping occasionally to glare at me with a steady dullness. "They're all the same thing," he said of Arabs in Israel and the West Bank. "They say that they're our enemies." As for the student at the university, "I said, 'What are you yelling for? Go to Saudi Arabia if you want to yell.' "

As a rhetorical device, this is convenient for escaping any Israeli responsibility, but it fails to see that Palestinians feel themselves a distinct minority group within the diverse, fractious Arab world, that their history is special to them, that their spoken accent identifies them immediately, that they face discrimination in many forms and often detest other Arabs as much as other Arabs detest them. Nationalist Palestinians in Jerusalem and the West Bank, for example, speak of their modern history as a series of occupations—by the Ottoman Turks, then the British, then the Jordanians, now the Israelis. In terms of that consciousness, the Jordanians were no more palatable than the Israelis, and perhaps less so: They were tougher and less tolerant of political expression than the Israelis, and being subject to their oppression was more complicated emotionally because they were Arabs. A Palestinian friend of mine in East Jerusalem explained that it was easier being occupied by Jews, who were naturally defined as enemies, whom you could hate without reserve, than by Arabs, who were supposed to be your brothers, and with whom you were not inevitably locked in conflict.

Just as the Jews of Israel have rejected the submissiveness of what they call the "Diaspora mentality" and have embraced a value of toughness, so militant Palestinians on the West Bank often see compromise as collaboration and look with distaste on their conciliatory cousins, especially those in Israel proper, who function as citizens of the Jewish state. Some Palestinians seek to emulate the Jews' resilience and perseverance. "For two thousand years you could not destroy the Jews," said Ibrahim Kareen respectfully. "They maintained, they persisted, they achieved." Now, some West Bank Arabs are trying to match the Jews' persistence by standing fast, by remaining on the West Bank, not moving out, and by rejecting both collaboration and radicalism. Such a man is called *samid*, meaning "the steadfast," "the persevering," and Raja Shehadeh has made it the theme of his book *The Third Way*, on life in the West Bank. "Between mute submission and blind hate—I choose the third way," he writes. "I am Samid."

In our conversation, Raja said he saw a symmetry between the Palestinian and Jewish uses of violence, at least in their psychological roots. "I think the experience of the PLO taking arms could be similar to the experience of the Jews when Zionism resorted to arms and strength as deliverance," Shehadeh said. "There has been a similar revolution among many people: We no longer are going to be submissive; we are going to take our fate in our own hands. Maybe there is a similar strain of stubbornness. It's a very strong and important psychological change which Jews in Israel completely refuse to deal with."

Against the broad sweep of human history, nationalisms are fairly recent, transitory political impulses, arising in western Europe after the French Revolution and going on to crystallize the aspirations to statehood that swept the post-colonial world. They emerge and then melt away with the shifting patterns of conquest and domination. But they are also heirs to the deeper tribal, religious, and ethnic forces that have defined the boundaries of group identity, moving peoples into hatred and warfare that have shaped the landscape of intolerance since the first recording of man's deeds. And especially so on this land, scarred by thousands of years through which the names of victors and vanquished have loomed large for a moment and then vanished.

Jewish nationalism is among those recent phenomena, developing as Zionism in the nineteenth century but drawing its intellectual and emotional context from the ancient history of the Jew in conflict with his surroundings. For the early Zionists, this was a continuum of suffering, a sense of apartness that found sustenance amid persecution, bigotry, and exile. From slavery and exile in Babylon, the Jews sang the psalm "If I forget thee, O Jerusalem, let my right hand forget her cunning. / If I do not remember thee, let my tongue cleave to the roof of my mouth; if I prefer not Jerusalem above my chief joy." Each Passover, the Seder, the ceremonial meal at which Jews celebrate the ancient Israelites' exodus from Egypt, has ended with the dream, the pledge, "Next year in Jerusalem." And when the movement known as Lovers of Zion developed in the early 1880s in Russia, it did so in response to the pogroms of

1881, but it found an ancient source of passion. A manifesto by one segment of the movement declared:

> Nearly two thousand years have elapsed since, in an evil hour, after a heroic struggle, the glory of our Temple vanished in fire and our kings and chieftains changed their crowns and diadems for the chains of exile. We lost our country where dwelt our beloved sires. Into the Exile we took with us, of all our glories, only a spark of the fire by which our Temple, the abode of our Great One, was engirdled, and this little spark kept us alive while the towers of our enemies crumbled into dust . . . and this spark is again kindling and will shine for us, a true pillar of fire going before us on the road to Zion, while behind us is a pillar of cloud, the pillar of oppression threatening to destroy us.[13]

Zionism gained momentum precisely where persecution of Jews was most severe, reaching a climax under Nazi Germany and opening the way to a large-scale exodus of Jews from Europe to Palestine. In this, the Jews were left entirely alone, without significant help even from Germany's enemies: Many Israelis whose nationalism shaped the early contours of the Jewish state, and many who remain in positions of influence in today's Israel, arrived by ships through a blockade set up by the British to curb the numbers of Jews entering Palestine. Those the British did not let through were met offshore at night and ferried clandestinely in small boats, or they jumped overboard and swam through the Mediterranean surf to the beach. Ephraim Sharir arrived that way and more than thirty years later became mayor of the town of Nahariya, which grew into a pleasant seaside resort right at the spot where he had landed. Others who were turned away by the British ended up back in Europe, still in the Nazis' grasp.

Theo Siebenberg came by a more circuitous route, but he then went to untold financial expense to establish connections. Born in Antwerp of a wealthy diamond family, he survived the Holocaust, went to South America, and moved finally to Jerusalem, where he built a house in the Jewish Quarter of the Old City, reconstructed by the Israelis after 1967. Once his modern house was up, he decided to excavate beneath it; years of digging and hauling dirt out on the backs of donkeys revealed a cistern, a ritual bath, and other remains of a Jewish house that had evidently been burned when the Romans destroyed the Second Temple in A.D. 70. Above, in his modern home, he placed a more recent artifact, a chandelier that he had retrieved from his parents' house in Antwerp, still intact when he returned after the war. And so the links were welded full round, from deep in the ancient earth to the crystal delicacy of survival.

In 1981, ninety-nine years after the Lovers of Zion had issued their declaration of survival—"while the towers of our enemies crumbled into dust"—the same theme reverberated through an address of remembrance and victory given by Menachem Begin, who stood near the Western Wall in Jerusalem as prime minister of Israel at the close of a gathering of survivors of the Holocaust. It was a soft summer evening, the throngs were hushed, the wall was bathed in glowing light beneath the golden Dome of the Rock of the Muslims. *"Mir zaynen do,"* he declared in Yiddish. "We are here. Where is the emperor? Where is his might? Where is Rome? Jerusalem lives forever. We are here."

Rarely does the victory of nationhood ring with such solemn tones of stirring nobility as it did that evening at the conjunction of ancient symbols and modern survival in Jerusalem. As the Greek dramatists knew, tragedy contains beauty.

But the Jews cannot see it in the Palestinians, and the Palestinians cannot see it in the Jews.

In essence, Jewish and Palestinian identities are now intricately bound up together. Palestinian nationalism has been used cynically by non-Palestinian Arabs as a spearhead against what they see as the alien implant of the Jews in the Middle East. And Jewish nationalism, after nearly forty years of success, owes its vibrance not only to the ancient trials and modern Holocaust, not only to global anti-Semitism, but also to the current confrontation with the Arabs. Each relies on the other.

Much of the Arabs' nostalgia for their pre-1948 Palestine, I came to feel, was the product less of sweet memories than of current anti-Zionism. Much Arab political commentary pictures Judaism as a religion, not a nationality, and Zionism is thereby portrayed as an artificial nationalism without logical basis. For the Arabs, the word "Zionism" has an ugly connotation that stirs a deep revulsion and dread, with overtones as heavy as those that "communism" carries for many Americans. " 'Zionist,' in Arabic is like 'Nazi,' " one Arab explained. "Since I was a child I have heard that the word Zionist is the worst. I didn't understand the meaning of it. I just thought Zionist was like criminal, thief, killer."

These emotions emerged on a winter evening at the Hebrew University campus on Mount Scopus, overlooking the Old City of Jerusalem. Under the auspices of the Jewish organization Hillel House, fifteen to twenty Arab and Jewish students gathered occasionally in a classroom for conversations—somewhat structured versions of college bull sessions. They sat around the edges of the room, facing each other in a lopsided ellipse. The subject this session—terrorism—eventually dissolved into a discussion of Zionism. "It always does," one of the student leaders said later.

Gamal, a thin young Arab, declared his opposition to the very idea of Zionism, which he portrayed as some evil curse with "a tendency to spread more and more."

Orna, a slim, dark Jewish student who had helped organize the meeting, countered that Zionism was not a monolith but a collection of varied ideas. "The one thing that unites all is that they believe in the right of Jews to a state. Within this there is a minority: I'm ready to give up the Golan Heights and to divide Jerusalem. But I see myself as a Zionist. I oppose the government completely, but I see myself as a Zionist."

"I was talking about *real* Zionism," said Gamal.

The group broke out into some good-natured shouting. "What's a Zionist? You saying that she's Arik Sharon?" said a Jewish man, referring to the hard-line former defense minister.

"What's a real Muslim? What's a real Arab?" asked another Jew, and the students laughed.

"What's Zionism for you?" an Arab wanted to know. And there followed a lengthy attempt at finding a definition, with many of the Jews, who were political liberals, arguing that just as socialism took many forms, so did Zionism, that as Israeli Jews they could be both Zionist and conciliatory about borders, about relations with Arabs, about the virtue of establishing an adjacent Palestinian state. Significantly, the Arab students found this almost impossible to accept. The Arabs knew most of the Jews fairly well, knew them as sympathetic and humane young people who simply did not fit their frightening image of Zionists. "You're not a Zionist," one said to a Jewish student who had just espoused a liberal line. "You're different from Zionists."

"I want to ask Monir," Orna said finally to one of the Arab students, "do you understand what my Zionism is?"

"I understand," said Monir, who then went on to demonstrate that he did not understand at all. "If you think a Palestinian state should be set up here, then you're against Zionism."

For most Israeli Jews—not the liberal-minded students in that classroom—Palestinianism is rejected with equally profound emotion. "I am a Palestinian," said a middle-aged Jew born in Palestine before the establishment of Israel. He smiled sardonically. In one quick utterance, he had affirmed his claim to the land and usurped the Arab Palestinians' identity. I heard this often from Israelis who wanted to underscore the absurdity of the Arabs' assertions of exclusive rights to the territory between the Jordan and the Mediterranean.

Partly, it is the newness of Palestinian nationalism, as distinct from older Arab nationalisms that developed at the beginning of the twentieth century, that draws dismissal and contempt from Israeli Jews. The Palestinians did not recognize themselves as a people until the most recent instant of history, and mainly in response to the establishment and growth of the Jewish state. This fact permits a derisive comment in a ninth-grade Hebrew-language textbook, *The History of the People of Israel*: "Only from the year 1959 and onward did these states—especially Egypt, Syria, and Iraq—raise in the meetings of the Arab League . . . the concept of 'the Palestinian entity' . . . and Palestinian rights in order to strengthen their propaganda against the state of Israel. . . . Israel is the only state in this region whose people—the people of Israel—has lived in the same land, spoken the same language, maintained tradition which has not been severed, and retained the same tie here for 3,000 years."

A more sophisticated approach is taken by a 1979 high-school textbook, *The Arab-Israeli Conflict*, which speaks of the "strong feeling of local identification which the refugees had—not as Palestinians but rather as residents of Haifa, Akko, Jaffa, and the other cities and villages from which they came." The passage continues, "The conflict is also a competition between two attachments. Our awareness that Arabs too have an attachment to this land doesn't have to detract from our attachment to the land."

Nevertheless, it is too threatening for all but a tiny fraction of Israeli Jews to accept the legitimacy of Palestinians' national striving. A 1980 study found only 11 percent of Jewish respondents in Israel favoring the recognition of a Palestinian nation.[14] There is a willful blindness reinforced by political and security concerns. The Palestinians are faceless.

During the 1982 invasion of Lebanon, for example, the Israeli estimates of casualties among the Arabs in southern Lebanon excluded Palestinians in the refugee camps, although they were hardest hit, and included only Lebanese in the cities. Even the 1982 massacres in the Beirut camps, and the outrage among the Israeli public that followed, failed to change the style of thinking in Israeli officialdom. When an explosion destroyed a multi-story building in Tyre, Lebanon, that was being used as an Israeli headquarters and interrogation center, the army, in providing casualty figures, simply ignored the Arabs who were killed. As bodies were dug out of the rubble, the army issued bulletins updating the number of dead; reporters finally realized that Arabs who had been held in the building as prisoners were not being counted, as if they had never existed. *

A subtler discrimination is practiced daily in the Israeli press, where Arab life is often rated as less valuable than Jewish life. An illustration came September 25, 1983, when a grenade went off on the West Bank, and Israel Radio reported on its English news broadcast, "Two Israeli soldiers were wounded this morning when a hand grenade was thrown in the center of Nablus." Then, almost as an afterthought, it added, "Three local Arabs were also hurt."

Occasionally a Jew runs against the current of denial that usually swallows Israelis' views of Palestinianism, but in doing so he serves only to illuminate the denial itself. After the Six-Day War of 1967, the Arabs of East Jerusalem wanted to erect a monument in honor of the men who had died fighting on their side. Naturally, the Israelis, as their new rulers, were emotionally opposed to symbols of Arab heroism in the wake of the warfare. But one Israeli official, Deputy Mayor Meron Benvenisti, of Jerusalem, endorsed the Arabs' request and finally persuaded Mayor Teddy Kollek and others to go along.

"I had the revolutionary idea of telling the Jews, 'Listen, these people who fought and died to defend their part of the city are heroes in the eyes of their people,' " Meron said. " 'And therefore their claim to put up a monument is justified, and therefore I'm going to fight for it.' And

---

* Initially the army attributed the explosion to a car bomb and later to a gas leak.

people said. 'Would you accept a memorial in the midst of Hyde Park for the Luftwaffe pilots who fell bombing London?' I said, 'If this is your perception of the situation, then this is precisely what I'm going to tell you: that these people are not invaders. They live here. These people are not murderers, they are heroes, like we are heroes killing their people.' And I forced Kollek to accept it."

But the arguments that worked were couched in terms of the Jews' self-interest. "I used pacification terminology," Meron explained with some feeling of guilt. " 'You need to give these people an outlet, a safety valve. If they want to demonstrate, this is where they will demonstrate. It is a good place because not many people can gather there. They cannot bring thousands there because it is a very steep slope.' " And so the small monument was erected in East Jerusalem, near the Rockefeller Museum of archaeology.

Israel attempts to draw a legal blank across the Palestinians' sense of national identity. The Palestinian flag is outlawed, as is any expression of support for the Palestine Liberation Organization, and the prohibition is enforced even by those Arabs who agree to work for the Jews. An acquaintance of mine doing army reserve duty on the West Bank once saw a Bedouin sergeant on the street grab an Arab boy who had drawn a Palestinian flag in his chemistry notebook, take him around a corner, rap him on the hands and the behind with a wooden club, and then let him go—a form of summary punishment.

The name "Palestine" is also usually prohibited, and some Israelis have a visceral objection to applying the term "Palestinians" to Arabs. Although a few Palestine Streets appear here and there on the West Bank, the Israelis have managed to purge most institutions of the name. To sing a Palestinian song, to scrawl the word "Palestine" on a wall, is a political crime. The Palestine Press Service, a pro-Fatah* news agency in East Jerusalem that gathers and disseminates information about Israeli oppression on the West Bank, was told by the government to drop the "Palestine" because it was "offensive to public opinion." The authorities would not register anything called "Palestine Press" as a company, so the agency filed suit, lost in a lower court and then abandoned the legal

---

* Al-Fatah is the main faction of the PLO, headed by Yasir Arafat.

struggle, leaving the matter in limbo—that is, remaining unregistered with the "Palestine" still in its name. The government took no further action. But Jewish reporters for the Jewish-owned, English-language *Jerusalem Post* sometimes get hassled by Jewish policemen and soldiers who check their press cards, which carry the formal name of the company that owns their newspaper, created under the British Mandate: the Palestine Post, Ltd. "I get a lot of trouble about that from young cops and soldiers who don't know the history," one reporter said.

The deep aversion to the word Palestine is an effort to dismiss the nationalist aspirations of the Palestinians as artificial. "We cannot stand a symmetry of claims," said Meron Benvenisti. "Israelis have a profound feeling that once they accept the symmetry that the other side is also a legitimate national movement, then their own feeling about their own right and legitimacy will be dimmed. They do not conceive of the conflict as a national conflict."

A dramatic Israeli move against Palestinian nationalism came when Israeli troops entered West Beirut in September 1982. Among their objectives was a concrete building housing the research center of the Palestine Liberation Organization. Inside were shelves and files of books and documents on the history of Palestine, on pre-1948 Arab villages and families, on major events of these turbulent decades. The troops entered and took everything, shipped it all back to Israel, studied it, and returned it only when required to do so fourteen months later as one of the conditions laid down by the PLO for the release of six Israeli soldiers who had been taken prisoner during the Lebanon fighting. It was as if Israel had tried to steal the Palestinians' past and identity, as if the Israelis could not stand to see the Palestinians have a historical archive. "This was not only to destroy them as a political or a military power," said Benvenisti, "but also to take from them their history, to erase that because it is troublesome. This was a profound need or urge not to allow the Palestinians to be a respectable or historic movement."

I visited the research center in October 1982, after it had been stripped. It was a sad sight—several floors of empty shelves and bare files and stark rooms from which the Israelis had taken even much of the furniture. The director, Sabri Jiryis, sat in the remains of his office. He described himself laughingly as "a hard-headed old terrorist," an Israeli Arab from Haifa who had studied at Haifa University, had gone to the Hebrew University law school, and had practiced law in Israel. "In 1967, after the war, I joined Fatah," he said. "I was responsible for some of their actions in Israel—responsible for northern Israel, supervising clandestine Fatah actions," by which he presumably meant terrorist attacks. In 1970 he left to supervise Hebrew-language broadcasts from the PLO's radio station in Egypt, which was soon moved to Beirut. His fluency in Hebrew made him a valued monitor of events in Israel, and he built up extensive archives—in other words, he was an Israel-watcher.

His center collected and published, putting out a journal and occasional books. "We wanted to document the Palestinian question and conduct research on it," he explained. "There is nothing like a Palestinian national library of politics, history, economics. We did our best to collect documents on the Palestinian question—newspapers, Mandate documents. We had microfilms of Israeli papers, Knesset records. We had 25,000 volumes, books dealing with the Palestinian question." All these were gone. Or were they? Jiryis indicated that much of the material had been microfilmed and placed in safekeeping somewhere in the United States. But some old books had been lost, he said, and they were irreplaceable.

The idea of Palestinianism stirs deep defenses in Jewish minds, observed Deborah Reich, an American-born Jew working on a program in Israel to promote Arab-Jewish cooperation. "As soon as you open the subject of a Palestinian state," she said, "you are attacking their dream, the Zionist dream people grew up with. People don't like their dream to be attacked. And it's sad, because the dream is a beautiful dream. Other people have other dreams. It's a different dream. I think that bi-cultural cooperation is more beautiful than a people who has been dispossessed for two thousand years having its own state. It's not that that dream isn't beautiful, but this dream is even more beautiful.

"I personally feel that the major psychological mechanism operating on both the Jewish and Arab sides for the past several decades now has been denial. Golda [Meir] said there is no Palestinian people; Arafat said the Jews are just a religious group. You're going to tell me who I am? That's what they do, on both sides. It really is two legitimate claims to the same square inch of turf. People don't understand, don't know about sharing it."

As Amos Oz writes, "Alongside Zionism, parallel to it and perhaps a byproduct of it, flowered the Palestinian experience. It may be a reflection of our own, a shadow. Perhaps it is a caricature, borrowing our symbols, emotional motifs, military and political techniques, our style, and even our poetic sensibilities. There is no copyright law for national experience, and one cannot sue the Palestinian national movement for plagiarism. Even if one were to claim that the Palestinian experience is nothing more than a parody, this would not suffice to nullify the fact of its existence. It has germinated and its growth presents a moral problem for us."[15]

I kept thinking of that immutable law of physics: Two bodies cannot occupy the same space at the same time. With that in mind, an Israeli friend in Jerusalem, a psychologist named Aaron Auerbach, had made a seductive and devastating argument to me shortly after I arrived in Israel. Aaron had immigrated from the United States a decade or so before. "You Americans," he said with a sparkle in his eye, "think that every problem has a solution. Well, this problem doesn't have a solution. Maybe you can control it, contain it, keep it from blowing up. But solve it? Never."

Danny Rubinstein, of the newspaper, *Davar*, put it another way. "If there were a partition," he said, "it would be an ethnic problem. Now, it is an existential problem between us and the Palestinians. The problem between us and the Palestinians is a problem between Jerusalem and Jerusalem. It's an existential problem. Which means either you or me." Thus does the clash between two nationalisms, each coveting the same land, shape the mutual perceptions of Jews and Arabs.

Conflict is comfortable to both sides. That is not to say that neither side wishes peace, or that neither could maintain its nationalism in the absence of confrontation. But for the present, the definitions are clean, easy, unambiguous. Everyone knows exactly where he stands. Even Israeli liberals who argue for humane policies toward Arabs are not all inclined to see legitimacy in Palestinian nationalism. In a 1980 survey of liberal Jewish leaders, only 58.8 percent accepted the idea of Palestinian nationhood.[16] Moderate Arab leaders would presumably be similarly resistant to Jewish nationhood. "Many doves are doves because the Arabs for them do not exist," Meron Benvenisti said of his fellow Israeli Jews. "So the whole thing is much more complex than people really think. Once you see that they exist, you say, well, they exist as individuals, but not as a community. They think, 'If I bring the Arabs into contact, if I give the Arabs more electricity, the conflict will be solved.' This is not an ethnic group that wants a bigger slice of the cake, but wants to make their own cake."

The competing nationalisms allow Jewish-Arab relations to move on two separate planes simultaneously. "One is communal, the other is personal," Meron explained. "The two levels never mix. You can see people who love Arab culture who are Arab-haters. People who were born here, in Israel or in Palestine, who know—even like—Arab customs and Arab ways of life, on the political level can be as chauvinistic as the other guy, even more, perhaps. And I think for all of us it is a constant conflict between two sets of interactions, the personal and the communal. That's why you can say, 'Ah, some of my best friends are Arabs.' And at the same time you can be the first to shoot an Arab."

THREE

Terrorism:
The Banality of Evil

Neither slay any one whom God
hath forbidden you to slay,
unless for a just cause.
—Sura XVII, The Night
Journey, Verse 35

THE CONCRETE PAVEMENT OF KING GEORGE STREET WAS SMEARED
with blood, drying in the sun, and strewn with glass fragments that
glittered like garish sequins. The injured lay on sidewalks as medics
crouched over them, holding plastic bags connected with tubing to the
arms of the victims. From time to time an ambulance would pull away,
taking the wounded across Jaffa Road to Bikur Cholim Hospital, just
up the next block. Crowds gathered grimly to watch the practiced,
efficient work of the men and women in the profession of rescuing and
cleaning up after terrorist attacks. Faces were set severely, with eyes
narrowed and lips pressed in tight, thin lines. Nobody cried.

King George is one of the main shopping thoroughfares in the western, Jewish part of Jerusalem, about half a mile outside the Old City walls. The intersection of King George and Jaffa Road is the area's downtown hub, crowded with strollers and shoppers in the middle of a warm, sunny Monday morning in early April. Newspaper sellers hawk their wares in the cadence of a singsong chant. In front of the florist's, bunches of flowers are arranged in puffs of bright colors. Fortunately, the children are in school.

Arabs rarely shop on King George Street. They feel uncomfortable among the Jewish crowds. They stick mostly to their own downtown area in East Jerusalem, that part of the city captured by Israel in 1967; its main thoroughfare is Saladin Street, boldly named after the Kurdish general who expelled the Crusaders and restored Muslim rule in the twelfth century. In Jewish neighborhoods, Arabs sometimes get hard looks, and moreover, many are afraid of being rounded up for long interrogations if a bomb goes off when they are in the vicinity. As one explained, "I will be either a victim or a suspect."

But on this Monday morning in April 1984, three Arabs drove down King George Street in a rented car and pulled over about fifty yards from Jaffa Road. On false papers, they had entered from Lebanon through an official border checkpoint during a period when Lebanese tourists were being allowed to visit Israel. They had been sent on a mission to take hostages in an Israeli government ministry, according to a communiqué that came later in Damascus from the radical Democratic Front for the Liberation of Palestine. They were about to bungle the job. While one stayed in the car, the other two walked into the Habira sporting-goods store and, speaking English with a heavy Arabic accent, asked to try on some jeans. They went into a dressing room, then suddenly emerged, one brandishing hand grenades and the other a small European-made submachine gun. He put the barrel to the head of Rani Cohen, a young man who worked in the shop, and said in English, "Don't move." The terrorist and the hostage were both about the same age. "I exchanged glances with him," Cohen said later. "For a few seconds he looked at me, and I looked at him, and suddenly, it was as if he passed me up, and he pushed me aside, as if he didn't want to kill me."

Someone outside apparently spotted the two terrorists and alarmed them, for without warning they rushed into the middle of the street, one shooting, the other throwing grenades. Israeli pedestrians and shopkeepers, many of whom carry pistols, drew their guns, fired back, and chased the terrorists down King George. Larry Tsach, a jeweler, wounded one of them. "He fell in the middle of the road," said Yishai Cohen, who has a clothing store on the block, "and next to him fell a canvas bag which he carried with him. He was lying for about a minute or two. And then suddenly he rose up, and his face was covered with blood, blood was also on the road. He had his hand in a fist, he cursed, he bent down, he took out a hand grenade, a yellow color, out of his bag." Blood streaming down his face, he ran toward Jaffa Road with the grenade in his fist.

"I shot at him," said Eli Cohen, a thirty-five-year-old insurance agent. But the Arab continued running, disappearing behind a bus. "I ran behind the bus, and he turned toward me," the insurance man said. "We ran toward each other, and I hit him on the head [with the pistol], and the grenade he was holding fell, and I shouted, 'Grenade!' and ran. I hid on the other side of the bus, but apparently that wasn't enough because I was hit by shrapnel." The young Arab said nothing. "He didn't shout anything. It looked like he was in a trance, as if he didn't care about bullets or anything." He died.

Soldiers and policemen swept into the downtown area, sealed off streets, and fanned out to search for the other two Arabs. Through the crowds raced rumors of a woman accomplice, either a blond Scandinavian or a Japanese; several foreign tourists were assaulted by angry mobs before they could be pulled to safety by policemen. A Finnish blonde who had spent about a month volunteering on a kibbutz was strolling with a dark Finnish man when she was attacked by a crowd. He was arrested, then released; she was badly beaten and hospitalized. Once she recovered, she left Israel immediately. A Japanese-American woman, in Jerusalem on holiday, was pushed and shoved by the mob before policemen rescued her, and at the Knesset, a guard fired at or above a Japanese tourist.

Arabs also became targets. Following their usual practice, the authorities rounded up all the Arabs they could find in the area, packing them into jeeps and paddy wagons and taking them off to the Russian Compound, a complex of buildings formerly used by the Russian Orthodox Church to house pilgrims, then by the British as a police command where Jews were often interrogated, and now by the Israelis as the Jerusalem police headquarters. Border policemen, in combat fatigues and green berets, slapped Arabs hard on the ears and the face as they took

81

them into custody. Angry Jews grabbed some Arabs before the police got to them; one red-faced, redheaded man pounced on an Arab worker from a construction site on King George Street, pummeling him with his fists as policemen, trying to arrest the Arab, pulled the Jew off again and again. The Arab worker shouted protests of his innocence as two officers locked their fists around his arms and hauled him off.

Venomous hatred poured from the crowd. A man yelled at the Jewish owner of a fast-food stand, "You are an employer of Arabs!" It was shouted as a deadly accusation, a lethal curse. Reporters' chaotic interviews with store owners and eyewitnesses were peppered with interruptions by passersby declaring earnestly that all Arabs should be exterminated, or that at the very least West Jerusalem should be closed off to them. A middle-aged man in a black beret announced that all Arabs should be killed. A younger man countered that you couldn't just kill them; you had to check first to see whether or not they had done anything.

"Check, check, check," the older man scoffed in an East European accent. "That's what they said during the Holocaust: 'Maybe there were no Jews being killed.' We should all just take a number and line up to die?"

Although the two other terrorists were captured soon after the attack, an hour or two later rumors circulated among the crowds on Jaffa Road that one had been seen on a roof. Police cars and jeeps raced up the street, the crowd following, and the mood rapidly darkened, appropriate for a lynching. People started yelling for the man—whoever and wherever he was—to be killed. Shots were even fired. But in the end it turned out to have been a false alarm. The figure with a gun that someone had spotted on a building was only a soldier making a final patrol of the area.

Two boys, about twelve or thirteen years old, said they thought terrorists should be tortured first and then killed. As for Arabs in general, one remarked, "Some are good and some are bad. Some are construction workers."

The shoot-out on King George Street, in which one died and forty-eight were wounded, was the most brazen and spectacular terrorist attack in Jerusalem for several decades. It came about two weeks before Passover, and its blow, delivered sharply against the malleable minds of children, carried into at least one family's Seder. An Israeli nursery-school teacher recounted what she thought was a cute little story about a three-year-old boy in her class. At the Seder, his mother told her, the boy dictated a note to be left, after he went to sleep, under the cup placed on the table for Elijah the Prophet: "Dear Elijah, let there be peace upon us, and let there be no more Arabs in the state, and may my Mommy and Daddy be blessed."

Ironically, Jerusalem is a safer city than New York. Debby and I never worried about our three children being subjected to street crime, for while apartments were often burglarized and other crimes against property were numerous, there were few acts of criminal violence against people. Nevertheless, we taught our children—Jonathan, Laura, and Michael—the standard and strict rule of Israel: If you see an unattended package or bag on a street or in a bus, don't touch it. Notify an adult immediately. So deeply ingrained did the lesson become that after we returned to the United States and I put some bags of newspapers out on the curb to be picked up, first Michael, seven, and then Laura, twelve, came dashing in to warn us insistently about the suspicious packages outside. Michael ran in another day to report a plastic cup of some sort on the street. I had seen it and asked him to throw it away. He adamantly refused to go near it, and he remained solidly unmoved by my extravagant assurances that we didn't have to worry about bombs on a quiet, tree-lined suburban street in America. At least not yet.

Michael and I did have a close call in Jerusalem, although I doubt that he ever quite realized it. He woke up feeling slightly unwell on a Monday morning in early April, and Debby and I decided to keep him home. As the morning progressed, he began to feel better, so I drove him to school along our normal route, which took us down King George Street, past the Habira sports store, to Jaffa Road. It was a few minutes before ten o'clock. The three Arab terrorists were just ten minutes behind us. I dropped Michael off at school a few blocks away and drove to my office, passing through the intersection again, minutes before the King George shoot-out began. For days afterward I replayed the two scenes in my mind—little Michael beside me driving along King George and the terrorists shooting and hurling grenades—wondering how it would have been if they had occurred simultaneously rather than a few minutes apart. What would I have done? Pushed him onto the floor? Gunned the car and raced away? Grabbed him and run from the car for cover? And what if he had been hurt or killed? Would I be sick with hatred for all Arabs? Would I, too, seek revenge?

The attack on King George Street was one of a spate of assaults by Palestinian Arabs on buses and stores in Jewish West Jerusalem, and Debby and I began urging Jonathan and Laura to minimize their bus travel and trips downtown. In addition, terrorist attacks by Jews against Arabs had erupted, making us nervous about Jonathan's frequent travel on Arab-owned buses to visit school friends who lived in East Jerusalem. Fear would be too strong a word to describe the atmosphere during our last winter and spring in Jerusalem, but the air was hazy with a sense of nastiness.

Terrorism is theater. Its real targets are not the innocent victims but the spectators. Those on the political side of the dead are to be frightened, intimidated, cowed, perhaps drawn into ugly retaliation that will spoil their image among the disinterested, who in turn are to be impressed with the desperate vitality and significance of the movement behind the terrorism. Those on the side of the gunmen, the bombers, the hijackers, are to be encouraged that the cause is alive. The goal of terrorism is not to deplete the ranks of an army, to destroy an enemy's weapons, or to capture a military objective. It seeks an impact on attitudes, and so it must be spectacular. It relies on drama, it thrives on attention, it carries within it the seeds of contagion.

If the reaction to terrorism were rational, there would be little fear of it among Israelis. As a rule, in the face of extensive intelligence, military, and secret-police efforts by Israeli authorities, Arab terrorists rarely manage to kill more than about twenty people in Israel each year, compared with two to three times that number of ordinary murder victims, more than 200 who commit suicide, and an average of about 425 who have been dying annually in traffic accidents in recent years. Between 1982 and 1985, a total of 654 Israeli soldiers died in Lebanon to prevent Palestinian guerrillas from continuing attacks that had cost a total of 29 lives in northern Israel in the four years from June 1, 1978, to June 5, 1982.[17] But terrorism plays on the emotions, not on the calculations; it penetrates the innermost feelings, shaping reactions, nourishing fears, influencing policy. It has a special bitterness for Jews who came to Israel seeking integrity of life, searching for the sense that they could walk openly and freely in the street as Jews, wear yarmulkes without shame, celebrate their religious holidays without awkwardness, connect the private realm with the public. Terrorism has stolen from them the cherished promise of normalcy.

Rarely has it advanced its specific cause, however. It may frighten, but it also deepens hatreds, hardens resolve, and radicalizes. Most severely, it becomes an ordinary part of life, like the raw rain that sweeps into Jerusalem during the winter.

Terrorism between Arabs and Jews, in both directions, has had a corrosive effect on the attitudes of average people toward each other, on their capacity to reject violence morally, on the low threshold of outrage that any decent society must maintain to be shocked by its own behavior and to prevent itself from degenerating into brutality. As terrorism becomes normal, it becomes acceptable. It grows into a routine.

Terrorism's ugliest successes have come when it has released an explosion of base violence from the decent people who are part of its target population. In November 1974, after Arab terrorists took an apartment house in the Israeli town of Beit Shean and killed its residents, the army killed the Arabs; an angry mob of Israelis burned the terrorists' bodies. In 1978, after a squad of Arab terrorists landed on the Israeli coast, commandeered a bus, killed thirty-three, and wounded eighty-two as they sprayed gunfire along the coastal road, Jewish students in a boarding school locked an Arab student in his room. "He didn't even know about the attack, hadn't heard what happened, and all of a sudden he couldn't get out of his room," said an American acquaintance, Susan Bandler. Years later, as a university student, he still couldn't talk about the incident with an Israeli Jew who had become a close friend. "It was hurting him, and it kept on hurting him, and he didn't know what to do," Susan said. He could talk to her because she was an outsider.

In the summer of 1985, after two Jewish teachers—a man and a woman from the Galilee town of Afula—were murdered by three West Bank Arab teenagers, Afula residents went on a rampage through the town, pulling Arabs out of cafés and beating them, assaulting Arab workers, stoning Arab-owned cars with blue West Bank license plates, burning Arab-owned shops. A Jewish youth, a student of one of the teachers, was mistaken for an Arab and was pummeled until someone identified him. For days, no Arabs dared go to work.

The rage had been building through more than a year of individual kidnappings and murders, including stabbing attacks on Israeli soldiers doing West Bank guard duty. More than a dozen Jews had been killed in these close-range assaults, which apparently drew their impetus from the Lebanese Shiite Muslim attacks that had been so successful in helping to drive the Israeli army out of southern Lebanon. As Palestinians took the Lebanese example into the West Bank, they hardened the Israeli right, promoting in particular the racist, expulsionist arguments of Rabbi Meir Kahane, the Brooklyn-born bigot with the sick eyes and the lucid, chilling logic that had been used against Jews in other places and other times. In the year after his Kach movement's election to the Knesset with one seat, Kahane's popularity soared to the point where, by the autumn of 1985, the public-opinion polls recorded enough support for him to win ten or eleven seats in a new election. Even allowing for Israelis' propensity to vent their frustration and anger more extensively on questionnaires than at the ballot box, the Kahane phenomenon alarmed the liberal-minded establishment enough to prompt President Chaim Herzog to tell a group of high-school students in a Tel Aviv suburb, "I think it is a disgrace to the Jewish people—and that is how it looks to the whole world—that a person could rise in the Jewish state and present a program that is very similar to the Nuremberg laws"—the measures promulgated by Nazi Germany in 1935 to strip Jews of their rights. Kahane satisfied the lust for simplicity that is fed by rage. He offered order as an antidote to uncertainty, complexity.

No Arab-Jewish relationship is entirely free of the scars of terrorism. Sometimes they refuse to heal, and in their rawness they inflame the mutual aversions. Sometimes they seal the wound in a toughness that disfigures. After a generation of this, Israelis look in the mirror and often cannot recognize themselves. Or, worse, what they see no longer bothers enough of them.

During the evening rush hour on Thursday, April 12, 1984, four eighteen-year-old Palestinians from two dusty, impoverished villages in the Israeli-occupied Gaza Strip climbed into a commuter bus headed south from Tel Aviv toward the coastal city of Ashkelon. About thirty-five Israelis were aboard. As the bus gathered speed on the highway, the Arabs pulled knives. One held a grenade under the nose of the driver and ordered him to continue past his terminal toward the Gaza Strip, saying that they intended to take the vehicle across the border from Gaza into Egypt, and from there to negotiate the release of 500 Palestinians held in Israeli prisons. As amateurish as the hijackers appeared—bent on pursuing an unworkable scheme and equipped with less potent weapons than terrorists usually carry—the passengers were justifiably terrified. They prevailed on the Arabs to let a pregnant woman off the bus; the hijackers did so, in a humane gesture that cost them the element of surprise. The woman flagged down a passing truck and reported the hijacking. Army and police roadblocks sprang up along the highway. As the bus sped into the Gaza Strip, soldiers fired at the tires, finally blowing them out, leaving the vehicle to continue slowly on its rims until it ground to a halt north of the border city of Rafah. As it stopped, the driver and several other passengers leaped out and ran to safety; the driver, a swarthy Jew of Middle Eastern origins, was mistaken by troops for one of the Arab hijackers, and was badly beaten.

Israeli military censorship imposed a complete blackout on the hijacking. The ensuing siege of the bus by Israeli troops, which continued through the night, went unreported by Israeli news organizations until it was over. This resulted in a bizarre scene at a central-committee meeting of the governing Herut Party in Tel Aviv. Even as word of the hijacking spread among politicians and reporters there, Israel's state-owned television station, the only one in the country, was broadcasting cheerful voices and faces from the convention, a surreal juxtaposition of fact and fantasy. Reporters and photographers left the hall and raced to Gaza, but no newsman or politician said anything on the air about the drama taking place sixty miles to the south.

Through the night, crack Israeli anti-terrorist commandos practiced running assaults on an empty bus parked off the road, out of view, while officers pretended to negotiate with the terrorists. At dawn the troops attacked, rescuing all the hostages except one—a young woman soldier who was killed when she failed to keep her head down during the assault. Foreign correspondents in Israel had been permitted to transmit heavily censored reports about two hours after the bus was hijacked, but not until the following morning, after the hijacking was over, did Israelis hear details from their own broadcasters. Israeli morning newspapers carried stories.

The officially stated rationale for the censorship, which was stricter than usual, held that the terrorists would gain confidence and information from listening to local radio broadcasts carrying details of the Israeli siege of the bus. But even after the episode, the censor's heavy hand was not lifted entirely. When the Israelis attacked the bus, the army said later, all four hijackers were killed, two immediately and two who "died on their way to the hospital." That official statement, as it turned out, was designed by an ambivalent, somewhat guilt-ridden ranking officer to conceal the truth without quite going along with the attempt by the army and the government to cover up a crime with grave implications: the double murder, after capture, of two of the hijackers by Israeli security men.

In fact, the two terrorists—cousins named Majdi and Subhi Abu-Jumaa—had been taken off the bus alive. They were led across the road to a field where a makeshift base and interrogation center had been set up for preliminary questioning, to determine whether or not they had booby-trapped the bus with explosives. Precisely which security authority had custody of them was somewhat unclear, although reports filtered out that both the border police—then acting under army command—and the Shin Beth, Israel's secret-police apparatus, were involved. The security men reportedly beat and threatened the prisoners in an effort to learn whether they had booby-trapped the bus with explosives. Beating Arab captives is pretty routine, but apparently the interrogators or guards lost their tempers, possibly, according to one account, because the terrorists were shouting, "Long Live Arafat!" and other, similar slogans. The Israelis began to beat their captives in a frenzy, as one official described it later, and both men died with fractured skulls. So many Israelis were involved that investigators had trouble determining precisely who landed the fatal blows. A group of policemen had turned into a lynch mob. Two years later, the attorney general was reported to have gathered evidence that the head of the Shin Beth, Avraham Shalom, was on the scene and personally ordered the prisoners clubbed to death.

The censor managed to suppress news of the murders for a while by banning the publication of selected pictures that had been taken by Israeli news photographers from three newspapers and a magazine. The photographs showed two men being led away from the bus, alive, by Shin Beth agents and soldiers; two of the photographers had pictures that were clear enough to enable identification of the prisoners, one of whom could be seen in handcuffs. Of all the Israeli newsmen and editors who knew of the photographs, however, only those from a fledgling new tabloid called *Hadashot* demonstrated enough outrage to pursue the matter. Israel's largest paper, the afternoon daily *Maariv*, did nothing, although it had a good shot of the other terrorist being led away; the photographer told me that he would not try to verify the identity of the man in his picture because he did not want to know a truth that would burden him with a choice between journalism and patriotism. By contrast, *Hadashot* took its picture to the terrorists' home village in the Gaza Strip—the location of which the army had revealed by blowing up the houses of the hijackers' families—and showed it to neighbors and relatives for positive identification. When *Hadashot* provided the information to me and showed me the picture, I visited the town as well, and, facing far fewer risks than an Israeli would in defying censorship, I wrote several stories for *The New York Times*.

The reaction in Israel was illuminating, and characteristically diverse. Many Israelis were disgusted by the murders and worried about undermining the longstanding policy of capturing terrorists alive, keeping them alive, and avoiding the death penalty even after conviction; the practice encouraged terrorists to surrender and release their hostages without feeling that they had no alternative but to fight to the death and take innocents with them. But many other Israelis expressed satisfaction that the hijackers had been killed; some offered the hope that they had been tortured first. And the Israeli press, with little exception, devoted more anger to *Hadashot* for evading the censor than to the authorities for trying to cover up. Editors generally accepted the apprehension of Defense Minister Moshe Arens and other officials that news of the murders would jeopardize Israeli soldiers captured during the Lebanon war and held by the Syrians and various factions of the PLO. The officials feared that the Israeli prisoners would be murdered in retaliation, a concern reinforced by a general Israeli view of Arabs as primitive and bloodthirsty. But it was a scenario without a recent precedent: Even an Israeli pilot, captured by the PLO and held in West Beirut while Israelis bombed and shelled the city during the summer of 1982, had been treated well and had been released unharmed, although in the prevailing tension under siege he could easily have become a target of brutality and revenge.

The publicity over the bus hijackers finally forced the defense minister to appoint an investigatory commission, which determined the causes of death, concluded that "some security-forces personnel may have broken the law" and referred the case to the military police and the attorney general's office for possible prosecution. More than a year later, in the summer of 1985, the attorney general, Yitzhak Zamir, called for the prosecution of twelve officials: Brigadier General Yitzhak Mordechai, chief infantry and paratroop officer, who had allegedly struck the prisoners with a pistol; five Shin Beth agents; three soldiers; and three police officers, all of whom were allegedly among a larger group that had beaten and kicked the hijackers after their capture.

However, the prosecution was slow in coming, and sixteen months after the murders, General Mordechai was acquitted at an army hearing. He had admitted pistol-whipping the hijackers—to learn quickly, he said, whether they had left explosives behind on the bus. But because so many people had struck so many blows, making it impossible for investigators to say precisely which blows caused the deaths, the general was cleared of any wrongdoing, even of lesser charges of "causing grievous bodily harm" and "undue use of force." Action pending against the eleven other security men was then dropped. The two hijackers were dead, but nobody was guilty of killing them.

Zamir, the attorney general, revived the issue in the spring of 1986, after the deputy chief of the Shin Beth and two other officials of the agency went to Prime Minister Shimon Peres to accuse Shalom, the Shin Beth head, of ordering the murders and then coordinating agents' testimony to pin the crimes on General Mordechai. The general and his troops, it seemed, had beaten the two hijackers but had then turned them over, bruised and alive, to Shalom and his Shin Beth men. Remarkably, Peres did not act on this information, and the three who complained were fired; Peres and Foreign Minister Yitzhak Shamir, who had been prime minister during the hijacking, opposed Zamir's call for a police investigation. The cover-up began to spread like a stain, tainting a broad spectrum of high-level Israeli political figures as Shalom swore in an affidavit that his actions had been approved by the political echelon.

To head off an investigation, Peres, Shamir, and other leading Cabinet ministers then made a deal designed to soothe the conscience and smother the truth. In June 1986, President Chaim Herzog issued a blanket pardon to Shalom and three of his deputies; in exchange, Shalom resigned as Shin Beth head. The three who were pardoned, two of them lawyers, were allowed to stay in their posts. The other three, who had brought the complaints, remained jobless.*

---

* Facing immense outrage from within his own Labor Party, Peres later acquiesced to calls for a commission to investigate the political leaders' behavior, but not the original crimes. The move was immediately blocked by Shamir and his Likud faction.

The official ambivalence was reminiscent of an incident in 1978 when Israeli army officers were treated lightly after having murdered Palestinian prisoners taken during combat in southern Lebanon. Lieutenant Daniel Pinto, convicted of strangling two prisoners and throwing their bodies down a well, was sentenced to twelve years; a military appeals court reduced the term to eight years, and the chief of staff, Raful Eitan, cut it to two. Pinto was released after serving sixteen months. Lieutenant Colonel Arye Sadeh, convicted of ordering a prisoner killed, received a sentence of two and a half years and a reduced rank of major. On the prosecutor's appeal, a higher court increased the prison term to five years and demoted him to private. Then Eitan reduced it to the original two and a half and restored Sadeh to major. Nor was this ambivalence about killing prisoners unprecedented. Menachem Amir, an Israeli criminologist, recalled an incident in which he was involved before the 1967 war. A terrorist, wounded and then captured, was told he would get no medical treatment unless he talked. "He told a very important thing," Amir remembered, "and died."

Understandably, Israelis who were disturbed by the murders in Gaza had more concern for themselves and their society than for the two terrorists, who did, after all, threaten innocent passengers on a bus. Had they met the same end as their comrades—death during the army's assault—not a flicker of dismay would have been seen. That would have been a fair part of the deadly game. But the spectacle of policemen beating them to death in hysteria provoked a new bout of gnawing self-criticism, at least in those rarefied, liberal-minded circles where such self-doubts are most active. Some wondered whether lawlessness and violence, so long a part of the Middle East, were working their way into the soul of Israel. Some Israelis of the old guard, who helped build the country on the ideals of humaneness, felt that the ground had shifted under their feet. They asked themselves whether the bloody tactics that had been accepted by mainstream Palestinians were coming gradually to be acknowledged as legitimate by important streams of Israeli Jews.

In some measure, the divide between Arabs and Jews who live under Israeli authority now begins with this violence and counterviolence. The bloodshed may stem from the political conflict, but terrorism and war have also become more than mere results. They are origins as well, and they have their own impacts. The intricate weaving of cause and effect has threads of attitude too tangled now to trace easily to their beginnings, even for an intelligent and introspective young man like Brett Goldberg. He had been profoundly affected by an act of terrorism against a good friend.

He was twenty-four when I met him, an American-born Yale graduate and a brilliant linguist who had "made *aliya*," which means, literally, "to ascend," the term Israelis use to describe immigrating from the Diaspora to the Jewish state. He was just finishing a stint in the Israeli army, preparing to fulfill his Zionist vision by gathering some like-minded idealists who would move to a poor development town in the Negev Desert and become the garbage collectors, street sweepers, and construction workers, doing jobs that Israeli Jews contemptuously label "Arab work" because it is left mostly to Arabs. Disturbed by what he called "the materialism that has swept over Israeli society," Brett wanted to recapture the earlier pioneering spirit of Zionism by returning Jews to manual tasks. "Jewish culture has been kind of corrupted by the fact that Jews disdain certain forms of labor," he said, "and Jews refrain from productive enterprise, which was the whole basis of their return to Israel." His project didn't work out in the end, but it provided a clear benchmark by which to measure his attitudes toward Arabs. He deplored the evolution of an Arab underclass. "The Arabs are becoming the coolies of Israeli society, along with all the hate and resentment that comes from a class society," Brett observed. He valued the relationships that he had heard existed in Palestine before Israel became a modern state. "You had Jewish intellectuals, you had Arab intellectuals, you had Jewish trades-men, you had Arab tradesmen, you had Jewish artisans, you had Arab artisans. Essentially you had two distinct ethnic groups, each one with its own culture, each one with its own modes of occupation. The Arabs had their own cities, the Jews had their own cities, the Arabs had their own urbane middle class, the Jews had their own urbane middle class. There was a very delicate embroidery of relations with the Arabs. But nowadays all that delicacy has left the picture and we're headed more toward a monolithic approach: the Jews against the Arabs. And that's our fault. That's a defect in our education; it's a defect in the precision with which we educate our youth."

This was the idealistic, tolerant, intellectual dimension of Brett's attitudes toward Arabs. But there was another side.

The Saturday before he came to sit and talk in my small office, he and his sister had been walking to a friend's house in Jerusalem. They were about half an hour late and still had a long way to go when they spotted a taxi and hailed it. They got in. "I asked him whether he knew how to get to a certain place in Talpiot," Brett said, referring to a Jerusalem neighborhood. "When I heard 'Tal-*bee*-ot,' we got out very fast. There are certain telltale signs of Arabicity, one of them being an inability to pronounce the *P*." His sister objected strenuously to leaving the cab. She thought he was being absurd. But Brett was adamant. I asked him why. "For me, with all the associations that I have, it's not a pleasant experience to enter into an Arab taxi," he said. "It's physically unpleasant, psychologically unpleasant. It's a very simple psychological phenomenon that negative experiences produce negative physiological feelings. And when I get into a taxi and don't realize until afterwards that I've gotten into an Arab taxi, I start to feel very uptight. I don't even know whether I consciously—whether all the associations of soldiers being kidnapped, people being kidnapped, run through my mind. It's just a very deep-seated fear for my own safety. And especially when I'm with any woman or with any unprotected person without weapons, it's a fear for their safety. That's a very hard thing to eradicate. I think even if all of a sudden Arafat were to sit down with Meir Kahane and terror were to be forsworn for generations, I think these fears would be a very hard thing to eradicate."

I could not fit this into the tolerant views he had expressed earlier, and neither could he. It was not an attitude he had brought with him when he came from the United States two years before, he said. "I would say this is learned behavior. The events have taught lessons of their own." And perhaps the most serious event for him, "on a gut level," as Brett put it, was the murder of a friend, David Rosenthal. Also American-born, Rosenthal lived on a Jewish settlement on the West Bank and worked as a custodian at the ruins of Herod's hilltop palace, the Herodion. He was alone there when five West Bank Arabs fell on him and stabbed him to death.

Brett was the one called upon to identify the body. "I was full of outrage simply because he was so defenseless and it was such a premeditated, cold-blooded act of violence," Brett said. "He was stabbed over one hundred twenty times.

"And his wife insisted upon seeing the body before it was interred, and she wanted to see it alone. And I'll never forget the scream."

.   .   .

Nurit and Etti Polak usually got home from school well before their mother returned from work, but they were not there when Geula Polak walked through the door in the afternoon of December 6, 1983. She was stricken with sudden concern. Her daughters were only eleven and thirteen, and they traveled to and from school by city bus. Mrs. Polak dispatched her older sons to the major hospitals in Jerusalem and then sat anxiously awaiting word. She had eight children, including a son in the army, and a husband who ran a street stand downtown where he sold felafel, the deep-fried balls made from a paste of chick-peas and served inside flat pita bread. Hers was a hardworking family, the salt of the Israeli earth.

At the central terminal, before the red and white bus began its run along route No. 18, Israeli troops went through their sad routine of combing it for bombs. Like almost all the buses they check, this one was clean. The driver was given the go-ahead to start his run, from downtown West Jerusalem out Herzl Street, through various neighborhoods where mixtures of Jews reside—survivors of the Holocaust and refugees from Arab countries, affluent immigrants from the United States and Israeli-born youngsters, college professors and auto mechanics. People from the entire range of this spectrum began to fill the bus. Among them were Nurit and Etti, who got on together near their school, as they did every day. It was shortly after noon, a rush hour of sorts, when many stores, schools, banks, government offices, and businesses close for the traditional siesta and crowds of adults and children head home. Many of the passengers who climbed on and off carried shopping bags and packages. One, apparently a Palestinian Arab, left his package behind on the floor when he stepped off. Nobody noticed.

The explosion was huge. It blew the roof off the bus, shattered windows in another bus behind, and sent an ugly column of black smoke billowing over the crowded thoroughfare. Wounded passengers remained sitting in their seats, stone still, blood on their faces. Two children sat together in the back. No one screamed. A strange silence hung over the wreckage. Then, slowly, motion and sound returned. Voices tore the cloak of quiet, urging help for this man or that woman or that child.

The final toll was six dead and forty-one wounded. It was the worst terrorist attack in Jerusalem in nearly five years. Two factions of the PLO issued statements claiming responsibility.

Most of the Polak sons who had been sent by their mother to various hospitals turned up nothing. But the one who had gone to Hadassah Hospital learned the awful news: Nurit was dead and Etti would not live long; half her head had been blown away. An ambulance was sent to Geula Polak's house, a common practice in Israel in case grieving relatives become ill or hurt themselves. When Aaron Auerbach, a psychologist and friend of mine, arrived to give aid, the house was full of neighbors. Mrs. Polak was lying on the floor, screaming. Aaron, who had brought one of the sons home from a hospital, put him in his mother's arms and sent the neighbors away.

In the swirl of grief that ripped through his house, the father kept his balance. When one of his sons told him, "I'm going to kill Arabs," the father replied sternly, gently, "No, you're not. You're going to grow up and, if you're a good boy, become a combat soldier."

"Gamal," a twenty-three-year-old Arab in East Jerusalem, heard about the attack on the bus from the news reports but did not realize until four days later that the two girls were sisters of his friend Ezra. When a mutual friend told him, he went to Ezra's house to offer condolences. Gamal was not a terrorist, but like many nationalistic Palestinians, he found it difficult to denounce such violence. Born in Jerusalem, he had gone to college in the United States and then, upon his return home, had been subjected to some unpleasant, brutal interrogation sessions with the Shin Beth, which held him for more than a month to find out whom he had contacted in the United States. Then they let him go without filing charges. When I first asked him about terrorism, he replied as if he were talking about an abstract political idea. "It's not terrorism," he said. "We are people who have a right, and this right has been taken away from us. And the only way to get it back is by violence. And that's not wrong."

But when I mentioned the No. 18 bus, he took a different tack. "I don't like this to happen," he said. "I have this friend Ezra. He had his two younger sisters killed. It really hurt me. But there's nothing I can do to stop it. When I went to his house to pay my respects, I could see the look of hate in his eyes. When I first came in, I thought, this is not the Ezra I knew. He said, 'You're an Arab! Get out of my house!'

"I said, 'I didn't have anything to do with it, and I know what you're going through, so I'll forget you said those words.'

"He said, 'Get out of my house!'

"I said, 'Look, I could have been on that bus going up to your house.' He started crying." Ezra had done his military service, but went back into the army after that, "obviously to kill to get even," Gamal said. "Who knows?" he added. "It might be me he kills. Hatreds can do so much."

Hatreds burn. They mix with sorrow and pride and helplessness and a furious zeal. For Matthew Liebowitz, who had arrived in Israel from Chicago just a few weeks earlier, the bus bombing was unbearable. Even though he did not know any of the victims, he wrote to his mother that he felt the loss personally. "I must let out and express my feelings through writing, especially to myself," he told her. "Last week a bomb planted by an Arab killed Jews on a Jerusalem bus. Two little girls, sisters, were killed. I read in *The Jerusalem Post* that their mother fainted repeatedly during the funeral. Why? My pain is too great to bear. Once again a Jewish mother must cry for her children—our children, because those girls were my little sisters. Jews die because they live. I can't endure the pain. A seventy-year-old man was also killed—my grandfather. Why?"

At dawn on March 4, 1984, Matthew, who had taken the Hebrew name Meir, joined three other newly arrived American Jews in a short ride into the hills overlooking a country road near Ramallah, on the Israeli-occupied West Bank. In the gentle light, they took up ambush positions and waited for a bus crowded with Arabs on the way to work. When one rumbled along, Matthew gave the signal and the others opened up with automatic rifles, spraying bullets through the bus windows and wounding seven of the Arab passengers.

The four Jews, arrested a few days later, were affiliated with the militant right-wing Kach movement of Rabbi Meir Kahane, whose platform of driving all Arabs out of Israel and the West Bank got him elected to the Knesset with about 25,000 votes the following summer. "Kach" in Hebrew is best translated as "thus," from Vladimir Jabotinsky's slogan, "And thus!" meaning with violence. Matthew, as a teenager in Chicago and during a year at Brooklyn College, had linked up with Kahane's American organization, the Jewish Defense League, his mother noted. After the bombing, she said, he wrote that "he had to go see Rabbi Kahane," that "somehow he had to find a way to deal with his inner pain." She denounced "the hold that Rabbi Kahane had" over her son.

Genese Liebowitz was a slim, dark psychologist who looked much too young to have a son in his early twenties. She came to Israel to help him after his arrest, and she came to my office in Jerusalem hoping to explain her son to the American public and thereby, somehow, to mitigate his punishment by an Israeli court. He was not a hardened terrorist, she argued, not a man filled with hate. He deserved punishment, she acknowledged, but not a long incarceration.

"Matthew essentially is a very idealistic Jewish nationalist," she said quietly, as if she were analyzing a client. "He's very much in love with the Land of Israel and has been since he was sixteen. He left home at the age of sixteen and came here for a year of high school. He's a religious Jew. He wasn't raised that way, but on his own he became a religious Jew at fourteen or fifteen. He's always been searching for some way to express his sense that the Jews had to be very strong in their own country. He's been a kid who has been looking for an image that would include a strong, powerful person who was also committed to Torah, to religion. He never was satisfied with either the military image alone or the religious person alone. Somehow he seemed to be looking for both."

When he joined the Jewish Defense League, his father objected vehemently. But his parents were divorced, Mrs. Liebowitz explained, and "when his dad rejected the whole thing, it made it more attractive." She herself had not understood Kahane's danger until she arrived in Israel. "What he offered Matthew was an image of someone who was not going to take it lying down. The slogan of Kach is 'Never Again.' The most painful thing is to see his people victimized. Rabbi Kahane's whole thrust is 'We are not going to be victims again. We are going to create a Jewish state in the name of God in which there will be nobody but Jews, so we will be totally safe from the influences of the non-Jewish world.' It's the image of a steel fist and the prayer on the lips that I think appeals to boys who are very sensitive to the victimization of the Jews and are very tied to the notion that Israel is essentially a religious homeland of the Jews."

Matthew (Meir) Liebowitz was sentenced to three years and three months in prison.

The threads of violence that ran through the bombing of the No. 18 bus extended on and on. One of those killed on the bus was the girlfriend of David Ben-Shimol, an Israeli soldier. Months later he took a rocket launcher and fired at a bus full of Arabs in Jerusalem, killing one and wounding ten. He was sentenced to life in prison.

It was a season of Jewish terrorism. After the bus bombing in December 1983, Jews began planting hand grenades at the entrances of churches and mosques and Arab houses. The pins were removed and the handles held down precariously by small piles of stones so that the slightest nudge would set off the charge. Altogether, fourteen grenades were rigged in and around Jerusalem, and although most of them were discovered before exploding, a few went off. Early one morning in Bethany, the town from which Jesus began his entry into Jerusalem on Palm Sunday, an imam opening a mosque was injured and a nun was hurt at a Greek Orthodox monastery. Another nun at a monastery in the Ein Kerem section of Jerusalem was wounded by shrapnel. After each incident, men would call Israeli and foreign reporters and claim responsibility on behalf of a shadowy organization called Terror Against Terror, whose initials in Hebrew were TNT. I got such a call myself; the man telephoned my home late at night, asked for me by name, and ended his brief message with the statement "When Jewish blood is spilled, Arab blood is spilled." Most Christians in Israel and the West Bank are Arabs.

The four Jewish residents of Jerusalem who were arrested admitted their guilt but denied knowing anything about the anonymous callers from "TNT." All were so-called born-again Jews, part of what is known as the *baalei teshuvah* movement, a strain of Jewish fundamentalism for formerly non-religious Jews who have found Orthodoxy. Yehoshua Caspi, the southern-district commander of Israel's national police, described the force that drove them to terrorism as "fanatical religious belief of some form that is not widely acceptable in religious circles." Again, as throughout the history of Jerusalem, religion and violence were intertwined. The Jewish terrorism that was committed and exposed that season contained an angry piety.

Just before one of those gentle Jerusalem dawns, three members of a militant, mystical, messianic Jewish cult crept out of an abandoned Arab village at the head of the Lifta Valley on the edge of the Holy City. Like many Arab towns, this one had been largely destroyed during Israel's War of Independence in 1948. The Arabs had fled, and their houses, built of stone blocks the color of the scuffed earth, remained empty and half ruined, perched on the back of a steep ravine that overlooked a biblical scene of terraced hillsides and olive groves. The small cult had taken up residence in one of the old Arab houses; neighbors said the members practiced a ritual of turning their faces constantly toward the sun, even while walking.

The cult believed fervently in the construction of a third Jewish temple on the plateau in the Old City of Jerusalem now occupied by the Muslim shrines of the Dome of the Rock and al-Aqsa mosque. The site, Mount Moriah, or Temple Mount to the Jews, is a flat, raised area of about 175,000 square yards just inside, and bordered by, the eastern wall of the Old City, facing Gethsemane and the Mount of Olives. There, Abraham is believed to have been prepared to carry out God's order to sacrifice his son Isaac. There in 960 B.C. King Solomon completed the first Temple, which was destroyed by the Babylonians in 587 B.C. The Second Temple was built on the plateau in 520 B.C.

It is a place of sacred conjunction for both Islam and Judaism: The vein of bedrock that breaks into the open there, that stone from which Muslims believe Muhammad rose on his horse to heaven, may also be the *Even Shetiyah*, the rock around which the earth was created, according to ancient Jewish lore, and which was probably enclosed inside the holiest part of the temple. Today the western wall of the mount is a focus of Jewish worship, but only out of frustration, for the Western Wall, or Wailing Wall, as it is also known, is nothing more than a massive retaining wall holding up the tons of earth and stone that form the plateau. In a sense, prayer there is a lamentation for the Second Temple, which has never been replaced since being burned in A.D. 70 by the Romans.

Modern Israel has possessed the Temple Mount only since 1967. After the war at Israel's birth in 1948, the Jews held West Jerusalem only. East Jerusalem, with the Old City containing the Western Wall and the Temple Mount, was in Jordanian hands. An ugly barrier of barbed wire and stone separated the Israeli and Jordanian zones, cutting through the heart of Jerusalem until the 1967 war; then, Jordan joined other Arab states in attacking Israel, which fought back and captured all the territory from its eastern border to the Jordan River. That gave the Israelis the West Bank, the Old City, and the Temple Mount. It was a moment of exultation, and David Rubinger's photograph of battle-worn Israeli soldiers gazing at the wall in tearful reverence became the famous image of the time.

But Israeli authorities then did what hardly any conqueror had ever done before in Jerusalem's thousands of years of bloody history; they refrained from putting their house of worship or their seat of power on the holiest spot. The Babylonians had destroyed Solomon's temple. The Greeks had plundered the Second Temple, had installed the image of Zeus in it, and had sacrificed swine on the altar. After A.D. 70, the Romans had replaced the Second Temple with a temple to Jupiter and statues of their emperors. The Muslim conquerors in 638 had put a mosque on the site, which the Crusaders had then converted into a church, which they called Templum Domini. The Muslims restored it as a mosque when they ousted the Crusaders at the end of the twelfth century. But the Jews, upon their return in 1967, ruled that existing religious institutions would not be disturbed and would be left under the control of their respective faiths. Some exceptions were made, notably in a congested Muslim area that was cleared of houses and small mosques to open a plaza by the Western Wall. But the Temple Mount, where mosques had stood since the first Muslim conquest of the seventh century, was left in the hands of the Waqf, the Muslim trust in Jerusalem.

In addition, Jews were proscribed by the chief rabbis even from setting foot on the Temple Mount, lest they inadvertently step into the area once occupied by the Holy of Holies, that chamber of the temple into which only the high priests, having been properly purified, could go. In the post-1967 period, many secular Jews ignored the injunction because they wanted to explore the elaborate Muslim shrines as tourists. Some religious Jews also ignored it out of their zealous desire to pray at that place; they sometimes snuck past Israeli soldiers and walked onto the grounds, where they held quick prayers before Muslim guards swooped down on them. One young man told me proudly that he had become the first Jew in nearly 2,000 years to blow the shofar, the ritual ram's horn, on the Temple Mount. He blew it and ran. Other Jews were determined to resist, however, and piously carried iron bars, stones, and bottles to prayer, concealing them in shopping bags in case of attack by the Muslims. The Jewish intruders were routinely arrested by the Israeli police and scolded like naughty schoolboys for playing with fire.

During my five years in Jerusalem, the idea of building a Third Temple in place of al-Aqsa and the Dome of the Rock evolved from a wild notion held by a very few fringe militants into a goal embraced and legitimized by parts of the established right wing. Some groups even had letterhead printed with a composite aerial photograph of the Old City as it is today and the Temple Mount as they wish it to be tomorrow; clear of mosques and dominated by a huge temple. A yeshiva was established in the Muslim Quarter, near the Temple Mount, to teach ancient rites of purification and other lost rituals connected with temple worship. None of this penetrated into Israeli government policy, which remained firmly devoted to leaving the Muslim holy places alone. But it heightened the Muslims' paranoia. When a demented Australian Christian set fire to al-Aqsa in 1969 and an Israeli soldier ran into the Dome of the Rock spraying gunfire in all directions in 1982, Muslim leaders and newspapers throughout the Arab world expressed the conviction that Zionist machinations were at work, not individual criminals.

True to the capacity of religious suspicion to infiltrate every crevice of civilization, archaeology also became, in the Arabs' eyes, a means of expanding Jewish jurisdiction. When Israeli archaeologists, rabbis, and yeshiva students opened a passage into an ancient cistern along the Western Wall, north of the public plaza, and followed it beneath the Temple Mount in 1981, the Muslims panicked, thinking the Jews were trying to undermine the mosque or retake the mount from below. When a leading rabbi encountered Arab workmen trying to seal the opening, he and some yeshiva students scuffled with the Arabs, scattering their cinder blocks. Israel's Religious Affairs Ministry then agreed to close off the cistern, and did so. But the Arabs weren't taking any chances; they built a wall of their own, of reinforced concrete, to block the alien advance, and another piece of historical knowledge was entombed, pending the arrival of the millennium.

When the cultists from Lifta moved in the pre-dawn darkness, then, they acted in a deep context. Equipped with ropes, ladders, and explosives, they went to the base of the eastern wall of the Old City and scaled it until they were on the Temple Mount, a few hundred feet east of the ornate Dome of the Rock, with its golden dome and its blue tile. They planned to blow it up to make way for a new temple. But one of the Muslim guards heard them, spotted them, sounded the alarm, and chased them away. They left their gear behind, which gave the police enough of a lead to arrest them a short time later. When I asked the chief of investigations, Yehezkel Carthy, about them, he minimized their significance as a group, though not the gravity of their intended crime. "They don't have any characteristics of an underground movement," he said. "Most of them are—I wouldn't say madmen but mentally unstable with messianic aspirations, with queer or abnormal thoughts or ideas. A small group—some of them are mentally deranged, some of them are on the verge of insanity—thought that with a small quantity of explosives they could raze the mosques and then the site would be clear for the construction of the Third Temple."

The next group that was arrested for planning to blow up the shrines was considerably more threatening, however. The plot came to light when twenty-five leading activists in Gush Emunim, the Jewish settlement movement on the West Bank, and two Israeli army officers from the West Bank military government were taken into custody a month later, in April 1984, and charged with several acts of terrorism against Arabs. According to the indictment, eleven of them had formed a "terrorist organization" whose violent plans and sophisticated operations spanned six years, from 1978 to 1984. Many of them had received extensive military training; they recruited and trained the others, equipped the group with weapons and explosives stolen from military depots while they were on army duty, and even set up a small factory on a West Bank settlement to manufacture bombs. They placed their targets under surveillance, planned the attacks, executed the assaults with cool professionalism, and escaped without injury. Sheltered by the milieu of fanatic religio-nationalism that prevailed at West Bank settlements, they existed for years beyond the reach of law-enforcement authorities, displaying immense skill both in operating clandestinely and in maintaining political ties in the governing right wing of Israel.

Their dramatic attacks were set in motion by an Arab terrorist act of particular viciousness on a Sabbath eve in Hebron, a fiercely nationalistic Islamic city on the West Bank. Hebron is another junction of Islam and Judaism, but one even more intimate than Jerusalem, for here is where the prophet Abraham, revered by both Jews and Muslims, is believed to have been entombed with his wife, Sarah, in the Cave of the Machpelah. Isaac and Rebeccah and Jacob and Leah are also believed to be buried here. The resting place, well underground, is covered by a large shrine built partly in the time of Herod—the distinctively framed Herodian stones are visible on the exterior wall, and the floor is Roman. It was then a synagogue and later, in the Islamic period, became a mosque. For centuries, a small community of devout Jews dwelled in a quarter of Hebron until Arabs rioting in 1929 killed many of them and drove out the rest. Some families returned several years later, only to be evacuated by the British in 1936 after renewed Arab riots. Under Jordan, from 1948 to 1967, Jews were barred from living in Hebron and from praying at the mosque and the cenotaphs inside; but in 1967, when the Israelis captured Hebron along with the rest of the West Bank, they established an intricate schedule of worship, allowing Jewish holy arks to be set up and providing certain times of exclusivity to Jews and Muslims. Occasionally, zealous Jews have tried to block Muslim access, and have assaulted Muslim guards. But usually the tension remains just below boiling, and between the assigned hours of worship, Jews and Muslims now pray simultaneously at the looming, marble cenotaphs that are cloaked in heavy weavings, the only place in the world where Jews and Muslims worship together.

The heady Israeli victory of 1967 brought a small group of nationalist Jews to Hebron in an effort to reestablish the Jewish presence in the city. Led by Rabbi Moshe Levinger, they first checked into the Park Hotel, owned by Fahd Kawasmeh, who was later to become the pro-PLO mayor of Hebron. The Jews refused to leave, confronting Israeli authorities who tried to remove them and finally exacting an important compromise in which the army would let them camp temporarily on the outskirts of Hebron. The makeshift encampment quickly grew into prefabricated house trailers, and from there to apartment buildings. Today the settlement, bearing the biblical name Kiryat Arba, is a satellite city and a center of Jewish extremism.

Gradually, too, Rabbi Levinger and his followers established themselves in the former Jewish Quarter in the center of Hebron, first sending their wives to sit in at the old Hadassah medical clinic there, then buying out Arab families in adjacent buildings—with both money and intimidation—and finally collecting funds from both the Israeli government and private American contributors to reconstruct the neglected and ruined stone buildings of the ancient quarter and its small, central synagogue. For the Jewish activists, the development contained the simple beauty of recapturing their lost and rightful history, of reconnecting the ancient and the modern across the disruptions of war. For the Arabs of Hebron, however, the fledgling Jewish resettlement, backed by the power of Israeli authority, represented an invasion by an alien force that seemed driven by fervent dreams of aggression against Arab land. The most radical on each side were lured to the confrontation.

This, then, was the background of religious and nationalist strife on that Sabbath eve in May 1980. It was a warm evening. By recent custom, a rather large group of Jews, after praying at the tomb of Abraham, walked through the darkened Arab city to the low stone building that was then the lone Jewish outpost inside the city limits—Beit Hadassah, Hadassah House, the old clinic where women settlers had prepared a Sabbath meal, where songs would be sung, where blessings would be made over the bread and the wine. Although many in the group were Israeli settlers themselves, there were Americans among them who were merely visiting for the weekend or studying for a time at the yeshiva at Kiryat Arba.

The Jews' Friday-evening routine was evidently well known among the Arabs of Hebron, and it was like a sore to many of them, rubbing against the smooth rhythms of the city's Islamic homogeneity. Few would deplore what was about to happen. Four Palestinians, originally West Bank residents who had been in exile and had stolen back across the Jordanian-Israeli border a year before, armed themselves with automatic rifles and hand grenades. Three of them climbed to the roofs of buildings across the street from Hadassah House, and the fourth stationed himself in the shadows of a doorway nearby. When the group of worshipers walked past, the Palestinians opened up on them with gunfire and grenades, then escaped quietly from the blood-drenched screams. Six Jews died; sixteen were wounded, and survived with awful memories.

By a strange twist of fate, almost all of the key doctors and nurses on duty that Friday night in the emergency room of Hadassah Hospital, in the Ein Kerem neighborhood of Jerusalem, were Arabs. And so, in the tangle of circumstance so common to the Middle East, the Jews wounded by Arab terrorists were rushed to a Jewish hospital to be treated and saved by Arab doctors.

On the West Bank, Israeli authorities feared reprisals against Arabs from Jewish settlers, and partly in an effort to lift a safety valve for the accumulating fury, the Defense Ministry expelled three visible West Bank Arab leaders: Mayor Fahd Kawasmeh, of Hebron,* whose Park Hotel had been the Hebron settlers' original foothold; Mayor Muhammad Mil-

---

* In 1984, Kawasmeh was elected to the PLO's executive committee and was then assassinated in Amman, apparently by Palestinian radicals.

hem, of nearby Halhoul, whose reasonable-sounding and eloquent defense of Palestinian nationalism had been a longstanding irritant; and Sheikh Raja Bayud Tamimi, the qadi, or chief religious judge, of Hebron, who had urged his followers to retake the now-Israeli cities of Jaffa and Haifa. The army also blew up the two stone houses, across the street from Beit Hadassah, on whose roofs the terrorists had laid their ambush; later, Israeli reporters discovered that the houses were owned by Arab families that had sheltered Jews during the riots of 1929. In any event, the demolitions and the expulsions did not serve their purpose. The leaders of the Jewish terrorist organization, most notably settlement activists named Menachem Livni and Yehuda Etzion, made plans to attack other prominent Arabs who had been condemned repeatedly by Israeli government officials for their radicalism and membership in the National Guidance Committee, a coalition of West Bank leaders advocating a Palestinian state. The placing of blame on local people constituted a misreading of the dynamics of terrorism, which was largely directed from outside. In addition, Arab rhetoric from abroad was sufficient to encourage violence without the words having to come from visible West Bank figures. There was no evidence that any of the Arab leaders had been responsible for ordering terrorist attacks on Jews—otherwise the Israeli authorities would surely have deported or imprisoned them—but the verbal assaults by high Israeli officials created enough of an inflammatory atmosphere to convince the settler-terrorists that they held in their hands the sacred terms of righteousness.

Retribution came precisely at the end of the thirty-day mourning period traditional in Judaism. Three bombs went off in various parts of the West Bank. Each contained 500 grams of high explosive stolen from the Israeli army. One, planted in the automobile of Bassam al-Shaka, the radical mayor of Nablus, blew away both his legs as he started the engine. Another blew off part of the left foot of Mayor Karim Khalef, of Ramallah, when he pressed the clutch of his car. The automobile burst into flames as Khalef screamed for help in getting out. A house painter rushed over, jerked the door open, and pulled the wounded mayor from the car just before the gas tank exploded. A third charge, meant for Mayor Ibrahim Tawil of El-Bireh, was attached to his garage, primed to go off when the door opened. After the other bombs exploded, Tawil was warned by the army to stay away from his car. An Israeli demolitions expert, a Druse named Suleiman Hirbawi, approached the garage, touched the door, and detonated the bomb, which exploded in his face and left him blind. According to the indictment, army major Shlomo Livyatan, thirty-four, had been called by a settler and told the location of the bomb; he in turn informed Captain Aharon Gila, thirty-five, deputy commander of the Ramallah district military administration, who accompanied Hirbawi to the garage. But Hirbawi, who was not a Jew, was never warned by Gila, the indictment charged. Instead, Gila allegedly stood by while Hirbawi approached the door. Major Livyatan was charged with providing intelligence information to the settlers on the movements of the mayors and the locations of their cars. The group's plan to bomb two other prominent Arabs, Ibrahim Dakak of Jerusalem and Dr. Ahmed Hamzi Natshe of Bethlehem, was aborted; Dakak's car was not there, and noise outside Natshe's house scared the settlers away. In all, fifteen Jews were indicted.

After the bombings, which were widely applauded by zealous Jewish settlers, the terrorist organization cautiously suspended its visible activities for some time. Then in the summer of 1983, a yeshiva student named Aharon Gross was stabbed to death in the Hebron casbah, the warren of twisting alleys and produce stalls that make up the city's main market. Retaliation from the Jews came swiftly. While the army confined Arab residents to their homes in a curfew, settlers rampaged through the market, burning stalls. Six settlers, including three of those involved in the attacks on the mayors, developed a careful plan to pose as Arabs and assault the campus of the Islamic College in Hebron. Some undertook surveillance, some drove getaway cars. Menachem Livni, Shaul Nir, and Uziah Sharabaf were later convicted of actually conducting the attack. They carried captured Soviet-made Kalashnikov automatic rifles, as Palestinian terrorists usually do, and they wrapped their heads in red-checked keffiyahs to enhance their Arab appearance. One of them, in an anonymous interview with the Israeli newspaper *Maariv*, said that he used the weapon that had belonged to one of the six Jewish worshipers murdered in the 1980 Hebron massacre. "When I held in my hand the weapon of one of the murdered," he declared, "I had a heavy feeling of duty toward the man who had had such a tragic death, and I said to myself, 'God will avenge his death.' " They walked calmly into the college courtyard, firing at a group of students in an adjacent grove, then spraying the courtyard with gunfire and throwing a grenade at a group of students standing near the entrance. Three were killed and thirty-three wounded. The three Jews were given the life prison sentence that is mandatory for murder.

Various members of the group were convicted of other acts. One, Shaul Nir again, planted two grenades on the stairs to the bleachers of a soccer field at a Hebron school in 1982; the explosions injured two Arab boys during a game. In 1983, three of the settlers planted hand grenades in two mosques in Hebron, wounding two Arab watchmen. In 1984, twelve of the group rigged bombs on five Arab-owned buses parked overnight in various parts of East Jerusalem. The charges, made from captured Syrian mines transported from the Golan Heights, were timed to explode when the buses were crowded with rush-hour passengers. But police discovered and dismantled the bombs, and the discovery led to the arrests. In the course of questioning, Shin Beth interrogators pretended to approve of the terrorism, some settlers told me, and gave such convincing performances that they obtained further information on the group's plans, including a plot to blow up the Dome of the Rock. And these men, some with army training, had the capacity to make it work. A detailed operational plan had been drawn up, according to the indictment; weapons and explosives were acquired; training was conducted; and containers to hold the explosives were ordered from a factory. Six of the settlers went to an army base in the Golan Heights and stole explosives from a military vehicle, took them to a settlement in the Golan* and later to Kiryat Arba, where they manufactured about thirty bombs. Posing as army officers on official business, they also bought silencers for Uzi submachine guns they would carry during the operation. Had they not been arrested before they had a chance to blow up the shrine, their act would probably have brought a reign of warfare and terrorism upon Israel and Jews everywhere. One official in the prime minister's office even estimated that Israel could not have survived the Muslim onslaught that would have come if the Dome of the Rock had been destroyed.

---

* The settlement is named Keshet, a word made from the initial consonants of *Kuneitra Shelanu Tamid*, Hebrew for "Kuneitra is ours forever." Kuneitra is a Syrian town captured by Israel in 1967 and returned to Syria as part of the 1974 disengagement agreements.

. . .

The Jewish worshipers in Hebron were machine-gunned by a squad of Palestinian guerrillas led by a slightly built man of thirty-two, Adnan Jaber. His brown eyes were disturbingly soft, too soft for a terrorist's. Indeed, when I met him after his arrest, everything about him contradicted my expectation that he be a crazed fanatic, wild with madness. No normal human being, I thought, could take an automatic rifle, climb onto a roof with other men on a Friday night, and open fire into a group of religious people returning from prayer. I needed to place him at the edge of civilization or beyond. I wanted his gaze to burn with fury, his speech to ring with zealous slogans. And as I drove south among the vineyards and olive groves from Jerusalem to Hebron, where he was being held by the Israeli military government, I imagined that I would have a tough time penetrating his shell of militant dogmatism. I decided in advance that I would not shake hands with him, and he must have picked up the cue, for he did not offer his hand when I was ushered into a small, bare, concrete office in the complex of cells, walls, courtyards, and barbed-wire fences from which the Israeli army administers the Hebron region of the West Bank.

What I found was something surprising, and the discovery remains with me as one of the most troubling in my five years in the Middle East. I would have been comfortable with Adnan Jaber as a wild-eyed lunatic. Instead he turned out to be an ordinary man of moderate intelligence who talked in a matter-of-fact way about his life, his military training, his cause, his politics. He was not inflexible, and he could analyze and reason maturely. His sanity bothered me deeply and has haunted me since. In essence, it was a statement on an important characteristic of the Middle East: Terrorism is not an aberration produced by demented personalities. It is an integral part of an existing subculture, encouraged and supported and approved by the mainstream of the society that forms the terrorist's reference points. He is not deviating from his society when he attacks; he sees himself as acting on its behalf and advancing its interests, and it probably sees him that way too. Some on his side may regard him with disgust, but to key elements of his culture he is noble and heroic.

My main interest in Adnan Jaber, and the reason the Israeli army made an exception to its usual rule barring contact between reporters and security prisoners, was that he had spent six months with other PLO guerrillas in a Soviet explosives and weapons course near Moscow. I wanted to talk to him about the Soviet training, a subject on which little information had reached the West. He was very responsive, providing a wealth of detail about the instruction he had received and about the training given Palestinian "freedom fighters" by other countries, including Vietnam, China, North Korea, and East European members of the Warsaw Pact. The interview ended up on the front page of the *Times*. Toward the end of our two hours, when we had exhausted the military subject, I tried to understand how he could have executed the Hebron massacre.

Jaber slouched over a table and spoke in quiet, somber tones. The positions he took were uncompromising, but he seemed cowed, even gentle. He certainly felt vulnerable as a prisoner who had not yet been tried, and perhaps he was softening his demeanor deliberately. Although no Israeli guards were present and he said he had not been tortured, he had the sadness of a whipped dog about him. And yet he presented himself as a professional military man who in Hebron had just been doing his job.

He had grown up in the West Bank village of Tayasir and had fled to the East Bank of the Jordan River with his father, a Jordanian army corporal, on the fourth day of the Six-Day War of 1967. They lived in Jiftliq, a town in the Jordan Valley that came under a reprisal air raid by Israel. His father died in that Israeli air attack, an event seared into Jaber's memory. He even recalled the date: "21 March 1968," he said. After that, he joined al-Fatah, the main wing of the PLO, headed by Yasir Arafat. "At that time there was a very bad situation," Jaber explained. "There was no land, there was no house, there was no anything. It was clear that the Arab nations weren't anything. And the reputation of the organization, especially Fatah, had grown greater." He received military training in Syria and Lebanon. On June 15, 1979, he stole across the Jordan River into the West Bank and lived mostly in caves before and after the Hebron massacre nearly a year later. He was caught four months following the 1980 attack while trying to recross the Jordan to escape.

What was his purpose in Hebron? Who were his targets? "There were soldiers and there were civilians," he said. "There were those who were armed, and there were those who were unarmed." So was he trying to kill any particular people? "There was a soldier standing in front of the building, and during the operation people came walking who were armed and unarmed, and we began having a clash with them. We couldn't attack the soldiers and not hit civilians."

"Tell me," I asked, "why is it that you think that attacking civilians— people who are innocent, not soldiers—what good does this do in solving the Palestinians' problems?"

He looked down at the table and spoke softly. "There were four of us and there were more than fifteen soldiers, and they opened fire on us." This was a lie; the first moment the Israelis knew that the guerrillas were there was when Jaber and his group, from ambush, sprayed the worshipers with rifle fire. "The same day," he continued, "there were a great number of soldiers in the Mosque of Ibrahim, and it was expected that they would attack us."

"But you were there to kill Jews, isn't that right?"

"I hope that you will publish this precisely. It is true that there were some people there who were not armed, but there were people who were armed. Maybe I should ask the public in America: There is a Palestinian people that is scattered throughout the world, in all four corners of the world. We are with American opinion and world opinion that people shouldn't be killed, but if American and world opinion are against people being killed, we Palestinians are being killed every day, if not by an Israeli tank, then by Arab nations all over the Middle East. I hope Americans will hear and know that we were killed and scattered in '48 and we were killed and scattered in '67, and the continuation of this story is in southern Lebanon."

But how can a man fire a gun into a group of unarmed civilians, killing innocent people?

"I'm like any man who has a cause. It is important for me to explain. We, as fighters, we fight not because we like to fight and like killing. We want the American people to know about the Palestinian case and the Palestinian people. This war, which we are in—I don't believe it is going to come to an end in the near future. There is no just political solution on the horizon. We as fighters hope that there will be a just solution to the question, but we see it as being very difficult. We are aware of the difficulties. The Hebron operation is part of the general operation that takes place between us and Israel. As a fighter, when they give me an order, I have to carry it out. We have internal feelings toward every person. Every person has internal feelings. My personal feelings are that I am sorry that the situation has reached this point."

Several years later I heard an echo of Jaber's words from a Jewish terrorist, one of those arrested in 1984 for the bombings of the Arab mayors that followed Jaber's attack by a month. The Jewish settler was interviewed anonymously by Meir Ben-Gur, of *Maariv*, who quoted him as saying of the bombings, "We didn't feel any feelings of victory or pride. We just did what we had to do. We felt sorrow and disappointment that we were forced to take such a step in an era when we have an Israeli government."

When I had asked Adnan Jaber my final question and he had given his final answer, a guard came in, handcuffed him, and took him back to his cell. He was sentenced to life in prison. Then, three years later, in November 1983, he was released and flown to Tunis when Israel exchanged 4,500 Palestinian prisoners for six Israeli soldiers captured during the war in Lebanon.

The measure of terrorism's evil victory, and the test of the society, can be seen most critically in the degree and nature of support that a culture or a people provides to its own terrorists. The act of terrorism evolves into a routine, accepted tool of combat employed by a subculture's well-integrated and highly regarded members. As Adnan Jaber said, it is just "part of the general operation that takes place." Or as his Jewish counterpart observed, "We just did what we had to do." Indignation wanes. The Arabs and the Jews have been quite asymmetrical on this point, with the Arabs generally hailing their terrorists and the Jews punishing theirs. And yet powerful countercurrents have run inside Israel from the late 1970s well into the mid-1980s, as Jewish vigilantes and terrorists have operated against Arabs on the West Bank, at first with impunity and later with mixed reactions from Israeli Jews who variously approved and condemned as the violence grew in scale.

On the Arab side, those who oppose terrorism usually do so quietly and in the confines of their own circles of family and friends. An unprecedented exception came after the December 1983 bombing of the No. 18 bus in Jerusalem, when five prominent Palestinians of the West Bank and East Jerusalem had a condemnation published on the front page of *Al-Fajr*, the East Jerusalem Arab newspaper that supports Arafat's Fatah organization. They made their denunciation broad, including not only the bus bombing against Jews but the Israeli artillery and air attacks on the Palestinian refugee camp of Ein Hilwe in southern Lebanon and the murder by a Jewish settler of an eleven-year-old Arab girl in Nablus, a major Palestinian city on the West Bank.

"It is our belief that attacks on civilian targets are detrimental to any Palestinian-Israeli understanding," their statement said. "Such acts, be they in Jerusalem, in Ein Hilwe, or in Nablus, are to be regretted. Violence against civilians, carried out by either side, is counterproductive to a just solution to the Palestinian problem. We believe that the PLO was not behind the incident, because it contradicts the political line which the legitimate leadership of the PLO is following." The statement was signed by Karim Khalef, the former Ramallah mayor who had been ousted from his post by the Israelis and who had lost part of his foot when Jewish terrorists set a bomb in his car; Mustafa Natshe, who had been removed by the Israelis as acting mayor of Hebron; Anwar Nusseibeh, former defense minister of Jordan; Hanna Seniora, editor of *Al-Fajr*; and Paul Ajlouny, who owned *Al-Fajr* and lived in the United States.

Raymonda Tawil, a writer and Arafat supporter from Ramallah, was amazed, especially so because she had been away from Israel and the West Bank for a year. She returned to find a pronounced moderation among her fellow Arabs, partly, she believed, out of fear that Jewish settlers would take revenge through terrorism of their own. "It's unbelievable," Raymonda said to me. "Everything has changed. People are not so happy about the bombing. We used to rejoice in the past; we used to be happy."

I remember one of those bouts of rejoicing. It followed a gruesome attack on a children's house at kibbutz Misgav Am in northern Israel, on April 7, 1980. The gentle hills of Galilee were still lush green from the winter rains, and wild flowers had sewn the slopes into crazy quilts of color. At dusk the hills softened, and from high points above the Sea of Galilee, the strings of lights that went on along the security fences encircling towns and kibbutzim looked like bracelets scattered on waves of dark velvet. In the full darkness, shortly after midnight, five Palestinians moved from their base in southern Lebanon to the fence along the Lebanese-Israeli border. The kibbutz, a pleasant landscape of stucco houses, walkways, barns, and fields, was hard on the frontier. Its 360 residents worked primarily in dairy farming. By ideology and tradition, the commune's children slept away from their parents, in special dormitories called "children's houses."

The five Palestinians carried Kalashnikov rifles, a grenade launcher, leaflets advocating the retaking of Palestine through blood and terror, and a list of names of Palestinian prisoners held in Israeli jails. They made their way through a mine field, cut a hole through a fence of jagged concertina wire, hacked a pathway through tall vegetation, cut an electronic fence, and crossed a fifteen-foot-wide road bathed in glaring light. Still undetected, they cut a hole through another barbed-wire fence, then cut through the chain-link fence surrounding the kibbutz. Army personnel monitoring the electronic alarms thought the signal transmitted by the breach in the fence was a malfunction, of which there had been many. The guerrillas crept about 100 yards to a small concrete building where four children were sleeping.

By chance, the kibbutz secretary, Sami Shani, was there. He had been notified by a mother who was taking her turn watching the children that the electricity had gone out; he and his wife, Esther, were seeing to the repairs when the terrorists burst into the house. As the two women locked themselves into the bathroom, Shani fought them with his bare hands. They shot and killed him. The men of the kibbutz, who all keep guns at home, bolted out of bed and raced up the hill to the house. Seizing two of the sleepy children, the Palestinians retreated to an adjacent children's house, where four other youngsters, ages two and three, were in their cribs under the care of a young father, Meir Peretz. The two women snuck out of the bathroom, swept up the two other children, and fled.

Now in the second house with Peretz and six children, the terrorists began shouting confused demands through broken windows. During the next nine hours, army officers talked to them through a bullhorn as the terrorists set and postponed deadlines for the release of prisoners and asked for the presence of an envoy from a Communist country. A regular army unit, the first on the scene, bungled an attempt at 2:30 A.M. to storm the house and free the hostages, with the result that a soldier was killed and a boy of two and a half, Eyal Gluska, died in his crib. Although the army's chief of staff, Raphael Eitan, announced that the boy had been murdered by the terrorists, Peretz's account and the autopsy suggested that he had been shot accidentally by the army.

As dawn came, the Palestinians asked for food for themselves. Army officers outside offered milk for the babies, the terrorists agreed, and packets of milk were placed on a windowsill. By then, one of Israel's crack anti-terrorist army teams had been flown in by helicopter, and at 10:30 A.M., the highly trained troops stormed the dormitory, killing all five Palestinians and rescuing the remaining children, four of whom were wounded. Peretz was shot in the leg by a guerrilla who forced him to shout to the Israelis to hold their fire.

Afterwards, Ezer Weizman, then defense minister, spoke to a gathering of sober, silent kibbutz residents. "For me it was one of the most difficult speeches," he said later, "when the dead were still lying and the wounded were being evacuated, to sort of explain to them why we didn't do more than we did, and trying to convince them that what we did was a hell of a lot. Just to emphasize the spirit of the kibbutz, nobody criticized, one or two asked questions, and then eventually somebody stood up and said, 'We would like to thank the Israeli army.' "

I was home in Jerusalem, 120 miles to the south, when the terrorists attacked. I awoke to the news early in the morning, raced to my car, and headed for Misgav Am, more than three hours away by the narrow roads that led northward. The *New York Times* photographer Micha Bar-Am had been spending the night on another kibbutz in the north and sped to Misgav Am ahead of me. I found him there, after it was all over, in the children's house. I had come to know Micha, my professional companion and personal friend, as a tough, sensitive man with the remarkable eye of an artist, the perspective of a historian, and the instincts of a veteran of too many wars. Since being brought to Palestine from Germany by his parents, he had fought and photographed Israel's battles. He had seen a lot. He could have grown hard. But when I found him in the children's house, he was standing, slightly stooped, as if he had been punched in the stomach by a rush of sadness.

Wind blew through the shattered windows of the nursery, whipping shredded, brightly colored curtains like torn battle flags. The walls behind the cribs were peppered with pockmarks. One side of a crib's mattress in a corner was soaked with blood. Toys on shelves stood cracked and splintered by bullets. Spent brass cartridges from the terrorists' Kalashnikov rifles lay scattered on the floor, among tiny shoes and toy teacups and books of fairy tales. Micha stood looking, his camera held down at his side.

Three days later I was on the West Bank talking with Palestinian students. Many of them approved of the terrorist attack on the children of Misgav Am. I can still see the twisted, laughing faces of the young Arab women from a vocational school in Ramallah. They stood in the middle of a narrow road that had been blocked with piles of stones and a few old tires. The tires had been set on fire, and black smoke rose in an ugly pillar. Their demonstration was being held to mark the day of the massacre of Arab villagers at Deir Yassin, but it took place in the immediate shadow of Misgav Am.

The young women's eyes flashed with angry pleasure. They laughed and shouted their delight with the terrorist "operation" against Misgav Am. I asked them what they thought of the terrorists, and they answered, giving only their first names and ages.

"We agree with them!" shouted Rawda, twenty-one, in a storm of laughter joined by other women.

Even when they threaten and kill children?

"The children will grow up to be soldiers," she explained. "It's the way to get our land."

"They don't care if they kill *our* children," said Suad, also twenty-one. She smiled, and everyone broke into giggles.

A similar demonstration at a nearby teachers' college for men was broken up brutally by the Israeli army after Arab students chanted at the soldiers, "We are going to do to you what they did at Misgav Am."

"We are not going to turn the other cheek," one army officer explained. "We are not Christians." The Israeli troops shot into the air, driving the students inside the walled campus. Then soldiers swarmed through the gate and over the walls, firing tear gas into the rooms, breaking down doors, and beating and hauling students to jeeps and paddy wagons. Soldiers shouted for revenge for Misgav Am. Saleh Najar had huge red welts on his shoulders and back and two superficial cuts on his right arm. He said he had heard a soldier say, "Yesterday, Misgav Am. Today, you!" Najeh Shahadeh reported that a soldier had clubbed him on the face and legs, crying, "You killed children, so blood is avenged in blood." Zakria Suror heard another shouting, "Every single droplet of Israeli blood will be retaliated for." Forty-one students were injured, six seriously enough to be hospitalized. Suror was arrested, and on the way to prison, he said, he and others were forced at knifepoint to repeat slogans with obscene names for Yasir Arafat, and were compelled to say: "Palestinians lost their land; we have no right to the land." At Ramallah prison, he reported, Israeli soldiers collected the students' watches, put them in a pile, and crushed them with stones. When the students complained of thirst, Najar said, "Some of the soldiers drank water in front of us and poured the rest on the ground."

These young Palestinians expressed a fairly common reluctance by Arabs to condemn terrorism against Jews, even while mouthing the accepted platitudes of humaneness. "I don't believe in bloodshed anywhere in the world," said Zakria Suror. "But at the same time I feel, as a Palestinian, that I should be treated as a human being with the right to live in my own land. But I stress that I don't believe in spilling the blood of anyone anywhere in the world. Israelis are every day killing children with attacks in southern Lebanon. This doesn't mean I am for bloodshed. I am absolutely and completely against bloodshed anywhere."

The acceptability of terrorism became apparent on an evening some years later at Hebrew University in Jerusalem, where sixteen Arab and Jewish students gathered in a classroom for a meeting sponsored by Hillel House, the Jewish students' organization. These were the most moderate and the most tolerant of the students on both sides of the cultural and national divide, and they came together periodically to discuss Arab-Jewish relationships. This night the subject was terrorism. There were Arab students on campus too militant to allow themselves to attend such a session with Jews; those Arabs who came were a self-selected sample with a strong bias in favor of political moderation. One could logically have expected them to denounce terrorism resolutely. But apparently the Jewish students had no such illusions. Through the whole discussion, no Jew demanded, and no Arab provided, a categorical rejection of terrorism. Right-wing Jews would undoubtedly have made the demand, but these young men and women adopted the delicate style of dialogue that has become customary when liberal Jews talk to moderate Arabs. The terrorism issue, so intricately woven into the political fabric of Palestinian nationalism and the PLO, is skirted adroitly, as if everyone tacitly agrees that demanding a denunciation is tantamount to making an accusation, to requiring the Arab to denounce the only institution that represents his nationalist aspirations as a Palestinian, and thereby to denounce the aspirations themselves.

Both the Arabs and the Jews spoke in Hebrew. They began by debating the definition of terrorism, noting its indiscriminate nature, its sophisticated organization. Eyal, a Jewish psychology student in worn jeans, read solemnly from articles of the Palestine National Covenant that endorsed "armed struggle" as the means to "liberate" Palestine. He noted that the covenant, the PLO's formal constitution, made no room for a Palestinian and a Jewish state to exist side by side. An Arab replied that Eyal was discussing terrorism in a vacuum, without the ideological factors that motivate it. Eyal answered that from what he had read, the ideological component had diminished. The Arab countered that all terrorist organizations were highly ideological and that terrorism was created from a lack of alternatives. "There are groups that never try anything else," countered another Jew. Then the students debated the PLO a bit, but gently. Asked to define the PLO in relation to terrorism, an Arab student replied, "I'd say the PLO is an organization which uses terrorism as one of its means."

"What other means do they use?" Eyal asked pointedly. A discussion about Arafat followed. An Arab threw it back at the Jews, mentioning the Jewish terrorism that had recently come to light with the arrests of the settlers. Eyal talked about the pre-state Jewish underground, whose attacks, he said, were aimed at troops and symbols of British power, not at civilians. But a young Arab woman in a pink sweater noted that the Jews of the underground hurt innocent people as well. "There is a difference between a nationalist struggle and terrorism," she said. "I call the PLO a nationalist struggle."

"And what about a bus and a children's house?" said Orna, a Jewish student who was leading the discussion. "That's a national struggle?"

"The bus [in Jerusalem], it wasn't the PLO that did it," said the Arab woman in the pink sweater. "Every violent action in the occupied territories is called national struggle. I don't agree with what happened with the bus. If it happened in Shechem," she said, using the biblical Hebrew name for the Arab, West Bank city of Nablus, "I'd say it wasn't terrorism, it was national struggle." In other words, attacking Jews on the occupied West Bank was justifiable, but attacking Jews in Israel proper was not. Remarkably, nobody in the room challenged her fine distinction between innocents dying on one side or the other of an imaginary line.

A few students tried to broaden the definition of terrorism to include conventional military action, such as the Israeli invasion of Lebanon. "Every act of violence is terrorism," said a thin, young Arab man. "I can justify the PLO. You can justify Sharon.* We all have logical motivations."

A Jewish woman in glasses, who until then had been sitting in silence, spoke up heatedly. "So you say that an invasion justifies anything? You can do anything? All I hear is about acts of terror. What else do they do? They're struggling for something. What do they do besides terrorist actions?"

A dark Arab woman countered, "Do you justify someone going into a church or a mosque?"—this a reference to the current spate of grenade attacks by Jews on Christian and Muslim holy places.

"I don't justify that," said the woman in glasses.

There was a fleeting discussion of Gandhi's nonviolence and the unreceptiveness of the Middle East to such a philosophy, and then the talk slid away from terrorism and toward Zionism, which occupied the rest of the session.

There was something good in this, that Arabs and Jews could sit down and air their feelings together. They seemed easy with each other. But at the end I felt depressed and dissatisfied, as if the words were mere slippery things gliding out of reach of reality. Most of the participants had an obvious aversion to terrorism. But nobody had really taken a moral stand of unconditional outrage at the killing of innocents, and nobody had really asked anybody else to do so. Most of these young adults had grown up in an environment where terrorism was such a part of the landscape that to wish it away seemed impossible. Instead it had to be analyzed, scrutinized, dissected, and understood. All very well, but it left me torn between anger and emptiness as I drove home through the Jerusalem night.

Some weeks later, an acquaintance at the university helped me gather a group of Arab and Jewish students to talk about their relations on campus. The conversation inevitably turned to politics and terrorism. They accused each other of letting political differences stand in the way of friendships. And when one of the Arabs, Shakeib Sirhan, declared, "If you ignore my political problem, you will not be my friend," a quietly

---

* Ariel Sharon, who was defense minister when Israel besieged, bombed, and shelled West Beirut in 1982.

eloquent Jewish student named Aviva brought a hush over the group in explaining her feelings. She cited an Arab woman student who had said to her that the attack on Jerusalem bus No. 18 had been done by "freedom fighters" but had called the Jew who killed an eleven-year-old Arab girl in Nablus a "terrorist."* Facing Shakeib, Aviva made a moving plea for a universal standard of decency that would spare all innocents. She asked him to oppose killing innocent people, no matter who they were. Otherwise, she said, Arabs and Jews would remain locked in violence and terror, divorced from all hope. When she finished, the group was silent for a moment. But Shakeib said nothing in reply.

It seemed an elementary question of morality, and I threw it at a man who lives among Arabs in the Old City of Jerusalem and teaches at Bir Zeit University on the West Bank, a place of militant Palestinian nationalism. "I tell you frankly," he said, asking to remain anonymous, "when you have a terrorist activity, the bulk of the people are happy. You walk down in the street, you ask the people, they are happy." He tried to explain.

"You have so much abuse, humiliation, dehumanization of people, that any act that hurts the enemy has the immediate impact of cooling off. The blood of the enemy—it's almost a cannibalistic attitude. Palestinians feel helpless. Any activity, including terrorist activity, is something to say 'We are still armed.' It's a reminder." But, I noted, there doesn't seem to be an appreciation on the Arab side, as there is on the Jewish side, of the corrosive effect of terrorism. "You know, it's where you are in a situation," he said. "You have lost so much, then you can afford being wild. You can afford being generous when you are in good shape. You can be tolerant to criticism. The Israelis are in better shape. The Palestinians particularly, they have been dehumanized. I'm not justifying it, I'm trying to explain it.

"You have two contestants; one is clearly holding the other down, grabbing him, but he cannot let go. The one who is on top cannot let

---

* A Jewish settler, infuriated when stones were thrown at him, left his car, ran into a back street, and fired into a bakery, killing the eleven-year-old and wounding her younger sister. There was no indication that they were the children who had thrown the stones.

go. He cannot say, 'Okay, I did it now. I can go and rest; I can rejoice in my achievement.' It's this kind of stalemate. The Palestinian is clearly held around the neck. But the other person, who is apparently the victor, is also held. And if somebody hits him from the back, the person who is down will not say, 'Oh, that's not fair.' On the contrary, he will rejoice in it."

His observations coincided with a survey's finding that 61.6 percent of a sample of 1,185 Israeli Arabs "rejoice at or justify fedayeen actions in which Israeli Jews are killed." For those described politically as radical, the figure rises to 93.6 percent, and for the most accommodating, it falls to 29.6 percent.[18] To many Arabs, terrorists are heroes. When Israel released several hundred from jail as part of a 1985 prisoner exchange, those who returned to their homes on the West Bank became celebrities; as they walked through town, crowds of Arabs would shake their hands and wish them well.

Danny Rubinstein, who covers the West Bank for the Hebrew-language newspaper *Davar*, had another perspective. "They don't have any way of coping with us," he said of the Arabs. "They say, 'We don't have Phantoms [jet fighters]. Give us Phantoms and we shall bomb Tel Aviv tomorrow morning as you bomb Beirut.' " He laughed. "They don't have any other weapon. To bomb a camp as we bomb the camps in Lebanon— it's worse than any kind of terrorism. It's war between both of us, and each side wields the best weapon it can. There is nothing wrong in terrorism. For me, what's important is the target, the aim. I'm not justifying it, but the Jews of this country, we used terrorism too. It was pure terrorism. They [the Arabs] use it, it was successful, and they got international recognition because of it."

When the bombs were placed in the cars of the West Bank Arab mayors, blowing off Bassam al-Shaka's legs and Karim Khalef's foot, a ten-year-old Israeli girl named Noah came home from school confused. "Mommy, are we glad or not glad it happened?" she asked. Her mother explained that they were definitely not glad, that violence was never the way. The next day when Noah came home, she said, "Mommy, you're wrong. We are glad."

A fault line of ambivalence cuts through Israel on the question of violence against Arabs. Every massacre or spate of Jewish terrorism sets off a spasm of painful soul-searching and self-flagellation. Some Israelis on the political left wonder repeatedly what has become of them, whether their Jewish values can survive within the heavy superstructure of a state that must be built and defended. Yet the violence continues sporadically; the introspection does not make it go away. High officials may issue formal condemnations, as did Prime Minister Begin in the case of the attacks on the mayors, but many Israelis suspect the police work of being less than vigorous. And while the culprits may finally be arrested and tried, they are sentenced to considerably less time in prison than their Arab counterparts who are convicted of terrorism.

When the three Israeli judges handed down the convictions and the sentences to the group of twenty-five Jewish terrorists, for example, they did so with mixed feelings they made clear in their elaborate rulings. Most of the crimes of which the twenty-five were found guilty, including attempted murder, manslaughter, causing grievous bodily harm, and activity in a terrorist organization, carried maximum sentences of twenty years, which is what Arabs in their position could have expected to receive. But in every case where the court had some latitude, it gave much lighter sentences than the maximum. Only the three defendants who had murdered the Arab students with automatic-weapons fire into the campus of the Islamic College received the maximum—life in prison—because the law allowed the court no discretion; it required life for anyone found guilty of murder.

Nine of the defendants were allowed to plea-bargain for reduced sentences running from eleven months to three years; a tenth received ten years. In the cases of those fifteen who stood trial, the judges found it possible to express compassion for the criminals and their families. In sentencing Yehoshua Ben-Shushan, for example, "one of the conceptualizers in the Temple Mount episode" who gave the perpetrators of the other attacks his blessing as they met at his house to plan and as they left from his house to execute their assaults, Judge Shmuel Finkelman had this to say: "The defendant . . . is married and the father of seven children. He himself is a scholar and a warrior, a hero of Israel's wars. Senior army officers testified [on his behalf]. Brigadier General Binyamin Ben-Eliezer told about Yehoshua as a soldier, a person, a friend and comrade. Brigadier General Meir Dagan spoke of Yehoshua as an exemplary officer. Yehoshua took part in the War of Attrition and thereafter in the Yom Kippur War, in which he was seriously wounded in hand-to-hand combat. Yet despite his wound he did not abandon the fight until the bunker was cleaned out. . . . In his final remarks to the court, the defendant asserted: 'As Yehoshua and as an officer in the Israel Defense Forces, I was faithful unto my last drop of blood to the point of risking my life, and I am faithful to my last drop of blood and my last breath to my army, my people, my land. And from this I will not budge.' Indeed. To pass sentence is hard as a rule, and especially so on such as these. But what is to be done? For the court can do only what it may do." And so the three-judge panel sentenced him to four and a half years in prison.

One of the key leaders of the terrorist ring, Yehuda Etzion, received only seven years, a fraction of what an Arab convicted of a comparable crime is usually given. The other terms in prison ranged from four years to four months, punishments administered with deep hesitation. In December 1985, President Herzog commuted the three-year sentences of Dan Barri and Yosef Tsuria, who had plotted to blow up the Dome of the Rock.

Throughout the brief history of modern Israel, and especially from the late 1970s, the notion of terror as a legitimate method against Arabs has found resonance among significant segments of the Israeli population, including some right-wing figures at high levels. The sentiment was expressed bluntly by one of the most extreme personalities, Yossi Dayan, second in the Kach movement only to Rabbi Meir Kahane. Dayan said of the bombings of the mayors, "These people who did this are very professional; they did very good work." Kach had no role, he said, then added, "But I can understand why people did—very good people. If the Arabs think they can hit us and be safe, they're wrong. They cannot go to sleep early without any worry. Just as we have to put guards on our houses, so they will have to put guards on their houses." Of the mayors, who had been elected by their towns in 1976, he said, "We called on them twice to leave the area; now they are paying the price. They can't call on everyone to revolt and at the same time not expect to be hurt. As soon as the Arabs leave the country, they'll have fewer troubles. There's room in this land for only one nation. Anyone who thinks Jews and Arabs can coexist is a fool." Significantly, it was just a few months after the Jews who did the bombings were arrested that Kahane and his Kach movement won a seat in the Knesset.

A poll published in *Haaretz* after the attack on the mayors found 36.6

percent of a sample of about 1,200 Jewish adults responding "yes" to the question of whether terrorism should be used against Arabs in response to terrorism; 54 percent answered "no." Chaim Herzog, before becoming president of Israel, characterized the poll results as "disturbing," saying, "There is a feeling that the only way you can deal with the Arabs is to pay them back in their own coin. There has been an undercurrent of this for a long time. It's something that cuts right across party and is based more on country of origin. He won't do it himself, but he doesn't mind if somebody else does."

Leaders of the Jewish settlement movement on the West Bank, even some who were relatively moderate, endorsed the assaults. "I remember people at the time quite pleased with it," said Israel Harel, a former journalist who became head of the council of settlements. "They claim today that they had leaks by documents from those who had bugged them [the mayors] or followed them that they were the real heads of the PLO and that they really gave orders for all kinds of sabotage, including the six yeshiva students who were killed at Hadassah House. They were sure that it was going to be a mini-Holocaust, and that they had to stop it in such a way that it would shock everyone." I knew Israel Harel as a humane and tolerant man, but even he admitted to some satisfaction at the time. "To tell you that I myself was in sorrow when it happened? I wasn't sorry. Today I reject this with all my mind. I say it, and I'm under criticism from some of my best friends for it, but I say it."

As a society, Israel was slow to acknowledge that some of the most idealistic, pious Jews in its midst, some of those at the leading edge of dedication to the welfare of the Jewish state, could be legitimately branded with the term "terrorists." In official communiqués, in Israeli newspapers and broadcasts, even in conversation, the word had become synonymous with the PLO and, in many quarters, with Arabs generally. It fit the stereotype of Arabs as bloodthirsty, less than human, and it obviated the need to see Palestinian nationalism as an authentic movement. Israel radio and television, and independent-minded papers such as *The Jerusalem Post*, almost always referred to the PLO as nothing other than a "terrorist organization" with "terrorist bases" in Lebanon containing "terrorist buildings," "terrorist trucks," and launching "terrorist boats." Palestinian refugee camps in Lebanon were merely "terrorist bases" or "terrorist headquarters." Of course, it was true that the PLO based its military there and used the camps as launching pads for terrorist attacks inside

Israel. But somehow the term became almost a catechism in Israeli discussion, a chant that masked the human faces behind the enemy lines. Furthermore, "terrorism," in the lexicon of war propaganda, could never be applied to Jews. It thus lost its intrinsic meaning and became a slogan of hatred.

When the first attacks were made by Jews upon Arabs, Israel tried hard not to believe the obvious. Officials, editors, experts, and ordinary citizens postulated that Arabs were once again killing each other in primitive, factional, or tribal feuds. Israelis on the political left were quick to see that Jews must have been responsible. But many from the center to the right proved adept at deluding themselves. After the mayors were hit, Israel Harel recalled, "I was sure for quite a long time that this was done by Jordanian intelligence." The rumor was bolstered by leaks from the Israeli military government on the West Bank. When Jewish settlers sprayed gunfire into the Islamic College in Hebron, Israeli military men suggested that it had been done by Arabs as part of the ongoing conflict between secularists and Islamic fundamentalists on the West Bank. Experts on Arab affairs immediately recognized this as patently absurd, since every major Hebron family had a child at the college who could have been killed or wounded, which would have produced a long feud among rival clans bent on revenge. Only in the winter of 1984, after the rash of grenades at mosques and churches, did Israelis begin applying the word "terrorists" to Jews. And when the twenty-five Jewish settlers and two army officers were finally arrested, the term became widely accepted, even in the official indictment. Nonetheless, some Israeli newspapers, and the state-owned television and radio stations, called them "the Jewish underground," a more benign term with heroic connotations from the period of the anti-German partisans in Europe and the pre-state days of Israel's painful birth. A final evolution in the use of the word came in 1985 when Brigadier General Shlomo Ilya, a commander of troops facing guerrilla attacks in Lebanon, was quoted by Israeli radio as saying that the army would "respond to terror with terror." In a short time, "terror" had moved from a term of opprobrium to an expression of official policy.

The settler-terrorists were repulsive to many Israelis and had been so for many years as they conducted vigilante operations against Arabs. Settlers smashed windows, broke into Arabs' homes, shattered furniture, beat Arabs, and shouted at them to get out of "Jewish houses." Young

Jewish toughs wearing knitted yarmulkes and carrying automatic rifles swaggered into shops, dumped over crates of oranges, and ordered Arabs out of what they claimed had been Jewish property before the 1929 riots. Settlers vandalized an Arab village's diesel generator by pouring sugar into the fuel tank. Others went on a rampage through the Arab village of Halhoul one night after a bus had been stoned and two Jewish women injured; the settlers smashed the windshields and headlights of twenty-five cars, five trucks, and two buses. After stones were thrown at an Israeli car passing near an Arab girls' school in the Jalazoun refugee camp north of Jerusalem, six Jews from the settlement of Shiloh returned to the school and hurled bricks and rocks through the building's large classroom windows. As glass flew, the girls, many of whom were only six and seven years old, huddled with their teachers in corners of the rooms, terrified as the settlers fired their automatic rifles into the air and into the building for about half an hour. Then the Jews went to private houses nearby, smashing windows with rocks and shooting holes into water tanks on the roofs. Liberal Israeli papers called it the Wild West Bank, for gun-slinging settlers were practically free to administer their own summary justice when they faced violence.

Although many of the settlers were decent people who refused to engage in such attacks, the freewheeling environment of self-righteous extremism attracted a smattering of demented personalities who, in a normal setting, would have stood out dramatically as violent misfits. On the West Bank, however, they blended in, finding acceptance in the Jewish settlements and license to exercise their combative impulses. It sometimes struck me that the whole settlement subculture had become so zealous and insane that insanity became unnoticeable there. One settler at Kiryat Arba tended to agree, but he saw some virtue in the wildness. "Ask yourself what was the type of people attracted to outpost places in America 150 years ago," he remarked. "Need I say more?"

The most vivid and telling case was that of Eli Haze'ev, an American-born Protestant who grew up in Alexandria, Virginia, as James Eli Mahon, Jr., the son of an air force colonel and World War II hero who served as an artillery-spotter pilot over Nazi Germany. Jim Jr. had no such war of universal commitment, and so he spent his entire, short life in a violent search through cause after cause, battle after battle, for a war to win, a victory that always eluded him. Raised to see and fight communists everywhere, he began in the army in Vietnam, fighting viciously, being wounded badly, then volunteering to go back again and suffering serious wounds as he battled his way up a hill single-handedly in the 1968 Tet Offensive. He lost a thumb, and the army wouldn't take him again. Frustrated and driven, he became an informant for the FBI, infiltrating anti-war groups he was convinced were communist. A chain of violence linked the episodes of his life in the United States; he was arrested at least eleven times in four states and the District of Columbia, there having killed a member of a motorcycle gang he had infiltrated. The FBI had the murder charges dropped. Then, on the fourth day of the 1973 Israeli-Arab war, Jim Jr. called his father from Tel Aviv. "Shalom, Pop," he said. He had gone off to join the Israeli army. When the Israelis told him they didn't accept foreigners, he spent a few weeks kicking around at a kibbutz and a yeshiva. He came home impressed, his mother told me, "that Israel would back its men, that they fought for what they believed in." Jim Jr. converted to Judaism in Washington, D.C., and changed his name, taking his middle name as his first and the Hebrew "Haze'ev," which means "the wolf," as his family name. He went back to Israel, becoming an Israeli citizen under the law of return, and there he told his friends that he had been called "the Wolf" in Vietnam. His parents said it wasn't true: He had been called "Killer."

At first he was rejected by the Israeli army because of his missing thumb and other old war wounds. Then he found someone who pulled some strings and got him in. But the army would not accept him as a career man, and he drifted a bit after his normal tour. He had a lust for motorcycles and a shyness around women, his friends said. He married twice, once in New Orleans and then to an Israeli policewoman in Jerusalem; they had a daughter before they too broke up. Eli Haze'ev gravitated toward Meir Kahane's extremist Kach movement, then moved to the settlement of Kiryat Arba, where he found his niche as a hater of Arabs, who he thought were all communists, his friends recalled. He was jailed for eight months for breaking into an Arab house, vandalizing it, and beating the occupants; he was one of the few settlers prosecuted for such activity. On another occasion he was stopped at Ben-Gurion International Airport, and his Israeli and American passports were confiscated, as he was about to board a plane for the United States to carry out what he had described to friends as an assassination plot against either a PLO figure or an American Nazi. He had a raw passion for violence.

Had he lived, he would have had considerable opportunity to play in the terrorist game constructed by his settler colleagues, partly as a result of his death. At the age of thirty-two, Eli Haze'ev became one of those gunned down by Adnan Jaber and his men after Friday prayers in Hebron. Jaber had no idea who he was and had never heard his name. Nor had most Israelis until his death. But, significantly, he became an instant martyr for the tough, ultra-nationalistic hard-liners of Israel. His funeral was held in Hebron with the city under curfew, Arab faces peering fearfully from behind curtained windows at the throng of militant, religious Jews, many with automatic rifles slung over their shoulders, who walked through the narrow streets in a defiant gesture of possession. Chief of Staff Raphael Eitan was there. A military salute was fired over Haze'ev's grave in the city's ancient Jewish cemetery. None of the other five who were killed—who were softer, more moderate, people of decency—was accorded these honors. The chief rabbi for the Ashkenazim,* Shlomo Goren, attended and made kind remarks to the parents.

"He told us Eli was dedicated to a cause extremely rare, such that he can only be considered holy, that without doubt his name will be remembered among the heroes of Israel," Eli's father recalled. "I told him I was grateful for his statement," the retired colonel from Virginia continued, "but that we regretted that he'd followed the tactics that he had. The old gentleman looked as if I'd slapped him in the face with a dead mackerel. I'm afraid I insulted him. He came back with some heat, saying, 'What do you expect?' "

Settlers felt insecure. Although the army was ostensibly responsible for order, the West Bank was not thick with Israeli troops, and one could drive long distances or spend long hours in the towns without ever seeing a soldier. This made many Jewish settlers uneasy and at times fearful, and when Arab youngsters would throw stones at their cars and buses, the settlers would often fire with their automatic rifles, killing or wounding the demonstrators. Or they would chase the children—usually high-school boys—and grab one of them, take him to their settlement, and beat him before turning him over to the army or the civilian police. One settler, a lawyer, held a mock trial of several Arab boys at Kiryat Arba, terrifying them with a snarling German shepherd before letting them

---

* Those Jews of European and North American origins.

go. Another group grabbed a boy, stuffed him into the trunk of their car, took him to the settlement of Shiloh, locked him in a room, and beat him before driving him to the police. I saw him covered with bruises. One Arab boy was seen being forced into a settler's car, was then reported in the custody of the military government, and later turned up lying dead in a field near his village. Nobody was prosecuted.

The settlers justified their actions on the ground that modern stones, like their ancient counterparts, were lethal weapons; in the days of the Old Testament, after all, stoning was a means of execution, and the Koran gives the practice a religious connotation, occasionally using "stoned" to mean "accursed," as, in Islamic tradition, Abraham drove Satan away with stones.[19] From the late 1970s to the mid-1980s, stone-throwing resulted in numerous injuries and one death, that of an Israeli woman soldier, Esther Ohana, who was hit in the head while driving through the West Bank. After she was killed, the settlers' newspaper, *Nekuda*, published an editorial that could easily have been read as incitement, especially if it had been judged according to the nervous standards used by the Israeli military censor to ban large quantities of material from Arab-language newspapers. "The voice of Esther Ohana's blood is calling us from the earth," *Nekuda* declared. "The inhabitants of Judea-Samaria will not stand any more non-action, because if we do, we will be transgressing the commandment 'Thou shalt not stand by your brother's blood.'" Such statements by Arabs were barred and those by Jews were not.

For most of the six years that Menachem Begin was prime minister, Jews could kill Arabs on the West Bank with impunity. Arrests were sometimes made, prosecutions sometimes begun. But somehow the cases rarely came to trial. The pattern of leniency was documented by an assistant attorney general, Judith Karp, who studied seventy instances of Jewish violence against Arabs during a year beginning in the spring of 1981. She found that even in cases of murder, the army, which administered the West Bank under Defense Minister Ariel Sharon, intervened to thwart police investigations or, at the very least, failed to press for vigorous police action. Settlers came to see themselves as living amid lawlessness. In murder cases, the report said, "the appropriate energy and required efficiency for investigations of this kind were not evident." Describing two incidents in which settlers killed Arab boys, Karp wrote, "The suspects received a summons to present themselves to the police station. They announced that they would not appear and that they would speak only with the military authorities. The police did not do anything to bring the suspects to the police station despite the grave suspicion." Where soldiers had shot Arabs, she said, "the soldiers' version was believed even though it did not seem reasonable, and the circumstances of the incident supported the complainant's version." Karp's findings produced no action by the Justice Ministry, the police, or the army, and she therefore resigned as head of a committee examining the problem. The report was suppressed for a year by the Justice Ministry; it was released only after Yitzhak Shamir became prime minister and a round of Jewish terrorism broke out.

Many Palestinians believed the Jewish settlers were laying the psychological groundwork for the Arabs to panic and flee should warfare erupt, just as the massacre of Arabs at Deir Yassin led many to flee during the 1948 war for fear that the Jews would massacre them as well. Indeed, the germ of this idea could even be found occasionally in the utterances of Jewish settlers. In 1980, *Nekuda* quoted a resident of the settlement of Ofra, Aharon Halamish, as telling a symposium on Arab-Jewish relations, "We have to make an effort so that the Arab people have a hard time in this country. If we employ them and develop them, we are undermining ourselves. We don't need to throw grenades in the casbah or to kick out the Arabs, but there is nothing wrong with our giving them a hard time and hoping they get killed."

Although Israel and the West Bank were teeming with rumors that Begin had inhibited the police and the Shin Beth from investigating the bombings of the mayors, I was never convinced that the four-year delay in making arrests was entirely the result of political interference. There were real administrative problems as well. Despite Begin's devotion to retaining the West Bank forever, his government did not treat it as an integral part of Israel. The policemen there, mostly local Arabs with Jewish superiors, were geared to cope with only common crime among the 750,000 Arabs, not with crime among the growing Jewish population, which reached about 30,000 by the time Begin resigned in 1983. No Arab policeman would dare to enter a Jewish settlement, and there were too few Jewish policemen to handle the problem. The army had overall jurisdiction, and the subordinate police units were not free to set their own priorities in conducting investigations. In addition, the Shin Beth and other security and intelligence agencies had focused not on Jews but on Arabs in an effort to combat Arab terrorism. The settlers, seen as idealistic Jews struggling for Israel's benefit, were not regarded by the authorities as a population that should be placed under surveillance. Furthermore, the Shin Beth's methods were hardly models of police investigatory skill; the agency recruited Arab informers by threat and bribe, beat and terrified Arabs they arrested, imprisoned them for weeks without lawyers or trials, and engaged in other shortcuts that they could not use when dealing with Jewish suspects. Avraham Achituv, who headed the Shin Beth when the mayors were bombed, wrote after his retirement that the failure to find those responsible was "first and foremost an intelligence failure." The settlement of Kiryat Arba, he reported, closed up solidly in the face of the investigators. No settler would speak with the authorities. "Apparently this was initiated spontaneously, and went to express, more than anything, solidarity with the perpetrators." It was doubtful, he said, whether Jewish terrorists who had operated against Arabs in the 1950s had enjoyed such wide sympathy.[20]

The sympathy for the militant Jewish nationalists of the West Bank extended into the higher reaches of government under Begin's Likud Bloc, which was devoted to keeping all of the land under Israeli sovereignty. The settlers thus stood at the cutting edge of the policy issue most vital to Begin's vision, the consolidation of Israeli control over the West Bank. This goal formed the core of his political being, the keystone in his mission to make and keep the Jewish people whole and strong on the entire land of Israel. In this atmosphere, some settlers were convinced that the attacks on the mayors had met with high-level approval. Meir Indor, an activist in the settlement movement, told Israel Radio that he had attended a closed meeting in which "a few high-ranking army officers and a few political figures," whom he would not identify, had reacted positively to the bombings and had expressed regret that two other Arab mayors, Fahd Kawasmeh of Hebron and Muhammad Milhem of Halhoul, had been saved from attack by having been deported. "They were sorry they sent the two mayors outside the country," Indor said. "If they had stayed one month more, they would have been included on the list."

When the arrests were finally made, it was clear that those responsible for the terrorism had not been fringe elements but central figures in the mainstream of the settlement movement, not its ideologists or religious interpreters but its activists, "quite religious people, very good people," in the words of Israel Harel, head of the council of West Bank settlements. They had close ties in the Cabinet; they frequented the corridors and members' dining room of the Knesset. The terrorist group's leader, Menachem Livni, was known as a disciple of Rabbi Moshe Levinger, the lean, scraggly-bearded mover of the Hebron settlers; Uziah Sharabaf, sentenced to life for participating in the Islamic College attack, was Levinger's son-in-law. Another key actor, Yehuda Etzion, was a major founder of the settlement of Ofra, north of Jerusalem, where Israel Harel resided. "They were the best," Israel told me after their arrests. "Not the leadership but the people, whenever you needed them, they would give their time. In our ethos, these are the most admired. The pioneers. They give the real weight to the settlement. Those people in hard times, you see them in the right places, by instinct." Israel made these observations not in admiration but in pain for what such "good people" had committed.

They "are not 'good boys gone wrong,' " countered Roy Isacowitz of *The Jerusalem Post*. "They are not the bad apples in the cart but the tastiest, freshest apples of them all. It is the cart itself that is rotten"—that is, the settlement movement itself.

After the arrests, Harel was on one side of a deep split in the settlement movement known as Gush Emunim, the Bloc of the Faithful, whose members were divided between condemning the terrorist acts and expressing understanding for settlers who "took the law into their own hands" when the army allegedly failed to protect them. The notion that "the underground" had taken "the law" into its own hands gained remarkably wide currency in the Israeli press and public, with few voices raised to note that nothing in Israeli law provides, for example, that Arab college students are to be sprayed indiscriminately with gunfire because unknown Arabs stabbed a Jew to death in a nearby marketplace. Yuval Ne'eman, a physicist and extreme right-winger who has been instrumental in developing Israel's nuclear-weapons program, saw the Islamic College assault in the context of the region's ancient tradition of revenge. "The students at the Islamic College were attacked for being Arabs," he said, "just as the yeshiva students [in Hebron] were assaulted for being Jews. No distinction was made in this case between guilty and not guilty. In the final analysis, this was an attack in the style of the Corsican vendetta or the common Arab blood feud. . . . This is the accepted moral code in Lebanon and is shared by Bedouins in the Negev and clans in the villages of Galilee . . . a tradition to which we have grown accustomed in our Middle East neighbors and in the entire Mediterranean area, but which we thought we, as Jews, had left behind in biblical times."

Ne'eman, who was then minister of science and technology and head of the Tehiya Party, caused an uproar when he distinguished between that indiscriminate shooting and the bombings of the Arab mayors. "Although it [the bombing] was an illegal act which I do not support," he said, "practically, there is a great difference between an assault on innocent people and an assault on people who hold responsibility." The bombing, he contended, was "an assault on individual persons who were, at the time, responsible for incitement. That was the National Guidance Council, which represented the PLO. And the fact is that after they were attacked—which, by the way, didn't cause death—we never again heard of the National Guidance Council." He did not raise the obvious question of why, if sufficient evidence existed to prove incitement, members of the council were not prosecuted. And since Ne'eman seemed to be saying that the results were positive, Israel Radio and *The Jerusalem Post*, among other Israeli papers, jumped to a conclusion, misquoted him as using the word "positive," and ignored his statement of opposition to the act. The erroneous impression was created in Israel that he had endorsed the assault on the mayors; significantly, two and a half months later, Israeli voters went for his Tehiya Party in greater numbers than ever before, making it the third-largest faction in the Knesset, with 5 of the 120 seats.

Although the Jewish terrorist ring provoked widespread revulsion throughout Israel, public-opinion polls also showed a substantial minority of Israeli Jews expressing some degree of support for the twenty-five Jewish terrorists. "The problem's not the twenty-five," said Rabbi David Hartman, a philosopher. "The problem is that they resonate in the hearts of the population." Of 1,200 Jewish adults interviewed by the Pori research organization nearly two months after the arrests, 31.8 percent found at least some justification for the attacks on Arabs, whereas 60 percent opposed the "underground."[21] Of 651 Jewish adolescents interviewed in August 1984, 38 percent expressed support for "private groups whose goal is to take revenge on Arabs for every attack against Jews." About 9 percent said they were prepared to join such organizations.[22]

The ambivalence was felt among Israeli officials and authorities as well. The proper prosecutorial steps were taken against the defendants, but the atmosphere in court was more like a picnic than a judicial proceeding. At one of the preliminary hearings, the accused, all in yarmulkes and full beards, sat among their relatives in the cramped courtroom on Arab East Jerusalem's Saladin Street. They chatted casually with their wives and friends, came and went at will from the courtroom, smiled frequently—though in a somewhat forced way, I thought—prayed, meditated, exchanged food and letters, and otherwise had a fine time. During recesses their police guards allowed them to mingle with their families in the hallway practically unsupervised, a leniency unimaginable in cases involving Arab terrorists. A policeman even stopped a defendant in the corridor and shook his hand warmly.

A year later, it was discovered that a high-ranking officer, Chief Inspector Meir Levi of the border police, had led the accused terrorists on some pleasant detours while transporting them between court and prison— once to a beach to let them swim and once for a meal in the police canteen at Ben-Gurion International Airport. He was dismissed.

At one early court hearing, the accused and their families and supporters erupted into a demonstration demanding the ouster of an Arab attorney, Darwish Nasser, who was observing the hearing on behalf of Karim Khalef, one of the bombing victims. When an army officer among the visitors' benches said that he recognized Nasser as a PLO suspect he had interrogated, the mother of one of the accused cried, "PLO, get out of here!" Her son and the other defendants picked up the chant. A defense attorney asked the judge to remove the Arab; the judge refused, saying that it was an open trial, and the relatives then left the courtroom noisily, declaring that they would not sit in the same hall with the PLO.

The court also instituted an unprecedented ban for nearly two months on the publication of the defendants' names, accepting the dubious argument by their attorneys that their families could become the targets of Arab reprisals. In fact, Arab villagers knew the faces, automobiles, and often the names of the most aggressive, antagonistic Jews from nearby settlements who smashed windows, grabbed children, and were quick to shoot. Ordinary Arabs feared them and avoided them, and Arab terrorists never pinpointed them or their families.

In the weeks and months following their arrests, the Jewish terrorists received expressions of both disgust and support from their colleagues on the settlements. Much was heard from the supporters about the danger in which settlers lived and the inadequacy of the army's protection. Rabbi Levinger, who was held in custody for a while and then released, rejected terrorism and in the same breath excused it, saying, "I can understand that Jews did what they do." Jews may be in danger in France or New York, he declared. But "in our holy country," he said, "there can't be such a situation, and the government must understand that it was its mistake, and the trial must be for the Israel government, not for them."

Benny Katzover, another Gush Emunim leader, remarked, "What is most important and most interesting is not what they did but what their motives were and the background of events that drove good, sober, and precious people to such acts." In the midst of this, a court gave life sentences to four Arabs convicted of the murder of Aharon Gross, the Hebron yeshiva student whose stabbing death had provoked the Jews' submachine-gun attack on the Islamic College. A classmate of the victim shouted in court, "What about the death sentence? That's why there's an underground!"

Some activists had the idea of running the whole group of defendants for the Knesset, and they began circulating a petition headed "To our brothers who are under arrest for their struggle to secure Jewish settlement in the Land of Israel." The father of Gilad Peli, thirty-one, said after his son received a ten-year prison sentence for plotting to blow up the Dome of the Rock, "The charge sheet omitted the basic point. Charge number one should have been 'love of Israel.' "

In 1985, after the government exchanged 1,150 Palestinian prisoners for 3 Israelis held captive by a Palestinian guerrilla group, extensive calls for the release of the Jewish terrorists were heard from the right. Among the Palestinians who were turned loose were hundreds convicted and sentenced to life imprisonment for terrorist attacks in which Jewish lives had been lost; those who wished were even allowed to return to their homes on the West Bank. Ariel Sharon urged amnesty for the Jewish terrorists, as did Yitzhak Shamir, who had been prime minister when they were arrested; Shamir, himself a terrorist in pre-state days, called them "basically excellent boys." Israel Harel, the settlement leader who had previously expressed revulsion over the violence by his compatriots, urged their freedom out of a fear that settlers would attack the newly released Palestinian terrorists. Some settlers did organize campaigns of surveillance and harassment of the Palestinians, including threats that were credible enough to induce a few to leave their West Bank homes for more congenial surroundings in Jordan or elsewhere in the Arab world.

Shortly after the arrests in 1984, I wandered one day through a small demonstration of support outside police headquarters. Between 100 and 150 people had gathered under some tall trees; many were holding placards: "We Demand Revenge! Death for Death! Blood for Blood!" "For the sake of my brothers and friends, for these I cry. We'll sit on buses, we'll walk on Jaffa Road, we'll tour the Galilee, and we'll walk on the streets of Nablus and Hebron." A sweet-faced young woman held one that read "The murderers are walking free, and the friends of the murdered are in jail." She was Sandra Stengel, who had immigrated from Brooklyn with her husband and seven children just nine months before. She used a dark-red kerchief to bind her head, in the religious tradition. "I know them," she said. "They're fine, upstanding people. It's a shame that the government wouldn't defend us and they had to take things into their own hands." In her few months living on the settlement of Kiryat Arba, she had become a quick expert on the "Arab mentality."

"The only language it seems the Arabs understand is language in kind," she explained patiently. "They don't respect reason. I hate to say what I'm saying, but it gets to the point where you've buried enough of your children and kissed enough of your men good-bye for the last time. We've tried everything. They just won't stop." As we talked, the mother of one of the six Jews killed in the 1980 Hebron massacre made a weeping, hysterical speech over a public-address system, mostly in Yiddish, salted with some broken English.

Sandra Stengel taught English to sixth-, seventh-, and eighth-graders at Kiryat Arba, but she made no attempt with her classes to condemn the Jewish terrorism. "A lot of the children have fathers arrested. All the kids say let's get them out." No children thought the violence had been wrong, she said. Their heads, and hers, were filled with myths about the freedom Arabs had to attack them and the restrictions on Jews' ability to defend themselves. "I was informed that if an Arab is ready to throw a grenade at me, I can't do anything until he hits me," she contended absurdly. "You get tired of mourning and crying. My daughter was on a bus that was stoned. It's a tragic, frightening thing." She then moved suddenly into an idealized vision of how thoroughly she belonged in this land, a conviction sustained by the mundane: She shopped at the Arab markets and was accepted there, she said. "I go into Hebron every day." Does she carry a weapon? I asked; virtually all men, and many women, carry pistols. She said no. I asked why not. "I'm not afraid." Her fear seemed rather abstract, an ideological fear. Her relations with Arabs were "very fine," she said. "I love children. I'm dying to learn Arabic. I say hello to the Arab women. I wish we could live in peace, I really do. That's my deepest wish."

The deputy speaker of the Knesset, Meir Cohen-Avidov, appearing at the rally to support the settler-terrorists, declared that any Arab who murdered a Jewish child should have his eyes gouged out. This brought a retort several days later from the Knesset speaker, Menachem Savidor, who admonished, "God forbid that we should advocate the use of the same brutal, bestial means employed by the terror organizations. There is no stronger guarantee for our security and survival than our moral strength. Violence and democracy cannot exist side by side. Anyone who supports violence, either tacitly or openly, as a spontaneous emotional reaction or as part of a world outlook, not only subverts the rule of law but also undermines the foundations of the government, the values of the state and the Zionist movement, and the prospects of peace and coexistence between Arabs and Jews."

Kiryat Arba's schools reflected the adult feelings. Kindergartners were pretending that the good Jews were the Smurfs and the Arab was Gargamel, the bad guy in the television program. The teacher, Ruti, explained to the children that there were good and bad Arabs. "The good ones are the ones who work for us in the settlement or the ones who come into the grocery store and you can say 'Shalom' to them. The bad ones are the ones who throw rocks at us, the ones that kill."

The children, confused and disturbed by the arrests of their fathers and their friends' fathers, drew pictures of weapons and built fighter planes, guns, and tanks out of blocks, declaring that they would use them to kill Arabs. When one boy pretended that he was holding his father's gun and said, "I'm going to kill the Arabs with this," another teacher, Margalit, asked where he had heard such a thing. "My father said it at home," the boy replied. "He said the Arabs are bad and have to be killed." Margalit did not know quite how to react. "It's a matter of education from home," she said. "In the kindergarten we try to ignore it." She told the boy that there were bad Arabs and less bad Arabs, who don't have to be killed. "We can live with them in the same land, as long as they know that we are the rulers," she explained.[23]

"My teacher thinks it's good what they did," a thirteen-year-old named Oren Edry told me. I had stopped him and his two friends as they were walking along a quiet street in the settlement, now a township of stone apartment houses and trees that were beginning to grow tall enough to give the community a well-established air. They were cute, bright boys in clean short-sleeved shirts and skullcaps, their pristine faces blessed with open gazes of sincerity. The three went to three different religious schools, both in the settlement and in Jerusalem, so they represented more than an isolated picture of what was happening in classrooms. Oren's teacher had been wounded in the 1980 Hebron massacre. "He felt what it's like," the boy said, "so we have to get up and do something." They talked for a long time in a torrent of slogans and arguments they had heard from their teachers and parents, assertions that the army does not protect them, that the world is angered more when Arabs are victims than when Jews are, that Arabs understand only force. Aharon Peretz, a blond boy with freckles, recited a justification of the attack on the Islamic College students: "One of them who was killed was an actual terrorist, and practically everybody there is a member of Fatah."

I asked the boys to pretend for a moment that they were the judges. What would they do to the Jewish terrorists?

"They should give them a punishment, but not a heavy one," Oren said. "I would give them ten years."

"No, that's too much," said Moshe Zilbert, eleven. "Two years."

"I would just let them go," Aharon said, "and tell them not to do it again."

These boys are taught that the Arab is Amalek, the Old Testament enemy of ancient Israel. "It says in the Torah that you have to destroy all the remnants of Amalek," said Oren. The Torah, the boys explained, accepts "foreign citizens" as residents of Israel only if they accept seven commandments. "We don't want them to live here at all," Oren declared. But if they do, then they must observe the commandments against eating uncooked meat, practicing idolatry, stealing, spilling blood, and engaging in incest. "They should be limited in area, not to provoke people," Oren continued, adding the sixth restriction. Aharon concluded with the seventh: "We have to be ruling over them and not them ruling over us."

FOUR

Religious
Absolutism:
Isaac and Ishmael

When ye are passed over Jordan
into the land of Canaan; Then
ye shall drive out all the inhabitants
of the land from before you. . . . And ye
shall dispossess the inhabitants of the land,
and dwell therein. . . . Those which ye let
remain of them shall be pricks in your eyes,
and thorns in your sides, and shall vex you
in the land wherein ye dwell.

—Numbers 33:51–53,55

"THE BIBLE DOESN'T TEACH YOU TOLERANCE; THAT I WANT YOU TO know," said Rabbi David Hartman. "The biblical framework is not the source of tolerance. That's not the place you go to for that. You go there for passion, for zealousness, for extremes. Biblical people are extremists."

We sat across a table in his Jerusalem study. It was a room laden with books and wrapped in a quiet mood of contemplation, but there was never tranquility in the ideas that burst from Hartman's mind. Laughing, shouting, whispering, adjusting his skullcap on the back of his head, he fired his thoughts as if to pepper you with joyous discovery. Clean-shaven and wearing a boyish smile, he delivered his most provocative and distressing conclusions with such a glowing search for inner morality that somehow I never went away from him depressed. He was one of Israel's most stimulating Orthodox philosophers. When we spent an occasional hour or so together, the subject invariably became the spiritual course of Israel, the nation's groundswell of religiosity and nationalism. The last couple of times I saw him, we discussed the religious traditions of Judaism, the Jewish settler-terrorists, and the struggle between absolutism and pluralism.

Intellectually, Hartman was a bridge between the fierce intolerance and the fervent morality of the religious tradition, a man who knew some of the settler-terrorists, had taught one of them, deplored their violence, and held accountable not only the individuals but Judaism: the failure of Judaism to experience a renaissance as the dream of Zionism had been translated into the reality of a Jewish state. He struggled to mesh the humanism of the religion with the exigencies of statehood. "It's not that the tradition is of one piece," he explained. "There are too many different strands in the tradition itself. There are deep intolerances in the tradition. So if you use the biblical model, you don't have pluralism, you don't have welcoming of the stranger. When you open up the Bible as a very careful framework from which you're building the foundations of your national identity, what you get there is not just 'Love the stranger,' it's not just pluralism and tolerance." It is also God's command to drive out the aliens—the pagan idol-worshipers—and to heed His warning that any who are allowed to remain "shall be pricks in your eyes, and thorns in your sides, and shall vex you in the land wherein ye dwell."

Even as a religious man, then, Rabbi Hartman had no illusions about the impulses of religious culture. "Religion is the source of utopian dreams," he declared, "and it is fundamentally reactionary, not pluralistic. I want you to know that the theological framework can be used in many ways. You can use God to expel the Arabs from every inch of this territory, and you can use God and the Bible and Jewish tradition to say that there shouldn't be Christians in this country and there shouldn't be any deviation from pure monotheism. The past can serve any purpose. So my question isn't what does the past awaken; the past can awaken anything. The major concern is who of the present are going to be making that decision. Who are the intellectual, spiritual leaders of the present? How are they going to use the tradition?"

.　.　.

In the Arab-Israeli conflict, the center does not hold. The moderate ground is eaten away, yielding to pious extremism on either side. Religion becomes a force of evil. It tears at the soul. It coats warfare and terrorism and hatred with a varnished righteousness.

In Judaism and Islam, as in man's other organizations of faith, anyone can find anything he wishes to sanctify his noblest and his basest actions. The strict moral code, the even justice, the glittering platitude, the elevation of the believer can foster both the beauty of generosity and the malice of exclusivity. Each virtue preached contains an antithesis within itself. Great wrongs are done in the name of morality, cruelty is advanced as a tool of justice, the holy platitude rationalizes the persecution, and the believer's certainty carries a curse against whoever stands outside. It is as true today as throughout the long history of this land, and of other lands as well, that the bloodshed and the conquest have often been performed in the service of God.

Much of the Arab-Israeli dispute is secular, relating to mundane issues of conflict over territory, military security, and cultural disharmony. And many of the Arab-Jewish tensions are nonreligious, following patterns of stereotyping, fear, envy, and wary friendship that are common to the prejudices between classes and ethnic groupings elsewhere. But religion does exist as a component of some of the frictions, giving them an added sense of scope and an aura of inevitability. Religion's role has grown as part of the widespread tendency toward fundamentalism that transcends societies and faiths: Some rabbis and imams lend their voices to the cause of violence.

The fundamentalism that has engaged Islam, beginning with the dogmatic fanaticism of Iran under the Ayatollah Ruhollah Khomeini, has spread into certain elements of Syria, Egypt, Lebanon, the Gaza Strip, and the West Bank. This has a considerably weaker—but no more attractive—parallel in Judaism, one that has led some secular Israeli Jews to denounce their fundamentalist countrymen as "Khomeinis." More diluted still has been the American and West European phenomenon of the born-again Christian, which contains, in some cases, a familiar self-righteous intolerance. All these developments have a shared affinity for absolutism, an inclination to impose their particular values on a broader population, a visceral aversion to diversity and pluralism. Each adherent knows with certainty that he is right and others are wrong.

A difference among them is the degree of state power each has to wield, a long-standing difference of relationship between religious and governmental authority. The scholar Bernard Lewis, a Jew who studies Islam, explained to a Jewish audience in Jerusalem one evening the variations among the Christian, Islamic, and Jewish interactions with politics. And he ended with a disturbing question.

"The Christian and Muslim positions are diametrically opposed," he said. "I speak of course of the classical Muslim position, not of the modernized, Westernized, liberalized, falsified Muslim position. And in the tradition of Islam, as the Ayatollah Khomeini has recently reminded us, religion is the state. The Prophet, during his lifetime, became a sovereign, commanded armies, made war and peace, collected taxes, dispensed justice, and did all the things that a head of state does, so that Islam, from its early inception, is intimately associated with the exercise of political power. And this has been a characteristic of Islamic societies from then until the latest movements of Islamic revival in Iran and Egypt and elsewhere until the present day. Islam is a political religion.

"Christianity, on the other hand—from the lifetime of its founder, who made a classical distinction between what belongs to God and what belongs to Caesar—Christianity has always recognized two authorities, church and state, to use the modern terms, sometimes joined, sometimes separate, sometimes in harmony, sometimes in conflict, sometimes one dominating, sometimes the other, but always two, quite distinct from one another. In Islam there are no such two.

"The Jewish position is very difficult to see since classical Judaism, rabbinic Judaism, evolved after the Jewish state had ceased to exist. And this now poses itself as a problem: Whether the Judeo-Christian or Judeo-Islamic tradition will predominate in this particular area remains to be seen."

The problems for Judaism, then, are bound up with the emerging shape and character of the young Jewish state. What is "Jewish" and what is "Israeli"? Where do the humanistic values of Judaism fit with the toughness essential to the survival of the Jewish people? Which strands of biblical morality should be used to weave the fabric of Israeli society? The questions have been illuminated by the rise of militant absolutism in Israel, by the growth of ethnocentrism, and by the proximity of religio-nationalism to the source of governmental power.

It is not that Israel is a land of fanatic religious fundamentalists; quite the contrary. Only 10 to 11 percent of Israeli Jews identify themselves in public-opinion polls as strictly observant religiously, and only a minority of that group are politically absolutist. But the impact of that small vanguard's biblical zeal, passion, and single-mindedness has been enlarged by domestic political circumstances and the fortunes of war.

The biblical arguments for holding the West Bank excite very few outside the ranks of the militant movement of settlers; most Israeli reluctance to relinquish the occupied territory rests on worries about security, not on God's deed to Abraham. Yet the Bible is the basic literature of Israel, even for the secularists. It is seen as the foundation of Jewish history, and so its themes have a resonance beyond the immediate circle of activists for whom the Bible is a living commitment. In the years following the capture of the West Bank during the 1967 war, these religio-nationalists seized the center of visionary activism from the old guard of Israel's founders. They captured Israel's romantic passion by joining a religious and nationalist fanaticism with a pioneering purpose. And they, not the secularists, then transmitted the pulse of Israeli policy as Menachem Begin came to power in 1977, injecting a spirit of righteous certainty into the posture of the Jewish state.

Israel passed through several stages of development to reach this moment. First came the dream, the ideological state, the vision, nurtured by the early, pre-state Zionists. Then came the building of the state, the stage of Ben-Gurion and the Labor Party Zionists. "Practice," Hartman whispered. "Tackle. Get things done. That's the Peres generation. That's Rabin. We gotta build roads. We gotta solve problems. I don't have time now for philosophers. Now's not the time to offer ideologies. Now's the question: Can I absorb 100,000 immigrants coming in from Yemen? How? I don't have housing. How do I get jobs? What do I do? How do I build industry? You have to build a national consensus. You have this enormous ingathering of such a variety of groups. The school of coping with reality, making things work."

That practical period lasted until the stunning Israeli victory in six days over the Arab armies in 1967, a war that placed the West Bank and the Temple Mount of East Jerusalem in Jewish hands for the first time in 2,000 years. A sense of grandeur followed. "The whole world fell in love with us," said Hartman. "To be Israeli was really sexy. Dayan's patch. 'There's nothing we can't do' type of spirit. We are really a power. We are the center now. People are interested in knowing, 'How do you people do it?' So I would say that both grandeur and decay set in, deep moral decay. We grew so fast into a visible central power that the seeds of arrogance as well came in. We were suddenly cast into the larger biblical drama of the larger Israel when we really weren't prepared for it. Suddenly we had a feeling that destiny was moving us. Besides the Rabins, who became popular international figures, there started to grow up in our dreams deep messianists, deep religious nationalists, deep dreamers of Ezekiel's vision. They were unprepared for it. And the very unpreparedness gave it some sort of religious quality, so you had the feeling that God suddenly said something has happened. Suddenly everything which we really dreamed about—Hebron, Shechem, Beit El, places [now on the West Bank] we revered in all our daily education—suddenly we were in our dreams. It was as if the Lord opened up the heavens and gave the Ten Commandments. So there was a deep sense that we were cooperating with destiny. It's not something we willed; it was willed for us. The messianic perspective on Israel suddenly surfaced. Something was given to us as a gift. Dare we not be up to this great divine gift? It would be like a divine betrayal. Dare I deny that which really Ezekiel understood, that which the prophets dreamed of, and here it's given to us? You have to understand, the Bible is not something preached, a Sunday sermon. It's the living picture of how you understand yourself. And this was a country of biblicism. The country was brought up on it.

"The country wasn't built by pragmatists," Hartman continued, enjoying the apparent paradox. "It was built by people with passion and a dream. Even though there was a surface practicality in the Ben-Gurion era, before that surface practicality lie the seeds of messianic dream. Practical people don't come to the Negev Desert. Therefore, deep down in this country is a receptivity to wild dreams. The people who created Israel were madmen, and therefore this country is receptive to mad visions, people mad like the prophets are mad. You never know when they will sprout. If we were realistic, we wouldn't come here. You want to be realistic? So live in California!" Hartman shouted, laughing. "Why do I have to stay here? I'm facing a potential hundred million Khomeinis. Why do I have to stay here?"

The messianists who arose after the 1967 war were a new breed of fundamentalists who created a dangerous synthesis of religion and nationalism, welding pious self-righteousness and military force into a potent single-mindedness. They formed the small hard core of the West Bank settlement movement, combining a literal reading of the Old Testament and an extreme political posture into an effort to close off the option, should it ever present itself, of relinquishing part or all of the West Bank in exchange for peace with the Arabs.

In a sense, they stepped forward to fill a void in Israel's national spirit. By the late 1960s, the country had become too comfortable to satisfy a Jew with a mission. The early, struggling, pioneering years had passed, and those who were driven by their ideals had to look to a new frontier. They found it on the West Bank, in the ancient lands of Judea and Samaria.

One American, immigrating to Israel with a deep Zionist conviction, realized once he arrived that he had merely exchanged an apartment in Brooklyn for an apartment in Tel Aviv. Searching for fulfillment, he then moved to the West Bank settlement of Elkana, where he believed he was finally acting out his commitment to the Jewish state. Varda Davidson, an Israeli-born mother of five, was pushed by a distaste for her own passivity. "We felt we had to do much more than just sit back in Tel Aviv, listen to the news, and wait for the next war," she said. "You have to do something—settlements, some sort of stronghold on the land. And that was something we could do besides war." Just as the Crusaders had built their fortresses and castles on hilltops in the eleventh century, so did the zealous Jews now place most of their new encampments and townships on the crests of the rough, stony hills that overlooked valleys and road junctions.

There were several waves of settlers. The bulk of the religious, ideologically driven Israelis took up their stations on the West Bank in the five years or so beginning with Begin's election in 1977, although small vanguards of them squatted illegally here and there from 1968 onward. That fundamentalist movement was bracketed, before and after, by mostly secular Jews who settled the West Bank for nonreligious reasons, both in the early years after 1967 and beginning in the early 1980s. Those who went first and established farms in the Jordan River Valley, where the flowing desert hills around Jerusalem plunge to an arid rift below sea level, had close contact with the earth itself, making it productive with modern irrigation and growing techniques. They turned the desert into a fertile ground for tomatoes, peppers, eggplants, cucumbers, and other vegetables, and they loved the land the way a farmer loves the land, not out of any mystical communion with their history. The third, 1980s wave of settlers went mostly in search of economical housing, made possible by government subsidies unavailable in major cities. They did not need a comprehensive system of faith to move them to the satellite towns that were serving as bedroom communities for Jerusalem and Tel Aviv.

The middle group was the important one in shaping the ideological framework of the movement. Led by the Gush Emunim activists, those settlers, most of them with higher education, forged an amalgam of religious and nationalist impulses that took them to barren, stony hilltops where they practically camped in small house trailers for several years until the government built them permanent apartments. They were driven by a search for biblical heritage, military security, and personal fulfillment, with the mixture of these components varying in each individual. Some stressed the secular, pioneering objectives, and many found a modest religious revival in the new communities.

Strangely, despite these settlers' avowed reverence for the land, I never encountered any who seemed to have any feeling for it. None had the farmer's devotion to working the land they claimed to love; they used it as a place of residence, a symbol of their faith and their history, an abstraction, but they almost never turned a spade or plowed a furrow. I never saw a pious settler in the hills of Judea and Samaria hold a clump of raw earth in his hand and watch it and smell it as he crushed it and sifted it between his fingers. As the Jewish townships spread from the rocky hilltops into the more arable valleys, advancing bulldozers cut swaths and scars through the Arabs' vineyards and small fields of winter wheat, which were then left fallow by the newly arrived Jews. One settlement I know kept a herd of sheep, another grew flowers in a hot-house. Some settlements built small factories on their land, but by and large their residents commuted to work in Jerusalem or Tel Aviv.

Their most aggressive champion in government was Ariel Sharon, a celebrated general and minister of agriculture in Begin's first Cabinet. I first met him as I was visiting the Gush Emunim settlement of Elon Moreh, named after the place that Genesis says God gave to Abraham and his seed. A Supreme Court decision later ordered the settlement dismantled because it was on privately owned Arab land, and it had to be reassembled some miles away. But on that warm July day, its few residents felt as if it were an outpost of permanent return. As settlers were patiently and eloquently explaining their deed to this land according to the Old Testament, Sharon zoomed up the hill in a jeep, preceded by a jeep full of soldiers brandishing automatic rifles. When he had stepped out and greeted everyone, and we had been introduced, he pulled out a map and gave me his reason for wanting Jewish families to settle these rugged hills. His argument had nothing at all to do with the Bible. "Security is not only guns and aircraft and tanks," he said. "Security first of all is motivation—motivation to defend a place. If people live in a place, they have the motivation to defend themselves, and the nation has the motivation to defend them. The fact that you are present, that you know every hill, every mountain, every valley, every spring, every cave; the curiosity to know what is on the other side of the hill—that's security. If you have all the guns and tanks in the world, you cannot do anything if you aren't motivated, if you don't know the area, if you don't feel that it is yours. Yes, I want to put the children before the tanks."

Through my years in Israel, every time I saw Sharon, he would recall our first meeting at Elon Moreh. He seemed to see it as a satisfying symbol.

The Gush Emunim settlers did not explain things in precisely the same terms as Sharon, however. "Jewish people came here not because of political reasons, not because of security reasons, but because this land was promised to them by the Lord," said Michal Shvut of Elon Moreh, a slender young woman who named her first son Shomron, which is Hebrew for Samaria, the area in which she lived. She spoke pleasantly, with the same quiet logic one often finds in an evangelical Christian: a simple, pure progression of reasoning drawn inside a circle of certainty untainted by the complex arguments of generals and diplomats. To anyone who did not know the Arab world in the cities and refugee camps beyond the gates of the settlements, the direct neatness of the appeal could be enormously seductive.

Listen to Benny Katzover, a Gush Emunim leader with a knitted skullcap, a black beard, and eyes that burn darkly. He is gesturing out over the ancient hills of Samaria, strewn with stones and scrubbed dry with a tawny summer green. "This is the beginning of all our connections to this land. For all our roots, this is a connection. This is the heart of Israel. This is much more Israel than other parts, and it is not only our roots but our values. In the last thirty years about 400,000 Jews left Israel because they lost their values, their connection with the land. If a Jew sits in New York or Tel Aviv, slowly, slowly, he forgets what makes him a Jew, why he has to keep himself as a Jew."

Or hear Varda Davidson: "Wherever you look you find Jewish remnants. You feel you're not on somebody else's land. You're giving the other an opportunity to stay in his home; you're not sending him away. He's got a right to be here as we have, and this can all be very, very nice and homey and cozy and all that. But let us be, let us build our homes, let us start living here, let us expand here if we want to, let people come up here if they want to. If the Arabs want to stay here on the top of their hills, or if they want to put up their houses wherever they do, as long as it's legal and as long as it's okay, we're not going to come and tear their houses down and build our own. This is a big land, and there's enough room for everybody." In a sense, she is right. When you travel through the West Bank, it seems mostly empty. If it were not for the exclusivity of religion or the anger and intolerance of nationalism, common sense would be on Varda Davidson's side: Arabs and Jews could live in contentment together on this ancient land.

I usually came away from conversation with settlers feeling a certain calm. They embraced you gently in a soothing dream, cleansing your thoughts of the complex ambiguities that swarmed through reality. Their honesty and idealism were attractive qualities that seemed softer at close view than from the distance of issues and headlines. "They're nice people," I once said to Micha Bar-Am, the photographer, as we pulled away from a settlement after some interviews.

"Yes," Micha said. "That's the trouble."

Many settlers professed to believe fervently in friendly coexistence with their Arab neighbors, and some seemed to have so much goodness in their hearts that they could not see the evil in their midst. "Nobody from here is going to go out and kill any Arab," Rachael Klein, of Kiryat Arba, told me on February 4, 1980. I think she believed that sincerely. But four months later, some of her neighbors did go out from Kiryat Arba and attack Arabs, deliberately, professionally.

"Kiryat Arba is the original name of Hebron," she explained, "so it is written in the Bible, at least fifty times. The rightful place of the Jew is in Hebron. Why? Because Hebron is the first city of David. Jerusalem was the second city. The Machpelah was bought by Abraham," she said, a reference to Abraham's purchase of the Cave of the Machpelah in Hebron as a tomb for his wife, Sarah. Mrs. Klein opened her Bible to Genesis and read: "In the beginning, God created the heaven and the earth. . . ." Then she stopped. "You see?" she asked. I can't say that I did.

"Why didn't God start with laws? God knew who he was going to give the land to." She turned to the present. "The government has been very weak. If the Arabs want to attack, they'll attack, and they won't attack if the Jews believe strongly enough in themselves. In Hebron, you'll find the Jewish houses are not being lived in by Arabs. They've been taken over as shops, but they're not living in them. The Arabs know they are Jewish houses and think they're inhabited by ghosts, and they won't live in them."

The streaks of fanaticism surfaced in multiple forms, sometimes in a mild paternalism toward Arabs, sometimes in a virulent bigotry, usually in a tendency to see Arabs as a hostile monolith rather than as the varied individuals they were. Until the 1984 arrests of Jewish terrorists, I never met a settler who would denounce the vigilantism and other violence practiced by Jews against West Bank Arabs. Conviction often took on a stormy ferocity.

Daniella Weiss lived in the settlement of Kedumim, which means "antiquities." She was a slight woman with short black hair and a gaze as steady as ice. In her cramped apartment, she had seated her guests at a table by a window that looked out over the stony hills of Samaria. "You must come and conquer it by settlement—not by war, not by fighting, but by holding it with your body, by living in it," she declared with cold firmness.

Religion and warfare were woven tightly together for her. She and her husband, a jewelry exporter, had moved with their children to the West Bank as the expression of what she termed "a religious awakening" that was stimulated by Israel's having nearly lost in 1973 to the Arab armies that attacked on Yom Kippur, the most solemn Jewish holy day. Indeed, the near defeat drove Mrs. Weiss into the avant-garde of the Gush Emunim movement. She was part of a small group that tried and failed seven times to establish itself on the West Bank, squatting here and camping there, each time to be evicted by Israeli troops. The eighth attempt succeeded as the army, under then Defense Minister Shimon Peres, let the group stay in what was to become the settlement of Kedumim.

Calling the occupied territories "liberated," Daniella Weiss envisioned the rise of a religious state under Jewish religious law and "a purely Jewish way of life" with a Third Temple built in place of the Dome of the Rock and al-Aqsa mosque in Jerusalem. She admired the fanatic impulses of the ancient sect known as the Zealots, who began the disastrous war against the Romans and held the mountaintop fortress of Masada, overlooking the Dead Sea, against a long Roman siege, and then killed themselves in A.D. 73 rather than be taken prisoner and enslaved. When a group of American visitors asked her whether she saw any parallel between her determination to stay on the West Bank and the defense of Masada, she said yes.

"You know what I'm ready to do for the idea I believe in?" she asked. "I'm ready to die for it." She spit the word with contempt for those who were not as ready as she. "The mentality of the people is the mentality of a nation that was scattered all over the world, used to persecution, pogroms, holocaust—and survival was the utmost achievement, and they learned that in order to survive, you have to bend. This is the Diaspora mind, and the process of changing from the Diaspora mind to the mind of an independent people will take a long time. The peace process [with Egypt] was terrible, like something that awakens the germs of a disease, a catalyst of Diaspora thinking—the idea that if you want the peoples of the world to be nice to you and let you live, bend a little, give a little. But the more we bent our heads, the more people oppressed us. Our bending does not result in the world respecting us. Just the opposite. Everybody despises us."

Similar sentiments were put another way by Dvorah Klein, who immigrated from the Bronx in 1973, as she stood on a rainy, windswept hill during the dedication of a new West Bank settlement. "This land was given to us by God," she said. "It was given to us in trust to take care of. It is not ours to give away." Then she glanced toward a group of Peace Now opponents of the settlements who were demonstrating nearby. "The government has made an error to think that democracy is the way to live in Eretz Israel.* It isn't. We have to live by the Torah."

In both Judaism and Islam a tension exists between the precept that the stranger must be welcomed and the impulse that allows him to be denigrated. Both extremes are inherent to the culture of the desert, where the tribal circle has clear and rigid definition, yet where the wanderer is

---

* The Land of Israel.

sustained and honored and protected by the host. This ambivalence—
between particularism and universalism—is debated today by religious
Jews, even those in Gush Emunim whose faith has become a vehicle for
militant nationalism. The conflicting values articulated in the Torah, in
the subsequent religious laws and scholarship expressed in the Talmud,
and in the centuries of politico-religious activity of the Jews have been
reflected also in the twentieth-century disagreements that have gripped
the settlement movement and Israel's Orthodox community, especially
following the arrests of the Jewish terrorists. Contradictions abound even
within the writings of the two main thinkers to whom Gush Emunim
has looked for spiritual and intellectual guidance. The movement's principal mentor, Rabbi Avraham Yitzhak Hacohen Kook, the first Ashkenazi
chief rabbi of Palestine, is often cited to justify the ultra-nationalism and
ethnocentrism of the settlement movement. He wrote of Zionism as an
instrument of God's plan for messianic redemption, phrasing his call for
temporal activity with such aphorisms as "Man cannot fly off to Paradise
merely by pronouncing his faith" and "The sacred and the secular together
influence the human spirit, and man is enriched by absorbing from each
whatever is suitable." Since he provided an ideological basis for a link
between the religious and the secular Zionists, his disciples—who included his son, Rabbi Zvi Yehuda Kook—used his teachings to interpret
the renewal of Jewish control over Judea and Samaria as evidence that
redemption was progressing. But as Rabbi Hartman noted, the senior
Rabbi Kook also displayed a tolerance quite foreign to the reflexes of
many of his followers. "Even Rav Kook said that the essence of being
Jewish is to serve some universal purpose," Hartman observed. "He saw
the return of the Jewish people as the first stage toward a larger, universal
love in the world."

In Hartman's view, this is a point on which Judaism has failed. "Can
Judaism stop living in its biblical, self-enclosed language of monotheism
and really begin to live in dialogue with the world?" he asked. "The
Bible doesn't give me a model for that. The Bible doesn't give me Judaism
in interaction: It's Judaism in alienation from the world, Judaism fighting against paganism. What is the Diaspora, two thousand years
of Jewish history? Judaism in alienation from the world. So finally
when Judaism does meet the world, what happens? It's the Reform
movement or assimilationist. We have no paradigm of the dignity
of a powerful nation living in dialogue with the world. You see, all

our paradigms are not that way; all our paradigms are exile, *galut*, stranger."

Another thinker important to Gush Emunim ideologues is Judah Halevi, a Jewish poet and philosopher of the twelfth century who wrote of history's selection process in his famous work *The Kuzari*. "The best-known things in it are racist," declared Elhanan Naeh, a professor of Talmud at Hebrew University and the Jerusalem branch of the Jewish Theological Seminary. "He says Abraham was the best of men but he contained in himself some bad elements, and these bad elements came out in the form of Ishmael." Since Ishmael is today considered a forefather of the Arab nation and the link through which the Arabs trace their origins to Abraham, his manner of treatment in religious sources has contemporary relevance. The Koran portrays him reverently without mentioning either the circumstance of his conception or his ultimate rejection as described in the primary Jewish source, Genesis.

Because Abraham's wife, Sarah, cannot conceive, she encourages Abraham to "go in unto" her Egyptian slave girl Hagar, who is then informed by the angel of the Lord, "Behold, thou art with child and shalt bear a son, and shalt call his name Ishmael. . . . And he will be a wild man; his hand will be against every man, and every man's hand against him." (Genesis 16:11–12.) The image of the violent Arab, reinforced by war and terrorism, remains in the minds of many Israeli Jews. And the elemental dynamics of jealousy and rejection contain a symbolism appropriate to today. In the power of human emotions that the Old Testament sketches with such bold strokes, Hagar, having conceived, begins to despise her mistress; Sarah, regretting what she has done, returns the contempt. And after Sarah finally conceives and bears Abraham his son Isaac, she urges Abraham to banish Hagar and Ishmael, saying, "Cast out this bondwoman and her son; for the son of this bondwoman shall not be heir with my son, even with Isaac." (Genesis 21:10.) God favors Isaac, the forefather of the Jews, by telling Abraham to do Sarah's bidding: " . . . in Isaac shall thy seed be called. And also of the son of the bondwoman will I make a nation, because he is thy seed. And Abraham rose up early in the morning, and took bread, and a bottle of water, and gave it unto Hagar, putting it on her shoulder, and the child, and sent her away; and she departed, and wandered in the wilderness of Beersheba . . . . And God was with the lad; and he grew, and dwelt in the wilderness, and became an archer." (Genesis 21:12–14, 20.)

Undoubtedly, the authors of Genesis never imagined their parable forming an ideological basis for an Arab-Jewish conflict thousands of years hence. Indeed, there is nothing in the Bible to indicate that Ishmael was the forefather of the Arabs, nor was this a belief held by the ancient Arabs. The tribe of Ishmael disappeared early in biblical history, but the term Ishmaeli lived on, evolving into a designation of a desert people, and eventually extending to Arab peoples as a whole. The idea that Jews and Arabs were "cousins," descended from Isaac and Ishmael respectively, was accepted in Jewish writings and included by Muhammad in teachings that became the Koran, and it is an article of strong conviction among many Muslims today.[24] Many Jews also accept the assumption, as Prime Minister Shimon Peres indicated in a 1985 address to the United Nations General Assembly: "The sons of Abraham have become quarrelsome, but remain family nonetheless."

To Professor Naeh, Judah Halevi's twelfth-century writings reinforce the Jewish ethnocentrism found in the Old Testament. "It's very dangerous," said Naeh of the Halevi thesis on the inferiority of Ishmael. "I'm not sure that in his time this theory had a very big influence with Jews, but it has in the last centuries, especially in Eastern Europe, in Russia, in Poland, etc. The Gush Emunim people see Halevi as their big prophet. They study each word, and they live with his ideas, the chosen people."

The Kuzari is written as a dialogue between the king of the Khazars, who is searching for a religion, and a rabbi who defends Judaism against the attacks of other faiths. In the end, the king finally converts from paganism to Judaism. And to help him toward that decision, the rabbi makes a number of arguments offensive to a tolerant mind. On the matter of divine lineage, he declares, "The details can be demonstrated from the lives of Adam, Seth and Enosh to Noah; then Shem and Eber to Abraham; then Isaac and Jacob to Moses. All of them represented the essence and purity of Adam on account of their intimacy with God. Each of them had children only to be compared to them outwardly, but not really like them, and, therefore, without direct union with the divine influence. The chronology was established through the medium of those sainted persons who were only single individuals, and not a crowd, until Jacob begat the Twelve Tribes, who were all under this divine influence. Thus the divine element reached a multitude of persons who carried the records further." By omission, Ishmael is condemned.[25]

Halevi's rabbi also denigrates Christianity and Islam, issuing the following denunciation: ". . . any Gentile who joins us unconditionally shares our good fortune, without, however, being quite equal to us. If the Law were binding on us only because God created us, the white and the black man would be equal, since He created them all. But the Law was given to us because He led us out of Egypt, and remained attached to us, because we are the pick of mankind."[26] And further: ". . . we are not even a body, only scattered limbs, like the 'dry bones' which Ezekiel saw. These bones, however, O king of the Khazars, which have retained a trace of vital power, having once been the seat of a heart, brain, breath, soul, and intellect, are better than certain bodies formed of marble and plaster, endowed with heads, eyes, ears, and all limbs, in which never dwelt the spirit of life, nor ever can dwell in them, since they are but imitations of man, not man in reality. . . . The 'dead' nations which desire to be held equal to the 'living' people can obtain nothing more than external resemblance. They built houses for God, but no trace of Him was visible therein. They turned hermits and ascetics in order to secure inspiration, but it came not. . . . Even in other instances of imitation no people can equal us at all. Look at the others who appointed a day of rest in the place of Sabbath. Could they contrive anything which resembles it more than statues resemble living human bodies?"[27]

Such ethnocentrism and religious arrogance feed a political mood today. And Naeh added another insight: "Halevi was born in Spain, spent most of his life there, and the legend says he tried to get here {to Jerusalem}. There is a famous legend that he was traveling through northern Africa to Egypt and Israel and that he got to the Western Wall and there some Arab horseman trampled him when he was praying. But scholars nowadays consider it as just as a legend, and they think that he wasn't here."

Gush Emunim activists take what they wish from the contradictory sources. As the eleven- and twelve-year-old boys in Kiryat Arba explained, they are learning in their yeshivas that the Arab is Amalek, the enemy tribe that God instructed the Jews to fight eternally and destroy: "Amalek was the first of the nations; but his latter end shall be that he perish for ever."(Numbers 24:20.) Hagai Segal, a settler from Ofra, was quoted in the settlers' paper Nekuda as declaring, "The Torah of Israel has nothing to do with modern humanistic atheism. The Torah yearns for revenge. Such a Torah is not humanistic."

Expressions of bellicose intolerance are given religious sanction and rationalization, which then filter into some segments of the lay population. Some rabbis, such as Eliezer Waldenberg, winner of the 1976 Israel Prize, declared that Halakha, Jewish law, required strict separation of Jews from Arabs, preferably an apartheid system or, better yet, the expulsion of the "goyim," all non-Jews, from Jerusalem. An American correspondent and his family became targets of some of this chauvinism in the Jerusalem neighborhood where they lived; the word "goy" was scratched into the paint of their car, and the children were hassled by Israeli youngsters on the street. Zohar Endrawos, an Arab in the mostly Christian Galilee town of Tarshiha, remembered Jewish youngsters in neighboring Maalot making crosses with their fingers and spitting on them. Another rabbi, writing in the student newspaper of Bar-Ilan University, near Tel Aviv, argued that the Torah prescribed genocide against the modern Amalek. At the Gush Emunim settlement of Elon Moreh, when security men went to investigate the murder of an eleven-year-old Arab girl by settlers, they were met with signs reading "Ishmaeli Police."

But others stress the humanism in the tradition. "When it comes to the Arab question," said Israel Harel, head of the council of West Bank settlements, "we don't have what we call one Torah. But I believe that the attitudes toward the Arabs here on the settlements, in general, you'll find less radical than among the general Israeli population. And I'll tell you why I say it and why I believe in it. The true believers in Torah believe in life first of all. The real true believers in Torah have a more humanistic approach than even those who are influenced by Western ethics. The law protects the outsider, the weak, the marginal. If people in an average Jerusalem neighborhood—even a better Jerusalem neighborhood, like Rehavia—would suffer what we have suffered all these years, I'm sure it would be like we sometimes see in Western films that a group of citizens are making law and order themselves."

Those prone to violence and revenge can find cause, but because they see themselves as civilized, and above the primitive culture of the desert, Harel observed, they must justify the bloodshed by wrapping it in ideology, especially socioreligious ideology. "If you want it, you find it," he said. "If you have a little bit disturbed personality, then it helps very much." Those Jews who planted bombs on buses were "mentally ill, completely," he added. "I could give you a list of two hundred reasons why it would damage the cause that they want. Only sick people could do it. Those people are educated in the Ten Commandments: Thou shalt not kill. If they are so religious and they study, every night, cabala* and so on, I just don't understand them."

Shifra Blass, a settler whose husband is a rabbi and specialist in Jewish law for the Justice Ministry, was equally categorical. "In Jewish religious ideology, there is no room for the kind of activity that we're speaking of," she said, "be it an attempt at mass murder at one extreme and at the other extreme these deviationist activities, taking the law into one's own hands. I feel these can all be called deviations from an ideology which is basically a moral and ethical ideology and doesn't allow for those kinds of things. We feel we are a community of people with a positive goal, with something creative and constructive to contribute to Israeli society, not just in terms of physical creations but also in values. I think that remains true. However, perhaps we have to check again if we've made our ideology clear to all. When we talk about an ideology, we have to admit there are wrong roads to take."

There was debate in the Gush Emunim movement, but no reform and little clarification. And Shifra Blass had her own blind spot. When I noted the similarity between Jewish and Arab terrorism, she replied vehemently that while she rejected Jewish terrorism as morally wrong, the differences were profound. "I must come back again," she said, "to the moral question underlying the ideology: Whose land is it? I believe this is our land, this is the Land of Israel, this is the land of the Jewish people. And I don't believe it's the Palestinians' country." But Palestinians, too, believe it is their land, I observed, and they also act out of a certain despair. "I would be willing to argue with you on that point, as to the purity of the motivations," she replied. "You have terrorists who are caught and say, 'I came to kill for the sake of killing,' like in the shoot-out on King George Street. People talk about anti-Jewish, anti-Israel racial hatred. At the end of both kinds of occurrences you can have innocent people dead, that's true. But if we're trying to speak more philosophically, the one who makes this moral blunder, who says, 'The

---

* A mystical system of direct contact with the Divine, based on esoteric interpretations of the Scriptures.

only way it can happen is if innocent people are caught up in it, and I'm sorry about it,' is a different kind of person from the one who says, 'Every Jew dead is a good thing.' "

In fact, one can find both kinds of people on both sides of the Arab-Jewish divide: There are the Adnan Jabers, who try to mitigate their deeds by talking disingenuously about innocents' being caught up in the struggle, and there are Jews who say clearly, "The only good Arab is a dead Arab." Mrs. Blass couldn't see the parallel.

There is no unanimity behind the rabbinical badge of Orthodoxy. A multitude of voices sings in disharmonious tones. Some have taken their ideas from the hardship of Israel; others have brought their perceptions with them from their particular backgrounds in the Diaspora: Rabbi Meir Kahane's racism from the streets of Brooklyn, another's liberalism from the 1960s of Berkeley or Cambridge. David Hartman carries his search for pluralism from his upbringing in the United States. In the wake of too much silence, the more tolerant were moved to speak after the rise and capture of the Jewish terrorists; a group of Orthodox rabbis gathered one evening in Jerusalem under the auspices of a politically liberal Orthodox group called Paths to Peace to discuss morality.

Rabbi Aharon Lichtenstein, head of the Allon Shevuth Yeshiva, declared, "These people reached what they reached not because they followed the Halakha [Jewish law] but because they abandoned it."

The president of the Israeli Academy of Sciences and Humanities, Ephraim Urbach, said categorically, "What worries me is their totalitarian approach—a clearly nationalistic, chauvinistic approach in the guise of religion, as if they know exactly what the intentions of God are, as if they stand above the law; any law that doesn't suit their opinions doesn't obligate them."

The rabbi of the settlement of Efrat, Shlomo Riskin, tried to draw a distinction between the frustrations of powerlessness and the obligations of power. "The vital challenge," he said, "is to be sensitive when the government is in our hands, to be humane when we are strong, to be neither murdered nor murderers."

Hanan Porat, a right-wing Knesset member and prime mover of Gush Emunim, pleaded for understanding that Jews were being driven to violence by Arab violence against them.

"But would you recommend the same punishment for your friends as for Arab terrorists?" asked Aviezer Ravitzky of Hebrew University.

"That's a question you should ask yourself honestly first," said Porat.

"My answer is an unequivocal yes," Ravitzky declared. A murderer is a murderer and must be punished as such, he continued. If there are any mitigating circumstances, the Arabs who commit terrorism have more justification, he argued, since they have no political power, and they might feel in real distress. "But us? The ones with the power? As if it weren't enough that we are sitting on top of them and governing them, we have to go and plant bombs under them in their buses?"

As a philosopher, David Hartman had another view. He saw Judaism itself on trial. He believed strongly in the theological right of Jews to hold the West Bank, although he was also willing to give at least part of it up to preserve morality. And he admired those at the leading edge of the idealistic settlement movement. But he also felt that something had gone terribly wrong: The land had become an idol, violence had become a means, and those embracing it were the victims of a tragedy in which Judaism had failed to evolve in its new context, that of state power. The young men who planted the bombs, machine-gunned the college, and plotted to blow up Islam's holiest shrine in Jerusalem "acted out of the purity of passion," he said. Therefore, he continued, "I have to condemn them more, because they're far more dangerous. They had the guts to do what we were really taught to believe in. They are sacrificial, ascetic, living without twentieth-century values. They transcended all the television, all the technological, twentieth-century civilization. There's a certain purity, there's an integrity, there's a straightness, they have the quality of the American pioneer. It's very Protestant. Do you know what it is, David, to mourn every ninth day of Av the destruction of the Temple, and you mourn in this city and each time you walk there it is a reminder that this is preventing redemption? How can you educate a community toward praying for the Temple, feeling the pain of God's home living in flames [and not expect people to do something about it]? These kids cried it and said, 'We can do something about it because we're Zionists.' They're not powerless. These are the best Zionists. They stopped praying and they started believing in the ability of the Jewish people to act. There's a new generation of Jews who have grown up who can act. These kids don't pray, they act. They have an enormous feeling for the dignity of the nation. They feel the pain. They can't stand an obsequious nation. They hate it. Dignity."

The reverence for power, which grows out of a history of powerlessness, reverberates through Israeli-Jewish society. As Rabbi David J. Spritzer wrote angrily to *The Jerusalem Post*, "One of the most important gains consequent to the establishment of the State of Israel has been the change in the traditional image of the Jew from the passive weakling who could be kicked about, robbed, and murdered almost at will. Jewish blood has been cheap for hundreds of years. . . . Not any longer. If someone hits us in the stomach, we will smash his head, perhaps those of his abettors too. . . . I am not altogether displeased that the Jew is viewed as actually dangerous, that even a small provocation will engender a massive reaction. We need the luxury of that image for at least a generation."

But Rabbi Hartman, by contrast, yearned for something beyond strength. "What happens when reality imposes itself on a dream?" he asked. "I have to say that the purpose of the Jewish return is to restore the dignity of particularism. The question is how do I treat the Arab, how do I treat Christians, how do I treat different people in my own society, and how do I treat Jews who are not religious? He who thinks he has the truth can be intolerant. We have not developed the pluralistic type. Jews here have not understood what I think to be the larger significance of the Jewish return: a pluralistic consciousness which feels that David Shipler and Hartman could really embrace each other as friends, knowing each other in their differences, and listen to each other. That is modernity in the most beautiful sense that I saw in William James. That's what America taught me. Unless fundamentalism gets healed, unless pluralism becomes a spiritual value, I don't see any future in the Middle East. There's no future for Israel unless pluralism—not just modernity in its cheap form but in its deepest form—becomes consciousness. Otherwise, I think the Middle East is going to be a place of civil wars, continuous ones of violence and murder and bloodshed.

"We have not built a cultural identity, we have not built a cultural renaissance," Hartman continued. "We have not built a dignity of a people who feel spiritually and culturally creative. And therefore the passion has been not the passion of creating a new idea but of creating a new land. Settling the land was the container of the whole passion, not rebuilding Judaism. And therefore the passion was land. Love of the land." He fell into an adoring whisper. "The land, the land. The country requires a totally new channeling of the romantic passion." And then, in full voice, rising to a crescendo, "I'm saying, damn it, we're here not to reclaim the land, we're here to reclaim Judaism! I'm here to correct the mistakes of Joshua. I don't want to live with Joshua as a permanent model of how Jews build the land. I'm here to find out whether, when Jews spoke about the dignity of minorities, did they really mean it or did they only say it when they had no power? I'm here to correct my own utopian myths. Can we build a society here that may save the Jewish people? Can we build a society which will say to Jews, 'It's something worthwhile to be Jewish; look what Israel has done to the Jewish people'?"

Once, David Hartman said these things at a seminar in Washington, D.C. In the audience was a young Arab woman, a consultant to an oil company, who approached him afterwards. Hartman described their encounter: "She said, 'What you said was beautiful. I wish we in the Arab world could have a philosopher like yourself talking. But we don't.' And then she started to give the Jewish business of 'You're the people of the Book and you've had that type of long experience.' I was crying. At that moment, the feeling that existed between me and that girl was something so precious, so tender, so gentle, I wanted to just hug her. I don't fool myself when this happens that this is reality. But it's also reality."

"Do you ever speak to Arab groups?" I asked him.

"They don't invite me."

The little girl, eleven years old, has freckles on her nose and wears a red ribbon at the top of a long braid that bounces back and forth across her back as she runs through the dirt pathways of the Dheisheh refugee camp. She has never met a Jew like David Hartman. She has never seen a Jew without a gun. Her name is Amal Abu al-Jamiyya. Amal means hope.

Dheisheh is a crowded slum, a labyrinth of concrete houses adjacent to the West Bank town of Bethlehem. In the winter, the chill of the raw rain sifts into bare cement rooms, mixing with the sick smell of burning kerosene from small heaters that glow and flicker in vain against the cold. In the summer, flies swarm. Children shout and play with toys and games they make themselves from old, bent bicycle rims and stones and pieces of rusty metal that lie around the alleys and the rocky fields nearby.

The poverty here is not profound, especially when compared with that of other slums in other parts of the world. But for the Palestinian-Arab residents, who fled from Israel proper during the 1948 war and then raised their children here, the camp remains a symbol of exile, a source of militant anger.

Since the 1967 war, six years before Amal was born, Dheisheh, like the rest of the West Bank, has been under Israeli military occupation, thus affording the youngest generation of Palestinian youth an opportunity to battle for their homeland in their own way: The children throw stones at Israeli cars and buses that pass the camp on the main north-south road between Bethlehem and Hebron. And then the only Jews whom Amal ever sees come running through the alleys—soldiers in their olive-drab fatigues, settlers in jeans and skullcaps, chasing youngsters who have hurled the lethal stones. She has never spoken to a Jew and says she never wants to.

"Do you like Jews?" she is asked.

"No."

"Why not?"

"They attack our homes, breaking everything, building settlements."

"Why wouldn't you want to talk with any Jews?"

"Because they are our enemies."

"What if you met a Jewish girl your age? What would you talk about?"

"Nothing."

"Wouldn't you be interested in learning about the Jewish girl's life?"

"No."

"Why not?"

"Because I don't know her, and she doesn't know me."

Does this cute Amal with the freckles on her nose have a dream in her life, I wonder.

"To get back our land," she says.

"How?"

"Demonstrate." Then, after a moment's thought, she adds, "We must use guns." The young men who brought her to talk with me explode in a roar of approving laughter.

The Palestinian Arabs who live under Israeli authority have no David Hartmans to conduct a philosophical search for morality. Neither the majority of Arabs, who are Muslims, nor the small minority who are Christians reveal any of the Jewish agony over the nature of their religious ethic. Perhaps because their culture is less introspective, because they now live in virtual powerlessness under Israeli domination, their debates are largely political, tactical. Furthermore, disagreements among them are often resolved by assassination, a practice that tends to discourage public breast-beating.

Jamil Hamad, the Palestinian journalist from the West Bank, analyzed the absence of moral debate and found it to be the source of much Arab weakness. His prescription: "Fight Israel with the same weapon that Israel is fighting you. The Arabs are for the easy answer. 'It's aggressive, it's Zionist, it's imperialist, it's an instrument of the U.S.' That's the easy answer. Until today I didn't find an Arab thinker who would isolate himself and write a book, 'Why we were defeated.' The easiest defeat is the military defeat. But I think the Arabs were defeated morally. Their morals, their values were defeated. And we will continue to be defeated by Israel and others as long as our values and morals are weak." Jamil was unusual in his candor. For the most part, if there is moral questioning it must exist only within the invisible chambers of private contemplation or in trusted circles of family and friends.

This blurs the religious component of Arab attitudes, softening the highlights that, on the Jewish side, cast factors of debate into sharp contrast. The religious and the political are considerably intertwined among both Jews and Muslims—and to a much lesser extent Arab Christians—but it is more difficult to identify and measure the religious element in the Arab calculus. It is as diffuse as the winter fog that sometimes settles among the Judean Hills.

The Christian Arabs who live in Israel proper, East Jerusalem, and the West Bank are mostly Greek Orthodox. Roman Catholic, Greek Catholic, and members of other, smaller sects. Their priests, some of whom are local Arabs, others of whom are sent from abroad to serve their churches in the Holy Land, sometimes deliver sermons in the traditional anti-Semitic idiom, blaming the Jews for killing Christ. So devoted are both Muslim and Christian Arabs to the accusation that "when the Catholic Church was considering the exoneration of the Jews from collective guilt for the crucifixion of Jesus," writes Yehoshafat Harkabi, "many furious protests against the proposal appeared in the Arab press, which saw in it a Zionist plot to push the Vatican into the move as compensation for Pope Pius XII's failure to oppose the Nazi extermination of Jews."[28] Blaming the Jews for the crucifixion reinforces religious hatred, but in the context of the Arab-Israeli conflict it seems to take second place to the secular impulses of Palestinian nationalism. Among Israeli Arabs, who are citizens of the Jewish state, the Christians are usually regarded as more moderate politically than the Muslims; Christians sometimes volunteer to serve in the Israeli army, an offer almost never made by

Muslims other than semi-nomadic Bedouin tribesmen. The army usually accepts the Bedouins, who serve as trackers, and rejects Palestinian Arabs, whether Christian or otherwise, as potentially subversive.

Islam is more pervasive in shaping attitudes. It, too, contains ambiguous and contradictory strains regarding the outsider, the nonbeliever, the infidel, and specifically the Jew, leaving individual Arabs to draw from Islam what suits them. "The attitude toward Judaism is very positive, the attitude toward Jews negative," said Salman Masalkha, a Druse graduate student who was researching Muslim mysticism for a master's degree at Hebrew University. Indeed, the Koran, based on notes and recollections of speeches by Muhammad and compiled as a book after his death in A.D. 632, contains an undertone of respect for the fundamentals and sources of Judaism while portraying Jews as unfaithful to the covenant and the Lord. Most of the Koran's negative references to Jews, which outnumber the positive ones, seem to derive from Muhammad's conflicts in the seventh century with the Jews of Medina, where he established his rule after moving from Mecca in 622. Because his own monotheism and preachings grew substantially out of biblical themes he is thought to have heard expounded by Jews and Christians, he hoped for the Jews' political and religious support. But he received only their rejection and contempt. The Koran relates, "Now hath God heard the saying of those who said: 'Aye, God is poor and we are rich.' [A declaration of the Jews of the tribe of Kainoka when Muhammad demanded tribute.] We will surely write down their sayings, and their unjust slaughter of the prophets; and we will say, 'Taste ye the torment of the burning.' " (Sura III, The Family of Imran, Verse 177.) Muhammad retaliated after he became powerful enough to lead a force on a successful raid against a Meccan caravan in 624, a turning point that led to attacks on the Jews and accusations that they and the Christians had "falsified their own scriptures in order to conceal the prophecies of Muhammad's advent," as Bernard Lewis has written.[29] When three Jewish tribes of Medina refused to convert, Muhammad drove out one, then another and exterminated the third, the Banu Qurayza.

"From the Muslim point of view, the Jewish revelation was a divine revelation that was corrupted," Lewis said. "Islam recognizes both the Old and New Testaments as authentic revelations, but they are superseded and replaced by the Koran in Islamic belief. They no longer have validity. They have been misused and corrupted by their unworthy custodians and they are, so to speak, withdrawn from circulation and replaced by a new edition—this total, final, perfect revelation."[30]

The Koran is shot through with this mixture of tolerance and rage for the preceding two monotheistic religions, which are perceived as vessels of God's word abandoned by those who received it. The ambivalence is reflected in verse after verse—one retelling a story from the Old Testament, another vilifying the nonbeliever and leveling colorful damnation upon him. In the vein of tolerance, for example, the Koran declares, "Verily, they who believe [Muslims], and they who follow the Jewish religion, and the Christians, and the Sabeites—whoever of these believeth in God and the last day, and doeth that which is right, shall have their reward with their Lord: fear shall not come upon them, neither shall they be grieved." (Sura II, The Cow, Verse 59.) The Jews are even acknowledged as the chosen people: "O children of Israel! Remember my favor wherewith I have favored you, and that high above all mankind have I raised you." (Verse 116.) Reverence for both Moses and Jesus is expressed prominently: "Moreover, to Moses gave we 'the Book,' and we raised up apostles after him; and to Jesus, son of Mary, gave we clear proofs of his mission, and strengthened him by the Holy Spirit." (Verse 81.)

The Jews' rejection of Muhammad engenders anger and bitterness, however: "And when a Book had come to them from God, confirming that which they had received already—although they had before prayed for victory over those who believed not—yet when that Koran had come to them, of which they had knowledge, they did not recognize it. The curse of God on the infidels!" (Verse 83.) The Jews are then condemned for straying into idolatry, as the Koran retells the story of the golden calf: "Moreover, Moses came unto you with proofs of his mission. Then in his absence ye took the calf for your God, and did wickedly." (Verse 86.) And all the prophets before Muhammad are seen equally: "Say ye: 'We believe in God, and that which hath been sent down to us, and that which hath been sent down to Abraham and Ishmael and Isaac and Jacob and the tribes: and that which hath been given to Moses and to Jesus, and that which was given to the prophets from their Lord. No difference do we make between any of them: and to God are we resigned." (Verse 130.)

But Abraham is clearly portrayed as a Muslim: "And when Abraham, with Ishmael, raised the foundations of the House, they said, 'O our Lord! Accept it from us; for thou are the Hearer, the Knower. O our

Lord! Make us also Muslims, and our posterity a Muslim people." (Verses 121–122.) "Abraham was neither Jew nor Christian; but he was sound in the faith, a Muslim; and not of those who add gods to God." (Sura III, The Family of Imran, Verse 60.) The last may be a reference to the Christians, whose notion of the Holy Trinity disturbed the Muslim sense of monotheism and rejection of idolatry.

The Jews are seen as having strayed deviously. "Among the Jews are those who displace the words of their Scriptures . . . perplexing with their tongues, and wounding the Faith by their revilings." (Sura IV, Women, Verse 48.) There were Jews who pretended to believe, the Koran says, "and they swear to a lie, knowing it to be such. God hath got ready for them a severe torment; for, evil is what they do." (Sura LVIII, She Who Pleaded, Verses 15–16.) Christians, as well as Jews, come under the scathing attack. "Make war upon such of those to whom the Scriptures have been given as believe not in God, or in the last day, and who forbid not that which God and His Apostle have forbidden, and who profess not the profession of the truth, until they pay tribute out of hand, and they be humbled. The Jews say, 'Ezra is a son of God'; and the Christians say, 'The Messiah is a son of God.' Such the sayings in their mouths! They resemble the saying of the Infidels of old! God do battle with them! How are they misguided!" (Sura IX, Immunity, Verses 29–30.) And closely following this, in one of the more imaginative prescriptions for damnation, a passage on Christians: ". . . many of the teachers and monks do devour man's substance in vanity, and turn them from the Way of God. But to those who treasure up gold and silver and expend it not in the Way of God, announce tidings of a grievous torment. On that day their treasures shall be heated in hell fire, and their foreheads, and their sides, and their backs, shall be branded with them. . . . 'This is what ye have treasured up for yourselves: taste, therefore, your treasures!' " (Verses 34–35.) The Jews come in for their own derision and punishment. "Of all men thou wilt certainly find the Jews, and those who join other gods with God, to be the most intense in hatred of those who believe." (Sura V, The Table, Verse 85.) The Koran accuses the Jews of "having spoken against Mary a grievous calumny." As if written in the voice of God, the book declares, "For the wickedness of certain Jews, and because they turn many from the way of God, we have forbidden them goodly viands which had been before allowed them." (Sura IV, Women, Verses 155, 158.) " 'The hand of God,' say the Jews, 'is chained up.' {i.e., God is no longer bounteous.] Their own hands shall be chained up—and for that which they have said shall they be cursed. Nay! Outstretched are both His hands! At His own pleasure does he bestow gifts. . . . But if the people of the Book believe and have the fear of God, we will surely put away their sins from them, and will bring them into gardens of delight." (Sura V, The Table, Verses 69–70.)

Arabs differ in their assessments of how much impact these verses have. "I don't personally think it's very strong, actually, partly because I don't think people read the Koran very thoroughly," said Sari Nusseibeh. He is the son of a former defense minister of Jordan, Anwar Nusseibeh, and has taught Islamic civilization at both Hebrew University in Jerusalem and Bir Zeit University on the West Bank. Sari speaks in gentle tones, his English accented with the purr of Arabic and the refinement of his British education. "A lot of people know the Koran, but not very thoroughly. If you're having an argument with someone who knows the Koran and is talking from the point of view of someone who knows the Koran, they want to defend the position that Israelis are terrible, the end is near, then they will go to a passage from the Koran that says how terrible the Jews are. Then you have the very same person who says, 'Well, God chose them, the Koran says.' The very same person can say that. I'm thinking of people like my grandmother, to whom the Koran is much more part of her upbringing. So I don't think the Koran as such creates anti-Semitism. Certainly as a young child I was never aware or given to any strident statements that were anti-Jewish. If anything, one feels all the time that Christians are more anti-Jewish than Muslims. I haven't felt that people are Islamically anti-Semitic. On the contrary, people will tell you that Islam accepts all religions. It certainly has been part of my upbringing to be taught that Islam accepts everybody else. I mean, Jewish prophets are Muslim prophets."

Sheikh Akrameh Said Sabri, one of Jerusalem's Muslim leaders, painted a similar portrait of a tolerant Islam. A man of forty-four years, he had the smooth, unscathed sheen of youth, giving him the glow of an ethereal figure devoted to affairs of the spirit. He displayed a certain political acumen, however, and his role in the Waqf, the Muslim trust that administers the mosques and other holy places, put him in daily contact with temporal affairs. He was head of the Waqf's Guidance Department, in charge of sermons. As such, he had extensive experience being warned and interrogated by Israeli police authorities who were sensitive to the inflammatory potential of imams' pronouncements during Friday prayers.

Sheikh Sabri received me in a formal reception room of his immaculate apartment in East Jerusalem. He wore a neatly trimmed black beard, a black suit and vest, a grey tie, and a snow-white turban with a centerpiece of maroon. His demeanor was reserved but pleasant as he replied to questions and squinted at me through his glasses. His son, about ten years old, brought thickly sweetened coffee in the tiny handleless cups that are integral to hospitality in Arab homes.

"Islamic doctrine is not an aggressive doctrine," the sheikh explained, "and when we say we want to solve this [Arab-Israeli] problem according to Islam, that does not mean we want to mistreat the other faiths. Islam is capable of dealing with other faiths clearly and fairly. It is an essential part of Islam that it is built on forgiveness and forgetting. What we do really hope is that the non-Muslims do really understand Islam as it is. We and they should not treat some of the Muslims' behavior as if it is part of Islamic doctrine." He had in mind some of the oil ministers, he said, but he also made a negative reference to Iran's Ayatollah Khomeini, who is of the Shiite sect,* which is more insular and militant than the Sunni, to which Sheikh Sabri and all Palestinian Muslims belong.

In assessing Islamic-Jewish relations, he endorsed the supposed common ancestry of the two peoples in Abraham, and he provided an intriguing version of ancient chronology. "There is no doubt that Isaac and Ishmael are [half-] brothers," he said, "and that Abraham is their father. But not all the Arabs descended from Ishmael, as not all Jews are descended from Isaac. The Arabs are two: The first is the original Arabs who used to live in the Arabian peninsula before Abraham came. Then Abraham came and married an Arab woman [Hagar, mother of Ishmael]. The second Arabs are those who came from Ishmael. Abraham was not

---

* The Shia movement began, in the seventh century, around the claim that Ali, the cousin and son-in-law of Muhammad, had been nominated by the Prophet as his successor and as heir to his divine legacy. It spread in the Umayyad period (A.D. 661–750) to a new, lower, urban class of Muslims, mostly non-Arab, known as the Mawali, to whom the orthodox, Sunni tradition was equated with the existing order of hierarchy and poverty. There were also Arab adherents to Shiism who carried the movement into Persia. The movement came to be known as Shi'at Ali; literally, the Party of Ali.

an Arab. Abraham is described in the Koran as not a Jew, not a Christian, but a Muslim. He followed the same doctrine as Muhammad."

The sheikh, too, attributed the tension between Islam and Judaism to the Jews' unwillingness to recognize Muhammad as a prophet, and he embellished the story somewhat. "The enmity of the Jews toward the Muslims has been mentioned in the Koran," he noted, speaking so slowly and calmly that he seemed drowsy. "The enmity started when the Jews were under the impression that Moses was the last prophet. In the Torah, there is a prophecy telling that another prophet for the Jews will come after Moses." Then Sheikh Sabri awoke to his next idea, smiling and leaning forward. "The Jews thought that the new prophet was going to be Jewish!" he declared with a laugh. "When Muhammad came with the message of Islam, he was, first of all, an Arab, not a Jew. Muhammad fulfilled all the criteria written in the Torah. They were disappointed and shocked. From that point, the enmity started toward Muhammad and Islam and his followers. Every time Muhammad had a truce with them, the Jews used to violate that truce, and the Jews got that reputation—as violators of agreements. In spite of this, the Jews were treated equally and gracefully, and under Islam, Jews had success in politics and literature. This is because of the liberal attitude of Islam toward them."

That historical image approximated what Muslim youngsters were being taught, even under Israeli authority. A sharper variation, found in some Jordanian textbooks used illegally on the West Bank, had the Jews of seventh-century Mecca plotting to assassinate Muhammad, a tale accepted by Arab schoolboys, apparently. "So, then, my children," reads one passage from a 1977 teacher's manual on Islamic instruction for first-graders, "you are aware of the Jews' aversion to our master Muhammad, God's prayer and peace be on his soul, and their endeavor to liquidate him when still a child. . . . We must be wary and circumspect so as to escape their perfidy."[31] An Arab friend of mine in his fifties who had never heard the story of the attempted murder asked his teenage son, whose entire West Bank school career had taken place under Israeli military occupation. His son knew the story well and had learned it in class; Israeli authorities, who recognize the power of the religious component in their conflict with the Arabs, do not always succeed in dampening its expression.

For all of the benign platitudes, however, it is a fact that Islam has also been a source of conflict with and rejection of the Jews. At the very least, its religious arguments have been called into service on behalf of the struggle. Fundamentalist Islam sets up a dichotomy between believers and infidels. It imparts a sense of divine righteousness to the makers of holy war. And it keeps alive the Arab yearning to retake Jerusalem. Thus, Israeli authorities watch closely the Muslim leaders under Israeli jurisdiction.

"The Friday prayers are always monitored by Israelis," Sheikh Sabri observed. "If an imam makes a leftist or extremist speech, he is summoned to interrogation and may be arrested. They monitor either through tape recorders or through collaborators who pass the information. What is not allowed is everything that contradicts the policy of occupation. For example, if we talk about confiscation of land, settlements, blowing up houses, these are hot subjects. On more than one occasion, when I talked on these subjects, they summoned me to police headquarters. Sometimes I am summoned a day or two before Friday, and they ask us not to talk on sensitive issues. I say, 'Everybody is talking about the subject, so we are the involved people, so we have to talk.' So they say, 'Don't use provocative language, don't incite the people.' " On such occasions, two or three Israelis speak to him in Arabic. "They treat me courteously," he said. They are the only Jews with whom the sheikh has ever conversed.

Outside Israeli control, Arab textbooks and newspapers have long used religious symbols and metaphors in their propaganda against Israel. The Old Testament is vilified as endorsing decadence, crime, and adultery. A 1964 Jordanian text for high-school juniors entitled *The Palestinian Problem*, for example, declares, "The Zionists used the spread of corruption and decay as an objective and as a means. Precedents for this were found in the Bible. . . . The Bible justified intercourse between the two spies and the harlot from Jericho. The Bible favored this since it aided them in their task of espionage, which in turn helped Joshua to conquer the town. . . . It is not surprising, therefore, that Zionism has made espionage its religion. It is nearly certain that Judaism is the only religion which has made a tenet of espionage. . . . Zionism exploits references to espionage in the Bible in order to transform espionage into a so-called religious service carried out by the Zionists with deep religious fervor."

Similarly, in his 1964 book *The Danger of World Jewry to Islam and Christianity*, Abdallah al-Tall, of Jordan, writes, "The Bible describes exactly the nature of the Jewish people and clearly brings out the character of the Jewish faith, which is built on treachery, baseness, barbarism, hatred, corruption, fanaticism, covetousness, arrogance, and immorality."[32] That is an echo from the medieval work of Ibn Hazm, the Andalusian author who lived from 994–1064 and who, according to Harkabi, "describes the Bible . . . as a shocking collection of immoral acts, such as the story of Lot's daughters; Sarah lying to God; Abraham refusing to believe God's word, feeding the angels as if they were flesh and blood, and marrying his sister; Isaac stealing; Jacob marrying Leah by mistake; Reuben lying with his father's wife and Judah with his son's wife; Moses born of a marriage between Amram and his aunt; David and the wife of Uriah, Absalom lying with his father's wives, and so on."[33]

Religious symbols are twisted. A passage in an Egyptian high-school reader from the 1960s declares, "O mother of Israel! Dry your tears, your children's blood which is being spilled in the desert will produce naught but thorn and wormwood. Wipe off your blood, o mother of Israel, have mercy and spare the desert your filthy blood, o mother of Israel. Remove your slain, for their flesh has caused the ravens bellyache and their stink causes rheum. Cry, o mother of Israel, and wail. Let every house be the Wailing Wall of the Jews."

During the 1967 war, a cartoon was published in Egyptian and Iraqi papers showing a bearded, long-nosed Jew being strangled with a Star of David around his neck. Another Egyptian text, used for training teachers in Islamic history, declared, "The Prophet enlightened us about the right way to treat them [the Jews], and succeeded finally in crushing the plots that they had planned. We today must follow this way and purify Holy Palestine from their filth in order to bring back peace to the Arab homeland."

The theme remains in a more recent Jordanian teachers' manual for Islamic studies in first grade. Published in 1977 and banned by Israeli military authorities, it still finds its way into West Bank classrooms. The text declares:

Deepening the hatred of racism and imperialism, and especially Zionist racism, in the souls of the students has become a compulsory command for every teacher. The teacher must not back down from this. Especially since he lived through and suffered the crisis of Zionist racism, he will instill the spirit of *jihad* [holy war] in the souls of the pupils. . . . Islam is a religion of unity. . . . Zionism occupied a large part of the Islamic land and evicted its people after making them taste bitter degradation. The teacher should strive to elucidate Islamic texts and their attitudes whereby Islam is embattled by its enemy and orders *jihad*, which preserves the nation's control over its land and the pride of its religion in the souls of its sons. The teacher should also strive to demonstrate to his students that *jihad* does not legitimize injustice and hostility but it does sanction the spreading of the message of God to his creation as well as uplifting them from the morass of error and deviance to the zenith of Islam. Likewise, it is necessary to implant in the soul of the pupil the rule of Islam that if the enemies occupy even one inch of the Islamic lands, *jihad* becomes imperative for every Muslim.

The concept of *jihad* derives from the classical Islamic division of the world into the "Abode of Islam" (*Dar al-Islam*) and the "Abode of War" (*Dar al-Harb*), meaning those areas that do not accept Islamic authority and are governed by infidels. As Lewis explains, "Between the realm of Islam and the realms of unbelief there is a canonically obligatory perpetual state of war, which will continue until the whole world either accepts the message of Islam or submits to the rule of those who bring it."[34] But within the dichotomy of hostility, non-Muslims can be tolerated as *dhimmis*, minorities under Islamic control. Thus, Jews can be accepted as subservient members of a Muslim society while a Jewish state, especially on formerly Muslim territory, is anathema.

How literally this concept is translated into attitudes and policy is another question, however, especially in view of the modern Arab states' willingness to forsake many other fundamentalist Islamic tenets. As late as the eighteenth century, Moroccan ambassadors always included in their dispatches a parenthetical remark following the mention of anyplace in Spain: "May God soon restore it to Islam." Islam, of course, had lost it 500 years before, and as Bernard Lewis noted wryly, "I'm not aware of any immediate plans for a reconquest of Spain."[35]

Islamic nationalists are as skillful as Jewish nationalists in citing religious sources to justify their claims to Palestine and Jerusalem. Islamic writings and commentaries contend that the ancient Hebrews ruled Palestine only briefly and incompletely; that the Arabs predated the Jews and were descended from the Canaanites, Edomites, Arameans, Jebusites, Phoenicians, Hittites, and Assyrians; and that the Western Wall was actually built not by the Jews but by the Phoenicians.[36] The Koran does not mention Jerusalem by name but refers to it as "the far distant place of worship" in describing Muhammad's night journey from Mecca to Jerusalem to heaven, back to Jerusalem and then to Mecca. Jerusalem is also called "the third of the sanctities" and "the first of two directions," a reference to Muhammad's initial practice of facing Jerusalem during prayer. Muslims believe this supports their integral rights to Jerusalem, although modern non-Islamic scholars tend to regard this as an early effort by the Prophet to induce support from the Jews. Muhammad initially included certain other Jewish observance in his religious ritual, such as a fast day for atonement on Yom Kippur, and only after the Jews rejected him did he abandon Jewish practices and substitute Mecca as the direction of prayer.

Muslim and Jewish writers often hold up mirror images of each other's faith, each portraying the other as absolutist and arrogant. In 1982, the *Jewish Chronicle* published an "analysis of Islamic strategy" by a journalist, Bat Ye'or, who described the concept of *jihad* and observed, "One is saddened to find, at the end of the twentieth century, forty leaders— representing one quarter of the world's population, most of them from the Third World—endorsing a creed which divides mankind into two hostile human groups. This makes a mockery of the expression 'just peace' and 'global peace.' "[37]

Similarly, Muhammad Ali Aluba writes from Egypt, "The Muslims recognize the faith of Jesus and the faith of Moses and regard their devotees as People of the Scriptures. But the Jews recognize neither the faith of Jesus nor the faith of Muhammad and regard their devotees as infidels and enemies of God."[38] The stereotype of the Jews as arrogant is given a religious basis. A 1960s brochure issued by the Egyptian Ministry of Foreign Affairs declared, "The Talmud considers the Jews equal to God, and as such everything on earth should by right be theirs." In a series of lectures in Cairo in 1963 and 1964, Raji Ismail al-Faruqi said, "The 'God of Israel' . . . is obsessed with his people, with the nethermost details of their daily chores. He watches their daily obscenities and their sins without moving a hair. After a few pretentious overtures in the first pages of Genesis, he spends all his time, energy and intelligence, while the rest of the cosmos rots, to dispossess a wretched little people of their land, put them to the sword and enter 'his people' into possession of land and whatever tree, beast or child who escapes his 'wrath.' The truth is that this god has never travelled, has never seen the world, not to speak of making it. He is a 'country' man whose world ended with his tribe, beyond which everything and everybody is equally foreign and equally an enemy. In short, he is a regional, tribal, separatist god, with whom monotheism has absolutely nothing to do."[39]

Even the notion of the Arabs as the Amalekites, taught to yeshiva boys at militant Jewish settlements on the West Bank, finds its parallel in a 1967 Arabic edition of *The Protocols of the Elders of Zion*, the fabrication that poses as a Jewish plan for world takeover. The edition's introduction "discusses the story of Haman, who, according to the Book of Esther, planned to exterminate the Jews. Following ancient commentators, [the author] traces Haman's descent to Agag, the Amalekite king who was slain by the prophet Samuel, and explains that the Amalekites were Arabs, thus giving the Arab-Israel dispute a dimension of great historical depth." The introduction "says that Haman's actions were a reaction against the Jewish aim of liquidating Amalek, and regards his plan as right and praiseworthy."[40]

Although the Jordanian textbooks that find their way into West Bank schools concentrate on political issues in vilifying the Jews, religion is a strong secondary theme. Israelis are accused of distorting the Koran in their own commentaries and school curriculum, for example. A third-grade Arabic-language book, published in 1975, asks the youngsters to write the following dictation: "Israel began to raise doubts about and deprecate the Holy Koran after it occupied parts of our land. It misrepresented its teachings and principles and tampered with its verses to stir up suspicion about the Prophet and His sayings." The Koran is also cited as an explicit source of anti-Jewish images. An exercise in a 1982 social-studies text for sixth-graders begins, "Mention a passage of the Holy Koran indicating the Jewish corruption vis-a-vis land." It follows a section discussing the Arab-Israeli wars and the Egyptian-Israeli peace treaty.

In a fourth-grade Islamic-studies text, published in 1973, Jews are condemned at length for rejecting Jesus:

> Our Lord Jesus—upon him peace—was born of a pure and pious mother named Mary, daughter of Imran. She gave him a proper upbringing. And when he grew up God sent him as a prophet to the sons of Israel. They had corrupted and blasphemed the commands of God which Moses—peace unto him—brought with him.
>
> And God sent to them our lord Jesus who upheld what was in

the Torah, and he revealed to him the Evangelical Book which called them to the oneness of God, His worship, and the doing of good deeds. They defied him and demanded from him proof that he was the messenger of God. He gave them many indications.

The sons of Israel saw these proofs and claimed that they were magic. They continued to rebuff him and began to harm him in speech and in deed. Only a few among them believed him to be the envoy, and they were the apostles who protected and helped him.

Our lord Jesus—peace unto him—still called the sons of Israel to the oneness of God and His worship. They conspired against him and tried to kill him, but God rescued him by making one of them in Christ's image, peace unto him, and the Jews thought that he was Jesus and they killed him and crucified him.

As an exercise, the children are asked, "What did the Jews do when God sent to them our lord Jesus, peace unto him?"

The allegation that the Jews crucified a likeness of Jesus, not Jesus himself, is contained in the Koran, and it helps reinforce the idea that the Jews, as cruel and clever as they are, can be tricked and defeated. The concept shows up in more political and anti-Semitic textbook passages as well. The mixture of politics and religion is inextricable. Warfare against Israel is often couched in religious terms. Thus, in the same fourth-grade Islamic-studies book, an assignment is given to write an essay on the theme of a pilot who "sacrifices himself and attacks the planes of the enemy of Islam and those who occupy our land." Similarly, a reading in a 1976 sixth-grade Arabic-language textbook declares, "The first condition for victory is to have faithfulness in God. . . . This belief will unite the Arabs . . . fire in them unswerving resolutions, incite in them heroism and sacrifice."

Claims to Jerusalem stand at the confluence of the religious and the political. A book of readings for third-graders contains the following dialogue:

Tariq: Look at the picture of the city of Jerusalem.
Rabab: Jerusalem is beautiful, Tariq.
Tariq: Indeed, it is established on the holy Palestinian lands.
Rabab: It is the pure city which God blessed.

Tariq: In it, the lord Christ—peace be unto him—lived.

Rabab: And to its land Muhammad—God pray for him and protect him—ventured and from it he ascended to Heaven.

Tariq: The blessed al-Aqsa mosque is there and so is the Dome of the Rock.

Rabab: The Church of the Resurrection is there, Tariq.

Tariq: Jerusalem is Arab. Our grandfathers lived there for thousands of years. The Muslims entered it during the reign of the just Caliph Umar Bin Khatab.

Rabab: But the Zionist aggressors occupied the city of Jerusalem and killed and evicted many of its people.

Tariq: Jerusalem is Arab, Rabab.

Rabab: And it will remain Arab forever.

Religion figures in the commentaries of periodicals throughout the Arab world, but they are less accessible to Arabs living under Israeli control. Some people who travel abroad smuggle them back in, and many can pick up readings from them on Arab radio broadcasts. Saudi Arabia publishes especially vicious attacks on Judaism, although the relatively low rate of literacy there reduces the size of the audience for such material. One paper carried an article headlined "The Torah as the Source of Jewish War Crimes," which began, "People who do not read the Torah and are not experts in it wonderingly ask about the love of destruction and the will to exterminate that characterize Zionism, while others are astonished by the devotion and enthusiasm the Jews demonstrate in carrying out their frightful crimes." It declared, "The Jewish religion is nothing but a collection of criminal racist principles, sowing cruelty, blood-lust, and killing in those who believe in it."[41] The Saudi daily *Al-Riyad* declared on October 25, 1982, "The Talmud and its writings maintain that the world is the property of God's people, the chosen, because the members of the human race are slaves to them. . . . These abominable ideas have led the Jews in the course of all of history to adventurism, espionage, and usury."

Egyptian publications toned down their anti-Israel and anti-Semitic attacks in the 1970s, and especially during the peace process, which began with Egyptian president Anwar Sadat's 1977 visit to Jerusalem. But the assaults resumed after a couple of years. The Cairo Book Fair in February 1981 carried such titles as *The Jews, Objects of the Wrath of God* and *The War of Survival Between the Koran and the Talmud*. In the fourth edition of *The Wailing Wall and the Tears*, published in 1979, Anis Mansur, editor of the prestigious *October* magazine, asserts that the Talmud urges Jews to kill any non-Jew. A 1981 volume by Kamil Safan, *Jews, History and Doctrine*, revives the blood libel circulated in Damascus in 1840, in which Jews were accused of killing non-Jewish children to use their blood for making matzot during Passover.[42]

The potent brew of religion and warfare found new possibilities in Lebanon after the Israeli invasion of 1982, as Shiite Muslim militiamen conducted guerrilla attacks on Israeli troops, claiming that Islam had managed to defeat the Zionist enemy where Arab states had failed. Shiite religious leaders called on their people to drive out the Jews. "Our people will not surrender to the enemy, because they were raised in the school of Muhammad and Jesus," said Sheikh Muhsin Atawi, a southern Lebanese leader. "The school of Muhammad and Jesus was your school, the place where we learn about revolution, rights, and justice."

Akif Haidar, head of the political bureau of Amal, the Shiite militia, declared, "We consider Israel an absolute evil, and any dealings with it a Muslim religious sin." The mufti of Lebanon, Abd el-Amir Qabalan, tried to dissuade Lebanese from cooperating with the Israelis. "Israel knows no friendship," he said. "She exploits friendship and then strikes out and flings her friends to the ground. Israel is a perverted creation which no true religion approves of, nor any person of pure conscience recognizes."

During the war of 1948, Arab troops that entered the Old City of Jerusalem and captured the Jewish Quarter destroyed twenty-two of the twenty-seven synagogues there. The Jordanians demolished the remaining five when they took over. In the years that they held the eastern part of the city, 1948–1967, the Jordanians burned and stole hundreds of Torah scrolls, books, and historically valuable Jewish manuscripts. Generally, Jews were not allowed to pray freely at the Western Wall, which can be seen, in one photograph, defaced by a political poster. In the ancient Jewish cemetery on the western slope of the Mount of Olives, overlooking the Temple Mount, some tombstones were broken and others were used as building blocks for latrines and barracks in Jordanian army camps. An Intercontinental Hotel was erected in 1964 just ten yards outside the cemetery walls, and graves were bulldozed to lay the hotel's access road.

Religious sites and symbols became junctions of rage. In 1982, when Alan Harry Goodman, an American-born Israeli soldier, charged onto the Temple Mount and started shooting into the Dome of the Rock, the word spread quickly through the Old City. Announcements of the emergency were made through the loudspeakers of al-Aqsa mosque, usually used to call the faithful to prayer. The faithful swarmed to the mount, and after Israeli troops and policemen had grabbed Goodman and dragged him off, the throngs continued to crowd the plateau, chanting, murmuring. Someone threw a brick at a line of policemen. Then another was thrown, and another, and soon the policemen were firing tear gas into the crowd. We were running, ducking, wiping our eyes when the first gunshots rang out. Tough border policemen in green berets were shooting, probably into the air, I thought. But then the bullets began to whine and ricochet off the stone. I dove behind a great pillar. Arabs jammed into the space as well, worming their way closer to the column than I. Suddenly I felt a push. I was being pushed out into the line of fire. I turned. It was a middle-aged Arab woman, her head bound in a shawl. *"Yehudi! Yehudi!"* she was shouting at me—"Jew! Jew!"—and the others started pushing too. I snapped at her, "I'm an American," and she let go and smiled sheepishly and made conciliatory noises.

Then the troops chased the demonstrators off the mount, driving them toward al-Aqsa, where noon prayers were in progress. The crowd had dispersed, but the border policemen were angry, and they kicked and punched some laggards. Finally, as their officer ordered the troops to withdraw, a couple of the policemen smiled devilishly to each other and exchanged some words in Hebrew. One reached for a tear-gas grenade and tossed it just outside, and upwind, of the door of al-Aqsa. The gas blew into the mosque. And the few worshipers came stumbling, coughing out as the Israeli troops walked laughingly away.

Religious extremism has attained a strange balance, once witnessed vividly by my colleague Allyn Fisher. A military court in Nablus, on the West Bank, had convened to sentence eight Arabs in the murder of a yeshiva student. On one side of the courtroom sat a group of Islamic fundamentalists; on the other side, fundamentalist Jewish settlers. Allyn watched, fascinated by the symmetry. There was no communication between them, she said, but they were so alike, as if someone had put a great mirror down the middle of the room.

Politically speaking, Islamic fundamentalists were sometimes regarded as useful to Israel because they had their conflicts with the secular supporters of the PLO. Violence between the groups erupted occasionally on West Bank university campuses, and the Israeli military governor of the Gaza Strip, Brigadier General Yitzhak Segev, once told me how he had financed the Islamic movement as a counterweight to the PLO and the Communists. "The Israeli Government gave me a budget and the military government gives to the mosques," he said. In 1980, when fundamentalist protesters set fire to the office of the Red Crescent Society in Gaza, headed by Dr. Haidar Abdel-Shafi, a Communist and PLO supporter, the Israeli army did nothing, intervening only when the mob marched to his home and seemed to threaten him personally. Yet I came to feel that the end result was pretty much the same no matter whether the force of fanaticism was religious or secular. In the cauldrons of political extremism, such as the Dheisheh refugee camp, young Palestinians were bombarded with a barrage of conflicting symbols: the crescent and the star, the hammer and sickle, the faces of mullahs and PLO leaders and Communists. One young man's bedroom had an entire wall, from floor to ceiling, painted in the black, green, red, and white of the outlawed Palestinian flag. Portraits of Lenin and Che Guevara were hung. Children were indoctrinated well enough to answer as if reciting a catechism. I asked a thirteen-year-old boy, Nadir al-Farat, whether he ever talked to Jews. Sometimes soldiers tried to make friends, he said, "but I refuse and run away."

What did he want to be when he grew up? *"Fedaye,"* he replied. "Freedom fighter."

PART TWO

Images

FIVE

The Violent, Craven Arab

The women who lose their sons or husbands in the
battle receive the hard news without weeping or
cries. The Bedouin mother is proud of the fruit of
her womb who fell in battle and died a death
worthy of a son of the desert.
—*The Arabs and Islam*, an Israeli textbook

THE INTERLOCKING STEREOTYPES THAT JEWS AND ARABS USE TO
categorize and explain each other have several origins. One is the relationship of power, in which Jews occupy the dominant role of the majority
and Arabs the inferior position of the minority within Israel and the
occupied territories. Another is the pattern of prejudices visible in classic
racism worldwide, made no less virulent by the fact that most Jews and
Arabs are of the same race. A third is the traditional anti-Semitism
acquired by Arabs from Christian Europe, an array of images also used
occasionally by Jews against Arabs. A fourth is the legacy of war and

terrorism that has led many Jews and Arabs to smear all members of the other group as violent, cruel, and bloodthirsty.

This last source, the ongoing military and political conflict between the two peoples, provides constant fuel for the fires of mutual fear and contempt. It serves as the rationale for bigotry. In its absence, many Jews and Arabs believe, the fervor of prejudice would die, leaving decent relations and only a smolder of minimal tension. So large does the political-military conflict loom as a maker of attitudes that hardly any Arab or Jew who has done serious thinking on the issue rejects the hypothesis—unlikely to be tested—that real peace would bring real human reconciliation.

I found it less easy to draw the lines of cause and effect. It may be, as those involved think, that the racism, anti-Semitism, and class prejudices are just corollaries to the main proposition, appendages of attitude attached to the essential confrontation of two peoples over one tract of territory. But now, after decades, just as war and terrorism have evolved into origins themselves, so have the prejudices and stereotypes worked their way so thoroughly into literature, education, history, language, and social mores on both sides that they seem to govern the conflict as much as they are created by it. Disease and symptoms intertwine.

Not all Jews subscribe to the whole list of prejudices against Arabs, of course, and not all Arabs hold all the negative stereotypes of Jews. Shadings of hardness and softness in seemingly infinite subtlety run across the spectrum between tolerance and bigotry, and exist even within the confines of narrow-mindedness. The patterns they form give shape to mutual viewpoints of immense complexity. But they do form patterns; certain images appear again and again.

For Jews, the most pervasive stereotype of the Arab is the fearsome, violent figure of immense strength and duplicity. Since bigotry rarely balks at inconsistency, the Arab of the Jewish prejudice is also imbued with a paradoxical cowardice. Capable of great cruelty, given to fanatical disregard for human life, he murders easily, either out of a crazed lust for blood or as an emotional animal easily incited and manipulated by murderous leaders. He can smile and serve you coffee and slip a knife quietly between your ribs. Or he can run whooping in frenzy in a wild charge on a kibbutz. But mostly he fights like a sneak and will rarely stand and face you like a man. He is more of a savage than a soldier, easily tricked and frightened.

Such images on both sides are integral to the dynamics of the Arab-Jewish conflict. "In order to be a victim," observed Danny Rubinstein, of *Davar*, "you have to create a picture of the enemy as a huge monster. Take a look at the Israeli hard-liners' perception of the Arabs—as a monster, as brutal, very powerful, very strong, very rich, everything. Then you are the victim, you have to survive, you don't have any alternative. If you see the other side as less powerful, there is a danger that you'll pity them, and then you'll understand their motives. Many times I get letters saying, 'If you're so good-hearted, don't go to the refugee camps; go to see how many problems the Jews from Russia have in this country.'"

The Hebrew-language textbook *The Arabs and Islam*, published by the Israeli Ministry of Education and Culture and used in religious Jewish schools for seventh- and eighth-graders, portrays the Arabs much as American Indians were once pictured for youngsters in the United States, as warlike and predatory. Indeed, the dominant theme of the book is war, thievery, and conquest, with relatively minor attention given to the Arabs' contributions in medicine, astronomy, geography, and architecture. Above a photograph of a line of Arabs riding camels, the caption reads "An armed group of men. It is possible that they are heading for a robbery raid." Below, the text explains, "In time of war, when the tribes' warriors go out from the camp to the battlefield, the daughters of the tribe accompany them with song and dance. The tribes' poets do not stop inflaming the warriors with poems about the tribes' wars and victories in the past, about the heroism of the leader, about hatred and vengeance against the enemy. . . . The women who lose their sons or husbands in the battle receive the hard news without weeping or cries. The Bedouin mother is proud of the fruit of her womb who fell in battle and died a death worthy of a son of the desert." This calumny of callousness is the standard stigma applied to supposedly inferior peoples, attached in other times by Westerners to the Chinese, Japanese, and Koreans, and used also in the 1960s by Americans who believed that the Vietnamese did not "value human life" as much as civilized white society did.

"The Bedouin man is proud to engage in robbery and so educates his children," the book continues. "Bedouin children like the game 'Ghazu' (robbery raids). They compete in running and wrestling and learn to use weapons at a very young age. . . . The tribes of the desert also busied themselves with robbery and looting. They attacked neighbors and wayfarers, and the booty enlarged their riches and possessions. It also happened that in these raids one of the members of a tribe would be killed, and then the whole tribe couldn't find rest until they avenged the blood of the killed one. The attacks and blood feuds caused the Arab tribes to be found mostly in a state of war." Then a perfunctory gesture of balance is made. "But not all the tribes in the desert were happy to go to war," the textbook explains. "Some of the Bedouin tribes settled permanently near the few places blessed with water. These places are called oases, and in them are springs of water, palms, and small areas of grain and vegetables. The tribes which ruled the oases preferred to live in houses and to quietly work their plots."

The book does not denigrate Islam at all; the life of Muhammad and the tenets of his religion are described in neutral terms. But the warlike image dominates, and no Jewish child who has not known an Arab personally, as most have not, could come out of reading the text with any image other than of the violent desert tribesman.

Israelis who have done studies of Arab stereotypes contained in their textbooks and children's literature have found that war is naturally a major topic. "The most important theme was the bravery, the patriotism, the willingness to sacrifice lives, the heroism of Israeli soldiers," said Daniel Bar-Tal, a professor of psychology at Tel Aviv University's school of education, who was researching elementary readers. "This was absolutely the most dominant theme in the Hebrew books. I would say 90 percent of the stories referred to this theme. Relatively there was a lack of reference to Arabs. When it was there, it was negative. Usually they don't know how to fight; they are almost always spies. At the same time, they are willing to destroy Israel; they hate Israel. There are some stories— very few—in which they are portrayed as very cruel, almost inhuman."

Another expert, Menachem Regev, examined an earlier vintage of children's books—those published before 1967, mostly in the '50s and '60s—on which a generation of Israeli Jews was raised. He found Arabs often portrayed as violent, hateful, and simple-minded enough to be incited by their leaders and wooed into peace by the more advanced and cultured Jews. "In the majority of children's stories," Regev writes, "the Arabs appear against a background of tension between them and the Jewish population in times of disturbance and war."

In one story, Arabs are depicted as running into battle with Indian-like war whoops: " 'Palestine—our land; the Jews—our dogs! Palestine—

our land; the Jews—our dogs!' Yelling and screaming these words the mob broke into the yard trampling underfoot those bushes that still remained."

Each war and riot generates its own children's literature, which then survives to carry the theme into the future. In 1958, two years after the Sinai campaign, in a story by M. Garin, *Devil 2 Leaves for the Border*, two children write a composition on their thoughts about the Israeli-Jordanian border: "Kalkiliya! The name alone was enough to make us shudder a bit, for we were well aware that it was a Jordanian town whose citizens had an implacable hatred for Israel and that two weeks before the Sinai campaign, our soldiers had blown up its police fort." In another Garin story, a Bedouin boy, Ahmed, makes friends with Jewish children hiking in the Negev Desert and takes them to his tribe's encampment. "Could it be that we had fallen into a trap? And maybe we were no longer in the territory of the State of Israel? Maybe Ahmed had taken us across the border? To enemy territory?" The fears turn out to be unfounded.

A 1939 story by Eliezer Smoli about a Jewish watchman in Hebron during the Arab riots several years earlier contains a frightening passage: " 'Daddy, Daddy, they killed so many Jews in Hebron . . . and children, too. . . . Daddy, Daddy, in Hebron and Motza! And other places, too,— It's awful!'—wailed Amaliya—'People were so sad and helpless. They told the most terrible stories, frightening, bloodcurdling . . . riots in Jerusalem, slaughter in Motza, dreadful murder in Hebron.' "

Highly charged vocabulary is used to portray Arab "gangs" and "rabble" drunk with violence. In 1963, Naomi Zoreia wrote in *Toward the Sand the Blue Sea*, "Jerusalem was totally encircled by Arabs intoxicated by the idea of war." And in B. Z. Yafet's *The Slogan "Courage,"* the following passage appears: "He was sure that the attackers belonged to one of the Arab gangs about whose cruelty he had heard so much even while on the ship. It wasn't hard for Tommy to reach this conclusion. As a practiced partisan he knew that only gangs of rabble with no discipline or brotherhood were capable of leaving wounded comrades on the battlefields."

Regev comments, "The cruelty of the enemy is reflected even in his attitude to his own people."

In a 1956 story by Ze'ev Domnitz, an Arab band takes three Jewish children captive during the 1929 riots and threatens to hang them if they lie. Ultimately, the Arabs leave the children unharmed and "the story goes on to tell of the friendship that springs up between an Arab and a Jewish boy who save each other's lives during the War of Independence," Regev writes. "The enemy, therefore, is shown as a rabble, hungry for booty, cruel and threatening," he continues. "This general outline becomes more pronounced when contrasted with the idealistic Jewish defenders, moderate and efficient."

In another passage, from a 1958 story by Binyamin Gal, the Arabs are shown as manipulated and undisciplined. "The Arabs attacked from the hills surrounding the kibbutz to the north and the northwest. They stormed the kibbutz, shouting wildly, without any plan or order. They weren't soldiers, but incited villagers, stumbling down the hills and waving their weapons." They are also depicted as frightening individually. A passage by Eliezer Smoli contains this fierce description: "The Arab teacher appeared at the door, a thonged lash held in his hand. He was tall and had a black pointed beard. His long cloak hung from his shoulders, his red tarbush was swathed in a white cloth and his feet were bare."

The importance of these images is heightened by the absence of personal contact between most Israeli Jews and Arabs after the establishment of the state in 1948, a characteristic of life illustrated by a conversation between father and son in Binyamin Halevi's *The Lost Tricycle*, published in 1960:

" 'I want to see an infiltrator! Daddy, what's an infiltrator look like?'

" 'Like any other Arab. There's nothing special about them. It's just their clothes that are different from ours. Anyway, you've seen pictures of Arabs, haven't you?'

" 'Yes—but I want to see a real Arab. Come on, let's go and see the infiltrators,' came the plea."

As Regev notes, "After 1948, the Arabs disappeared from the personal scene of many Israelis. Gradually, the 'Arab' became unreal, something seen in photographs. It is just this lack of opportunity to see 'real Arabs' that gives added importance to literary descriptions of the Arab. Even if the author entertains no such ambition, the picture which emerges in the pages of children's literature becomes the only picture of an Arab that the child knows." Regev condemns "the creation of a stereotype of the Arab as the enemy," observing that the writers fail to distinguish between the description and the evaluation. "Thus the appearance of the Arab as shown in these stories is one which inspires fear long before it is established whether he is friend or foe." An occasional "good Arab" appears in the literature, but he is an individual exception to the rule, "the Arab who links his fate with the Jews and who, presumably, is regarded as a traitor by his own people."[43]

Many of these children's books remain currently popular and available in libraries. Eliezer Smoli's *The Frontiersmen of Israel (Anshei Bereshit)*, about a Jewish family living in Galilee, was in its tenth edition in 1984 and had exerted "a profound influence on the thinking of two generations of young readers," according to Uriel Ofek, a writer and translator of children's books. The story could have been about noble, heroic pioneers of the American West facing the cruel savagery of the Indians. Arabs have burned down the Jewish family's farm. Smoli concludes:

> Everything was burned. A pile of glowing ashes was all that remained of the threshing-floor. Hanging their heads, father and son stood silently weeping . . . suddenly, Hermoni bent down and raised the plow. They stood still. "Come on, Eitan," Hermoni cried impatiently. "Harness it to the horse! Quick, get some rope!" Eitan fetched a length of rope and handed it to Hermoni, who tied both ends to the plow, looping the middle around the pommel on the horse's saddle. "You lead the horse, Eitan!" he called, as he dug the plowshare into the rich soil. "Get along there, boy!" he called to the horse. Slowly the plow moved forward, churning the black soil over and leaving behind a trail of freshly-turned earth. "There, Eitan! We've opened a new furrow," Hermoni said. "Everything has to have a beginning."

The Gideonites, a 1968 novel for teenagers by Devorah Omer, tells a melodramatic tale based on the true story of the Nili, a Jewish underground in Palestine that spied for the British against the Turks in World War I. The Arabs in these pages are drawn severely as primitive, brutal, violent, unfeeling. Turks and Arabs are mixed together into a dark, sinister force; no Arab individuals emerge at all. Instead, Jewish children are constantly demonstrating how much cleverer and tougher than Arabs they are, how adept they are at making Arabs look like fools. The heroine, Sarah, cuts loose a string of camels and steals them to show the Arabs what strong will the Jews have. When "a big, burly Arab" lets his flock into a Jewish field, a Jewish boy protests.

"Let them eat in peace," replied the Arab rudely. "This our field!" Alex did not let the Arab scare him. The Arab raised the stick he was holding. It was a thin stick with a round knot at its end. Alex knew that a bashing from such a stick could be quite serious. The Arab raised the stick over the boy's head, but Alex stepped nimbly aside. The Arab lost his balance for a moment, and Alex ran a few steps back and faced him again. When the Arab came at him, Alex bent again. The stick hit his head but he managed to push the Arab back. The shepherd, who had been standing with his back to the slope, slid and fell backwards, rolling down toward the valley. When he got up he was very upset and ran toward his village calling his herd, who followed him.

Adult literature has also portrayed Arabs as hostile and violent, but with a richness and variety that often introduces contradictory images. Gershon Shaked, professor of Hebrew literature at the Hebrew University in Jerusalem, sees the Arab in Israeli fiction as having taken the place, and many of the attributes, of the gentile in the experience of the European Jew. "Of all possible non-Jews," he observes, "it is the Arab who is most common in Israeli Hebrew literature. This is hardly surprising, since it is the Arab who plays that role in the life of the average Israeli Jew which was formerly played by gentiles in the Diaspora. . . . In the early days of literature in Palestine a basic, paranoid attitude was maintained as it was brought to Israel by immigrant writers with Ukrainian-Bolshevik experiences, and this attitude surfaced once more in the figure of the Arab persecutor. . . . He is also a symbol of the entire hostile environment. The Arab continues in the role of the oppressor who made the Jew into a persecuted soul." In Yosef Aricha's *Nocturnal Landscape*, Shaked notes, the Jewish hero, captured by a band of Arabs, "expects Abu Yussuf, the leader of the gang, to treat him the way Cossacks dealt with Jews, and when Abu Yussuf does not behave as expected because a photograph of the Jew's daughter resembles his own child, the stereotypical expectation proves momentarily false, although in fact it is immediately confirmed by a young member of the gang who violates the leader's command and takes Giladi's life." Other writers, including Amos Oz, construct what Shaked calls "mythical figures of the gentile," which serve as an abstraction of the undefined threat of strangeness. "Thus," Shaked writes, "just as the social incarnation of paranoia from the Diaspora found new life in

THE VIOLENT, CRAVEN ARAB

the Land of Israel, so did an introjected, mythical embodiment of that fear." Some writers, including A. B. Yehoshua, have played with the notions of persecuted and persecutor, blurring the definitions and roles. Of *Opposite the Forests*, a story of conflict between a Jewish forest warden and an Arab watchman, Shaked writes, "Yehoshua makes clear that there are no pursuers and no pursued: everyone is pursued in his own way, and the covenant between the two 'guardians' of the forest is that between two victims."[44]

"Arabs, I think, only understand the language of force, and to deal with them by favors doesn't help." Arye Attia flashed a boyish smile and leaned over the table in my office to take a sip of his black coffee. I asked how he felt about the massacre of Palestinians in the Beirut refugee camps by Lebanese Phalangists. "I'll tell you the truth," he said, grinning. "I don't feel sorry for them. I don't feel sorry for them. I simply say, it's too bad that all the world is against us. And it will interfere with us. But I don't feel sorry for them. I think in general that we have to let them bust their own heads together, let them kill each other."

Arye Attia, who operated a construction crane, was born in Jerusalem in 1953. His parents, who had come from Libya, raised him on tales of pogroms, telling him "about how they hid in their houses, all the Jews, and how some Jews were killed if they were found in the street." Later, as an Israeli soldier, he had his own experiences to reinforce his hard attitudes toward Arabs. During the 1973 war he was captured by the Egyptians in Sinai and held for forty days. "I spent seven days in hand-cuffs, behind my back, and my eyes covered, in a room by myself. When they kept taking me out for interrogation and then would return me, taking me on circular walks to just beat me, they would walk me around and just beat. Or, during the first days, they would have us all get down on the floor together, and they would walk over us and beat us with a whip."

That Arabs understand only the language of force has become the cliché in Israel by which the tough-minded assert their understanding of the "Arab mentality." Meir Cohen-Avidov, deputy speaker of the Knesset, made the argument in sympathy with the Jewish West Bank settlers arrested in 1984 for terrorism against Arabs in the occupied area. "It is unthinkable to continue with the soft-hand policy in these areas," he declared. "People don't know the Arab mentality. They weren't born here, they didn't live with them, they don't know them. I know them. Without a strong hand, there won't be quiet here in the state of Israel."

Inherent in the concept is the notion of the Arabs as cowards, a theme found in literature and enshrined, for one Israeli army recruit I knew, in basic training. A sergeant told the new soldiers seriously that if they were ever attacked by an Arab plane, all they had to do was to aim their rifles at it and the pilot would turn tail and be gone. Thus, many Israelis were taken by surprise when the Arabs made an impressive military showing during the 1973 war, and some Israeli troops in armored units during the 1982 Lebanon invasion expressed astonished admiration at the tenacity of Syrian tank crews during hard battles.

The image of Arab cowardice is the other side of a Jewish fear so powerful that it penetrates even the superior force that Israeli authorities have over their own Arab citizens. A small group of Jews and Arabs have seen this vividly as they have worked in a program called Interns for Peace to bring together residents of several neighboring Jewish and Arab towns in the Galilee. The resistance to joint meetings, social events, school visits, and playground-construction projects has come mostly from the Jews, many of whom are appalled that young Jewish interns, mostly from the United States, are living in Arab villages. "A lot of Jews I speak to make absolutely no distinction between Israeli Arabs, who are loyal Israeli citizens, and Arabs on the West Bank. They think I'm living with eight thousand PLO terrorists," said Peter Schaktman, a twenty-three-year-old native of Buffalo, New York. The immense differences in attitudes, with Israeli Arabs generally more willing to live peacefully with Jews, are bleached out by the blinding glare of hostility. Raphael Eitan, who as chief of staff of the Israeli armed forces treated the country to repeated derogatory remarks about Arabs, once told me that he saw no difference between those in Israel and those on the West Bank. When I asked him whether he ever talked to any Arabs, even those living close by his farming community in Galilee, he growled, "I don't need it."

A 1980 survey of 1,223 Jewish adults found 51.6 percent judging that a large part of the Israeli-Arab population—that is, Arabs who lived as Israeli citizens inside the pre-1967 borders—hated Jews. Fifty-three percent said they thought a large segment of the Israeli Arabs were happy when there was an attack on Israel. Only 15 percent judged the Israeli Arabs as largely loyal to Israel.[45] (In fact, Israeli Arabs have been shown by studies as considerably more accommodating than Jews believe. One survey of 1,185 Israeli Arabs found that only 11.8 percent of them advocated replacing Israel with a Palestinian state; the rest agreed to various forms of partition, mostly along the pre-1967 lines, with Israeli and Palestinian states existing side by side.[46])

Violence was a major theme in the images of Arabs held by Jews questioned in the 1980 study. Israeli Arabs were categorized as violent by 40.7 percent of the Jews and as nonviolent by 22 percent. Syrian Arabs were judged violent by 57.6 percent and nonviolent by 16.9 percent, indicating that some differentiation among Arabs does take place. Egyptian Arabs, in the wake of the peace treaty, were labeled violent by only 20.7 percent and nonviolent by 30.9 percent, which was close to the way Israeli Jews categorized themselves (22.2 percent violent, 35 percent nonviolent). Americans came out the best, with just 12 percent of the Israeli Jews labeling them as violent and 48 percent as nonviolent.[47]

The sense of all Arabs as hostile and dangerous is easily brought to the surface. Israeli security men, accustomed to spotting Arabs in a crowd and regarding them as potential threats, practically went crazy in Cairo while protecting the first Israeli delegation in Egypt after Sadat's 1977 visit to Jerusalem. Everybody around was Arab, and the old rule of thumb was rendered useless.

The anxieties operate on more mundane levels as well. After a terrorist attack in Jerusalem, Irith Gubbay, a Jewish Intern for Peace, called to have her phone repaired in the Arab village of Tamra and got a Jewish clerk on the line. "[The clerk] gave me this long lecture about what happened in Jerusalem—how could I still be living in Tamra, and don't I see that Arabs are just out to kill us and we should oppress them and why should we give them anything?"

Anxiety is heightened by language problems. Although most Israeli Arabs speak Hebrew, only a tiny fraction of Israeli Jews speak Arabic; some imagine that when the Muslims chant prayers, they are really saying, "Kill the Jews, kill the Jews, kill the Jews," Peter Schaktman observed.

"It's easy to get paranoid," said Susan Bandler, another intern living in Tamra. "On the radio, three quarters of the stations they don't understand, and they're sure there is planning, they're sending transmissions to each other all the time." Of course, Israel is the perfect place for that old crack that even paranoids have real enemies. Susan told of a Jewish friend's experience at an Arab's wedding: "Everyone's singing and dancing, and everybody's clapping and clapping, and he's clapping. Finally somebody tells him, 'You know what it is? This is an old PLO song for the destruction of Israel.' "

An initial fear also grips some of the interns when they begin their two years of living in Arab villages. Esther LaFontaine, an Israeli Jew whose parents had immigrated from Libya, said that she "felt Arabs were very dirty, very bad, and very dangerous" when she arrived in Tamra accompanying her American-born husband. "I was afraid that men would shoot me in the street or rape me. The first day we came to the village I couldn't sleep. All night I was shaking. Now I'm comfortable, with open doors." When she went off on this adventure, she didn't tell her parents where she was going to live. But months later, after she finally let them know, her mother visited the village and found herself able to spend pleasant hours cooking and singing with the Arab women; they had language, music, and cuisine in common.

The interns have had to work hard to overcome the fears of Jewish schoolchildren and their parents about visits to Arab villages. A scout troop of ninth-graders in the Jewish town of Pardes Hanna, just down the road from the Arab town of Kfar Qara, expressed a kind of nervous curiosity, saying, "We're interested, and we're willing to try, but you should know that we're scared," according to one of the interns. The scout leader was also afraid, but the visit took place successfully in the end. At a joint Arab-Jewish summer camp run for eight days, the Jewish boys were so frightened that they moved their beds out of the rooms where Arabs were staying and couldn't get up the courage to bunk with them until the last night. Jewish tour guides and bus drivers often balk at taking American Jewish groups to visit the interns in Arab villages, according to the head of the program, Rabbi Bruce Cohen. "The Israeli tour guide tries to dissuade them," Bruce said: " 'I don't know how to get to Tamra.' 'The roads aren't paved.' 'I won't be responsible for security.' "

Many Jews who have lived for years in Jerusalem imagine such danger that they avoid going to the eastern, mostly Arab part of the city and rarely gather their nerve to wander through the exotic alleys inside the walls of the Old City. The fear was heightened by a series of stabbings there in 1985. Many others do go, of course, and nothing usually happens to them other than an occasional hard stare. But the sense of being at risk is a deterrent to most. I did not realize this when I first arrived; I asked a Jewish employee to buy a King James version of the Bible, which I thought should be standard equipment in the *Times* Jerusalem bureau. I was thoroughly puzzled when she returned empty-handed, announcing that none of the bookstores had one. That night at a dinner party I expressed amazement that a King James version was not to be had in Jerusalem, of all places. An American friend smiled knowingly, guessing that my employee had been afraid to venture into East Jerusalem, where there are Christian bookstores, and had looked only in Jewish West Jerusalem. Sure enough, when I checked back with her, she admitted that she had stayed on the Jewish side of the city. I asked her to try in East Jerusalem, and I kept asking over the next few days, but nothing ever happened. She simply would not go there, and I finally went and bought the Bible myself.

Other Jews complain about having to go to East Jerusalem to conduct business with the United States consulate, whose passport and visa office is located in the Arab sector. Especially galling is the fact that almost all the clerks, who do the initial screening of applications, are Arabs. Although I never knew them to be anything but courteous, some Israeli Jews found them uncomfortable to deal with, possibly because the Jews were not accustomed to Arabs' having the authority to tell them what to do—to fill out this form or to supply that document.

The images of hostility and violence that are attached to Arabs lead sometimes to fantasies about plots and schemes where none seem to exist. When an eleven-year-old Jewish girl, Nava Elimelech, was abducted and brutally murdered and her body dismembered, Raful Eitan used his position as chief of staff to assert that the crime was part of an Arab initiation rite into a radical terrorist cell; although there have been several cases of Arabs' sexually assaulting and killing Jewish children, in this instance the general appeared to be speculating. Police officials and the interior minister, Yosef Burg, immediately denounced him, saying that no such evidence had come to light. Israeli newspapers gave prominent display to Eitan's unfounded assertion, which the Israeli journalist Yehoshua Sobel likened to the infamous blood libel charging that Jews murdered Christian children to use their blood in making matzot during Passover. "Raful joins a large and glorious tradition, in revealing his detective revelations close to the Passover holidays," Sobel wrote with acid sarcasm. "Who is more accustomed than us Jews to the many discoveries of child murder for ritual purposes?"

Later, when officials in the Tel Aviv city government spread rumors of an extremist Muslim attempt to take over Jaffa—once an Arab city and now part of the Tel Aviv municipal area—by purchasing apartments with PLO funds, a quick denial came from the prime minister's adviser for Arab affairs, Binyamin Gur-Arye, who called the rumors "exaggerated and untruthful" and declared that "such irresponsible reports hurt Arab-Jewish relations and cause unnecessary unrest."

Similar fears of PLO money being used to buy apartments lay in the arguments of Alexander Finkelshtein and his group of Upper Nazareth citizens who organized to keep Arabs out of their town. Their views of Arabs, touching every stereotype, also contained a strong element of anxiety and anger over Arab hostility. "If my flag goes up, the Arabs spit on it," said Avraham Cohen, a forty-six-year-old veteran who got his army shirt out of the closet to show me his battle ribbons, then pulled up the shirt he was wearing and pointed to a scar on his belly: "That was the Sinai in '56." Then he added, "All they want is to take these areas from the Jews, and if they have the opportunity, they'll throw us into the sea."

Perhaps most frightening is the specter of Jewish men going off to a war and Arab men remaining with the unguarded Jewish women and children. "If I have to go to war, our women will sit in shelters and the Arabs will kill them," Cohen declared. "So our hearts will be here all the time."

Even if Arabs didn't kill them, it would be offensive just to have Arabs around not fighting for the country and expressing contrary political views, explained another member of the group, a high-school teacher and guidance counselor named Galila Barkai. She seemed to be saying that the mere presence of Arabs would spoil the fervent unanimity of a wartime atmosphere. "Let's think of a situation of wartime," she said, "and my husband and all husbands go to war, and I stay here with my kids, and I have to go to the shelter, and I have an Arab neighbor, and he doesn't go to war, and my husband is fighting. The Arab doesn't fight; he stays with his family behind. And we all go to the shelter. And he's sitting with me in the shelter, and all of a sudden he wants to talk politics, and it happens, and he talks politics about what happens in the war. He talks politics about what happens in the battlefield. And my husband is there, and all other husbands are there, and he's there in the shelter, and my husband is protecting him, as he's protecting me. And all of a sudden he talks about the PLO and he talks about the Arab problem, and how the Arabs are very right with all they want and everything. How do you think I would feel?"

For some Jews, these images translate into harsh prescriptions for dealing with the Arabs. Finkelshtein's Upper Nazareth group wants expulsion. An Arab woman doctor who lives there is harassed by a Jewish neighbor who parks his car in front of her driveway and tells her, "You belong in Amman. This isn't your place, it's mine. Go back to Amman."

An Arab teacher and politician, Walid Sadik, recalls his encounters with Jewish schoolchildren to whom he is sometimes invited to speak: "What you hear in the questions is terrible. For example, 'Why do you have to settle here? This is our own country. You have to be expelled outside the country. You have a lot of land, and we have a very tiny piece of land. This is for Jews, so you have no right to stay here, and if we let you, you have to thank us for that.' Or, one of the students said to me, 'Why are you complaining? I am complaining that the Likud Party didn't do the same as Nigeria did to the Indians, Asians. We have to expel you just like that. Or if you stay here you have to work only in manual labor.' When I complained that we didn't get into government institutions, they said to me, 'You have all the rights. Your task is to work.' "

A Hebrew University faculty member, Shlomo Ariel, writes to *Haaretz* about disturbing attitudes in discussions with young Jews who are about to enter the army:

I met with about ten groups of fifty young people each, which represents to a certain extent a random and representative sample of the Jewish population of Israel of this age level, with all its strata and ethnic origins. . . . The young participants, almost unanimously, expressed full identification with the racist positions of Finkelshtein toward Arabs. To the claim that the latter are Israeli citizens with equal rights according to the law, the typical reaction was that Israeli citizenship should be denied them. In each discussion group there were a few who proposed physically liquidating the Arabs, right down to the elderly, women, and children. They received the comparison between Sabra and Shatila [the Beirut refugee camps] and the Nazi destruction favorably, and said with full candor that they would carry out such destruction with their own hands with no inhibitions or pangs of conscience. Not one expressed shock or reservations about these declarations, but there were those who said that there was no need for physical liquidation; it would be enough to exile them across the border. Many supported apartheid on the model of South Africa. The idea that to the Arabs of Israel this country is their country and birthland was received with amazement and mockery. Any moral claim was rejected with scorn. In each group there were not more than two or three holders of humanitarian, anti-racist views on this question, but it could be seen that they were afraid to express themselves publicly, and indeed those few who dared to express their unpopular opinions were immediately silenced by a chorus of shouts.[48]

Stereotypes of unrelieved Arab hostility are also held by some Jewish specialists on Arab affairs, who somehow enjoy dealing with Arabs from a posture of power and superiority. Moshe Sharon, who has been chairman of the Hebrew University's department of history of the Islamic countries, has also served as an adviser on Arab affairs to Prime Minister Begin and to the Defense Ministry's military government on the West Bank and Gaza Strip. He approaches Arabs with a mixture of paternalism and contempt. "From personal experience," he wrote in *The Jerusalem Post*, "I have found that almost every Arab is a propagandist. In an amazingly short time, an Arab will turn any discussion with a foreign visitor into a monologue on Israel's oppressive policy toward the Arabs under its control. In this respect, there is very little difference between Israeli Arabs and those who live in the administered territories." Professor Sharon's lack of discernment does not carry over into the practice of carrying weapons to the West Bank, however. While many Israeli Jews feel compelled to have at least a pistol when they travel there, Sharon takes a tear-gas canister the size of a beer can, which he regards as a more humane way to deal with any threat that may arise. "It doesn't get them into trouble, and it doesn't get me into trouble," he said. And when he's in his office at the Defense Ministry in Tel Aviv, he puts the silver canister up on a bookshelf.

There is a difficult ambivalence in having to live as neighbors with people deemed as unremittingly hostile and violent. Among the most sensitive to the problem is Shifra Blass, the religious settler on the West Bank, who believes both in humanism and in the rights of Jews to the land.

"On the one hand," she said, "we're at war with the Arab nations, and we are aware of terrorism. And every time the children go out we tell them, 'Don't pick up suspicious objects.' When you go to Jerusalem, your child has to know he doesn't pick up a wallet he sees on the street. And you have to explain why. On the one hand, you're forced to instill in him certain suspicions and fears. For children it's frightening. The children go on trips sometimes to Jerusalem, and occasionally the bus is stoned. Once, two months ago, a school bus coming here had a Molotov cocktail thrown on it. Thank God it didn't explode. That's what you're dealing with on the one hand, and for survival you can't ignore it. You can't tell your child that it's nothing.

"On the other hand, we live in an environment with Arab neighbors, most of them the same kind of people we are, in terms of living. They have a day-to-day life and want to do it peacefully, and we also have to prepare our children for living in that. This is a very thin line to tread, and children don't understand subtleties. You have to come right out and say things. There are Arabs who don't want us in Israel, who try to kill us. But most of the people you see are good neighbors, and we don't have trouble. You can visit them, you can see how they live. In order to do that, because it's a different culture and a different standard of living, you have to explain it in a way that won't bring the kind of attitudes which are very easy to have in such a situation, this kind of stereotype: They are dirty, there are smells coming from the village, they're with the sheep. If you teach them, and you take them out on school trips, and the Arab explains how he makes pita [flat bread], and he makes it for them, and he brews them tea, and they sit and they're his guests, there's no thought of this kind of stereotype, because he's being hospitable to you, and you're his guest, and you can understand something about him as a human being. That's the one thing in which we have an edge over people who live in the cities, because they have one stereotype: the Arab who comes to do the garden or to clean the street; and that's who does it in Israel today. And we simply cannot afford that kind of stereotype."

The dilemma was put another way by Ze'ev Chafets, who served as director of the Government Press Office under Begin—until he resigned out of disgust at Begin's reluctance to name a state commission to investigate the Sabra and Shatila massacres. We were talking one day about bigotry against Arabs, he was telling me of a disturbing discovery about the attitudes of someone close to him, and his thoughts drifted to his son Shmulik, then about a year old. The great challenge, Ze'ev said, the great difficulty, would be how to instill a balance in the boy, how to raise him so that he would be "ferocious enough to be a soldier, and gentle enough to be a citizen."

SIX

The Violent, Craven
Jew

He who splits open the wombs of pregnant women
and massacres children is capable of dirty acts of
deception . . . as is every underhanded coward who
seeks to catch his enemies unprepared.
—Yusuf al-Sibai, *Twelve Men* (short stories)

T HE POLITICAL-MILITARY CONFLICT SHAPES ARAB IMAGES OF JEWS AS
decisively as it does Jewish images of Arabs. Of all the anti-Jewish themes
in Arab textbooks, newspapers, and literature, none has more prominence
than the portrait of the aggressive, brutal Jew who embraces violence
without remorse. Here the Arab and Jewish stereotypes of each other
attain remarkable symmetry, even down to the counter-image of Jews as
cowards, which mirrors the Jewish notion of the Arabs' lack of courage.

Among Arabs, the stereotype of the violent Jew becomes increasingly
pronounced as contact between Arabs and Jews decreases: It appears most
strongly in material written in the Arab world beyond Israeli jurisdiction.

It exists in more varied forms in the attitudes of Arabs living under Israeli occupation on the West Bank and Gaza Strip. And it seems weakest among Israeli Arabs, citizens of the state who often have jobs with Jewish employers and relatively little confrontation with the police authorities. Among West Bank and Israeli Arabs, stereotypes seem to fluctuate with an individual's immediate experience and his membership in a peer group or subculture. Thus, the hardest views on the West Bank can be found either among residents of refugee camps, who are exposed to constant political indoctrination and personal hardship, or among highly politicized urban residents and university students. Softer attitudes are visible among rural Arabs, particularly the relatively apolitical farmers, provided their land has not been confiscated for Israeli settlements. Among Israeli Arabs, land is a major factor in shaping perceptions of Jews; studies have found that the most hostile are the Bedouins of the Negev, whose goat herds and encampments have been driven off ancestral land to make way for Israeli army bases and firing ranges. Then, in descending order of hostility, come the non-Bedouin Muslim Arabs, the Christian Arabs, the Galilee Bedouins, and, finally, least hostile of all, the Druse.[49]

Israeli authorities exert considerable effort to prevent Arabs in Israel, the West Bank, and the Gaza Strip from having access to the virulent printed Arab propaganda that circulates outside Israeli borders. Most newspapers and many books from the Arab world are banned from general circulation in Israel, but a good deal of material gets smuggled in and passed hand to hand, and Arabs are occasionally arrested for possession of it. Arabic-language papers and magazines published in East Jerusalem and Haifa are subjected to the tight strictures of the Israeli military censors, who examine every line of copy, including obituaries, for hints of political "incitement." Even translations of sharply worded articles that have appeared in the Hebrew-language press are often barred from the Arabic papers, and the Arabic news on Israeli radio and television is usually scrubbed free of the kind of tough reporting on official Israeli behavior that is customary on Hebrew newscasts. But Arabs get around the obstacles by picking up Jordanian television, some Syrian television in the north, and radio stations from throughout the Arab world.

In addition, although West Bank schools follow the Jordanian curriculum, the Israelis try to keep textbooks published by Jordan out of the classrooms. Israeli authorities purge the books of offensive passages, then reprint and reissue them. Technically, only those Israeli versions of the

Jordanian volumes are supposed to be used by West Bank teachers. In practice, however, enforcement is impossible. "There are one thousand schools and three inspectors," said an Israeli official who oversees the texts. "Every two to three years we can get one to each school." As a result, Arab youngsters on the West Bank get a healthy dose of anti-Israel material. By contrast, Israeli Arabs are taught in Arabic-language schools under an Israeli curriculum, which stresses Jewish history and virtually ignores Arab history and the Arab-Israeli conflict, with the counterproductive result that the youngsters usually acquire their political views from the street, untempered by the careful perspective and accurate background that can be provided by a responsible teacher.

The Jordanian textbooks that filter into West Bank classrooms—whether on the subject of reading, mathematics, social studies, or Islamic studies—deal with Jews mostly in terms of the Arab-Israeli conflict, a yearning for Palestine, an adulation of Arab military heroism, and a description of the Jews' cowardice. A fairly typical passage, in the *Diary of Arabic Language* for high-school juniors, also includes a rather clumsy rationalization for the Israelis' military victories over the Arabs:

> They fight only when they stand behind fortified villages or behind walls, according to their inherent behavior in all times and at the present time as well. Even now, when they use warplanes in fighting, these in themselves serve them as a shield to protect them. Similarly, the tank, and any implement of modern warfare, all put in their hearts the audacity to fight us. These implements used by the Jews do not indicate that they have courage and have nothing to do with the objective situation. And yet we should not infer from this that we can abstain from using modern means of warfare, for if we use them in addition to the daring and courage with which the Muslim soldier is blessed, we would be able to defeat them. Courage alone cannot yield victory on the battlefield, and the cowardice of the Jews is not adequate to overthrow them.

The opening passage of that excerpt is taken from the Koran, which is frequently cited to bolster the cowardly image. "They will not fight against you in a body save in fortified villages or from behind walls," the book says of the Jews. (Sura LIX, Exile, Verse 14.)

The massacre at Deir Yassin comes in for detailed treatment with elevated rhetoric. "The women of the village stood side by side with the men in the battle," reads a passage on page 54 of the Arabic-language text for fifth-graders. "They bandaged the wounded and the injured, and some of them died and thus won the *shihada* [the promise of God to those who die in a holy war]. One of those women was Hayat. . . . On that sinister day of slaughter, Hayat was stirred to respond to the call of the homeland . . . and suddenly she heard a moan of a wounded man and hurried to bandage his wounds. But the criminal hand that struck the wounded did not let the victim escape death, and shot him with bullets, and the daring Hayat was struck by ignoble and perfidious shots, and was soaked in her purified blood."

Reading and grammar exercises are infiltrated by military themes. A reading book asks children to write sentences responding to questions about Acre (in Hebrew, Akko), an ancient Mediterranean port now part of Israel: "How did the people of Acre vanquish Napoleon and repel him from the city? Acre is a usurped city; mention the names of the other Arab cities which Zionism usurped." In a grammar book, pupils are asked to give the accusative form in the sentence "The Arabs will liberate Palestine." A manual for teachers of beginning Arabic provides a series of pictures entitled "The Little Hero" and a description of the scenes:

Ziad's mother was doing the laundry. She called to Ziad and asked him to buy soap. Ziad carried a shopping basket and went to the market. The market was closed off, the enemy soldiers carrying arms. The Zionists were making the rounds of the market. Ziad passed through the market and looked at the soldiers. He saw a store in the quarter. Ziad bought soap and chalk. Ziad stood in front of the fence and wrote on it: "Palestine is my home."

The Zionist soldiers cried out, "What are you doing?" Ziad remained silent. The Zionist looked at the gate. The Zionist read, "Palestine is my home."

The pictures are followed by a story to be told to the children by the teacher: "The Arabs lived in Palestine. Palestine is beautiful. It has oranges, lemons, and beautiful cities: Jaffa, Lod, Ramle. The Zionists attacked the Arabs. Zionism stole Palestine. The Arabs and the Jews have fought each other many times. The Arabs still fight to this day. The

Arabs will be victorious, and the Palestinian people will return to Palestine. The children will return to their sweet homes."

In falsifying history and romanticizing Palestine, the passage blends some of the major themes of Arab textbooks into an emotional brew: Israelis are rarely Israelis—which would lend their statehood some legitimacy—but Zionists, with all the overlay of ugliness that the word conveys to Arabs. The Arabs did not attack the fledgling Jewish state; the Zionists were the aggressors. The Arabs are heroic fighters moving toward victory, toward a recapturing of a sweet life that is made to seem real, although it never was and never can be.

Exaggerations are frequently used to describe the "Zionists' " aggressive intentions and behavior. A favorite is the charge that "the Jews consider Palestine as a point of departure for the building of their state from the Nile to the Euphrates," an allegation found in a 1982 fifth-grade social-studies book published in Jordan, and one that derives from numerous Arab writings and speeches over the years. In 1959, for example, Nasser declared, "Israel has a certain policy, and it is that she must establish the State of Israel, the Holy State, from the Nile to the Euphrates, and take parts of Lebanon, Syria, Jordan, and Egypt. We must take this talk seriously and never laugh at it." Some Arab writings contain the fabrication that a huge map showing such an extended Jewish state hangs in the Knesset.

The charges are being updated constantly. The 1982 Jordanian social-studies book has Israel explicitly ordering the massacre of Palestinians in the Beirut refugee camps and makes no mention of the Christian Arabs who actually did the killing. "On June 5, 1982, Israel launched land, air, and sea attacks on Lebanon in which its troops occupied the city of Beirut, blockaded it, and annihilated large portions of it," the textbook tells fifth-graders. "Israel proposed a massacre in the Palestinian refugee camps."

A book of short stories, *Twelve Men*, by Yusuf al-Sibai, contains an account by an Egyptian soldier of his unit's attack on Kibbutz Yad Mordechai in 1948: "The enemy began to wave white flags, but we had little faith in his honor. For he who splits open the wombs of pregnant women and massacres children is capable of dirty acts of deception designed to bring about an end to the shelling and then to attack us, as is every underhanded coward who seeks to catch his enemies unprepared."

Another textbook portrays Zionism as a formidable force that should exhort the Arab to unity and loyalty, "especially since his enemy continually strengthens the ties of loyalty and the feeling of belonging together . . . until this loyalty has become supreme selfishness, blindness, and fanaticism, dangerous not only for the Arabs but for all humanity."

The texts are replete with passages exalting Arab military resolve and glorifying violence against the Zionist enemy. A social-studies textbook instructs the pupils, "Paste in your notebooks several pictures representing the weapons of the Jordanian Arab army." Peaceful reconciliation goes unmentioned as a goal, and any Arab parent who might want his child to see less warlike options has to look outside the classroom. This poses an especially hard problem for moderate West Bank Arabs who often feel their sons and daughters drifting away into radicalism, pushed both by the militant atmosphere in their schools and the capricious arrests and interrogations to which they are subjected by Israeli soldiers and secret policemen. In the milieu of zealous nationalism that envelops Palestinian youth, it becomes unfashionable, even dangerous, to question the propriety of a poem entitled "The Blood of the Martyr," which appears in an Arabic-language text for sixth-graders:

A bullet in the chest of the criminal aggressor
Is more delicate than the whisper of the poem and more merciful. . . .

Other poetry, notably by Tawfik Zayyad, an Israeli Arab who serves as a Communist Knesset member and mayor of Nazareth, urges Palestinian steadfastness in stirring terms that could not be published in Israel but find their way into a Jordanian Arabic-language text for vocational-school students. His poem "Here We Are Staying" appears on page 37 of the text. The term "blue fangs," in the second verse, comes from the Arabic expression "His fangs are blue," meaning that he is untrustworthy and evil.

In Lod, Ramle, and the Galilee,
At your throats
We are a piece of glass like a thorn

In your eyes
We are a storm of fire

Here on your chests we will remain
As walls
We will clean plates in hotels
We will fill the cups for the owners
And we will wipe the floor tiles in the black kitchens
To extract a mouthful for our little ones from out of your blue fangs.

We will challenge
We will starve
We will be stark naked
We will hurl poetry
We will fill the angry streets with demonstrations
And we will fill the prisons with pride.

We will make our infants a generation of revolutionaries
One after another. . . .

Just in case the students are a little slow to get the point, the textbook hammers it home with an assignment to discuss the statement " 'Withstanding and challenge' are the two main ideas expressed by the poets of the occupied land."

An especially vicious passage appears in *Twelve Men*, one of whose stories has an Arab fighter saying to an Israeli soldier, " 'I shall kill you and drink your blood! But your blood is filthy . . . disgusting . . . and it is not enough to kill you once. Let me kill you the way I want.' And then he began to tighten the grip of his fingers around the throat of the Israeli soldier until the soldier's face turned blue, his eyes began to pop out of their sockets, and his tongue came out. At this point he loosened his hold, so as to let him breathe, only to repeat the procedure, saying, 'Well, what do you think of this game: Entertaining, isn't it?' "

In many readings and drawings, youngsters are pulled into the fight and the cause. Fathi Ghabin, a Palestinian painter from Jabaliya camp in the Gaza Strip, was sentenced to six months in prison for an exhibition of paintings depicting the death of his seven-year-old nephew, who was shot by Israeli soldiers during a demonstration in 1982. The boy lay on his side, blood flowing from a chest wound, as a crowd of protesters stood in the background with arms raised defiantly. The painting's dominant colors—the red of the blood, the green and white of the boy's shirt, the black of his pants—were the colors of the banned Palestinian flag. Other works showed a broken Star of David and an old man with a bleeding boy, in a mélange of violence and nationalism that infuriated Israeli authorities. "First it is the colors; you have the colors of the PLO flag," an Israeli official told Edward Walsh of *The Washington Post.* "That is considered inciting material because it insinuates the ongoing armed struggle."

Textbooks also strive to make children feel involved. A beginning reader for first-graders, published jointly by Syria and Jordan in 1976, tells a story of a little boy, Said, receiving a signal of help from a hilltop garrison of Arab soldiers who have run out of food while fighting the enemy. The father prepares food and sends Said to take it through enemy lines; he is shown in drawings hiding behind a rock from ugly soldiers with Stars of David on their helmets. The boy, reaching the Arab soldiers, is embraced by them thankfully.

A fourth-grade reading book contains letters to sons from fathers at the front. "When the great attack started, our Arab jets struck and blasted thunderously," reads one, purportedly from the Golan Heights during the 1973 war. "My son, Qusayu, from the summit of this mountain I now see the fiercest battle in the Hauran Valley and the Golan Heights. Oh, here they are, our Arab brothers, the Iraqi, Jordanian, Moroccan, and Saudi soldiers, participating in the battle of liberation. My son, I did not write you everything because the battle is long and your turn will come one day. You and your generation will be the rising future soldiers."

The contemporary Arabic press is also loaded with articles and commentaries that reinforce the violent image of the Jews. Listing towns and refugee camps that had been the targets of Israeli attacks over the years, *Al-Jazira* of Saudi Arabia declared on September 6, 1981, "All the massacres against helpless, innocent women and children at Deir Yassin, Qibya, Baher al-Bakr, as-Salt, Irbid, Sidon, ar-Rashadiyeh, and al-Fakahani were carried out without any guilt feelings or pangs of conscience."

The inflated argument of the printed word is not always translated literally into Arab attitudes, especially among Arabs who have contact with Israeli

Jews. A softening, a shading takes place, a gap opens between the idea and the reality, and the contrast between the murderous image and the subtler fact sometimes causes considerable confusion, even despair.

A Syrian army captain was once caught in this limbo between what he thought he knew and what he then learned. After the Six-Day War of 1967, he was held by the Israelis along with other captured Syrian and Egyptian officers in a prison at Atlit, on the Mediterranean, south of Haifa. In an effort to counter the propaganda these men were fed at home, the Israelis decided to take them on tours of the country, to show them Israel. The project was coordinated with Beit Ha-Gefen, a joint Arab-Jewish community center in Haifa, whose founder, Yaacov Malkin, remains haunted by the episode. Most of the captured officers were invited to dine with Jewish families, Malkin told me, but the Syrian captain refused. He insisted on being driven around by an Arab, and so an Israeli Arab who was affiliated with the community center was asked if he would pick the captain up at Atlit and take him out for a day.

As the two drove away from the prison compound, the captain told the driver to stop the car. And then the Syrian laid down his ground rules for the trip: The Israeli Arab was to take him wherever he said, and if he did not agree, the captain would insist on returning immediately to the prison. The driver said fine. To the market in Haifa, the Syrian commanded. And off they went.

When they arrived in the crowded streets, the captain ordered the driver to stop, got out of the car, chose a small store at random, went in, and asked for eggs. When the merchant nonchalantly produced a carton, the Syrian was astonished. "I believed you were starving," he told his guide.

Then he ordered his car to the lowlands below the Golan Heights, on what had been the border with Syria until the fighting that June had yielded the heights to the Israelis. The captain gave the name of a kibbutz. The driver took him there, and the Syrian stared out the window as they wound slowly through the kibbutz grounds, seeing children at play, families, children's dormitories. The captain asked for a second kibbutz by name, and they went there as well. In all, he had his driver take him to five kibbutzim below the high plain that rises above the Sea of Galilee. On the way back to the Atlit prison, Malkin said, the Syrian officer sat in silence.

Shortly before reaching the prison, the captain told his driver to pull over and stop. The driver did so, and the captain got out, asking to be left alone for a moment. He walked a short way from the car, off the road, and there he stood and wept. Then, after a while, he came back and slipped in beside the driver again. For fifteen years, the captain explained, he had sat in hilltop military positions overlooking those kibbutzim. He had not just thought, he had *known* that they were armed fortresses, pure military bases. He had not just thought, he had *known* that Israelis were all starving. Now, he said, he could never tell anybody back in Syria what he had seen here.

When the Arab driver told the story to Yaacov Malkin, who had devoted enormous energy to bringing Jews and Arabs together to break down mutual stereotypes, Malkin suddenly felt the heavy weight of ignorance pressing against all efforts. "I realized how huge the gap was," he said in sadness.

Egyptian officials got something of an education from Jamil Hamad, the West Bank journalist, when an Egyptian delegation visited Jerusalem after the 1979 peace treaty was signed with Israel. In the lobby of the Hilton Hotel, with swarms of journalists milling around talking with the Egyptians, an Israeli security agent zeroed in on Jamil, an Arab. "He picked me just like that, and he approached me and he said, 'Give me your identity card.' " Jamil recalled. "I was going around, I was talking with the Egyptians, and so he got suspicious. I said, 'Look, this is my press card I have on my chest; you can read my name.' He said, 'I need your identity card.' I said, 'No,' He said, 'Come, I'll give you a hard time.' I said to him, 'Fuck you. I'm not going to give you my identity card. This is discrimination. Why do you choose me? There are hundreds of journalists.' He said, 'Look, I warn you.' I said to him, 'To hell with you.' And I went with the car with an Egyptian high official outside the hotel, and he chased us. We went to another hotel, we sat at a table, we had dinner, we talked, and he was watching. And then the Egyptian security officer who was responsible for the Egyptian delegation said, 'I can't believe it. He's going to smash your head tomorrow.' I said, 'No. You have to realize that.' "

Similar readjustments of attitudes and images were imposed on West Bank and East Jerusalem Arabs by their sudden contact with real Israeli Jews following the 1967 war, when the Israeli army took over East Jerusalem and the West Bank from attacking Jordanian forces. Many Arabs remember that they fully expected the Jews to massacre them.

Israeli soldiers who entered Hebron found the population terrified and braced for death as their leaders surrendered in an effort to save them. A young Arab woman in East Jerusalem recalled her brothers' and father's being rounded up by soldiers, blindfolded, and assembled with other men on the Mount of Olives; Israeli troops clicked their rifles to make them think they were about to be shot, she said. That the Israelis did not kill those men in Jerusalem or massacre the population of Hebron is not to say that the war was free of unwarranted violence. But as some Arabs will now admit, the Jews of reality turned out to be considerably less evil and more varied than the Jews of imagination.

Under Jordanian rule, Palestinian Arabs were presented with as harsh a picture of Jews as now exists in the Jordanian textbooks, and so residents of the West Bank and East Jerusalem were entirely unprepared for living with the Israelis. Many remember vividly their first encounters with Jews, and although the freshness, the surprise, of the initial meetings has been dimmed since by the haze of rough treatment under military occupation, sketches of amazement can still be seen in the recollections.

Raja Shehadeh, the young Arab lawyer from the West Bank, regarded Jews as a monolith, despite the cordial relations that his grandfather, a judge, and his father, a lawyer, had with Jews in Palestine before 1948. "Before '67 I had never seen a Jew," Raja said. "It was completely another land out there. You know how it was in Jordan—I suppose it still is. There isn't an attempt to make the Jew a human being or help people come to terms. I suppose my ideas came from school and from the books. I wasn't thinking of individuals. I thought of a group of people who were deceptive, perhaps like a band of robbers—what the child thinks of a band of thieves who would steal at night." So strange and sinister did the Jews seem to Raja that he clamored to be allowed to watch the weekly convoy that Israel was permitted to send between 1948 and 1967 from West Jerusalem to Mount Scopus to retain the Israeli claim over the spot where Hadassah Hospital had operated before the 1948 war. He wanted to catch a glimpse of Jews.

He was sixteen in 1967. "From the first week of the occupation," he said, "we had Israelis in our house because my father had Jewish friends from before '48. He was never the kind of person who saw it in black and white. He was saying we have to make peace. Some of the Israelis, including some in uniform, were extremely cultured, nice, and so forth." Among the first visitors were David Kimche, later to become director general of the Foreign Ministry, and Dan Bawli, a Tel Aviv lawyer who had apparently known the Shehadeh family from earlier years.

Sari Nusseibeh, the Oxford-educated philosophy professor whose father, Anwar, was once defense minister of Jordan, had something of the same disorientation, moving from image into reality: "What sticks out in my mind is a lecture my father once gave in Petah Tikvah. I think it must have been in '67 or '68. It must have been very early on. This was a strange feeling of traveling into the midst of the enemy, of the enemy's society. And everybody who was around you was the enemy. You were actually inside them. It was a very strange feeling. He was invited to give lectures from early on, actually. It was an open meeting, and there were a lot of Yemeni Jews. It was part of a festival, a festive kind of meeting. I remember, a lot of the people who were present were very happy; they responded happily and positively to my father's speech."

Few Arabs had such benign first encounters, however. Abed Samara, now a sociologist at an-Najah University in Nablus, was a boy when he saw his first Israelis, soldiers, in 1967. "My brother was *mukhtar* in our village, twelve kilometers west of Ramallah," he said. "Our house is very close to the main street, which passes through the village. So they used to come and ask for tea and coffee, the soldiers. So, you can't say that we don't have. So we gave them, the first day or the second day, and after the second day they stopped asking. The officer stopped it or something. Our feeling was a mixture of fear and generosity. They were very, very polite. They just knocked on the door: 'Good morning, please can we have tea?' or something like that. They spoke in Arabic to us, three or four phrases: *sabaah al-khayr* [good morning] or *biddna shai* [we want tea] or *biddna gahwa* [we want coffee], something like that. After that it was the Israelis who would pass by and ask the way to Ramallah or something. One asked, 'Do you know Hebrew?' I said no; he said, why? I said it's not necessary. I was thirteen at the time. Then it was the army who were coming to make curfews if something took place. It was common to see Israeli soldiers."

I wanted to know what had been his first real conversation with an Israeli, and he laughed. "The first real conversation was in interrogation," he said. "It was in 1969. I was a student in the high school, and I participated in a demonstration. 'Why did you make this demonstration and put out these leaflets?' And they did catch some leaflets in my house.

And I said, 'I am a student and a Palestinian; this is my way.' They said, 'Do you want to destroy Israel?' I said no. Of course, I was lying.

"By the way," he added, "our house was destroyed twice, in 1967 and 1968, and two of my brothers were arrested. Even my mother was arrested for one night. My first brother was arrested for cooperating with some fighters, giving them food and shelter. He was arrested for five years and the house was blown up. The second one, they found on our land two boxes of hand grenades from the Jordanian army. They destroyed the house, but in the court he was found not guilty. They were not {his hand grenades}. For a peasant it is a tragedy. It sometimes takes a lifetime to build a house, and to destroy it in two or three minutes. They came and asked us to evacuate the house in half an hour. And they destroyed it. I remember that we were all weeping, most of the women in the village and all the kids. And my brother was arrested four days before. We thought they might kill him. I was thirteen."

I asked Samara how all this had shaped his views of the Israelis. "The Israelis or Israel?" he asked, making a distinction that came to him only after years of informed contact. And then he gave his own reply, which was surprisingly moderate, considering his experiences. "All of this helped me to know the Israelis more. I did have relations with many Israelis, more on the left camp. I know the history of the conflict, the Israeli-Arab conflict. The history of the Arab weakness, and also of Israeli oppression. So what I can say now is that I can accept the idea of coexistence between these two states. Israelis came to this land and in fifty or sixty years developed very quickly into a new nation. So to say we must destroy Israel or the Israelis must leave this country, there are many generations now in Israel. They don't know any other place to go other than Israel. Some Arabs say, 'Even so, we want a state with all of them living together.' It might be achieved, it might not be achieved. Maybe the Israelis will refuse to live in a state with us. So I think the best solution is a two-state solution."

Now, in retrospect, some Arabs try to find reinforcement in their recollections for the violent images they carried of Jews, to see the brutality then as an argument against the military occupation now. Jamil Hamad, the West Bank journalist, divided his images into the Jews of his nostalgia and the Jews of the occupation; he put them into two basic categories separated by the creation of the state. "There are the Jews of

1945, '46, '47," he said fondly. "But the Jews of 1967 were a mixture of the Jews offered to me by the Arab media and the Arab literature and the Jews whom I saw coming to my house, burning it, setting it on fire, and beating my wife. A Polish Jew we'd known from before '48 came in '67 and said to my father, 'Abu-Ata, the Jews you knew before '48 no longer exist. Keep away from the Jews of today.' It will be very gloomy after ten or fifteen years, when people who lived in coexistence are gone."

The stereotypes are not all-inclusive, not for Jamil or some other Arabs who have had enough contact to provide them with friendships across the Arab-Jewish divide. "Mahmoud," who works in a travel agency and meets many Jews, was a boy when the Israeli troops came to his family's pleasant house in Jericho. "It was a Sunday morning," he said. "I remember the whole family—my uncles, cousins, the whole family—we had to evacuate the house and go down to the basement. I remember there was this new veranda my father had built; it had glass windows all around it. And then this bomb came down. I had this toy machine gun on a cupboard, and it was destroyed. I remember this food we had—in a big bowl—and the food was full of glass, and most of it was black.

"The Israelis came and took all the men out of the house and searched for weapons," Mahmoud continued, "and had them kneel on their knees. They had their hands over their heads. They took some meat and bread and some cooked rice. I was scared. I remember this other soldier, he had a beard, he came and started speaking Arabic and said, 'Do you have any cigarettes?' My aunt said no. He looked at her hand, and she was holding a pack, and he grabbed the pack and walked away. We had a brand-new car, a Dodge. They asked my father for the keys. They took the car and drove away. Two weeks later my father found it on the road to Jericho, completely burned up."

And how has all this added up for Mahmoud in his view of Jews? Not so simply, he said. He has been held and interrogated by the Shin Beth on some unspecified suspicions, but never charged. A classmate of his from East Jerusalem who had gone to Jordan and then to Lebanon was shot dead during the Israeli invasion of Lebanon. "He was one of my best friends," Mahmoud said quietly. "He was twenty-three years old. His photo was in the newspaper. This guy wouldn't go to fight. This guy wouldn't kill a bird." Mahmoud was not sure where this left him. "I've had friends killed by the Israelis, but I can't say that I have to get even with all Israelis or that I have to kill every Israeli I can get my hands on," he said. "It's just that not all people think the same. I have an open mind. I don't hate them. I hate the ones in uniform who are controlling the place."

The Jordan River has considerably less grandeur and might than its legend and history convey. In New England, it would be called a brook. At some seasons of the year it is little more than a trickle as it runs southward among ochre desert hills and cliffs and flatlands. But today, as in ancient times, its dimension of symbolism is far greater than its physical size, for along part of its length, it forms the border between the Hashemite Kingdom of Jordan and the Israeli-occupied West Bank.

In the first weeks after Israel captured the West Bank in 1967, the Jordan River became an obstacle more formidable and dangerous than its mere measurements would suggest. Palestinian Arabs who resided on the West Bank, but who happened to be outside the area when the war ended, were technically barred by the Israelis from returning. Some exceptions were later made for the sake of family reunification. But in that early period, no one knew what the future held, and many Arabs risked their lives to cross the Jordan into the West Bank to rejoin parents, spouses, children. Some died. Ibrahim Kareen was arrested.

He is a slim man with sad eyes, as if he has taken on the burden of the Palestinian people as he runs his East Jerusalem press agency, geared to publicize Israeli outrages against West Bank Arabs. As we talked in his office on Saladin Street, a loudspeaker from the minaret of a nearby mosque blared a muezzin's mournful call to prayer.

Ibrahim's family lived in a suburb of Jerusalem, and he was a college student in the Jordanian capital of Amman when the 1967 war broke out. Unable to contact his family, he heard rumors brought by fleeing West Bank residents that his parents had been killed. When his sister managed to get word that they were alive, Ibrahim resolved to make the risky journey to see them in Jerusalem. He and five other university students spent most of a day walking along the river, looking for a place to cross, finding only fortifications and watchful soldiers. Then a Jordanian smuggler with a small, tinny truck offered to take them over at night for five dinars apiece, about fifteen dollars. They agreed, he picked them up, found the right spot, and drove his battered vehicle through the shallow water and up the opposite bank. An Israeli army patrol spotted them when they were just twenty yards from the main road.

"They searched us and took us into an Israeli vehicle," Ibrahim said. "It was my first contact with Jews, ever."

The Arab students and the Jewish soldiers were about the same age. "We were five young people from the university, and of course we saw five young Israelis looking at us, while we were looking at them. And then no one knew what would happen, where they were taking us—to kill us? As difficult as it is to remember those feelings, I think it was as if you were traveling to the unknown. You don't know what they are going to do."

They were taken to a military camp of some sort, and there Ibrahim had to begin revising his images of the efficient, disciplined Israeli soldier. He had never imagined that such a powerful army would look so slovenly and display such individualism. In his suit and tie, Ibrahim was a bit overdressed, even for such a momentous occasion as his infiltration across the border, and he looked a lot more presentable than the troops who were guarding him. "It was the first time in my life I had seen soldiers wearing shorts, no shirts," he said. "All the time the soldiers were drinking juice—I thought it was alcohol. The first day, there were very young soldiers and an officer playing Ping-Pong, and everyone was cursing the other, you know. My God, in Jordan such a thing would not happen, a soldier cursing the officer.

"Before this, we knew nothing," Ibrahim continued, meaning nothing about the Israelis except the standard arguments: " 'The Israelis came to our country, blah, blah, blah, blah, blah. We are going to get back what we lost. We will send them to the sea.' You know, all the Arab rubbish, propaganda they sold to us. In the beginning, you worry how these people who are not disciplined—not the discipline we know—could defeat us. Then you start to think that discipline, saluting, polishing your shoes, is not important. Now we always make fun of the Arab armies, which are good for exhibitions, for parades," he continued. "You need this kind of discipline for parades. You look at the Jordanian army, the Syrian army, and see what good parades they do. They celebrate the army day, and the victory of the army, and you start wondering, What victory? We haven't seen any victory." The raspy wail of the muezzin's call to prayer faded, and the busy noises of the street filled the office. We sipped hot, strong coffee from tiny cups.

The students were taken to Nablus prison, Ibrahim said, and their heads were full of dire expectations. "We were wondering if they wanted to come and kill us," he recalled. "Was there any spot [in the cell] for cover? There was not. There were windows in every part. We thought that they might kill us. The next day this high-ranking officer came over and took three people from Nablus—the driver and his colleagues. And I knew they were released because they were from the Masri family [an influential, wealthy West Bank clan]. So then I knew that the bribe does exist!" Ibrahim's regard for the Israelis seemed heightened by this discovery of their potential for corruption. After nine days in jail, during which some of the prisoners were badly beaten, he said, he was fined thirty dinars and released once his father came to pay.

In the grinding viciousness of the Middle East, the stereotypes of violence and cruelty are often fashioned by real events, and the malleable attitudes of children are shaped with a flowing ease. "Three weeks ago they came at twelve o'clock [midnight]," Ibrahim said, "knocking at my door, three Shin Beth people, just to hand me a piece of paper saying I am summoned the next day at eight o'clock to the Russian Compound [police headquarters]. I asked them, 'Why do you come to inform me of this at this time?' They said, 'When do you want us to come?' They terrified my children, my wife, myself. I was interrogated, and all the time I knew they might put me in jail. My two-and-a-half-year-old boy said, 'I am afraid of the police.' This is just the age when his tongue starts to speak all kinds of things and he starts to absorb."

For many Arabs, the most radical, hostile, violent Jews become typical of all Jews. "Arabs tend to identify Jews and the army as one and the same," said Peter Schaktman, an American Jew working with Interns for Peace in the Israeli-Arab village of Kfar Qara. And religious Jews are regarded as especially hostile to Arabs. When Schaktman and other interns explained their program and mentioned that it was run by a rabbi, Bruce Cohen, Arabs often said, "A rabbi like Meir Kahane?" The generalizations are present even in casual remarks, which have their impact on children. When jet fighters flew over, possibly on their way to Lebanon, Arab grandmothers in Israel would often say to the little boys and girls, "The Jews are going to kill our brothers." The evening that the Israeli state commission reported on its investigation of the 1982 massacre of Palestinians in the Beirut refugee camps, Schaktman was visiting the home of an Arab villager who had the television news turned on. The father had told his children, "The Jews did it." So the three-year-old daughter of the house, knowing that Schaktman was a Jew, asked him, "Did you kill them too?"

Against the brilliant, gleaming Mediterranean Sea, the corrosive grit and disintegration of war had made Tyre a broken city. Every street was strewn with crude chunks of concrete, splinters of glass, burned skeletons of windowless automobiles. No structure was untouched. Roofs had been blown off by bombs. Whole facades had been stripped away by the concussions of air strikes, revealing room after room of torn curtains and shattered furniture that made the apartment houses look like the dollhouses of careless children. Buildings whose walls remained standing had been pockmarked by shrapnel and gouged by rockets. Windows and doors were surrounded with chips and holes from gunfire. There was rubble everywhere, crumbling into a cruel dust insinuated by the summer humidity into every corner of the spirit. It was the end of June 1982.

Tyre lay sweltering, thirteen miles up the Lebanese coast from Israel: the defeated command post of the PLO, which had ruled over the city's Lebanese inhabitants for years before the Israeli army had roared through on the way to Beirut. The battle had died angrily, leaving shocked elation, suspicion among the Lebanese who were finally rid of the hard hand of Palestinian occupation but now had the Israelis to confront.

"This is the first time I have spoken with an Israeli," said the young woman. Defiantly, she faced an army colonel on the steps of a Muslim school that had been founded by her grandfather. The Israelis had bombed and damaged the school and had then turned it into a temporary headquarters for Israeli troops. Now the army unit was pulling out, leaving the building empty again, turning it back to the principal, the woman's father, who stood on the steps making a little speech thanking the Israelis for driving away the PLO.

She began her conversation with the Israeli colonel by gathering the courage to interrupt her father and contradict his message of gratitude. The colonel found her intriguing. She wore a white summer dress printed with tiny blue flowers, so pristine that she seemed like an apparition of calm against the dusty rubble. Her hair was short and jet black, her gaze steadily curious and intelligent. She was twenty-one years old, and her name was Zainab Sharaf al-Din, from a prominent Tyre family.

"I can't bear to see anyone occupy my country," she declared in clean, clear English. "From my childhood, I know that Israel is my enemy. And now I keep this opinion. You came, you destroyed our land, you killed so many people, and this is not good for us." A look of nervousness flickered across her face. She said she knew she had just placed herself in danger of arrest. "This is the first time I have spoken with an Israeli," she said.

"And you can speak freely," said the colonel. "There is nothing to fear." He was not what she imagined an Israeli army colonel to be. He did not believe in this war.

His name was Mordechai Bar-On, a veteran and the former chief education officer of the army. He had retired after twenty-two years in the service to become an historian and had now been mobilized to guide journalists into the battle zone; he was my escort officer that day. In civilian life, he helped organize anti-war demonstrations for the Peace Now movement. His daughter was married to an Arab who ran a coffeehouse in Jerusalem. But to Zainab Sharaf al-Din, he was the image of an Israeli army colonel in his baggy, olive-drab fatigues, a representative of all that she had been taught to detest. And yet something in her brightness, her alert openness, enticed the colonel into an insistence that we sit with her in conversation, even though it was late afternoon and dangerous not to be back in Israel and off the Lebanese roads by dusk.

We found chairs in a dim, grimy office of the school, stripped of all other furnishings. Her father admonished her, "Speak from your head, not from your heart." The colonel let her begin, for he was interested in knowing how she felt. And I sat silently, scribbling notes, suspended in wonder at the delicate encounter amid the rubble of war.

The young woman had had no friends in the PLO, she said, but her best friend in school had been a Palestinian girl with strong nationalist feelings, which she too could support. She excused the violence of the Palestinian guerrillas against the townspeople of Tyre. "The bad behavior grew up because of the way they were treated," she explained. "They were hardened from the way they were treated. They were refugees, they had no permanent jobs, they were living in poverty. I love them. I don't hate them at all. I would like to see them living in their land and have their own government and coexisting with the Israeli people. I don't say they should be eliminated from this world."

She did not want to see Lebanon sign a peace treaty with Israel. "Of course I would like all the Israeli army to leave Lebanon," she said. "I think the Israeli government doesn't like Arabs to be good, to be developed, to progress, so they will not do anything for our benefit." A treaty would just give Israel license to keep part of Lebanon, she believed. "Israel will enforce a certain situation which is far from our nationalism." She smiled, as if she were both apologetic and pleased to be saying these things to an Israeli colonel. "I believe Israel is my enemy," she continued boldly. "The peace with Israel is not peace. It is war. Because Israel wants to dominate the largest area, as large as they can, and for their own benefit, not for the benefit of another nation."

The colonel watched and listened, captivated. Then he spoke quietly, slowly. "You are a very beautiful human being," he began, "and it gives me a lot of pain to hear what you say. On Palestinian self-determination, you're right." He, too, favored a Palestinian state. He, too, opposed his government's policies. "But on the subject of Lebanon, you're very wrong. I love the way you speak, and it gives me pain that your education has not allowed you to make a very important leap. If you have an enemy, you must try to find a way to make peace, not to keep that enemy an enemy."

She looked surprised. "But you want to solve it?" she said. "You don't want to eliminate them from this world?"

"No, no," the colonel answered. "Without this uniform, I go to demonstrations for the rights of the Palestinians."

"I'm happy to meet you," she said, astonished.

"I'm not alone," the colonel continued. "We are a democracy. And we are fighting within a democracy. I think you have to think a little bit in terms of defusing the prejudices you have. Lebanon, you said, will not benefit from the peace. I think you're very wrong about that, just because Lebanon will be reunited, will not have to struggle with Israel. I have to know more people of your kind, and you have to know more people of my kind."

Zainab Sharaf al-Din was smiling in a glow of revelation, as if some curtain had been lifted.

"In the meantime," said the colonel, "thank you very much. You have touched my heart."

She replied, "And you too."

They exchanged addresses. "If you ever get to Jerusalem . . ." he said, and she laughed and stood on the steps of the school and waved and smiled as we drove away.

Two years later, Mordechai Bar-On was elected to the Knesset on the leftist Citizens' Rights slate, Israeli troops were still in Lebanon, no peace treaty had been signed, and no peace had come to Zainab Sharaf al-Din's battered country. Only an image had been revised, and that perhaps only for an hour of a summer afternoon.

Many Arabs are so deeply convinced of the inevitability of Israeli violence that they cannot imagine anything else. Atallah Mansour, an Israeli-Arab journalist who covers the Galilee for a Hebrew-language paper, expressed this in a remarkable statement. "Jews are used to having enemies," he said. "If someone tries to be their friend, they get suspicious." Less sophisticated Arabs often conjure up the most conspiratorial, sinister interpretations to explain unwelcome events.

At 7:20 A.M. on August 21, 1969, a fire was set in al-Aqsa mosque on Jerusalem's Temple Mount. Burning for three hours, it damaged the dome and destroyed the carved wooden pulpit that had been placed in the mosque on October 9, 1187, on the occasion of Saladin's prayers after the capture of Jerusalem from the Crusaders. Meron Benvenisti, deputy mayor of Jerusalem, felt the tragedy deeply. "I, a non-Muslim infidel and a hated occupier, stood there with tears in my eyes, overwhelmed with grief," he wrote. [50]

Michael Dennis Rohan, a young, blond Australian Christian who belonged to the fundamentalist Church of God, was arrested the next night, and he confessed to the arson. But although Muslim guards had seen him running from the scene just after the fire began, Arabs were—and are, to this day—widely convinced that it was a plot by the Jews to destroy one of the holiest Muslim shrines in Jerusalem. As Arabs rushed to the mosque, a religious leader shouted to the crowd that Jews were responsible. The Jewish police let the arsonist into the compound, Arabs argued; he was in Israel for months before the fire, being trained; the Jews paid him $50,000; the police caught him quickly because they knew about him all the time; the fire department came late and worked slowly; and so forth.

Even among non-observant Muslims, the destruction of the pulpit and other artifacts evoked a surge of nationalist and religious feeling that translated into demonstrations and vitriolic anti-Israel declarations. "One eyewitness reported that a piece of the [pulpit] on which was carved 'Allah is Great' fell to the ground in the fire," writes Gerald Caplan. "When this fragment was carried outside the mosque into the compound and was seen by the crowd, they began to chant the phrase and surged toward the outlet to the Western Wall. They turned back only when the Israeli guards shot in the air." Caplan, a psychiatrist who studied Arab-Jewish relationships in Jerusalem, concluded that in this and other situations, Arabs' public expressions were not necessarily relevant to private belief. The Arabs "manifest a coexistence of two selves," he writes, "the private self that is shrewd, pragmatic, and fairly objective, and the public self that is self-deluding, vague, idealistic, and emotionally expressive. When, as often happens, these two selves are in conflict, the individual is not upset, for his acts are primarily motivated by his private self, whereas his words, especially if other Arabs are within earshot, express the attitudes of his public self."[51]

That the arson was an official Zionist plot has been so enshrined in Arab belief that it crops up as an undisputed fact in both casual conversation and political writing. The Middle East News Agency in Cairo declared, a few months before Sadat's 1977 visit to Jerusalem, "It has been eight years since the Zionist occupying forces set fire to al-Aqsa Mosque in the framework of a well-educated scheme to . . . annihilate the Islamic heritage and place all holy places under Zionist control. This act of provocation, which encroached upon the sentiments of the Islamic world and constituted a blow to international law, was designed to alter the status of Jerusalem."

A similar assumption about the sinister conspiracies of the Jews operated in March and April 1983, when hundreds of West Bank schoolgirls were overcome by dizziness, headaches, fainting spells, and stomach pains. Mayor Ahmed Shawki of Jenin, where the sickness began in the Araba School, accused Jewish settlers of spreading some sort of poison, "a wild gas." He spun out his theory in some detail. "I think the government knows that it's the settlers. It was done at night, and no one can go out except them. They have the weapons and can go freely. After it happened the first time the government should have put some soldiers to protect the other schools, and it didn't." Demonstrations broke out, stones were thrown at Israelis, and protesters were shot. As the mysterious sicknesses continued into April, affecting girls at schools sixty miles apart, Palestinian leaders stepped up their accusations that the Jews were poisoning the Arabs. The deposed mayor of Anabta, Wahid Hamdallah, said the Israeli government and army were spreading the poison. Israeli officials were infected by hysteria of their own, speculating that radical Palestinian factions had spread some substance to implicate the Israelis and provoke Arab students into protests. Brigadier General Shlomo Ilya, who headed the military government on the West Bank, declared, "We found a pamphlet in one Jenin school saying that if the students didn't go out to strike on Land Day, the fate of the Araba School would be their fate too. So we have one clue, although only one, that shows a connection between forces that want to cause unrest and this incident."

The Israeli Health Ministry could find nothing abnormal in the blood and urine of those affected. Officials reasoned that the initial outbreak might have been caused by some external substance but that subsequent symptoms seemed to have had no organic basis. Similar mass psychosomatic ailments had been observed years earlier among schoolgirls in England, the Israelis noted. But the panic and outrage grew so acute that the authorities invited a team from the Centers for Disease Control in Atlanta to perform an investigation. The Americans came and conducted their examination.

The diagnosis: hysteria.

SEVEN

The Primitive, Exotic
Arab

They only understand force and strength.
They work on their emotions.
They're not rational.
—Batia Medad, a Jewish settler

For many Israeli Jews, the Arab dwells at the heart of darkness, deep in the recesses of fear and fantasy. He appears almost as another species, marching to the beat of some primordial drum whose resonance stirs an ancient dread and fascination. He is backward, uncivilized, a man of animal vengeance and crude desires, of violent creed and wily action. He is also the noble savage, the tribal chieftain, the prince of the desert dispensing a cruel justice enviable in its biblical simplicity. Somewhere in the core of Israeli anxiety, he seems more authentic, more intrinsic to the brutal, circuitous ways of the Middle East, where the Jew yearns to belong.

The image of the Arab as primitive evokes both contempt and romance among Israeli Jews. Many are disgusted, others patronizing, a few infatuated. And some indulge themselves in all of those contrasting emotions simultaneously, always yielding to the invincible stereotype. Rarely— even among Jews with great affection for Arab culture—does the Arab emerge as an ordinary human being living in a modern society. Usually he is enveloped in a glow of exotic tradition so bright that it obscures the shadings of modernization that now color much of Arab life.

Arabs are repeatedly confronted with this primitive image of themselves, and often in surprising circumstances. Rifat Turk, an Israeli Arab who has become a celebrated soccer star on the Hapoel Tel Aviv team, had it thrown up at him by a woman who should have known better, an Israeli Jew living in Tel Aviv and working as a reporter for the Hebrew-language newspaper *Yediot Ahronot*. Turk is fluent in Hebrew and has a following of Jewish fans who have made him a major part of Israel's soccer craze. He is an urban boy by background, from Jaffa, once a teeming Arab city in its own right and now the Arab quarter of greater Tel Aviv; he lives in a spacious old house in Jaffa with his wife and little daughter, whom they have given the non-Arab name Natalie. In sum, he has become as much a part of Israeli society as an Arab can be without trying to pass as a Jew. Yet the reporter evidently harbored a certain suspicion, or conviction, that an Arab could never quite move into her advanced, Western world, for when she met him for an interview at one of Tel Aviv's chrome-and-glass beachfront hotels, she looked at his jeans and colored T-shirt and asked, "When you come to meet Jews, do you dress like this, and when you're with Arabs do you wear a keffiyah?" He was taken aback. "I dress like this all the time," he said, and it was then her turn to be astonished. "She asked me, 'Does your wife wear a veil?' I said, 'You're taking me back fifty years.' "

It seemed remarkable, and a measurement of the isolation of many Jews, that an Israeli newspaperwoman would be ignorant of the fact that veils are worn by exceptionally few Israeli-Arab women, that practically the only veiled women in Israel are the semi-nomadic Bedouins who live mostly in the desert. A drive through Jaffa, any Arab village in the Galilee, or any part of the West Bank would have told her as much. Yet the Jews' ignorance of their Arab neighbors is profound. An Arab woman who teaches Arabic to Jewish children in the town of Afula gets constant questions from her pupils: "Is it true that Arab girls' fathers arrange marriages?" And the teacher answers, "Once, the fathers forced their daughters to marry this man or that man, but now it's changed." The traditions that do remain in Arab culture—the circumscribed role of women, the power of the extended clan, the elaborate ritual of hospitality—lay the groundwork for daily exaggeration and stereotyping by Israel's newspapers, which unconsciously reinforce the primitive image, even through their choice of vocabulary.

"In the papers we use different terms for Arabs and Jews," said Danny Rubinstein, who has spent more than a decade covering the West Bank for the daily *Davar*. "We say there was a meeting in Jerusalem of Israeli leaders and Arab notables. *Nikhbadim*, notables." This is practically a universal style in the Israeli press, and most Jews would find nothing offensive in it, believing that it accurately conveys the tribal aspect of Arab society. But Danny and some others have become sensitive to such subtle slurs. "So I wrote a story," he said laughingly: " 'Some Arab leaders from the West Bank met yesterday with some Israeli notables.' And, well, the editor just changed it. He thought that I had made a slip. He was laughing afterwards. You say Israeli 'intellectuals' and Arab— we don't use the term 'intellectuals'—we say *maskilim*: 'educated.' So I mixed those up too: 'some Palestinian intellectuals and educated Israelis.' " The expression "educated Arabs" is slightly pejorative, implying that Arabs are uneducated and that educated Arabs are something extraordinary. "Arabs are always villagers," Danny said. "But Israeli kibbutzim or moshavim [farming communities] members, we never call them villagers. They are members of a moshav or a kibbutz. But with Arabs, it is an image of something very tribal: *kafriim*, villagers."

As usual, some of the stereotypes contain seeds of truth. The Arab village is, indeed, different in social and economic structure from the Jewish kibbutz, although both are bound by a certain cohesion and insularity. And while the village's municipal officials are elected, some Arabs attain prominence by virtue of their seniority in large, influential families; the terms most often used by the Israeli press—"notables" and "elders"—summon up images of old men in white keffiyahs and robes, puffing on water pipes, sipping coffee, and murmuring Arabic pleasantries. These are not wholly inaccurate pictures, for such scenes are certainly part of Arab life. But they exclude the skillful, professional Arab in the business suit; they romanticize those portrayed while denigrating their talents; and somehow they enable the Jew to take Arab leadership less seriously, regarding it as quaint, colorful, tribal, and somewhat illegitimate—a product of inheritance rather than merit.

I was once struck by the dramatic conflict between image and reality when I attended a reception given for East Jerusalem Arabs by the United States consulate. It was held by the pool at the American Colony Hotel, a former pasha's mansion of old stone and graceful arches and courtyards. The crowd was a prosperous, well-groomed cross-section of Jerusalem Arab leadership, including dark-suited businessmen, trade-union officials, lawyers, physicians, professors, and writers, virtually all of them fluent in English, and many with a sophistication about international politics that gave the gathering a worldly ambience. Since many Jerusalem Arabs refuse to attend such affairs with Israeli Jews, the consulate usually entertains Jews separately—even to the point of having separate Fourth of July receptions—which means that few Jews ever get to see such an Arab crowd. I wandered around the pool, nibbling hors-d'oeuvres, drinking gin and tonic, and imagining how dumbfounded most Israelis would be if they were suddenly led into that party, into an Arab culture they never realized existed, one where they would have to search in vain for their primitives. The only Israeli Jew I encountered at the reception told me how uncomfortable he felt being practically alone among Arabs. I suspected that his discomfort may also have come from the kind of Arabs who surrounded him, Arabs who did not fit neatly into the derogatory categories fashioned by long years of strife.

Some of the early writers in Hebrew who lived among Arabs, either in Jerusalem and Hebron or in Damascus and Baghdad, portrayed Arab culture with a fairy-tale romanticism, a sort of *National Geographic* awe and wonder that has been passed down to some of today's Israeli Jews. The exotic customs and dress, the vivid scenes of Arab bazaars and weddings, the utter strangeness of the society were conveyed with both respect and, just as often, aversion. Yehuda Burla—who was born in Jerusalem in 1886, served in the Turkish army during World War I, and then lived for several years in Damascus—drew sharp sketches of Arab characters as real human beings, but he tended to denigrate Arab culture as revengeful, scheming, and intolerant. He also played out his comparison of Arab and Jewish (Western) culture through Arab women, who displayed a lust for the Jewish world of permissive modernism, a striving to break free of their crippling culture and move into Western society.

Yitzhak Shami (1888–1949) wrote in constant streams of primitive stereotypes. In *The Vengeance of the Fathers*, a short novel about tribal conflict, Shami makes Islam into something akin to superstitious paganism as his Arab characters act out vicious feuds in the medium of a religious pageant and procession. He writes of the Arabs:

> Actually, they're just big happy children, all excited about making this pilgrimage together and about meeting their brethren from near and far, from Jerusalem and Hebron, from the Negev and the North and the East. Like children they kick and scratch at each other over nothing, simply in fun and mischief. Mostly it all depends on the leaders of the processions, the flag-masters, who are also the sheikhs of the young men. If these show a strong hand, and if their eyes take in everything and hold all their wild and hotheaded young men in tow, if their ears are sharp and can distinguish from afar between fervent song and screams of pain calling for help from kinsmen or neighbors, if they're always ready to spur their horses into a gallop quickly enough to separate the fighters in time—then you may be sure that with the help of God and his prophets the caravan will continue on its way according to plan. The swords will return to their sheaths, the raised stones will be thrown away, the angry eyes will smile again in reconciliation, and the stragglers will catch up with the caravan.

The writing is fast and exciting, the descriptions vivid with detail. But the Arabs are cardboard characters, props on Shami's stage of exotic primitivism, hardly human in their sounds and motions: "Agitated now, all burst into violent uproar. Like a herd of bulls which, having smelled the blood of one of their number, pack together in a circle around the place, bellowing, raising their noses and their horns and then bursting into stampede, so they all packed around the brothers of Abu Faris with dreadful cries, brandishing their staves and clubs and swords, and then moved forward like an advancing storm." And their social system's severe treatment of women is taken as the basis of a grim portrait—not a lie but an embellishment:

> The only ones who were silent and angry were the young women. On this day they had allowed themselves some laxity with the

precepts about covering the face and not raising the voice. The celebration had finished so quickly: the spectacle was over, and they again felt their enslavement. Ahead of them stretched a long line of gray, monotonous working days, with no spark of joy or consolation to illumine them. Again they would have to close themselves up in their homes and continue bearing the yoke; again they would have to suffer in silence at the hands of their rivals and mothers-in-law, to submit to having their every movement watched and used as a pretext for hints and slanderous remarks against them to their husbands, who severely punished any wrong move or error, and beat them for the slightest motion of their eyelids, or for any superfluous dallying by a window or a door.

Occasionally a piece of writing combines Jewish ethnocentrism with a picture of Arabs as profoundly alien, primitive, and hostile. In "Hebron," a story by Y. D. Berkowitz, a group of Jews visit the ancient city of Abraham's tomb and find "fortified yards with peeking houses, built like pyramids, with high stone walls." The narrator continues, "The feeling of being strangers also came to us because as we entered the city of our forefathers we were not met by any Jewish faces. From out of the yards and stone houses tall, bearded Arabs stared at us, and their looks were withdrawn and reserved from all those who weren't 'theirs,' like that of a primeval tribe, living alone in its fortified nest high among the rocks, peeking out at the world with an ill-tempered and suspicious eye." At the end of the day, the Jews return to Tel Aviv with relief.

The notion that Arabs cannot distinguish between fact and fantasy is also a recurrent theme of the primitive stereotype; it is found in Hebrew writing from the turn of the century up through comments made today by prejudiced Jews. Shami, writing about Arab literature in 1911, declared, "Within the Arab soul there are two centers of authority. In his daily life he is practical and clever, weighing everything on the scales of cold logic and analyzing it minutely; and he is not easily fooled. However, that same Arab is a different person in his spiritual life: no people in the world has developed the power of imagination and fantasy as has the Arab people. For them there is no distinction between fiction and an event that actually happened. Overstatement and exaggeration are second nature to them. Their figures of speech and descriptions are enlarged seven-fold. A story told in simple language, without extraordinary disputation, does not capture their fancy or arouse their interest."[52] A similar assertion appears in Devorah Omer's *The Gideonites*, a children's novel about Jews spying for the British against the Turks in World War I Palestine. "Pay special attention to information from bedouin camps," the author has one Jew advise another. "They are blessed with great imagination, every roving unit seems to them like a division and every shot is an attack."

The Bedouins came in for the same ridicule from an attorney for the Green Patrol, a squad of tough young Israelis who were organized by the Agriculture Ministry to chase the semi-nomads off desert grazing land that Israel wanted for military bases, kibbutzim, and nature reserves. Some Bedouins complained that the patrols were using intimidation and violence, to which the lawyer, Herzl Kadesh, replied that such charges could never be confirmed "because the polygraph doesn't work with Bedouins." He explained the reason to me with a patient smile, as an insider educating a visitor on the mysterious ways of the exotic Middle East. "You see," he said, "the imagination is very broad, and sometimes they mix imagination with facts." The Bedouin tribesmen are so convinced of the truth of their fantasies, Kadesh asserted, that they do not display the physiological signs of mendacity—the elevated blood pressure, the higher pulse and breathing rate—to which a lie detector responds. So, he said happily, there is no way to verify their stories.

Even a Green Patrol inspector, Yaacov Shmul, who was hardly sympathetic to the Bedouins, gasped at the lawyer's remark. "That's racist," Shmul snapped.

A companion view, found in textbooks, newspapers, Israeli government propaganda, children's literature, and contemporary conversation, sees the backward Arabs as blessed by the Jewish advances they have had the good fortune to touch. The Jews have brought them material progress, educational improvement, social reform. The Arabs earn more money than before, receive better medical care, and send a higher percentage of their children to school. Arabs experience democracy, and Arab women—denied the vote in most Arab countries—have been enfranchised by the Jews. The West Bank, even under military occupation, has prospered materially as it never did under Jordan. The influx of Jews to Palestine in the nineteenth century first attracted Arab migration into the area west of the Jordan River, since the Arabs believed, as did the early Zionists, that the Jews were bringing "civilization" to a region of heathens. Thus, the Arabs must be grateful to the Jews.

Again, a great tangle of nonsense grows from a seed of truth. Although the material and social progress of the Arabs can be attributed partly to the contact between Arab and Israeli Jewish society, much of it is also the result of an industrious Arab labor force, a Palestinian obsession with education as a way out of inferior status, and a general rise in living standards in that part of the Middle East, beyond Israeli borders as well. But in the most rigid Jewish bias, the Arabs are given neither credit for the advances nor sympathy for the gap they still endure.

A 1982 high-school civics textbook used in Hebrew schools contains a chapter of straight propaganda on this point, without any effort to provide a fair-minded description of the status of Israeli Arabs. "With the intention to aid the Arab economy to take its rightful place in the national economy, the rate of development of Arab agriculture was accelerated. . . . Arab agriculture enjoys all the same services as Jewish agriculture. . . . The Israeli legal framework, and the equality which dominates it, brought a revolution in the status of the Arab woman. The Israeli law forbids minor marriages (under age sixteen) and also forbids polygamy and divorce against the woman's will; it opens the possibility for equal education for the Arab girl, who is generally deprived in this area in Arab countries. . . . Many hundreds of Arab activists now take part in the system of local rule. . . . Also the Arab lists for the Knesset, with all their dependency on various Jewish parties, bring familiarization to the democratic lifestyle." The chapter also contains a section on "the decline in the influence of the village elders," which is written on the assumption that traditional village life is a negative being cured by contact with Israeli modernism.

The notion that Arabs benefit from contact with Israeli "civilization" is fairly widespread among even politically liberal Jews. Teddy Kollek, the mayor of Jerusalem whose accommodating policies give the city administration a tolerant tone, made a quick visit during his 1983 reelection campaign to a wholesale outlet in an East Jerusalem industrial park, run by the big Hamashbir Hamerkazi department store. As he was strolling through the building shaking hands, one of his aides whispered to me that only Arabs were allowed to do retail shopping there as part of a Jewish effort to educate them in the advanced techniques of consumerism. This sounded strange, and his vision of Arabs as backward beneficiaries of Israeli modernity seemed a bit too pat, so I checked his story with the manager of the outlet. Not true, the manager said. Anybody could shop there.

Studies show that Arabs who have accepted Westernization tend also to be the most susceptible to political radicalism, something that leads some Israeli officials who work on the West Bank to value traditional, rural Arabs as less militant than many of their urbanized counterparts. The categories do not always hold up, however, either in reality or in the popular Jewish view. The degree to which Arabs are interested in emulating Jews is often cited as an optimistic mark of progress toward peaceful coexistence: As the Arabs climb up out of their primitive state, thanks to the Jews, they grow less hostile toward the Jews—or at least they ought to. An illustration was provided by Adi Halpern, an official of the right-wing Herut Party in Tel Aviv who was accused in an Israeli newspaper (falsely, he insisted) of endorsing apartheid, South African style. He explained to me at length how hopeful he was that Arabs and Jews could live together. As evidence, he asserted that Arabs were copying Jewish architecture in building new villas. (Although values run the other way: Israeli Jews tend to admire the old Arab architecture.) Furthermore, he said, his argument had a clincher: Arabs are putting two toilets in their new houses—just like the Jews.

These biases are also prevalent in fiction. In one children's story, the differences in material levels between Jews and Arabs are cause not for the activation of social conscience but for a smug, patronizing attitude toward a subservient Arab who sings the praises of the Jews. An Arab teacher in Eliezer Smoli's *The Sons of the First Rain* takes his class on a visit to a Jewish school, where he is so struck by what the Jews have built that he makes a speech:

> By God, we have very much to learn from you, the Jews. This place was abandoned and desolate—and then you came along with all your energy and transformed it into a veritable Garden of Eden: green, filled with flowers and shady trees. Space like this, and even bigger, is left empty in our village, serving only as a tethering ground for the donkeys and the camels, where not so much as an onion is grown. See how much water there is here, and how pure it tastes! Every day I read diatribes in the newspapers against the Jews, and there are a lot of agitators who stir up trouble between us and you! But as I walk through your streets and as I see the

tremendous labor you have invested in these desolate abandoned sand-dunes, which you've turned into such flourishing land, I have to say to myself that it was God who sent you here to serve as an example to us, so that we could look at what you do and do likewise ourselves. Let us only live in peace together, as good neighbors. You came to visit us, and now we've come to see you and your school. May our hearts meet together, and may hatred cease. What will all this strife and trouble achieve? For hundreds of years this country was under Turkish rule and now it has woken up to a time of blessing. It's to you that we owe the prosperity, to your capital, your energy, to all the good things you've given us.[53]

A variation on the theme of Jewish superiority appears in Zvi Zaviri's 1958 story "Sheikh Abdullah" when Jewish children capture the Arab sheikh who has been responsible for attacks on their settlement. "We want peace," one Jew tells the Arab, "not just in order to be able to receive something, but also to be able to give something, and even more than this: We're ready to teach you things, to make you a partner in what we're doing." The humane and patronizing connotations are caught also in Yosef Haim Brenner's "From a Notebook," in which he writes of a walk through citrus groves at night and converses with a downtrodden Arab peasant: "Then it was that I pronounced myself guilty—very guilty indeed—for never having learned to speak Arabic. If only there had been words to say it. . . . Orphaned laborer! Young brother! It matters not whether the theories of the learned are correct or not, whether you are my blood kinsman or not. For on my shoulders is placed the responsibility for your welfare. It is for me to show you the light, to nourish you with the milk of human kindness."

Physical descriptions often mix splendor with ferocity. In *The Wild One*, published in 1966, Pessah Bar-Adon gives speech to a horse describing the commander of an Arab band saddling up: "In the hours that remained before nightfall, he devoted himself to his dress, his pistol, and his rifle. He combed his moustache and curled it upward. His servant washed and curry-combed me and decked me out in finery: colored reins decorated with glass beads, an embroidered woolen saddle—in short as befits the mare of a commander. Toward evening they led me out and he mounted me, dressed in the finest military khaki, with medals on his breast, the decorated pistol belt around his hips, his rifle in his hand and a bandolier of bullets across his chest. He wrapped his abbayah round him, covered half his face with the edges of his keffiyah and set off for the rendezvous accompanied by his aides, they, too, mounted on their own steeds."[54]

Adir Cohen of Haifa University found that children's literature tended to describe the Arab as having a "narrow forehead, a scar and a moustache." In adult literature, too, Arabs often make fleeting appearances in vignettes of primitive mystery, as in Brenner's novel *Breakdown and Bereavement*: "The black-skinned wife of the Arab watchman focused on him with the whites of her eyes, then opened the small gate in the fence for him with her huge key."

Very little is taught in Israeli classrooms about modern Arab civilization. *The Arabs and Islam*, the major textbook on Arab and Islamic culture for Jewish seventh- and eighth-graders in Israeli religious schools, begins, "You have surely asked yourself more than once, Who are the Arabs who live with us in Israel? What is their origin? What is their religion? In the coming lessons we'll try to answer these questions." But the answers are anachronistic, at best, not so much for what they contain but for their omission of the urban, twentieth-century Arab society that has made the Arab world into a collage of the modern and the traditional. The book portrays mainly Bedouin nomads and desert settlements. All the photographs and drawings in the text and its accompanying workbook show a primitive, tribal Arab culture of desert life, tents, camels, and bandits, having little to do with most Arabs who now live with the Jews in Israel. Published under the imprint of the Ministry of Education, the books create no respect for the culture; they convey only an image of a strange, backward, warlike society full of sheikhs, caliphs, and revenge, profoundly alien in its most basic mores. Even in sketching the old desert society, the text fails to convey the dignity and elaborate beauty of Arab customs, the intricate civilization that flourished against the vast wilderness. Although the book avoids cultivating explicit hatred, and provides one brief lesson on Arab achievements in mathematics, astronomy, and architecture, it also avoids describing any aspect of society with which Jewish children are able to identify. And thus it leaves an impression of Arabs as a breed apart.

The stereotypes are not universally held by Israeli Jews, of course, but they are prevalent enough to infiltrate many levels of discourse, from the mundane conversation to the carefully constructed political analysis, from the graffiti on lavatory walls to the highest-ranking general's testimony before a Knesset committee. Phrases, epithets, images flicker through the daily lives of Israeli Jews like stray bullets that whistle and whine and wound.

Yosef Goell, a *Jerusalem Post* editorial writer and usually an astute observer of Israeli politics, made a slur against Arabs as he wrote about the qualities of Israel's leadership: ". . . in a crunch, our leaders proved themselves to be better, and of a higher intellectual and moral caliber, than their opponents, by whom I mean not the outclassed and corrupt Arabs, but the much more dangerous Americans and British."

Army reservists, doing guard duty on the West Bank, spend idle hours vilifying Arabs, and among the multitude of conflicting stereotypes, one emerges straight out of the storybooks: "They are likely to sneak in at night and cut your throat," said one soldier, reporting the fears expressed by two men in his unit.

An Israeli radio reporter, discussing the imminent return to Egypt of the Sinai's ecologically delicate Red Sea coast, asked Avraham Yoffe, head of Israel's Nature Reserves Authority, about envionmental protection in Arab countries. "Is there something about Arab society which is inimical to nature conservation?" the reporter said on the air. In essence, Yoffe answered yes, there was some cultural inability to appreciate such issues.

On the Jewish settlement of Shiloh, Batia Medad, a young, soft-spoken mother of two children, talked with the direct simplicity customary among the religious and fervent settlers. But when she gave a long, pejorative dissertation on the Arabs, whose neighboring village she can see from her hilltop apartment, her placid features dissolved into a superior smile, and she spoke with a sneer. "They're not educated American academics," she said. She waited for laughter that didn't come. "Maybe you can learn something from them about herbal medicine." Her smile became knowing, contemptuous, and she suddenly lost her quiet beauty. "They only understand force and strength," she declared. "They work on their emotions. They're not rational." I asked whether she and other settlers had any relationships with Arabs. "Oh yes," she said. "An Arab man comes and sells fruit." Her husband is active in the right-wing Tehiya Party.

Emotionalism and irrationality are among the hallmarks of the primitive stereotype. I was surprised one day to hear the slur from one of the highest officials in the Israeli Foreign Ministry, who was giving a briefing to half a dozen foreign correspondents. Asked whether he thought Syria would withdraw from Lebanon, he said, again with that unpleasant, knowing smile, "Rationality is not necessarily a factor in this part of the world. Rationally I'd say yes, but they don't often act rationally in this part of the world." In the end, however, it was Syria, not Israel, that acted rationally, for as events subseqently proved, Syria's decision not to withdraw was an act of calculated rationality that scored an important victory over an Israel that had been gripped by rampant emotion in its Lebanon adventure.

Similarly, the stereotype assumes that there exists a certain childishness and stupidity in the Arab personality. The Israeli writer David Shakhar once remarked to me, in what I hope he realized was hyperbole, that Jews did all the PLO's publicity work because the PLO people were too stupid to do it themselves.

Incidents that reinforce the stereotype are often greeted with a strange delight. In October 1983, during a celebration in Damascus of the tenth anniversary of the Yom Kippur War—known in Arab countries as the October War—President Hafez al-Assad presided over a bizarre military pageant and ceremony in which teenage Syrian girls fondled live snakes while martial music played in the background. As the music rose to a crescendo, the girls bit into the snakes, tore off the flesh with their teeth, and spit it out. Blood ran down their chins. Syrian leaders applauded. The girls then skewered the snakes with sticks, grilled them over a fire, and ate them. Syrian militiamen strangled puppies and drank their blood. The ceremony, broadcast on Syrian television, was recorded by Israeli television, which transmitted the snake scene on the nightly news but regarded the puppy episode as too gruesome. *The Jerusalem Post* then ran a story expressing annoyance that American television networks had not seen fit to show Americans either scene.

Many Israelis said they were disgusted but not surprised by the sick pageant in Damascus, and they wished the rest of the world had seen it as evidence of the style of base cruelty Israel faces from the Arab countries. To some it seemed further proof that Arabs were essentially subhuman, a notion that received wide distribution in a comment by General Eitan, who as Israeli chief of staff was severely condemned by the state commission that investigated the Beirut massacre. As Eitan was retiring in April 1983, he testified for the last time before the Knesset's foreign affairs and defense committee. He told the legislators that many more Jewish settlements had to be built on the West Bank, that if there were 100 settlements between Jerusalem and Nablus, Arabs would not be able to throw stones. "When we have settled the land, all the Arabs will be able to do about it will be to scurry around like drugged roaches in a bottle," declared Israel's highest military officer. The remark triggered a storm of outrage among many Israeli Jews, but it also prompted expressions of admiration for Eitan, who showed up in public-opinion polls a month later as the country's leading choice for chief of staff. In 1984 he was elected to the Knesset.

The epithets can get pretty raw. Daliah Shhori, writing in the Hebrew-language newspaper *Al-Hamishmar*, recorded the anger, the hatred, the denigration of Arabs that she found scrawled in the women's lavatory at the Hebrew University's social-sciences building on Mount Scopus:

First toilet, on the inside door, in red ink:

ARABS

DOGS

DONKEYS

HORSES

CATS

MICE

Framed, in green ink:

DEFEAT, EVICT, DEPORT THE ARABS

On the inside partition wall, in red:

KILL ARABS!

And in green:

OPENING A COURSE FOR THE IDENTIFICATION OF ARABS.
RULE NUMBER ONE—OPEN YOUR EYES LOOK STRAIGHT
AHEAD AND YOU WILL SEE.

Second toilet, on the inside door (in red):

ARABS GO FIND A STATE, HERE YOU WON'T STAY.

On the inside partition, in blue:

HUNDREDS OF BILLIONS ARE SPENT BY ISRAEL ON THE
ARABS. MONEY TO JEWS NOT TO ARABS.

In darker blue:

ARABS OUT!

Third toilet, on the inside door:

ARABS LOOK FOR A STATE, HERE YOU WON'T STAY.

In red:

ARAB DOGS!

In blue:

ARABS OUT!

. . . On the inside wall was written:

BLOW UP HASSAN BEQ [a mosque in Jaffa] AND BIR ZEIT!
[the West Bank university]

It is possible that the author was one single student. It is hard to
determine by the handwriting if it was the work of one woman or
more. It is also possible that I saw the writing a short while after
it was done and that it was removed the next day. . . . If I were
to come across similar writing directed against Jews at some university, say in Cairo or Paris or New York, I wouldn't delve too
deeply into the question of whether the author was a single student
or an entire group and whether the cleaning service of the university
was working properly.

The images often have direct impact on the behavior of Israeli Jews beyond
the mere expression of attitudes. After the Israeli invasion of Lebanon,
for example, as the Joint Distribution Committee began to use donations
from American Jews to deliver blankets, mattresses, heaters, and other
emergency supplies to Palestinian families who had lost their homes
during the fighting, a committee official, David Harman, encountered
fellow Israelis who thought the Arabs were tough and could get along
with less than Jews would tolerate. During a discussion of which thickness
of mattress to buy—five or ten centimeters—David remembered one
Israeli, an upper-class Egyptian Jew with a degree from the Sorbonne,
saying, "Oh, they're Arabs. Five centimeters is plenty." Similarly, Jewish
nurses treating Arab patients at Hadassah Hospital in Jerusalem have
made remarks about Arabs needing less anesthesia because they didn't
feel pain as acutely as Jews, or about Arabs being able to pull through
a tough illness because they were somehow genetically more resistant.
"What people sometimes say is that the Arabs are stronger than the
Jews—'You don't have to worry; he'll come out of it'—which I find very
offensive," said Dr. Mayera Glassman, an anesthesiologist at Hadassah
in Ein Kerem. As a South African Jew, she was sensitive to the racism

implied in such a statement. "I once had an argument with someone, and he said, 'Well, it isn't a racial remark. They really are stronger.' "

The image of Arabs as primitive and backward has also contributed to the reluctance of Jews to be treated in Arab hospitals, an aversion that reached a pitch of anxiety from March 1983 into that summer, when months of sanctions and hunger strikes by Israeli doctors threw Israel's system of medical care into chaos. Despite the closing of clinics and the dangerous neglect of hospital patients, very few Jews took their medical problems to Arab clinics and hospitals in neighboring East Jerusalem, the West Bank, or Gaza, which continued to run normally. Because of economic disparities between the Jewish and Arab populations, some of the facilities in Arab areas are ill equipped and poorly operated, to be sure, and they generally practice a lower level of medicine than the Jewish-run system. But there are private hospitals and clinics, many of them administered by Christian religious organizations, that are clean and well staffed and provide decent treatment. Most Jews in need during the strike were oblivious to the existence of these Arab institutions, and Israeli authorities made no apparent effort to coordinate with the Arabs and refer Jewish patients. On the contrary, the idea of transferring Jews to Arab hospitals was used as a threat by striking doctors. At one point, a scare was thrown into government officials by Dr. Naphtali Shani, a spokesman for doctors at Beersheba's Soroka Hospital, who described plans to send patients to a hospital in the Gaza Strip if the government failed to negotiate an accord. This seemed to many Israeli Jews like the rough equivalent of a plan to send virtuous people into hell. After the strike ended, Shani admitted that there had been no such plan but was glad his statement had frightened officials; a Knesset member from the right-wing Likud Bloc, Michael Kleiner, replied with a demand, never carried out, that Shani be brought to trial for his threat.

Elsewhere, not a single Jew seeking care took advantage of an arrangement between Israeli and Arab doctors to refer patients from the Jewish-run Meir Hospital in Kfar Saba to Arab-run hospitals in the West Bank cities of Nablus and Tul Karem. The Jews' reluctance to make the move rendered moot a decision by the West Bank military government to block the arrangement by invoking a rarely used ban on Israelis' spending the night in the West Bank, a prohibition ignored in the case of Jewish settlers and visitors to settlements.

A crude humor sometimes attends the granting of inferior status to the Arabs. Although political jokes between Arabs and Jews are rather scarce, and considerably less inspired than, say, political humor in the Soviet Union and Eastern Europe, occasionally a joke captures something of the contempt that governs the relationships.

One, told by Jews, concerns the chief rabbi who goes to heaven and is welcomed by God, who invites him to dinner. At the table, God introduces him to the other guests. "This is Jesus Christ," God says, "and this is Moses." The rabbi, suitably humbled, shakes hands and takes his seat. They begin with the soup course, but the rabbi notices that he has no spoon."

"God," says the rabbi, "I have no spoon."

God looks over his shoulder, snaps his fingers, and calls, "Muhammad!"

Another joke, also told by Jews, indulges the common misperception that Arabs and Christians are two separate categories of people, ignoring the fact that many Arabs are Christian. And it contains both a primitive stereotype of the Arab and an anti-Semitic portrait of the Jew: An Arab, a Christian, and a Jew are sitting on a train. A fly buzzes in through a window. The Arab grabs it and pops it into his mouth. A second fly comes in. The Christian smashes it against the wall, and the Arab peels it off the wall and pops it into his mouth. A third fly buzzes in. The Jew grabs it, holds it up, and says to the Arab, "You want to buy?"

This ugly humor represents bigotry distilled. Many Jews would find it reprehensible. Yet it does tap a real attitude toward Arabs, one whose more precise measurements were taken in a 1980 survey of 1,223 Jews chosen to provide a representative sample of the Israeli-Jewish population. Asked to rank Arabs, Americans, and Israeli Jews on a scale of one to five from the most progressive and developed (one) to the most primitive (five), 41.7 percent put Arabs at numbers four and five, the most primitive end of the spectrum; only 5.6 percent put Israeli Jews there, and 2.8 percent judged Americans similarly backward. When the middle value, number three on the scale, was added to the totals, 75.5 percent put Arabs in the middle-to-low categories. Seen the other way, 72.1 percent found Americans advanced enough to be placed at position number one, the most progressive on the scale; 50.7 percent placed Israeli Jews there, and only 6.5 percent gave Arabs the most progressive, developed rating.[55] Interestingly, while the primitive label proved to be widely accepted as appropriate for Arabs, the Israeli Jews thought more highly of Americans than of themselves.

The stereotype plays a curious role in intra-Jewish relationships as well, for some of the tensions between the Ashkenazi and Sephardi Jews in Israel can be attributed to the dynamics of prejudice against Arabs. The Ashkenazim are Jews with origins in Europe and North America; some of their fathers and grandfathers settled as the original Zionist pioneers in Palestine before the creation of the Jewish state. The Sephardim, a term initially applied to the Jews in Spain, now include those with origins mostly in the Muslim countries of North Africa and the Middle East, as well as those from Sephardi communities in Greece, Bulgaria, South America, India, and elsewhere. Colloquially, they are also known as Oriental or Eastern Jews. Although some families from Yemen and elsewhere in the Muslim world can trace their presence in Palestine back for six or eight generations, Sephardim began arriving in Israel in large numbers only during the 1950s, well after the Ashkenazi establishment was firmly in place. As relative newcomers they were subjected to discrimination and relegated to poverty, where many of them remain today. While individual Sephardim have since risen into the ranks of higher education, private enterprise, and government, as a group they are still regarded with contempt by many Ashkenazim. And one of the leading stereotypes attached to the Sephardim is that they are primitive, tribal, crude—that there is something Arab about them. Their music is infused with the keyless quarter-tones of Arab music; their families are extended, and infatuated with elaborate tradition; their food is decidedly Middle Eastern. Much of their culture has been absorbed from the Arab countries in which they have lived. Many speak at least a mangled Arabic, and because they generally have black hair and olive skin, they bear a physical resemblance to the Arabs.

"If Israelis would value and honor the Arabs, there might be a change in attitude toward Eastern Jews," said Eli Padeh, a Jew who helps supervise Interns for Peace in the Galilee. "Newcomers from Arab countries behave like people in traditional societies. Sometimes Western people don't feel comfortable listening to Arab music. But go to Eastern [Jewish] weddings and the orchestra is often Arab. They sometimes play nationalistic songs, but the Jews don't listen to the words and don't care what they mean. They just like to listen to the music. It's the culture of our enemy. Because of wars, anything connected with Arabs is bad. So if you come from an Arab country, you are seen as similar to Arabs, and you are discredited."

The bigotry's awful depth was plumbed in a 1976 trial in Tel Aviv. The son and eighteen-year-old daughter of Masuda Mato, a Jewish woman from Iraq, had had an incestuous relationship, resulting in the girl's pregnancy. When the baby was born, the daughter placed it in a pail. And when Mrs. Mato—the baby's grandmother and the mother of both parents—found the infant, she poured boiling water into the pail, killing the baby. She was arrested for murder. In court, her defense attorney argued successfully that because she had been schooled in Arab culture before coming to Israel, she had merely acted "in accordance with Arab ways her family had brought from Iraq," which allegedly included tolerating incest but then killing any child that resulted from the sexual relations between brother and sister. She had carried out the infanticide "with the concept of family honor uppermost in her mind," her lawyer declared. The court was evidently undisturbed by the contradiction inherent in the notion that Arabs—and therefore Jews from Arab countries—accept incest but regard the family's honor as tainted by its results; the prosecution's demand for a heavy sentence was denied, and Mrs. Mato, who was forty-nine at the time, was given eight years in jail. The Israeli news agency, Itim, reported the story, and *The Jerusalem Post* printed it, as if it were all undisputed fact, without even a phrase to question the accuracy of the brutal stereotype.

At some stages of Israel's early history, the transfer of negative images may also have gone in the other direction—from Sephardim to Arabs. David Harman believes that the original characteristics applied to Sephardim after their massive influx in the 1950s—that they were dirty, slovenly, primitive, unwilling to work—were then used against Arabs on the basis of the Sephardim's having come from Arab countries and been schooled in Arab cultures. David remembers as a boy using the idiom *avoda Kurdit*, meaning "Kurdish work," a derogatory reference to supposedly inferior work done by Kurdish Jews, and a companion or precursor to the current insult *avoda Aravit*, "Arab work."

Significantly, some of the Ashkenazim most contemptuous of the Sephardim are politically liberal on Arab issues; they denigrate Sephardim as unrefined, anti-Arab racists who have taken Israel around a crucial corner away from humaneness and toward a rowdy intolerance. But what appears at first to be a political judgment emerges finally as a matter of class, ethnicity, and culture. Sephardim are rejected ostensibly because they are branded as viciously anti-Arab—much as white middle-class American liberals of the '60s denigrated white blue-collar workers for being anti-black—but the main Ashkenazi stereotypes of Sephardim are precisely those used against Arabs by other Jews, both Ashkenazi and Sephardi.

This struck home one evening when Debby and I were sitting in a cozy Jerusalem restaurant with some liberal Ashkenazi friends who had been quite active on behalf of Palestinians and Bedouins. They asked me what I was working on at the time, and when I told them a series of articles on the Sephardim, they snorted with contempt. Just then, some angry yelling was heard from the street, beyond our view. "There," said one of my liberal friends, nodding toward the shouts. "There are some of your Sephardim you can go and interview." As we left the restaurant later, a couple of young men outside were playfully, noisily pushing each other around, their voices echoing through the darkened street. "There are some more Sephardim you should interview," one friend said with a laugh. And the other added seriously, "The only answer is more Ashkenazi immigration." The Ashkenazim had unwittingly borrowed images and arguments from the Jewish-Arab dispute and applied them to the Ashkenazi-Sephardi tension. Just as many Jews see Arabs as loud and uncouth, so my refined Ashkenazi friends saw Sephardim; just as many Jews find the answer in more Jewish immigration, so my friends wanted an influx of more Ashkenazim.

One of the leading liberals in the Knesset, Shulamit Aloni, who heads the Citizens' Rights Party, caused an uproar in 1983 when she denounced Sephardi demonstrators supporting Menachem Begin as "barbarous tribal forces" that were "driven like a flock with tom-toms" and who chanted " 'Begin! Begin!' exactly like a roll of tom-toms in a savage tribe." She denied being a racist.

So did Amnon Dankner, a columnist for the liberal newspaper *Haaretz*, who dismissed Sephardi traits as akin to Islamic culture. He would resist being "trampled beneath the feet of the wild," he wrote. "Western culture, with or without Jews, is the developed culture, the culture from which we have adopted most of our political values and concepts of aesthetics, and which we are trying to continue to adopt here. The fact is that while Western culture developed over the last several hundred years, Islamic culture waned. . . . The kissing of the hand by the father, the wonderful hospitality, the authentic longing for Zion, the naive messianism are perhaps beautiful things to one who loves such things, but for me they are not the symbols that I want to see in the society that my spiritual fathers and I fought to establish here; an exemplary humanistic and progressive society, interwoven with the niceties of humane liberalism."

Since Arabness has become a disability in Israeli values, its use against Sephardim helps stimulate their anti-Arab attitudes. Many Sephardim try intensively to detach themselves from any cultural association with the Arabs, to divorce themselves from the object of Ashkenazi contempt. And so some of them denounce Arabs with ferocity.

"Many of the Oriental Jews really feel good in Arab culture," said Danny Rubinstein, the Israeli journalist. "They eat Arab food, they used to wear Oriental dress; to listen to Oriental music, and so on. But because of the political problems and because of the fact that they were less prestigious and not in the Ashkenazi establishment, they tried to reject the culture. For them it represented something inferior, something bad, something that characterized the enemy. I remember when Sadat came to Jerusalem. I speak quite fluent Arabic and many times I used to joke with Knesset members in Arabic. You have about ten or fifteen Knesset members who know Arabic very well, but they never spoke to me in Arabic. When Sadat came to Jerusalem, and he came to the Knesset and he delivered a speech in Arabic, all of them started to speak Arabic. It was something to be proud of, that they spoke Arabic. I was amazed because I didn't know. They said, 'Well, I finished school in Baghdad,' and so on. Until then, not one of them admitted that he knew Arabic well. It was something to be ashamed of: 'Well, you are like them.' And all of a sudden because Sadat came, because the enemy stopped being the enemy for a couple of minutes, a couple of days, then it wasn't shameful to speak Arabic."

The Arab perspective on Sephardi Jews mixes political resentment with cultural affinity. Many Arabs have accepted the stereotype of Sephardim as hatefully anti-Arab, but others see the dynamics clearly. Sami Mari, an Israeli Arab who taught psychology at Haifa University, lived in a mixed Arab-Jewish apartment complex in the seaside city of Akko; there, he saw Arabs able to maintain smoother relations with Sephardim than with Ashkenazim, and the Sephardim seemed more comfortable with Arab neighbors than with Ashkenazim. "There is a cultural sameness," Mari explained. "An Oriental woman doesn't have to apologize, as in front of a Western family, if she does everything and her husband sits like a king. They don't feel that they are being criticized." Arabs also seemed less threatened culturally. "At an Oriental wedding I feel at ease," he said. "Some of the rituals are different from ours, but I feel at ease. I enjoy the food; I enjoy the singing and dancing, even the looks of the people, the spontaneous behavior. Ten, fifteen men are dancing with each other. Men are hugging each other and kissing each other. Or women are getting isolated and having their own chat."

When the Lebanon war began in the summer of 1982, an Arab woman went for her usual morning coffee with a Sephardi-Jewish woman on Mari's block in Akko. "They sat down, and the Arab lady said, 'Oof, we are tired of wars and wars. Why not let the Palestinians have a state on the West Bank and Gaza Strip?' And the Jewish lady said, 'You can't put a Palestinian state in my home.' And the Arab lady became insulted, and she left her coffee and went out. It's typical of Oriental culture: You don't drink coffee when you are insulted." The Arab's woman's revenge came in refusing the coffee, a symbolic act relevant to both Sephardi and Arab culture. Hearing of the spat, Arab and Sephardi neighbors arranged a *sulha*, a reunion based on compromise and apology, done ceremonially by Arabs to resolve differences and restore the relationship. "And now she realizes, 'Okay, I'm against a Palestinian state, you are for, we are neighbors, we can disagree,' " Mari said. "I doubt whether a Westerner could have helped solve the problem."

The Sephardi anger at Arabs stems from the Sephardim's position in the society. "Everywhere they read about and absorb, unfortunately, the superiority of the Western culture and the inferiority of their own," Mari explained. "The Israeli system tried to homogenize them in order to control them, to de-Arabize them, to de-Easternize them so they would be easier to manipulate. To me there has been a cultural rape. I think it's two oppressed people; each is oppressed in a different way. They are loaded with frustrations and animosities and so forth, so they explode."

Jews from Morocco, Tunisia, Iraq, Syria, Egypt, and elsewhere in the Arab world want to be seen as Jews, not Arabs, to be integrated into Israeli society as full members, not left by the Ashkenazi establishment on the periphery. That is why they gradually deserted the Labor Party,

as the embodiment of the establishment, and flocked during the 1970s
to the Likud Bloc of Menachem Begin. Although he was an Ashkenazi
of Polish origin, he embraced the Sephardim as Jews in a way that no
Labor leader had, and so made them feel part of Israel, part of the Jewish
people. His right-wing positions were less vital in this shift of the Sephardim's political allegiance than his recognition of and admiration for
their intrinsic Jewishness. And so to highlight their Jewishness, their
belongingness in the Jewish state, their status as not quite on the bottom,
many Sephardim attack the group closest to them in class and culture:
the Arabs, who exist just below and outside Israeli society.

This begins to explain the quality of Sephardi attitudes toward Arabs,
but it does not address their extent, nor does it necessarily bolster the
conventional wisdom in Israel that "Sephardim hate the Arabs" because
of their miserable experience of having lived as Jews in Arab countries.
Throughout much of history, Jews—with some exceptions—had an easier
time in Islamic than in Christian societies, and while many suffered
abuses under the Arabs, others led lives on which they now look back
with nostalgia. Public-opinion surveys on their attitudes about Arabs
have been contradictory. A 1971 study found Sephardim holding more
negative images of Arabs than Ashkenazim. But a 1983 sample failed to
discern any difference in attitudes between Ashkenazim and Sephardim.
Research from 1978 demonstrates that when Sephardim have a positive
self-image, their image of Arabs is no more negative than that held by
Ashkenazim, a key finding that seems to establish a link between the
stereotyping of Arabs and Sephardim on the one hand, and Sephardi anti-
Arab attitudes on the other. As the self-esteem of Sephardim rises, in
other words, so does their opinion of Arabs. Both Arab and Jewish social
scientists have speculated that the most tolerant Sephardim are those who
have gradually begun to move upward into Israel's mainstream and who
have started emphasizing a new pride in their cultural origins. "A rise
in their social status and their satisfaction with their situation . . . results,
among other things, [in] a reduction in their fanatical rejection of the
Arab as part of running away from everything connected to the East and
its culture."[56]

In any event, in Israel as elsewhere, ethnic prejudice is often greater
at lower socioeconomic levels, which are dominated by Sephardim who
are especially sensitive, because of their low status, to being seen as Arab-
like. Among those with higher education, however, I found that the

stereotype of Sephardim hating Arabs broke down with practically every step I took. Sephardim cropped up again and again as I moved through liberal-minded political areas and circles of Israelis devoted to fostering Jewish-Arab understanding and cooperation.

Eli Padeh, who is working to promote joint Arab-Jewish trips, building projects, school visits, and other such contacts, was born in Algeria of Moroccan parents, and he is as tolerant a man as one can hope to meet. Ran Cohen, who escaped as a boy from Iraq by stealing through the desert and across the border into Iran, is a left-wing Knesset member who, as a colonel in the paratroopers during the Lebanon war, argued vigorously against sending the army into West Beirut and held back his artillery unit from extensive shelling that had been ordered against civilian neighborhoods. Michele Ohayon, who did a liberal-minded film on a love affair between an Arab man and a Jewish woman, came from Casablanca, where her father's shop was burned down by Moroccan Arabs; he supported her film and helped her with advice. When Arabs in Nazareth tried to organize a meeting of Arab and Jewish mayors to discuss mutual problems, the Ashkenazim were the least interested, according to Atallah Mansour, the Arab journalist. "It was a Moroccan from Afula who ran around and told all the mayors to come," Mansour recalled. Yaacov Gatigno, the principal of an elementary school in the Jewish town of Kiryat Ata, came from Tunisia when he was eighteen, and he has pushed hard for visits and meetings between his Jewish pupils and those from an Arab school in a neighboring town. "In Tunisia," he said, "the relations between Jews and Arabs were normal, so it was very easy for me to continue and nurse this. When I was a boy, I played with Arab boys in school. My father was town clerk, and also a lawyer, so Arabs visited us all the time. We found a common language, and we knew how to get along with Arabs. They were natural and good relations there—we played and we fought. Here, it's different. The Jews live far from the Arabs here. They're not neighbors. So the encounter is always planned; it's not natural. So we want the children to meet as many as possible, so it will be natural."

These images of Sephardim and Ashkenazim also got jumbled for Palestinian prisoners in the Israeli-run Ansar camp in Lebanon. After their release, some of them told a Palestinian acquaintance of mine that they had entered with fixed ideas that Sephardim hated Arabs and Ashkenazim were more tolerant. Their experiences with Israeli soldiers doing guard duty shattered all generalizations. Occasionally, a Syrian Jew, recognizing a Palestinian from Syria by his accent, would single him out for beating and harassment. But just as often the Sephardim would display moderation and sensitivity, and Ashkenazim would indulge in brutality. The prisoners could not discern any pattern at all.

The stereotype of Arabs as primitive and tribal seems a peculiarly European one. It is especially visible in photographs and paintings by European visitors of the nineteenth century, who emphasized the colorful exotic costumes and settings of the Arab natives they saw. According to Yeshayahu Nir of the Hebrew University, some photographers even took props and backdrops along—a scene of a European forest appears in a photograph behind a desert Bedouin. And generations of Westerners, both in Europe and North America, were nourished on biblical images provided by those early artists, images of Arabs in their flowing robes and keffiyahs in the narrow streets of Jerusalem, in the fields with their flocks. Perhaps those images were little changed from biblical times; at least they now create in today's visitor a sudden rush of feeling that when he walks the Jerusalem cobblestones and looks at shepherds in the stony hills, he has stepped directly into the Bible.

But the pernicious effect is to plant the caricature in the mind as the whole reality. Even if you can regard the image with neutral emotions, you cannot identify with it. The Arab of the imagination seems possessed of a remote mystery and moved by primeval forces. And if you are a Jew living in Israel, indifference is practically impossible. You must have strong reactions, for there, even tolerance is a conviction, an ideology that must be formulated, articulated, and defended. And so an Israeli Jew, who may endure mixtures of attitude even within his own single self, can find the specter of the primitive Arab not only repulsive but also attractive, exotic, fascinating, infatuating.

I met a few Jews who were afflicted with what some of their compatriots derided as the "Lawrence Complex," after T. E. Lawrence, or "Lawrence of Arabia," the British military genius of World War I who came to identify so with the Arab that he wore Arab dress and led Arab armies into Damascus against the Turks. In no case did I know Jews who abandoned their own identity as Jews in the course of moving into a fascination with Arab life. Rather, they devoted their professional endeavors to studying the Arabs, explaining them to their fellow Jews through the media of the university and the press—and sometimes as advisers to the army and government—and serving as the Arabs' advocates in some conflicts with the Israeli establishment.

Unlike their Israeli critics, I never found anything offensive in these Jews. Most of their interest was directed at the desert Bedouins, not the urban Palestinians, and I could easily see why Bedouin life seduced them so. They may have romanticized the Bedouins somewhat, and in the process glossed over some of the negative features of that tribal society, but that is about the worst one can say. Essentially they were interested in collecting folklore and studying customs and simply spending time in Bedouin villages and encampments. One Jewish environmentalist who lived in Sinai until it was returned to Egyptian control assembled Bedouin sea myths by driving his jeep to coastal camps, sitting around open fires, and listening to old fishermen—whose grandfathers used to travel in open boats as far as the Horn of Africa—tell him the stories that had been passed down, generation after generation, about the gods of the wind and the land and the sea. Another traveled throughout Sinai and the Negev with a tape recorder, having Bedouins recite into his microphone the oral poetry that has existed as the culture's memory of wars and drought, love and unfaithfulness, feuds and friendship. The poems are laced with sadness, humor, and heroism. One man, who became a leading expert on the Bedouins, abandoned his Jewish first and last names and took instead the Anglo-Saxon-sounding names of the two streets at whose intersection, in his hometown in upstate New York, his father owned a gas station. This was to mask his Jewishness from the Arabs and reduce their inhibitions about welcoming him. I doubt that many were fooled, but he asked nonetheless that I not betray his pseudonym in print, for it has become his real name now, the one by which he is known to his Israeli friends as well. In other respects, he has retained his complete Jewish identity, including Sabbath dinners and bar mitzvahs for his sons.

Occasionally, Jews with this Arabist bent learn the rituals of Arab tradition and follow them so scrupulously that they behave more like Arabs than the Arabs themselves. In Hebrew literature, this translates into an emulation of the "noble savage" much as the heroic pioneers of the American West were seen to have survived by learning the ways of the Indian. Ed Grossman, an American-born journalist who has lived in Israel for many years, told me that Jewish experts on Arab affairs advised him, when sitting with Arabs, never to let the sole of his shoe face anyone else. It is true, in Bedouin custom, that the soles of the feet or the shoes are tucked under the knees or pointed away from others when sitting on the floor of a hut or a tent, for to aim your sole at a man is to insult him. Similarly, at mosques, worshipers often place their shoes sideways, sole to sole, so that they do not roll over with the soles upward, which would be regarded as an insult to God. The tradition is still respected in more conservative areas of the Muslim world, such as Yemen. But this custom has long been abandoned among modern, urbanized Palestinians, and Ed said that many Arabs have crossed their legs and faced him with the sole of a shoe without meaning offense. Similarly, although Israeli Jews often experience friction because they are too brusque and businesslike with Arabs, dispensing with the usual gradualness of conversation over relaxed cups of coffee, at least one Jew had the opposite reputation. He was an official in the West Bank military government who spoke Arabic and fancied himself an expert on Arab culture. Ed once asked a West Bank Palestinian his opinion of the official. He was all right, the Palestinian said, but he had one defect: When you went to see him, it would take him so long to get to the point. He would offer coffee and talk and ask endlessly about the family before getting down to business!

In these cases, the Jews were able to deal with the storybook Arab of desert ritual but not with the Arab who had stepped out of his past and into the egalitarian, modern world of the Jew. The primitive Arab, though frightening in many respects, was also safer somehow, fitting into a neat box of easy definition. Even as the Israelis saw themselves lifting the Arab out of backwardness, they felt themselves less equipped to cope with him in his new standing. They could respect and admire him rooted in his own culture, but they could not accept him as an equal in theirs.

I knew an Israeli Jew who had grown up in Haifa with Arab neighbors, who had taught himself to speak the language and had a canny appreciation and respect for Arab customs. He had some good Arab friends in Galilee and could read a situation in an Arab town or refugee camp with the quickest streetwise instincts. He was politically liberal—though not enough so to advocate a Palestinian state—and he often railed against the Orthodox religious establishment and the intolerant religio-nationalism that governed the Jewish settlement movement on the West Bank. Arabs liked him and welcomed him warmly. He liked Arabs too, but in a traditional, tribal category where their customs were rich and quaint and decidedly unlike those of the Jews. He never said as much in clear words, but the articles he suggested I should write were mostly on these themes of tribal tradition, ceremony, revenge, the practice of murdering the daughter or the sister who sleeps with a man before marriage. He seemed most comfortable with the Arabs who were rather simple and traditional—shopkeepers, farmers, shepherds—and ill at ease with those of higher education and advanced professions who had become considerably Westernized. Knowing the Arab ways, gliding into Arab culture, was somehow a way into the essence of the Middle East, a testimony to the struggle of rootedness against the fear of apartness. Here were all the complexities of the Jewish view of the traditional Arab, the multiple shades of admiration and denigration, of respect for the customs that threw into relief both Jewish superiority and, at the same time, Jewish alienation from this land.

At the heart of darkness dwells a cold doubt about Jewish belongingness among these terraced hills and vineyards, among the dry desert wadis and citrus groves. How, after centuries of absence, does he shed his strangeness and dig himself into this fickle earth? As Gershon Shaked writes in his appraisal of the Arab in Hebrew literature, "The Jew of literature—conscious that he is living in a foreign land—sees the Arab as the true native, born of the soil, flesh of the land's flesh, and bone of its bone; he perceives himself as a strange and estranged foreigner trying to strike roots in a hostile environment. In that view the Arab is shown as a kind of desirable anti-norm. He represents all those qualities that the Jewish soul most yearns for, qualities which are in complete opposition to the 'blemished' heritage brought by the Jew from his country of origin. To some extent the Arab becomes the authentic Jew—the ancient pre-exilic Jew—before he was tainted by his wanderings."

EIGHT

The Alien, Superior Jew

Israel is the cancer, the malignant wound,
in the body of Arabism,
for which there is no cure but eradication.
—Cairo Radio, 1963

ELIAS FREIJ, THE MAYOR OF BETHLEHEM, CAN SEE THE ENTIRE PIC-
ture from his large, glassed-in front porch. Across the road that runs in
front of his home, the scuffed hills climb through olive groves until they
reach the charming Arab village of Beit Jala some distance away. A slender
minaret rises gracefully from a cluster of houses, all built of a rough
brown stone so close to the color of the earth that the town seems to
have grown directly out of the sacred soil. Rooted to the land, the Arab
village nestles in suspended time, a classic portrait of Middle Eastern
antiquity.

For many years, Mayor Freij could look out on this entrancing scene with tranquility and satisfaction. Nothing disturbed his harmonious view. And then, in the early 1980s, there appeared on the crests of the hills above and behind Beit Jala a squadron of gleaming white apartment houses erected by the Jews, the leading edge of a vast new neighborhood called Gilo, which had been under construction for some time, out of sight, on the outskirts of Jerusalem. With a quickening pace, Gilo had spread until the box-shaped buildings marched step by step into view across the hilltops and down the slopes, forming a clashing backdrop to the picturesque Arab village in front of them. They did not look rooted to the land; they did not seem part of the sacred earth. Their colors were too bright, their designs too crisp, and their lines too clean; they seemed to have been imposed on the stony hills in dissonance, like interlopers perched precariously on the surface of history.

For Elias Freij, a moderate Palestinian, a man who preaches dialogue and compromise, the view from his porch now captures the essence of the West Bank's disturbing evolution under Israeli expansion and Arab political incompetence. While the Jews grab, the Arabs squabble among themselves. But Freij is just a pragmatic survivor, not a bigot. He does not hate Jews for what they are; he merely dislikes what they do. Something deeper is involved for many other Arabs, and that, too, is contained in the multiplying scenes of modern Israeli houses sitting incongruously next to old Arab villages. The Jews are regarded as aliens, outsiders, trespassers trying to graft their foreign cultures onto indigenous Arab land. And they don't fit. They don't belong. Their presence in the Middle East is artificial, a contamination of Arab purity. The image ignores the ancient ties of the Jews to this place.

From time to time this searing rejection of Jews in their essence burns through the Arabs' intricate arguments about recognizing Israel, creating a Palestinian state, suffering under military occupation, regaining some of the West Bank. And in those moments it illuminates the core of the conflict, casting a harsh light on the obstacles to reconciliation. My introduction to this element of hatred came very early, soon after I arrived in the Middle East. I went to the West Bank village of Halhoul to see the mayor, Muhammad Milhem, an articulate orator with the presence of a charismatic politician. As we talked, I posed the basic questions of a newcomer. I asked whether Milhem differentiated among Israelis, whether he found any who appealed to him. He replied with an eloquent, disturbing statement that drew the line between those Jews who seemed to him to have come from this land, who felt close to the land and respected it, and those who had come from outside, particularly from Western cultures. He placed Moshe Dayan, foreign minister at the time, in the favored category, accepting him as a man born in Palestine, a son of the earth, a Jew with some sense of respect for the Arabs. He placed Menachem Begin, then prime minister, in the outsiders' camp, deriding him as an alien immigrant from Poland and sneering at all Jews with origins in Europe. How, he asked, could anyone regard them as rightful residents of the Middle East?

The comment was sharpened by the fact that Milhem was not a militant radical by Palestinian standards. He spoke openly to me in strong criticism of specific radical PLO leaders, endorsing a more moderate approach. But this ingredient of his attitudes, so smoothly blended into his basic outlook, had an ugly odor. And it was repeated to me often enough by other Arabs, sometimes with embellishment, that it seemed a significant theme in Arab images of Jews. Perhaps for some, even for Milhem, it was thoughtless reflex, as many prejudices are, for several years later, after the Israelis had deported Milhem from the West Bank, he and Mordechai Bar-On, the former Israeli colonel and Peace Now activist, traveled together across the United States, speaking jointly before groups at synagogues and elsewhere on behalf of peace. In 1984, Milhem was elected to the PLO executive committee.

In some measure, the Arabs' branding of Jews as inherently alien is part of the general sectarianism that reaches a high pitch among all ethnic and religious factions in the Middle East. In Jerusalem, hardly anybody can deal with you until he knows what religion you are. Then he can put you neatly into a box, define you, and determine the degree to which you deserve to be hated. The passion with which Jews hate other Jews and Arabs hate other Arabs certainly rivals the antipathy between Jews and Arabs. The closer the groups, the more corrosive the tension seems between them, between Orthodox and secular Jews, between rival ultra-orthodox Hasidic movements, between Arab Christians and Muslims— who tell bigoted jokes about each other—between desert Bedouins and urban Arabs, between Muslims and Druse. So it is no leap of logic and no betrayal of an ethical norm for Arabs to regard Jews as alien. By and large, Arabs refer to Israelis as "Jews," not "Israelis," and this helps categorize them.

On certain occasions, the notion of the Jew as outsider is even twisted into acceptance because an outsider is needed to end fraternal strife. Yaacov Malkin, the Israeli Jew who founded the joint Arab-Jewish community center in Haifa in 1958, recalls that the center's first director, a Greek-Orthodox Arab, was so disliked by Roman Catholic and Muslim Arabs that they followed him around town, found he was going early in the morning to the home of a Jewish mistress, and forced him to leave his post. He moved to the United States, and the directorship was taken by a Jew, who was still there more than twenty-five years later.

Some Arabs see Jews' prejudice against them as an attempt to impose alien, Western values on the region. "Equality to me is an intellectual value." said Jamil Hamad. "I can't be an equal to the Israeli, to the Jew in Israel, without understanding his background, without knowing his history so I could argue with him. And from this point, you can see how some Israelis look down at the Arabs. They don't treat them equally because they never make the effort to understand the Arabs, how an Arab lives. What are the values in an Arab house? What is the status of a mother, of a father, of the boys? How do the boys treat their father? These are the little things which the Jews should understand if they have in mind to continue living in this part of the world. If I go to Philadelphia, I can't take everything from the Middle East back to Philadelphia. I have to understand the environment there. So if the Israelis want to continue living here and they have plans to have peace with the Arabs, so they have to understand the system, the technique of the Arab mentality. Now, whether you accept it or reject it, that's another question. But at least when you see this Arab jump and kill his daughter because she had a love affair with somebody, don't jump and say those Arabs are brutal savages. You should say, I disagree with that, but, it is in their roots."

Homogeneity, so elusive in this land of intense variety, becomes the salve of certainty and comfort. Some Jews yearn for it, although many do not, having come from cultures that value pluralism. Some Arabs discard it by going abroad to study and work. But in the eyes of many Arabs, the presence of Jews who have power ruins the internal harmony of Arab life; it is often just as simple and as brutal as that. You feel it if you go to a small village like Jibya, on the West Bank, just fifteen miles north of Jerusalem. The Arabs there—who have grown up in their fathers' houses, have picked the olives and planted the winter wheat, have studied and married and had children who play among the same rocky hills and pastures—know and love the rhythms of tradition. Jews are outsiders, unwelcome in the extreme.

I went to Jibya with an Arab-American friend on a warm afternoon in May. The town, with seven families, was nothing more than a short string of stone houses along a road flanked by olive groves and stony fields; it had a pleasant, remote air of laziness and impoverished simplicity. No taint of slick, fast-paced modernity had visited here. There were no Israeli soldiers in view. An old man with deeply lined, weather-beaten skin had wrapped a tattered white rag as a keffiyah around his head. His black shoes, which he wore without socks, were fastened with wire instead of laces. A middle-aged woman wore a floor-length white dress embroidered in red.

The village had no phones, so we arrived unannounced at the home of a family my friend knew. We were greeted with effusive warmth, were seated on square rattan stools on the small porch, and then inundated with conversation. The talk began with news of the family's relatives in the United States, then turned to land confiscations by the Israelis. Villages that had lost land were named, and the coming of a new settlement was discussed with bitterness. The family said their village had lost communal acreage where they had once planted wheat, lentils, grapes, figs. The old man's teeth were stained brown. A thin woman emerged from the kitchen carrying tea on a silver-colored tray, which she put down, carefully balanced, on the frame of a stool whose webbed seat had rotted through. She dumped lots of sugar into the bottom of each small glass, then poured steaming amber tea on top of it.

I asked if they saw many Jews here. "Two men came—Jews," someone said. "We suspected they were settlers. They had a map, and they went to look at the land."

Green sprigs of sage were brought, and the thin woman put a sprig in each of our glasses. *Maramiya*, they called it, which is derived from the word *Maryam*, or Mary, a reference to the Virgin Mary. "When she was having pains with Jesus, they gave her *maramiya*," the woman explained. They wanted to offer this to us now, she said, because it was from the land. It gave the tea a spicy, metallic flavor against the sweetness.

Do you have any contacts with the Israelis? I asked. "Not a single individual. We are afraid to go out in the surrounding countryside because of the settlers."

A boy carrying a school briefcase wandered in and listened to my friend translating my questions into Arabic, the answers into English. I asked, Do you see soldiers? "Yes," said one of the women. "Soldiers came here in the past with tanks, others on foot with guns, and looked around the area, looking for 'troublemakers.' The villagers rolled some rocks out there and tried to stop them. They took some things from the village. Two years ago, they took an old olive press and an old grinding stone. They came at night. People here knew what was going on, but nobody wanted to go outside—afraid. Now we see them quite regularly—at night, for maneuvers."

Any friendly contacts with Israelis? "Not at all," said the old man. "Not at all. Never. We have never met any good Jews."

The thin woman, holding an egg in her hand, asked what we wanted for lunch. We protested politely that we could not impose. She insisted, explaining that the village grows its own olives and figs and from its own wheat bakes bread in a communal *taboun*, a round oven. She was not to be talked out of producing a meal, and after a short time served scrambled eggs; flat bread; cooked broad beans known as *fuul*; a dish of olives; plenty of olive oil; and green powdered thyme, called *zaatar*. We tore off hunks of bread, dipped them in the olive oil and then in the thyme, which clung to the oil and coated the bread with powdery green. Afterwards, she served tea with sprigs of mint.

"Some of our better *zaatar* fields are gone now," said the old man. But some things had improved, he added. Two years ago the village had been hooked up to the electric lines and also now had running water. "We used to get water from the spring," said one of the women. "We used to carry it on our heads. One of our cousins went to Jordan and got rich and came back and put it in."

Around their stone house, almond trees grew. And from the backyard, I saw the object of their anxiety about the encroachment of the alien world of the Jews: Across the stony valley was a new Jewish settlement with its concrete boxes scarring the hillside. The people in Jibya did not know the settlement's name.

The image of the Jews as alien is formed against a background of theological and historical argument in the Arab world at large. In textbooks, scholarly works, and press commentary, Jews' links to Abraham, to

Semitic ethnicity, to divine right over the land are challenged with intricate and detailed rhetoric.

"Jews have no right or title in Palestine because they are not the offspring of Abraham, Isaac, and Jacob," declared *Al-Akhbar*, an Egyptian newspaper, in August 1977. "Jacob is not Israel, and the latter is a different person who had nothing to do with the Patriarchs or the Prophets; he was the forefather of the Jews. . . . It is a pure act of arrogance on the part of the Jews, the killers of Prophets, to advance the claim that they are the Prophets' descendants." And so the Arabs try to build a case in religious history for their interpretation that the Jews are strangers to this land.

It is the Jews' strength that seems to rankle. "While the Jews may be hated because they are regarded as different and alien," writes Yehoshafat Harkabi, the Israeli expert on Arab affairs, "Islamic society was founded on the recognition of religious groups existing side by side, with power and superiority reserved for the Muslim faith. For the Christians, the very existence of the Jews, who refused to accept the Gospel, was a provocation, while Islam accepted their presence in its midst, though under conditions of subordination." In other words, the Jews have become the objects of rejection by virtue of having acquired the power of statehood. Moreover, Harkabi observes in depicting Arab attitudes, "The bond between Israel and imperialism is not accidental, but historical and cultural. The antagonism between Arab nationalism and Zionism is presented as not merely a clash between a natural and an artificial nationalism, but as parallel to the antagonism between Islam's universalism, broad outlook, and tolerance and its teachings on the equality of man, and the narrow, particularistic, tribal, jealous, and selfish attitude of Judaism."

Therefore, Arab broadcasts and writings have tended to label Israel as an illness. "Israel is the cancer, the malignant wound, in the body of Arabism, for which there is no cure but eradication," said a commentator on Cairo Radio in April 1963. A lecturer in 1961–62 at Cairo's Institute of Higher Arab Studies declared, "The existence of Israel nullifies the unity of our homeland, the unity of our nation, and the unity of our civilization, which embraces the whole of this one region. Moreover, the existence of Israel is a flagrant challenge to our philosophy of life and the ideals for which we live, and a total barrier against the values and aims to which we aspire in the world."[57]

Arab scholars have also asserted "that there is no racial continuity

between the ancient Hebrews and the modern Jews," that "in all generations a mixed multitude was converted to Judaism," Harkabi notes,
a line of argument that opens the way not only to the historical rejection
of Jewish rights in Palestine but to the more diffuse sense of Jews as
alien outsiders. These contentions have been spun into detailed elabo-
rations of history, which argue that many modern Jews descend from the
Khazars of the Crimea, who converted to Judaism in the eighth century
and therefore have no Semitic origin.

The pseudo-scholarship translates easily into virulent propaganda. Symbolism by an Arab poet, Fadwa Tuqan, is explained in a current Jordanian
textbook for high-school freshmen: "The poetess is alluding to the usur-
pationist Jews with words such as 'owls' and 'phantoms.' " An earlier
Jordanian textbook on Arab society, published in 1963 for high-school
freshmen, contains a reading entitled "Like Carthage, Israel Must Be
Destroyed," which includes the passage "Thus Israel was born and thus
the malignant cancer came to infect the Arab Homeland. King Abdullah
called it 'a cataract in the eye, a thorn in the living flesh, and a bone in
the throat.' Like the cry of Cato, the famous Roman orator, 'Carthage
must be destroyed,' so you Arab boys and girls must cling to the slogan,
'Israel must be destroyed.' "

A 1963 Egyptian reader for junior-high-school students has a passage
entitled "Israel—Asylum for Criminals," which contends, "Every Jew
who committed a crime somewhere and wished to escape from the hands
of the law hurried to Palestine. . . . Salem said, 'Are not the Jews who
stole our land the scum of the nations with nothing in common between
them?' "

In *The Growth of Modern Arabism*, published first in 1943 and reissued
in 1971 in Beirut, the author, Mahmoud Azat Darwaza, gives the following assessment of early Jewish migration to Palestine: "The Arabs are
aware of the danger which lies in their [the Jews'] reappearance, of their
greed, of the fact that they are concentrating in the very place which
links the Arab countries of Asia with those of Africa. They are a racial
and geographical obstruction between the Arab countries, and this forces
the Arabs, who surround them on all sides, to continue to fight them
and to tighten the siege around them until this new phenomenon will
be destroyed."

The notion of the Jews as a "racial geographical obstruction" is embellished in bizarre fashion by portraying them also as irreligious agents

of imperialism and communism, sometimes all in the same sentence. ". . . capitalist materialism and communist materialism are nothing if not Jewish institutions, whose principles were ratified by Zionism in order to sacrifice the non-Jewish world by distancing religion from life," wrote Saad Guma'ah, a doctor of jurisprudence who served as Jordan's ambassador to the United States in the 1960s and was prime minister in 1967. His book, entitled *God or Destruction*, contends that Zionism's "aim is to destroy the concepts of humanitarianism and morality of all nations," and that "the Talmud encourages murder, exploitation, robbery, and immorality."

In January 1984, the Saudi paper *Al-Gumhuriya* expounded upon this theme of the Jews as communists, a slur also found in anti-Semitic tracts in the United States. "The idea of communism began with the Jew, Karl Marx," the paper declared. "The Red Revolution in Russia was begun by the Jews. The communist attack in the Middle East was launched by Jews who came to Syria, Lebanon, Palestine, and Egypt, in order to propagate communism. The Jews still oversee the communist movement in Egypt . . . . Most of the Soviet espionage networks in America contain Jews. They are the strike force of the USSR everywhere. . . . We know well that communism and Zionism are two sides of the same coin. From the establishment of Israel up to the present, only the USSR has derived benefit from it." The argument must confuse the Syrians, not to mention the Russians.

In branding Jews as aliens, Arab commentators often rely on religious arguments. Assertions are made that the Jews forfeited their rights to the land by having broken the covenant with God. Jordanian textbooks accuse the Israelis of distorting and denigrating the Koran in the secondary-school curriculum that is imposed on Arabs under Israeli control. "The Israeli curriculum is dubious regarding the rectitude of the respectful Koran and underrates its importance and value and distorts its statements and arouses doubt about the biography of the Messenger—peace be on his soul—and his discourses, and perverts the principles and instructions of Islam," says a junior-high-school text used in the study of Arabic. The Jews "lost religion and this world as well . . . at the hands of the righteous Muslims," says a Jordanian grammar book. And the Arabic text goes on to blame the Israeli curriculum for attempting "to sever the Arab pupil from his roots, his origin, and civilization."

As in other areas of stereotyping, there is a question here of how directly the printed polemics translate into private attitudes. Given the large problem of illiteracy in parts of the Arab world, the published stereotypes may be more significant as expressions of existing attitudes and of an elite political catechism than as vehicles for spreading bigotry. The propaganda is also most important among Arabs who have no contact with Israeli Jews. Sana Hassan, daughter of an Egyptian ambassador to Washington, discovered how imbedded the alien image was when she took the initiative to visit Israel three years before Sadat's dramatic journey to Jerusalem. "Contrary to the myth, and my own expectations, Israel is a very Middle Eastern society," she told Tom Friedman of *The New York Times*. "I grew up with Nasser's image of Israel as a foreign, European body that had 'to be plucked like a thorn' from the Arab heartland. I came here visualizing a small Paris. When I got here, I found that Tel Aviv looks just like Alexandria, so much so that it makes me nostalgic. I find that Israel is basically a Mediterranean state with certain European enclaves, like the kibbutzim and universities."

In reality, however, Israel is a mixture: Tel Aviv is neither Alexandria nor Paris but a sultry, Levantine blend of wily, hot-blooded street life and a slick, thin veneer of luxury. Consequently, Arabs who live with the Israeli Jews between the Jordan and the Mediterranean tend to have less categorical impressions than Miss Hassan. For some West Bank and Gaza Arabs, and especially for Israeli Arabs who are exposed to Jewish life, the picture of the Jews' foreignness is painted in considerably subtler tones. Often it is expressed in terms of cultural differences—real ones, to which the Arabs attach heavy value judgments.

Enter an Arab home and you are likely to be greeted by a rich and warm hospitality that begins with effusive statements of welcome, goes on to strong Turkish coffee, and continues into an extravagant meal. If it is evening, you will be urged to stay the night, and if it is daytime, you will have to invest hours in visiting before you can get away. Although this is largely ritual, most Arabs I've encountered convey their welcomes with such convincing sincerity that visitors feel truly appreciated. By contrast, Israeli Jews generally display a Western reserve in their approaches to guests, offering a cup of coffee and perhaps a piece of cake but little else to sweeten the occasion. This can be as pleasant and hospitable as in an Arab home, just without the formal outpouring that Arabs prefer; it is a question of gradation and style. Jews recently arrived from Arab countries carry with them the more elaborate Arab practices, but these have often disappeared by the next generation, and the informal, casual, direct method of entertainment prevails.

The Arabs' gestures of friendship and hospitality sometimes take on remarkable dimensions. Clinton Bailey, an Israeli Jew who speaks fluent Arabic and teaches Palestinian affairs at Tel Aviv University, made good friends with many southern Lebanese when he served as an adviser on Arab affairs to the Israeli army there. He argued, usually in vain, for a politically sophisticated and humanitarian policy toward the Shiite Muslims in the area. One morning, after Clinton had been released from his reserve duty and was back home in Jerusalem, two Swedish soldiers from the U.N. force in Lebanon knocked on his door and handed him a package. Their truck had broken down in southern Lebanon one evening, they said, and they had asked a man at a local gas station if they could park it there and spend the night in the cab. "No," the man said, "come inside." He insisted that they sleep in his house. And when he learned that they were going to Jerusalem, he gave them a big tin of baklava to deliver to Clinton.

When Jews fail to be as generous, the contrasting styles can create friction. Arab youngsters, for example, often felt cheated by the Jews when small numbers of Arab and Jewish children began visiting each other's schools in Israel under the auspices of a few modest programs aimed at promoting mutual understanding. Under the normal routine, the Jewish children would spend a morning in the Arab school and then divide up for visits to the Arab children's homes. Then, a few weeks later, the Arabs would make a return trip to the Jewish school and visit the Jews' homes. The Arab youngsters often found the visit with the Jews terribly disappointing. The Arab families had poured out their hospitality on the Jewish youngsters, but the Arabs just did not get the same treatment when they then visited the Jews. Although this appeared to result more from cultural styles than from prejudices, the Arabs often felt insulted. "They don't care about us," the Arab children would often say of the Jews.

An Arab teacher in a Jewish school recalled a conversation she had on this point with a teacher in an Arab school who told her, "The problem is that you came to us, and we made you meals and had you in our houses and made you cakes, and when we come to you, you make nothing for us. And the children see that." As a result, organizers now have Arabs visit Jews first so that the Arabs don't go in with high expectations. If on the return visit they better the Jews in providing hospitality, that becomes a source of pride rather than resentment.

Nevertheless, many Arabs hold firm to an image of Jews as cold and inhospitable, as less oriented than Arabs toward the family. Often, Arabs assert that Jews are less ready than Arabs to lend a helping hand to others. Some Arabs, even those with extensive contacts and years of experience with Jews, take undue offense at imagined slights. "If I pass someone in the morning and say hello, and he doesn't say hello in the same way and with a smile, I feel bad the whole day," said Atallah Mansour, the Israeli Arab who covers the Galilee for the Hebrew-language paper *Haaretz*.

At the same time, Jewish society is seen as having qualities of skill, education, and permissiveness that the Arabs admire and sometimes envy. One study found that both Jewish and Arab adolescents agreed on certain characterizations of each other and themselves—that the Jews are more educated than the Arabs, and the Arabs more hospitable, modest, generous, and dedicated to their work.[58]

Some Arabs emulate Jewish styles, associating them with things Western and modern, regarding them as superior to the traditional Arab culture, which they come to see as "backward." Bishara Bisharat, the Arab physician who worked in a Jewish-run hospital in the Galilee, sees a certain convergence as Western Jews adopt some Eastern ways and Arabs become Westernized. "It's changing from the two sides," he told me as we sat in the living room of his small apartment in Afula. "We are going to be less hospitable than before. Of course, if you come to my parents', you will not go without eating a meal. But here," he said laughingly, "I'm afraid that you'll go without eating. There, you cannot escape, even if you explain that you have just eaten and so on—no, you will be there all afternoon." Then he added, "My wife and I visited a Jewish family in Tel Aviv; it's not different from us. Maybe they make more hospitality because they know they are entertaining Arabs. And we make less because we try to be Western, modern."

Young Arabs from the West Bank and East Jerusalem found themselves with sudden access to "Western, modern" culture after the 1967 war, when Israel captured the territories and traffic began to move fairly freely back and forth. Some were so infatuated that they tried to copy the Jews, dressing in jeans and altering the pronunciation of their names. In the company of Westerners and Israelis, Yusuf became Yosef, Ibrahim became

Avraham. To a considerable extent, this remains an active phenomenon among some upper-class Arab youths. A few Israeli Arabs have even legally changed their names, both first and last, to Hebrew names, and their spoken Hebrew is so fluent that they "pass" as Jews. Albert Aghazarian, who was an East Jerusalem teenager in 1967, went through the phase of attraction to the Western culture represented by the Jews after he was suddenly able to go out of the Old City into West Jerusalem and Israel beyond. Now, even as an Armenian, he has come to identify fully with the Palestinian cause, and he seems quite sensitive about the issue of his flirtation with Israeli Westernism. An expansive talker on most subjects, he spoke somewhat elliptically on this one. I asked him how he had been affected by Westernization.

"The first kind of reaction to this kind of cultural contact is to copy it," Albert said. "How do you copy it? First to find yourself an Occidental girlfriend, to be up to date with the new book of the month, to be familiar with the new films, by trying to force yourself to love classical music, even if it's alien, it's not natural. Until now I have to admit—the vulgar part, if you like—classical music is not my music. It's not something which is really natural. I listen to it because I have to. You don't distinguish, so you try to be Westernized, modernized. These are the concerns when you are seventeen, eighteen. Then you reach a phase of transcending. It's like you consume something to the end, then you transcend it. And by transcending, maybe for a while you pass, *en passant*, through a degree of irrationally rejecting your experience. It's irrational, you know, moving 180 degrees to the other side, until you find the balance, where you can see that type of world that you lived in as beautiful. But in certain context, with reservation. And I like to think that more or less I have reached that phase. For me, Western culture is neither God nor the devil. It's sort of a balanced thing. But to reach this, you have to exercise the ultimate indigenous mood and you have to experience being a maverick, being over-Westernized."

In some Arab circles, Western culture, as represented by the Jews, emerges as immoral, and there are Arabs who consciously avoid contact and discourage their children from having relationships with Jews because they are afraid they will promote the decay of Arab society. This backlash is visible across the spectrum—in the rise of Islamic fundamentalism, in the Palestinian nationalist movement, and in the traditional older generation.

Nevertheless, emulation, copying, and looking up to the Jews have also been functions of the power relationships since the establishment of the Jewish state—or, in the case of East Jerusalem, West Bank, and Gaza Arabs, since they came under Israeli control following the 1967 war. Before that, Sari Nusseibeh of East Jerusalem recalled, "We felt superior and looked down on Jews, especially when you talk about or think about religious, Orthodox Jews. I knew an old woman who worked with my grandmother, she's as old as my grandmother. I remember her making statements about Jews, racial statements, especially about Orthodox Jews. 'Those dirty Jews,' and that sort of thing.

"This has changed, I think. The [earlier] situation encouraged it. The Jews were a minority. The Arabs were stronger. They [the Arabs] looked down upon them, whereas today people don't think of Jews, Israelis, as weak. On the contrary, if anything they sort of look up to them as being superior, having proved themselves to be stronger than the Arab nation, and so forth. Jordanians admire Jews for what they have done. The picture of the Jew held by my grandmother's maid, the picture she had of the Jews, is totally different from the picture her granddaughter would now have of the Jews. This changed to being a picture of somebody to be respected or admired. This was after '67. The admiration was for the military might rather than for the cultural. After '67 and the war there was an image of the superman, the Israeli superman." Arabs who grew up in Israel experienced the evolution of these attitudes much earlier. "When I was a kid, the Jew was something unreachable, a superman," said Hashem Mahameed, the middle-aged mayor of the Israeli-Arab village of Um el-Fahm. "You couldn't beat him in a war—he's the strongest, he's the cleverest."

Stereotypes, like coins, have their opposite sides. And Sari put the contradiction in terms of phases of image and attitude: "But this has changed again, I think. The superhero of '67, the Israeli superhero soldier, his stature has diminished considerably since '67. The Israeli soldier you see on the street, he doesn't very much contribute to the image of a superman." Sari laughed. "A lot of soldiers, especially the ones you see on the West Bank these days, look rather lost and rather incompetent, and illiterate in many cases, uneducated. And this is for the Arab who has been working in Israeli factories, and so he's managed to sort of learn to speak Hebrew and has managed to understand a little bit about Israeli society. And so he probably feels he's once again cleverer than the Israeli soldier. The Israeli soldier is more lost than he is, in many ways." Hashem Mahameed agreed. "Now we don't glorify the Jews as much," he said. "The Jewish image in the eyes of Arab kids is not that superior now."

Nevertheless, immersed in the swirling countercurrents of competing images of the Jew as alien, as superior, as illicit, as powerful, the Arab learns the special techniques of staying afloat. An Israeli Jew, Zvi Bar-El, wrote of this, about Jerusalem Arabs, with rare empathy as a correspondent for *Haaretz*:

. . . between the Temple Mount and the water pipe there are a thousand other details that you need to know in order to live in the united city. You need to know to cross to the other side of Jaffa Road before the policewoman stops you and checks your identification. You need to know how to lower your gaze in time in front of a border policeman. You need to know what to write in the Arab newspaper in order for it not to be suddenly closed down. You need to know what to say to whom in order to get a loan for housing from the municipality, and what to say to whom in order to receive Jordanian funds, and at the same time not expose yourself to the danger of the nationalists. To work in groups near the yeshivas in the Muslim quarter, and to leave prayers on the Temple Mount alone. To come to the mayor's receptions and to shake Jews' hands for a specified length of time, so as not to be suspected of excessive love or of lack of courtesy. To chisel in your heart the names of the new neighborhoods in Arabic, but to tell the bus driver their names in Hebrew. And to hope that your son or daughter will someday learn in Hebrew University, but to know that the continuation from there will be in the Abrahami garage or the Tenuvah warehouse.

NINE

Segregation and
Class

A man who's a fool is a fool,
whether he's an Arab or a Jew.
—Tewfik Abud,
an Arab plumber

T HE SCANT POLITICAL HUMOR GENERATED BY THE ARAB-JEWISH CON-
flict usually has a raw, racist texture. There is nothing to savor in the
wit, little that plays on self-deprecating subtleties; when the punch line
has been delivered, the laughter is angry, leaden. Anyone looking for
joke-telling that elevates and enriches would do better with the Russians,
for Jews and Arabs carry too much bitterness about the mutual hostility
that locks them together. They can sometimes laugh at each other, but
rarely at themselves.

I heard only one joke that deflated an absurdity and poked fun at a
revered legacy with the required touch of fine, disturbing pleasure; it

was so clever that I have a sneaking feeling it must have been thought up by a Soviet émigré. The setting is a most esteemed Israeli kibbutz founded by those brave Zionist pioneers who drained the swamps and carved a new nation out of hostile land. A venerated old founder is standing with his small grandson, looking out over the settlement that has grown and prospered.

"See that road?" the old man says proudly to the boy. "I built it. See that house? I built it. See that field? I plowed it."

"Oh, Grandpa," the boy says, "did you used to be an Arab?"

Arabs have become the manual laborers of Israel, a fact that brings shame to many idealistic Jews and bolsters negative images that bigoted Jews and Arabs hold of one another. In Arab eyes, the Jew is the owner, the boss, the man of power who exploits his workers. Or he is seen as uneducated and arrogant, one of the "chosen people" who is unwilling to stoop to menial work and so leaves the jobs of garbage collector, janitor, dishwasher, construction worker, fruit picker, citrus packer to the underclass whom he despises, the Arab. In Jewish eyes, the Arab is dirty, lazy, thieving, incompetent, and at the same time uppity, wealthy, and brash. These are the hard ribs of prejudice that form around the factor of class in the Arab-Jewish relationship.

On one of Teddy Kollek's campaign stops for reelection as mayor of Jerusalem in October 1983, a large group of Jewish factory workers unloaded a lot of gripes about life in the city. During the friendly give-and-take of debate and argument, one of them objected loudly to the universal ailment of high taxes and low services. As a clincher, he threw in the ultimate complaint to the mayor: "We're worse off than the Arabs!" But the rest of the crowd interrupted the man with shouts of "No! No!" He had gone too far, even for a disgruntled bunch of Jerusalemites hardly inclined to restrained discourse. To be worse than the Arabs would require a certain adjustment in self-image by working-class Jews who are accustomed to having another group of people to look down on.

Netivot is a blue-collar Jewish town of low apartment buildings and unkempt gardens about eleven miles southeast of Gaza. Some 60 percent of the residents are from Jewish families that originated in Morocco, about 30 percent are from Tunisia, and the rest are a smattering of British, French, Soviet, and Hungarian Jews. Unemployment is fairly high, and a resentment seethes against Arabs from the nearby Gaza Strip, who come to do menial work that the Jews do not want at wages lower than the Jews will accept.

In 1983, after a Netivot resident was murdered by Arabs in Gaza, the mayor of the Jewish town banned all Arab workers from his community for a day. It was a gesture of anger, and also one of precaution, for he was afraid that his townspeople might attack any Arab they happened to see. "You have [Arab] laborers willing to do all kinds of dirty work," said Shlomo Abitbol, director of the community center there. "People who live here aren't willing to do it. The people who clean the streets here are Arabs. The people who work in agriculture are also Arabs." The Jewish employers pay them less than they would have to pay Jews to do the same work, which seems to foster more resentment against the Arabs who take the jobs than against the Jews who employ them.

Indeed, one of the real annoyances to many Jews near or below the poverty line is that some Arabs, especially on the West Bank, are well enough off to build ostentatious villas many times the size of the cramped apartments of the Jews themselves. Since relatively few Jews visit the West Bank, the first time many of them see these elaborate homes comes when they are assigned to the West Bank for a month of army-reserve duty. Then the shock and dismay erupt in ugly locker-room talk among the soldiers. Some of the attitudes were recorded by Arthur Kutcher, an architect with a degree from Yale, who served in an irregular guard unit made up of those who were either too old or physically unfit for regular combat details; many were lower-class high-school dropouts. Fascinated and appalled by the stereotypes of Arabs harbored by these men, Kutcher kept a notebook of conversations, comments, and impressions.

"The basic attitude of our chaps was, What are they complaining about?" Kutcher told me. "They've got it good, they've got money, they don't have to pay taxes, since the Israeli occupation they've been much better off, we treat them much better than the Jordanians—that's probably true." He read from the remarks about Arabs that he had jotted down in his notebook: "All rich, living well under Israel, receiving money from oil states, animals, sons of whores, dogs, ready to put a knife in your back, stupid, suitable only for physical labor, objects of contempt, subhuman, suitable objects to be shot or beaten." In other words, he observed, "You heard that they were rich, that they were deceitful, that everything was going well for them, that you couldn't trust them, and besides that, that they were dogs and sons of whores and characters on a lower level of existence. And it really reminded me of the kind of things you could expect a Russian peasant to be saying about the Jews in Europe, the same kind of arrogant, malicious superiority, coupled with a fear of their deceit and an envy of their wealth."

A lot of the talk was tough-guy, machismo stuff, embellished to impress, and tailored to reinforce the image of Jewish power over the Arabs. In this milieu, any Arab challenge ignited deep fury. Two soldiers, whom Kutcher called "marginal types," told men in their unit about being absent without leave and driving into Jerusalem from the West Bank. An Arab taxi driver in front of them, going down the middle of the road, would not let them pass. Finally they managed to get by him, forced him onto the shoulder, got out with their rifles, opened his door, dragged him out, and threatened him with their guns. They were quite proud, Kutcher said, that the Arab turned white and pleaded with them to spare him.

The stereotypes of Arab laziness, dirtiness, and incompetence work their way into Hebrew slang, where "Arab," either as a noun or an adjective, has come to have a pejorative connotation. *Avoda Aravit*, "Arab work," has two meanings: menial work that nobody else wants to do and also a job that is poorly done; it is an expression so ubiquitous that a Jewish friend of mine heard it from an Arab, an East Jerusalem mechanic who asked what kind of repair my friend wanted on his car, "good work or Arab work?"

The epithets fly around school playgrounds and classrooms, taking virulent forms that offend Arabs who hear them and disturb some liberal-minded Jewish children and their parents. Zohar Endrawos, an Arab from the Galilee village of Tarshiha, used to play soccer on a team with Jews from the adjoining town of Maalot. "If I made a mistake, didn't pass to somebody," he recalled angrily, "my own teammates said, 'Dirty Arab!' " My son Jonathan noticed that an Arab teammate of his playing basketball for the Anglican School in Jerusalem used to get a lot of hard, special opposition from Jewish kids on opposing high-school teams.

"Moshe," a slight, sensitive thirteen-year-old who wears a black skull-cap and attends a respected religious Jewish school in Jerusalem, told me that he heard bigoted remarks "almost every day" from both children and teachers. His mother, who has gone into school to complain, was fearful enough about his safety in raising objections that she asked me not to publish his name, a request that conveyed something of the atmosphere in a significant segment of Israel's religious community: Speaking against anti-Arab bigotry is deviant behavior—uncomfortable and possibly risky.

Moshe gave a few examples. When the boys play basketball and somebody misses a basket, the others, including teachers, say, "Don't shoot like an Arab." The remark "Don't _____ like an Arab" has many applications as a condemnation of any poor performance; all that needs to be done is to fill in the blank. During a playground fight, when a boy spit at Moshe and he spit back, a teacher scolded him: "Don't spit like an Arab." On another occasion, a teacher said to a child, "Don't wipe your nose on your sleeve like an Arab." Generally, "When somebody does something not nice, they say, 'Don't act like an Arab,' " he noted.

Arabic language is a required course in Moshe's school, and although "some of the children think it's silly" to study it, "others think it's quite good," according to Moshe. "One child said he thought it was good because then he could say things to Arabs, meaning not very nice things. A lot of children say, 'Why do I need to learn Arabic? This is a Jewish state. We don't need to learn Arabic.' "

I tried to get some picture of how widespread this was. Did most kids express anti-Arab feelings? "A lot." Did he have friends who thought differently? "Yeah, but some of my best friends also say those things." Does that bother him? "Yeah, quite a lot. Sometimes I make comments about it, but it doesn't seem to make any difference. When somebody says, 'Don't shoot like an Arab,' I say, sometimes I say, 'I've seen the Arab basketball players playing better than a lot of players,' or I say, 'Arabs are people as much as we are.' " And what do the kids say back? "They don't." No argument? "No." It doesn't affect them? "No, they don't give it any particular notice." Did he ever talk to a teacher about this? "Uh, no. I never thought of it." Are there teachers in the school who he thinks would support his viewpoint? "Sure, yeah." Do the teachers ever bring this up with kids at all, talk about it? "No." Then, after further questioning, it emerged that Moshe had drawn some reaction to his defense of Arabs: Other children had accused him, "quite a few times," of being a traitor. "They said that I was a communist and that I hate the country and I want to help the PLO get us out."

Moshe's parents, immigrants from England, were terribly upset, and they found sympathy among some of the school's staff. "Outrage and shock and anguish on our part, I think, are not too strong words to describe our reaction," said his mother. "It sort of made us feel that everything we held dear was being trampled in the mud, and we couldn't bear it, and we couldn't bear that it be visited on [Moshe] in this way. We never imagined that we would come across this kind of thing— prejudice of the most bigoted kind, lack of tolerance of dissent, the lumping together of dissent with treason. A lot of teachers want to tackle the problem where they believe it begins. For example, a history teacher, an excellent woman from a kibbutz, said her own contribution is to teach history the way she sees it rather than tackle the thing front on. There is a kind of feeling that's been creeping into Israeli education for a few years now that puts less emphasis on other world civilizations, and she has put her finger on this ethnocentrism." In the religious schools especially, the beauty of ancient Greek and Roman civilizations is often submerged by a strong emphasis on their oppression of the Jews. "She said all of these civilizations have a history of causing the Jews a lot of trouble—Babylon, Greece, Rome, and so forth," Moshe's mother observed. "But she said her concern was to make sure the civilizations came across to the students as magnificent civilizations. She would teach them language, art, literature, philosophy, architecture."

Fighting parochialism is a long and lonely struggle in the face of everyday experience, where most Israeli Jews see Arabs only in menial jobs. "They see an Arab worker who has been working in construction all day, sweating, covered with dirt," said Laura Franklin, an American Jew who served with Interns for Peace. "Of course he's dirty. But if they would go into his house, it's immaculate. Those women scrub the floors every single day, and they shine." The repulsive image prevails. I was surprised to hear it from another American-Jewish woman, who had immigrated and had married an Israeli. She was dreading an upcoming week when her office was to be painted. She assumed that the painters would be Arabs, and she remarked, "I don't want to be stuck in this office all day with a bunch of Arab workers."

Public-opinion surveys show mixed attitudes among Jews. The 1980 study by Mina Tzemach found that among a sample of Jewish adults, 36 percent labeled Israeli Arabs "dirty," and 17.9 percent judged them "clean." The remainder put them in the middle of the scale between the two extremes. Only 8.5 percent of the respondents said that Israeli Jews were dirty, and 44.6 percent called them clean. On a scale between "diligent" and "lazy," however, the results were reversed, with Israeli Arabs getting higher ratings than Israeli Jews, owing probably to the impression of Arabs as willing to work at the most menial tasks—including, interestingly, pouring the concrete and laying the pipe for the hated Jewish settlements on the West Bank. Only 20.6 percent called the Arabs lazy, and 40.9 percent said they were diligent, whereas the results for Israeli Jews were 29.1 percent lazy and 26.3 percent diligent. On both questions, Americans came out the best, with 51.1 percent of those interviewed judging them clean and 61 percent diligent.

Walid Sadik, an Israeli-Arab social-studies teacher and politician, encounters some startling comments from Jewish students in schools where he visits and lectures. "They are superior, the Arabs are inferior," he said, summing up the remarks. " 'We can do whatever we want with the Arabs. What are you speaking about, about these human norms? We have no need for you.' This is the trend. One student said, 'Are Arabs really as nice as you look?' Kfar Saba [a Jewish town] is about eighteen kilometers from here geographically, but socially it is very, very far. We have no social relations with the Jews. And if you ask a person what are the relations between you and an Arab, he says to you, 'Yes, I have a worker, I have a gardener, I have someone who cleans the stairs of the house or a woman working the field.' So there are no relations. I gave a seminar two months ago in Haifa. I asked, 'Have you ever met an Arab?' Of thirty teachers in the room, only four said they had. This was the first talk they had ever had. For this reason the image of the Arab is very false. The image is extracted from the PLO fighter or the bombs or the primitive worker. In addition to that, there is some literature, and this, as kids, makes a profound impact."

Hebrew stories for children often contain the expressions "Arab work" and "Don't behave like an Arab," even where Arabs are not substantively involved. In Devorah Omer's *The Gideonites*, a Jewish boy, Alex, says, "Don't you think it's terrible that all our watchmen are Arabs? They're supposed to protect us, but instead they steal our property." At another point, Absalom whispers, "The Arab watchmen have gone to sleep as usual." Then, later in the pages, a Turkish Jew named Aaron recounts his unfortunate service under an Arab officer in the Turkish army: "We were cold, the rains beat down on us, there were lice and bugs, and we were beaten by the ignorant Arab commander. You should have seen how he enjoyed being in charge of educated Jews."

Yigal Mossensohn, in *Hasamba and the Big Secret*, has an Arab whisper
to a disguised Israeli as they watch Egyptian soldiers burst into anger
over a card game, "They'll let themselves be killed for something that's
utterly worthless—but they're not prepared to work." In Yossi Margalit's
The Friend from Abu Hammam, a different light is thrown on the stereotypes
in a story of a Jewish boy befriending an Arab boy from a nearby village.
"One day Avner turned to his father and asked: 'Daddy, isn't it true that
all the Arabs are thieves?' 'Who told you that?' his father replied crossly.
'That's no way to talk!' 'But when you bring Arabs into the house, you're
always on the watch that they don't steal anything. And you tell me to
keep my eyes open, too. But when Jews come, you're never afraid they'll
take anything. . . .' His father looked embarrassed: 'There are all sorts
of Arabs,' he said, 'and some of them may be thieves. You can't know
who is and who isn't.' "[59]

As thoroughly as the blowing sand of the desert sifts into every crevice,
the image of the Arab as sneaky, smelly, and dishonest insinuates itself
into all areas of perception. In the analysis of government policy-makers,
in the street talk of children, the notion that Arabs cannot be trusted is
often a fixture of conviction, unquestioned and immutable. A Foreign
Ministry expert, once briefing reporters on Israeli-Arab competition in
black Africa, noted that Arab countries had made big promises of aid
and low-cost oil to the Africans but had not followed through. That
would have been enough to make his point, but somehow he had to add,
with a thin smile, a generalization about the Arab character: "The Arabs
promise very easily," he said, "but there is very little behind it."

Much of the discourse in Israel, whether on high questions of policy
or matters of everyday life, contains an assumption that Arabs are unpleasant to the senses, uncomfortable in the social order, and impure as
elements in the Jewish state. There is a faint parallel here between the
Arab notion of the Jew as an alien cancer in the Arab world and the
Jewish notion of the Arab as alien to the integrity of the Jewish nation.
In addition, there are two parallel counter-currents—the Arab view that
Jews represent an attractive Western modernity and the opposing Jewish
perception of Arabs as indigenous and authentic natives of this coveted
land. The way these strands are woven determines an individual's pattern
of attitudes. Just as the Arab may be infatuated with a permissive, exciting

Jewish society, the Jew may envy the Arab as a true son of the earth, integral to the wily, mysterious ways of the Middle East. And how that thread of admiration appears among its opposites—the Jew as foreign, the Arab as unwholesome—gives the perceptions their many shadings throughout the two populations. For Israeli Jews, the repulsive, fascinating Arab becomes a strand of argument that can take some interesting twists.

The Labor Party, for example, has opposed Israel's annexing the West Bank less for what the move would do to the Arabs there than for what it would do to Israel. The key argument is essentially ethnocentric; it holds that the 750,000 West Bank Arabs, added to the 500,000 Gaza Strip Arabs and the 600,000 Israeli Arabs, would constitute a population of nearly 2 million Arabs who, with their higher birth rate, would eventually overwhelm Israel's 3.5 million Jews. "We have to offer a way that will lead to a Jewish Israel, and not to an Israel that dominates two, maybe three million Arabs," said Haim Bar-Lev, a former chief of staff and the secretary of the Labor Party, speaking on Israel Radio in 1983. "Please don't forget that right now Israel is responsible for over three million Arabs, and even if we get free of the responsibility for the Lebanese Arabs, according to the Likud philosophy, we are still stuck with two million Arabs. And for every Jew and for every Zionist this to my mind is a crucial factor."

Most liberal Israeli Jews, those who generally reject anti-Arab bigotry, would undoubtedly subscribe to Bar-Lev's fears for the integrity of the Zionist enterprise. Their position seems far from the ideological pillar of the extreme rightists, such as Rabbi Meir Kahane, who want to expel the Arabs to maintain and enhance the Jewish character of Israel. The basic difference is that Kahane is a racist and Bar-Lev is certainly not. In addition, some Jews in Labor's camp want out of the West Bank for altruistic reasons. Yet despite the obvious moral contrasts, the liberals and the rightists share an anxiety. Bar-Lev wants not to absorb the Arabs in the first place; Kahane wants to take their land and expel them. As repulsive as liberals find Kahane, neither is satisfied with large numbers of Arabs living under the Israeli umbrella. Distilled to their ultimate essence, both viewpoints embrace an ethnic, national purity as an ideal.

The pluralistic, integrationist approach that has been the standard for American society has no relevance here. In nobody's mind can Arabs and Jews be simply individual human beings, divorced from their identities as Arabs and Jews. Nationhood in the American concept may transcend race, creed, and ethnic origin, but in the Middle East the nation attempts to serve as an embodiment of those traits—not to promote harmony among diversity but to emphasize and express those differences. This is a regional phenomenon, not simply an Israeli one. Neither Arabs nor Jews want integrated schools, for the most part, and neither culture looks favorably on the occasional instances of Arab-Jewish intermarriage. Each side strives for cultural, religious, and ethnic integrity while its most enlightened members seek good-neighborly relations, a middle course between the extremes of integration and apartheid.

A nationalist Jewish settler on the West Bank, Shifra Blass, spelled this out in lucid terms. "Both nations have a very strong, dominating culture that they're interested in perpetuating," she said. "Both nations are very religious. We're interested in keeping our children inculcated with our own values, which means that we wouldn't be interested in an integrated school which would dilute them. However, it doesn't mean either that we're interested in a kind of ghettoization, or certainly not dehumanization. I think what we're trying to do is teach respect for people who are not like us, who don't want to be like us, whom we don't want to be like, a respect that says, 'Just as you want to be Jewish and you want to observe your holidays, you want your culture to be pure, so do they, and they have the same right to respect that we expect for ourselves.' It's not ambitious, it's not grandiose. I think if we can get that across, though, that's a very good first step."

Unfortunately, however, the segregationist impulses are not usually signs of benign neutrality; often they are accompanied by very strong emotions among settlers and other Israeli Jews. And sometimes the feelings burst from unexpected sources. An American-born Jew from the political right who worked as an official in Begin's Likud government was astonished one evening by his eleven-year-old daughter's expression of what he considered racist attitudes. She said that Arabs were smelly and dirty, that she would not want to live in the same building with Arabs, and would object if an Arab girl joined her class at school. The odd thing was that Arabs had lived without incident in their previous apartment house; her father's guess was that she was picking up these attitudes from school and friends.

One day on a hilltop at the edge of Jerusalem, a small group of Sephardi Jews from a poor neighborhood set up a "settlement" to protest the government aid given to West Bank settlements and denied to impoverished city residents. Many of those involved were hardly tolerant of Arabs, and their opposition to settlements was not based on any altruism for their West Bank Arab neighbors. If anything it was the opposite, and they explained their aversion to living on the West Bank in anti-Arab terms. "I came from Morocco to live in a Jewish society," said Moshe Montenegro, a truck driver. "I don't want to go and live in a hostile Arab society."

Nor do many Jews want Arabs in their society, as Yoram Binur, a thirty-one-year-old Jewish reporter for the Jerusalem weekly *Kol Ha'ir*, discovered when he posed as an Arab and tried to make his way in Jewish West Jerusalem. He let a bit of stubble grow on his chin—"about the same length as Yasser Arafat's," he told Tom Friedman in an interview for *The New York Times*—wore a black-checked keffiyah around his neck, carried an Arabic newspaper and kept a pack of Farid cigarettes, a brand sold in East Jerusalem. He is fluent in Arabic.

"The passengers on line 15, first bus in the morning, avert their glances," he wrote. "They wonder what an Arab is doing at this hour on a bus leaving Palmach Street. I stare at a pretty woman soldier. We exchange glances for a moment or two. Then two male soldiers sitting next to her join the glance game. Their looks are provocative, threatening, and they caress their Galil rifles. My place at the bottom of the ladder is made clear to me without us exchanging even one word, and I lower my stare."

He continued: "Friday night, a singles club in Kiryat Hayovel. People move away from me as though I have AIDS, and wherever I move a vacuum is created around me. I sit next to a single woman, offer her in English a Farid cigarette and express my appreciation of the place. 'Tomorrow, I will recommend this place to the guys in East Jerusalem,' I say. Then I ask her to dance. I didn't get a dance out of her. She went up to the manager and complained about their letting an Arab enter. The answer she got, we later learned, was: 'This time we didn't have a choice, but it won't happen again.' "

Segregation is sometimes enshrined in religious declaration. In 1983, Chief Rabbi Yosef Yashar of Akko, a coastal town with a mixed Arab-Jewish population, issued a formal ruling that Halakha, Jewish law, forbids Jews to live in a place with Arab neighbors. The statement was made in an effort to block Arabs from continuing to move into a particular

Jewish neighborhood; the chief rabbi feared that contact would "Islamicize" the Jews. Akko's Jewish mayor, Eli De Castro, tried to calm the atmosphere, recalling that Akko was an Arab city before Israel was founded, that Arabs and Jews had lived together there in neighborly fashion. A Muslim leader made similar observations about the good relations in the city and expressed hope that rifts would not be created by the chief rabbi's ruling.

Akko's only integrated neighborhood, Kiryat Wolfson, was studied in 1979–80 by Akiva Deutsch, a sociologist at Bar-Ilan University, and other researchers at a time when 67 Arab families lived there among about 500 Jewish families. Deutsch was hesitant to make generalizations about Arab-Jewish relationships on the basis of his findings, but the results shed some light on attitudes. "They had lived together for three to five years," he reported. "Most wanted to stay. Those who wanted to leave said they wanted better living conditions. Very few Jews openly confessed to wanting to leave because Arabs lived in the neighborhood. There was no feeling of tension, but there was a feeling that there might be tension. The relationship was a little bit more hesitant on the Jewish side. People wanted their cultural autonomy."

Personal contacts between the two groups, most of which took place in courtyards and apartments, appeared to generate slightly more satisfaction among Arabs than among Jews. Ninety-seven percent of the Arabs said they felt good when they met Jews, and 87 percent of the Jews said they felt good when they met Arabs. Ten percent of the Jews rated their feelings as bad, and no Arabs said that. But Deutsch added cautiously, "It might be the truth that it's no good, and Jews might be more open about saying it. The Arabs are living there, and they don't say. It might be."[60]

Overall, Israeli Jews were divided on the acceptability of integrated housing. A 1984 survey[61] found that 53 percent of Jews questioned opposed Arabs and Jews' living in the same apartment house, 5 percent said that it depended on the circumstances and the neighborhood, and 33 percent supported integration. Those opposed gave as reasons the social-cultural gap; the "different mentalities" that would lead to friction; the Arabs' hostility to the Jews; their untrustworthiness; their desire to rule the Jews; their bad influence on children; and the dangers of common education, Jewish assimilation, and mixed marriage. The attitudes varied with political persuasion: Among those who supported religious parties and the extreme-right-wing Tehiya Party, 75 percent opposed mixed housing; 68 percent of the Likud voters opposed it. Among Labor Party voters, 43 percent opposed and 44 percent approved integration.

A more detailed picture emerged from the 1980 survey by Mina Tzemach, which asked Jews to indicate their degree of readiness to mix with Arabs in various situations. As in studies of ethnic and racial relationships in other societies, the resulting scale demonstrated considerably more openness to integration on the job than in the neighborhood. Following are the percentages of the 1,223 respondents who said they were ready, without qualification, to have contact with Arabs in various circumstances:

Common workplace	52.7
Visit Israeli Arabs	48.2
Work in same room	47.8
Host Arabs at home	47.1
Friendship with Arabs	43.6
Participate in social events	42.4
Homes in same city	42.4
Children study together	41.8
Homes on same street	29.8
Homes in same building	26.2
Mixed marriage by relative	3.7

An additional 12 to 14 percent in most of the situations said that they were unsure but that they thought they were ready for contact with Arabs. The major exception was mixed marriage, which another 3.6 percent endorsed with uncertainty and 87.5 percent rejected unequivocally.

The hypothetical Arab to whom Jews are asked to react in such studies is usually the Israeli Arab, a citizen of the state and therefore a somewhat less threatening figure than the more nationalistic Arab resident of the West Bank or Gaza Strip. Furthermore, Israeli Arabs' attitudes have been studied more solidly than those of West Bank and Gaza residents. One result is that in the social scientists' research, Jews and Arabs come out looking and thinking much like any majority and minority anywhere, with the majority interested in protecting its privileged status and the minority, seeking the society's benefits, somewhat less resistant to contact. Sammy Smooha's 1980 survey of a representative sample of 1,185 Israeli Arabs found 41.9 percent favoring segregated neighborhoods, a lower proportion than among Jews interviewed. A correlation existed for Arabs, as for Jews, between attitudes toward politics and toward Arab-Jewish contacts. Neighborhood segregation was endorsed by 86.7 percent of the Arab radicals, 54.2 percent of the less radical hard-liners, 33.6 percent of the moderates, and 15.5 percent of those categorized as accommodating.[62]

Another study, published in 1985 by the psychology department at Haifa University, found that Israeli Arabs sixteen and seventeen years old were expressing markedly less interest in having contacts with Jews than those questioned a few years earlier. "The Arabs try to get close to the Jews, but Jews prevent them from doing so," one interviewee explained. This fit a pattern in which the minority, seeing itself as weak, blames the majority, seen as powerful, for not wanting good relations. Israeli Arabs, whose images of Jews usually have more political content than Jews' images of Arabs, often answer questions about their perceptions of Jews with statements about what they imagine Jews think of them. So an Arab high-school boy who is asked what comes to mind when he thinks of a Jew often makes such comments as "He hates Arabs" or "He wants to kill us." In answering similar questions, Jews also mention Arab hostility, but less prominently; as the majority, they are somewhat less fixated on what Arabs think of them.

The ancient city of Nazareth lies cupped in the curves of the Jezreel Valley west of Mount Tabor. The crooked streets wind among the brown stone houses of the Arabs, beneath the confusion of domes and cupolas that crown the multitudes of churches and monasteries. The alleyways are filled with the clatter of crowds, the constant motion of shoppers, merchants, tourists, and priests.

Nazareth is an Arab city, and so the Jews have erected Upper Nazareth, which stands on a high bluff above as a fortress of gleaming white concrete apartment buildings. The structures there are bland and regular, the streets broad and quiet, embracing a suburban mood. Built in the 1950s as a Jewish town for the working class, Upper Nazareth has evolved into one of Israel's few integrated communities as Arab families have gradually moved in. And thus it has also become a crucible of Arab-Jewish antagonism, a place where the tools of bigotry are forged. The friendships between Arabs and Jews are few and fragile. Distaste has proved powerfully corrosive. No collection of Israeli Jews can provide a more comprehensive catalogue of the multiple, overlapping, and contradictory stereotypes applied to Arabs than those residents of Upper Nazareth who have organized to kick the Arabs out. And although Arabs who choose to live there are, by the process of self-selection, fairly moderate politically, they are learning bitterness.

Tewfik Abud, a slim Christian Arab who works as a foreman in a Jewish-owned plumbing company, was thirty-two years old in 1973 when he and his wife, Monira, were living in a small, rundown house in Nazareth. They could not find decent housing in the Arab city, and since he was commuting anyway to his job in an Upper Nazareth factory, they began to consider the unthinkable—a move into Jewish territory. "I talked with my friends, and especially with my brother-in-law, who is a lawyer," Abud recalled. "He said, 'Are you ready to live there?' Our family said, 'The children, how will they grow up? How will their security be?' " He had no ready answer except that he was willing to take a risk. He found a Jew who agreed to rent him an apartment, and Tewfik Abud thus became one of the first Arabs to settle in Upper Nazareth. "I rented it for two years." he said. "After two years he came and said to me, 'I want to sell.' I'd already invested a lot, and I didn't want to move, so I decided, yes, I wanted to buy."

His problem was raising the money. If he had done a stint in the Israeli army or had served as a policeman, he would have qualified for a government-supported loan or another apartment directly from the Housing Ministry at a price well below the market value. But the army does not take Arabs, except for Bedouins and Druse, and Abud was not among the few Arabs who have worked as policemen. So he went to a commercial bank for a mortgage. "I had to go there many times," he said. Threading his way through the financial checks and the bureaucracy, he finally arrived at the last step. And then he received a shock. "The bank man said, 'No, because you're an Arab, and Arabs in Upper Nazareth cannot get mortgages.' I said, 'Why didn't you tell me from the first day?' He said, 'This is a new law.' " It wasn't true, of course. There was no such law. But Abud had no alternative that would work quickly enough. "I sold my wife's gold, took loans from relatives and friends," he said, and he managed to scrape enough together to make the purchase.

The apartment is small, but exquisitely neat and clean. The living room is done in lacy curtains, a couch and chairs upholstered in deep red, and an Oriental rug. The kitchen is modern and shiny. Their twelve-year-old daughter, Chinaz, a crisp, pretty girl with her dark hair cut short, breezes through with a friend, Ronny Awat, a Jewish boy from upstairs who has lots of Arab pals. He is a handsome lad with black, curly hair—his mother is from Algeria, his father from Morocco—and he tries to combat the anti-Arab feelings among his peers. When another Jewish boy cursed an Arab kid's father who had just died, Ronny organized retaliation. "The whole neighborhood ostracized him [the Jewish boy] and didn't let him participate in our games," Ronny said, his dark eyes flashing. "He's beginning to understand."

But Ronny is an aberration among the Jewish children. "When we play with them, sometimes they say things we don't like," Chinaz observed, "like 'dirty Arabs.' They say we smell as if we don't have soap and water."

"There are some Jewish friends, but there are not many nice Jews," said Lama Fahum, a ten-year-old Arab girl. "I have no close Jewish friends. They always fight with us. They don't let us play with them." Lama is so blond she looks Scandinavian (probably a vestige of the Crusader blood introduced here nine centuries ago) but her mother says that some Jewish children call her "black Arab."

During Succoth, the Jewish festival in which meals are taken in an outdoor hut called the *succa*, the Arab children are sometimes invited, sometimes not. "There's a boy from the neighborhood and also a girl, and they say, 'If these Arabs participate, we won't participate. We'll leave the *succa*.' Their father beats them if they play with us," Chinaz said.

Chinaz's mother added, "Children ask us, 'Mommy, why can't we go inside too?' A girl told her if they play with Arabs, the rabbi punishes them."

"Apparently their education is not okay," said her father. "I'm not condemning the children. They're small. They have to teach that we are people and we have to live together. They're yelling about peace. Where are they making peace?"

The Arabs have their own prejudices. Monira Abud served up two common stereotypes of Jews: their conspiratorial violence and their lack of communal concern. "They burned the mosque in Jerusalem and said it was a crazy person," she said in reference to the Australian Christian who set al-Aqsa mosque on fire. "We can also do something and say it is a crazy person," she added threateningly. "What they can do we can do." Then she denigrated the Jews as less neighborly than the Arabs. "Many people [Jews] got used to coming to me for something, to borrow something," she said. "They don't have that custom, but Arabs do. A Jewish woman came to the Arab family, not the Jewish residents, to borrow dishes for a bar mitzvah," she asserted. "I didn't mind. She's my friend. I'll give her anything she wants. She didn't take anything from other [Jewish] neighbors."

Monira explained that she would rather live among Arabs if she could find housing, but she insisted that she had every right to be there, especially since Upper Nazareth was built on formerly Arab land. "We didn't come from Arab countries," she declared. "I was born in Israel, I want to live here. When the children are playing, they say to my daughter, 'Go out of Israel. It's a Jewish land, not for Arabs.' Did we steal our apartment here? We came, we invested money."

Parents suffer most on behalf of their children. Amira Fahum, Lama's mother, sat in one of the deep red chairs of her friend's living room and spoke with indignant pain of her daughter's summer nightmare. "When my girl was still small, she wanted to go to a summer camp," she said. "A bus came. I paid money, paid for the camp. She cried that she didn't have any friends there. Every day she would come and say, 'They beat me, they beat me because I am an Arab.' I went to the summer camp and to the counselor and said, 'The children are making problems.' The counselor said, 'She's a child like any child,' that the kids are in the camp to enjoy themselves and not to be yelled at. I said, 'My girl is a child too. Why do you make problems for her?' The counselor said, 'Why do you send your daughter here if you know there will be problems? Send her to lower Nazareth.' I said, 'I'm a teacher. I educate children to be good and loyal Israeli citizens.' The head of the camp told the counselors [who were about eighteen] to watch the situation. The next day the children were supposed to go to a pool. My girl came and said, 'A boy took me by the back of the neck and pushed me underwater and wouldn't let me up. Bubbles were coming up. I almost died.' I complained, and they said, 'Children are children.' I took her out and now send her to an Arab summer camp." It is a long trip of an hour or so every day on two buses.

Lama would also prefer to live in lower Nazareth, among Arabs. That is where she goes to school, rather than to the Jewish public school near her house. Monira, Chinaz's mother, explained succinctly why she pays twenty dollars a month to send her children to St. Joseph's school in Nazareth, to be with other Arab youngsters. In the Jewish school, she said, "They'd lose their language. They [the Jews] would break them."

How would they break them? "From a spiritual, emotional point of view," said Lama's mother. "From the soul."

Tewfik Abud had listened to the children and the adults, and now he had something strong to say. "Arab friends ask us, 'How do you manage to live with the Jews? How do you feel? How do you get along?' We explain. It is possible to live with the Jews. Arabs in East Jerusalem haven't entered into Jewish society. They're even afraid to enter a Jewish café. I go into West Jerusalem, I eat and drink and sing—I'm a man. It's a democratic state, and I know my rights. I've lived forty years with the Jews. There are good Jews too. There are very good neighbors. They behave toward us like other Arabs do. They are very good to us."

On his job, where he is the only Arab foreman and supervises Jews as well as Arabs, relationships are fairly good. "A man who's a fool is a fool, whether he's an Arab or a Jew," Abud said. "If he doesn't understand, I say, 'You're stupid.' I don't say, 'You're a stupid Jew.' The boss calls me to the office, we drink a cup of coffee, he doesn't say, 'You're a bad Arab.' He explains it to me like a man. But there are other people who ruin it, put ads in the paper and put signs over doors, say Arabs are dirty, knock on the door and say not to let Arabs buy, knock on doors of Arabs and say, 'If in two days you're not out, we're going to destroy you.' "

The campaign has effect, for some Jews are unwilling to sell or rent to Arabs. Lama's father had been trying to find a place for a relative. "I talked with a few families. They tell me, 'Yes, of course.' But when they ask me my name and I tell them, they hang up."

In all of the friction, the attack taken with the gravest offense is the assault on honor. "I read in one of the newspapers that the Arabs are dirtying the stairways," Abud declared. "So what I asked was to photograph the Arab houses and photograph the Jews' and see whose is cleaner. I don't want to see even a speck of dirt here. Cleanliness is in our blood."

.   .   .

"There are two kinds of cultures," said Rafi, a pale, bald Jewish militant with a needle face and severe, piercing eyes. He was an activist in Alexander Finkelshtein's group Mena, which sought to keep Arabs out of Upper Nazareth. "There are two kinds of cultures," Rafi said, "the Jewish-Israeli culture and the Arab culture. The Judeo-Christian versus the Muslim. The foundations of the cultures are very different. The whole setting, the outlook on life, the attitudes are very different. Everybody where Arabs live complains about urine smells in the corridor, shouting, the radio at two o'clock in the morning. The whole quality of life is going down. The value of apartments is going down. Arabs moving in will pay more to get a foothold. The second Arab tenant will pay 20 to 30 percent more than the full value of the apartment. Later, when the block is 30 to 40 percent Arab, Jews won't buy anymore. Later, when the value of the apartment goes down, you must sell to an Arab because no one else will buy it."

Alexander Finkelshtein's apartment is in disarray. The combative veteran who has organized Jews into their strident campaign to keep Upper Nazareth pure and free from dirty Arabs lives in filth and disorder. His flat is approximately the size of the Abuds', but with none of the Arab family's attention to housekeeping. The floors are unswept, the furniture worn. The bathroom stinks. A bookshelf holds a jumble of dusty rocks and fossils; on the walls hang snakeskins and a bandolier of bullets. Dirty dishes fill the sink of the grimy kitchen, which seems to spill into the living room, for it is in the living room where, inexplicably, the Finkelshteins keep their refrigerator.

"In the beginning, they came drop by drop," Finkelshtein said of the Arabs. "We were very tolerant. But now it's reached levels so that the proportion of the population, the danger, is that this will turn into a mixed city, and that we don't want. We tell Jews about to leave Upper Nazareth not to sell or rent their apartments to Arabs."

As Lama's father noted, this works in some cases, but economic considerations seem to prevail in many others: The Arabs' demand for housing is higher than the Jews', and Arabs are often willing to pay more. Even the mayor of the town sold to an Arab family, and not because he thought it would advance his political career. "It's legal," said Rafi, "but from a moral point of view we're against it."

Ironically, these conditions were created by the Israeli government's discrimination against Arabs, for while Jewish housing was being built

283

with government funds over the years, little aid was provided for housing in Arab towns such as Nazareth; the resulting shortage for Arabs forced them to look to Upper Nazareth. Furthermore, the intensive construction of West Bank settlements after Begin entered office in 1977 made so much inexpensive housing available to Jews that Jewish demand dropped in towns such as Upper Nazareth, creating a softer market and a higher vacancy rate. Arabs were simply carried into Upper Nazareth by the natural flow of the marketplace.

But they have not arrived in such numbers as Finkelshtein and his group think. In their fears, the Mena group imagine themselves being overrun by hordes of Arab children, women, and men. "Forty percent of Upper Nazareth residents are Arabs!" said one of the group, Avraham Cohen, a forty-six-year-old retired military man dressed in white pants, a white shirt open halfway down his chest, and a gold chain. "The vision of Ben-Gurion was that this be a Jewish-only city. There are places where you don't even hear Hebrew! Jews are afraid to buy apartments here. We're interested in a pure Hebrew city only." Finkelshtein claimed that Upper Nazareth had 18,000 Jews and 7,000 Arabs. But the official government figures at the time, in 1983, showed only 3,000 Arabs among 25,000 Jews.

In any event, the Arabs are seen in contradictory roles: They lower the standards and depress property values, it is argued, but at the same time, they have become wealthy and uppity and pay more than Jews for the apartments, possibly with money provided by the PLO. What the Arabs see as discrimination—that the Jews charge them higher prices than they do other Jews—the Mena Jews see as part of a wily Arab conspiracy to take over the Jewish town by buying it. "It's an Arab way, and I know the Arab mentality," said Galila Barkai, a high-school biology teacher. "When you want to grab, to stick to the place, first you come and rent for a few years. And then you buy. It's sneaky. Arabs believe that when you plant a tree, this is yours. I respect the Arab mentality very much. If Jews had this mentality, they would have known that when they buy these apartments, they are theirs. If it is mine, I have to keep it. Otherwise, slowly but surely I will give the whole country back. I don't hate Arabs," she added. "But my sacred cause is that this city should be a Jewish city."

The Jews in Mena are clearly uncomfortable with confident Arabs, and they see the benevolence of Israeli society as a cause of the Arabs' cockiness. "If the stomach is satisfied, the head works," Avraham Cohen complained. Finkelshtein added, "Because of the birth rate, the Arab area is getting stronger numerically. They get health insurance. They are using money that comes from Jews all over the world [as contributions to Israel]. Their children grow under the protection of the state and the flag. Our soldiers also protect them. And what happens? They don't salute the Israeli flag, don't recognize the state of Israel. Arab students who receive stipends from the state of Israel demonstrate their identification and sympathies with the PLO when they declare, 'With blood and fire we will liberate Palestine.' They spread propaganda poison against Israel." Then he added an important point: "Their confidence is growing," he said. A bit of Hebrew slang has developed to describe this phenomenon: *Tufso rosh*, "They've gotten airs." The extremist Kach movement of Meir Kahane even put up posters in Jerusalem sounding the alarm: "Arabs from the territories have taken over the night life in Beersheba!"

Rafi elaborated: "As long as an Arab is alone or with just one other, he is better behaved than Jewish residents. He pays his rent and pays without any problems. But when they get stronger and stronger, they start to hassle the Jewish neighbors. A Jewish sociologist says in Europe you can tell a Jew by the way he behaves. In Israel you can tell an Arab because he behaves the way a Jew does in Europe. An Arab can be very nice, quiet, cooperative, humble, submissive. But on the other hand, when they are together, they get a lot of self-confidence." Rafi left no doubt about which manner he preferred in Arabs.

These Jews are at the extreme; they are the spokesmen of apartheid, the unalloyed racists, the victims and purveyors of the most corrosive fantasies. They are certainly not endorsed by the majority of Israeli Jews. Yet many elements of their attitude toward Arabs can be found, somewhat diluted, in the broader reservoir of Israeli Jews, for even the most repugnant methods of stereotyping are connected to larger questions of nationalism, military security, and religious homogeneity that find responses in the larger population. The Jews of Mena, for example, begin where many Arabs and many other Jews of Israel begin: They are segregationists. And this grows out of a search for cultural integrity, a yearning for a sanctuary of comfort in being Jewish, a striving varnished with the sheen of morality. "After the Holocaust," Finkelshtein explained, "[we sought] to create a warm corner in this small land to absorb all the Jews who wanted to be absorbed in it. The dead gave us the mission of creating the state."

I asked if any Arabs lived in his building. "Two, to my sorrow," he replied. Then he went on a counterattack. "In Nazareth, they don't allow even one Jew to live in the city. *They* are the chauvinists, and *they* are the racists." His theory has probably not been tested; these days, Jews generally do not try to live in Arab cities and towns. But Finkelshtein touched a point of accuracy about Arab notions of exclusivity. Even those Arabs who endorse mixed neighborhoods are usually thinking in terms of their own freedom to move into better, Jewish areas, not Jews' freedom to move into Arab communities. And beyond Israel's pre-1967 borders, in the occupied West Bank, the Arabs' rejection of Jewish presence takes on a virulent, militant tone as elementary anti-Jewish bigotry is combined with fears of Israel's power to acquire Arab land.

The mood of argument in the Mena organization is one that stimulates revulsion in more moderate quarters where Jews value Jewishness without considering themselves anti-Arab. But the central idea of Jewish homogeneity is one that has broader appeal, and even many of those who bridle at Mena's racism would not find fault with the essential concept as expressed by Mehave Zaharia, thirty, a Mena activist who wears a thick black beard and a knitted kipa, as Israelis call the yarmulke. "I was born in Jerusalem," he said. "I have been here [in Upper Nazareth] seven years. We came from Petah Tikvah [a suburb of Tel Aviv], and they told us it was a Jewish settlement. If we had thought for a moment, even in a million dreams, it would turn even into 10 percent Arab . . ." This is an anti-gentile chauvinism, which focuses on Arabs as the most prevalent non-Jewish group in Israel.

Perhaps the most startling, disturbing version of this viewpoint came from Galila Barkai. She was a handsome, well-groomed woman who spoke fluently and directly in English and who talked persuasively on the subject after classes with students from the high school where she taught. My question on relations among Arab and Jewish children in Upper Nazareth set her off on an explosive, angry, anxious discourse. "My child, my third one, is going this year to the kindergarten, and there are two Arab kids in the kindergarten," she said. "I'll tell you what my fears are. He's a child. They are children. And they don't understand politics and everything else. What will happen if he likes this child and they start playing together and they become very good friends? This is what's happening in Upper Nazareth. When kids are playing together, you can't say anything. How can you tell a child not to play with a kid because he's an Arab? This is the problem." Her voice had been rising steadily, her speech quickening, and she was practically shouting now. "Therefore, I don't want them to come here, because they create this problem! I can't go to my child—he is three years old, and I can't go to him and say, 'Don't play with this kid because he's an Arab.' And they are bringing me to do it someday, because I won't have any other choice!"

Personal friendships, she worried, can soften political resolve. "I have a friend who has a son—he's twelve years old now—and they live in a building where many, many Arab families live, and she is like me, she is against it, and she doesn't want them. But he plays with the Arab kids. So he quarrels with her every day, and he tells her, 'Mother, what do you want? These Arab kids, they don't understand politics, they don't understand anything, and I don't care. I like them, and I play with them, and they are my best friends.' And this is what's going to happen, because you can't stop these kids from playing together!" She was red-faced, shouting. "If they don't move here, there won't be a problem!"

Galila Barkai's two older boys, ages eight and ten, appeared to have gotten the message. "I don't have to tell them not to play with Arabs," she said. "Because they live in my house, they hear my opinion and my husband's opinion. My husband lost a brother in the Yom Kippur War. They are very clever kids. I'm sure they would never go and play with an Arab kid." If anything, they go a little too far, as became clear when one son objected to being treated by an Arab doctor at the local clinic. "But he's an Arab," the boy said to his mother, and she replied, "He is a very good doctor. I just don't want the Arabs to live here, because it is a Jewish city."

"I never talk about politics at school," she said. "I tell them, 'If you want to talk with me about it, later, at my house, after school.' Three days ago a pupil of mine came to me and said, 'Why is it forbidden to sell an apartment to an Arab when he is a citizen of this country?' I said, 'He's a citizen, that's true. I don't say no. But think about if all of us are going to sell our apartments to Arabs. What will happen to Upper Nazareth? One day, in four or five or ten years, one morning we'll open our eyes and we'll find out that Jews in Upper Nazareth are in a minority. What will happen then? We can close the door and take out the key and go away to Europe or Tel Aviv or to Haifa.' " Was the girl persuaded by the argument? "Very much, very much. And her mother met me a day later, and she said, 'You know, we argue about these things very much at home, and we think like you, but the child doesn't think like you, and she didn't think like you, but after she talked to you she was so persuaded.' I talked to her about an hour. I was sitting and talking to her very slowly."

The Jews at the vanguard of Mena's exclusionary efforts also use a powerful amalgam of security, class, and sexual issues to form their images of Arabs. Concisely stated, they argue that young Arab men, freed from any military obligation, have a three-year advantage on their Jewish counterparts in getting started in careers. Working while the Jews are off in uniform, the Arabs make some good money in those years—although they are simultaneously accused of accepting low pay and constituting cheap labor that competes unfairly with Jewish workers. Then they get rich and seduce Jewish girls. "They are richer than us," said Galila Barkai in repeating a common view. "They have money. Three years they don't go into the army. Young soldiers come back here from the army after three years, and sometimes they don't have work because there are no jobs, jobs in many cases occupied by Arabs." She did not seem to know anything about the discrimination that Arabs encounter in the workplace.

"The Arab mother sleeps very well at night," said Finkelshtein. "Nobody takes her sons to war. Her son, when he gets to army age, doesn't go to the army. He makes money. Our sons, Jewish sons, give the best three years of their life and serve until fifty-five [in the reserves], and some of us go on to serve until death releases us."

He added the final concern. "One of the problems we consider very grave, both from a religious point of view and a national point of view, is that already in Israel there are thousands of Jewish girls who have married Arabs," he said, again using figures that are probably exaggerated. "There is no opposite process. Arabs don't allow their daughters to marry Jews. Children born to mixed couples won't want to fight against their relatives, so the Israeli army will lose whole divisions of soldiers."

Rafi then spoke up with a slight smile on his lips, though his eyes were as cold as bullets. "Love is more dangerous than hate," he said. "It's dangerous to our existence."

TEN

Sexual Fears and Fantasies

Daughter of Israel! . . . Beware of the Arab,
who seeks only your shame
and disgrace.
—A handbill of the Kach movement

"LOVE IS MORE DANGEROUS THAN HATE." RAFI'S STRANGE SMILE
hardened the mood in the room, and none of the other Jewish Defenders
of Upper Nazareth winced. I stared at the man. He was thirty-eight and
thin, intense. His pasty skin was stretched tightly against his bald skull.
"I have a B.A. in psychology," he declared, providing the credentials
that enabled him to hold forth on the danger of love. Far from provoking
revulsion, his remark released a burst of passion from the others on the
obscenity of intermarriage, on the risk of rape. It quickly became clear
that the aversions to Arabs as dirty, noisy, rich, violent, primitive, lazy,
uppity, and thieving were laced with a powerful fear of the alleged sexual

prowess of Arab men and the designs they were imagined to have on Jewish women. There was a strong sexual tint to the recurring specter of Arabs sitting with Jewish women and children in underground shelters while the Jewish men were off at war. It had never happened in significant scope as far as I could determine (since the last war that had sent Upper Nazareth residents into shelters had been in 1973, before significant numbers of Arabs began moving in), but the Defenders painted the picture so vividly in the imagination that I could see it myself: Here were the Arabs, dark and rough and good-looking, stuck for hours below ground with lithe, gentle Jewish girls and women unable (or perhaps unwilling?) to defend themselves against the advances of the Arab men. How the Arab rapists were to do their dastardly deeds with their own wives and children present in the shelters was a question never addressed. The fearsome picture simply excluded Arab women and children; they would have disturbed the wonderful flow of fantasy.

It is a remarkable fact of prejudice that the features applied to the hated group become universal. The dirtiness, laziness, sneaky greed, and sexual prowess have been attributed to many targets of bigotry in quite varied circumstances and cultures. The sexual stereotype in particular has been used against American blacks by whites, against Europeans in China and Japan, against European Jews by gentiles, and now against Arabs by Israeli Jews. The theme can also be found in some Arab images of Jews.[63]

Sexuality acts like a subtle magnet in talk about Arabs, drawing the conversation along an unrelenting path to the lurking fears. Again and again, discussions begin at one point and end at the sexual threat. This happened on the morning of my second visit to Upper Nazareth, when I went to see a high-ranking police officer. He spoke too candidly and without the required approval from his superiors to be comfortable with his name in print. My purpose was to get a clear, official report on allegations that Jewish militants had stood in front of apartments and physically prevented Arab families from moving in, had broken into Arabs' homes and threatened them if they did not get out. The officer began properly, carefully. "No one wants the Arabs here," he said. "But it's forbidden for us {the police} to have a position. We're set up to enforce the law." Two months earlier, he confirmed, Jews had organized a break-in of an apartment on Israel Street being rented by an Arab family. More recently, about twenty or thirty Jews had stood at an apartment entrance and denied entry to an Arab woman and her son who already lived there. It had happened in the quiet light of a September Friday afternoon, the calming hours before Shabbat Eve. The officer went personally, and told the protesters: "It's Friday afternoon. Let's leave the status quo. Everyone go back to your houses, and on Sunday we'll deal with it." So, he continued, "Sunday morning I summoned the [Jewish] group, and I said to them unambiguously that from the point of view of the law, they have no case. The moment they break the law, we'll arrest all of them. If Arabs complain, we'll protect them."

Gradually as we talked, the officer dropped his mask of formal impartiality. "As a man, I understand these people, not as an officer of the law," he said. "As an officer of the law I summoned them and warned them that if they broke the law I would arrest all of them. But there is a problem of culture. On Yom Kippur, when everyone is walking, the Arab will go in his car when it's clear that it will be annoying. They [the Jews] complain that 'we go to reserve duty, and they stay and make parties, bring all kinds of people, we don't know them, have lots of children,' and they say, 'Would they accept me down there?' " meaning in the Arab city of "lower Nazareth." And then the officer leaned forward, as if he were going to express the final, ultimate truth of the situation. "There hasn't been a case of an Arab girl getting involved with a Jewish man. But there are many cases of Jewish girls of fourteen pregnant by Arabs."

"Oh," I asked, "how many?"

"Many."

"How many?"

"A lot."

"Yes, but what are the figures?"

"I don't have the figures here. But don't forget, when a Jewish boy goes to the army at eighteen, and he comes home every two weeks, they [the Arabs] are working. He [the Arab] has a nice car, he strolls around. I have lived in Upper Nazareth for twenty years. Twenty years ago an Arab didn't dare to go up after dark to Upper Nazareth. Today a Jew doesn't dare to go down to Nazareth after dark. Twenty years ago a girl wouldn't dare to go with an Arab. There was one case eighteen years ago, and they shaved her head in the center of Upper Nazareth. Today in the middle of the day they dare to fool around with girls and yell that we're a democracy and we do what we want." Arabs had moved into the high-ranking police officer's block, and he planned to sell his apartment and get out; he had recently begun building himself a house on the edge of town.

"Now," scoffed Monira Abud, the Arab woman who had lived in the town since 1973, "they're saying, 'Arabs are going after our Jewish daughters.' " She sniffed. "If she wants an Arab she can go to Nazareth, she can go to Hebron." In other words, a loose girl doesn't have to wait for opportunity to move next door.

Indeed, the Jewish fears seem to divide into two parts—the fear of rape and the fear of naive girls' being easily seduced. The specter of seduction is a major theme of the incessant campaign against Arabs by Meir Kahane's Kach movement, which distributes leaflets on university campuses warning Jewish women not to date Arab men. One in Hebrew reads:

> Daughter of Israel!
> You are the daughter of a great people, chosen and special, the People of Israel. Don't befoul yourself. Don't bring shame upon yourself.
> Don't go out with Arabs and goys of any kind. . . . Beware of the Arab, who seeks only your shame and disgrace.
> Daughter of Israel, befriend only sons of Israel!
> And son of Israel—
> You are called to join the "Jewish honor patrol" in your region. The patrol will take the responsibility of reducing the contamination and assimilation of Jewesses and Jews.

Another Kach handbill, in English, is directed at American Jews and others from the Diaspora who study for a time at Israeli universities. One side is printed with huge letters: "JEWISH WOMAN WE WANT YOU!" Below is a quotation purportedly from an Arab student named Hussein: "Arab students in Israeli universities fare somewhat better with foreign Jewish girl students, who are perhaps attracted by the handsome and exotic foreignness of the Arab," and then a comment from an unidentified "lecturer": "The best way of screwing the Jewish state is to screw a Jewish girl and broadcast the fact as widely as possible." On the back, a detailed message appears:

Welcome home! Welcome to your land of Israel. . . . We wish to draw your attention to a very immediate danger that is ever-present. THAT DANGER INVOLVES THE ARAB, AND ESPECIALLY STUDENT, WHO QUITE OFTEN POSES AS A JEWISH IS-RAELI, for the purpose of sexual relations with Jewish girls from foreign countries. This is NOT merely fear of what MIGHT happen; it already has, many times, to the girl's great grief.

Jewish woman! You did not come to Israel to be LESS Jewish or to live the life of a gentilized person. You came here to be part of the Jewish people, YOUR people, in your Jewish state. . . . If you meet an Israeli who asks you to go out with him, ask him for his TEUDAT Z'HUT, identity card. There is a place for his name. All too often, the one who says his name is MOSHE is really the Arab, Musa. There is a place, too, for "nationality" (in Hebew, *leum*). See if it says the word *"Yehudi,"* Jew. If you cannot read Hebrew, ask someone. DON'T BE ASHAMED. Believe us, you will save yourself great heartache. . . . If you do meet an Arab, DO NOT GET INVOLVED WITH HIM AT ALL. Do not feel sorry for him. Remember that their classic line is to win your sympathy. . . . DATE ONLY JEWS. And date the kind of person you would want to marry because he RESPECTS you. The Arab does not. He wants you only for sex and . . . because this is his way of getting at Jews.

Some right-wing Jews, including Kahane's followers at Hebrew University, harass Jewish women they see walking with Arab men. So zealous are the assaults that an Arab woman student I knew became a target because her light hair and complexion usually led people to mistake her for a Jew; when she strolled or stood talking with Arab male students on campus, she was often taunted and threatened by Jewish toughs who didn't realize she was Arab, who thought they had come across one of those scandalous Jewish-Arab couples.

Part of the aversion to Arab-Jewish sexual relationships is based on a general apprehension, particularly strong among the Orthodox, about the dilution and assimilation of the Jewish people. Opposition exists to Jews' marrying any non-Jews, Arab or otherwise; as the most numerous gentiles in and around Israel, Arabs therefore become the main focus of the anxiety. In 1980, for example, the Hasidic movement Agudath Israel passed a resolution expressing concern that the open Israeli-Egyptian border, which resulted from the peace treaty between the two countries, could "stimulate assimilation and intermarriage for Israeli Jews" and Egyptian Arabs. In a similar vein, a leader of Agudath Israel, Rabbi Eliezer Shach, who was co-chairman of the Council of Torah Sages, once told a small meeting attended by my friend David Harman that wars between Israel and the Arabs were good; otherwise, he said, Jewish girls would be studying in Cairo, Arab boys would be studying at Hebrew University, and look what would happen.

Nevertheless, considerably more emotion is aroused by Jewish women's involvement with Arabs than, say, with American Protestants or European Christians who volunteer on kibbutzim. The threatening image of the macho Arab is deeply ingrained in Israeli Jewish society, and outrage over promiscuity by Jewish girls is intensified if their partners are Arabs. Sometimes it even becomes news, as it did for Israeli Army Radio, which reported once that Arabs with fancy cars were seducing fifteen-year-old Jewish girls. A leading Hebrew-language newspaper carried a story about Jewish girls' selling themselves for drugs—to Arabs! The emphasis of alarm was less on the drugs or the prostitution than on the fact that the clients were Arabs. And as David Harman noted, "If a Bedouin rapes a Jewish girl, it's a sensational story for the papers, but if a Jewish beach bum rapes a Scandinavian tourist, it's just a little story."

Rumors fly wildly. During the 1973 war, Israeli troops were telling each other that a Syrian army unit had surrounded a kibbutz full of women and girls. "It was auto-suggestive," said an Israeli intelligence officer. "What would I do in a case like that?"

Adi Halpern, a Likud politician in Tel Aviv, even came up with a story about a Jaffa rabbi locating some 500 Jewish women who had been kidnapped and/or raped by Arabs and taken into the West Bank before 1967, when the territory was still under Jordanian control. There, Halpern said, they bore children and continued living with the Arabs as quasi-prisoners. I tried mightily to find some thread of truth to this tale, and finally concluded that at most, it may have been woven extravagantly out of an incident or two.

Given the strong feelings about Arabs' raping Jews, police statistics might be expected to give an accurate picture. But officials do not seem interested in getting past the myths and into the facts. Yehezkel Carthy, chief of investigations for the Israeli national police, had nothing to offer except his "impression" that "almost half" of all rape cases that are taken to court, when they occur between strangers, involve Arab men attacking Jewish women. There were no figures to back up his estimate, Carthy said, because official policy bars the collection of crime statistics on the basis of ethnic, national, or religious origin. The Justice Ministry gave the same reply.

Even if Carthy's impression is accepted, however, it emerges as less dramatic than it sounds. The percentage of cases involving Arabs would naturally be greater in the category of rape involving strangers—the basis for Carthy's estimate—than in the other major grouping, those where rapist and victim know each other; very few Arabs know Jews intimately enough to be accused of raping them, and so the overall proportion of Arab involvement in both categories taken together would have to be considerably below Carthy's "almost half." And since Arabs in Israel, the West Bank, and the Gaza Strip constitute about 36 percent of the total population under Israeli control, the incidence may not be disproportionately high.

Cultural taboos and other attitudes probably distort both the pattern of rape and the reporting of the crime. Because Arab society is fraught with sexual restrictions, and Jewish society is relatively permissive, Jewish women present greater opportunity to the rapist, Carthy observed. "Many [Arabs] own cars and drive to work every day," he said. "Whenever they encounter a girl hitchhiking, they would offer her a lift. The habits of the Arab girls—conservative dress, even fear of strangers," work against their traveling alone or being in a situation conducive to rape, he explained. "Our Jewish girls wear negligible clothing, speak to strangers, agree to go to a café or a discothèque." In addition, the penalties exacted by Arab society are considerably more severe than the Israeli legal punishments for rape. "They would hesitate to do anything to one of their own girls because of fear of revenge," Carthy said; an Arab girl's brothers or father would be likely to murder a man who raped her. In very traditional Arab households, the girl herself would be killed if she had premarital intercourse, even against her will, to restore the honor of the family; it is a custom that deters Arab victims from reporting rape. "We do have such cases sometimes, but very seldom," Carthy said.

Israeli police and prosecutors also seem inclined to take complaints about Arabs' raping Jews more seriously than those about Jews' raping Jews. In Israel as elsewhere, a male bias infects police work, with officers often implying that the woman somehow invited the attack by her suggestive dress or manner. If a Jewish woman accuses an Arab stranger rather than a Jew, this innuendo of female responsibility for rape is much less credible, and one that law-enforcement officials are less likely to want to believe. Consequently, it is reasonable to suspect that a higher percentage of Jewish-Arab accusations than Jewish-Jewish accusations are prosecuted. Finally, Jewish women are more inclined to report rapes by Arabs than by Jews, according to Menachem Amir, a criminologist at Hebrew University, and women soldiers who are raped almost always report the crimes if the rapists are Arabs. "I think it seems much more of an affront," he said. "There are some cases of university girls' sleeping with Arabs who pass as Jews. Then they discover it and cry help."

Suggestive comments by Arabs on the street seem to provoke considerably more annoyance among many Jewish women than do similar remarks by Jews. A Jerusalem secretary disliked walking past a certain construction site near her office. "The Arab workers make comments," she said. Sara Widlanski, a Jewish teacher of Arabic, found waiting for buses every evening in Tel Aviv quite uncomfortable because at her stop— a collection point for Arab workers—groups of Arab men made remarks loudly among themselves and sometimes to her, perhaps not realizing that she understood their Arabic but at the same time wanting her to know that they were talking about her. Somehow, the brashness of the Arabs struck her as possessive, her husband, Michael, said, and since she felt this was her country, not theirs, she found the behavior more offensive than when it came from Jews. At times, however, the antics reached a level that would have been intolerable from Jews or anyone else, she said, as when an Arab once walked out of his group of friends at the bus stop, came close to her, and urinated on the sidewalk.

Michael felt that from time to time a kind of group psychology of brash ribaldry operated among Arabs when enough of them encountered lone Jewish women. In broad daylight while waiting at Jerusalem's central bus station, he saw a group of five Arab workmen "walking along the sidewalk accosting every lone woman they could find. Usually the woman would briskly walk away, and the Arab workers would follow. I couldn't hear what they were saying, although I would assume they were making remarks that amounted to a proposition. The apparent fear or discomfort of the woman produced laughter among the workers."

"The way they look at a woman," said Sara, "they're very, very erotic the way they look, your eyes, if they are a light color. If I go to the market, the *souk*, I get a great price just because of my eyes. They would say, "I take 10 percent off for your eyes.' I would start to speak Arabic, and they would say, 'Another 10 percent.' They're very physical. Arab students in the university, when they talk to you, they go like this." And she put her hand on Michael's knee. "They wouldn't do it to an Arab. That's why I'm so insulted."

The image of the sexually aggressive Arab is so overpowering that young Jewish women are often advised against going into Arab neighborhoods and villages. Jewish women who live in Arab towns as part of their work with Interns for Peace are greeted with sheer astonishment. "Jewish bus drivers, Arab bus drivers, practically everybody will say to a woman intern who is going to Kfar Qara, 'What? That's an Arab village, you know that? What are you doing there?' " said Deborah Reich. "If it's a Jew, they'll go on and say, 'It's dangerous. What's a woman doing alone there?' The oddest assortment of people bring this up with me."

Policemen and soldiers sometimes stop and question mixed couples they see. Raja Shehadeh, the Arab lawyer from the West Bank, was halted by Israeli policemen in a jeep while he was strolling in the hills with a Jewish woman after dark. "They started asking her if she was Jewish," he said. "They made very strong insinuations of sexual relations. We walked around, and then they met us once again on the way to my house. They said, 'Be healthy, look after your health,' implying a lot of sexual things, which was very disturbing, so much stressing that she was Jewish." This became more explicit one evening when Raja was driving a Jewish woman home. Two Arab policemen stopped them in Jerusalem, he writes in *The Third Way*. "We have orders to take in for questioning any Jewish woman seen with an Arab," he quotes one of the policemen as saying. When Raja asked the officer what kind of orders, "he became a bit incoherent, but it turns out that these are unofficial, standing orders, issued by the military to the local civilian police." Finally the couple was allowed to drive on after promising "never to do it again."

To some extent, the image is reinforced in Israeli cinema and Hebrew literature. A 1983 film entitled *Drifting*, about the homosexual scene in Tel Aviv, contains two Arab workers who are given an aura of super-masculinity. "Arabs as phallic symbols," Dan Fainaru wrote in a *Jerusalem Post* review, "recall the similar use of 'black studs' in a certain kind of American literature, and not the best one." The image shows up occasionally in children's literature as well, which sometimes portrays Arab attackers as bent on raping Jewish women. Zvi Lieberman's *In the Hills of Jerusalem* has a conversation between Arabs on the warpath. "Someone asked: 'Will there be enough women for each one of us?' '*Inshallah*, there will be enough. The brilliant fighters who excel in the battle will get an additional one as well.' "[64] Gershon Shaked, writing about the Arab image in Hebrew literature, saw Arab characters not only as "the mythical embodiment of Jewish fears" but also as "the mythical embodiment of Jewish yearnings for the true masculine strength which is to be found in the anti-norm . . . because it is not found in the norm."[65] In this vein, of course, sex is not merely sex; it is also possession and power.

Similar stereotypes of Jews occur occasionally in Arab attitudes, although with somewhat less prominence. A 1979 edition of *The Wailing Wall and Tears* by Anis Mansur, editor of the Egyptian journal *October*, asserts that Jews are instructed by their faith to "ravish all women of other religions." Among lurid propaganda paintings found after the 1967 war at a girls' school in Khan Yunis, in the Gaza Strip, was one of Jewish fighters attacking Arab women. The Jews look like pirates with their wild beards, hooked noses, and sinister eyes. One holds a rifle in the air; another leans over a girl, choking her; and a third, glaring salaciously from under a helmet emblazoned with a Star of David, is clawing at a woman's blue robe. One of her shoulders is already bare, and one arm covers half her face, which is frozen in a look of alarm and terror.

Raja Shehadeh writes of the Israeli occupiers of the West Bank in sexual terms, then abruptly apologizes for doing so and blames his state of mind on the state of occupation. "Since the occupation, I have begun to think of our hills as 'virginal', 'molested' by the Israeli bulldozers—the bulldozers that have for me become the symbol of the Israeli power over us. I am sure that my imagery would not be so replete with sexual-political symbols were I left to the privacy of my feelings. I can thank our occupiers, then, among other things, for instilling in me a political pornographer's eye for this land."[66]

Sometimes, but not often, Arabs accuse Jews of making sexual advances. After Israeli border policemen were stationed on Jerusalem's Temple Mount to protect the Dome of the Rock from Jewish extremists' bombs, the mufti of Jerusalem, Sheikh Sa'd Eddin Alami, issued an angry accusation against the troops: "[They] conducted themselves in a manner which is inconsistent with the sanctity of this holy mosque. In other words, some of them have been noticed making unbecoming gestures to passing girls, for instance."

Jamil Hamad told me at length about a conversation he had in 1975 with the head of an Arab government—whom he asked not to be named—who believed the most fantastic nonsense about Israelis' locking up Palestinian women in a prison and raping them every night. Jamil, who travels throughout much of the Arab world, was sent to the Arab prime minister, "Mr. J.," by a mutual friend who felt the leader needed to be better informed about Israel. " 'Go and educate that idiot,' " Jamil quoted his friend as telling him. " 'But I warn you, be a good listener, and don't use English expressions.' I said, why? 'They have a very terrible complex about people using English words mixed into the Arabic. They start hating you.' I went, he was very cordial, he offered me tea, and he began to chat, etc., etc., and he said to me, 'Tell me what's going on on the West Bank.' I said, 'It's very difficult for me to review the situation on the West Bank; I know you are a very busy person; I appreciate the fact that you're giving me ten minutes.' He said, 'No, no. I'm giving you two hours.' And I began to tell him things about the West Bank and Gaza. And I intentionally tried my best to be objective, very objective. He said to me, 'How many Palestinian prisoners in Israeli jails? I said, 'Mr. J., let me be honest with you. I had a chance to have a dinner with the Red Cross representative in Jerusalem two months ago in one of the Arab houses in Ramallah. . . . He felt free, he was so friendly, we were drinking, and he said to me, "I don't know, I feel I can trust you." I said to him, "Look, I know this is a Western approach: You want me to keep this trust, I promise you." And he gave me the number—in those days something like 6,200 Palestinians.' The reaction came just like that," Jamil said. The Arab leader was skeptical that the figure wasn't higher, and the dialogue that followed provided an insight into the high-level convictions about Israeli monstrosity.

The prime minister interrogated Jamil about the Red Cross representative. "Where is he from?" he asked.

"I don't know," said Jamil, "but I think he is either French or Swiss. And, Mr. J., you know those people are picked very carefully."

"I'm sure he's a Jew," the prime minister declared.

"I don't know."

"What about the Israeli prison for Palestinian women in Ramallah?"

"Mr. J., what are you talking about?"

"Do you know where Ramallah is?"

"I think so," Jamil replied sarcastically.

Here Jamil paused to explain. "Now the conflict started to emerge. He wanted to give me a slap, spit in my face. 'Do you know where is Ramallah?' I said, 'I think so.' "

From there the conversation continued:

"How frequently do you go to Ramallah?" the head of government asked Jamil.

"Twice a week, sometimes every day," Jamil replied, "and I know Ramallah as I know my bedroom."

"Have you seen the newly built Israeli prison for the Arab women in Ramallah?"

"No, Mr. J., I know the military prison in Ramallah, which is located in the building built by the British Mandate authorities, and it's a very small prison, can accommodate only fifty people or something. The main prison on the West Bank is in Nablus, unless they take prisoners to Israel."

"I'm talking about the prison for women."

"There is no such prison in Ramallah. There is an annex in the Russian Compound prison for women, and it's against the laws in Israel to put a woman behind bars with men. I tell you, anyone who did it would be kicked out."

"I'm not talking about that, I'm talking about a prison."

"Look, Mr. J., I don't have any idea about it, so please tell me."

Jamil sighed and smiled and told of what followed.

"He told me the following: that Israelis built in 1971 a huge prison near Ramallah, two kilometers from Ramallah, and it's only for Arab women. He looked into papers in front of him and said, 'Something like 6,500 Arab women are jailed there, and it's guarded by Israelis, and in the evenings, the doors of the cells are opened, and the Israeli soldiers get into the cells where they can make love with the Arabs. You did not hear that?'

"Now, David, at that point, I was facing a very terrible psychological conflict with myself. It was in my mind, and I knew if I was going to come to him, he would give me trouble. And if I would say to him, yes, then I'll feel guilty all my life, because I lied, because I bought a lie. And it was a real war inside me. And a minute passed, a minute of silence passed. And I said to him, 'Mr. J., I have to tell you something. If you want to screw Israel politically, to scandalize Israel at the United Nations Security Council, in the nonalignment conferences, come to me. I'll give you stories. I'll give you facts. But please, Mr. J., don't take this story to anyplace, because they will make a big joke at you. This is an unfounded story, no grounds, no merits. It's imagination, and I'm sorry, I have to tell you that he who sold you this idea deceived you, cheated you.'

"And he got angry at me. He said, 'This is our intelligence.' I said, "If your intelligence can count Palestinian women in jail, how many settlements have been built on the West Bank?' He said three hundred. I said, 'No, ninety-eight.' He said, 'I'm so sorry that Israel has succeeded in making a Palestinian defend the Zionist entity.' I talked back to him and said, 'I am a very nationalistic Palestinian. After living under oc-cupation, I know the weapon I can fight Israel with—the facts.' And I left. That evening my friend came to me with a bottle of Scotch and said, 'Jamil, you made him so angry. He hated you.' "

Since each side believes that the other is eager to rape its women, calm assessments of actual attitudes and practices become difficult. To some extent, the cultural taboos and the political emotions seem to enhance the attraction of sex across the Arab-Jewish barrier, lending an additional bit of excitement to the fantasy and the encounter. On the other hand, certain ingredients of prejudice, especially Jews' negative images of Arabs, also repel and inhibit desire for sexual contact, and many Jews are adamant in their conviction that Jewish men have no interest in Arab women. A different assessment came from Arthur Kutcher, the Yale-educated ar-chitect whose army buddies on the West Bank were so vocal in their contempt for Arabs. Amid the storm of hateful images ran a current of lust. "The myth among the boys was that the greatest prize one could get was an Arab girl," Kutcher said, "because they're so hard to get, because their own society keeps them under such close control." One morning, the Don Juan of the unit, on guard at the building used in Nablus by the Ministry of Interior, "struck up a conversation with an Arab girl who was reported to be very 'white'—that is, looking like an 'English girl'—and this was apparently an even greater prize. Later in the morning he went to his duty post, which was on the roof of the building, and she threw him her gold necklace, which was quite a suspicious act. The border policeman who was on duty noticed this," and when the two were about to meet, he was taken into custody by the military police and transferred elsewhere. The military commander of Nablus, who confirmed the account, told me that soldiers are under strict orders not to fraternize with Arab women, both to avoid entrapment and blackmail and to minimize the possibility of violating Arab mores.

Paragraph Five of the classified instructions to Israeli troops on the West Bank is headed "The Arab Woman." It declares:

> The residents of the occupied territories have a very special sensitivity to the behavior of others toward their women, and so you must observe the following rules:
>
> A. You are forbidden to touch the body of the women.
>
> B. You must refrain from any connection—overt or covert—with Arab women.
>
> C. You don't search the bodies or clothes of women.
>
> D. If you are compelled to stop women and bring them to a place of detention, do this with all necessary firmness, but without any injury and all in the presence of the family.
>
> E. Do not say anything or do anything or make hints that could be construed as hurting women.

Some Jews with military experience expressed skepticism that Kutcher's soldiers were typical. Danny Rubinstein, the West Bank correspondent for *Davar*, and Ze'ev Schiff, the military correspondent for *Haaretz*, doubted that Israeli troops were attracted to Arab women, citing as evidence the absence of rape (hardly conclusive, since sexual attraction can take forms other than rape). Menachem Amir, the criminologist, agreed that few Arabs were raped by Jewish soldiers. During the 1948 war, there were about twenty reported cases, he said, six during the 1956 campaign, six during the 1967 war, and no more than twenty since the occupation began in 1967. Local Lebanese officials, including the mayors of some of the cities occupied by the Israeli army after the 1982 invasion, told me that there had been no problem of rape. Even allowing for the Arab women's fear of reporting rape, Amir said, studies showed that "Arabs rape Jews, and Jews rape Jews, but very few Jews rape Arabs. It is very rare. One of the reasons is the distaste of Jewish boys for Arab women, especially when they are Muslim, as if they are not clean." This stereotype of Arab women as unclean has created some bizarre behavior. Amir helped investigate one case in which three soldiers who raped an Arab girl provoked a disgusted reaction from other men in their unit. "They said, 'How can they do it? They are dirty,' " he reported. In another incident near the road that descends from Jerusalem through the Judean Desert to Jericho, "Three soldiers raped a Bedouin woman," Amir said, "and before, they washed her."

The *hamsiin*, an irritating, dusty desert wind, blows for several days at a time, mostly in the weeks following Passover. It pesters Israel with a dry, gritty heat that scratches away freshness, turns the air yellow, sifts into the parched crevices of the skin. Its smothering annoyance even conquers the evening and the night, making the darkness stale, and stifling the usual coolness that comes with sundown. As the wind nags, the days and nights hover, unmoving, squabbling into electric tension, raising tempers. Voices crack and sharpen shrilly.

Hamsiin is the Arabic word for "fifty," used because the wind traditionally blew for a total of about fifty days out of the year. And it drives people a little crazy after a while. Once, in Jerusalem, on the second or third day, someone said that a biblical scholar had developed a theory that a *hamsiin* had been blowing when Jesus was judged and crucified. We all nodded, understanding.

For months, it seemed that all of Israel was talking about the film entitled *Hamsiin*, a powerful vignette of Arab-Jewish friction, comradeship, and lust. Produced by Jews with both Jewish and Arab actors, it represents part of a recent genre that has begun to address the pathology of hatred with a frank sensitivity.

The film starts with music by a flute and drums, and then the first line is spoken, in Arabic, on the eternal issue: "It seems that they're going to seize the land." The land is in the Galilee, where the scene opens in a vision of harmony broken by anger. As Gedaliah the Jewish farmer and his handsome Arab farmhand Khaled work together with cattle in the fields, Khaled's hot-headed cousin Ibrahim sneaks up to a surveyor's hut, setting it on fire, to fight the first step by the government toward confiscating his family's acreage. Gedaliah chases Ibrahim, catches him, and puts him into a jeep, but instead of turning him over to the police takes him back to be reprimanded by his family in the neighboring village. The family is grateful to Gedaliah, and the father lectures Ibrahim sternly: "They're Jews, but they're our neighbors." The young man replies, "They just want to take our lands; they shake our hands and throw us out." Gedaliah suggests that the Arab family sell its land to him before the government takes it; he wants to expand his holdings into his dream—a full-fledged cattle ranch. The Arab family considers, visiting Gedaliah, exchanging blessings in Hebrew and Arabic, and finally agrees to sell.

Hamsiin explores Khaled's divided loyalties as an Israeli Arab working for a Jew, and it peels off the layers of Gedaliah's tolerance until the core of ugliness is revealed. No other film during my five years in Israel made such an impact, stirred such conversation and debate. It laid bare the profound pain of the Arab-Jewish struggle.

Khaled and Gedaliah are bound by the kind of friendship men have when they work together in the fields, a rough fellowship and admiration in which they joke and horse around, wrestling and laughing; once, they spray each other playfully with a water hose. But as the specter of land confiscation looms, Khaled's friends, a group of young, unmarried Arab men, begin to criticize his closeness to Gedaliah, calling him a Jew-lover. Hostility grows. Arabs begin to vandalize farming equipment. Some newly planted avocado trees are uprooted from Gedaliah's fields. His water pipe is broken. He asks Khaled if he knows who is responsible; Khaled replies that he does not. Strains then develop between the two of them, and between the two communities. A Jewish theater owner kicks Arabs out of a movie. Khaled and a friend stab an Arab who has been serving as an informer to the Jews. A group of Jewish toughs comes in the night to the shack on Gedaliah's farm where Khaled sleeps, awakening him and threatening him. Gedaliah comes to his rescue, throwing the thugs off his land, and Khaled runs to warn an Arab friend that they are coming his way. Moments later, the Jewish thugs swagger up to the friend's watermelon stand and force the Arab to cut open a watermelon for their inspection, like Southern rednecks harassing their "nigger." Haughtily, they reject the watermelon and make him cut another, and another, and then start pushing the Arab around; in the struggle, the Arab stabs one of the Jews in the shoulder, and the Jews beat both him and Khaled.

The next day, Khaled stays away from work; Gedaliah goes to the village to find him, to persuade him to return. "What has happened here?" he asks Khaled. "People have lost their heads. But you and I, we're different."

As the friction rubs raw like the irritation of the *hamsiin*, Gedaliah's sister Hava, a music student, arrives home from Jerusalem for the summer. She has done little during the year but sleep, does not want a career in music, and now decides sullenly to move into and rehabilitate an old house nearby that used to belong to her grandfather. Khaled offers to help her. Slowly, gently, the film portrays their growing affection in smoldering glances, gestures of infatuation against the tightening background beyond them. Once she is undressing when she notices Khaled watching her through the window. She meets his eyes and continues to disrobe completely, looking at him the whole time. She plays with him a bit, driving him at night into an abandoned part of the farm, letting him kiss her, hold her, then abruptly instructing him, "I want you to get out now, Khaled." As they ride one day in her jeep past a group of Jews, one asks, "Who was that in the jeep with Hava?" The reply: "Her Arab."

Gradually, the ardor between them builds as the tension rises between the Arabs and the Jews. The Arab family, afraid of retaliation, calls off its deal to sell land to Gedaliah. Gedaliah finally realizes that Khaled is falling for his sister. And finally, Gedaliah watches through the window as Khaled and Hava make love, Khaled writhing on top of her like a great, muscular bull. You see only her face, not his, as if he were nothing but a hunk of animal flesh. Gedaliah, nauseated, waits for revenge against his friend.

It comes the next morning. Khaled is fixing a fence inside one of the narrow, barred cattle runs. And in deliberate madness, Gedaliah opens a gate to let a bull in from the pen. The bull lowers its horns and charges down the length of the run, plunging into Khaled, goring him to death, emerging with a bloody horn. Gedaliah, shaking, climbs into the jeep and hides his eyes behind a pair of mirror sunglasses that reflect a distorted image of the land. At last, the rain washes clean the spot where Khaled has died. Little wild flowers are beginning to grow there. The film ends, and the audience is silent for a long moment.

"The movie is not about Khaled and Hava," said the director, Danny Waxman. "It is not a love story. The part that's more important to me is about the Khaled-Gedaliah relationship. Some people say I'm not optimistic enough. By nature I am optimistic. But the longer I live here, the less optimistic I get."

Arab-Jewish love stories do have a place in Israeli film and Hebrew literature, but they are almost always burdened by tragedy. *Hamsiin*, for example, was followed by *Pressure*, a film by Michele Ohayon about free-loving students who confront the security apparatus of the state. After a romp of lovemaking, Raif, the Arab, has left Yoma's bed, and she is alone. Suddenly Israeli security agents burst into her room looking for her lover on the suspicion that he is part of a planned terrorist attack. After they find and arrest him, Yoma searches in vain for help from her friends, from her father. "We kept telling you this would be nothing but trouble," her father says when she stops by his textile shop. "He'll drag you down with him. People here don't get arrested for nothing. You are killing us. Your mother is sick. She won't be able to stand this." Yoma replies, "You always taught me not to abandon friends," and she goes on trying until she herself is picked up by Shin Beth agents who want to use her to make Raif talk. They take her to headquarters at the Russian Compound. "You can't keep me here," she says. "I'm not Arab." But she is dumped into a cell with foul-mouthed Jewish prostitutes who talk obscenely about Arabs: "They're ass-fuckers, all of them," one says. Yoma protests the slurs, saying she would date an Arab. "You Arab's whore!" one of the prostitutes shouts. "You're worse than an Arab!"

When Yoma is later released, she finds refined Jewish society more polite but no more helpful. She goes to a liberal Jewish advocate of Arab rights, who explains that his group can't appear to be supporting terrorists. A sympathetic professor says he hasn't been able to find a lawyer who will touch the case. Her landlord terminates her lease. In desperation, she tells the Shin Beth she will help them if she can see Raif. They give her the questions to ask him, and she is led in. She and Raif hold hands across the table.

"I love your eyes," Yoma says.

"The only part of me they haven't touched." His face is bruised.

"They say you see terrorists."

"You, of all people, mustn't question me."

In the end, the Shin Beth decides he is not involved and sets him free. But the love affair cannot survive. When Yoma goes to his village to find him, she overhears friends talking about his imminent marriage to an Arab woman. She watches him from a distance, and then departs.

There is grinding fury, lacerating guilt, in this contemporary Israeli treatment of personal lives torn by the larger conflict. Blame has an edge, but it includes both sides, for the films often respond to the concerns of both the Jewish and Arab actors who play the roles, and who sometimes rewrite the scripts as they go.

By contrast, earlier works, especially books and stories written before the creation of the state, have an apolitical, *Romeo and Juliet* quality about them, diffusing blame into a blurry cultural conflict. Yehuda Burla, a writer in Hebrew who was born in Jerusalem in 1886 and resided in Damascus after World War I, accomplished moving portraits of Jews and Arabs in love. In "Secret Love," he draws a delicate picture of an unresolved affair between Gideon, a young Jew lounging against a fig tree, and Hamda, the younger sister of his Arab partner, who has returned after four years. Gideon suddenly finds her grown, and beautiful, and they fall into a furtive lovemaking embellished by beautiful words. The story ends with a speech of warning from Gideon's friend that he is toying with danger.

Burla's *In Darkness Striving* is a powerful novel set in Damascus, where an itinerant Jewish peddler of dresses and jewelry, Rahamo, a merry man who always eyes the girls, falls in love with a Muslim woman, Shafikah. She is divorced, but her former husband's brothers have sworn to kill anyone who marries her. Rahamo, who is already married, contrives to visit her village often, where her father puts him up for the night and welcomes him warmly. The Jew makes loans to her father at generous terms, and the family grows fond of him, not suspecting the surreptitious love he and Shafikah share. But when the brothers discover their affair, they waylay Rahamo on the road and blind him by pouring a scorching substance into his eyes. Shafikah loses her sanity, her family ties her to the bed to keep her from slipping out of the house, and she finally drowns herself in a river. Like Job, Rahamo struggles with his faith, his God, and his affliction, and under the tutelage of a wise and kindly Muslim sheikh, he attains spiritual freedom in the end. In stitching his rich embroidery of culture and scene, Burla also attains something unusual: His Arabs and Jews are not the ordinary cardboard characters but real people, each with his own defect and strength, wickedness and generosity.

．　．　．

The Arab village of Peqi'in is very relaxing. Surrounded by olive groves and tobacco fields in Israel's northern Galilee, the ancient town enjoys the slow tranquility of bucolic beauty among gardens and patios wild with woven grapevines and flowers. The old stone and concrete houses spill across a wadi and climb a terraced hillside in the warm, comforting sunlight of spring. A few miles north of here, in Lebanon, Arabs of various religions and groupings are enmeshed in bloody warfare among themselves, but in Peqi'in the same Arab factions—Christians, Muslims, and Druse—live in relative tolerance of one another, their friction limited to social separation and innocuous political maneuvering in the city council. A synagogue even remains, a proud monument to Jews who also lived in the town with the Arabs—harmoniously, the Arabs say—for centuries before the birth of modern Israel.

The idyllic village is pretty dead, though. Night life is not Peqi'in's strong point. And so when Samir Sabag hit his late teens and early twenties and wanted to have a little fun, he sometimes got out of town and went looking for bright lights, loud music, and girls—Jewish girls.

"When I was a young guy," he said, grinning, "I used to drive around in a jeep and go into discos in Tiberius," the tourist city on the Sea of Galilee. The young women there were not Arabs, of course, since most Arab families remain strict about their unmarried daughters' dating, dancing, and otherwise cavorting with eligible men. Samir had to step from his restrictive culture into permissive Jewish society and, in the process, expose himself to the most emotionally burdensome contacts Arabs and Jews can have, contacts between the sexes. Here, the potential for hurt is keen, the vulnerability deep.

Jews have trouble identifying Samir as an Arab. He is an Arab Christian who builds houses for a living, and unlike most Israeli Arabs he wears a full black beard; his Hebrew is fluent, cleared of all flaws of accent and pronunciation. His easy smile and friendly charm diminish the odd effect of his cloudy left eye, blinded when he was a boy by the explosion of an old mine or grenade he and other children found near the village. As Samir tells it, he never tried to "pass" as a Jew, although other Arabs do so at times. But he especially liked "soldier girls" and saw them as something of a challenge. "Once, I was dancing with a girl soldier," he recalled with a smile, "and she heard me speaking Arabic to a friend. She said, 'What? You're an Arab? I won't dance with you! I can't dance with you!' She backed away." Samir put his palms up in horror to mimic her shocked expression. "I said, 'You're not dancing with an Arab. You're dancing with a person.' " His smile broadened. "It took me two to three weeks, and she was begging me to take her out."

In talking with Samir and other Arabs about the joy of conquest, I couldn't shake the feeling that getting an Israeli woman soldier into bed must bring particular satisfaction. It is just about the only way an Arab has of "screwing" the Israeli army. Arabs tell a joke along this line— more interesting than funny—about four men of different backgrounds engaging in a little one-upmanship. The conversation goes like this:

The American: "No one does anything without the CIA knowing."

The Iranian: "We have the best carpets in the world."

The Israeli: "We have the toughest women soldiers in the world; they can never be raped."

The Palestinian: "I've raped an Israeli soldier on a Persian carpet, and the CIA didn't know."

The urge to break loose from the sexual inhibitions of Arab culture found expression in patterns of prostitution. Michael Elkins, of the BBC, researching organized crime in the late '60s, discovered Jewish prostitutes working in East Jerusalem because Arabs, regarding Jewish women as a special treat, were willing to pay more for the pleasure than Jews were. The prostitutes had simply moved to the area where they could make the most money—the Arab part of town. Ultra-orthodox Jews—another group of men barred from sexual freedom within their own culture— have also become a major part of the clientele.

Sara Widlanski was once involved in an unpleasant episode with her husband Michael's acquaintance Muhammad, an Arab merchant in the Old City who sold beads and trinkets from a small shop on the Street of the Chains. Sara passed by the shop with Michael's brother one day and stopped for a chat. While the brother-in-law was outside in the alley, Muhammad began talking to Sara about his alleged affairs with Jewish women. Once, he said, a woman from Ramat Gan, near Tel Aviv, almost raped him. "I didn't feel comfortable with this subject," said Sara, "so I started talking about his wife and his children." But Muhammad kept returning to the topic, asking Sara, "Why did the woman want to rape me?" Then he insisted that she try on a necklace. "He tied the chain on me, forced me to try the chain by putting his hands all over my body. I didn't want to scream, so I pulled his hands away and went out." Still, she did not want to insult him by leaving immediately, because he was her husband's friend, so she asked her brother-in-law simply to come inside the shop and be with her. She left after a few minutes.

Most Arab-Jewish sexual liaisons seem doomed to short life and intense pain. A young Jewish woman told me of a brief affair with an Arab waiter in a kibbutz guest house where she was spending a weekend. The young man tried hard to hide his origins and yet felt constantly ashamed of his masquerade. She guessed immediately that he was an Arab and did not mind in the least. But she also did not tell him that she had guessed, and as he pursued her, he became increasingly consumed with his unstated lie. He would say that there was something that she did not know about him, that perhaps she would not be interested in him if she knew. Finally the truth came out, and still they continued seeing each other. She tried to reassure him, but he would not be reassured, and the relationship eventually broke up over his constant tendency to blame the small disagreements between them on her reservations toward him as an Arab. His inability to believe that a Jew could deal with him as a human being, independent of his Arab identity, corrupted the friendship.

Falling in love is often a difficult process of discovery, as Zohar En-drawos learned when he went with a Jewish woman from a neighboring town. They were both twenty-two, and they dated openly for more than a year. "Then I found out what racism was," he said. The opposition to her going with him was intense and enveloping. "How many times I heard 'dirty Arab' from her parents, friends. I never thought about getting married, but I think she did. Every Jew who knew about it talked to her; even the head of the [city] council talked to her." The ethnic tension seeped into their relationship, finally surfacing during a lovers' quarrel. "Even my girlfriend said to me once, 'This will teach me to get close to you barbarians,' " Zohar recalled painfully. "I could never have said that to her about her Jewishness."

Perhaps not, but many Arabs are hardly delighted by Jewish-Arab dating. Deborah Reich, an Intern for Peace, encountered several well-educated Arab men who frowned on the young Arabs' rush to Jewish women and imagined it was happening even when it was not. She once told an Arab politician about an illuminating, warm conversation she had had with a young Arab who said that he had never thought he would meet a Jew who understood him. The politician interpreted it as "a female-male dialogue," Deborah recalled, "that we'd coupled up some-how, physically or not. And he launched into this whole diatribe on the phenomenon of Arab men with Jewish women and the whole problem of Arab youth today being drawn to the city to try to get laid and so on. To me it's funny, almost, because it reminds me of middle-class American Jewry of thirty or forty years ago: Who did the nice middle-class Jewish boy practice on? Certainly not on girls like his sister. It wasn't acceptable to go to bed with a nice Jewish girl who was going to be somebody's wife someday.

"I've had one or two other educated Arab men phrase it this way," Deborah continued. "I think they identify with the problem of the young Arab guy kind of caught in the middle. He's out there, but then he's got this other life at home. But to me the idea that young, presentable, good-looking, well-spoken Arab guys go out and find Jewish girls in Tel Aviv—I don't see why that's so surprising. Anytime you have a juxtaposition of a sexually repressive culture with a sexually open culture, the boys from the sexually repressive culture are going to be hanging out with the girls from the sexually open culture. Some percentage of those girls are always going to be open to that, be not prejudiced enough or be thrill-seeking enough or be in rebellion enough or be just open-minded enough that it's acceptable to them. What's the big deal? I mean, it's not new."

The universities are often the meeting grounds, and while only a minority of students seem to mix across Arab-Jewish lines, the few who do so describe the relationships as always complex. Some Arab men tell a woman who refuses to have intercourse that she is anti-Arab, a bit of pressure that explains why some Jewish women, including political liberals, will have nothing to do with Arab men sexually; they feel coerced. "Many Arab men have Jewish girlfriends," said a Jewish woman who is married to an Arab. "They go to bed with Jewish girls and then marry [Arabs] in the village."

"Not many," countered her husband. "Most of my friends [at the Hebrew University] wanted to have Jewish girlfriends, but very few of them had. Jewish girls didn't want to have an Arab boyfriend. The stereotype is that the Arab is looking for sex and that's all."

"The stereotype," his wife interjected, "is that all men are looking for the same thing but that Arabs use the fact that they're Arabs. 'Oh, you don't want to go to bed with me because you're against Arabs.' "

Orna Sasson, a student who has worked hard to organize meetings and dialogues between Arabs and Jews at the Hebrew University, has better relations with Arab men than with Arab women because the women on campus are "very closed, very conservative, traditional—stay in their dorm rooms, rarely go out," she said. "I once asked an Arab woman whether she minded Arab men going with Jewish women. She said, 'No. They have sex drives they cannot satisfy with us, so they might as well with Jewish women.' I asked, 'What about you? Don't you have sex drives?' She said, 'Yes, but the traditions are stronger than I am. I'd like to feel free, but I have to wait until I get married.' "

In practice, Arab society, and especially urban culture, may be somewhat less Victorian than it appears. A young, single Arab-American who has spent considerable time in the Middle East collared me one day after reading a line in a story of mine about Arab society's being "fraught with strict sexual taboos." Politely but firmly, he disagreed, offering as evidence a rather detailed account of his own social life in several Middle Eastern cities. He found Arab women quite interested in limited premarital sex, although many avoid actual intercourse, since they are generally considered undesirable as wives if they lose their virginity. Those from wealthier families fly to Europe to get their hymens sewn up, he said. Because of the frustrations of Arab men, he added, many visit prostitutes and a minority engage in homosexuality: blond foreigners—both men and women—are particularly desirable.

But in the villages of the Galilee, it is doubtful that free love is around the corner. In recognition of the sensitivities, Interns for Peace instructs Jewish women who spend two years living in Arab villages to observe the most conservative guidelines in their social behavior. "For example," said Deborah Reich, who lived in the Arab town of Kfar Qara, "it is not acceptable for me, as an intern, to be sitting alone having a conversation in the living room with a young guy when the family's in another part of the house. You don't sit alone in a room with a guy. He, being progressive and maybe being from a progressive family, says, 'Oh, come on, Deborah, that's ridiculous. You know, this isn't the Middle Ages.' He has nothing to lose. He's decided he's going to be progressive; that's his role in that village. He's a son of the village, and they're not going to ostracize him as long as he stays within reasonable limits. But I can kill Interns for Peace in that village if I do that. For example, I'm not supposed to walk alone at night. If I'm being accompanied home by somebody from the family because I stayed too late and it got dark, unless he's, like, over fifty and married, it's not a good idea for the husband to drive me alone in the car. I once was given a ride from down the road by a post-university, mid-twenties guy, and the kid sister came along as the chaperone. She fell asleep in the back of the car, and he and I were having a conversation in front of my house with the motor idling, and when she fell asleep and plunked down below the profile of the window, I felt uncomfortable, and so did he.

"Listen, guys are guys, man," Deborah said. "The look that I would get standing out waiting for a bus in daylight at Kfar Qara from the guy standing next to me isn't any different to me from what I get in Tel Aviv standing there."

ELEVEN

Mirrors of Semitism

A Jew is forbidden to charge interest
on a loan to a fellow Jew, but,
as far as a non-Jew is concerned,
it is permitted to lend with interest.
—*Al-Nadwa*, Saudi Arabia, 1981

THE TERM "SEMITIC" WAS COINED IN 1781 BY THE GERMAN SCHOLAR
A. L. von Schlözer to identify a family of related languages, including
Hebrew, Arabic, Aramaic, and others. He derived the word from Shem,
one of Noah's three sons, giving the unintended impression that all those
who spoke Semitic languages shared a common ancestry, and thereby
setting in motion a process of labeling that may have distorted biblical
history and anthropology. In the nineteenth century, the narrow linguistic
definition of "Semitic" gradually broadened into the concept of race, and
the notion grew up in European writings that a Semitic group of people
existed with quite specific characteristics of appearance and culture. Mod-

ern archaeological excavations and other research have led some contemporary scholars, most notably S. D. Goitein, to break that link between language and race, to conclude that there is no basis for the idea that the varied peoples who spoke Semitic languages also shared physical and social traits. "We know the outward appearance of the ancient peoples who spoke Semitic dialects from their pictures, as well as from bodies found in excavations," Goitein writes, "and they were as different from each other anthropologically as any people could possibly be. Their economic and social conditions differed even more widely. What they had in common in literature or religious ideas can be proved to be the outcome of a long process of cultural integration."[67]

The true tribal and familial relationships of Arabs and Jews lie somewhere in the mists of history, susceptible to the reinterpretations of the centuries. But the concept and the vocabulary remain intact; by custom, Jews and Arabs are still regarded as Semitic peoples linked by more than language. And this creates difficulties in using the term "anti-Semitism," which seems illogical when applied to attitudes between Arabs and Jews. I have heard a witty Palestinian on occasion condemn the anti-Arab bigotry of Jews as "anti-Semitism." As he puts it, "I am a Semite."

Conventional anti-Semitism has a place in Arab images of Jews, but only as a minor undertone. It can be found in Arab books and newspapers, but rarely in conversation, and it does not appear to translate heavily into everyday attitudes. The negative generalizations made about Jews by Arabs who live under Israeli authority are dominated more frequently by the themes of brutality, cowardice, alienation, coldness, immorality, and the like, leaving to Arab propagandists the notions of Jews as usurious, exploitative, stingy, hook-nosed, and bent on a conspiracy for world domination.

This old pattern of stereotypes that has been known in the West as anti-Semitism originally took shape not in the Muslim world but in the Christian countries of Europe and North America, from which the Arabs then imported it, embellished it with a certain Islamic coloration, and used it as a convenience once Arab-Jewish conflicts arose. "The Arabs did not oppose Jewish settlement for anti-Semitic motives," writes Yehoshafat Harkabi. "Their opposition aroused anti-Semitic emotions among them."[68]

The Protocols of the Elders of Zion, for example, have been translated into Arabic and published extensively in Arab countries. A colleague of mine once saw a copy, in English, on the shelf in the home of a prominent Palestinian Arab in Gaza. Israeli authorities seize copies periodically from West Bank residents. Tom Friedman of *The New York Times* had a copy presented to him by a Pakistani he was interviewing in Bahrain. The Pakistani, Tom said, "was one of these guys who I'm sure anytime he talked to anyone came to that subject—a hard-core anti-Semite. He didn't know I was Jewish, and I didn't disabuse him of that. He said, 'I can smell a Jew a mile away.' I said, 'Oh, yeah?' He looked at me and said, 'You're not Jewish, are you?' He didn't know I was."

The Protocols, fabricated by a Russian priest, originated in 1903. They were first published in a Russian newspaper as the purported minutes of secret deliberations by Jewish leaders in Basel, Switzerland, supposedly held in 1897 to plot the destruction of Christendom and the takeover of the civilized world by an empire of Jews and Freemasons. They appeared in book form in 1905 and circulated throughout Europe in various translations. In 1921, Philip Graves, a correspondent for *The Times* of London, discovered that they had been largely plagiarized from an 1864 satire on Napoleon III by Maurice Joly, *Dialogue aux enfers entre Machiavel et Montesquieu*. But they were widely believed, and some of their assertions about the far-reaching tentacles of Jewish influence can be seen in Arab writings today on the specter of a powerful, satanic Zionist conspiracy that explains history and excuses Arab defeats. Under Nasser, Egyptian writers frequently cited the Protocols as if they were incontrovertible evidence of all the despicable qualities of the Jews, as much a guide to Jewish behavior as the Bible. Some picked apart the allegations that they were a forgery, and Nasser himself used them in an interview with the editor of the Indian English-language paper *Blitz* in 1958, saying, "I wonder if you have read a book *Protocols of the Learned Elders of Zion*. It is very important that you should read it. I will give you a copy. It proves beyond the shadow of a doubt that three hundred Zionists, each of whom knows all the others, govern the fate of the European Continent . . . and that they elect their successors from their entourage."[69] In 1974, Henry Kissinger told a small gathering of Israelis during an evening at Golda Meir's house in Jerusalem that he had just been presented with a beautifully bound copy of the Protocols in Saudi Arabia. A 1964 Jordanian textbook contained eight pages of quotations from the Protocols, whose recommendations on the use of spying, corruption, and immorality were shown to have parallels in the Old Testament, Harkabi reports. I did not find a reference to them in any of the current Jordanian texts I examined, however.

Another anti-Semitic import from Christendom is the blood libel, the medieval calumny that Jews use the blood of Christian children in rituals, such as the baking of matzo for Passover. Its antecedent appears to have been an accusation by pagans that the early Christians used human blood for ritual purposes, Bernard Lewis writes in *The Jews of Islam*. Later, after Christians made the charge against Jews, it was broadened to include among the victims any gentile children, Muslims as well—although Harkabi notes that centuries earlier Jews were accused of killing Muslim children without making ritual use of their blood. The blood libel appeared in the fifteenth century in the Ottoman Empire but was not documented again in the Muslim world until the nineteenth century, when it sometimes provoked violent attacks against Jews. In Damascus in 1840 and in Deir al-Qamar in 1847, the malicious story was spread by Christians, and it recurred in Jerusalem in 1849, in Constantinople in 1866, and Jerusalem again in 1870. Other instances in the nineteenth century have been documented in Aleppo, Antioch, Tripoli, Beirut, Izmir, and elsewhere. Six allegations arose in Egypt between 1870 and 1892, again made by Christians. The libel, adopted by Muslims, has been kept alive into the twentieth century; in 1962, the Egyptian Ministry of Education published *Human Sacrifices in the Talmud*, a reprint of an 1890 volume by Habib Faris in Cairo. An Egyptian editor summarized part of the book: "The innocent one was a boy called Henry Abd al-Nur, who had not yet passed his sixth year, whom the Jews slaughtered in Damascus and sucked his blood to mix it with the dough from which they prepared matzo for the Festival of Passover. The affair did not end with the condemnation of a single one of the Jews, despite the conclusive proof of the extraction of the boy's blood."

The End of Israel, published in 1960 in Cairo, quotes a "Rabbi Taunitus," who converted to Christianity, as saying, "The Zionists believe that Christian blood is essential for the performance of several religious rites." He claimed that the bride and groom at a wedding are presented with an egg stained with Christian blood; that the rabbi at a circumcision ceremony mixes a drop of Christian blood into a glass of wine and puts a drop into the child's mouth; that when the Jews mark the destruction of the Temple, they smear their foreheads with ashes of flax stained with Christian blood. The book contends that these rituals may also be performed with Muslim blood if Christian blood is unavailable, since many Christians have converted to Islam, with the result that Muslim blood contains some Christian blood as well. Abdallah al-Tall, in *The Danger of World Jewry to Islam and Christianity*, quotes a 1958 volume by a Turkish general, Jawad Rifat Atil Khan, describing how Jews place a child in a barrel with many hollow needles, which pierce the body and drain the blood. The pain of the dying is a good thing, the author writes, for the Jews believe that the blood is purified by suffering.[70]

More recent examples of Arab anti-Semitism have a heavy religious component, portraying the Jews as scheming enemies of Muhammad who broke their covenant with God and became immoral in their lust for wordly goods. "Their vices and corrupt ways were noted as far back as the Koran," wrote Marwan Muhammad Ali in the Saudi magazine *Al-Nadwa* in 1981. "The first and most important of these characteristics is their arrogance, and their claim that they are a chosen people and that God singled them out. . . . The second characteristic is their hard-hearted cruelty. The Jewish heart has no mercy for one who is not Jewish. The Talmud commands the Jew to roll a stone over the mouth of the pit where a non-Jew lies so that he cannot be rescued. . . . The third characteristic is the broken covenant. . . . Treachery is the Jews' most prominent feature. They are unable to make commitments and obligate themselves. The fourth characteristic is that the Jews keep the best things for themselves alone. . . . A Jew is forbidden to charge interest on a loan to a fellow Jew, but, as far as a non-Jew is concerned, it is permitted to lend with interest." And so on, through "miserliness and envy," "instigation and war-mongering," "hypocrisy," and "the belief that they have more rights then others."

Thus, Islamic ingredients are mixed into the traditional European anti-Jewish attitudes, views of the Jews as arrogant, sneaky, scheming, and untrustworthy. Much current writing tends to focus on Jews as greedy and exploitative. Jews are portrayed as controlling the international banking system, Western news organizations, and political forces. They plot in secret and work clandestinely to spread their power. A weekly magazine in Saudi Arabia even published an accusation that Jews were trying to take over international sports organizations.

A Saudi Arabian paper printed a story in 1984 about a man named Israel, whom it described as "a usurer who exploited situations of weakness in order to extract as much interest as he could. The village usurer was familiar with the situation of all the villagers, and was able to intervene at the right time—not in order to save someone from hardship, but so that he could profit from the sweat of the toilers and the tears of those drowning in the sea of need." The right time was the cotton-picking season when the man Israel could "give any of the villagers who were in difficulties the money they needed at usurious rates. The cotton owner found himself forced to accept any proposal because if not, the 'white gold' [cotton] would turn into lost wealth."

In another article criticizing the Egyptian peace process with Israel, the paper reported, "The [Egyptian] children today sing, 'The Jews are thieves and have the smallest of consciences.' The children represent an aspect of the national conscience and give it very clear and detailed expression. A child does not have manners or fear, and he says what he thinks and feels, and what happens around him. Adults should learn from him, and leave him to speak for them."

A teacher's guide to third-grade Islamic education in Jordan that has infiltrated into the West Bank contains the following story, which the teacher is supposed to tell the class:

In Medina the Muslims used to drink from a well called Roma's Well. This well belonged to a Jew who sold its water to the Muslims. One day the Prophet [Muhammad] said to his comrades, "Which one of you will buy this well and allow the Muslims to drink from it? His reward will be a spring from the springs of paradise."

Othman Bin Afan heard what was said and went to the Jew to bargain with him on selling the well. The Jew knew what had gone on between the Prophet and his comrades, so he thought that it was his opportunity to sell it for a very high price, according to the well-known custom of the Jews every time and everywhere, since they are greedy. He said to Othman: "I'll sell you only half the well." Othman asked, "For how much will you sell it?"

Here the teacher asks his students, "Do you know what the Jew did?" The Jew started raising the prices until he sold half the well for twelve thousand dirhams. Othman paid for it with his own money and gave half the well to the Muslims to drink from, to carry as much as they could to their houses and to irrigate their palm trees.

Then he said to his Jewish partner, "I want to arrange for my half and yours, so if you wish we can have one day for me and one day for you, or if you prefer, one jar for me and one for you."

The Jew answered, "I accept the first proposal." So they made a deal. But the Muslims took enough water from the well on each of Othman's days to satisfy them for two days, and no one was ready to buy water from the Jew on his days. The Jew understood that his half of the well would do him no good anymore. So he decided to sell it to Othman and asked him, "Will you buy my share of the well?"

"We don't need it anymore," replied Othman, "but if you wish I'll pay eight thousand dirhams for your share." The Jew accepted the eight thousand dirhams, and the well became a well for the Muslims, and they could drink from it for no charge.

In that story and much of the stereotyping, the Jew is portrayed as not only greedy but also stupid and easily fooled. The double theme was given prominence in a series of anti-Semitic jokes published by the Saudi Arabian daily newspaper *As-Sharq al-Awsat*, in a section called "Good Morning":

How do you kill a Jew? Throw a coin in front of a speeding bus.

How do you drive a Jew crazy? Put him in a round room and tell him you left a coin in a corner.

How do you tell a Jewish house? By the toilet paper drying on the clotheslines so that it can be reused.

How can you tell a Jewish park? By the bolt and lock on the trash can covers.

How do you know you're in a Jew's house? By the fork in the sugar bowl.

What did the Jewish Santa Claus say to the boy? "You want to buy a toy?"

A Jew went up to the top story of the Eiffel Tower in Paris and looked down at the street and saw a round piece of metal. The Jew decided that if he went down in the elevator it would take a long time, and almost certainly someone else would pass by, see the coin, and take it. Thus, the Jew saw no alternative but to jump onto the coin from the top of the Eiffel Tower. The next day the newspapers published: "Jew Commits Suicide by Jumping from the Eiffel Tower onto a Trash Can Cover."

Ugly jokes of this kind are rarely heard from Arabs living inside Israel and the West Bank, who seem to be finely tuned to the dangers of expressing anti-Semitic attitudes. One of the few I was able to get an Arab to tell me has a Jew walking with his wife past an outdoor stand that sells *shwarma*, grilled meat on a spit that is flaked off and eaten in pita, the flat bread. As the couple stroll by, she says, "Oh, that smells good," and looks expectantly at her husband. He replies, "Oh, would you like to walk past it again?"

When an Israeli Arab in the Galilee village of Tarshiha told this with a few of his relatives sitting around, everyone laughed.

Another that is popular with some Palestinians examines the different reactions to a fly floating in a bowl of soup. The Palestinian won't eat the soup. The Jordanian takes out the fly and eats the soup. The Israeli eats the soup as well, but first forces the fly to spit the soup it has swallowed back into the bowl.

The image of the gullible Jew seemed to prevail among at least some merchants in southern Lebanon after the Israelis invaded in 1982; special pleasure was taken in outsmarting and cheating the Israeli, who was supposed to be so strong and clever. David Harman, who supervised relief programs funded by the Joint Distribution Committee, speaks Arabic and heard Arab shopkeepers saying to each other, "Here come the Jewish soldiers. Prices up by 50 percent." One store owner remarked, "These smart Jews think they're so good at conducting war, but when they come into our shops, how we rob them!" Others laughed at the Israelis for giving aid. "Some thought the Jews were stupid," David observed. "First they shoot up the place, then they bring in cement to rebuild it."

Michael Widlanski once witnessed a reversal of the stereotypical roles during a bargaining session in the Jerusalem shop of his Arab friend Muhammad. A Jew came along trying to sell the Arab some lockets, hearts made of plastic to look like wood. "I don't have any money," said Muhammad. The Jew asked fifty shekels each, about twenty cents at the time. "I don't have any money."

"Forty shekels, forty," said the Jew. "It cost me forty-five to make them. I can't lose money on them."

"I don't have any money," said Muhammad. "I could pay you next week."

Finally they agreed on 920 shekels for the bagful. Muhammad gave him a thousand-shekel note. "I don't have any change," said the Jew, and gave him a hundred-shekel bill.

"I don't have any change," said Muhammad.

"That's okay," said the Jew, and he left.

Then Muhammad turned to Michael and remarked, "He's too nice. He's crazy. He believes people who say they don't have money. He loses all the time."

Tom Friedman encountered very few expressions of anti-Semitism during the nearly five years he spent covering the Arab world from Beirut. Aside from the Pakistani handing him the Protocols in Bahrain, there was a very senior official of Kuwait Radio. "Every time I went to see him, year after year after year, he had the same lecture about how [Defense Secretary Caspar] Weinberger was Jewish, and there was a Jewish cabal, etc., etc., etc." But the Kuwaiti was an exception, Tom said. "I really felt I had much more anti-Semitism in high school than I ever had in the Arab world," he told me. "Oh, God, I was called dirty Jew and kike and people used to throw pennies at us. They'd throw a penny in the hall and see if we'd pick it up. Minneapolis. Minneapolis was a hotbed of anti-Semitism. I'll never forget in grade school, a kid with a lisp calling me 'Dirty Dew' because he couldn't say 'Jew.' It's that kind of nastiness, with a hard edge to it, that I never felt in the Arab world. I always felt comfortable there. The Sunni Muslims in particular were tolerant."

Tom did not hide his Jewishness, but neither did he advertise it while he was in Lebanon or other Arab countries. "I became very adept at deflecting the subject away from religion in any conversation," he said. "People assume you're not Jewish. Your name could be Goldberg; they assume that if you're there, you're not Jewish. I was applying for an Algerian visa. The guy was filling out the form for me, and when he got to the place for religion, he just wrote Christian. Or they'd ask, 'Friedman— what kind of name is that? Oh, you're not Arab? You're American? Well, what were you before you were American?' And I got very adept at dancing around it and changing the subject. It was second nature. Get it off the subject, next subject. But there was always a tension in me.

There was always a knot in my stomach for five years. Do they know who I am? If they knew who I was, what would they say?"

Once, at a fancy Beirut dinner party, seated next to the wife of the minister of public works, Tom got the usual questions. " 'Friedman. What kind of name is that?' And finally I think she established that I was Jewish, and I went into my changed-subject routine. And she said, 'Oh, you're trying to change the subject.' Not in a vicious way, but she wanted to talk about it more, and I didn't, and she picked it up immediately. I wasn't subtle enough. We just laughed. We both laughed. I had to admit that she caught me in my own game. It was hard enough living and working there; I didn't want it to be an issue. I also never sought out [Lebanese] Jews there, never did a story on Jews in Beirut. Low profile. But don't deny who you are. It was a very careful line that I kept. I didn't hide it. If somebody said, 'Are you Jewish?' I'd say, 'Yes, I am.' And with certain people I could talk about it, talk about my feelings—with my close friends, most of whom were Greek Orthodox or Sunni Muslims."

One of his friends was Saab Salam, a Sunni and former prime minister. "He used to love to introduce me as 'He's Tom Friedman and he's Jewish.' I was the court Jew there. But it never had that hard edge on it where it really was frightening. Saab was proud to have a Jewish friend and always looked after me. It was more amusing to all of us. Because they knew Jews in Lebanon and they interacted with them, these are people who are used to coexisting. Yet they had the same stereotypes, and I could never disabuse Saab of that notion that the Jews control America, that they control all the wealth, that they control all the banking. The only anti-Semitic remark I ever heard in Lebanon was from our French neighbors, who were diplomats, and they once referred to our landlord—who ironically was a Palestinian—after he had raised the rent: '*Comme ça avec les juifs.*' " Just like the Jews.

Then Tom remembered another incident, one that saddened him. "Two nights before I left I was invited to the home of a young Lebanese girl who was in the Red Cross. There were three of them I'd interviewed during the years I was there. I got to know them because they cleared out my house [after it had been blown up]. And one of them told the worst anti-Semitic joke. It made me realize she didn't know I was Jewish. She said, 'What is this?' " And she held out her hand without moving it. " 'It's the hand of a dead Jew, because if he were alive, he'd be going like this.' " And she rubbed her fingers in the gesture meaning money. "Oof, it just really hit me. And this is from a liberal Red Cross volunteer—a Christian. That hurt me very much because it was from someone whom I would have expected not to have those kinds of feelings. So I never had any illusions that it wasn't out there." Especially among the Maronite Christians, the ostensible Israeli allies. Once, during the 1982 war, Tom went to Christian East Beirut and took a break at a swim club to lie in the sun. "And some Israelis walked into the pool, five of them in uniform, to take pictures: 'Oh, crazy Lebanon, people at the beach, fighting in West Beirut.' And they kind of walked around like they owned the place. People smiled and posed for pictures, but after they walked out, I saw people cursing them, making gestures, 'These farmers from Israel.' I always felt with the Maronites that their ancestors persecuted my ancestors somewhere along the way."

Jews are not the world's only victims of the "anti-Semitic" stereotype, of course. The image of the wily, money-grubbing exploiter, the merchant and banker who cheats and schemes to control and manipulate, has been applied to hated groups in many cultures, by the Laotians and Cambodians to the Vietnamese living in Laos and Cambodia; by the Vietnamese and others to the Chinese living in Vietnam and elsewhere in Southeast Asia; to the Indians in some parts of Africa; and, with a few variations, by the Russians to the Soviet Georgians.

Occasionally, like the quick flash of a mirror, the stereotype is also slapped on the Arabs by the Jews.

As an undercurrent of belief, some Israeli Jews see West Bank and East Jerusalem Arabs as profiting unduly, as cheating them in the markets, as evading taxes, as secretly importing money in an effort to improve their political leverage. Bargaining to buy something in the Old City is not always fun, as it should be, and Jews often come away feeling that they have been taken, as they often have. But beyond this cultural clash, the more malignant images appear from time to time in Hebrew literature and children's books, some dating from pre-state days, when Jews in the Middle East lived in predominantly Arab societies. As in the Arabs' images of Jews, these "anti-Semitic" stereotypes represent only a minor theme in the overall Jewish attitudes.

Breakdown and Bereavement, a novel by Yosef Haim Brenner published in 1920, includes Arabs as mere props to add color to the scenes of Jerusalem, and usually in fearsome or exploitative vignettes. A Jew who journeys from Hebron to bathe in the springs of Tiberius is asked whether the waters have done him good. " 'The waters are fine, but they're not in good hands,' winked the Hebronite in allusion to the Arab manager of the springs, who took advantage of him, as he did of all Jews, by charging four whole piastres for every bath."

Yehuda Burla, though more discerning and respectful of Arabs in his novel *In Darkness Striving*, reverses the usual direction of the anti-Semitic stereotyping. He portrays the Jew as generous and the Muslims as vicious moneylenders. Burla has his Jewish hero, Rahamo, who narrates the story, offer a loan to an Arab farmer who explodes in gratitude. " 'May God strengthen you, Rahamo,' he replied. 'I was ashamed to trouble you again, particularly as I fear I might not be able to pay it all back out of the crop—and now you yourself offer me a loan! By Heaven, you're better than the Muslims.' He then went on to tell me that some effendis who lent the peasants money took up to forty percent interest out of the crops. I myself had never lent out money on interest, nor had my father."

Turning standard patterns of prejudice upside down, children's books have sometimes given Arab characters the same negative physical traits with which Jews are tarnished in other literature. Menachem Regev's survey points to a few of these, including Zvi Zaviri's 1958 portrait of a sheikh in *Yuval's Adventures*, for example: "He was tall, broad-shouldered and narrow-hipped. A trimmed beard covered his dusky, bony face. His eyes burned perpetually and beneath his well-groomed moustache there always played on his lips an arrogant, intelligent smile." The image of smug arrogance is particularly effective in triggering some of the same reactions and apprehensions about quiet, secretive plotting that have long accompanied anti-Semitism.

But perhaps the most remarkable parallel of all is the use of the hooked nose to characterize fierce Arabs. In *The Cadillac Goes Down South* by M. Garin, two Jewish children meet a Bedouin in a market:

"On one hip there hung a very sharp short Bedouin dagger, and from the other swung an enormous revolver attached to a decorated belt. In addition, his fingers were occupied with a sharp flick-knife with which he picked, every now and then, at his enormously long teeth. His face was thin, sharp and very wrinkled, a golden-brown color like burnished copper. Beneath a keffiyah as big as a sheet, showed fierce long black curls; his eyes flashed like the glint of a dagger. But the crowning touch to the whole picture was his nose—a real eagle's beak of immense proportions."

Eliezer Smoli does the same thing in *The Men of Early Days*, which was published in 1939 but is still read today. He describes a member of the Arab bands:

"The rider dismounted from his horse in one light leap. He was a man of about forty, tall and broad shouldered. Two angry eyes glinted out of a stern face beneath a small narrow forehead. The ends of his moustache curled upward, stiff, pointed and sharp as two horns. His hooked nose made his face look even more like that of a bird of prey, murderous and evil-hearted."

Baptism of Fire, written by Ze'ev Domnitz in 1956, even contains an Egyptian spy named Ramadan Eagle-Nose, "a man who looked more like an eagle than a human being." He contemplates the pleasure of "the final slaughter" in Israel, and beneath an ugly drawing of him, the caption reads "The enemy's chief spy, a loathsome character, cunning and full of devilish plans, whose base is in Cairo from where he plans murder and sabotage."

TWELVE

The Holocaust

Nothing afterwards can be the same.
And when people come along and use it
for their own purposes—trivialize, vulgarize,
in effect violate those who have
vanished in smoke there—
you want to shake them.
—Irene Eber

GREY METAL TOWERS APPEARED ON THE PLATEAU WEST OF NABA-
tiyeh, Lebanon, within a couple of weeks after the Israeli invasion. I first
saw their ungainly silhouettes as I drove quickly from the coast, dodging
in and out of the Israeli military convoys that littered the narrow country
road with armored vehicles, trucks, and jeeps. The long-legged towers
suddenly cut an incongruous geometry against the large, smooth curve
of blue sky; they were the same sort that stood around kibbutzim in the
Galilee, settlements on the West Bank, and Israeli army bases everywhere.

Nobody in the army would say what the towers were for, and the
official silence remained long after the answer became obvious. Each time

I drove past, there was more activity to be seen beneath them. Bulldozers began to work the earth. A chain-link fence was erected and then topped with rolls of barbed wire. Finally, tons of dirt were piled and pushed until high earthen dikes rose along the road to hide the place from passersby. And then this barren stretch of scruffy land, fenced and guarded, came to have a name. It was called Ansar, after the nearest village, and gradually the name penetrated the vocabulary of all of southern Lebanon, and of Israel as well. It was learned by the Palestinian and Lebanese women in the coastal cities and refugee camps who pleadingly held out snapshots of their missing young men, begging you to find them, saying in the beginning that perhaps their sons and husbands and brothers had been taken "to Israel." Later, they knew that their men had been imprisoned in Ansar, and they spoke the word with a vile hiss, as if it were a curse.

The Ansar prison camp was not on the Israeli army's standard tour of southern Lebanon. The distinguished foreigners who visited the area—politicians, celebrities, avid American contributors to Israel—were usually whisked up the coastal road to be shown how many buildings had not been destroyed in the fighting, how unlike the television pictures the reality was in fact. Ansar would have proved a very different point, and so it was kept out of view behind the earthen dikes, a makeshift outdoor complex of tents, barbed wire, and guard towers. Few journalists were allowed inside, and by the time I was called by the army in September 1983 and told I could go, I could not even remember when I had asked, it had been so long before. To avoid a synthetic show's being put on, I had requested permission to enter the camp and to speak with any prisoners I might choose at random, in addition to a couple of inmates I named in advance. When the army once offered to let me just look at the camp from the outside without interviewing prisoners, I refused to go. Now the authorities had finally agreed to an open visit.

I had two companions: our photographer, Micha Bar-Am, and one other reporter, Cordelia Edvardson of the Swedish newspaper *Svenska Dagbladet*, a smart, sensitive woman in her middle fifties who had grown up in Germany, surviving the concentration camps of Theresienstadt and Auschwitz. Cordelia had strong feelings on behalf of Israel, a powerful compassion for the Palestinians, and a personal history that deepened her reactions to what she saw at Ansar. "If I were on their side, I'd be a fighter too," she said later. "And if I survived and prisoners were taken, I would be in there."

What we saw first were the faces, haunting stares through barbed-wire and chain-link fences, faces of dark anger, of vacant defeat, the tough faces of seasoned Palestinian fighters, the weak faces of those swept up innocently by the storm of war, aging faces, boyish faces whose youthful freshness was already tarnished by an early hardness. They watched us closely, fastening their gazes on us as inmates do when any novelty breaks the heavy boredom of imprisonment. They wore a motley assortment of clothing: sweatsuits, bathing suits in the September heat, Israeli army uniforms that the authorities had turned into prison garb by dying them brown instead of the usual olive drab.

About 4,700 men were being kept there at the time—mostly Palestinians, plus some Lebanese picked up in the Israelis' sweep that followed the fighting fifteen months before. There was a constant turnover of prisoners, with some being released after investigation and new ones arrested by the troops occupying southern Lebanon. Israel was anxious to release them all in exchange for Israeli soldiers being held by the PLO, but it was not until two months after our visit that the PLO's Fatah faction agreed to an exchange and Ansar was nearly emptied: 4,500 Palestinians for 6 Israelis.

The camp was a squalid sore. The prisoners lived in large, crowded army tents on several fields of bare ground. Around them they could see only barbed wire, guard towers, and armored personnel carriers. The compounds were smothered in an awful stench of sewage and garbage. Gritty, amber-colored dust from the plateau sifted into everything, coating the tents, filtering into hair, tinting the prisoners' skin and clothing. During the winter rains, the dust turned to mud, and the Israelis were busy making new compounds with asphalt floors and small shower rooms and latrines to improve conditions during the approaching rainy season. Although each prisoner was issued three blankets, the first winter began as raw and miserable, without heaters for the tents, without sufficient clothing. A Red Cross inspector told me privately that tuberculosis had been a problem for a while, but then he shrugged with the weary resignation of a man who has seen too much. Ansar was a prison camp, he said, and prison camps are unpleasant places. He had found worse conditions in Syria and elsewhere.

The Israelis treated prisoners with a blend of brutality and humaneness. Some of the Israeli guards, soldiers who had been court-martialed for various offenses and were serving sentences themselves, returned to their base prison in Israel talking about how they had mixed laundry detergent into soup being prepared for the Arab prisoners.[71] Inmates complained of being beaten and insulted during interrogation in the early months, a practice that apparently waned as protests were made and prison routines were established. A few men were killed, however, some during what the Israelis said were escape attempts, others under murkier circumstances. Three died and three were wounded when an armored personnel carrier went through a ditch and a machine gun fired a burst into the camp, apparently by accident. Two officers and two sergeants were court-martialed on charges ranging from negligence to negligent homicide; one officer received a reprimand, and the three others were given suspended jail sentences. Another prisoner was shot in the head and killed as he reached through the barbed wire to retrieve a letter he had dropped, according to the leader of the prisoners' committee, Salah Taamri.*

Letters were allowed in unlimited numbers by Israeli authorities, and prisoners were writing about 10,000 a week, a ceiling set by the quantity that the Red Cross was able to handle. Technically, every incoming and outgoing piece of mail was subject to censorship, although one officer confided that many were passed unread because of the sheer volume. Evidently, however, at least one Israeli censor indulged himself in a streak of sick humor. Taamri showed us several snapshots of prisoners' children that had been sent into the camp by families outside. The pictures, too, had been cleared by the censor, who had carefully pressed his ink stamp of approval on each child's face.

As the months wore on, the prisoners grew restive. They engaged in political indoctrination, made Palestinian flags which fluttered from tent poles, and sang Palestinian songs. They busied themselves by making bracelets out of stove pipes, chain necklaces out of electrical wire, cigarette holders out of wooden vegetable crates, and canvas bags from tents. To keep his spirits up, one man even built a glider in the hope that he might escape by air; it was left in one of the compounds, a kind of monument

---

* His name has also been rendered as Tamari.

to whimsical determination. The prisoners also organized, electing a four-man committee to represent them to the Israeli authorities, who heard their complaints and responded to some of them. All four, led by Taamri, met with us for about an hour. One objective, Taamri said, was to get Israel—which did not regard them as prisoners of war—to treat them as such under the Geneva Convention. They finally obtained a copy of the convention through the Red Cross. "But when we got it," he said, "it made it even worse, just like reading the Ten Commandments, the Bible—just a fiction."

Taamri had a disturbing knack for taking the symbols most precious to Jews and twisting them into biting attacks. He was a tall man of forty, fluent in his English and facile in his rhetoric. Married to Dina, the former wife of King Hussein and the former queen of Jordan, Taamri carried himself with an aristocratic air. His hair, nearly black with wisps of grey, hung almost to his shoulders, and his beard and moustache were neatly trimmed. His light-blue eyes locked on people with a discomforting steadiness as he lectured, gestured, wagged his finger, made his points with slick, practiced argument. Originally from a Bedouin settlement near the Herodion, the great hilltop fortress of King Herod on the West Bank, he had changed his name from Assad Suleiman Abdel Khader, had studied at the University of Cairo, and had become the head of the PLO's youth corps and reputedly a commander of PLO units in southern Lebanon. When he surrendered to the Israelis on July 16, 1982, in Sidon, he gave a moderate speech to other Palestinian prisoners, telling them that the time of armed struggle had passed. A couple of years before, he had guided John le Carré around the Palestinian refugee camps in Lebanon, earning himself a mention of gratitude in the foreword to le Carré's *The Little Drummer Girl*. And some who knew him thought he was the model for the novel's Khalil, the urbane Palestinian revolutionary who favored fast cars and fast women.

We met him in the hospital tent, although in a sense we had met him just before. We had come from a tour of the camp. At one compound, where he was being held and was clearly the leader, prisoners who saw us approach their fence crowded together, shouted, whistled, waved their hands in V signs, and burst into nationalistic Palestinian songs. They then had begun to chant in heavily accented English, "Ansar is Auschwitz! Ansar is Auschwitz! You are Nazis!" I looked at Cordelia. She had been fifteen when she was moved from Theresienstadt to Auschwitz, just six months before the Germans, in retreat, started to force prisoners out on long marches, death marches in which many perished. I watched her face as the Palestinian prisoners compared Ansar with Auschwitz. She stared through the barbed wire, into the mass of men in huddles of amber and brown who searched for resilience in the obscene slogan. Ansar is Auschwitz. Cordelia seemed in pain, but she said nothing.

When we then sat across the table from Taamri, he spoke with pride, almost arrogance. "If the Israelis want to turn Ansar into a graveyard of our ambitions, of our hopes to go back, of our dreams," he declared, "it will be Israel's graveyard of their own hopes." He called Jews "the chaotic children of God," and said, "What is striking is the hypocrisy. They speak of their purity of arms. They raise the banner so pure, under which they wage the most ferocious war. The Jews are chaotic and arrogant." He said, "I think this last war has created more grudges than in 1948. There will be a qualitative change." Then he added, "In Lebanon an era has ended where armed struggle could be waged." But as long as there is injustice, he said, the struggle must continue in some form. "One of the challenges we meet during this imprisonment is not to have our faith in coexistence between Arabs and Jews perish."

Cordelia, who had visited Ansar a couple of months before, pulled out a striking photograph of a reunion she had arranged between a father and his two sons in the camp. When she met the man, he told her that he did not know where his sons were. She had asked the camp commandant if he would find them, and he had, and when the three were brought together, a photographer had snapped a picture. Now she wanted to give it to them. Taamri missed the point, did not tune in on Cordelia's compassion and effort. He simply said that he did not recognize the men, and he scoffed that arresting sons was the "special Jewish way of family reunion." Then he glided back into his rhetoric. "But I still ask: Why should Israel keep such an appalling camp, which at least in appearance resembles some bitter experiences the Jewish people have been through?"

Cordelia mentioned the chants, "Ansar is Auschwitz," and asked him, "Do you agree?"

"I can't agree and I can't disagree," Taamri said smoothly. *What?* Suddenly I wanted to scream at him. *Do you know who sits here in front of you? Do you know what she has seen? Ask her, if you don't know the difference. She'll tell you about Auschwitz.*

"What Begin said about us—animals on two feet," he continued in a calm voice. "Doesn't it bring an echo of what Hitler said about the Jews? When you ask children in Sabra and Shatila, 'How did you survive?' Because they were short. Well, many Jews survived because they were short."

Tell him, Cordelia. Tell him who you are. Say something! Roll up your sleeve: show him the number tattooed in blue ink on your forearm. I ached for her to do it, to throw it in his complacent face. *Tell him. Educate him. Let's see how he confronts truth.*

"To someone whose family got killed, the whole world is a holocaust," Taamri went on, obviously pleased with the idea he was developing and polishing. "We have a headmaster of a school who lost eighty-two members of his family in one air strike. For him, that was a holocaust. Should anything be special because you are Jewish? Are the Israelis Jews? Are they the chosen people of God, or are they the chaotic people of the devil? Pretty soon you will have more battlefields than synagogues."

Oh, Cordelia, tell him! But she sat composed, and all she said was, "Auschwitz was an extermination camp. Children and elderly people did not come out alive." He did not argue with her, did not try to justify his analogy. He simply did not know who she was, and she never told him. Not a word, not a hint. He sailed past without being touched by her. And I felt like a kettle with the lid on, boiling. I yearned to say something myself, and I came to the edge of speaking out, telling him her story. Now I think that perhaps I was wrong not to have delivered a simple, calm sentence to him: *Mr. Taamri, you are sitting with a survivor of Auschwitz.* But Cordelia was there; it was her interview as much as mine, her experience that day more than mine. It was up to her. I just couldn't stand it, but I had no right to push her private trials onto the table, to turn an interview into an argument; she had to be the one to speak.

When we left the camp and were driving to Jerusalem, I complained and scolded with the warmth I felt toward her, and I asked her why she had kept her silence, why she had not let him know that he was facing somebody with whom he could not manipulate the symbol as if it were just an image in a history book, a piece of propaganda. Why, why? I wanted to know. Her answer was simple, yet it contained all the depths of her suffering and her survival. "It would have been unfair," she said. "He was behind bars, and I was free."

. . .

"I understand her," said Irene Eber, a good friend of mine who had also gone through the Holocaust, in Poland. Irene listened to the story of that day at Ansar. "I understand her. It is hard to throw it in someone's face," she said. "It is hard to lose your compassion for someone whose fate you can empathize with. It is really hard to see people behind bars. When I go by a prison, my heart stops. I think it gets into a real tangle of emotions there. It is so close. And if it's that close, you don't go up to strangers and tell them what's going on in your head."

The Holocaust has become a vehicle of hurt and outrage between Arabs and Jews, a symbol of immense grievance on both sides, an event without analogy, yet one used often as analogy to inflate the scope of each side's transgressions. Arab propagandists frequently liken Israel to Nazi Germany and the Palestinians to the Jews of Europe. Menachem Begin, for his part, routinely accused the PLO of aspiring to commit genocide against the Jews. The respectability of the forum has been no deterrent to this sort of nonsense.

During a 1985 debate on Israel's attacks on villages in southern Lebanon, for example, the Saudi Arabian representative to the United Nations, Samir S. Shihabi, told the Security Council, "Hitler preceded them [the Israelis] with his Nazi destructive machinery in the ways of brutality and murder, collectively and individually, and even though they have surpassed them now, his end was inevitable, and their end will be inevitable if the world does not stop them before it is too late." A Saudi Arabian newspaper, *Al-Gumhuriya*, editorialized in 1983, "Now one can ask the leaders of Israel: 'Did not the Nazis torture you or in previous generations did you not represent the Nazis before the world as wild, cowardly beasts? And is what you are doing less than what the Nazis did?' " A similar parallel was drawn in a 1984 issue of the same paper. "Just as Hitler behaved with conceit, so too Israel behaves," it declared. "Why did the Jews of the world fight Nazi Germany while they are doing the same thing which the Nazis did against them? Israel enslaves the Palestinian people in the West Bank and Gaza more harshly than the Nazis fought the Jews." A 1977 commentary in the Syrian paper *Al-Baath* was apparently written on the assumption that its readers accepted the parallel and that Israel hoped to exterminate the Arabs. "Zionism ought to realize that it can never attain the strength of Nazi Germany," the paper said, "neither will the Arabs in Israel ever assume the status of the Jews in Hitler's Germany."

In earlier years, an explicit affinity for Hitler was expressed by some Arabs. *Mein Kampf* was translated into Arabic and circulated extensively. Haj Amin el-Husseini, the mufti of Jerusalem, wrote in 1943 to the German foreign minister, Joachim von Ribbentrop, requesting German intervention in the Balkans to prevent Jews from migrating to Palestine, a fact noted on a small panel in Jerusalem's Yad Vashem memorial museum to the victims of the Holocaust. Especially during the first twenty years of Israel's existence as a modern state, some Arab scholars and politicians wrote approvingly of Nazi efforts at extermination, blaming the Jews for attempting to subvert Germany. Abdallah al-Tall, of Jordan, declared, "The blame applies first and foremost to the Jews themselves and their characteristics of treachery, deceitfulness, crime, and treason, and in the second place to European civilization, which apparently could not long suffer the vile Jewish character, and in the course of time hatred of the Jews and loathing for their vices led to a movement of collective killing." Others have branded as an exaggeration the figure 6 million as the number of Jews exterminated in massacres and death camps. In 1960, after the Israelis had kidnapped Adolf Eichmann, the Lebanese paper *Al-Anwar* published a cartoon of Eichmann and Ben-Gurion shouting at each other, with a caption:

Ben-Gurion: "You deserve the death penalty for killing six million Jews."

Eichmann: "There are many who argue that I deserve the death penalty for not finishing the job."

During Eichmann's subsequent trial in Israel, the Jordanian English-language paper, *Jerusalem Times*, printed an open letter to Eichmann bemoaning his failure to kill all the Jews but praising him for getting 6 million, who otherwise, the writer asserted, would have committed atrocities against Arabs in a second part of the Middle East.

The memory of the Holocaust is a potent weapon in the hands of Arabs, and some enjoy using it as tool to shock Jews. An Arab student, Samir Zrake, once told me how he needled a class at Hebrew University. "They asked a question, 'Who was the most idealistic person in history?' My answer was Hitler, a man who stood for his principles. All the Jews looked at me. The teacher intervened."

Jews react variously, and not always with predictable outrage, when

Arabs draw parallels between Israelis and Nazis. After our Ansar visit, Cordelia and I gave a lift to an Israeli army officer who listened to me boil and rage for a while about Salah Taamri's glib use of holocaust terminology, and then spoke up. The officer said he didn't blame the Palestinians. They were merely wielding the best weapon they could find to attack Israel, he said, and he would do the same if he were in their position. That is how the game is played, he explained: It is a war of emotion and propaganda, not only of guns.

A very different response came from an American cardiologist who read my account in the *Times* and was so enraged by the chant, "Ansar is Auschwitz," that he called me long-distance from New York City one night to talk about his feelings. He had been in Auschwitz at thirteen, he said. His parents and his brothers had perished there, their bodies burned in the huge crematorium. "I can still remember the chimneys, the smoke coming out of the chimneys," he told me. "I will never forget that my whole life."

Irene Eber saw the parallel as infuriating, but she also understood it in another way, as a search for a Palestinian history. "It's not only a Jewish experience, I think it is a human experience," she said. "It has such implications for all humanity, it is such an event in history. Nothing afterwards can be the same. And when people come along and use it for their own purposes—trivialize, vulgarize, in effect violate those who have vanished in smoke there—you want to shake them. And you want to say, 'Look here, you've got to understand what you're talking about. You can't talk in these terms. You must get your terminology straight. Learn about it and then come back. But don't say such things because that's not what the Holocaust means, that's not what it's about. You cannot do that.' That is, to call Israelis Nazis may release tension, but it is not the same thing. The trivialization—it's staggering. Why is everybody latching on to this as a symbol? I'd say because of the power of the images. You say 'Holocaust,' and anybody who's ever seen a picture, and anybody who's seen a film immediately has a certain image, and you don't have to say anything more."

It has been natural for the Palestinians, pitted against the Jews, to use the Holocaust as a device for building their own history. "This establishing of history is a very powerful impulse in people generally," Irene observed. "People must search to establish their history. It becomes extraordinarily painful to watch it when you see that they're establishing the wrong history for themselves."

Irene, who teaches Chinese philosophy at Hebrew University, is a delicate woman who speaks with a quiet, charming lilt that seems too light to carry the weight of her thoughts. She was just a child when invading Germans massacred Jews in her hometown of Mielec, Poland. "They came into this town, made a pogrom, and burned down a large portion of the Jewish section," she said, "burned the synagogue, burned the butcher, burned the bath house, and killed the people, because it was Erev Rosh Hashanah—it was Eve of New Year—killed the people who were in the bath house and the butcher. They came on motorcycles. I was nine years old, and I remember it. That is what is so uncanny. It is so clear to me. I remember the next day when they buried the people who had been killed, in a mass grave. They apparently weren't allowed to bury them in the Jewish cemetery, so right across from where we lived there was a field, and then there was the back of where a house had burned, and they dug a big, big pit and they buried the people there. That was in 1939."

In March 1942, the Jews were deported from Mielec to the Lublin district, where Irene and some of her relatives lodged with Jewish families in a small village. One by one, they made their way back to Mielec, were deported again to a ghetto, and again elsewhere, and finally they knew that in the next deportation they would be going to Auschwitz. "People write books and say nobody knew. We knew. Other people knew. If they now say they didn't know, it is memory. We knew. I knew, and I was a child. What we did is we all made a false wall under a roof in the attic. We left a little hole in it. And it was supposed to be just for our family, my father's two sisters, and we had a cousin living with us and so on. The day of the deportation, everybody's frantically running to hiding places—other people had also prepared hiding places. We rushed up there, but other people knew about it, so other people rushed up there too, and there were in that space, I don't know, a hundred people? I can't tell you. There wasn't enough food, and there wasn't enough water. We took turns sitting and standing. They were flushing people out and shooting people. And we kept hearing the shooting. The Germans came searching, of course; we could hear them; they came with dogs. And, you know, the familiar story: A child started crying; the mother took a pillow and smothered the child. It happened there. I've never seen anything quite so awful. When she came down, her husband was allowed to stay, and she handed him the dead child."

The ghetto was converted into a camp, and eventually Irene escaped. "I dug my way out under the barbed wire, and I just went to the railroad station and bought a ticket—I was twelve—and got on a train. I went back to Mielec and asked Polish people to hide me." Much of her family, including her father, perished.

Many years after the war, Irene finally found the strength to go back to see her town of Mielec. The buildings were there, just as she remembered them, every house in its proper place along every little street, practically unchanged, as if a war, a holocaust, had never happened. But all the people were gone, the Jews had disappeared, and others were living in their place. That eerie physical sameness inflicted the return with hardship. And in her generosity, Irene could see the parallels between her pain and that of Arabs who return and are wounded by the physical destruction they find. I was moved to tell her about a middle-aged Arab professional I had just met who worked in Amman, Jordan, and had lived before 1948 in Jaffa. There was no parallel in the departure, of course, for Arabs fled from Jaffa; they were not deported to ghettos and death camps. But going back seemed to have something of the same quality of suffering. In 1984 he returned for the first time and went back to find his house, his neighborhood. It had become a slum. His family's citrus grove was a dump. I asked what he had imagined, and he said, "I had remembered it the way it was."

"Had you felt a yearning to go back all these years?"

"Oh, yes," he said.

"And now?"

"I realize I can't go back, I don't want to go back, it's finished."

"How does this sit with you emotionally?"

"It's too early to tell. It's only been a day. One thing I can say now is that it's resolved something for me, something that was nagging at me for all these years."

Irene listened to the story and talked about her own return. "It was just like the whirlwind swept them all away," she said of the Jews of Mielec. "And there were the signs, the mezuzoth—not the mezuzoth but the indentations where the mezuzoth had been on the doorposts. It was all there. Again, it is the same and it is different. Both are equally powerful. Because in one case you realize that that past is so gone for the Arabs, they can't go back naming the streets as they had been doing in the camps after Jaffa, where they had lived; it just won't work anymore. The more Arabs come here, the less this kind of imagery will work. And it is for this reason that other kinds of images have to be invented for their past. That past doesn't work because that past is so gone, is so finished. Going back, to me, was that I remembered everything with such uncanny clearness, such clarity. I see the pictures over and over. There came one moment when I said to myself, Maybe I invented it all. Someone once asked me, 'Please draw me a picture of where grandmother's house was, where you lived, where the baker was, the butcher and all that.' I sat down and I took a pencil and I drew it. The proportions were probably all wrong because, you know, distance is so much greater for a child. I drew it all, I remembered it, and then I said, Maybe it didn't happen. Maybe I'm just fantasizing everything. And for me, this going back and finding this shock of recognition was, I think, equally powerful as that shock must have been for him of nonrecognition."

Very few Arabs seem to know much about the Holocaust. Its full horrors rarely seem to penetrate. It goes unmentioned in the Jordanian curriculum that governs teaching in West Bank schools, for example, and it is skimmed over quickly in the Israeli schools for Arabs. Even the best informed and most sophisticated and moderate of the Palestinian Arabs cannot bring themselves to gather the experience of the Holocaust into their understanding of the Jews. That essential feel for the trauma, the tragedy, the aloneness of the Jews in that dark period is simply missing from the Arabs' sense of history and from their grasp of the present. And therefore they cannot understand Israel. They cannot understand the fierce sensations of vulnerability, the lusty devotion to military strength, the stubborn resistance to international criticism, the waves of guilt that soften the core of the hardness. They cannot comprehend the gnawing fear of powerlessness that grinds beneath the arsenal of tanks and planes, the lurking conviction that it could happen again, and that again the world would look the other way.

Raja Shehadeh, who grew up in the West Bank schools under Jordan, knew absolutely nothing of the Jews' sufferings under the Nazis before 1967, when his territory came under Israeli control and he found himself in contact with Israelis. "Certainly we had never heard of the Holocaust before '67, all over the Arab world," he said. Now, at least among his circle of relatively knowledgeable friends on the West Bank, he observed, "I do hear much more said about the Holocaust. I think there is much more awareness of the Holocaust than there ever was in pre-'67 and in Jordan." But the awareness translates more easily into self-pity than into a sympathy for the Jews, as Raja himself demonstrated in choosing the title of his book, *The Third Way: A Journal of Life in the West Bank*. On the back cover, the origin of the phrase "the third way" is explained: "From the wisdom of the Treblinka concentration camp: 'Faced with two alternatives—always choose the third.' Between mute submission and blind hate—I choose the third way. I am *Samid* [the steadfast]." And so Treblinka becomes a metaphor for the West Bank. How did he come to this? I asked him.

"An Israeli friend of mine told me about this, a Canadian Jew," Raja explained lightly. "It struck me as something interesting, so I used it."

There are no courses on the Holocaust at Bir Zeit University, a bastion of Palestinian nationalism on the West Bank. And in the Israeli-Arab schools, teachers often race through the chapters on the Holocaust in a couple of days, giving the subject the kind of pro forma treatment that just doesn't stick in kids' heads. An Arab teacher told me that he had no grasp of the magnitude of what had happened to the Jews until he had been teaching for some years and happened to see films and photographs on Israeli television of the ghettos and the concentration camps. Then, and only then, was he awakened to the scope and the severity of the event.

Something of the same thing happened to a militant Arab in his early twenties who had gone to Israeli schools for Arabs but expressed himself in vehemently anti-Jewish terms. He even equated Israel with the Nazis and said that what happened in Germany was the same as what was happening on the West Bank. Several American Jews in the Interns for Peace program challenged him, asked him what he really knew about what had happened in Germany, and then took him to a museum established by ghetto fighters. He was deeply moved, seeing what Jews had suffered. In his lifetime he had seen the Jews only in command; to him, Jews were the powerful. On his job at an ice-cream factory, he told some of his Jewish co-workers about his visit to the museum, about his reactions, and they began to open up to him, to accept him as they had not before.

For many others, however, even knowledge fails to open a clear view through the corrosive Arab-Jewish conflict; neither side can truly see the other through the veil of grief and anger. And so, many Arabs who know something about the Holocaust tend to interpret it in their own terms, in their own interest. "I think they are aware of the brutality the Jews have suffered," Albert Aghazarian of Bir Zeit said of his Palestinian students, "but being aware, I think they are surprised and say, 'How come these people, who have suffered, are doing the same thing?' " I asked him how anyone could reasonably argue that the Israelis are doing the same thing. "Two hundred thousand Palestinians have been imprisoned since 1967, " Albert contended. "That is one out of six of the population. Many of them are arrested after a bomb; you collect five hundred people or one thousand people. But that is still the experience of prison, even it if is for ten hours, even if it is for six hours. You have to consider that as being in prison. You have forty-eight percent of the land taken, you have ten thousand houses demolished, including the three villages near Latrun, including the esplanade of the Wailing Wall, including the detonation of houses. You have over one thousand two hundred leaders of the community who have been deported. These were leaders who were not involved in any kind of activities that even subjectively you can call terrorist. These are church leaders, university presidents, union leaders—they threw them out. You have a thousand two hundred laws that have been implemented, arbitrarily controlling every aspect of life in a very racist and apartheid way. You need a permit to plant tomatoes and to plant eggplants and to plant vines. You have to get a permit if you want to plant a plum tree in front of your house. If you lose your ID [card], you are in vital trouble. If you do not follow all this trickery in paperwork you are out and the border is sealed. If it is accumulated, I think it is enough brutality to call it genocide."

I asked him if he didn't see that genocide was an exaggeration, since the word's literal meaning, the intention to murder a whole people, had no application here. "It's the form of murder which is changing," Albert replied. "Let's agree on the term 'mass brutality against a people.' Once you start seeing a group of people as less human, anything becomes possible."

Courses on Israeli society and Jewish history, including the Holocaust, are given by Arab faculty members to Arab students at an-Najah University on the West Bank. "We teach about the Zionist movement, the first five immigration waves that came here, the settlement before 1948, the state," said Abed Samara, a sociology professor, "about Israeli institutions, the [political] parties, the Histadrut [the nationwide federation of labor unions], the political differentiations, the social stratification of Israeli society, the political movements, industry, agriculture, all aspects of Israeli society. We teach about anti-Semitism in Eastern Europe, the history of the Jews in Europe. Most of the students are very interested. They say it's the first time they hear such analysis of Israeli society." One result, he felt, was that some of the Arab students began to abandon some of their stereotypes, or at least refine them by differentiating between Jews in Israel and Jews outside. Others resist; most of those are extreme nationalists or members of the Islamic fundamentalist Muslim Brotherhood. "I have four or five out of fifty who say, 'What's the use of this?' They say, 'Why learn this? We know their history. They are all against us, and they will continue to be against us, so what's the point of this?' But after four or five lectures they take it and they become more understanding."

But does this newfound knowledge, especially of the Jews' suffering under the Nazis, alter the way in which the students interpret Israeli behavior? Samara's answer was discouraging. "They say, 'The Holocaust was a very bad thing for us Palestinians, because the final development of the Holocaust was the creation of Israel in this part of the world against the Palestinians, which means we were the main losers of the Holocaust. Even more than any other people, we are against [the Holocaust] because we are the victims, the final victims, the ultimate ones.' It was the way they reacted."

Palestinian Arabs who see themselves as paying for the crimes of the Germans explore the theme frequently. In *The Third Way*, Raja Shehadeh tells of a "a waking nightmare" that once took possession of him.

The soldiers burst into my room and as they surrounded me their uniforms faded away and turned into striped rags, and their cheeks and their eyes hollowed out and their guns dissolved. They bared their arms and on each one was a concentration camp number. They surrounded me in a tight circle, pointing their tattooed arms at me.

As they stood there, all their flesh withered away, and they were just skeletons, interlocked skeletons, gripping each other, encircling me.

"Your turn has come," they whispered.

"Why? What have I done?"

"You are *Samid* [the steadfast]. We know all about you, we have been watching you. No one, let that be known, no one will ever get away from us. We are the survivors of our six million brothers.

"We are here on earth to avenge our brothers' deaths. This time we shall exterminate every one, before they get a chance to touch us."

"But what have I done?"

"What have you done? Don't look so innocent.

"You seek our destruction—as does everyone. You, the Arabs, are the new Nazis. But we shall get you first. Never Again. . . . You cannot hide. Remember what we say. Never Again. Never Again. Never Again."

As their voices faded out, one reached out and stamped my arm with a number. And then they were gone.

Raja goes on to write, "Sometimes I think I am the victim of the victims of the Nazis. Fate has agreed that I also pay the price of the Holocaust; fate—through nightmares, through the great subconscious—has decreed that I inherit the memory, the fear, and the horror of Auschwitz. . . . I have the horrible suspicion that I am more aware of the concentration camps, think about them more and dream about them more than the average Israeli of my age does. He acts, and I dream the dreams that he should have."

It is impossible to see Jews as victims when you are being victimized by them, even where your suffering has no parallel to theirs. And the defenses you set up to screen out the suffering of your enemy are quite effective, it seems. Jamil Hamad doubted that knowledge of the Holocaust induced Arabs to see things any differently. "I'll tell you why," he said. "First of all, I think the Arabs are aware of what happened in the Holocaust, and they intentionally disregard it. They don't want to talk about it. They minimize it. Because the Holocaust to them represents the case which made the Jews establish their state on their land. But if you talk to them on an intellectual basis, they would say, 'We condemn what the Nazis did to the Jews.' At the same time they would say, 'We are not responsible for that, we are not the ones who massacred the Jews, so why do we pay the price?'

"If we bring more young people to see the films of the Holocaust, that would not change the situation. Why? Because the political conflict between the Arabs and the Israelis has reached a point, a degree, at which the human factor does not count too much. We are involved in a political confrontation, military confrontation, so the talk about the human-life value, the loss of the human lives, this and that, does not count."

Jamil also stressed the attempt to dismiss the Holocaust as something less in reality than it has been portrayed, or something that the Jews brought on themselves. "Many Palestinians believe that the numbers of Jews massacred and killed was and still is exaggerated," he observed. "They say that the numbers of the Jews massacred in Germany was exaggerated by the Zionist movement just to promote the idea of establishing a Jewish state at this time. Secondly, they see it from a different angle, that, okay, the Germans did that to the Jews, but the Jews may have provoked the Germans into doing this. When the Palestinians talk about the Holocaust, they can't take the Holocaust as an isolated issue and talk about it—it's impossible. They have to link it with the political developments and military developments that came in Palestine. To see the Holocaust the way the Americans and Europeans see it? It's impossible. There you are not party to a political and military conflict with the Israelis. Here we are a party to it."

In their insensitivity to the proportions of the Holocaust, Arabs are often annoyed at what they see as the Jews' wallowing in their grief and suffering. "Now let's talk about it frankly," said Jamil. "You Americans have faced in the past terrible times, more or less massacres—the Civil War. Now, it's a good subject for a film, but not an issue which you keep feeding up to your children. Why don't the Jews stop talking about the Holocaust? My theory is that the conflict is badly needed for the survival of the Jews. I feel sometimes that the Arab-Israeli conflict is also needed badly to crystallize, to strengthen the national spirit among the Israelis. It's trying to make use of the Holocaust—which is a very disastrous event, disgusting, I admit that—again, it's trying to make use of it for political reasons. Blackmailing. It's like trading my personal pain, my personal tragedy, to get something. That's why I don't like it, personally."

In practice it is not so calculated, of course. The scars of the Holocaust are deep, and they form the background against which the Arabs' pledges to drive the Jews into the sea are seen. But in Israel, of all places, the memory of the Holocaust is also frequently cheapened by Jews who use it for political propaganda. My first encounter with this was a poster, pasted to a building in downtown Jerusalem by Kahane's Kach movement, which opposed the periodic summit meetings between Begin and Sadat. The poster featured a doctored photograph of Begin and Sadat together, Sadat wearing a tie emblazoned with swastikas and Begin wearing a big Star of David on his lapel, like a Jew under Germany. As I stopped and gawked, Israeli Jews walked past unfazed, accustomed as they were to such tactics.

But Begin would have been wounded most painfully, for he was deeply rooted in that traumatic history, imprisoned in its agony. It was Begin, more than any other Israeli leader, who saw contemporary events through the prism of the genocide that had been practiced against the Jews. When he ordered Iraq's nuclear reactor bombed, he did so citing the potential for another attempt to exterminate the Jews, and he made that vow of resolution: "Never again." Even his involvement in Lebanon was governed by the memory and the fear, the conviction that the PLO, from its bases in southern Lebanon, was bent on exterminating the Jews and that the Christian Arabs of Lebanon faced extermination by the Muslims. That concern for the Christian minority as potential victims of a holocaust framed Begin's secret commitments to Christian leaders to defend them against the Syrian air force, if it were used; in part, the obsession was responsible for drawing Israel into the quagmire of vicious Lebanese factionalism.

Begin reacted vehemently during the Israeli siege of West Beirut when President Ronald Reagan called him and asked him to stop the bombardment. "What hurt me deeply was that the president said, 'It's a holocaust,' " Begin told me during a later interview. He was sitting on a couch in his office. "He hurt me very deeply," he said, "and I answered him in my answer to his letter. I said to him, 'Mr. President, I know what is a holocaust.' " Then Begin turned to his press secretary, Uri Porat. "Will you please bring me the picture?" Uri didn't have to ask which one. He picked a framed photograph from the prime minister's desk: the famous picture of Jews being rounded up in the Warsaw Ghetto. Begin held the photograph in front of him. "This is holocaust," he declared. "This is the Warsaw Ghetto, 470,000 Jews already taken out and brought to Treblinka. And these are the children and the women. Look at this child. Look at the fear in his eyes, how he tries to raise his hands, and look at this mother, looking at the other Nazi soldier lest he open fire at the child. Such children were killed—one and a half million for six years, brought to Auschwitz, Treblinka, Maidanek, etc. This is holocaust. And I later wrote to the president that he hurt me deeply and personally by using that word."

On occasion, the Holocaust has also become a weapon used by Jews against other Jews. A couple of Israelis who had been children of the Holocaust remembered, when they first arrived from Europe, being called "soap" by other Jewish children who were already in Palestine. The cruel taunt was a reference to the Germans' making soap out of the bodies of murdered Jews. In 1982 and 1983, in the throes of severe ethnic tension, Sephardi Jews scrawled slogans on buildings and shouted epithets at Ashkenazi Jews who were demonstrating against Begin. "They shouldn't have rescued you from Hitler in 1945!" one man yelled, and somebody wrote on the Jerusalem Theater "Ashkenazim to Auschwitz, Treblinka, and Dachau." At a Haifa art exhibition in 1985, Meir Kahane became the victim of his own tactics; a Jewish artist, Harold Rubin, hung a painting entitled "Homage to Rabbi Kahane," showing "a Nazi-like bully with Jewish features, his *tefillin*-wrapped arm raised in a Nazi salute," *The Jerusalem Post* reported.* An inscription read "Judenjugend," or "Jewish Youth," a takeoff on the Hitler Youth of the Nazi era. A right-wing Knesset member, Meir Cohen-Avidov, pulled the painting off the wall, demanded that the exhibition be postponed, and promised to work for the cutoff of public funds from the Chagall House of the Haifa Painters and Sculptors Association, where the show was held. The offending painting was put on display again, however.

The Holocaust never quite leaves Israeli Jews alone. Arabs use it against them, and they use it against Arabs. Jews use it against other Jews. Even

---

* *Tefillin* are the leather thongs and other phylacteries worn by Orthodox Jews during prayer.

the president of the United States, it seems, can use it against the minister of Israel. And finally, in spasms of outrage and guilt, some Israeli Jews use it against themselves. "Even when Begin didn't talk about the Holocaust," said Irene Eber, "it was there as an underlying ghost." And it haunts Israel at every step, shaping attitudes quietly, fundamentally.

Holocaust survivors can be found at all points on the Israeli political spectrum. No particular position seems to attract them more than another. They stand on the extreme right, advocating Jewish settlement on the West Bank and tough military measures against Arabs. They stand on the far left, calling for withdrawal from the West Bank and the establishment of a Palestinian state. Some, such as Israel Harel, the settlement leader, combine conflicting views of nationalism and humanitarianism into an idiosyncratic synthesis. Harel is a resolute believer in the Jewish right to integrate the West Bank into Israel, but he was disgusted by the emergence of Jewish terrorism against Palestinian Arabs. Born in Rumania, he was seven when he and his mother were sent to a concentration camp in the northern Ukraine. His father, taken away to be shot, fell among others who had been killed, and thus survived beneath the heap of bodies. "Right after the war we tried to make our way to Eretz Israel, at that time Palestine," Harel recalled. "A British ship, I remember, stopped our way. I remember the British soldiers' jumping on the deck, and we were taken to Cyprus. They released us because I was sick, and they took sick children to Haifa."

How much does this experience bear on him now? A friend of his who was sitting with us as we talked said that she had never heard this story; she had assumed that he was a sabra—Israeli-born—and never realized that he had been through the Holocaust. "I wonder how deeply the Holocaust still drives people," Israel mused. "I would say that in some way, even myself but definitely others, we put up big gates [to fence off] the Holocaust. If it influences, it's so deep you cannot distinguish it. My feeling is that the Holocaust has less effect on our life—political, spiritual, moral—than it should have. I think in some way we passed it too quickly, too easily, and I include myself, too. If I look very deeply into myself, I cannot find very definite marks." Then he immediately qualified his observation. "Maybe the way I eat," he said, laughing. "Until today, I can see my father. Once my father wouldn't let me not finish bread. It's holy. Because for a piece of bread he worked a week.

Up to today, even this Shabbat, 'Well, why don't you finish your bread?' "

Nevertheless, some of the Israelis' moral agony about being occupiers, about being military victors, about being political oppressors—some of the guilt about being strong—finds its roots in the Holocaust. Albert Aghazarian did not quite seem to understand this as he concluded his catalogue of grievances against Israel and his argument in favor of the application of the term "genocide" to Israeli behavior toward the Arabs. I pressed him repeatedly to revise his terminology. As an Armenian, could he not see the difference between Turkey and Germany on the one hand and Israel on the other? He talked in vague circles for some time, but finally concluded, "What I have a grudging admiration for—grudging—is that in spite of everything, you still have moral forces in Israel. What you may broadly call the 'peace camp.' You have some forces in Israel that have not been numbed, surprisingly." And he did not seem to see that this came at least partly from the Holocaust, from the Jews' sense of obligation, having once been victims.

Remarkably, images of the Holocaust kept flashing through the minds of some Jews as they fought in Lebanon, and others, such as Dov Yermiya, an old veteran of the good fight in and before 1948, groaned and fumed under the weight of the history and the present. "I was in the Great War, World War II," he said. "I was in the British army, and I fought in the Middle East and then in Europe. And when we first met the remnants of the Holocaust, and just started to help them, to gather them, to ship them to Israel with the Haganah, I remember, already then, thinking and conversing with my close friends who were together with me in this business, saying that what happened to you Jews and your Holocaust will affect us, Jews in Israel, for the bad. First of all, we lost a lot of good people. Millions and hundreds of thousands of those who could have done something better. But also something has happened. The victim has gained some of the character of the victimizer. And it's hard to believe, but I see it."

Dov pointed to a photograph of a high-ranking Israeli general. "He is supposed to be my friend because he was in the Palmach, and we come from the same origin. But I see him as more or less a fascist warlord who is capable of doing things that have been done to us. The idea of taking the Arabs and shipping them in lorries or on foot out of this country is there somewhere. And if it becomes possible, or feasible, it might happen.

That's why I see that we have been influenced by the victimizers, and we have become more or less similar to them."

It was hard for an outsider to argue with someone who was so deeply and purely Israeli, but I could not let it go at that. I asked first why he thought the Arabs used the Holocaust as an argument. "Because they know that they would have done it to us if they could," he said sharply. "One doesn't have to be a big fool to know that some Jews do think it and some Jews do say it. Now, certainly, both sides use that harsh idea for propaganda. But they all have some kernel of truth in them." But surely it's an exaggeration, I said. Nobody has suggested taking Palestinians off to gas chambers. "No. Well, certainly, what the Nazis have done, there's nothing to compare. But for me it's bad enough that somebody thinks of taking them from their places and putting them on lorries and throwing them on the other side of the Jordan. It's bad enough. It needn't be as bad as it was with the Germans."

For an idealistic old veteran who imagined his country forsaking its ideals, the Holocaust became the only container large enough to hold the grief and the guilt, the only metaphor atrocious enough to accommodate the shame. In the autumn of 1982, after the invasion of Lebanon, the siege of Beirut, the massacre by Israel's Lebanese Christian allies in the Sabra and Shatila refugee camps, many of the old veterans and the new veterans who searched for a denunciation had to use the Holocaust. Nothing else seemed sufficient to capture their deep agony and anger. They recognized the differences, of course; they were trying to measure not the objective events in Lebanon but their feelings about what they, their army, had done there.

Just as Shimon Avidan, the famous brigade commander from 1948, sat on his kibbutz during the war and saw, flashing in front of his memory, the photograph of the Warsaw Ghetto that Begin kept on his desk, so younger warriors kept seeing images from Nazi Europe. Gidon Shamir, a thirty-four-year-old book publisher, served as an officer in his elite unit in 1982, as he had in 1967, 1973, and the War of Attrition against Egypt. He went into the villages, the refugee camps, where he never knew who was going to shoot him. "It can be a ten-year-old kid. You can't take a chance. You can't wait and ask him, 'Say, do you have a gun?' On the other hand, you can't kill him. He is a kid. He's really innocent. You see all these young boys fighting. You have two choices: one, not to fight and take the chance that they will kill you, or to fight, to kill them, and after that you have time again to think and say, 'What's going on with me? Who am I fighting against? Why? What for? Is it necessary to fight?' " When his unit went into the town of Nabatiyeh, the Israeli army made an announcement over loudspeakers. "Everybody should come out of their houses and come to this big yard, men on one side, women on the other side," he recalled. "And it was a terrible shock. It looked like the trains in the '40s in Germany, one side children and women, one side men, a very hot day, not enough water, from the morning till the evening, and the army started researching. That's a system to keep the people from getting wounded, on the one hand; on the other hand it looks very ugly." Gidon Shamir was born in Israel, a highly trained, skilled combat officer.

Ran Cohen, a lanky, balding kibbutznik and colonel in the paratroopers, found the same analogy. "The government decided to make selections among the whole Palestinian population," he said. "That means you have to take all the Palestinians—and there are hundreds of thousands of Palestinians—and to go to every one to see if he's a member of the PLO or not. That means you have to go to every family, every household, everyone, and to make a selection. We remember the selection from other places, from our history in Europe, where the Nazis used to make a selection from the Jewish people. It's not the same, I know, but after all, that means that we have to go to Rashadiyeh, to Ein Hilwe, to other refugee camps, and to make a selection. That means that we have to kill many, many people, to wound many, many people. Little by little we become more and more ugly, not in the character we want to be. For the Jewish people, who have suffered, it is more critical than for other nations." Ran Cohen, born in Iraq, became a member of the Knesset two years after the war.

These soldiers are men of extensive experience both in combat and in human affairs. They are tough and sweet, men of justice who know how to kill. "I want to keep my army morally the best," said Ran Cohen. "I think this makes us stronger, more unified, more ready to go and fight. And this makes our army the best in the world. Without that it would be another army. No, I don't feel guilty. As a citizen of Israel I feel bad, not guilty. Bad."

But the Holocaust? Selections in the camps? Trains disgorging their passengers on their way to death? The boy with his hands raised in the Warsaw Ghetto? I sat over these questions with my friend Hillel Goldberg, a young lecturer at Hebrew University in Jewish ethics and intellectual history. He was a religious man with a graceful, fine precision of compassion in his reasoning, and our long discussions brought a valuable clarity to my own thinking. We rarely conversed except at length, and this time we met after the massacre of Palestinians in the refugee camps of Beirut.

"There is quite clearly a segment of the population of Israel—how large one cannot really know, but certainly a significant segment of the population—for whom this event is a turning point in the moral context of Zionists and Israeli history," he began. "There was, quite clearly here, a failing of massive proportions. Jews have been sensitized over the centuries, and particularly since World War II, to the notion that the ultimate evil is twofold: the killing of innocent people and the stance of the bystanders, the standing by in indifference to the killing of innocent people. Jews have been almost reflexively conditioned to regard the 'outside world' as morally inferior on account of either its active participation in or indifference to the fate of the Jews during the Holocaust. As research gets uncovered year by year, it becomes increasingly clear just how widespread that indifference was. It becomes quite clear how truly insignificant the fate, or the murder, of the Jews was to people who had the power, in at least some way, to change that fate by bombing the rail lines to Auschwitz. All this has simply increased the sense that Jews are morally superior—not necessarily inherently, racially, but simply by what's occurred, simply by historical fact. In the slaughter of millions of Jews, the people who did it were obviously guilty, and the people who could have done something about it were, in another sense, guilty.

"The Jews struggled along the best they could," Hillel continued, "created a state against formidable odds and of course made mistakes in varying degrees of severity along the way, but essentially maintained Israel as a moral enterprise. Now, this massacre is one incident; it doesn't retrospectively change all that was done. The scope of this massacre was quite small compared to the kinds of massacres that were perpetrated against the Jews in World War II. Notwithstanding all that, the point has been reached where it becomes clear that even if only by crimes of omission, we are capable of those very sins against which we have rightly objected so reflexively, strongly, vociferously, and with such great and justified righteous indignation. And when the tables are turned on you in that way, you reach a great—we reach a great moral crisis. That moral crisis cannot be wished away; it has to be confronted. It's not like the recitation in the Yom Kippur service, where one says that one has sinned before God and then one is absolved. With respect to sins one commits against God, God himself can absolve you completely, providing that your remorse is sincere and complete. That's all it takes. It can be instantaneous. However, with respect to sins committed against man, God as it were removes from himself the power to absolve you until you have rectified those sins. The only absolution that can occur can occur only after the wrong has been righted."

Hillel had been a supporter of Begin and was sorely disappointed with him. "Here was a man who, on almost every public occasion, dragged in the Holocaust as a justification for whatever Israel was doing at the point," he said. "And I thought they were inappropriate, but I never thought they were insincere. I thought they were politically unwise but heartfully felt. I certainly can't say at this point that he wasn't sincere. But what I can say is that if all that he learned from the Holocaust was that it's wrong when it's done to the Jews but it's not wrong when something similar is done to other people, then he's ignored the universal side of Jewish thought, which clearly links the Jew to mankind."

I told Hillel what one soldier's mother had done after the massacre. The story was powerful, and it left him sitting in silence for a long moment, meditating, gathering his thoughts. "What happened out there was somehow of a kind with what happened in the Holocaust," he said finally, "at least in the consciousness of those people who, in fact, went through the Holocaust and know it better than anyone else."

The mother lived in Jerusalem. Several days after a Lebanese Christian Phalangist unit entered the refugee camps and slaughtered men, women, and children, her son came home from the army on leave. She met him outside the door and would not let him into the house until he answered some questions.

Was he there during the massacre? Yes, he said, outside Shatila. Did he hear anything, see anything? No, the young man replied, but his friends did. And what did they do? Some did nothing, he answered. But had he known anything himself? No, he repeated.

His mother was not sure that he was telling her the truth, and she is not sure today. But she let him come home. It was her most painful moment in all the years she had had this boy, she said to friends. She was a survivor of Hitler's concentration camps.

PART THREE

Interaction

THIRTEEN

A Mingling of Cultures

> The nations shall rush like the rushing
> of many waters: but God shall rebuke them,
> and they shall flee far off, and shall be
> chased as the chaff of the mountains before
> the wind, and like a rolling thing before
> the whirlwind.
> —Isaiah 17:13

SOME FIFTY MILES FROM THE TOWN HOUSES OF JEWISH JERUSALEM, where refined sophisticates gather for wine and cheese and talk of politics and cinema, Bedouin semi-nomads of the Azazmah tribe roam with camels and camp in tents on the arid wasteland of the Negev Desert. No distance between two societies could encompass a more profound journey from the modern to the ancient. Yet once, for an instant, I had the curious experience of seeing them overlap.

The rectangular goat-hair tent of the Abu-Bilaya family stood in the full darkness and silence of the desert. Flat, unleavened bread had been baked on a scrap of smooth metal balanced on stones over a crackling fire of twigs. Now the host, preparing to serve dinner, had his son carry a pitcher and a towel from one guest to another, pouring water onto our hands, then holding one end of the towel as we dried with the other. It was just a practical method of washing up before a meal in the wilderness, and it slipped quickly into the background of a thousand impressions from a visit to the Bedouin camp.

But a few months later, on the first night of Passover, I found myself in the Jerusalem apartment of a Jewish family, immigrants to Israel from the United States who had gathered for the traditional Seder to mark the deliverance of the Israelites from slavery in Egypt. Flat wafers of unleavened bread, matzo, were set out for the ceremonial meal as a throwback to the desert ways that were imposed during the Israelites' forty years of wandering through Sinai, as a symbol of the hasty flight of the ancient Jews whose dough had not had time to rise. And as we took our seats around the big table, the children of the house brought a pitcher, a basin, and a towel to each of us, pouring water on our hands as we held them over the basin, then holding one end of the towel as we dried with the other. Suddenly the images merged and time collapsed; history touched the present, as it so often does in this land of connections across centuries. The everyday life of the desert Arabs, practiced now as in the biblical eras, had been transformed into Jewish ritual, coexisting and crossing and tangling the crucial lines that mark the vital definitions.

Contemporary scholarship has gone to some lengths to demonstrate that Jews and Arabs have no ethnic links, that while the Isaac-Ishmael lineage is widely accepted in popular belief, it has no basis in anthropology. But beyond the issue of ethnicity lies a rich historical affinity of culture and religious tradition. For Arabs and Jews, those cultural roots are intertwined; Judaism and Islam, interacting through thirteen centuries, have made significant impact on one another. And the resulting bonds, invisible to most Jews and Arabs against the glare of the conflict, have a tensile strength that keeps the two peoples in a contact of strained and awkward intimacy.

The connections run along multiple strands. The Old Testament, for example, is full of intricate descriptions of customs that are virtually unchanged in Arab desert life today. The Jews were a sedentary and agrarian people quite different from the camel-breeding nomads who made their life far out in the desert, and the Jews' sojourn in Sinai was a mere interval between periods of static settlement in Egypt and Canaan.

356

But many of the cultural traits detailed in the Bible bear strong resemblance to that continuing desert tradition. At the heart of Genesis, the patriarch Abraham followed an elaborate ritual of hospitality now practiced in precisely the same way in Bedouin encampments, where the stranger is to be welcomed effusively, fed lavishly, and protected. When the three messengers of the Lord visited Abraham, he rose to meet them, then "Abraham hastened into the tent unto Sarah, and said, Make ready quickly three measures of fine meal, knead it, and make cakes upon the hearth. And Abraham ran unto the herd and fetched a calf tender and good, and gave it unto a young man; and he hastened to dress it. And he took butter, and milk, and the calf which he had dressed, and set it before them." (Genesis 18:6–8.) Similarly, Lot insisted on a lavish welcome at Sodom when two angels approached. "And he said, Behold now, my lords, turn in, I pray you, into your servant's house, and tarry all night, and wash your feet, and ye shall rise up early, and go on your ways. And they said, Nay; but we will abide in the street all night. And he pressed upon them greatly; and they turned in unto him, and entered into his house; and he made them a feast, and did bake unleavened bread, and they did eat." (Genesis 19:2–3.)

Anyone who has encountered Bedouin hospitality will recognize these Old Testament verses as familiar portraits of a durable tradition. A Bedouin today beseeches a traveler to enter his tent, partake of a meal prepared much as the Bible describes, drink his sweet tea and bitter coffee, and spend the night amid the cushions and quilts that are spread out for him. The ethic of welcoming the stranger remains so powerful that it is often captured for contemporary Bedouins in oral poetry. One recited now in Sinai gives a lecture on being a good host:

> Take from me, Salman,
>   some weighty advice,
> And accept it, Salman,
>   though it's told you in verse.
> If you spot strangers traveling
>   from lands far away,
> Stand in front of the tent
>   till they see you and turn.
> Then shake out the carpets
>   and make yourself mild,

So your guest may sit down
    in the tent and feel sure.
Then the fire do kindle
    though never too hot,
Lest the coffee beans burn,
    when the pan is held near.
Fight fiercely for the right
    to sup the camp's stranger.
God gave us hands and fingers
    and will keep us in store,
And if your guests themselves
    do lapse into joking,
Let your eye laugh with them,
    but add nothing more.[72]

The first recorded contact between Arabs and Jews occurred, appropriately, in war. But in that initial encounter they fought on the same side, joining forces in 853 B.C. at the battle of Karkar in Syria as part of a rebellious uprising against the Assyrians. An inscription by the Assyrian king Shalmaneser III names the Arab as Gindibu the Aribi, who led 1,000 camel riders while King Ahab of Israel commanded 10,000 foot soldiers and 2,000 war chariots. The Assyrians emerged victorious.[73]

The term "Aribi" is regarded as one of several variations that have finally come down in modern times as "Arab." Some linguists have postulated that it is derived from an ancient word meaning "west," first used in Mesopotamia to denote the peoples west of the Euphrates Valley. Bernard Lewis prefers an etymology containing the idea of nomadism, as in the Hebrew *arabha*, which means "dark land" or "steppe"; or the Hebrew *erebh*, which means "mixed" or "disorganized," in contrast to the organized sedentary life; or the root *abhar*, which means "to move" or "to pass" and which may also be the origin of the word "Hebrew." In any event, Assyrian and Babylonian inscriptions refer to Aribi, Arabu, and Urbi peoples. Tributes from the Aribi often included camels, according to the ancient records, and drawings also show them with camels, indicating that they were desert dwellers, probably nomads in northern Arabia whom Lewis believes to be the same as the Arabs who appear in the later books of the Old Testament. Around 530 B.C., Persian cuneiform documents include the term "Arabaya," he notes, and Aeschylus mentions Arabia in *Prometheus Bound*.

Talmudic literature is replete with references to Arabs. Ancient Jews had longstanding relationships, sometimes of enmity, sometimes of co-operation, with the Nabateans, a neighboring people of Arab origins who resided just on the east of the Jews during the Maccabean, Herodian, and Roman eras. The modern Israelis have carefully excavated some Nabatean settlements in the Negev, reconstructing the ruins of one hilltop town that was used to extract tolls along a trade route between the Mediterranean and the Arabian peninsula. An Israeli agronomist nearby has even experimented with desert agriculture using only the rainwater accumulated in ancient cisterns built under the arid, gravelly hills and wadis by the Nabateans, who apparently farmed successfully with the method.

But the full flowering of Arab-Jewish symbiosis came with the rise of Islam in the seventh century A.D. and the extension of the Islamic empire throughout the Mediterranean basin. This, forming what Lewis calls the Judeo-Islamic tradition, represents one of three great interactions between the Jewish people and other major civilizations. Of the three—with the ancient Greeks, the Arab Muslims, and the European Christians*—Goitein sees the Arab-Jewish associations as the most important in shaping each party's cultural and religious traits.

The Jews' close contacts with the ancient Greeks in Palestine and elsewhere endured for a thousand years and created internal strife among the Jews over their Hellenization, their assimilation into Greek culture. Important Jewish thinkers wrote in Greek, including the philosopher Philo of Alexandria and the historian and Second Temple priest Flavius Josephus. But Greek civilization did not deeply penetrate Jewish culture, and the writings in Greek were not translated and did not reach the Jews generally until modern times.

The later association between the Jews and the Romanic and Germanic peoples of Europe also lasted approximately a thousand years, attaining a peak from the nineteenth century until it faded and was then crushed

---

* A fourth may be added centuries from now, when enough time has passed to satisfy the patient historians: Jewish culture in the English-speaking democracies.

359

by the Nazis in the middle of the twentieth century. It produced two Jewish languages: Ladino, based on a Romanic foundation; and Yiddish, based on the German. The rich Jewish scholarship and literature that grew out of the German-Jewish culture, rendered in German and Yiddish, induced some scholars to place the German-Jewish and the Arab-Jewish symbiosis on equal levels of significance.

But others see the Arab-Jewish as a more complete cultural relationship. "Despite their great relative importance," Goitein declares, "none of the creations of the Jewish authors writing in German or conceived under the impact of modern Western civilization has reached all parts of the Jewish people or [has] influenced the personal inner life of every Jew to the profound degree as did the great Jewish writers who belonged to the medieval civilization of Arab Islam. The reason for this difference is self-evident. Modern Western civilization, like the ancient civilization of the Greeks, is essentially at variance with the religious culture of the Jewish people. Islam, however, is from the very flesh and bone of Judaism." As a result, Judaism could take from Islam without losing its own character, without facing the dilemma presented both in Hellenistic society and Christian Europe, where the path to enjoying the benefits of the host society lay through a certain assimilation, and the price of cultural integrity was paid in alienation from the dominant society. Goitein notes that while German-Jewish writers in the nineteenth and twentieth centuries were extolling Judaism as "essentially identical with the highest attainments of German thinking," Jews writing in Arabic during the Middle Ages "never had the slightest doubt about the absolute superiority of Judaism." In other words, "Judaism inside Islam was an autonomous culture sure of itself."

Islam, like Christianity, is a daughter religion of Judaism. Its prophet Muhammad, born in Mecca between A.D. 570 and 580, is thought to have been unable to read but to have gained knowledge of the Bible orally from both Jewish and—to a lesser extent—Christian travelers and traders. As a result, the Koran contains a multitude of references to biblical characters, stories, and themes, many of them retold with an embellishment and variation expected of tales passed by word of mouth. The Koran's heavy echo of the Books of Moses, combined with Muhammad's adherence to a monotheism against the predominant, pagan culture of idol-worshipers, suggests that his religious views were strongly influenced by Jewish thought. Goitein postulates that Muhammad's mentors were Jews, since fewer Christians appeared in the Arabian peninsula at the time. Evidently, he expected considerable Jewish support for his teachings. Also, one of Muhammad's wives was Jewish, a fact seldom mentioned by Muslims.

After failing to meet success with his preaching in Mecca, he moved 280 miles north to Medina, which had been settled by Jewish tribes. Ultimately, the cohesion that Muhammad provided the Arabs resulted in their attacking and driving the Jews from Medina. But initially he looked to the Jews as his natural followers. Perhaps in an expedient effort to gain their favor, he absorbed some Jewish practices into his ritual. These included prayer facing Jerusalem, observance of the fast day of Kippur (Yom Kippur), and the old Jewish custom of bowing and prostration during prayer, a practice later abandoned by the Jews (except for its vestige, the five prostrations during the Yom Kippur service). Although prostrations remained in Islam, Muhammad removed the other overt Jewish practices after the Jews of Medina reacted contemptuously to his preaching. He substituted Mecca for Jerusalem as the direction of worship, although Jerusalem was retained as a slightly lesser light in the constellation of Islam. After his death and in early Islamic times, some authorities denounced the concept of Jerusalem's holiness as a Judaizing infiltration. Later, of course, when Islam accepted Jerusalem's holy status again, the city ceased to be Jewish in Islamic eyes.

Muhammad also took the concept of the Jewish Sabbath, but only as a day of communal prayer, not of rest, for a complete halt in activity would not have been convenient either in the life of the Bedouin goatherds and camel-breeders or for Arab merchants who were constantly shipping goods and traveling. The day of rest was rejected as a Jewish perversion until centuries later, when it became too attractive to resist.

Despite the Medina Jews' dismissal of Muhammad's teachings, it was the presence of the Jewish community that helped provide an environment conducive to eventual Arab acceptance of monotheism. Where Judaism had developed in conflict with everything that had gone before, Islam grew out of existing monotheistic faiths; Muhammad preached in the context of Jewish and Christian doctrine. The doctrinal intimacy was summarized in one of Muhammad's famous sayings, contained in collections of Muslim oral traditions: "You will follow the traditions of those who preceded you span by span and cubit by cubit—so closely that you will go after them even if they creep into the hole of a lizard."

The emerging Islamic faith shared many, but not all, of Judaism's religious practices and theological themes. Both Judaism and Islam barred pictures and statues from their synagogues and mosques, although Islam went a step further by refusing liturgy, poetry, or music in worship, embellishments for which Judaism and Christianity share an affinity. While Islam and Christianity embraced evangelism, Judaism did not. Both Islam and Judaism firmly rejected the Christian concept of the Trinity, regarding the Father, the Son, and the Holy Ghost as bordering on idolatry, as undermining Christianity's monotheism. As a consequence, during later periods of forced conversion, Jewish authorities considered it less blasphemous to pretend to regard Muhammad as the prophet of God than Jesus as the Son of God. This dissembling practice was adopted by the Jews from the Islamic doctrine of *taqiya*, which suggests that one can lie about his religious beliefs for the sake of survival as long as he holds them firmly in his private convictions. Since Judaism's theological conflict was less severe with Islam than with Christianity, Jews in Yemen, Iran, and Morocco used the method during tough periods there while those in Germany and England did not.

A striking Judeo-Islamic parallel appears in the system of oral religious law, a divine regulation of the minute matters of morality and custom in everyday life. This is entirely alien to Christianity, but it forms the core of both Judaism and Islam. The body of law, called Halakha in Judaism and Sharia in Islam, functions with a process of responsa (*fatwa* in Islam), or answers by learned clerics to questions posed on matters of ethics, family life, and the like. The Islamic concept appears to have grown directly out of Judaism. As Goitein observes, it was principally in Iraq, the major center of Jewish studies, that Muslim religious law developed. Study of the law is considered worship both for Jews and Muslims, and each now has religious courts in Jerusalem to adjudicate disputes and administer the translation of the oral tradition into practical living. Although contrasts abound in the specific legal provisions—the rules of inheritance, for example, are quite different—many of the laws are similar, including dietary rules that forbid the consumption of "that which dieth of itself, and blood, and swine's flesh," in the Koran's words (Sura II, The Cow, Verse 168). The Jewish laws of diet are stricter, and so Muslims are permitted to eat meat prepared by the People of the Book, but Jews who keep kosher may not eat meat prepared by Muslims. The exception to the pattern comes with Shiite Muslims, in whose strictest doctrine, Lewis observed, anything touched by Jews is unlawful.

"Islam is much closer to Judaism than Christianity," Rabbi David Hartman observed. He saw in this the prospect for dialogue. "Much more sense of the transcendent God, the non-image God, the imageless God," he said. "Its tremendous concern with law. Law and theology are much closer. And the place that the community plays in spiritual life. And on a cultural level, the family, the role of the family, are all ways in which we can be talking to each other."

Just as Islam drew from Judaism and absorbed much of its theology and organization, Judaism also felt the impact of Islam. Between antiquity and modernity, as Jews were dispersed throughout the world, the richest Jewish life and history took place in Christian and Muslim lands, where Judaism adjusted and emulated the host religion. "If we compare the Jews of Christendom with the Jews of Islam," said Bernard Lewis, "we find that they tend to follow the practices of the dominant religion even in matters which one would have thought are very intimate and of profound religious significance. For example, in marriage, where in Islamic lands Jewish marriage is polygamous, in Christian lands it is monogamous. This is clearly following the practice of the dominant creed. It is remarkable that in a matter as central and important as the family, given the centrality of the family in Jewish life, the two communities should both follow the host society. For the Jews of Christendom, of course, this involved a change, while for the Jews of Islam, it didn't."

For both Jews and Muslims, Judeo-Islamic interaction reinforced the practice of travel for religious study or pilgrimage. "Journeys whose aim was a visit to famous scholars and schools were an old Jewish custom, most conspicuous in talmudic literature," Goitein observes, "and this tradition received new impetus under Arab rule, where travel for study's sake became a characteristic aspect of Muslim civilization." As a visit to Mecca or another holy place became an obligation for a Muslim at least once in his lifetime, so a Jew living in Spain or North Africa in the eighth or ninth century would aspire to "behold Jerusalem" before he died. Pilgrimages were made to the tombs of saints, with Muslims visiting those of Jewish saints, Jews visiting those of Muslim saints, and the two religions sharing as many as thirty-one saints in common, according to one account. Some Muslims in the ninth century criticized these pilgrimages as practices borrowed from the Jews, and in the tenth century one Jewish scholar attacked them as an idolatry that had come from the Muslims.

In other respects, however, Jews were often the subject of enormous admiration. The Koran puts an amusing twist on the biblical story of Joseph, for example. After his jealous brothers have left him to be taken into slavery in Egypt, Joseph resists the attempted seduction by Potiphar's wife. In the Koran's version, he is initially exonerated. She becomes the object of gossip among the ladies of Egypt. So to prove how devastatingly handsome the Jew is, she invites the ladies to a banquet, gives them knives to cut their food with, and then has Joseph enter. So stunned are they by his beauty that they cut their hands.

Among rural Arabs, Jews of learning, as well as Muslims, were sometimes respected with superstitious faith as healers and magicians. Goitein tells of a Yemenite Jew who was asked by the wife of a Muslim villager to write her a charm so that she could bear her husband a child. He declined since he did not believe in such sorcery, but she persisted and finally persuaded him to write something out in Hebrew. "Obviously fortified by the Hebrew charm, she regained the love of her husband and eventually bore him a son," Goitein writes. When the Jew returned to the village a year later, having forgotten the incident, he was surprised with an elaborate greeting of festivities and presents.

In another story, a famous Jewish scribe, diligently copying a Torah, was interrupted by an Arab shepherd demanding an amulet for his sick sheep. Annoyed, the scribe wrote a curse in Hebrew on a piece of paper. When the sheep got well, the Jew was given the fattest ram in the flock.

There was a great cross-fertilization in customs and superstitions between Jews and Arabs. Messianic movements appear to have risen in both Judaism and Islam at the same times. In 1121 in Baghdad, for example, both a Jew and a Muslim declared themselves religious leaders who would bring redemption and an era of justice; the same year, a Jew in Palestine proclaimed himself the Messiah. Shortly thereafter, wealthy Jews of Baghdad were promised by a false Messiah that they would be miraculously transported to Palestine. They gave up their riches and climbed to the roofs of their houses. They wore green clothing, just what Muslims imagine they will be wearing when they reach Paradise.

· · ·

The experience of Jews under Islam varied widely, but as a whole it fulfilled neither the stereotype of perfect tolerance and harmony nor that of cruel oppression and extermination. The situation stood somewhere between the two, a deference to the dominant culture but rarely the kind of persecution that Jews suffered under Christendom. So difficult was the Jews' position under the Church that they welcomed the Muslim conquests and helped the Islamic invaders in Palestine, Syria, Spain, and elsewhere, for at least under Islam they were permitted to exist as a subordinate minority. Whereas practice in Christian countries was worse than precept, in Islamic countries it was generally the other way around: Practice was better than the doctrine preached. "There is enormous variation," said Bernard Lewis, "ranging from a very large measure of tolerance, to situations of acute persecution and forced conversion. If we mean by tolerance an absence of discrimination, then the society was never tolerant, never pretended to be tolerant, and indeed the absence of discrimination would have been regarded not as a merit, but as a dereliction of duty. If, however, by tolerance we mean the absence not of discrimination but of persecution, then we have a very different answer. In general, the record, I would say, was a fairly good one. There are areas of persecution. But generally speaking there is nothing resembling the violent persecutions, the massacres, the pogroms, the repressions which we find in Christian Europe. Nor do we find the kind of economic restraints or restrictions which were imposed on Jews, though of course there were some, on a limited scale."

Discrimination was quite explicit in some parts of the Islamic empire. Jews were prohibited from holding government offices. If they passed Muslims on the street, they were required to dismount from donkeys so their heads would not be higher. Special clothing or colors were forced on Jews—and Christians—as a means of identification in some Muslim countries, where Jewish women had to wear one black and one white shoe, for example; in Yemen and elsewhere, yellow badges were required centuries before the Nazis used the yellow Star of David to designate the Jew. Heavy taxes and tributes were collected from non-Muslims, and in Egypt the tax receipt constituted a pass permitting the Jew or Christian to leave his village. In Iraq, non-Muslims had to attach the receipt to their necks, and the penalty for failing to do so was death. Forced conversions in Yemen reached a point where Jewish children whose fathers had died were torn from their mothers and taken into Muslim homes.

The logic held that everyone was born naturally into Islam, that children were diverted to other religions only by the parents, and when the father was absent, the children reverted to Islam.

The Muslims also inherited a law from the Eastern Roman Church banning the construction of new synagogues while protecting those already in existence; both provisions were ignored in various parts of the Islamic empire, where new synagogues were sometimes permitted and old ones sometimes burned. It was the common practice of Muslim schoolboys to stone Jews—a venerable tradition that has acquired a political edge today on the West Bank—and "when the Turkish Governor asked an assembly of notables [in Yemen in 1872] to stop this nuisance," Goitein writes, "there arose an old doctor of Muslim law and explained that this stone-throwing at Jews was an age-old custom . . . and therefore it was unlawful to forbid it."

All three religions had prohibitions against consulting each other's physicians. Christians were not to use Muslim or Jewish doctors, Jews were barred from using non-Jewish doctors, and Muslims—arguing that non-Muslim doctors could control one's soul through the control of his body—were enjoined from going to Christians or Jews for medical treatment. In practice, however, there is documentary evidence of considerable interchange in medicine, with Muslims teaching, learning from, and being treated by Jewish physicians, with Christians and Jews as court physicians to Muslim caliphs, with a collegial fellowship emerging among doctors, at least until the decline of the Islamic empire in the late Middle Ages, when government decree reinforced the Muslim religious authorities in their declarations against non-Muslim physicians. Generally, the situation of the Jews under Islam worsened from the Middle Ages into the twentieth century.

When Islam flourished, Jews participated rather fully in the pursuit of medicine and other sciences, including astronomy, mathematics, and physics. They wrote in Arabic, and their work became integral to the society's scientific literature. Jewish philosophers and religious thinkers also absorbed significant elements from Muslim thought. "In the literature of philosophy and even of theology," Lewis writes in *The Jews of Islam*, "one may say without hesitation that the influence flowed from Islam to Judaism and not the other way around." Goitein sees Muslim mysticism, especially Sufism, the pietist movement of the ninth and tenth centuries, as having had considerable impact on Judaism. Although early

Muslim mystics apparently benefited from contact with Hasidic Jews, the Islamic mysticism ultimately became a richer, more fluent system of thought than the Jewish. Because of the Muslim conquests, the imposed slavery, and the mixing of huge numbers of diverse people, the ground for philosophical enterprise had a fertility among the Muslims that was absent among the Jews, who retained relatively closed communities and married within them. Sufism's tenets were ascetic, advocating the renunciation of individual personality and the worldly elements of life to achieve oneness with God. The ecstasy that accompanied man's passing through higher and higher levels of perfection did not penetrate Judaism. But the basic Sufic ideas shaped Bahya's *The Duties of the Heart*, written in 1075 in Arabic; translated into Hebrew, it became a highly popular Jewish book of devotion.

Maimonides, one of the most illustrious thinkers of Judaism, was also profoundly influenced by Islam. A physician, astronomer, philosopher, and religious scholar, he was born in Córdoba, Spain, in 1135 and spent much of his life in Cairo, where he died in 1204. He lived, learned, and wrote deeply within the context of Islam; his major work of philosophy, *Guide of the Perplexed*, rests its central argument—that life's only worthwhile purpose is pure, abstract thinking—on Greek philosophy as interpreted by Islam. "Thus, the *Guide of the Perplexed* is a great monument of Jewish-Arab symbiosis," Goitein observes, "not merely because it is written in Arabic by an original Jewish thinker and was studied by Arabs, but because it developed and conveyed to large sections of the Jewish people ideas which had so long occupied the Arab mind."

In Maimonides, who codified Jewish oral law, David Hartman sees a basis for Judeo-Islamic accord. "Maimonides, who lived with Islam, wrote a major responsa about Islam not being paganism, and had a very high regard for Islamic monotheism," Hartman noted. "So there is a very, very interesting tradition in which the Jewish philosophers, in which Maimonides, the greatest Jewish Halakhist philosopher of Jewish history, lives with intense dialogue and respect for Islamic philosophy. So there is a precedent now for a rich intercultural, spiritual theme. There is enormous ground on which that could be possible."

Arab and Jewish cultures have also been mutually enriched in poetry and language. Before Islam, the notable Jewish poetry that existed was almost entirely religious, and it was the rise of florid, secular Arabic poetry that influenced the creation of a similar branch of Hebrew literature—verses on love, satirical works—a secular poetry written prolifically by the prominent Hebrew poets of the Middle Ages. Modern scholars see such development as having been made possible by the heavy influence of Arabic on Hebrew, which had existed only as a cloistered religious language without everyday application.

By A.D. 1000, about 300 years after the Muslim conquests, most Jews living under Islam were speaking and writing in Arabic. "Arabic itself became a Jewish language," Goitein notes, and "was employed by Jews for all secular and religious purposes, with the sole exception of the synagogue service." This Jewish input contributed to Arabic literary tradition, and the Jews' intensive contact with Arabic was, in turn, responsible for the shape of modern Hebrew, which "developed its grammar and vocabulary on the model of the Arab language," he observes. "The revival of Hebrew in our own times would be entirely unthinkable without the services rendered to it by Arabic in various ways a thousand years ago." Jewish philology grew out of immersion in Arabic as well. "It was the contact with the Arabs—'the worshippers of language,' as they have been called—that directed the Jewish mind to a field of activity, for which, as it was proved subsequently, it was particularly gifted, and which bore its mature first fruits to the benefit of the national language of the Jewish people itself."

This now seems a misty past whose shapes and shadows, scarcely discernible in the garish hostility of the moment, linger only in the quiet dawns and dusks of contemplation. Few Jews or Arabs would acknowledge this wealth of common heritage, the pervasive movement of influence back and forth between the cultures and religions. Yet even today, despite the conflicts, the interactions exist beside the frictions. Each side takes cognizance of the other; each is part of the other's vital sphere of life.

This begins with the most elementary words that Jews and Arabs speak. As Semitic languages, Hebrew and Arabic share vocabulary and grammar, and now, as close neighbors under the Israelis, they also share some important slang. In Arabic and Hebrew, the number "one" is *wahid* and *ehad* respectively; "five" is *khamseh* and *khamesh*; "seven" is *saba'a* and *sheva*; "twenty" is *ishrin* and *esrim*; "one hundred" is *miyeh* and *me'ah*. In both languages, "four" is *arba*; "day" is *yom*; "night" is *layla*; and the right side is *yamin*. The word for "house" is *bayt* in Arabic and *bayit* in

Hebrew; "sun" is *shams* and *shemesh*; "hand" is *id* (in spoken Palestinian Arabic) and *yad*; "milk" is *haliib* and *chalav*; and "water" is *mayeh* in Arabic and *mayim* in Hebrew.

For Jews who grew up in Jerusalem in the 1930s and early 40s, Arabic was a source of slang. Danny Rubinstein was taught street games by Arab children, games for which only Arabic words existed. Arabic names were used for fruits and vegetables that the Jewish immigrants to Palestine had not known from Eastern Europe. Much of this terminology has now been lost to Jews, except to that generation of Jerusalemites. But other Arabic words have crept into today's colloquial Hebrew. Many Jews now use the Arabic *fashla* for "failure" instead of the Hebrew word, *kishalon*. Since Hebrew has no curses—unless one counts the biblical "harlot" or "son of a whore"—many Israeli Jews have borrowed Arabic obscenities and now use them frequently instead of the Russian epithets that permeated the spoken Hebrew of the early Zionist pioneers who made their way to Palestine from Russia and Eastern Europe. "*Kus ummak*," a vile Arabic curse meaning "your mother's cunt," is now such an integral part of the verbal landscape that Jewish drivers who know little else in Arabic shout it fluently at those who cut them off on the highway.

Two-way linguistic contamination has occurred around the Arabic greeting "*Ahlan wa-sahlan*," meaning "welcome." It is a contraction of the longer Arabic saying "May your way to our tent be through a smooth valley." Many Jews have now adopted only the first part, *ahlan*, which they pronounce without the aspirated H, so that it comes out sounding like *aalan*. This corruption, in turn, has filtered back into the colloquial Arabic spoken by some Israeli Arabs who are fluent in Hebrew, and who now also say to Jews—and even to each other—"*Aalan*."

Jews who lived under Islam adopted Arab first names in many cases, just as Jews in the West have been given Western names. Occasionally an Israeli Jew—a West Bank military officer or a police operative who interrogates Arabs—assumes an Arab code name as a kind of *nom de guerre*. The Arabic and Hebrew are often very close in any event: Musa and Moshe (for Moses), Yusuf and Yosef (for Joseph), Ishak and Yitzhak (for Isaac), Ibrahim and Avraham (for Abraham), Yaacub and Yaacov (for Jacob), Maryam and Miriam, Daoud and David.

Arabs eager to melt into Israeli society sometimes Hebraicize their names at convenient moments, or even change them legally in a few rare cases, a practice approved only reluctantly by the Interior Ministry in view of the difficulty it creates in identifying them as Arabs. Others make strange combinations. Mahmoud Azzi, an Arab actor who has played roles in Israeli films, became Mahmoud Artzi on the screen, keeping the Arab name Mahmoud and taking a last name that had a Hebrew sound to it.

The vast majority of Arabs are easily identifiable to most Jews by accent or appearance. But uncertainties have grown as Arabs have gained fluency in Hebrew and as Sephardi Jews—many of whom share the Arabs' traditional facial features, dark hair, and olive skin—have become predominant in the Israeli-Jewish population. One right-wing Jew complained that he could not always tell an Arab from a Jew anymore unless he asked his name, the ultimate giveaway. Another, less troubled, said confidently that he could always tell "by looking in their eyes." What he imagined betrayed them in their eyes he seemed unable to define.

Arabs find it easier to spot a Jew, since few Jews speak Arabic fluently enough to pass. One who does, Naftali Sappir, is a Jerusalem native who befriended an Arab family until they discovered that he was Jewish; in their distress, the relationship cooled. Naftali, however, seemed to feel less offended at their turn of mood than elated that his Arabic was good enough to fool them.

A multitude of sad and comical episodes spring from the driving need to attach the Arab or the Jewish label firmly and at first glance. Rabbi Bruce Cohen and another Jew, standing one day at a fast-food stand in Tel Aviv, were arguing over Bruce's ideas for projects to promote Arab-Jewish cooperation. Bruce's companion was skeptical. "You can never trust an Arab," he told the rabbi. "Don't you agree?" he asked the man behind the counter. "Don't you agree that you can never trust an Arab?"

"I can't agree," said the man, "because, you see, I'm an Arab."

Confusion over identities has given Michael Widlanski, an Arabic-speaking Jew, some moments of acute discomfort when he has occasionally encountered Arabs, using Hebrew names, working in stores. "I'll try to speak to them in Arabic, and they'll answer in Hebrew," he said. "I get very scared because their Hebrew is so good that I think they might be Jewish and if I continue speaking Arabic it would be an insult."

Policemen get mixed up as well, with ugly results. In one incident, officers on patrol beat two Ethiopian Jews severely and then said, "Oh, we thought they were Bedouin," according to Menachem Amir, the Hebrew University criminologist. In other words, Amir noted, "It's okay to beat Bedouin." One Saturday, other officers stopped a man whom they thought was an Arab and ordered him to produce his identification card. When he said he didn't have it with him, they beat him up. Later, when they learned that in fact he was an off-duty Jewish policeman, they gave the excuse that they felt exonerated them: They had honestly believed that their victim was an Arab.

Crime has grown into a bizarre area of Arab-Jewish interaction, a fertile field of cultural penetration and cooperation that enhances the criminals' flexibility and efficiency. The most common pattern, according to Yehezkel Carthy, chief of investigations for the national police, is for Jewish and Arab criminals who have met each other in prison to divide their labors once they get out: Jews steal and Arabs fence. Jewish criminals break into Jewish homes and stores and then transfer the stolen property to Arabs, who sell it on the West Bank and transport it through Jordan to other Arab countries, or take it to the Gaza Strip and from there to Sinai and Cairo. "Crime doesn't recognize political borders and differences in political views," Carthy mused.

Sometimes, mixed Arab-Jewish criminal bands perform the burglaries together. In Negev Desert towns, a team of Bedouins and Israeli Jews broke into several factories, made off with large quantities of goods, and in one incident murdered a watchman who had surprised them. Burglaries in Arab neighborhoods of East Jerusalem rely on more elaborate cooperation, with the Arabs casing the Arab homes and businesses. "The Jewish parties will supply the arms, the transportation—usually a stolen car—and the Arab parties will supply the information, the victims, the entrances and exits from the house," Carthy explained, adding that the home of a prominent and wealthy East Jerusalem Arab had been burglarized by just such a group of Arabs and Jews.

The Jewish criminals, who are generally right-wing patriots, choose their partners out of simple opportunism, apparently attaching no political significance to working with Arabs. Some are Sephardim who speak Arabic; others are Georgian Jews who are alienated enough from Israeli society to merit the Arabs' trust. "In all the cases that I can recall," Carthy noted, "the parties were hardened criminals with previous convictions who just cooperated in some stage of their criminal careers. It's not that they started together."

Other areas of crime besides housebreaking also foster some cooperation across the Arab-Jewish divide. In the lucrative hashish trade, the goods come in from neighboring Arab countries, especially Syrian-controlled areas of Lebanon, and pass into Jewish hands for street sale. Cattle-rustling, thefts of fruits and vegetables from the fields, and other such agricultural crimes inside Israel involve Jews who do the stealing and then Arabs who put the goods into the economy of the West Bank, Gaza, and the Arab towns of Israel.

In a 1975 survey, Menachem Amir found that 40 percent of all pimps in Israel were Arabs managing Jewish prostitutes. When he asked the women why they preferred Arab pimps, they told him that although the Arabs sometimes beat them, they were fairer than their Jewish counter-parts.

One could imagine that an Arab, always vulnerable to police pressure as a suspected terrorist, would make a rather untrustworthy partner in lesser, common crime. "If I were in the underworld," said Amir, trying to think like a Jewish criminal, "I wouldn't trust an Arab. I would not be sure that he would not talk. You can just bring the Shin Beth and say, 'You're not just a criminal, you're PLO.' It's better to buy a gun from a Jew because if you're caught you can say, 'He sold it to me.' Otherwise it's from the PLO." This, he reasoned, strongly motivates the Arab criminal to spill the beans.

In at least one case Amir knew of, the Jews were the ones not to be trusted. It was a breakout from Ramle prison. Seven Jews and one Arab made it beyond the walls, and then the Jews pushed the Arab aside, refused to take him with them, and left him to go to the only place he could—his own village, where he was captured in a day and a half. The others weren't found for a year and a half.

The two cultures have made some impact on each other in social mores and esthetic values. Young Arab women, especially Christian urban residents whose families are Westernized enough to let them attend college, often wear tight jeans and other scanty dress in a tendency frequently denounced by elder Arabs in the villages, who blame the Israeli Jews for corrupting their youth. Similar criticism has come from an extremely orthodox Hasidic sect, the Neturei Karta, whose women shave their heads at marriage and cover their arms and ankles. In their Jerusalem neighborhood of Mea Shearim, big signs in English and Hebrew warn tourists to dress conservatively or face violence, and some European and American women visitors have had stones thrown at them for ignoring the admonition. In 1984, Mea Shearim residents felt compelled to hang pink posters with black lettering giving the same message in Arabic:

REQUEST AND WARNING

TO WOMEN VISITING OUR NEIGHBORHOOD

NOT TO APPEAR IN OUR NEIGHBORHOOD

IN SHORT GARMENTS (NOT COVERING THE KNEE)

IN SHORT-SLEEVED CLOTHES (NOT COVERING

THE ARM).

THE TORAH OBLIGATES TO DRESS

IN MODEST ATTIRE THAT COVERS

THE ENTIRE BODY.

—Residents of the Neighborhood

The Neturei Karta opposes Zionism on the conviction that a Jewish state has no right to exist before the coming of the Messiah. It is a very small sect, and Rabbi Moshe Hirsch, its "foreign minister," enjoys trying to get its views into American newspapers. He explained to me why Arabs now had to be warned about clothing, and of course he blamed Zionism. He himself wore the traditional broad-brimmed black hat, black coat, black trousers and shoes, a white shirt without a tie, a wispy grey beard, and curls that hung down in front of his ears. From New Jersey originally, he spoke English with an American accent, always with the slightest suggestion of an ironic smile touching his lips, as if he were vaguely amused by the role he played and the things he said. "The world-renowned modest Muslim dress," he observed, "has deteriorated sharply after having been affected by the ways and customs of the Zionists' uncivilized dress. The adherence to the request to conform to the mode of the Jewish Orthodox residents of Mea Shearim will further the peaceful and amicable relationship and coexistence between the Muslim and Jewish people, as had been the rule before Zionism had infringed on the Jewish way of life."

Arabs have also adapted commercially to the proximity and buying power of Jewish society. In Mea Shearim, which is reminiscent of an East European shtetl of the nineteenth century, extensive intermingling occurs on the level of trade. Arabs wishing to buy and sell used goods walk down the street calling in Yiddish, *"Alte zachen"* (old things). A tall Arab smoking a cigarette lopes through the market looking for work. A sign on a storefront, handwritten in Arabic, announces that a textile shop has moved "to 40 Shivtai Yisrael Street, near the No. 11 bus stop."

Even the most nationalistic Palestinian merchant in East Jerusalem and the Old City will place Jewish artifacts on sale for Jewish tourists. On Saladin Street just a few blocks outside the Old City walls stands a small souvenir shop owned by Farah and Naim Terzi, brothers of the PLO's observer at the United Nations, Zehdi Labid Terzi. Among the trinkets and beads for sale are Stars of David, menorahs, and metal plates reading "Shalom."

Israeli-Jewish values and interests have been shaped extensively by Arab tastes. Many Jews have come to admire Arab copper and brass plates, baskets, embroidery, food, and architecture. The most expensive and prestigious houses in Jerusalem are the old Arab-built houses made of weathered stone with graceful arches, thick walls, and high, cool vaulted ceilings. Nestled behind hedges are small gardens flowing with flowering bougainvillea. The lush Jerusalem neighborhoods of Talbia and Rehavia, erected mostly by Arabs in the 1920s and taken into Israeli custody after the Arab residents fled during the 1948 war, are considered prime areas of real estate, where the finest houses sell for $400,000 to $1,000,000 and individual apartments can go for $300,000 and up. Anyone who mentions that he is living in an Arab house in Talbia hears Israelis ooh and aah with envy.

Out of genuine regard for the styles of Arab creativity, the Israelis have set up an Islamic Museum in West Jerusalem to display the art and handicrafts of Islamic societies. They have integrated into their restaurant menus the thick, black Turkish coffee favored throughout the Middle East and the chick-pea paste known as *hummus*, a dish that the Jews seem able to make decidedly less deliciously than the Arabs. Rather than seeing this imitation as a compliment, however, some nationalistic Palestinians find it annoying.

"The Israelis have stolen a lot of the Palestinian culture," said Ibrahim Kareen of East Jerusalem. "For instance, many dances. The Hora. This is Palestinian. Many dishes. You go to Israel and the style is Arab. Architecture. You go to old Jaffa, no matter how hard they try to make things look different, you can see it. Except for Tel Aviv. I now have Jewish friends who come and ask for iron windows, grillwork. Most of them are made by Arab blacksmiths, protection bars. From Tel Aviv they come to Jerusalem and ask for this kind of Arab style. Two years ago, El Al wanted to make their hostesses wear dresses with embroidery. This was Palestinian. Now we go to souvenir shops in Israel, and in some cases they will tell you these dresses are Israeli, when they're Palestinian."

Kareen goes a bit far. The roots of folk dance are old and tangled, and while the Hora does bear resemblance to Arab dances, the origins are too deeply buried for any side to make clear proprietary claims. In a sense, what he sees as theft is merely acculturation, interaction, symbiosis.

In many respects, Arab and Jewish cultures complement one another. Each softens the other's rigidities. The social permissiveness of the Jews gives Arabs a chance to escape from their stricter mores, and the ready supply of Arab "goys" can be used by Orthodox Jews to run a modern society while observing religious law. In Israel, the Arab often serves as the *"shabbes goy."* Hotels manage to conform ostensibly with the injunction against work on the Sabbath by employing Arabs to wait tables, clean rooms, and carry bags. Hospitals under Orthodox religious administration use Arabs for many Sabbath chores (although Halakha explicitly permits Jews to do life-saving work on the Sabbath). Absurdity quickly gains ascendancy in this area. My son Michael, hospitalized one Saturday in Jerusalem with pneumonia, was being admitted to Shaare Zedek Hospital by a Jewish doctor wearing a yarmulke, who examined him but could not take pen in hand to write out instructions on his chart. The doctor called on an Arab nurse whose knowledge of Hebrew was, shall we say, incomplete. As he dictated to her, she attempted to get unfamiliar terminology down in some legible form, asking how to spell every other word and putting each one painstakingly on paper in what Debby and I dearly hoped was an accurate and comprehensible fashion. Treatment at Shaare Zedek turned out to be professional, caring, and flawless, but the religious-cultural acrobatics at the beginning were not very comforting.

Arabs sometimes figure in Jewish religious ritual as well, although not always as the Talmud would prescribe. My secretary, Julie Somech, noticed that every year before the autumn holiday of Succoth, when each family takes meals in a *succa*, an outdoor shack erected for the occasion, a wealthy Hasidic neighbor of hers did not bother to go out and gather branches and wood and put up his own *succa*—he hired an Arab to build it.

In more accepted routine, Arabs have become part of the Jews' Passover ritual as the symbolic custodians of all bread products that are removed from homes before the week of celebration. At an annual pre-Passover ceremony, a ranking rabbi entrusts the products to a selected Arab—usually an elderly man with a tanned, seamed face framed by a white keffiyah—in exchange for a token payment, which is then returned with a modicum of interest as the products are symbolically taken back at the end of Passover. Individuals also may go through the ritual, finding a non-Jew—often an Arab—to be the temporary custodian. When Michael Widlanski, an Orthodox Jew, delivered a bottle of Scotch whiskey to an Arab acquaintance, the Arab—an observant Muslim who did not drink alcohol—asked mischievously why the Jew could retain wine at home but not whiskey. A theological repartee ensued in which Michael noted that whiskey, but not wine, was made from grain, all products of which must be cleaned out of the house before Passover.

Rigid faith does not always reinforce the militance of the conflict. Devout Muslims and devout Jews often respect each other's religiosity, and Michael, who studied in Egypt for a time, encountered many Egyptians who seemed to admire him both for being religious in his Judaism and for saying so forthrightly.

The Muslim Quarter of the Old City of Jerusalem is a warren of cobbled alleys that twist through arches and around crooked corners, then suddenly become stairways as they climb and descend along the ancient contours formed by the land and the centuries of ruins that lie below. Behind the stone walls of the houses that crowd along the edges of these narrow passageways, tiny, unseen courtyards provide spots of green, perhaps a lemon tree and a stable for a donkey, and a common center of gossip and friendship and family.

In daylight hours, the main alleys ring to the cries of vendors and the pleas of merchants and the abrasive cackle of radios tuned to the dissonance of the world outside. After noon prayers at al-Aqsa mosque, a torrent of worshipers floods through el-Wad Road toward Damascus Gate in a festival of faces and robes and headdresses. By dusk, the shops are mostly shuttered, the alleys empty, and the light soothing.

As the configuration of Jerusalem has shifted under successive conquerors, Jews have found various places to live and study and pray within the Old City walls. Although the Jewish Quarter was the center of Jewish residence in Jerusalem from antiquity, Jews spread later into the adjacent area that came to be known as the Muslim Quarter. In the nineteenth century, Hasidic religious groups from Eastern Europe established yeshivas and synagogues there, as close as possible to the place where the Temple had stood, had been burned, and—many believed—would stand again. After 1967, which ended the Jordanian period in which no Jews were permitted to reside in the Holy City, efforts to reestablish a Jewish presence centered on the Jewish Quarter. But some Jews also had their sights on formerly Jewish buildings scattered among the Arabs of the adjacent Muslim Quarter.

The old Jewish presence was clear to anyone with a keen eye. The shadows could be seen in many of the doorways—a shallow hole carved in the stone, a blotch of concrete or plaster smeared by Arabs to cover the place where Jews once fastened the mezuzah, the small case containing a piece of parchment inscribed with two passages from Deuteronomy. On the third story of one stone building, a small, inconspicuous synagogue even survived thanks to the Arab custodian who lived in an adjoining apartment. The Torat Hayim Synagogue, as it is known, was established in 1887 and abandoned abruptly in 1948 when the Arab Legion conquered Jerusalem; the Jews there fled in such haste that they left holy books open on the tables. The Arab neighbor, from the Abu Lachim family, stacked the 20,000 books in a small room and thus saved them all; they included dusty Hebrew commentaries on the Talmud that were printed in the 1820s in Warsaw. The Holy Ark remained intact, and the original furniture was preserved. When the Israeli army entered the city in 1967, the Arab custodian presented surprised soldiers with the key.

In the late 1970s and early 1980s, about 200 Orthodox Jews took up residence in the Muslim Quarter once again, reestablishing yeshivas and creating new ones to study Temple rites in preparation for what they believed would be the coming of the Messiah and the construction of the Third Temple where al-Aqsa mosque and the Dome of the Rock are now. And in a gesture of pragmatism, one group also installed plastic windows to thwart Arab children who periodically stoned their building.

Some of the Jews were able to insinuate themselves into a wary, somewhat accommodating relationship of neighborliness with the Arabs. As I walked through the quarter with Eliezer Gorodetzer, a twenty-eight-year-old nicknamed "Eli" who had immigrated to Israel thirteen years earlier from Brookline, Massachusetts, Arab youngsters called, "Shalom, Ali!" He chuckled at the Arabic rendition of his name. And he carried a pistol beneath his jacket. At first, Arab families tried to lock him out of the courtyard through which he had to pass to get to his apartment; they used the excuse that they did not want him to see their women. They relented when he threatened to break the door down, and the subsequent relationship evolved into one of benign courtesy.

But other Jews created trouble so serious that Mayor Teddy Kollek, fearful that the precarious balance of Jerusalem's calm was being disturbed, appealed to the chief rabbis to press them to leave the quarter. His concern centered on one yeshiva that took ex-convicts and turned them religious. The pious thugs, bearded and dressed in black, repeatedly beat up Muslims with clubs, hammers, and iron bars and got beaten up by Muslims as well. A stroller through the area could see both Arabs and Jews bearing bandages and scars. Yeshiva residents even beat an elderly woman unconscious in an effort to take over and expand into her apartment. Just as the Jews periodically objected to the high volume of the amplified muezzin's call to prayer in al-Aqsa mosque, Arabs also complained that the Jews in the offending yeshiva would pray loudly all night long, keeping them awake. Normal Jewish families would be welcomed as neighbors, many of the Arabs told me, but just get the crazies out of there.

In essence, this was a clash of proprietary interests: The Arabs thought that the Jews were moving in to demonstrate rights of ownership in the Muslim Quarter, and the Jews thought so too. But much of the everyday friction at the points of Arab-Jewish contact is cultural, a conflict of East and West, a bad chemistry of mixed styles. Two areas of frequent encounter have the special capacity to inflame mutual distaste. One is bargaining in the marketplace; the other is the confrontation between the individual and the bureaucracy.

Few Jews who shop among the alleys of the Old City seem to grasp the finest nuances of agreeing on a price. In its best form it is a dancelike duel, a graceful feint and parrying, a pursing of the lips, a bit of flattery, a touch of humor, a smiling nod of accord in which both sides feel victorious. When Arab merchants bargain with Arab customers, there is a good-natured tone not always present when the customer is Jewish, as documented by the psychiatrist Gerald Caplan, who studied Arab-Jewish interaction in Jerusalem.[74] He found that Arabs usually assumed that they would get the goods for about 20 to 25 percent less than the merchant asked, and so they usually offered half of his original price "as a joke."

Perhaps a shopkeeper would flirt with a woman customer, proposing a discount for her pretty eyes. The Arab customer would praise the merchandise but note that the wonderful carpet or leatherwork had been on sale elsewhere for far less. The purchaser would add, however, that he dearly wanted to buy from this shopkeeper, not his competitors, since he was such a fine man with a kind and honest face. "He begged the merchant to enable him to acquire these excellent goods at this most excellent shop by lowering his price," Caplan observed. "In response to futher pressure from the seller, the customer might express the liveliest appreciation for the goods while explaining, with suitable embellishments, his regret that his own limited means at the moment prevented his paying as much as he would otherwise like in order to oblige the merchant." The shopkeeper would give a "special price" because he liked the customer so much, and "the transaction thus ended with mutual compliments."

Caplan found quite different dynamics when Jewish customers were involved. Where Arab buyers considered it anathema to express disdain for the merchandise, insult the merchant, or dispute the fanciful stories that he spun to justify his high price, those were precisely the steps urged by many Western Jews on one another, and even promoted as official advice in a pamphlet by the Israeli Ministry of Tourism. The recommended method, and one I saw practiced by many visitors to the Old City, had the customer assuming that the merchant was an unscrupulous rogue determined to cheat. The purchaser was encouraged to catch the shopkeeper in his fraudulent claims, make disparaging remarks about his products, and walk off in a superior gesture of contempt, hoping to be called back with a lower price. There was little appreciation of the fact that the merchant never imagined that anyone would believe his tales, little understanding of the etiquette, humor, and gamesmanship involved. A sale would probably be made, but with it came bruised feelings, quite the opposite of the good sense of mutual benefit that dominated the complimentary negotiating between Arabs.

The other field of abrasive contact, the bureaucratic encounter, has pitched the Arabs' sense of honor and class consciousness against the Israeli Jews' egalitarianism, creating a clash of values. After 1967, when members of the Arab community's power structure in East Jerusalem and the West Bank were suddenly subjected to Israeli government agencies, they were deeply offended by being forced to wait in lines or outer offices for hours with the common Arabs of the lower and working classes. They were also insulted by being strip-searched as they crossed the Allenby Bridge from Jordan into the West Bank, and especially by the Israeli requirement that they dump their shoes in the same pile with those of lower standing. All this was a bitter affront to their dignity. Members of the local aristocracy were accustomed to priority handling, to a favoritism and bias that came from their social status and their personal connections with the sources of official power. Their attempts to establish such ties with the new official structure did not work. And while the Israeli bureaucrats initially acted out of the simple instinct of treating everyone equally and enlightening Arabs with this value, some of them—especially police investigators and military commanders on the West Bank—quickly tuned in on the Arab devotion to honor and began to use humiliation as a weapon. Thus, Israeli officials developed the practice of summoning a leading Arab nationalist or a member of a prominent local family to local military headquarters at eight o'clock the following morning, only to make him wait in a crowded anteroom for three or four hours with swarms of common workers, just to whittle him down to size. More often, the result was corrosive bitterness and resentment.

Cultural misunderstandings figure so prominently in Arab-Jewish tensions that Israelis organizing school and home visits among Arab and Jewish youngsters have drawn up a list of guidelines for each:

Modes of Behavior in an Arab House

1. Preparations
Try to dress in a proper and respectable way. It's not acceptable to wear shorts or revealing clothes. It would be nice to bring a small present to show consideration. Bring sweets to Muslims and Druse. To Christians it's also possible to bring wine.

2. Entrance and Sitting
At the entrance of the host's house, put out your hand to shake hands. The hostess, if she is traditional, doesn't shake hands. Sit in the place you have been given by the host, and don't move to another place. An upright style of sitting which is uncomfortable to you is preferable to a negligent way of sitting which may express a lack of respect for your hosts. Don't sit with your legs apart and don't sit in such a way that your host can see your soles. If you came as a

couple, refrain from sitting too close together and from outward displays of affection like caressing and hugging.

3. The Conversation

The host initiates the conversation and not you. He may say many times *Ahlan wa-sahlan* (Welcome) and every time answer him *Bikum* (A blessing on you too). Don't press him and don't start up with questions before he opens the conversation.

In the course of the conversation you will hear new and interesting things and may even be asked your opinion. Refrain from such expressions as "Wrong" and "You don't understand," even when you express a disagreeing opinion. Try to listen and understand and in the end you'll be able to say, "Like us, but . . ." Start with the commonalities and only after that pass on to the differences.

Remember that older people express their opinions before the young, and no matter what, don't interrupt anyone. Let people express their opinions right to the end.

4. The Meal

The conversation will continue until you're invited to the meal. Don't go first to the dining room. Let the older people lead the way. If you're not told where to sit, sit in the center—you're the guest. When the food has been brought out and it's tasty, it's important to praise the hostess. The girls can find the hostess in the food-preparing room, even if she doesn't participate in the meal. The hosts' happiness will grow if you ask for more. Sometimes, only the guests receive fork and knife while the residents take their food with their hands. You will show your appreciation for your host if you, too, eat like them.

If you need the bathroom, ask the host. The girls should ask the hostess. After you ask, wait until they show you the way. The hosts will not be satisfied with simply giving directions.

5. Goodbyes

When coffee has been brought the visit can be ended.

There are those who offer very bitter coffee in a small quantity in a cup that passes among all those seated. If the taste of the coffee is too bitter, you do not have to drink it, but don't clean the cup and don't ask for sugar. After the bitter coffee comes the sweet coffee. When you return the cup to the platter (tray) say to the host, *"Daiman"* (May your house always have it good).

Thank the host for the hospitality, shake hands, and don't forget to invite them to your house. The hosts will accompany you up to your final exit.

Modes of Behavior in a Jewish House

1. Preparations

Dress in a nice, but not exaggerated, way. For instance, there is no need for a suit or tie. It's possible to dress in a traditional or modern way. The main thing is that you feel comfortable with your dress.

It's not necessary, but it's possible, to bring a small, not exaggerated present. They will surely be happy to receive it, especially if it's a home product. For example, a jar of olives or baked goods.

2. Entrance and Seating

In the entrance to the host's house, hold out your hand and present yourself in a formulation like, "Shalom, my name is Hassan."

It is possible that the house you enter may be different in some ways from the houses you know. Don't be afraid of difference—in the whole world there are people of different cultures whose houses are different from each other's, and the best way to deal with this is to accept with respect both ways of life, yours and theirs, without assigning grades to these and those.

Many—if not all—Jews have very free hospitality customs. That is to say, they expect the guest to feel himself at home from the first minute. In general they will invite the guest to sit, and if they don't suggest it the guest can ask where to sit.

It is completely permissible for the guest to take an interest in his surroundings. For example, to ask for an explanation of a picture, or an appliance, or how long the hosts have been living there. If the guest admires anything in the hosts' house, it is certainly worthwhile for him to express his impressions, in humble words, without exaggeration.

3. Conversation

There are no set rules for conversation. Sometimes the host asks questions, sometimes he wants to hear from you. The hosts will certainly be happy if you show interest in them: How is the family made up, what are its members involved in, what interests them, what are their problems? They will be equally happy to hear about your family, its doings and problems. In the conversation, it's worthwhile to show interest in what you are told and to express sympathy for the host family's problems.

It's possible to discuss anything, but it's preferable to raise political topics only after personal recognition has been created and some level of personal trust has been achieved.

4. The Meal

The hosts will certainly tell you where to sit. If they don't, ask if it's okay to sit in a place you choose for yourself.

If you liked the food, praise it, and again—without exaggeration. If the hosts offer more, they will certainly be happy if you take it. At the end of the meal, thank whoever served it.

5. Goodbyes

There are no set rules about the time for leavetaking, but in many places it is acceptable to leave about one-half hour after the end of the meal and the drinking of coffee. If the hosts really insist that you stay, and if you have free time and you're enjoying the visit, they will surely be happy if you stay a little longer.

On exiting, make sure to say goodbye personally to each of the hosts. Thank them for the hospitality—in simple words. And invite them for a return visit at your house.

Between the hard, flat walls of cultural intransigence stand a few Jews with the unusual experience of having grown up among Arabs in pre-1948 Palestine. In those years Jerusalem formed a crucible where Arab and Jewish cultures adapted to each other with a spirit of coexistence and accommodation amid the friction. "My father still tells me stories," says Naftali Sappir, "of when he was a kid in the Old City and Arabs used to come every Rosh Hashanah and Pessah {Passover]. They would cover copper dishes with new tin, and twice a year they would walk through the streets and shout, in Yiddish, '*Weissen kesselah!* Whiten the kettles!' "

Those Jews who were not confined within the parochial circles of the Hasidic yeshiva world, who mingled with Arabs and played in Arab streets, found in themselves a more fluid approach to Arab society. Some even came to feel that the reflexes of Arab culture ran deeply within them, a sense that has persisted into adulthood, despite the religious antagonisms and anti-Jewish riots that burst out most dramatically in 1929 and 1936, and through the succeeding decades of warfare and terrorism.

These are not qualities that are easy to define or measure. "My wife claims that I am a complete Arab," said Rafi Horowitz, but he offered a less categorical appraisal of himself. He was one of those who had grown up among Arabs in Jerusalem, a toughly built, balding man in his middle fifties now working in Israel's Government Press Office after a long military career. Journalists knew him casually as an Israeli hard-liner, and that was true on a purely political plane. But it was only part of a more profound, less visible complexity that surged beneath the surface. "I'm antagonistic to Arab nationalism and very, very friendly to Arabs as human beings," he said. "I'm Dr. Jekyll and Mr. Hyde, to some extent." And then he explained.

His mother's family had lived in Palestine for eleven generations, and his father had come from Germany in 1921. "My mother was a doctor and had a clinic in the Old City, and I was born in the middle of the riots in 1929. I lived in Jerusalem. We lived in different places, but mostly either next to Arabs or among Arabs. Arabic was the language that was spoken at home. My mother spoke Arabic fluently. I learned Arabic from playing with kids. I went to school with Arabs. And I almost cannot get away from my embrace or entanglement with the other residents of this big condominium.

"I grew up in a very strict home with a German education," Rafi continued. "But just on the other side of the door there was a world one hundred and eighty degrees away from my home with black furniture, a piano, education, and so on. I couldn't play with the kids outside if I had shoes on, so I used to hide my shoes, play with the kids, and when I came back I would put my shoes on very quickly. This was another world. I am somehow exactly in the middle. I have a split personality."

The entanglement he feels with Arab culture, the affinity for the rhythms of Arab life, are so much a part of him that he cannot quite tell where his Arab impulses end and his Jewish ones begin. This is not a blurred identity but an affirmation of his legitimacy as an Israeli Jew, a Zionist son of the Middle East. Born amid Arab riots, toughened and softened by both war with Arabs and friendship with Arabs, Rafi has gained a hardness without hatred.

When he was eighteen, he and his Jewish classmates joined the Haganah. The Arab Legion besieged his unit in the celebrated Etzion Bloc, a cluster of settlements between Hebron and Jerusalem. "The atmosphere was that we were doomed," he recalled. "I remember a night when the commander gathered us and we walked to a stony spot. We were only eighteen, most of us. And he said, 'We can't run away from our Jewish history, and this is going to be Masada.' And I didn't want to die." Then the Arab troops overran the Jewish unit. "In less than twenty-four hours most of my friends—schoolmates—disappeared," he said. "My company was composed of a class from my school. So I lost more than eighteen members of the same class I went to high school with in less than twenty-four hours." Rafi was badly wounded, and lay bleeding. "I saw the others being cut to pieces, castrated, the eyes cut out. Some of my friends were raped next to my eyes." Later he was in a Jordanian prison camp. "We had groups coming in the middle of the night, captured, and most of them suffered the trauma of being raped, not by one or two but by companies. It's a way of disgracing your enemy." He was taken to a desert camp in Jordan near the Iraqi border, where he spent eleven months as a prisoner of war. He minimizes the hardship. I asked how he was treated.

"Objectively, not so bad," he said. "I was wounded, and we were treated very badly as wounded, but as one lives according to criteria of the time and space and doesn't compare that to anything else, I think, looking back on it, it wasn't that terrible. Yeah, we suffered very bad— how would you call it?—residential conditions in the middle of the desert. Tents, of course. Terribly hot days and terribly cold nights, which broke every bone in you. And we didn't eat very well for the first, let's say, half a year, but by and large I don't think it was that terrible. I don't think the Arabs treated their own soldiers any better, because we watched Arab officers beating the guards around us. So I have perspective. I'm not complaining that much."

After his release as part of a prisoner exchange in March 1949, Rafi joined the Israeli army. He commanded a Druse unit that made long-distance patrols in the Negev against hashish smugglers and infiltrators and then, after the 1967 war, became an officer in the military government on the West Bank. He implemented the plan to open the bridges across the Jordan River to allow Arabs to travel between the West Bank and Jordan, and he helped facilitate a program of family reunification under which some 40,000 West Bank residents, abroad at the end of the war, were eventually allowed to return.

"It's difficult for me to explain why I don't hate," he told me. "First of all, I'm a by-product of all the Jewish national aspirations. I carry on my back an experience of many centuries of Jews in this country passed over to me by my mother with basic, elementary, twenty-four-karat Zionism without the slogans. On my father's side I'm a son of a true Zionist who in 1921 left a very well-to-do home and came to live here. I grew and had those aspirations as part of my mental tissue, physical tissue. But very realistic. Not a day has passed in my personal history without realizing that the Arabs are in this reality. I didn't live in a period where the Arabs didn't exist, where my nationalist dreams could have been artificially swollen up both territorially and mentally, where the Arabs never played a major role. There were Arabs all the time. And I don't see any solution without Arabs.

"The Arabs were a part of my childhood, a part of my scenery," Rafi continued. "They were my friends, they were the children I fought with but made friends with. In my pigment there is a lot of the essence of the East, whether it's food, dress, and I don't know what part of my brain is really Oriental. The only context I knew with human beings all my life was with Jews and Arabs. So they're there. First of all, you can't hate. You cannot hate. I'm not even boasting. I'm not that nice Jew who says I don't hate Arabs and I don't know why. I know why. Because in my cognition, the Arabs are a part of a family. They're too close."

Rafi struggled to define the elements in Arab culture that he found in himself. "First of all, warmth," he said. "Personal warmth. The physical confidence that we have from touching each other. It's a closeness. This closeness is a very dangerous closeness. Look how an animal plays with its offspring. It sometimes beats it with its paw, but it licks it all the time. That is a very physical thing. I think the Western world created a sort of distance that drives people away from each other. Try to get Western people together, too close. They need that distance, what they interpret as their privacy, which is their protection."

Rafi's denunciation of separateness, privacy, and his embrace of the familial intimacy that marks Arab life put him into an ironic contrast with a young Arab-American I knew, Christopher Mansour, who came from Michigan to visit his Arab relatives in Israel for a year. The lack of privacy in Arab homes gnawed at him, given his American background. "Families are very close, and you have to put up with a lot of things," Christopher said. "I was just up in Nazareth visiting relatives. They're very nice people. You can't just come in and sit down and say, 'Hi, howya doin'? How's things goin'? Everything's exciting,' talk a bit, and then leave. You've got to come in and sit down and eat and sit and stay the whole five days. I mean, it's kind of nice, I like the hospitality, but it's taken to the nth degree. It can get to be painful. My upbringing has been in the United States where relationships have been a little more inpersonal. You can have more personal space, I guess is about the best way to put it. You have privacy when you want privacy. And in Arab society they don't really understand the idea that you want to be alone. That means that you're mad, you're angry at something, or you're upset, and you should have somebody with you."

Here, then, was an Arab-American finding Arab society rather smothering, and a Palestinian Jew finding it harmonious with his inner rhythms. "It creates another mechanism of the mind," said Rafi Horowitz. "The mañana mentality." Quoting an Arabic saying that means "Speed comes from the devil," he said, "The wisdom of time. Even in my tiny family my wife is completely different. She says, 'Why do you prolong that?' Processes have to take longer. It gives you the possibility of not being very precise in the sense of what you hope to do, not hoping for immediate results but waiting. I don't know if these qualities would serve any other reality in another part of the world. But here I sense that this is a training that is needed in this part of the world."

Then Rafi searched again for a way of explanation. "Somebody like me who spent long, long nights in the middle of the desert listening to a Bedouin *mawal* that lasts for about an hour and a half, which could be a monotone, with a moon the size of the scene from Apollo when you approach very close. Me, the voice, and the moon in a flat, stony desert that goes from here to eternity. I think that Bach or Beethoven would have been a tremendous dissonance. That's a part of it. The music, the voices, the smells. The capability of making friends very quickly and not demanding too much privacy for myself."

FOURTEEN

Fire in the Desert

The Day when men shall be like scattered moths,
And the mountains shall be like flocks of carded wool,
Then as to him whose balances are heavy—
his shall be a life that shall please him well.
—Sura CI, The Blow, Verse 1

T HE COLORS ARE A FANTASY ACROSS THE SWEEPING PLAINS AND PEAKED
mountains of Sinai, an impossible spectrum of tans and greys and browns
and rusts shifting into copper greens and pastels as the sun moves and
the light changes, the only motion in a landscape of stillness.

Our jeep turned inland from the shimmering Gulf of Aqaba, leaving
the single, slender pencil line of blacktop road that marks the fragile
trace of human civilization along the flowing coast of sand and gravel.
The tires growled against the dry hardness of the desert as we headed up
Wadi Watir, a broad valley that forms a channel for the angry, rushing
flash floods of winter. Behind the wheel, Clinton Bailey smoothly shifted

gears and found the solid ground, practiced as he was in the ways of this wilderness.

Clinton, known to many of his Israeli friends by his Hebrew name, Yitzhak, is a tall, clean-cut American Jew who immigrated to Israel in 1958 and has now become one of the Western world's foremost experts on the Bedouin tribesmen who live in the Negev and Sinai deserts. In the years of Israeli occupation of Sinai, from 1967 until the final portion of the peninsula was returned to Egypt in 1982, he and a few other Israeli Jews were seduced by the mysterious beauty of the desert and were drawn into an affection and fascination for the culture of the Bedouins. Clinton learned their slang-ridden Arabic, studied their customs, collected their oral poetry on tape, defended their rights against the Israeli bureaucracy, and formed many strong friendships. There was hardly an oasis, a tent, or a hut where he would not be welcomed with warm greetings of "Doctooor Bai-lee!"—the title had some tenuous connection with his Ph.D. in political science—followed by elaborate rituals of hospitality and food.

He represented one side of a schizophrenic Israeli attitude toward the Bedouins. In Sinai, relations were admiring, paternalistic, respectful. But in the adjacent Negev Desert, which lies inside Israel proper, they have been tense, condescending, and abusive, as Israeli authorities have chased the tribesmen off their lands, confiscated their goats, confined them to reservations, and denigrated their way of life. Like the sweet tea and bitter coffee that Bedouins serve their guests, these contradictions take their place in the complex mosaic of Arab-Jewish interactions.

The wadi gradually narrowed and climbed almost imperceptibly as we drove. The ground grew finer, and incongruous rivulets of water meandered down through the sandy track we were following. Suddenly at a bend we saw the palms of Ein Furtaga, an oasis whose spring was plentiful enough in March, right after the winter rains, to trickle into the hot sand as an omen for travelers.

In the shade of the palms, a ramshackle hut had once served as an enterprising Bedouin's rudimentary café to serve warm soft drinks to groups of Israeli campers, who often toured in the backs of open trucks. A couple of Bedouin families were living in the oasis. An old man with three yellowed, snaggled teeth gave "Dr. Bailey" a grizzled smile of welcome, took us into his hut, and poured us glasses of sweet, steaming tea. There were two others in our small band besides Clinton and me—

Lucia Moffet, a friend of Clinton's visiting from Massachusetts, and the *New York Times* columnist Anthony Lewis. We sat and drank, and then continued south through Wadi Ghazala, named for the gazelle, on our way to the oasis of Ein Hudra for the night.

Desert wadis can be valleys, dry riverbeds, gorges, or the faintest depressions in the earth. They are the highways of Sinai for Bedouins and their camels, for outsiders and their jeeps and trucks. Clinton drove alternately in front-wheel and four-wheel drive, and at times we all had to get out and push the jeep through deep sand. Somehow he lost his bearings and failed to keep right at the confluence of three wadis— Ghazala, Lathi, and Hudra—putting us on the wrong "road." It was late afternoon by the time he realized his mistake and turned around, and the sun was getting low when we arrived back at the intersection where we had gone wrong. We needed to find a Bedouin who knew every peak and canyon.

I remembered a story that Micha Bar-Am had told me of giving an aged Bedouin man a ride on a desert road. The old man was blind, the desert nothing but an endless stretch of emptiness that he could no longer see. But somehow he could feel it, for after a while in the car he tapped Micha on the knee to indicate that this was where he got out. Amazed, Micha stopped and watched as the man walked slowly off into the wilderness, somehow knowing exactly where he was going.

Clinton spotted a Bedouin boy on a camel, asked directions to Ein Hudra, and the boy offered to go the whole distance with us, make us bread, and spend the night.

He was just sixteen, a quiet, sinewy lad named Salim who reminded me of the nicest streetwise kids in New York, with a mature competence and steadiness on his familiar ground of arid cliffs and plains. He ran to ask his mother's permission, then clambered aboard the jeep and proceeded with calm assuredness to take us through steep and difficult terrain. Salim worked occasionally at the Israeli beach resort of Neviot, on the Gulf of Aqaba, but he preferred the tranquility of the inland wadis. His only worry was that he would be drafted into the Egyptian army after Sinai was returned, and so he was considering journeying to Saudi Arabia to find a job.

The wadi narrowed as dusk came slowly. On each side rose sheer cliffs of rust red, tan, grey sandstone smoothed and scooped into ripples and whorls by millennia of wind and blowing sand and swirls of raging floodwater. The light changed constantly, fading into delicate pastels as a half moon, up above the mountains on our left, turned silver.

Toward the waning of the dusk we saw a dark thicket against the cliffs: Ein Hudra, the oasis believed to have been a place of encampment for the ancient Israelites in their Sinai wanderings. As we approached, the tops of the palms rose in jagged silhouettes against the last, fading light of the sky. The jeep came to a stop, and the engine died. We were alone.

We unpacked our gear and chose places on the sand under the palms. Salim quickly gathered twigs and branches and made a fire. Then he was kneading the dough, rolling it into perfect round loaves, spreading and rolling with his hands and frying it on a piece of scrap metal that had been left from some weapon in some war. The big, flat, browned slabs of bread were soft and hot. We ate beef stew from cans, flavored with wine, washed down with wine and coffee. And for dessert, Lucia concocted a dish of bananas flambé. She used Jack Daniel's, pouring it into the pan and then dipping the pan toward the fire. When it burst into flame, Salim jumped back as if he were witnessing some pagan ritual.

The growing darkness cooled the desert, and Clinton taught us how to fold and drape keffiyahs to protect our heads and necks. And when the night came with a final thoroughness, we were carried into another bewitching world. The white stone and sand were silver in the moonlight, and the stars were so bright they looked as if they were sitting on the tops of the mountains. I walked to the edge of the oasis, against the cliffs, and there felt the most complete silence I have ever known, so total that I began to hear the humming inside my head.

I woke up at 5:20 when the first hint of pale dawn touched the sky. The others were still asleep, and I crawled out of my sleeping bag, put on my shoes, and walked slowly, slowly, around the oasis. The day came softly, like a curtain rising gradually on a spectacular scene. Four large groves of date palms made up the oasis; around them stood waist-high walls built of small stones held together with wet sand. These were the gardens of the Bedouin tribesmen who came in season to tend the trees and gather the dates. Clusters of stone huts were perched on high, broad, flat rocks sloping up from the palms, lush green against the barren cliffs.

When the sun was high and warm and the dawn wind had died, three camels and two riders, a father and son, came out of the silent wilderness of the desert and paused. The two dismounted gracefully. The boy led the camels to a stone trough fed by a clear spring, and the animals drank deeply. The father, squatting in the sand, lit a small fire of dried twigs. He made tea in a blackened pot. The scene could have been as ancient as the Bible. Only the slightest details betrayed the encroachment of the modern world on the timelessness of desert life. The father used wooden matches from a box labeled in Hebrew letters—made in Israel—and as the sleeves of his traditional robes slid back, the glint of a stainless-steel watch with an expansion band could be seen. Large water containers, strapped to the camels' backs, were made of plastic.

But the fire was an eternal, civilizing ritual. One of the first things a Bedouin does when he comes to a new place is to light a little fire to make a center, a focus that structures and diminishes the vastness, that creates a circle of intimacy in the wilderness and seems to reduce the wild desert to manageable size. So it is also with the Bedouins' hierarchy of values and customs: the veiled women; the arranged marriages; the sign of ownership in which the Bedouin hangs his possession in a tree to ensure that it be left untouched; the biblical justice of revenge; the elaborate hospitality that requires the honored guest, for example, to set the pace of eating, to eat until he is satisfied and then stand up to signify that the rest of the company may end the meal. In an empty desert, with few tangible goods, the Bedouins have surrounded themselves with re-markable intricacy, a complexity amid simplicity, an edifice of mores that organizes and defines existence in a hostile, sweeping, limitless land.

On our way back from Ein Hudra, Salim insisted that we stop for tea. Clinton deftly declined—although the conversation in which he did so probably took as long as the tea would have—and Salim then insisted on bringing us a goatskin filled with sour, curdled goat's milk, a thick liquid that tasted like a wonderful cross between yoghurt and cheese. We drank, and the boy's duty to make us welcome was fulfilled.

As we continued along the wadi, we were flagged down by a Bedouin girl dressed in a black robe and cape that made her look like a deep spot of darkness in the blinding desert. She wanted a ride back down to her flock. Her eyes danced from behind a colorfully beaded veil. She was fifteen, the daughter of a man Clinton knew, and when she asked us not to tell her father that we had given her a ride, Clinton suspected that she had snuck off on a tryst with some young lad up the wadi. When we came to her flock of goats, which were perched up and down a precipitous cliff, the girl got out and quickly gathered broomweed, which she chopped into pieces with a rock. Then she knelt over it, pulled her cape over her head to shelter the weed against the wind, and lit a small fire—her hearth in the wilderness. She brewed tea, and we drank. From time to time, she shrieked a piercing call at her goats, telling them to come down off the cliff.

Clinton knew her family well. Her brother and cousin had been arrested by the Israelis for selling hashish to some hippies on the beach. But since her father's brother was a chief who collaborated with the Israelis, providing intelligence, Clinton was surprised that his official contacts weren't able to get the young men out. Clinton wrote a couple of letters and went to see an intelligence man in Beersheba, and they were finally released after a year. Thus did the Israeli Jews mesh their society and government with the timeless Bedouins.

I asked the girl if she would like to go to school. "Now I'd be embarrassed," she said, with Clinton interpreting. "I couldn't go to school now. I'm a big girl. A boy would see me, I'd see a boy. I couldn't go to school now. The girls would like to learn. I'd like to learn. If somebody sends us a letter, we look at the letter and we don't know what's written there. If I went to school, I'd understand every single word." Besides, she added, tending goats wasn't so great. "They run up the mountainside, and you have to run after them. They break their legs sometimes, and they get scratched." She pulled out a plastic bag of tobacco and rolled herself a cigarette.

Nowhere in the contemporary Arab-Jewish relationship has there been as much harmony and compassion as among Israelis and Bedouins in Sinai from 1967 to 1982. The desert tribesmen, identifying with their own interests and not some larger political or military objective, had a long history of conflict with the settled Arabs and never seemed very threatening to the Israelis. Nor did any competition exist between them over the land, as it did in immense bitterness between Israelis and Bedouins of the Negev, adjacent to Sinai. The desert also drew a special breed of Israeli Jew, not one who reveled in the militant nationalism of his country's larger conflict but one who treasured more the marvels of Bedouin culture, the human contact with a people who could perform the miracle of scratching a life out of the vast, spectacular wasteland. A passion for the Bedouin was mixed into a passion for the desert: The man and his environment converged; the desert was alive; its people were part of the landscape. And then, for some Israelis, Bedouin society evolved into an intriguing aspect of human civilization.

Elia Sides, for example, an Israeli ecologist who lived in Sharm el-Sheikh, discovered from talking with old men that among the fishermen who once journeyed in open boats as far as the Horn of Africa, a highly developed oral sea mythology had grown up stikingly similar to Viking tales. It was dying as fishing became less important and as the men who knew the stories passed away. Elia rushed up and down the coast in his jeep to sit and listen and collect as much as he could before Sinai was returned to Egypt.

Clinton's attraction operated on several intellectual levels. "Among Bedouins I find a tremendous lack of materialism, an emphasis on social values, which definitely takes predominance over material values," he explained. In a deeper dimension, he was captivated by the continuity between biblical life and Bedouin life, by the Bedouins' similarity "to my own biblical ancestors," as he put it; he found that by studying the culture, he gained insight into the Bible and the main actors in the Bible's dramas. "There's a lot of behavior in the Bible that I would say is Arab, if not Bedouin, behavior," he observed. "In that sense the Bible is a rather accurate record of life when the Israelites lived in the desert."

Over the years, his studies and contacts have also given him a sense of perception about the cultural components of the Arab-Israeli conflict and of its Middle Eastern context. To understand the region, he observes, one must understand the Arabs, for they are integral to the region. And even their governmental behavior strikes him as often being based on the desert ways. There is, for example, an important interaction between Arab nationalism and pride, a chemistry in Arab governmental attitudes that he sees coming from the stark existence of the desert, where a man, a tribe, must not appear weak, for the only defense is the appearance of strength. Revenge, therefore, becomes a form of deterrence. "The reason that he has to retaliate, the reason that he has to force retribution out of the other side, is that other people will see that essentially he is strong," Clinton notes. "If he has been violated in the conflict, he has to show that it was foolhardy to violate him, that essentially he is a strong person. There's no long arm of the law; there's no police force, no army that you call on the telephone and they send over two squad cars. It's what some-body else thinks that you can do to him, you or your family or the people who protect you, that will deter him from violating you. And that is the essence of pride. That's the basis of it. The word 'justice' is 'balance,' and they compare it to the side sacks of a camel. A camel can go on as long as he's balanced, and once he's tilted he can't move. Balance is justice and tilting is injustice. As long as a person feels he's been violated, he can't go on until he feels it's been balanced."

The Sinai Bedouins' attitudes to the Israelis were less obvious. But it seemed clear that the Israelis dealt more humanely and justly with Sinai Bedouins than the Egyptians had. Furthermore, the Bedouins had no ideological aversion to reaping whatever benefit could come from contact with Israeli society. As a result, Israeli modernity touched their lives significantly. By building a road along the Gulf of Aqaba, the Israelis opened a desert that had been accessible only through days of rugged travel by jeep or camel or foot. Suddenly tourists could get there in two or three hours of driving from the southernmost Israeli city of Eilat; this brought the outside world into Sinai as never before.

The Bedouins found that although the Israelis disrupted smuggling by patrolling the coast—depriving some of the tribesmen of a major source of livelihood—the latest conquerors of Sinai would pay them to work around the hotels and restaurants taking out garbage, cooking, washing dishes, or mixing cement for construction. They learned that tourists would pay to ride on camels and would give candy and ballpoint pens to their children. The young, dark men of the tribes, who had grown up knowing only women heavily cloaked and veiled in black, were stunned by the sudden appearance of blond Scandinavians in bikinis. The shift from herding to wage labor was intoxicating. The newfound cash could be traded for a portable radio or a cassette recorder, a truck, a jeep, or even a Mercedes-Benz. Families began to move their goat-hair tents from the remote wadis down to the coast, where they put up ramshackle huts made of the Israelis' trash—scrap metal, plywood, orange crates.

A seed of change was planted, and the father schooled in the ways of the desert no longer found a ready pupil in his son. In Dahab, a coastal settlement that grew from 40 huts in 1967 to about 140 in 1982, Sheikh Abu-Abdallah, a reflective chief of the Muzzeina tribe, spoke quietly with us about what had been lost. He gathered with other elders at dusk, for sweet tea and evening prayers and talk, near a simple mosque they were building out of crude desert stone.

"For us to go to Cairo in the past was eighteen days by camel," said the sheikh. "Three times a year we went to Suez to get what we could carry and came back. It was just a little, but because we knew what we had, there was peace of mind. The older people are sorry that it's past, because they know the value of peace of mind, the power of peace of mind, the importance of peace of mind. Now you can have everything. The young people see these things, and they want them too, and these young people don't know what it is to go to Suez three times a year. They can get things whenever they want. I am sorry that the new generation doesn't know anything about what their ancestors' life was like. Those who grew up since 1967 have no experience in the desert. That is fifteen years now. They don't know the old world, only the new. They are not educated in this way. They desire cars, but they are not really educated."

The old chief relaxed as darkness closed in around the glow of the embers. The stars were so bright that Tony Lewis stared up at them for a long time. "Don't you have stars in America?" asked the sheikh.

During its occupation of Sinai, Israel established schools and hired Bedouin teachers in the major encampments, and although the pupils were mostly boys, a few families began to break tentatively with tradition by sending their daughters. Medical clinics were set up, paramedics were trained, and itinerant Jewish doctors made periodic visits. Friendships developed solidly enough to cause considerable sadness when the goodbyes were said and the Israelis pulled out in accordance with the Israeli-Egyptian peace treaty.

I saw some of these farewells near St. Catherine's, the remote Greek Orthodox monastery at the base of Mount Sinai. In November 1979, a week or so before that section of the desert was returned to Egypt, an Israeli Agriculture Ministry employee named Moshe Sela (nicknamed "Moshe-and-a-Half" because of his height) drove back and forth across the hard-packed desert earth to the scattered huts of Bedouin friends. Sela had been responsible for building a cluster of tastefully designed stone houses in the area to serve as a school, a clinic, and so on. To the end, the Israelis' generosity was met with some puzzlement.

"You'd send a car for everyone who got injured," one Bedouin told him, "a helicopter for every pregnant woman in danger. I don't understand why you take it so seriously when someone gets ill. Why do you get so excited? It comes from Allah. Why do you send so many helicopters?"

I went with him to some of the huts spread widely among the arid peaks. At one, the man of the family was not at home, yet the women invited us in anyway, a violation of normal etiquette they found acceptable only in the case of this tall Jew whom they valued and trusted. Their feelings were heightened in their last-minute anticipation of the Egyptians, who they knew would be less kind to them. In hut after hut, Moshe Sela sat on their earthen floors for a final talk and a last sip of steaming tea, and as he rose to leave, the embraces he received were almost anguished. Even the women, veiled and cloaked in the deep black robes that make them shy shadows in the desert, said their good-byes with emotion. Moshe Sela brushed the sleeve of his khaki jacket across his eyes.

Fear of the Egyptians was a mainstay of the Bedouins' sorrow and had apparently been taught to their children. The fifteen-year-old girl who hitched a ride with us to her goats had never lived under Egypt, since she had been born in 1967, but she told us with blunt certainty that if we had been Egyptians coming along in a jeep, she would have preferred walking. "Egyptians always start up with the girls," she said. "They'll screw donkeys."

Bedouin adults expected to be accused by Egyptian authorities of "collaboration" with the Israelis. During one farewell, when Moshe promised to return to visit his friends after Egypt took over, a Bedouin asked that he be understood and forgiven if he did not greet the Israeli with warmth when the Egyptians were watching. His affection for the Jews would have to be concealed. Pressures did come to bear, in fact, and some Israelis who traveled later into Egyptian-run Sinai encountered an atmosphere of apprehension. During one such trip, an Israeli was sitting with a few young Bedouin men when they suddenly spotted Egyptian plainclothesmen in a nearby jeep. Quickly the Bedouins changed out of their jeans and Western shirts and into traditional robes, and then ignored their Israeli friend.

Israeli tourists sometimes found their Bedouin guides and drivers using the Hebrew they had learned to hurl coded insults at Egyptians. One driver, after passing each Egyptian checkpoint, would say to the policemen as he drove away, *"Shukran, ben zona,"* a mixture of the Arabic for "Thank you" and the Hebrew for "son of a whore." Thus, "Thank you, you son of a whore."

A couple of weeks after my last visit before the Israeli pullout from the Mount Sinai area, I returned there for a ceremony led by President Sadat to inaugurate construction of an interfaith house of worship at the base of the mountain. Egyptian officials had erected garish banners and flags on the plain where the ancient Israelites had waited for Moses to descend from his encounter with God, and raucous music played over loudspeakers, setting up discords against the vast and wild beauty of the desert. Inside a roped-off area, the princes of the wilderness had been assembled, aging sheikhs in white keffiyahs and headbands of black and gold, kingly men, survivors with leathery faces and keen eyes, whose long lives had spanned a run of conquerors and wars. They stood in regal dignity for hours in the relentless sun, waiting for Sadat to arrive by helicopter. When one or another would squat in the sand or talk to a comrade, young Egyptian soldiers with fixed bayonets would snarl and bark to silence them and get them on their feet.

In an Israeli courtroom in the Negev Desert town of Beersheba, princely Bedouin men, wearing their finest, flowing robes of gold thread woven into black, sat proudly and erect before a fussy, nearsighted judge who peered through his spectacles and muttered at the papers in front of him. At the side of the courtroom, five young, beefy members of the Israeli Green Patrol, whispering among themselves, smirked and sneered at the Bedouins. In search of protection, the tribesmen had come from the ancient desert into the alien culture of Western law and justice.

The Green Patrol, an arm of the Agriculture Ministry whose powers were enhanced when Ariel Sharon was agriculture minister in the first Begin Government, had launched a war of attrition against the Bedouins. In an effort to drive them off desert tracts designated as nature preserves or military zones, the Israeli toughs first ordered them to leave and then, if they stayed, swooped down on their camps, fired guns into the air to frighten children, shot their herding dogs, ripped down their tents, and trucked their flocks of goats off to slaughter without even so much as the due process of a hearing. With Clinton Bailey's help, some of the Bedouins engaged Israeli attorneys who fought for them in court and sometimes—if they moved quickly enough—obtained temporary restraining orders against the slaughter of the flocks, the Bedouins' major possessions. The patrol usually sold them for slaughter the same day, paying the Bedouins one third of the market price minus the costs of trucking and confiscation. But the ultimate legal argument—that the Bedouins had a right to graze their goats and wander on the desert land—was usually made in vain, for no title deeds have existed in the culture of the wilderness. Bedouins have simply known all their lives which clan and tribe live in which wadi; they have nothing on paper to state the obvious. And so the concept of formal land ownership, imported (but largely ignored) by the Ottomans and the British and now enforced and made part of the Israeli structure of law and authority, has excluded the semi-nomads and left them practically defenseless in the courts, which have interpreted rules that are irrelevant to the Bedouins' ways.

In essence, this has been a clash between antiquity and modernity, a conflict once again between the desert and the settled agrarian life. The Bedouins have wandered the Negev since migrating from the Arabian peninsula, probably in the eighteenth century, according to Clinton. Now competing interests struggle over the land, even the desert land, and especially so after Israel has had to relocate its military forces following its withdrawal from Sinai. Three new air bases had to be built in the Negev; army firing ranges and fields for maneuvers had to be established. Kibbutzim want to irrigate and cultivate. And preservationists want desert zones made into reserves; some argue that the Bedouins are over-grazing and that their black goats damage the fragile desert vegetation by cutting plants too low, although this is disputed by other experts.

Israeli government policy has evolved on the assumption that the sedentary life represents a positive advancement from the rather unsavory, backward, and undesirable existence of the nomad. Many officials see themselves as catalysts in the inexorable process of progress. Far from trying to preserve traditional Bedouin life while resolving the problems over land use, they think they should help history along by structuring deterrents to the old ways and incentives to the new. Clusters of houses have been built with closed courtyards, too little space for entertaining guests, no place of privacy for the women, and too little land for grazing. "Bedouins like space," said Clinton. "When they sit in front of their tent and look out, whatever they see is considered home."

Compensation was paid to Bedouins evicted from the sites of new air bases in such stingy amounts that the tribesmen could not support themselves and were forced in many cases into wage labor. This has undermined their sense of independence and honor, which is based on a free roaming, subsistence agriculture, not on a boss or a labor product. Living in a community and being forced into the cash economy, the Bedouins are no longer the masters of their own fate.

As in Sinai, some Bedouins have welcomed the change, for cash can buy what barter has never been able to. And since the Israelis have cracked down on cross-border smuggling for security reasons, the semi-nomadic Bedouins in the Negev have been reduced to the rudiments of desert agriculture for their livelihood. Many have also joined the Israeli army as trackers, but even they are not spared the calloused hand of contempt. The Bedouin tribes that had lived in the desert for many years before the Jews established modern Israel are dismissed by the Green Patrol and its supporters in government as "squatters" on "state land." In a revealing comment to the newspaper *Davar*, the head of the Green Patrol, Allon Galili, declared, "The Bedouin takes advantage of the good will of other people. This is the nature of nomadism. The strong one wins. As nomads, they deal in robbery. They have legitimate laws: robbery as a means of making a living. We call it theft. What they call vengeance we call murder. A legitimate custom of theirs, such as having a number of wives, we call polygamy, and it is against the law. If we want a proper country, then there's no room for nomads."

Galili's patrol met considerable frustration. Some Bedouins allowed their goats to graze in kibbutz fields. Others ignored orders to move from desert wadis they felt were traditionally theirs. Or, having moved, they filtered back again. The patrolmen often responded with anger and violence. "First of all, they're children," Swaylim Abu-Bilaya said of the Green Patrol members when I visited him in his camp with Clinton. "They're young, not from the point of view of age but from the point of view of behavior. People who go around bothering other people aren't men. That's one reason they cannot be the government. Second, they're stealing from people. They're taking their flocks away. Third, they're damaging relations between two peoples, the Bedouins and the Jews. They know this is our land, but they want to push us out into these settlements. We can't live in the settlements. We'll die in the settlements. They scare our children away and shoot our dogs. You call that a government? That can't be a government."

We spent a December night in Swaylim Abu-Bilaya's goat-hair tent, an ingenious shelter whose fibers were woven loosely enough to allow smoke to pass through them but to keep the heat in. It was cold that night; there was frost on the ground at daybreak, and as we settled in to sleep, Abu-Bilaya brought mats and pillows and quilts that were the colors of blood and ivory. He laid them out and smoothed them and arranged them for us and kept asking solicitously if we were comfortable. The fire crackled and the air smelled of smoke and the words were all spoken softly.

Abu-Bilaya had another guest that night, Muhammad el-Khishkhar, whose family was in its own tent a few miles away. Two of his camels had wandered off, and he was out looking for them when darkness approached. He slept in the tent, and in the morning relaxed around the fire as his host, using a can as a mortar and an iron bar as a pestle, pounded coffee beans with a rhythmic tap, tap. El-Khishkhar told long stories from his grandfather of the days of tribal wars and blood feuds, and only when the sun was high did he walk off to look for his camels. He did not know that during that dawn, the Green Patrol was pouncing on his camp a short distance away, driving his family into the cold, tearing down the tent, and packing the two women and ten children into three jeeps for a long ride to a closed area where they were permitted to live. They were allowed to take only three blankets, according to his wife, Fatma, and although she pleaded to be permitted to leave her two-month-old baby with another family because of the cold, the Green Patrol refused.

The baby died the following night. An uproar ensued in Israel, and an official autopsy was ordered. Dr. Bezalel Bloch, director of the Institute of Forensic Medicine, found "signs of interstitial pneumonia" and a "slight thickening of the endocard," which is the inner muscle of the heart. The report did not discuss the possible effect of exposure to cold on an infant with such illnesses, and Dr. Bloch said the police had ordered him not to elaborate, even though they also decided not to recommend prosecution.

Other Israeli doctors were less restrained. "When a two-month-old infant takes ill and is exposed to low temperatures without appropriate protection," said Dr. Shimon Moses, "the combination of the two factors, the illness and the cold, is liable to be to his detriment. From my experience with infants suffering from a known infection, they tend not to retain their body temperatures when they are exposed to the cold. It is not good for a sick infant to be in other than optimal conditions." Dr. Moses was head of pediatrics at the Soroka Medical Center and a professor in pediatrics at the Beersheba Medical School.

Nobody was prosecuted, disciplined, or reprimanded in the affair. The Green Patrol announced triumphantly that its practices would be continued unaltered.

FIFTEEN

Secret Police in an Open Society

Thou shalt not go up and down as a talebearer
among thy people: neither shalt thou stand against
the blood of thy neighbor.
—Leviticus 19:16

THE JEEP CARRYING TWO PLAINCLOTHESMEN AND TWO UNIFORMED
soldiers drew up to the ramp of the airliner that had just arrived at Tel
Aviv's Ben-Gurion International Airport. As the passengers filed down
the steps, the plainclothesmen searched for a face—the pleasant face of
a particular twenty-year-old Palestinian Arab. They saw their man, watched
him descend, intercepted him on the tarmac, asked for his documents,
put him into the jeep, and drove away. No fuss, no muss. Very smooth,
clean, quiet. Let us call the man "Gamal."

They had about an hour's ride, enough time for one of the agents in
civilian clothes, a gentle interrogator named Elias, to brief Gamal on the

outlines of their suspicions about him. In that conversation and subsequent sessions of questioning, Gamal was to learn something of the extensive scope and efficiency of Israel's intelligence apparatus.

Elias informed him, correctly, when and where he had met in Chicago with a Palestinian known to be active in the PLO, what date the Palestinian had visited Gamal in another American city, and in which restaurant they had dined.

"Yes, he's an old friend of the family, and we talked about family matters," Gamal said nervously.

"I don't buy your story," Elias snapped. They took him to police headquarters at the Russian Compound in Jerusalem.

Israeli agents told Gamal many details about himself and his family. They knew that his brother had lived in the United States for the last seven years and had married an American woman. They mentioned the name of her father, the name of her mother. They knew that Gamal had been born in East Jerusalem, that he had grown up under the Jordanians and had been seven years old when Israel conquered that part of the city during the 1967 war, that he had gone to a particular college in the United States for the previous three and a half years, and that he was now coming home to his family in Jerusalem.

Indeed, his parents were waiting for him at the terminal. They watched as people surged through the gate that opened from the customs area, and they waited until the last passengers from the plane had trickled out. Their son never appeared. Knowing that Arabs were often detained at the airport for special searches and interrogation, they stayed a while longer. Then, when they made inquiries, Israeli police authorities provided no information. Only six hours later did they learn what had happened to their son, and only after forty-five days did they see him when he finally got home. What should have been a twelve-hour flight became a six-week journey for Gamal into a netherworld of Arab-Jewish conflict.

Clearly, any Arab who imagined that he could escape Israeli surveillance by journeying beyond Israeli jurisdiction, whether to the United States or Europe, would eventually learn otherwise. One man who vacationed in Europe returned to a confrontation with Israeli interrogators who played back to him the particulars of his rather complicated itinerary; he had obviously been tailed everywhere. In Gamal's case, the tight spotlight of Israel's Mossad, the country's main overseas intelligence agency, had apparently been following the Chicago Palestinian, illuminating all who came within his circle, including Gamal. That piece of intelligence was enough for a presumption of guilt by association, igniting official anxiety that a potential PLO operative was arriving in Israel. Once back in the country, Gamal became the responsibility of the Shin Beth, also known as Shabak, the internal police apparatus that operates in a shadowy and often brutal secrecy, largely insulated from the normal restraints imposed by the judicial system. The Shin Beth and Mossad report directly to the prime minister.

The agents took a long time to accept Gamal's innocent version of his meeting. The man in Chicago, originally a West Bank resident and "an active guy" in the PLO, came from a family with close ties to Gamal's. "I went to his house for dinner in Chicago," Gamal said. "It was just family talk—nothing. Then he came to [my city] and called me, so I invited him over. We had dinner in a restaurant," catching up on conversation about mutual friends, Gamal remembered. "I said [to the interrogator], 'If you know all this, you must know what I was talking to him about,' and he slapped me and said, 'I ask the questions here.' I said, 'If I'd known this would happen, I never would have seen this guy.' All of a sudden he starts yelling and slaps me. I never had that hard a one before, even in a fight."

The repetitive questioning and the physical abuses fell into a pattern common to the experiences of other Arabs who have described their imprisonment. "They wanted to know if I was related in any way to the PLO or if I had special training," Gamal recalled. Elias served as the "soft" interrogator, with the harder role filled by a huge, ugly, powerfully built man whom Gamal dubbed the Monster. "He was almost seven feet tall with muscles—just like the ones you see in the movies," said Gamal with a wry amusement that he managed to muster up three years after the fact. "Once you get to know him, he's a real nice guy. He called me names: Dog, Animal, Sucker, Son of a Bitch, Son of a Whore, all in Arabic."

Serious interrogations took place in Room No. 6 in the Russian Compound, Gamal said, where he was taken with a hood over his head. "That's where they show you what hell's all about. I think it's underground. I could feel the humidity of the place. I got down there by steps. I could hear people screaming and yelling, people in agony, all over the place. It was like a madhouse. I was kicked everywhere—in the balls, even. I had an ulcer operation in the States—I was kicked in the stomach. I was whipped on the back, with my shirt off. I passed out. They had a cold-water tub. They would put my head in the cold water first and then hot water, then cold again and then hot water. I'm a chicken; I would have told everything if I'd known anything."

Gamal was held incommunicado for forty-five days. He was never brought before a judge, never allowed to see a lawyer, never permitted a visit from his parents or even from the International Committee of the Red Cross, which tries to keep tabs on the treatment of Arab prisoners. "They told Daddy's lawyer that it's just routine, not serious. 'If it gets to something serious, we'll let you see him, but it's not serious.' " Finally the Israelis seemed satisfied: Either he was not associated with the PLO or they had scared him enough to drive him away from any involvement. They halted the interrogations. "They let me rest for four days before they released me."

Such methods lend the Shin Beth a specter of omnipresence and envelop the young Palestinian in a smothering cloak of vulnerability; the aim, of course, is to deter him from any political or violent activities he might be contemplating. And although the Shin Beth has faced a growing shortage of fluent Arabic-speakers, as those Jews born in Arab countries have reached retirement age, the preemptive approach remains central to the strategy.

When Zohar Endrawos, the twenty-five-year-old Israeli Arab, was studying in Rome and went to the Israeli embassy to renew his passport, he was held for hours of questioning. When he flew back to Tel Aviv, he was kept at the airport and interrogated for three hours, then a week or so later arrested and held for three days. "At the beginning of the investigation the interrogator told me, 'I have no legal basis to hold you, but I want to break that mind-set.' Every Palestinian Arab who lives in the state of Israel feels free to express his political opinions," Endrawos observed, "and I think that is the mind-set he wanted to break. He wanted to break me as deterrence. He limped in his right leg and was a prisoner of war in Syria in 1973. He said he was tortured in Syria and wanted to do the same to me. He said they pulled out his fingernails. He said, 'From a physical standpoint I won't torture you, but from a psychological standpoint we will. We'll hit you a little and you'll faint, and we'll give you only a little water. From a physical standpoint it will leave its mark.' "

Perhaps so, but not as the Israelis intended. When I asked Endrawos what he thought he would be doing if his family had fled in 1948 rather than staying in Israel, he gave a crisp answer: "I would be in a refugee camp and would be a guerrilla."

Following such captivity, even freedom does not feel entirely free. After Gamal's release, he said, "I got called twice to go and see those guys for interrogation. This guy Elias suggested I should report at the Russian Compound daily for three months. I said, 'I can't do that. I've got things to do.' I was working in my father's office. Elias said, 'Okay, but don't leave Jerusalem. Go from home to the office, office to home, that's all.' Then, the second time, one month later, he called me and said, 'Okay, you can go wherever you want.' "

Gamal is an open, soft-spoken young man, but the shadow of the experience still darkens his mood, makes him cautious, keeps him home at night, moves him to plead with me to avoid using his real name. "I talked to a *Jerusalem Post* reporter, and three days later they came back to me. If I were outside the country, I wouldn't care. I'm here. I'm under their thumb. They can get me in a matter of minutes." And that is precisely the state of mind the Shin Beth seeks to induce.

The system can produce some bizarre moments. When Gamal's incarceration ended, he recalled, "The Monster came and shook hands with me and said, 'I'm sorry if I caused any inconvenience. It's my orders from above.' " A few months later, Gamal saw him again, near Jaffa Gate in the Old City of Jerusalem. The Monster walked over and invited his former prisoner to have a cup of coffee at a nearby café. As they sat together, the brutal interrogator smiled and said, "Be a good boy and don't get involved in anything. You're a nice guy. I like you."

Gamal was flabbergasted. "Okay," he replied, "but do me a favor. If you see me on the street, don't come near me."

As in the underworld of crime, Arab-Jewish interactions at the sordid levels of secret-police work are murky, complex, and extensive. Constant efforts are made to recruit Arabs as informants and spies through enticements, threats, and punishments. Many Palestinians, applying for exit papers from the West Bank to travel and work in the Persian Gulf states or other parts of the Arab world, are told by Israeli agents: You will get your papers only if you work for us. Look around, and when you return, tell us what's going on. Some have been promised money if they cooperate, imprisonment if they do not.

Gamal's first encounter with this came when he was just fifteen and applied for a laissez-passer to leave for the United States. As a Jordanian citizen, he could not pass through Israeli border control using his Jordanian passport lest it be stamped by the Israelis and thus rendered invalid by the Jordanians. So he was at the mercy of the Shin Beth man who interviewed him on his application. The time came for him to go see the agent. "My mother, who is a little superstitious, said verses of the Koran over my head." It didn't work. The Israeli agent made a tough proposition. "He asked me why I was going, was I close to the PLO," Gamal recalled. "And then he said, 'Well, if you see anything, would you tell us?' I said, 'What do you mean?' 'Well, work for us. We'll take good care of you. If you need money . . .' I said, 'No, I'm going to study.' They refused the laissez-passer." A year later, he applied again and was interviewed by a Sephardi Jew who called himself by the Arab name Abu-Daoud ("Father of David"). "He said, 'Work for us. That's what's good for you.' I said, 'I know what's good for me. I don't want any part of it.' " Two weeks later, without explanation, they issued him the laissez-passer anyway. "My daddy said, 'You did good.' This thing was going above my head. I couldn't really understand it." Perhaps his arrest when he returned was the Shin Beth's final try.

How many Arabs acquiesce and agree to spy is anybody's guess, but Palestinians in the West Bank, the Gaza Strip, East Jerusalem, and Israel proper tend to feel that schools, workplaces, villages, and even militant refugee camps are pervaded by informers. The impression is reinforced by the rapidity with which the Israelis are often able to move from arresting a single terrorist to scooping up an entire cell, a process that relies on contacts within the Arab population, physical abuse, and trickery in interrogation.

The lack of informers among Jews represented a handicap to the Shin Beth's investigation of Jewish terrorism against Arabs in the early 1980s, but some of the other techniques were used effectively once Jewish suspects were in custody. Genese Liebowitz complained that her son Matthew confessed to involvement in an attack with automatic weapons on an Arab bus only after the police tied a hood tightly over his head. He had asthma and told his guards that he was having trouble breathing, but to no avail. "They shackled him and hooded him, took away his shoes and shirt for two solid days," she said. "They made him sleep on the floor. They gave him about five or six hours of sleep every twenty-four hours." They planted one of the other assailants in his cell to tell Liebowitz that they had enough evidence for a conviction. And during interrogation they told him a lie that they knew would break him: that the driver of the bus had been shot dead through the heart. "He freaked out over that," his mother said, and signed a confession somewhat broader than the actual scope of his participation warranted.

These methods do not always substitute adequately for solid police work. When applied to Arabs, they crack many important cases, but they also hold a certain probability of error, since a prisoner may confess falsely just to end the physical or psychological pressure. The legal basis for the suspension of customary rights lies in emergency regulations imposed on Palestine by the British in 1945; directed mostly against Jews in those years, the draconian provisions are now used mostly by Jews against Arabs. Inside Israel proper, someone accused of a security offense may be held for up to fifteen days without seeing a defense attorney, and in occupied zones—the West Bank and the Gaza Strip—the time can run to six months. But these limits are frequently ignored, as in Gamal's case. Lea Tsemel, one of the few Jewish attorneys willing to defend Arabs in security matters, told me that 90 percent of her clients have confessed by the time she reaches them. In the main, the confessions are true, she said, although "very often there are extra things added that are not accurate." In major cases of terrorism, she noted, the authorities have a strong interest in being extremely careful to capture those who actually committed the attacks.

In less serious offenses, however, including stone-throwing, possession of banned literature, hostile political activity, and membership in or support for a "terrorist organization" such as the PLO, a good many capricious arrests, summary punishments, and acts of collective intimidation occur in a way that tends to diffuse the police activity and thus dilute its deterrent effect. So constant is the mist of precarious existence that hangs over West Bank residents that being hassled or arrested is practically like getting wet in a rainstorm: It happens to you from time to time, and rarely as the result of anything you do.

West Bank children suffer high anxiety as a result. A 1981 study comparing eleven-year-old Israeli Jews and West Bank Arabs requested each of them to write a caption for a drawing of a mother asking her son, "What happened in school today?" The Jewish children wrote, "Nothing special," "The teacher was angry because I didn't do my homework," and other, similar replies. But the answers of almost all the West Bank Arab youngsters contained violence: "Soldiers burst into the classroom and sprayed us with tear gas," or "We held a demonstration and threw stones at the soldiers."[75]

The random nature of arrest was graphically illustrated to Arthur Kutcher, the American-born architect, as he guarded the Nablus city hall on the West Bank during his army-reserve duty. One afternoon, on the street in front of him, Arab schoolchildren were gathering to wait for a bus. Suddenly, two Jewish settlers carrying Uzi submachine guns and wearing civilian clothes and skullcaps came around the corner to Kutcher's left in a rapid walk, then burst into a run. Shouting and whooping, they "ran past us, in front of us," he said, "and seized an Arab kid of about sixteen or seventeen. One of them grabbed him by the arms and the other pointed his Uzi at the kid's head." Kutcher's commander, a border-police sergeant, ran to separate them, pulling the Arab boy back to the steps of the city hall to protect him. The settlers, activists in the right-wing Gush Emunim movement, were hysterical, and the commotion brought a crowd of Arabs out of the building, as well as the Israeli army colonel who was acting as the city's chief administrator in the aftermath of the Defense Ministry's ouster of the elected Arab mayor. The colonel, a Druse, looked the situation over and told the settlers that if they had a complaint against the boy, they should lodge it with the police across the street. "So the kid and the settlers were taken off to the police," Kutcher said, "and our commander told us that it was quite peculiar; from what we could see, the kid had simply been standing there. He'd walked in front of us and had gone to the bus stop and stood there. It certainly didn't look like he was being pursued by anyone, and [our commander said] that as soon as we were off duty all three of us should go to the police and testify to this."

They did so, but the police were not interested in testimony, even from Israeli soldiers, that would undermine the settlers' accusations against the boy. "We were told by the desk officer [an Arab] that evidence had been given by the two Gush Emunim people that they had seized the boy red-handed with a stone in front of the municipal building, and as far as he was concerned the case was closed. We told him this was not the case, we saw no stone, he didn't throw any stone, he was standing quite calmly." The officer replied that they would have to wait for the police commander, a Jew, to return, which he did after about forty-five minutes. "The commander said that as far as he was concerned, the evidence was conclusive that the boy had thrown stones. He said, 'As far as I'm concerned, their testimony is sufficient to convict him, and there's no point for you to hang around.' We asked him if our testimony would be required, and he said, 'There's no need.' "

In the Jalazoun refugee camp, a labyrinth of bare concrete houses jammed together on crooked alleys north of Jerusalem, a spate of stone-throwing at Israeli cars in the winter of 1982 brought a barrage of nighttime visits from Israeli troops. They came about 8:30 P.M. to the damp, two-room house of Isa Abd-Rahmen el-Kheldi, a Palestinian construction man who was working for seven dollars a day building the central synagogue in downtown Jerusalem. His wife and the smallest of his thirteen children were asleep; the oldest were sitting on the cold floor watching television. Sounds came from outside. Mrs. Kheldi stirred, thinking she was dreaming. Half awake, she asked her husband to check, and as he approached the door, it burst open and seven soldiers crowded into the tiny room.

"What is your name?" a soldier asked. He was told.

"That's right," the soldier said in Arabic. "This is the name we want. Where are your children?"

The father took them into the room with the television set. A soldier pointed to a boy sitting at the end of the line and asked his name. It was Fadel, and he was fourteen years old.

"Come with me," the soldier said to the boy. "Put some clothes on him," the soldier commanded the parents. Then handcuffs were locked onto Fadel's hands in front of him and he was led out the door.

"Put them on my hands, not his!" shouted his mother, weeping.

For more than a month, his family was not allowed to see the boy and heard nothing from the Israeli military government about his condition or the charges against him. The father hired an Arab lawyer for $300, about two months' salary. A Red Cross representative was permitted to visit the boy about two weeks after his arrest, in accordance with the Israelis' normal procedure, and the family finally saw him several weeks later. Israeli officials were vague about his alleged offense, saying only that he belonged to "an illegal organization" and had given a confession, the contents of which they were not prepared to reveal.

This is the pattern. When stones are thrown, when slogans supporting the PLO are painted on walls, when demonstrators block roads with rocks and burning tires, the Israelis get jittery and tough. They sweep up Arab boys and imprison them for days or weeks without contact with parents or lawyers, hoping to scare them into naming others, hoping to scare others into caution. But the efforts are so unfocused, the suspicions so fragile, the threads of evidence so thin that innocents are inevitably caught with the guilty. Informants can be vitally accurate, or they can mislead, naming names just to pursue feuds and settle scores. And the boys themselves name other boys simply because they are terrified. "Sometimes they take anybody and start asking questions, and under threat he says any names, any names just to be free," explained Moussa Ahmed Masaoud.

He was fifteen, already beginning to fill out into a young man's physique, but his eyes were young, and he kept wiping them as he told of his own arrest. The soldiers came for him at night, about 11:30. He was blindfolded and handcuffed and taken to Ramallah, just south of the Jalazoun camp, where he was placed alone in a small cell. In the morning, interrogation began. He was put in a corridor made cold by an open door and an open window. He was stripped, and cold water was poured over him as four Israelis questioned him in Arabic.

"Tell us what you've done."

"I did nothing, I did nothing."

"Tell us what you've done."

"What can I tell you if I did nothing?"

They contended that he had thrown stones and painted slogans. He denied it. "They hit me but not very hard," he said. "They used bad words about my mother, my sister, my father," and those about his mother angered him the most. After forty-nine days, he was released without charges for what the Israelis said was lack of evidence. "I never imagined that jail was such a thing," he said. "It's much worse than I thought, both in their treatment and in my thinking that I was cut off from the world, lost my school, my family."

To the extent that Israeli behavior on the West Bank is calculated, the theory appears to be one of preventive strikes: If you can't co-opt, terrify. If you can't find the guilty individual, harass and punish the society in which he operates. If a Jew is killed, place the entire village under an around-the-clock curfew for at least a few days, preventing anyone from going to work, enabling the Shin Beth and the army to search and interrogate. If a stone is thrown, turn the entire population of a neighborhood out of their beds at night, make them stand in the street for hours.

It was early April, a cold night in the West Bank city of Nablus. Arthur Kutcher was assigned to guard a unit of Israeli border policemen called because stones had been thrown at a police patrol. About 1 A.M., he said, the border policemen—who are dressed and armed like soldiers and, on the West Bank, serve under army command—began banging on the doors of a row of houses on the street where the incident had taken place. All men, women, and children were ordered out. "They were told to come out as they were, in their nightclothes, and told to stand in the street in the cold," he said. Until about 3:30 A.M., the forty or fifty people stood while the border troops checked their identity papers and waited for Shin Beth agents to arrive. "The Shin Beth people went along, and, of course, they knew people who might be suspect, and they simply examined who was standing in the street," Kutcher recalled, "and they came across, finally, one youth who they knew had a history of this sort of thing, and they were going to arrest him. But he became quite panicky, and he pointed out another youth of about sixteen, who was then apprehended, physically seized, and from what I could see he was not resisting. He was just simply grabbed and beaten." Kutcher saw a border policeman hold the boy from behind while a Shin Beth man slapped him in the face and punched him in the chest and stomach. "It wasn't an extensive beating, but it was enough to make an impression; that is, a lesson." The boy's family and neighbors looked on passively, as if going through a frequent routine. "When they were rounded up, there was very little required to get them out. They had been through this before. They took this as a matter of course, including the beating. I don't think it was a terribly serious beating. Obviously the point was humiliation. He was put into the jeep and taken off to detention."

Assaulting an Arab's honor has become an accepted tool of antagonism. "Whoever shows any sort of political uppityness has to be humiliated," Kutcher observed. Arabs have told of being made to sing the Israeli national anthem and shout "Down with Arafat!" A squad of border policemen, arriving at the village of Halhoul after an Israeli bus had been stoned in 1982, were later brought to trial for rounding up all the men in the town, forcing fathers and sons to slap each other, making residents crawl on the ground and bark, and ordering them to shout praise for the border police.

A free society can never be content as an occupier, for injustice corrodes the vision and gnaws at the sense of moral well-being. And so Israel endures its occupation of the West Bank with profound ambivalence. Its rough handling of Arabs brings a strain of shame.

A ranking military commander on the West Bank, a professional officer, once told me of the pain he felt in his assignment, of how he would rather have been training his men to fight a war than to battle Arab children staging demonstrations. He was angry at stories of brutality and wanted to prosecute any soldier involved. But nobody, not Arabs and not Jews, would give him the details he needed before he could act. The Arabs were afraid, the Jews inured. New draftees, born only eighteen years ago, have never known a time when the West Bank was not under Israeli occupation. Many regard it as a natural state of affairs. Some, of course, chafe against the burden. When I left the commander's office, two of his men outside asked me for a lift to Jerusalem. One said, "Would you give a ride to two soldiers who hate what they're doing here?"

Occasionally, though rarely, Jews come to the defense of a Palestinian they feel has been unjustly treated. In 1984, the entire kibbutz Kerem Shalom conducted an unsuccessful campaign on behalf of a Gaza Strip Arab, Abdul-Aziz Ali Shahin, who had been placed under house arrest apart from his family after completing a fifteen-year prison sentence for serving as the Fatah commander in the Hebron area of the West Bank. Arguing that Shahin had infiltrated into the area from Jordan right after the 1967 war, Israeli authorities moved to deport him, and in the interim restricted him to the village of Dahaniya and prohibited him from communicating with anyone. His lawyer claimed that he had been in the Gaza Strip in 1967 and had been registered there by the Israeli census that followed the fighting. His Jewish defenders, arguing that Shahin was just the kind of moderate Palestinian whose search for coexistence Israel should encourage, denounced the lack of due process contained in the army's order. "In our eyes this isolation is in total opposition to the principles of democracy," the kibbutz wrote in an open letter. "If the State of Israel suspects that Mr. Shahin is violating a law, this can be dealt with through the court system." The protests managed to win nothing for Shahin but the right of a weekly visit from his wife. However, it illuminated the pockets of intense idealism and conscience that remain in the Israeli population.

Palestinians on the West Bank and the Gaza Strip have lived under one or another oppressive system since 1948, with the Jordanians and the Egyptians exercising tough control over the West Bank and Gaza respectively. If anything, there is perhaps more ambivalence under the Israelis, for now the system is neither a democracy nor a police state but a little of both. The Israeli Defense Ministry governs in a volatile mixture of humaneness and oppression, reflecting the contradictory impulses of Israel: an open system that fears for its security. Again and again the government has tried to limit the very freedoms it has granted to the 1.2 million Palestinians living there. It has allowed colleges to operate in a highly charged political atmosphere of support for the PLO, then tried to restrict the political content of textbooks and lectures to eliminate expressions of that support. It has allowed virulently anti-Israel professors and teachers to work, then assigned to itself the power to dismiss them, a power that stimulates protests by Arabs but is rarely used. Poets may write, but their books are sometimes taken from shops and barred from school libraries. Painters may paint, but some works are banned from exhibition. The authorities permitted West Bank residents to elect mayors in 1972 and 1976, when the voters chose PLO supporters over moderates, but beginning in 1980, the Israelis moved to oust every elected mayor of every major town and city except Bethlehem.

Troops and policemen have, on occasion, been prosecuted for brutality, but only halfheartedly after much public uproar, and their sentences have usually been light. Strict guidelines on opening fire during demonstrations have been promulgated, but little or no training has been given in crowd control, leaving every inexperienced soldier at the mercy of his fears with only a deadly rifle as his protection from angry stone-throwers. A grinding guilt works at the bowels of Israeli consciousness. Or, worse, a callous frustration numbs the young Jew and carries over into his own open democracy. He has grown up thinking that Arabs are good for beating.

The infectious brutality festered and then broke into an open sore in the Tel Aviv civilian guard, which patrols streets and watches for suspicious characters who might be planting bombs. Jewish high-school students from Herzliya, north of Tel Aviv, were shocked at what they witnessed when they volunteered for night duty in 1984. Under the supervision of Sarah Rahamim, the chief of their base, bands of volunteers from Tel Aviv schools drove through the city, spotted Arabs, pushed them into stairwells, slapped and punched them. "We were driving in the area of the central bus station," one girl told *Haaretz*. "Suddenly we saw three Arabs in front of us. One of the volunteers asked them what they were doing here and where they worked. He instructed them to enter a stairwell in a nearby house and to wait there. . . . I told Sarah that I had heard that they were beating them, and I wanted to know what was going on. Sarah said to me: 'Go look. When my daughter sees it, she gets a good laugh.' I got out of the patrol car and went to the building door. The three Arabs were facing the wall with their arms raised. One of the volunteers asked one of the Arabs: 'Where do you live?' The Arab answers, and he yells at him: 'Why are you lying?' and hits him. Another question and another shout: 'You're lying!' And a blow." During another patrol, she said, "We saw an Arab running. We didn't know if he was running because of us or because of the rain. We all got out of the patrol car and stopped him. Everyone was armed even though we had not passed the firing range [test] and it's forbidden. . . . I came to the door of the apartment house. . . . The student leader was holding the Arab's identity card. In front of him stood the Arab with his hands up, and behind him stood a volunteer with drawn rifle with the cartridge in. I heard the student leader say to the Arab: 'If we see you again, that will be the end of you.' And he slapped him. They make a real thing out of the beatings. They talk about this experience to everyone. One guy broke an Arab's teeth, the second forced another Arab to crawl. Another boasted that he broke two of an Arab's teeth."

Another student, a boy, told the paper, "The guys on the base prepared me by saying that you have to beat Arabs because Arabs rape girls and are a criminal nuisance. When you beat them, they go away. When we drove in an area without Arabs, what's called a 'clean area,' the volunteers explained to us that it was clean because they were beaten and they fled." The volunteers mocked Arabs for their accents and tried to make them cry. The commander, Sarah Rahamim, was forced to resign, but no criminal action was taken.[76]

The conscience of the country is always there, yet wrongs are done as a matter of routine. A system of military courts hears security and political cases in the occupied territories, and many of the judges are attorneys and law professors, not career military men, who preside during their month of reserve duty each year. But the ostensible judicial protections are easily foiled by the latitude of the Shin Beth to force confessions, by the fear of Arabs to charge publicly that they have been tortured, by the reluctance of the courts to throw out confessions that are challenged, by the inability of many Arab families to afford defense lawyers, by the fact that laws on the West Bank and Gaza Strip are made by military decree with no legislative input.

In practice, the Shin Beth appears to operate with little supervision from the political level and few restraints from the judiciary. Kutcher remembered vividly how his path touched the secret police activities just fleetingly, as a tangent makes only the slightest contact with a circle. "A friend asked me to change guard duty with him," he recalled. "He asked me to guard the Shabak cells and he would do the front gate. I said, 'Why?' He said, 'Well, first of all they keep them in windowless cells for a day, a day and a half, two days, without any toilet facilities, and every time the door opens there's a terrible stench. Sometimes they get hysterical, try to get out, and besides that, when they're brought in, they're often beaten.' He had seen them beaten, and although he hated the Arabs, he himself couldn't stand to see them beaten, and could I please do it? And I thought, well, I don't want to see them beaten either, but it's something I should do. That evening, when I stood guard duty, no one was brought in, so I in fact didn't see this. But I don't see why he would lie about this. This is sort of an inner room where you can see the door to one of the cells, and from the outside you can see that the windows are blocked off. We were not allowed to go into the cells at all. We were strictly told to stay outside because someone might try to seize our weapon. Was there a stench? Yes. It had the smell of a very unclean lavatory." He had heard that the cells were to be demolished shortly thereafter.

The Shin Beth and the army have little problem breaking through the flimsy legal protections that exist on paper in the West Bank, which is governed by Israeli military decree against a legacy of Turkish, British, and Jordanian law. The Israeli authorities pick and choose the statutes left by previous conquerors as the situation happens to suit them and often ignore the restrictions on police activity that they have imposed on themselves. Although many cases conform with the formal guidelines on, for example, the number of days a suspect may be in custody before being visited by the Red Cross, his more substantial rights are frail indeed. Arrest without cause, detention without trial, and summary punishment are all part of the Arab's common experience with Israeli authority under military occupation. The abuses seem to transcend politics, existing under both Labor and Likud governments.

Twice a year, in January and June, a flurry of arrests takes place. Those targeted seem inevitably to be twelfth-grade boys and a few twelfth-grade girls. They are taken in for questioning, held for four or five days, and then released, often without charge or explanation. The detentions seem insignificant given what is possible, but they can be calamitous for these teenagers, for their arrests coincide with the administering of the *tawjihi*, the matriculation examination required by Jordan to signify the successful completion of high school and the eligibility for entrance into a university in the Arab world. The sittings in January and June are both compulsory parts of the test, and any youngster who misses any part has to wait a full year to take it again. Otherwise he lacks a credential vital for access to professional life.

Palestinian activists and some of their Western supporters, most notably Law in the Service of Man, an affiliate of the International Commission of Jurists, began to discern the pattern in 1983 and to call on the Israelis to halt what was evidently a deliberate practice of placing *tawjihi* candidates in custody just long enough for them to miss their exams. The Israelis then became more blatant. Some students were arrested, held until the exams were over, and released without ever having been questioned. The authorities ordered others expelled from their schools or transferred to distant schools difficult to reach because of inadequate public transportation from their villages.

Khaled Ajamiyya, of the Dheisheh refugee camp, was picked up by soldiers the night before the exam. There had been no riots or stone-throwing, but no matter. "They had all kinds of secret police and military people floating around here," he said. "They handcuffed me, put a cover over my face, and pushed me out the door and took me to a detention room in the Russian Compound. I spent the night there. The next day the secret police came, interrogated me about alleged activities with the PLO, accused me of having stabbed somebody in the Bethlehem market. I said no. I was very nervous. They put me in a chair and hit me in the back of the head with a wooden club. They strapped me to a water pipe and kicked me four times in the head. I was held for eighteen days." And as he was about to be released, "the secret police said, 'Don't even bother to take the *tawjihi*. Anytime you try, we'll bring you here.' "

Palestinians go through a lot of speculation about how the Israelis choose their targets. "People who have been a little more cooperative with the Israelis—not collaborators, but cooperative—were allowed to take the exam," said Khaled. Perhaps those who were arrested were more overtly nationalistic and strident. The Shin Beth does not discuss its methods publicly, however, and even if the Israelis functioned with a calculated rationale that lent a precision to the selection process, the results came through to many Palestinians as practically random.

Few Israelis, even the liberal-minded who feel discomfort over being occupiers, would deny their security agencies the most flexible tools to combat terrorism. The bomb on the bus, the shooting in the market, the taking of a child hostage renders the finest principles into little more than delicate abstractions. As the years have passed, the threshold of outrage has risen. Rarely do the violations of human rights on the West Bank stir revulsion by more than a fraction of the Jewish population, and mostly among those old enough to remember a time when there was no occupation at all to nag at the spirit of righteousness. In some measure, Israeli Jews have stopped seeing the issues, a development predicted by Amos Elon, the Israeli author and journalist known for his disturbing and biting prescience. He remarked after the massacre by Israel's Lebanese allies in the Beirut refugee camps how difficult it would now be, in the shadow of that atrocity, to mobilize Israelis' indignation at the lesser evils being perpetrated on the West Bank. He recalled the protests a few years earlier when the Palestinian writer Raymonda Tawil was placed under house arrest in Ramallah; how loud was the outcry from liberal Jews, he remembered, when soldiers stationed outside her house began writing down the license numbers of cars as both Arabs and Jews drove up to visit her! Amos was right on target. Only the most contentious newspapers—*Haaretz* and *Davar,* for example—cover the West Bank with the acerbic perception it deserves. The larger-circulation papers do not often present the Palestinian view. The single television channel, state-owned, has devoted progressively less attention to the West Bank Arabs, especially since its foremost West Bank correspondent, an Israeli Druse named Rafik Halaby, was forced off the air in the early 1980s by what he called "political pressures," specifically: "You're not allowed to interview personalities identified as PLO supporters in the territories. You can't use the term West Bank. You can't do feature stories on the territories. In short, the journalistic coverage of the territories was limited. Personally, I also suffered from a wave of threats on my life and attacks by political elements, and to a certain degree my life was endangered by the settlers on the West Bank." Practically all news organizations shun the word "occupied," preferring the euphemism "administered" to describe what are increasingly called "the territories." An oblivious numbness has set in.

Still, there is that Israeli conscience, and even if it often seems to lurk too far beneath the surface of toughness, it has tempered Israeli behavior and has influenced the ways in which the Palestinians respond to their hardships. Candid Arabs will confide that the police state under Jordan from 1948 to 1967 was considerably harsher than the occupation by the Israelis has been since 1967. And the techniques of coping, resisting, are different. "Jordan was tight," said Albert Aghazarian. "But under Israel, the more you yell, the safer you are. In Israel, the more you talk, the more protected you are. If he touches you like this, on your hand, you should say, 'He's massacring me!' You should exaggerate in order to protect yourself, whereas in Jordan if he's massacring me and I say, 'He's touching me,' then I'm in worse shape. You say you're all right."

Those Jews who are sensitive to the precarious Arab relationship with police authority have to make hard decisions, even inside Israel proper, where Arabs are supposedly afforded the protections of an impartial judicial system. Meron Benvenisti, the former deputy mayor of Jerusalem who lives in the city's Abu-Tor neighborhood with Arab neighbors, explained the difficulties. "When they [Arab youngsters] smashed the windshield of my car for the second time, I was faced with a dilemma," he said. "Should I call the police? They'll probably arrest six or eight or ten; they'll see this as a political, as a terrorist, act. Or should I go to the local power structure, to the mukhtar's, and explain the situation? And I made a decision: that if I'm going to live in this neighborhood, I should approach the local power structure and not use my own connection with the external power structure, which is not only something that the Arabs don't do, but also because it's Israeli, Jewish, it's even worse. It was the right decision because from then on nothing happened. I told the mukhtar, 'Look, I can do it [call the police], but I've come to live here. I don't demand any special privileges, but at the same time you have to understand that I'm a neighbor, and therefore I'm under your protection.' "

Meron feels a duality of roles. "You are a neighbor and an enemy at the same time, and the question is when to activate one identity and when to activate the other one," he said. "Our [Arab] neighbor did some work in his garden, and he found an old '67 mortar shell, live, when he excavated. So he called me and I came and I saw what it was, and I had to make a quick decision: Should I call the police? The shell is there, and then his kids will most definitely be arrested because the police will think that this is just a hiding place. Or shall I move this thing to my garden and call the police? Well, that was risky because it was an old thing, and rusty. So I decided to risk it, and I took it and put it there and called the police."

Both edges of the Israeli sword are finely honed, and they cut deeply. The easy arrests, the official violence, and the strategy of humiliation may intimidate much of the West Bank population, deter some Palestinians from anti-Israel political agitation, and unravel incipient plots of terrorism. Undoubtedly, the repugnant methods are partly responsible for foiling many would-be attacks on civilians. But Israeli interests have been wounded as well. Just as the army is now drafting young Jews who have never known their country without a subordinate Arab population subject to martial law, so the PLO and other militant groups are now recruiting young Arabs who have never known a life without the hard, superior hand of the Israeli military occupation.

The toughness sows a bitterness and lends a luster to the nationalist impulses that Israel seeks to quash. What possible use can it be, for example, to take paintings out of galleries and books of poetry out of stores and libraries? "What did those poets write?" asked Yehuda Litany, formerly the West Bank correspondent of *Haaretz*. "Who was hurt by the verses they composed? Does the banning of those books or pictures prevent those feelings? It only exacerbates and deepens them. It seems that the Israeli government is not aware of the fact that works of art which are distributed underground merit increased circulation and are received with heightened enthusiasm, more than if they had been published openly. The feeling of participating in a sin, the secretiveness, adds to the pictures and poetry of the underground a magic that they would not have were they distributed and sold openly."

So there are West Bank fathers who are afraid of losing their sons, losing them to anger and absolutism, to the radical milieu of the "freedom fighters." When the fathers remember having known Jews in more amicable circumstances, when they preach compromise, conciliation, moderation, the sons simply throw the day's events back at them. It is like shouting into the wind.

One night, a Palestinian friend from Bethlehem called me at home. In a weeping voice, he told me that his teenage son, demonstrating against the occupation, had been hit in the head with a tear-gas canister. The injury was serious. A soldier had apparently fired the canister from a gun aimed directly at the crowd rather than shooting it above the heads so that it would travel along a gentle arc before falling to the ground. The boy's skull was fractured above the forehead, and splinters of bone were being removed by Jewish doctors at Hadassah Hospital in Jerusalem. He was conscious when he was rushed to the emergency room, and when his father appeared beside him, distraught, the boy looked up and said, "Dad, don't let the Jews see you cry."

My friend's son recovered physically and now wears a plate in his head. There was no brain damage. But the wound widened the gulf between the generations, and the father finds himself arguing frequently with his boy. They still talk, at least. When he told his woes to another West Bank Palestinian, that man replied that he was lucky. His own son had gone to Amman and then to Beirut to join the PLO.

One who followed that route and then returned to his home in East Jerusalem was Husam, a young man who seemed soft and naive as he talked to me in the grocery store where he worked. He had been a boy in 1967 and remembered the Israeli troops with confusion. They came giving out sweets and saying, "How are you? How are you?" to the children in Arabic. "We thought they were Iraqi troops," said Husam. But later, he added, they would grab children who were playing, ask them where they were going, hit them, and shoo them home.

Husam joined a Palestinian theater troupe that did plays tinged with political messages about the occupation, about Palestinian nationalism. Frequently Israeli authorities interrupted performances, refused permits, and interrogated actors. But through the medium of the stage, Husam came to feel something about the Palestinian issue he had not felt before. "I began to feel that it was not enough for me to write poems. I wanted to give more," he said. "It was not enough for me to step onto the stage and tell the people this and that." In 1980 he went to Lebanon and registered at a university in Beirut. The overwhelming presence of the PLO there in those years stirred him, and he was drawn into their organization, reading their literature, talking to their leaders. He was most attracted to the Popular Front for the Liberation of Palestine, the organization of the late Ghassan Kanafani, who had written one of the plays Husam had performed, *Return to Haifa*. "So I applied to them, and they took me. The people involved with the theater here were for the PFLP, and they sent reports every month. So when I went to Beirut I found they knew everything about me—a whole file—so I had no trouble being accepted."

After a period in Beirut going to college and doing "special training with the PFLP," Husam returned to Israel. He was picked up immediately by three of his Arab friends. "Everyplace I went they were there: 'How are you?' " Finally they approached him wanting to join the Popular Front. "We think you are a leader of the PFLP," they said, and asked to become members. "I said, 'Leave me, let me think.' I began to watch them in the cafés, in the streets, in their houses. I made visits to their houses to watch not just them but their sisters and brothers and cousins. Then I invited them to my house one by one. I took from them their pictures, names, histories, and I told them they were now in the Popular Front. I told them about my friends, who was good and not good, who was a spy in the West Bank and the Galilee. So we began to work together, the four of us."

Husam had no inkling that one of the three was an agent of the competing Fatah organization, the main branch of the PLO headed by Yasir Arafat. The agent and another man were dispatched by Husam to Syria to contact the PFLP, met secretly with Fatah people instead, and brought back money to finance an "operation," a terrorist attack that was to be made to look like the work of the PFLP. One Saturday morning when Husam was home sick in bed, his three friends gathered in the apartment belonging to one of them. The provocateur brought the makings of a bomb and told them that Husam had ordered an attack. "I didn't know anything about this subject," Husam insisted. The three began work, and the bomb exploded. Husam, whose home was nearby, heard the blast.

"One of our neighbors came to me and he told my mother that he wanted to talk to me secretly. She got out and he closed the door. He told me that my three friends were dead. My sister went out to see what happened. I went to the roof and saw many soldiers with dogs. All of them were bloody." As it turned out, only one died; the two survivors were interrogated and told the authorities about Husam. "They left me alone for a week after that. They arrested all my friends in the street. They wanted to watch what I would do. Would I go out? They closed the bridge [across the Jordan River to Jordan]. I was very careful. I went to my job normally, to the places I normally go. The explosion was Saturday. Wednesday they opened the bridge. So I went to visit all my friends and my family and told them I was going. At 1 A.M. Thursday they came to my house—secret police and Israeli soldiers—came and conducted a search. They asked where I was going. I said university in Jordan. They asked, 'Have you been in Lebanon?' I said no. My father was very ill. They said, 'Say good-bye to your father.' I said, 'I don't have to because I know I am in the heart of my father.'

"They took me out, blindfolded me, and handcuffed me, and stopped to get *shwarma* [grilled meat] and cola."

They beat him on the back with the butts of their rifles and took him to the Russian Compound, where he was stripped, searched, and handcuffed to a water pipe just at the right height so that he could neither stand nor sit. After fifteen hours of that, they put him in a cell, where a policeman came and told him, "There is a strong man, he wants to hit you, he wants to kill you. So you must tell us everything."

The interrogator, a Jew from Yemen, spoke perfect Arabic, Husam observed. "He said, 'I want to ask four questions, and I want the answers to be yes: One, did you go to Lebanon? Two, did you organize these three men? Three, did you make the bomb? Four, did you receive weapons training?' I said no to all the questions. He said, 'I'll leave you. You don't get out.' " Husam's hands were handcuffed behind his back and a small board was inserted behind his elbows and across his chest so he could hardly breathe. Two hours later, the interrogator came back and asked the same four questions. Husam said no again. "He spat in my face." This went on for sixty-three days.

"They went to my home [at one point] and said to my mother, 'Your son was a terrorist in Beirut.' She said, 'No, my son just studied there.' They said, 'If you give us something your son studied in Beirut, we'll let him go.' She looked in my room. Before that, after the explosion, I had ripped up everything. She found one thing, an ID card from the university. They came and asked me, 'Have you been in Beirut?' I said no and he started to hit me. He pulled out my ID card and put it down. I said I was in Beirut but I was studying there. So he said, 'I've grabbed the first thread: You were in Beirut, you returned, you organized these men, you made the bomb.'

"They brought my friend out of the hospital. He had been strong and big. When I saw him he was like this," and Husam held up one finger. "He had fourteen pieces of iron in his body from the explosion. I didn't recognize him. I greeted him and said, 'Be a man.' The secret police asked, 'Did Husam take you to Lebanon?' I looked at him. He said no. The secret policeman hit me and said, 'Don't look at him.' My friend had a broken thumb they had put a pin in. The policeman put the thumb under a table leg, sat on the table, and said, 'Did he organize you or not?' He cried, 'Yes! Yes! Yes!' After that, they brought to me the confessions my friends had written. I asked for a lawyer; they allowed him to speak to me after forty-three days. By then I answered yes to three questions: I was in Lebanon, I was in the Popular Front, I organized these men. But I didn't know anything about what they did."

Although Husam had been arrested where he lived in East Jerusalem, which was annexed by Israel in 1967 and is subject to Israeli, not military, law, he was tried before a military judge, not a civilian court. The prosecution asked for twenty-three years. In the end, however, the judge accepted his story: He was convicted not of making a bomb or planning a terrorist attack but of belonging to an illegal organization, and was sentenced to three years in prison and three suspended.

Strangely, as Husam and other former inmates describe things, Palestinian nationalists have more freedom of political expression in Israeli prisons than outside. He served his time in a new prison in the desert near Beersheba, "a political prison," as he called it, where Arab "security prisoners" were kept separate from the Jews and Arabs who had been sentenced for common crimes. There the inmates received political indoctrination from fellow inmates, sang banned nationalist songs, and celebrated Palestinian political holidays. "It is part of our big front with

Israel. My friend is on the front in Lebanon," Husam said. "I am on the front in prison. Every organization had its inside organization—Fatah, PFLP, etc." There was no direct communication with leaders outside of prison, but indirect messages were passed through visiting families. "We worked making furniture, camouflage nets for tanks. This is something political, if I'm in the PLO making nets for Israeli tanks. The prison administration takes pictures of you as you make a net, and put it in the newspaper. When you work eight, nine, ten hours, you return to your room, and you're very tired. They want us to forget about our revolution."

To keep their fervor alive, the inmates organized committees on Palestinian culture, food, holidays, and the like. "First, we sang songs of the revolution," Husam said. "Then, talk. Third, some revolutionary slogans. And the policemen see all that. They start to say this is not allowed. Sometimes they use the [tear] gas, sometimes. When Brezhnev died, we made a party; we discussed his policies, how it was in the Kremlin."

The security and political prisoners were not allowed to have radios, but they bought them clandestinely from Jewish inmates, who could get anything from the canteen; the Jews met the Arab prisoners in the kitchen and the hospital. "For us, we decided, no hash, no drugs," he said. "We'd get drugs from the staff nurse and use them to buy radios. Also, from prison to prison—put it under your eggs and go.

"We had many books inside that they don't have outside the prison," Husam added. "Your family can bring you books and change the first pages, make it the Koran or something so the policeman looks and says okay. We read about all the revolutions in the world: Mozambique, Vietnam, South Korea, North Korea. We made a program for new prisoners: You want to read these books, you must discuss them and understand them. We can't leave you to waste your life. We have a communal life."

Husam also studied English and Hebrew in prison. "You must learn your enemy's language to know what he says."

Husam was released on August 15, 1983, at the age of twenty-five. He had already learned his enemy's language.

SIXTEEN

Arab Citizens of the Jewish State

Verily, God will not change his gifts to men,
till they change what is in themselves.
—Sura XIII, Thunder, Verse 12

WHEN ISRAEL DECLARED ITS EMERGENCE AS A SOVEREIGN COUNTRY on May 14, 1948, the founders knew that they were heading into war. The years leading to this moment had been shredded by communal violence between the Jewish immigrants to Palestine and the Arab residents who sought to resist and repel the Jewish settlement. Now, a crescent of Arab armies was poised to invade from Syria, Transjordan, and Egypt as soon as the British Mandate came to an end the following day. Yet on the eve of the inevitable battle, visionary Jewish leaders held fast to an idealism that has endured as a beacon, as a challenge, and as a haunting standard by which a generation of nationhood has been constantly measured. The Provisional State Council in Tel Aviv, the fore-runner of the Knesset, included in the Proclamation of Independence a pledge that the fledgling Jewish state would "uphold the full social and political equality of all its citizens, without distinction of religion, race, or sex." Addressing those Arabs who were about to become citizens of Israel, the document declared, "In the midst of wanton aggression, we yet call upon the Arab inhabitants of the State of Israel to preserve the ways of peace and play their part in the development of the State, on the basis of full and equal citizenship and due representation in all its bodies and institutions—provisional and permanent."

Since 1948, the appeal has been met more fully than the promise. It is no exaggeration to say that at least 99 percent of Israel's Arab citizens have never been involved in a terrorist act. Their reported rate of common crime is also low—thirty criminal files opened per thousand Arabs annually compared with sixty-two per thousand nationwide. They participate extensively in elections, about half of them voting for Zionist parties. The vast majority have adopted a malleable political posture of loyalty to Israel and affinity for the larger Arab people, an emotional ambivalence that represents much less hardship for the Israeli government than for the Israeli Arabs themselves. Indeed, anyone who prefers to see the glass as half full instead of half empty can credit both the Jews and Arabs of Israel with maintaining their country whole in the face of fundamental divisions. For the most part, they have kept civility in daily relations. In large measure, they have overcome the logic of violence and nationalism by preventing Israel from becoming victim to the kind of factional blood-baths that have torn its neighbor Lebanon. But the pledge and hope of the Proclamation of Independence went far beyond the minimum ne-cessities of orderly statehood, and to the Arab citizen the emptiness between the level of achievement and the brim of promise is a yawning gap of disappointment, hurt, and often anger.

Today, one out of every six Israelis is an Arab, but the Arab is not Israeli in the full sense. His citizenship is shallow. It taints his self-identity with complication. He exists at the edge of a society that can never, by its nature, accept him as a complete member in disregard of the religious and ethnic identities that set him apart. He is an alien in his own land, an object of suspicion in his own home, torn between his country and his people.

After the 1948 war, the Arabs who remained in Israel numbered

156,000, about 18 percent of the entire Israeli population. In 1983 they were more than 600,000, or 16 percent of the population, and by 1993 their number is expected to reach 1 million, or 20 percent of the population if birth and migration rates remain steady. About 75 percent of the Arabs have been born in Israel since the establishment of the state. Educated in Israeli schools, fluent in Hebrew as well as Arabic, well read in Bialik and the Bible, they make their dreams, measure their opportunities, judge their chances, and formulate their dissatisfactions largely in an Israeli context, comparing their lot to the Jews, not to the Arabs outside, and yearning for the original promise of "full and equal citizenship and due representation."

The pledge has never been embraced wholeheartedly by Israeli authorities. In 1961, for example, the government's adviser on Arab affairs, Uri Lubrani, told a meeting of a Jewish youth organization, "If there weren't Arab students, it might have been better. If they had remained hewers of wood, it might have been easier to rule them." They were seen as inherently hostile to the state, deserving of subjugation, and dangerous to educate.[77]

The Arab-Israeli conflict and its attendant terrorism cast a deep shadow over the standing of Israeli Arabs in the Jewish state. Plagued with attempts at political violence against innocent civilians, Israel searches for shortcuts to security, and so Arabs become automatic targets of scrutiny, distrust, and restriction in the understandable obsession with public safety. Just being an Arab in appearance is to wear a badge that commands the attention of the security services. Showing the official ID card with "Arab" written in the space labeled "Nationality" is to announce, "Suspect me. Watch me. Check me. Search me. Question me." Despite some relaxation over the years, controls remain. The military government that once supervised Israeli Arabs—requiring them, for example, to obtain passes from the army just to travel from one region of the country to another—was dissolved in 1966. But the Shin Beth and other Israeli authorities still keep a close eye on the country's Arab citizens, engendering both the submissiveness that is desired and the antagonism that is feared.

Although freedom of movement is the rule, police and army checkpoints spring up on Israel's main roads from time to time to stop vehicles and examine their occupants and contents at random—or what seems to be at random. Actually, the checks are fairly methodical: Jews are exempt.

As the automobiles and trucks are forced to slow and weave gently through a gantlet of metal spikes set first across the right lane and then the left, the soldiers wave down almost anyone with a blue West Bank or silver Gaza license plate, and they peer closely into the windows of cars with yellow Israeli plates. If the drivers or passengers look Arab, they can plan on a stop. So routine has this become that many Arabs automatically pull over when they come to a checkpoint, while Jews whiz through undisturbed.

Israeli security is based on probabilities. There is no fine net that can screen out the weapons and explosives, no seal that can insulate the innocent from the terrorist. And so at the permanent checkpoint on the road to Ben-Gurion International Airport, the border policemen on duty are trained to stop Arabs, not Jews, on the reasonable calculation that Jews are unlikely to carry weapons in for a terrorist attack on their own airport. The trouble is that Arabs are also unlikely to do so—that is, only a tiny fraction of the Arabs who pass through the checkpoint would have any such inclination. The authorities would argue rightly that it takes only one, that the checkpoint is a deterrent, that innocent Arabs are often victims of terrorism as well and should welcome the protective measures. All true, but somehow the supreme rationality of those arguments fails to touch the feelings and attitudes of the Arabs wishing to think of themselves as normal human beings who are no more involved with planting bombs than their Jewish countrymen.

For those Arabs who are also Israeli citizens, the search often creates indignation. "At the gate of the airport, two Moroccans in the border police stopped us," said Halim Endrawos, a Galilee Arab who worked for the Histadrut, the federation of labor unions. "One came and said, 'Get out of the car, get against the car, open the trunk, take out the spare tire.' I said, 'I don't have the strength for it; you do it.' They took our suitcases and made rags of the things." Then one of the policemen called to a colleague with a sneer, " 'Come see the little Arabs,' " Endrawos complained. "I felt for the first time that I was an Arab of the twentieth class," he said. "I smoked my cigarette from the wrong end—that's how upset I was. It was the first time since the founding of the state I felt like that."

But it was nothing new to many others. His son, Zohar, believed that he was watched closely whenever he flew on El Al, the Israeli airline, as he had done about half a dozen times to and from Rome, where he went to college. On every occasion, he said, he was assigned a seat over a wing, with a security man behind him. "Every time I would go to the bathroom, the security man would follow."

Inside the terminal, an infallible courtesy prevails among the young Israeli Jews who check passengers. A glance at the passports and a few key questions usually provide enough guidance for the security women and men to decide whether to open suitcases and search with their infuriating thoroughness. No questions have to be put to Arabs, though; their bags are almost always opened, emptied, examined closely, and repacked item by item by the watchful guards. It is even worse at the Allenby Bridge coming over from Jordan. There, Arabs are shunted away from the air-conditioned international terminal into a sweltering building where their bags are examined and they are often strip-searched. One young Jewish woman, assigned to this task for her army-reserve duty, was so repulsed by having to inspect the naked bodies of Arab women that the next time her reserve obligation came due, she simply ignored the call-up notice and failed to appear. It was not that she thought the checks unnecessary—she knew of one Arab family found to have stuffed explosives into the body of a dead baby they were bringing back to the West Bank for burial. But she detested the duty and preferred to risk some punishment from the army to avoid it. Nothing happened to her.

A certain cultural harassment sometimes takes place through the means of security, an obvious effort to intimidate into a degree of assimilation. Monir Diab, who runs the community center in the Arab village of Tamra, recalled going with his father to the airport to see his brother off on a trip. The father was stopped and searched thoroughly. "I said, 'If he hadn't had a keffiyah on, you wouldn't do this.' The official said, 'So if you know that, why do you wear the keffiyah?' " Yet Diab retained faith in Israel's democracy. Just three years old in 1948, he remembered as he grew up having to get permission from the army to travel from Tamra down the road to the Jewish town of Kiryat Ata. "Today it is not the same," he said. "Then there was a military government. Now there is more democracy for the young people. They can say what they want. Everyone was afraid to speak. Now they can say anything."

Perhaps, but the Shin Beth hears what they say and often intervenes to curtail incipient political activity. Arabs observe that their mail from overseas often arrives looking as if it has been opened, read, and resealed. Telephones are tapped; one young Jewish woman who spoke good Arabic told me that she had been assigned during her army service to monitor Arabs' conversations, a task she found unpleasant and, for the most part, uninteresting.

The Shin Beth's favored method of intimidation is the search and the interrogation. After Nawil Salah, the radical secretary of the Arab student union at Hebrew University, moved into a Jewish apartment house in Jerusalem, two policemen knocked on the door at eleven one night and said they had come to check on an anonymous report that Arabs were living in the building. Although they did not show any search warrant, they began to walk around the apartment, Salah later told the local newspaper, *Kol Ha'ir*. When the student protested and started to phone a lawyer, the policemen threatened him with "a settling of accounts," as he put it, and then left.

A week later, he was interviewed on Army Radio about the situation of Israeli Arabs, particularly at the university. That evening, two policemen arrived again at his apartment, this time with a search warrant. They were to look for "material connected with incitement or the committing of a crime." They found nothing.

More systematic and concerted efforts are made to undermine organized activity that has a political overtone, even where it poses no security threat to the state. When Nakhle Shakar, an Arab who works as a civil engineer for the city of Tel Aviv, assembled some neighbors to promote the preservation of Arab Jaffa where he was born and raised, the Shin Beth began to summon him repeatedly for interrogation. The issue as he saw it was quite simple: Israeli authorities were denying Arabs permits to renovate lovely old houses in Jaffa while granting building permits in the same area to Jews. Apartments and houses vacated by Arabs were quickly sealed by the city with brick and mortar so that no new Arab families could move in. Many fine old buildings were being demolished. Most of old Jaffa was becoming a slum-ridden neighborhood of school dropouts, delinquents, and drug addicts, and every Arab move to revive the town was rebuffed. The only renovation tolerated was a Jewish revival, which was turning the seaside section into a cute, quaintly refurbished tourist attraction of art galleries and restaurants. But the Arab areas were models of decay.

"We call it a kind of constructive protest," said Nakhle of his neighborhood organization. "The people are in a dream of despair. We want to take them out of their dream. We created the League of Arabs of Jaffa, and we had a big meeting—six or seven hundred people who elected a committee of nine. And then they sent the Shin Beth to make us afraid. We were called in for questioning many times. Why? Because we are asking for education and housing." So relentless was the Shin Beth in harassing league members that people began to drop out. "A lot of those who agree with us don't want to participate. Three teachers were with us. They left the league. Why? Because the Ministry of Education told them to leave. We are not extremists," Nakhle pleaded. "We only want to ameliorate the situation. We are an Arab people. We have our history, we have our past."

When it became clear that the Israeli authorities would simply not allow a solely Arab organization to operate as a pressure group, Nakhle and the others took a path that has long been familiar to Arab politicians who want to run for office: They found some sympathetic Jews to lend legitimacy to their effort and joined with them. This pattern has prevailed in politics. No Arab party has existed on a national level; Arabs have run for the Knesset on lists of Jewish-led parties, mostly the Rakah, or Communist Party, but also the Labor Party and, in the 1984 election, a small group called the Progressive List for Peace. Arabs who have contemplated forming a uniquely Arab party have found themselves spending a lot of time with Shin Beth interrogators.

It is easy to explain the Israeli authorities' nervousness. Arabs cast 9 percent of the votes in the 1984 election, enough to seat 10 of the 120 members of the Knesset if they had voted in a bloc. The Israeli political system has always relied on coalitions. No single party has ever won a majority, and all governments have been dependent upon a few small groupings added to the leading party to make a slim majority in the Knesset. Thus, an Arab list of nine or ten Knesset members would probably be the third-largest party in the legislature, with pivotal power to determine which major party leads the coalition. As it is, however, the Arab vote is quite fragmented, with 35 percent going to the Communists in 1984, 21 percent to the Labor Alignment, 18 percent to the Progressives, 11 percent to the Likud-led coalition parties, 6 percent to a small group led by former defense minister Ezer Weizman, 5 percent to the centrist Shinui, and the rest to other tiny groupings. The five Arabs who were seated in the Eleventh Knesset in 1984 were scattered so thinly through various parties as to be ineffectual.

According to Shmuel Toledano, who served from 1966 to 1977 as the adviser on Arab affairs in the prime minister's office, this is the result of a conscious decision. "The government decided that it would be much better for the Arabs to be integrated into the existing Zionist parties so as to prevent an Arab party," he said. "But it wasn't easy, because every party was closed." So the Arab integration came very slowly and incompletely, producing no significant Arab input into the policy-making of any major party.

Of course, the existence of an Arab party would be no guarantee of a bloc vote by Israel's Arabs, for their political views are more diverse than many Jews seem to realize. A representative sample of Israeli Arabs questioned in 1980 was quite divided on the virtue of the Israeli-Egyptian peace treaty, for example, with 49.2 percent supporting it, 28 percent expressing reservations, and 22.8 percent in opposition. On the question of Palestinian statehood, 64.3 percent supported establishment of a state on the West Bank and Gaza Strip, 20 percent did so only under certain circumstances, and 15.7 percent opposed it; ideas about how much territory it should include varied widely, from all of Palestine to a small sliver of the West Bank. The PLO got approval from 68 percent as the representative of the Palestinian people, was accepted by 22.9 percent with reservations, and was rejected entirely by 9.1 percent.[78]

Jewish uneasiness about Israeli Arabs runs quite high, and the hand of the secret police can be felt even in local politics. In the Galilee village of Um el-Fahm, two members of the town council elected in 1983 were "interviewed" shortly thereafter by Shin Beth agents in an effort to dissuade them from joining a coalition with the new mayor, Hashem Mahameed. He was elected on the list of Hadash, a leftist grouping that included the Communists, and he heard about the attempt from one of those who had been approached. Since his council was divided evenly between the Hadash and the more moderate political groups, it did not take much for the Shin Beth to nudge the balance against him.

Some Israelis would find this terribly threatening to the democratic process, but many others approve of such tactics. Raphael "Raful" Eitan garnered support from a considerable minority of Jews with his idea that no citizen who failed to do "national service"—meaning military or some sort of civilian voluntary work—should be allowed to vote. This would exclude extremely orthodox Jews, who are exempt from the army on religious grounds, and almost all Israeli Arabs, who are rejected even in the few cases where they offer to serve. In my conversation with Raful in his backyard, I suggested that this might undermine Israel's democratic principles. "Why?" he asked gruffly. "In America, he who doesn't serve in the army doesn't get voting rights." If Israel is too open, he added, "They'll say, 'We were democratic,' but the whole democracy will be under flowers.'" I explained to Raful that there was no such restriction in the United States. We don't even have a draft, I pointed out. "Well, earlier, when you had a draft," he persisted. No, I said. Many Americans never served in the army; they didn't lose their right to vote. He looked at me with a stubborn blankness, this senior officer who had been an official guest of the Pentagon more than once. It took some time to persuade him. Finally he said, "Well, we're a young state. Sometimes we have too much democracy." He had just completed serving as Israel's top military man—a sobering thought. But the tough attitudes on civil rights were not unique to Raful. Jewish high-school students meeting with Israeli Arabs have often expressed amazement that Arabs could vote; their image of Arabs in relation to the state has been shaped by the military occupation of the West Bank and Gaza, whose Arab residents are not Israeli citizens. The 1980 survey by Mina Tzemach found 40.7 percent of 1,223 Jews questioned agreeing that preventive arrest of Arabs was "justified for security reasons, even when there is no proof against them." Another 37.4 percent disagreed, and the rest didn't care. To the question of whether Israeli authorities should be "exploiting every opportunity to encourage Arabs to leave in order to reduce their numbers," 34.6 percent said yes, 41.9 percent said no. Another 1980 survey, by Sammy Smooha, of Haifa University, found 64 percent of a sample of 1,200 Jews advocating increased surveillance over Arabs.

Probably few Jews are aware of the extent to which surveillance is now conducted; if they were, they would be either relieved or appalled, depending on their political convictions. Every Arab who teaches in the Israeli Arab schools has to have clearance from the Shin Beth, for instance, a fact well understood by Arabs but rarely known by Jews. In the Arab department of the Education Ministry, where almost all employees except the director are Arabs, "the guy who sends out letters for the Shin Beth is a Jew," explained Gershon Baskin, who worked in the ministry on programs aimed at increasing Arab-Jewish understanding. By law, every government employee is required to have a clearance, but the rule is enforced vigorously for Arabs and generally ignored for Jewish teachers. Gershon knew a case of a man who was denied clearance because his brother was involved with Rakah, the Communist Party, which is legal in Israel and always has several seats in the Knesset. "They didn't hire him," Gershon said, "and told him if he could get his brother into line he could have the job."

This produces extensive fear and caution among Arab teachers who, convinced that informers are everywhere, usually avoid discussing political issues in the classroom, or even outside. The impact on both education and Arab political life is significant. Since half of all university-educated Arabs are teachers and since Arab political leaders come largely from among those with higher education, the more moderate—the teachers— tend to exclude themselves from visible activity, leaving the field to more radical figures. Similarly, the schools are removed from involvement with the Arab-Jewish conflict, leaving children's political questions to be answered in the streets, where the moods can be unthinking and militant.

Even innocent, intelligent, and well-intentioned actions by teachers can lead to trouble, as an Arab high-school counselor once discovered. The Israeli basketball team Maccabee Tel Aviv was about to play a big game against Italy. The counselor overheard students asking each other which side they were going to root for. "I'm supporting the Italians," one said. "Anybody who's against Maccabee I'm for." Another replied, "Heck, I have nothing to do with the Italians. At least I know these people. I can go to Tel Aviv and I know their names and so forth. So I support Maccabee. I don't necessarily love them or support their movement, but at least they're closer to me." The students knew the historical significance of the team's name, and that complicated their feelings. Judah Maccabee led Jewish rebels in the victorious uprising against the Seleucids in the second century B.C., seizing the Temple Mount from Greek rule and restoring Jewish worship in the Temple.

The counselor thought this would be a good occasion to let the kids elaborate on their feelings about their place in the society. She organized a discussion to air attitudes about identity, an important concern for young Israeli Arabs. She followed it with a questionnaire asking the students which team they favored, how they saw themselves. Apparently there were informers, for the authorities sent five telegrams—to her home, to her parents, to her brothers, and to her school—and telephone calls were made, including a telephone call to her mother, who then was seventy-five years old: Tomorrow morning at eight o'clock she should be in Jerusalem to meet with functionaries of the Ministry of Education. She was scared, so she went. And the official who summoned her ignored her, keeping her sitting outside his office for two hours. When he finally called her in, he said, "Oh, that's you. What do you want to do with politics? You want to advance, you want mobility, you want to keep your job?"

Official apprehension exists about Arabs in a good many jobs. Shmuel Toledano, who served as adviser on Arab affairs to prime ministers Levi Eshkol, Golda Meir, and Yitzhak Rabin, made strenuous efforts to bring more Arabs into government positions, although he found all three leaders indifferent. "The trouble with the three of them was that they had no attitude," he told me. "They didn't care about the Arabs. This problem didn't bother them, the general problem of the Arabs of Israel. Everything was quiet, everything went smoothly. The problem of the Arab Israelis was not pressing."

Curiously, the attempt to find Arabs more government jobs came partly at the initiative of the head of the Shin Beth, Avraham Achituv. "He said that more Arabs employed is better for the security of the state of Israel: 'I don't want Arab unemployed,' " Toledano recalled. "He was the one who approached me and told me, 'Please, have an assistant, an Arab, a Muslim.' Although in my office there were many [secret] documents, I did it. People are afraid. They ask me, 'Could you promise that this Arab will not put a bomb? Could you promise that this Arab will not marry, will not start with a secretary?' Of course, nobody can promise. There is a psychological fear much bigger than reality. One thing just reinforces these fears: One bomb is thrown somewhere."

Significantly, perhaps, Toledano had served as an intelligence officer of the Haganah (and was therefore arrested by the British), a major in military intelligence during the 1948 war, and then for twelve years a ranking officer in the Mossad, dealing partly with Arab affairs. Growing up in the mixed Arab-Jewish town of Tiberius, he spoke Arabic at home with his mother, who was the eighth generation of her family in Palestine. "Originally we are from Toledo [Spain]," he said of his family, "but went to Morocco. Four hundred years in Morocco. For one hundred fifty years we were living in Tiberius. And in Morocco we spoke Arabic, so we continued this and spoke Arabic in Galilee. For years, until she died, I spoke to her in Arabic."

Toledano is a tough, compassionate man who sees Israel's relations with its Arab citizens as a mixture of success and elusive aspirations. "Sometimes I am amazed," he said, "from the pure security point of view, at how 600,000 Arabs—with intellectuals, with people suffering, with people thinking that they're second-class—have such quiet behavior. People are living—not loving each other but living together. Six hundred thousand are really practically loyal citizens. This is one point.

"On the other hand, I don't think that we succeeded in real integration. We have coexistence, but not integration. I want to see more Arabs at parties. In Tel Aviv, if I'm going to a Jewish party, I want to see Arabs. I never see them. If I go to Nazareth, to a party of Arabs, I want to see Jews. Integration means more Arab activity in all things with Jews, side by side, more living together in mixed towns. With the Israeli Arabs we don't have a national conflict. We have a minority that is fighting for equality and nondiscrimination. When I was looking for an assistant, tens of Arabs were fighting for this job, which is a purely political job of the state of Israel. I think this fight is legitimate and even positive. The minute he wants to be equal and fights for a job in the government, fights to be in the Knesset, excellent." It was evidence of the Arab's loyalty to and identification with the state, Toledano felt. "The problem is that you can't make him equal 100 percent, you just can't. Equality means an Arab can be in the Cabinet. Equality means that an Arab can be in the foreign office. Equality means that he'll be in the security services and everything. Can he? The answer is, he can't. And if he can't, he's not equal. And this is the tragedy."

Non-Jews are excluded from sharing authority and participating fully by the basic fact that Israel is a Jewish state, conceived as a sanctuary and vehicle of Jewish life and representing a culmination of Jewish power and self-reliance. Israel has never resolved the contradiction inherent in having an Arab population in a "Jewish state." But two other forces also bolster discrimination against Arabs. One is the obstacle of military preparedness and security, which in a defense-oriented economy closes off important avenues of advancement to Arabs. The other is the culture of poverty, in which a cycle of inferior education, impoverished living conditions, low motivation, and a lack of investment capital renders Arabs economically dependent on Jews. As a result, the Arabs have become Israel's underclass, a continuation of their inferior position that grew out of the 1948 fighting, when those Arabs who fled were often the wealthiest urban residents who could afford to go and those who stayed were generally the most rural and the least privileged.

This does not suggest that Arab life is desperate now, for many villagers live in simple comfort with their own houses and abundant gardens and extended families. Some have their own small businesses and a certain economic security. But a sense of rising expectations has gripped many of them as they have come to think of themselves as Israelis as well as Arabs. "We ask, 'To whom do you compare yourself in terms of achievements?' " explained Sammy Smooha, the sociologist who has studied Arab attitudes. Those questioned are given five reference groups. The majority, 58 percent, say they compare themselves to Israeli Jews; that is, to the majority in the society where they live, not to Arabs elsewhere. Only 14 percent see Arabs in Arab countries as their standard of reference; 13 percent cite Arabs in pre-1948, Mandatory Palestine; 9.5 percent cite residents of Western countries; and just 5 percent see West Bank Arabs as the group with which they compare their achievements. Smooha observed, "I think there is an element of intense contact with the Jewish population. Comparing yourself with the most advanced population, you feel deprived."

Among urban households, Arabs had about 68 percent of the average family income enjoyed by Jews in 1984, and considerably less if rural residents were included in the figures. Large families and poor housing have led to overcrowding, with more than three people per room in 30.6 percent of the Muslim homes and in only 1.1 percent of the Jewish homes. As of 1983, only 16.8 percent of the Arab households had telephones, compared with 75.8 percent of the Jewish households. Private cars were owned by 46.4 percent of all Jewish families and only 25.9 percent of Arab families; 92.5 percent of the Jewish households and 66 percent of the Arab households had television sets.[79] The proportion of Arabs in the population as a whole is about 1 in 6, but it is only 1 in 60 in senior government posts, 1 in 300 in university academic positions, and 1 in 16 on the executive committee of the Histadrut federation of labor unions. As of the early 1980s, there was not a single Arab among the 625 senior officials of the prime minister's office, the Bank of Israel, the state comptroller's office, or the Ministries of Finance, Housing, Health, Industry, and Communications. There were 2 Arabs among the 109 senior officials in the Education Ministry, 1 of 104 in the Agriculture Ministry, 1 of 114 in the Ministry of Labor and Social Affairs, and 1 of

133 in the national police. "There has never been an Arab Supreme Court justice," notes Alouph Hareven, a former army intelligence officer turned scholar. "No large economic institution in Israel is headed by an Arab—no bank, industrial enterprise, or agricultural undertaking."[80]

Israeli Arabs have been rather successful in medicine, mostly by studying in the Soviet Union or elsewhere abroad, then returning to practice in Israel. A few also get into Israeli medical schools, although the experience is not always pleasant. "We weren't accepted as well as we wanted," said Dr. Bishara Bisharat, a soft-spoken and politically moderate young man who went to the Hebrew University in Jerusalem as both an undergraduate and a medical student from 1971 to 1978. "In the first year, when we had groups in the laboratory, sometimes I was standing alone," he recalled. "Nobody wanted to join my group. After the fourth year I had more friends among the Jewish students, and it was easier to be one of them. But during the first year it was difficult. It's a closed society."

In the fourth year, he said, the students were divided into subgroups of twelve each to work together as interns in the hospital. None of the Jews was willing to be with any of the eight Arabs among the students, so all eight clustered together, leaving four more places to be filled on their team. "No one wanted to be with us," said Dr. Bisharat. "One said, 'I don't want to be a bad doctor because of the structure of the group.' So they decided that the eight of us couldn't be in the same group, and they divided us and forced us to be in other groups." In other words, giving the students a choice resulted in no mixture at all, and the faculty had to step in and impose the group organization, with two Arabs in each. "We became friends," the doctor noted, "and we are friends until now from this group." He then went to the Jewish town of Afula to practice in the local hospital.

Security rules bar Arabs from defense-related industries, an especially damaging prohibition for engineers. Although the Technion, Israel's leading engineering school, accepts Arab students in small numbers, after graduation they often have to go abroad to find decent jobs. Nakhle Shakar, who could not get into the Technion and studied in Italy, looked for six months and counted himself lucky to land a position with the Tel Aviv city government. But a friend of his with an engineering degree turned to farming in his village of Tira because he was unable to find anyone to hire him in his specialty. The difficulty extends into nonmilitary areas as well. A toiletries manufacturer "didn't want an Arab engineer," Shmuel Toledano recalled, "because the owner said, 'He might put something into my toothpaste.' "

Arabs also carry a stigma for not serving in the Israeli army, where they are unwelcome because of official uneasiness about their loyalties, and where most of them do not want to be because of their aversion to fighting for Israel against their kinsmen from Arab countries. So they are naturally exempted from the conscription that applies to Jewish men and women. Practically the only non-Jews accepted into the army are Bedouins and Druse, two peoples that have become adept at deferring to the dominant group in whatever part of the Middle East they happen to be. Even those few Palestinians—Christian Arabs and non-Bedouin Muslims—who may volunteer are almost always rejected.

It would be simple enough if it were left there. But the Israeli army has taken on an unusual role for a military organization in a democratic society; it has become something akin to the country itself, a noble institution of national commitment whose universal membership and lifetime ties signify a pervasive joining of the national purpose. The effect is to demilitarize and democratize the military rather than to militarize the civilian democracy, for the army is a gathering of the community, and anyone left outside remains something of an outsider in his civilian life as well. Prospective employers inevitably ask about an army tour and tend to raise an eyebrow at those who have not served. Some Jews, such as the very religious, are exempt. But those Jews whom the army rejects because they have police records, for example, can be marked forever as unworthy.

Many Israeli Arabs argue that they should not be relegated to inferior status for failing to do military service. "I say if you are afraid to include us, is it our problem?" remarked Safwat Audeh, the deputy principal of an Arab high school. And there are other ways to contribute to the society, reasoned Halim Endrawos. "When the Jews went to the army," he said, "Arabs went to the fields, picked the fruit, worked in the gas stations—that is national service. Instead of taking a rifle and going to kill Arabs, I helped here."

Nevertheless, many explicit privileges are granted to those who have performed military service. The Technion, for example, began in 1984 to give applicants who had been in the army a six-point credit toward the eighty-eight-point average in matriculation and entrance examinations required for admission. Subsidized Housing Ministry loans of about $10,000 are available only to those with military experience, making the purchase of apartments much more expensive for Arabs, who have to borrow from private lending institutions. Welfare payments called "child allowances" are slightly higher for families with a member who has been in the army or the police force. In 1983, the Knesset initiated a raise in such payments only for veterans with at least four children, and then—under pressure from religious parties—added an amendment applying the increase to yeshiva students who did not serve in the army. Government administrators went a step further by making the extra payments to new Jewish immigrants who had not been required to do military service, thereby leaving Arabs as the main group excluded from the higher benefits. Although the increments were so small as to be symbolic, the Supreme Court later struck down the provision as discriminatory because it had been extended to yeshiva students but not to Arabs; limiting it strictly to veterans would have been acceptable, the court declared.

A conspiracy theory—that government was keeping public payments lower to push Arabs into leaving the country—was given credibility in 1976 when an internal memorandum by two Israeli officials came to light in the Israeli press. Known as the Koenig Report, the document was written primarily by Yisrael Koenig, who had important authority over the disbursement of funds as the Interior Ministry's representative in northern Israel; the co-author was Zvi Alderoty, mayor of the Jewish town of Migdal Ha'emek, in the Galilee. Out of a fear that the Arab population in the Galilee would soon exceed the number of Jews there, the officials urged that government subsidies to large Arab families be reduced, that young Arabs be encouraged to go abroad to study and not to return, that authorities begin a harsh crackdown on Arabs who evade income taxes, that the number of Arab employees in Jewish-owned enterprises be restricted, and that increased surveillance be conducted of the Communist Party and other politically recalcitrant groups. Whoever leaked the memorandum to *Al-Hamishmar,* the paper of the Mapam socialist party, apparently did so out of rather narrow political motives: to torpedo the imminent appointment of Alderoty as head of the Labor Party's Arab department. The leak accomplished that and also provoked a broad outcry. The pro-Labor *Jerusalem Post* denounced the report's recommendations as "a scheme tainted with nationalist fanaticism," Arab leaders termed it racist, and some Jews called for Koenig's dismissal. But many prominent Galilee Jews, frightened after riots by Arabs protesting land expropriations, expressed sympathy for the proposals. Koenig, who had served in his powerful post since 1964, remained in the job through the right-wing Likud administrations of Menachem Begin and Yitzhak Shamir and into the Labor-Likud government led by Shimon Peres. He resigned in 1986.

Indeed, significant support among Jews for discrimination against Arabs was documented by Mina Tzemach's 1980 survey. Of 1,223 Jewish adults selected as a representative sample from throughout the country, 47.3 percent said that in most or all cases they would favor giving preference to Jews over Arabs for access to higher education, 40.7 percent would discriminate in private employment, 44.5 percent in public jobs, 48.5 percent in housing subsidies to large families, 49.7 percent in social-security payments, 42.7 percent in loans for agricultural development, and 65.8 percent in high government offices. Another 10 to 14 percent said that they could imagine some cases in each job or payment category where they would favor Jews over Arabs. In every sphere of endeavor, more Jews opposed equal opportunity than supported it.

Coupling "rights" with "obligations" when referring to Israeli Arabs is a popular official slogan in Israel, meant to imply that disloyalty to the state must not be rewarded and that Arabs must somehow earn their rights of citizenship. Seventy-one percent of the Jews interviewed, for example, said they objected to universities' accepting any Arabs "who openly declare that they are unhappy about the existence of the state of Israel but don't incite hostile activities." Of all the reasons for justifying limitations on Arabs, security emerged as the most often cited—by 75.9 percent of the respondents. The second reason given was the possibility that because of natural multiplication, Arabs would eventually constitute a majority in the state. Religion was mentioned as a basis for restrictions by only 13 percent. But while 60.3 percent of the Jews endorsed equal obligations for Arabs, only 47.8 percent supported equal rights.

A drive down a country road between a Jewish and an Arab town is a journey between privilege and neglect. In the Arab villages, there are no public swimming pools, no neat parks, and often no sewage systems. The narrow streets are sometimes unpaved, often surfaced poorly, and pitted with potholes. Schools have little science equipment, much scarred and broken furniture, and so many pupils that some classes have to be held in rented rooms. In many areas, the government has confiscated land in such tight rings around the villages, and has barred the issuance of building permits for new houses, that the communities have no place in which to expand. Arabs frequently build without the necessary permission, thereby risking their future if the authorities should decide to have the illegal houses demolished.

Living standards have improved dramatically since 1948 as Israel has linked Arab villages to electricity and water networks and as residents have gone to work increasingly in the Jewish sector for wages considerably above their previous earnings in agriculture. But discrimination in the allocation of public funds between Jewish and Arab municipalities has been a longstanding practice in Israel. In the 1983 budget, for example, the central government provided the Arab city of Nazareth with the equivalent of $629.40 per capita, compared with $1,688.00 per capita in Upper Nazareth, the largely Jewish town on the bluff above. The Arab village of Kfar Qara received $231.17 per capita in public funds, while the neighboring Jewish town of Pardes Hanna got $1,540.90 for each resident. In addition, Israel welcomes private contributions from Jews abroad but not from Arabs. While Jews in the United States and Europe have maintained a rich tradition of philanthropy toward Israel, the bulk of Arab attempts to send money have come through the PLO or other organizations that Israel considers hostile. Suspicious that outside radicals are trying to buy influence with Israeli Arabs, the authorities have banned most such funds, putting Arab villages at a financial disadvantage.

Yisrael Koenig may have wished to maintain or enlarge this discrepancy, but at least one of his colleagues in the Interior Ministry, Arieh Hecht, head of the local government department, deplored the discrimination. "It is an embarrassment to the state of Israel that the Arabs get less," he conceded. "I don't deny there is a gap," he added, "but the gap is closing. [In the last few years,] we have been making a great effort to make progress in the Arab sector and to give as much as possible to the Arab villages in recognition that the Arab villages are not what they should be yet. We're taking serious steps, although we're not satisfied yet. Only over the years will equality come."

The Arab towns are caught in a vicious circle. Because their leaders see themselves as standing outside the mainstream without significant political influence, they do not make forceful or sophisticated demands for money from the central government. In a highly competitive scramble for limited resources, they yield by default to the more active Jewish towns. And those few Arabs who do lobby have less impact than the Jews. A Likud leader from Upper Nazareth obviously runs on an inside track with decision-makers in Jerusalem, whereas a Communist from Nazareth can easily be ignored by the country's political establishment. Furthermore, Hecht observed that Arab towns and cities have been less willing than Jewish localities to raise the local taxes required to receive, and repay, government and bank loans for capital construction; the creation of public areas such as parks has remained less important in Arab culture than it has to the Jews. But without that capital development in sewage systems, schools, playgrounds, and the like, operating expenses have been less and services have been sparse.

In the far north of Israel, just five miles from the Lebanese border, a unique partnership exists between the Jewish town of Maalot and the Arab town of Tarshiha. Alone among the scattered and separate communities of Arabs and Jews that are strewn throughout the flowing hills of Galilee, they have been paired under a joint municipal council and operate as a single entity of local government, as if they were two neighborhoods of the same town. The unification took place in 1963 for reasons that Jewish town officials have already forgotten, although as I soon discovered, Arabs remember the circumstances quite clearly.

After more than twenty years of this partnership, the result is hard to characterize. It lends itself neither to rhapsodies of optimism about Arab-Jewish fraternity nor to convictions of gloom and despair. It is not a model that anyone else in the country seems inclined to emulate. It bolsters no particular political viewpoint. In its ambiguity and self-contradiction, it seems quite representative of the relationships between the Jews and the Arabs of Israel.

Physically the two towns are typical of their respective segments of the society, the newer, expanding Jewish Maalot containing box-shaped apartments and manicured parks and modern schools, the older, stagnant Arab Tarshiha honeycombed with mostly narrow streets, small shops, and houses built of brown stone. Groves of gnarled olive trees with silvery green leaves stand between the two. Schools are separate, of course; although as in other parts of the country Arab children are free to go to Jewish schools and Jews to Arab schools, they don't exercise the choice to cross the lines. The Arab and Jewish kindergartens do exchange visits and engage in some common play. A summer day camp for a mixed population of Arab and Jewish children has been successful. But otherwise, social interaction is practically nonexistent, according to those on both sides. No Arabs live in Maalot; no Jews live in Tarshiha. Community centers with their clubs and sports and handicrafts are separate; in Maalot, Jewish girls come under strong pressure not to date Arab boys.

Nevertheless, both towns seem better off with each other than without. Although Maalot was once the target of one of the most brutal terrorist attacks to hit Israel, it has also enjoyed more security as a result of its proximity to Tarshiha. In 1974 a squad of Palestinians crossed the border and murdered twenty-one children who were spending the night in a Maalot school while on a trip from their hometown of Safed. Three members of a single family also died. A soldier and three terrorists were killed, and sixty-two civilians were wounded. But in the late 1970s and early 1980s, Maalot was subjected less than other northern towns to shelling from the PLO's bases in southern Lebanon. Town officials speculate that the Palestinians did not want to risk hitting the adjacent Arab area of Tarshiha.

For its part, Tarshiha benefits financially from Maalot's ability to get government funds and private contributions, although the Arabs complain that the pie is not sliced fairly. Politically the Arabs are at a disadvantage, both because they number only about 2,500 to 3,000 compared with the 6,500 Jews and because as Bedouins, Christians, and Palestinian Muslims they fragment their votes around clans, religious divisions, and narrowly based parties to the point where they managed to elect only one Arab to the eleven-member town council in 1983, the last balloting before my visit there. Other elections, held every five years, have yielded more equitable results. In 1978, for example, six Jews and five Arabs were seated, with three Jews and three Arabs in the governing coalition and three Jews and two Arabs in the opposition. But the center of political influence has remained steadily on the Jewish side. The Arabs have never been able to get together to field a candidate for mayor, leaving the post entirely to the Jews.

"Theoretically," explained Danny Ceisler, the city manager, "if Tarshiha had one candidate and everyone voted for him and Maalot had many, he could win. But Tarshiha is always more divided than Maalot." Ceisler, a pudgy, friendly man wearing glasses and a yarmulke, is sympathetic to the Arabs' complaints that they lag behind, and he fights with the central government on the issue. But he also draws a line. Much housing needs renovation, he said; a kindergarten is in danger of collapsing (although another, brand-new kindergarten has been built); the water system is poor; erosion on the mountainside where Tarshiha is perched constitutes a serious problem that requires expensive retaining walls. "You'll see that Tarshiha is more developed than other Arab villages, but it is not enough," he said. And when I asked him what would happen if Arabs tried to move into Maalot, he replied, "I think there would be opposition. Here there would also be a great yelling. Even personally I would oppose it." Why? "My attitude is based on the fact that I am a religious Jew and he is a non-Jew. Also, assimilation." Did he mean intermarriage? I asked. "Yes."

One fight that was won brought the construction of a new regional Arab high school in Tarshiha to replace an aging building that had served Arab villages in a wide area. The victory was attained with the unwitting help of a group of American-Jewish contributors, Ceisler explained, smiling. Under an anti-poverty effort known as Project Renewal, American-Jewish communities pair up with impoverished Israeli-Jewish neighborhoods. The Americans visit the Israeli communities, help plan physical renovation and social programs, and give money, which is matched by the Israeli government. The Arabs in Tarshiha were getting some money for roads, a sewage system, and the high school out of the Project Renewal funds donated by Jews from eastern Pennsylvania, Ceisler said, although the American Jews were unaware of this and never met with the Arabs on their visits. Ceisler confided, "Since there are matching funds, you can say that it's the government money that's going to Tarshiha."

He regards the Arabs in the village as relatively moderate, observing, for example, that they did not participate in Land Day, the nationwide strikes and demonstrations organized annually to protest Israeli expropriation of Arab land. "During the Lebanon war," he added, "people from Tarshiha came to help and to hand out food to the shelters. They were prepared to help as much as they could." He felt no tension—"not at all." Then he added, "It could be that they felt it in their hearts."

The tension is there, not far below the surface. It is a mixture of frictions: the difficulties of a minority's relation to the majority combined with the ambiguities of identity that inflict the Arabs who are citizens of the Jewish state.

I drove from the expansive Danny Ceisler to his counterpart in Tarshiha,

Ghassan Haddad, who managed the municipal offices on the Arab side
of town and who proved to be an opposite character in every respect. My
appearance in his small room was apparently enough to ruin his entire
day. Rarely have I provoked such a nervous and unhappy look on the
face of anyone. He immediately rushed off to find some established
community figure to lead the way through the minefield of a newspaper
interview, leaving my translator and me alone in his office for half an
hour—an unprecedented breach of Arab etiquette. He failed to persuade
the man he sought to come, so he collared Safwat Audeh, the English
teacher and deputy principal of the high school who displayed none of
the political hesitation inherent in most Arabs who depend on the Education Ministry for their livelihood. A man of fifty-three, Audeh wore
a grey suit and a yellow and blue tie with a beach scene painted on it.
He gave his short version of the history of Maalot-Tarshiha.

"Before there was any Maalot here," he said, "there were Jews from
Rumania here, and with those Jews we managed quite well, even under
the military government. Even after Maalot was founded in '57, until
'63, we had no problems with Maalot." Then, about 1962, Audeh was
delegated by Tarshiha residents to press the military authorities to allow
the establishment of a town government to obtain improved services and
a high school. The military officials replied that the only way Tarshiha
could have its own local government would be in combination with
Maalot. "I said, 'This is a choice? This a false choice,' " Audeh recalled.
The Arabs were divided, with those least opposed agreeing only "in
principle, on the basis of equality," he explained. Arabs were appointed
by the military to the first town council. "The first mayor was a good
Iraqi Jew. His name was Sasson. He was a writer in Arabic, a poet. After
one year he couldn't stay in Maalot. Why? He believed in parity. Then
came another one. He didn't give us our rights. We had to write petitions.
In this country you have to make noise." He gave a good grade to the
current mayor and a mixed appraisal of the overall results. "In the short
run we are having better services than other Arab villages," he said, "but
in the long run we are losing our identity as a village. Maalot will expand
more and more, and we won't. So in the long run we will be like Katamon
[a Jewish slum] in Jerusalem, Acre [the Arab section] of Akko."

In such a sensitive spirit of pride and identity, everyday problems take
on the scope of callous or conspiratorial indifference. Audeh complained
about a water cutoff that had occurred the day before. As the nervous

Haddad hastened to explain, it was merely a temporary difficulty by the national water company. But Audeh saw it in different terms, and perhaps he was partially right too. "In Maalot they announce in advance when they turn off the water," he observed. The authorities have no respect for the Arab residents of Tarshiha, he said, and the ordinary Jewish residents of Maalot have no interest in the Arabs. "We have tried to arrange meetings for schoolchildren with the Jews of Maalot," he complained. "The kind of people in Maalot, with all respect, are not sociable enough with us. If we had had no partnership in the municipality, we would have been better neighbors. When we are partners, we want equality."

The rising expectation, the striving for equality, is a major theme of frustration for Israeli Arabs, and others in Tarshiha had similar assessments of the relationship's destructive potential. "I think in a partnership like this we're only damaging both people," said Mouin Daoud, an Arab accountant and former town council member. "I have an office in Maalot. My two daughters came to Maalot and saw the public gardens and said, 'Daddy, we want to play there.' They went, played, came back, and asked, 'Daddy, why don't we have this in Tarshiha?' I can't lie. It is a small girl; it's forbidden to lie. And if I tell her the truth, she'll say that Jews don't give it to us. The partnership should be dissolved."

The same bitterness came from the only Arab currently on the town council, Hanna Sussan. After running through the litany of complaints about Tarshiha's being shortchanged in public funds, he turned to the tone of the relationship. He recalled a hurtful incident under the previous town council, which met to consider a proposal by the mayor to give a medal after the Lebanon invasion to Raphael Eitan, the outgoing chief of staff who had just made his infamous remarks about West Bank Arabs' scurrying around like roaches in a bottle. "I got up and said, 'I speak in the name of the Arabs of Tarshiha,' " recounted Sussan. " 'We will not give good certification to such a man. He killed Jews and Arabs together. He killed Jews in Lebanon, and he killed our brothers in Lebanon.' " The mayor asked for a vote. One Jew was absent, and one sided with the Arabs, so the proposal lost, six to four. But Sussan and the others were wounded that it had been made at all.

"The first thing that should be corrected is the social aspect," he said. "There's no hatred, but there's no closeness. It's like a paper partnership. Why won't I have [Jewish] friends? Why won't my children have friends?"

His married daughter was unable to find housing in Maalot, where she works at a bank, and so moved to Nahariya, a Jewish town twelve miles away on the coast, where she lives without problems in an apartment house with Jews. "Why in Nahariya and not in Maalot?" her father asked. "There should be people in the local government who believe in the partnership. One member of the council, instead of calling me Hanna, calls me 'the Arab from Tarshiha.' Is that the education of a representative of the public? What matters is that a human is a human. This circle must be broken."

Mouin Daoud put it another way: "My question is, somebody who comes from Morocco, someone who comes from Ethiopia—does he deserve an apartment for free, and I, who am willing to pay, don't I deserve one? He who suffered from discrimination must not discriminate. The Jewish people suffered. They must not do this."

As Israeli Arabs yearn for an end to discrimination, they commit themselves to an identity as citizens of Israel. They rely on that identity, use it as a basis for their demands, find in it a ground for dialogue with open-minded Jews, and begin to see their fate as tied less to the Arab people than to the Jewish state. Yet, as they are reminded daily, they are also Arabs, and few try to flee from that fact. And so the striving masks and complicates the turbulent attachment to being Arab, allowing it to churn unresolved, to erode the sense of belonging. What do the Israeli Arabs want from the Jews? "We would like to be like them," said Safwat Audeh, the high-school teacher. "You know what 'integration' means. It comes from *integer*, which is Latin meaning 'whole.' Keep me whole. Don't split me off."

Another answer came from Halim Endrawos. "We want to live here the way the Jews live in America," he declared. "They don't feel that they're second-class there."

The desire for full participation in Israeli society means a wrenching journey into foreign territory, for as Arabs look out from the security of their stone villages at the Jewish world that surrounds them, they gaze into the alien culture of a more powerful people. To Susan Bandler, after two years of living in the Arab village of Tamra, a bus ride from Haifa served to illuminate the contrast between the communities. "If one needed a passport to travel between Haifa and Tamra," she wrote, "it would legitimize the feeling of displacement one has during that trip. . . . Along the way it is known as the Arab bus; the ticketseller in Haifa looks questioningly at Jewish travellers, and the driver is liable to pass by unfamiliar faces waiting at roadside stops along the route." The bus goes through an industrial zone east of Haifa, then through the Jewish town of Kiryat Ata, then down a country road, "until it reaches the sharp right turn into Tamra where I often expect to find passport control. It is at that point that one leaves the modern Jewish society so often thought of as embodying all of Israel and enters a different, more traditional world— different in sights, sounds, and smells, in the architecture of the buildings, the dress of the inhabitants and the language they are speaking.

"The bus entering Tamra will not drive through the village but will circle it," her account continues, "exiting through the entrance. No one drives through Tamra, no one gets lost in Tamra, no one is there who doesn't have a reason for being there, and that includes very few who do not live there, other than the travelling salesmen who often come from the West Bank or Gaza. While a Kiryat Ata youngster will see all those who pass through, his counterpart in Tamra will see only those who come to visit him."

But the harmonious, insular comfort of the village must ultimately be left behind, for "the Arab child grows up with the added burden that he, unlike his counterpart in Kiryat Ata, will have to leave the security of his home, his village, and venture into Israeli-Jewish society, whether it is to study, to work, to go to a government office or to the movies. There he must learn the workings of a foreign culture, including a new language, of which he, an Israeli, is a part." Complicating the transition, Susan observed, is the fact that "Israeli Arabs view Jews as victors; it is the Jews who control the country, who serve in the army, who win the wars. The attachment that Arabs feel to their homes, their villages, and their land becomes increasingly important in light of a relative insecurity they feel outside of these places."

At the same time, however, some Arabs welcome the chance to move away from the suffocating life of the village. Jalal Hassan, twenty-two, grew up in Mashad, near Nazareth, and went to the Hebrew University in Jerusalem. "I stayed at the university only one year," he said, "because I realized that I went to the university only to leave the village. I hated being there in the village. I felt myself very limited. In a Jewish city it's very hard also. People relate to me as an Arab. I had a good relationship with a Jewish girl, and she didn't want to continue it because I was an Arab."

Stepping outside into the wider world of the Jews can be frightening. "In general," said Zohar Endrawos of Tarshiha, "Arabs are afraid of Jewish things. Anything that's Jewish they're afraid of." And then, unconsciously drawing a parallel to the Jewish tactic of survival in the Diaspora, he added, "The education I received from my mother was to walk next to the wall and not cause any problems."

The Arab sense of alienation is reinforced by the rhetoric of some right-wing Jews. In December 1984, when the leftist Green Party sent a delegation from West Germany to watch proceedings in the Knesset, two rightist legislators, Geula Cohen and Raphael Eitan of the Tehiya Party, raised placards in protest from their seats in the chamber. Tewfik Toubi, an Israeli Arab who has been elected repeatedly as a Communist Knesset member, grabbed Cohen's poster, shouting, "Shame on you! They are guests."

In a revealing outburst, Cohen replied angrily, "How dare you! You are yourself a guest!" Toubi flew into a rage and scuffled with another Tehiya member, Yuval Ne'eman; the two had to be separated by the sergeant-at-arms.

It is citizenship that complicates the question. Somehow, every Israeli Arab must arrive at his own formula giving weights to his Israeli and Arab identities. Arabs on the West Bank and the Gaza Strip have no such problem; for them, Israeli Jews are simply military occupiers, and Arabs who live under the occupation rarely understand the attitudes of their relatives who live under the rubric of Israeli citizenship. "Our feelings are very moderate," said Nakhle Shakar, the civil engineer from Jaffa, "not the feelings of my uncles on the West Bank, because they never lived with Jews; they live in closed Arab towns. Here we always lived with Jews. I began my life living with the Jews. I speak Hebrew like the Jews. My uncle [on the West Bank] is a merchant. He has commercial relations, and there it stops. He never invites a Jew to his house for dinner. He doesn't know the difference between North African and Ashkenazi. He sees people of different races and doesn't understand how they can belong to the same people. On the West Bank, they are under military occupation; they can't see them as human. They have no social relations with them. For them, Jews are only soldiers."

For Nakhle, however, the issue is not who the Jews are but who he is. "The political situation is that you must be a member of a country," he observed. "You cannot be a member of the world. You must belong to something." And where does he belong? "In Jaffa there is a very strange situation," he replied. "The Arabs speak Hebrew like the Jews. They put on the same clothes, they have the same habits. But when I ask myself who am I, I always turn back to my origins. I feel myself an Arab. I speak Arabic at home, I eat like Arabs, I have my church. I am an Arab—a Palestinian Arab. I am an Israeli. I have rights."

In reaching for a synthesis between what is Arab and what is Israeli, Arab parents have trouble finding a balance for their children. "I have to explain very sensitive things to my son," said Monir Diab, director of the Tamra community center. "I try to be as clear and accurate as possible. I have to explain to the kid that on the one hand he's Israeli, on the other he's connected to the Palestinian people. I don't want him to be torn."

And Safwat Audeh faces the eternal debate between generations. "I have two kids in Hebrew University, in law school. They say, 'Father, come and see extremism here. Come and see how Rabbi Kahane comes and brings people from Katamon [to fight] against us.' And I say, 'But there are good Jews.' They say, 'Come and see.' The more educated our kids are, the more disappointed they are. We have been teaching our kids to find the good Jews and talk to them. The open Jews are very few."

Every spring, as Israel approaches the celebrations of its Independence Day, Arab schoolchildren are drawn into marking the event halfheartedly with readings and Israeli flags: the blue Star of David and two blue bars against a background of white. One year, Walid Sadik, an Arab politician from the town of Taibe, noticed his nine-year-old son painting an out-lawed Palestinian flag on his arm and tearing up the paper Israeli flag he had been required to make in school. "I felt very bad," the father said. "I don't want the Israelis to suppress the Palestinian flag, and I don't want my son to tear the Israeli flag. I want something in between." Then he added, "This is our fate. I am a Palestinian and an Israeli. My fate, my task, is to build a model that will enable both sides to come together." Did he tell his son of his feeling? "No, because he will not understand it. He has no rational motives. It's a fashion. And not only my child. I see all these youngsters with Palestinian flags. My child always asks when he sees a detective film on TV, 'Who is killed, Jews or Arabs?' He thinks the whole world is Jews and Arabs."

In Sadik's view, based on his years as a teacher, Arab schooling in Israel contributes to radicalism by ignoring the historical and political context in which the Israeli Arab finds himself. The curriculum contains little study of Arab literature, no admiration for Arab culture, and no comprehensive lessons on events in the Middle East after 1948. Arabs deride the educational program in their schools as "Bialik and the Bible" in its emphasis on Jewish culture and religion. A blank is left where the Arab youngster's sense of his own position in history should be. "From kindergarten, they teach them Israel, Israel, Israel, brainwashing about Israel," he said, "but in their daily experience, they see the border police attacking their parents or making rude behavior. Hatred can be smelled in the air. I asked my pupils, 'What is the PLO?' They said, 'The representative of the Palestinians.' But who are *they*? They do not know."

"The educational system tends to de-Palestinize us, then to de-Arabize us," said Sami Mari, an Arab psychologist at Haifa University. "The goal is a yes man who accepts the superiority of Western culture vis-à-vis his own background. It is a computer model of social training. Their rationale says if you can control the input—curricula, content, experiences, teachers, and so forth—you can achieve your desirable output, which is a yes man, a conformist, a submissive person. They forgot what goes in between, in the brains of these people.

"When I was in high school," Mari continued, "that was in '56, '57, we had a Jewish Iraqi teacher of Hebrew. I think he distorted the Hebrew language and literature because he was learning it with us, so that was a disservice to us and to the Jewish culture at the same time. He came with a text of Ahad Ha'am, an excellent piece on imitation and assimilation. The core of the essay is that Jews are dispersed all over the world; there are a lot of pressures for them to imitate the great goyim and assimilate. But the way out: Continue being yourself, so the way is not imitation and assimilation. If you imitate continuously, you wind up assimilated. If you go off creatively, you wind up competing with them and then enriching your own group. It is written in the Education Ministry curriculum, why Arabs should study Hebrew literature: to sympathize, to appreciate. Here the teacher was explaining, look how Jews have made themselves and so forth and so on—true. And then something switches, something turns on. I want the article to continue to be taught in our schools."

In a sardonic essay on Arab education, Hana Abu-Hana of the Arab Orthodox College in Haifa begins with a sketch of a sad little exchange in an Arab school's eighth-grade classroom. The teacher asks the children what they want to be when they grow up. A boy named Said replies, "I want to be a pilot."

"Let us, together, try to teach Said's teacher how to clip his pupil's wings," Abu-Hana writes, "help him find the 'educational' arguments to explain to Said that his ambition is impossibly grand. Said must be taught to be a 'realist.' Said is attentive to the frequent calls on television to the youth in Israel to enlist in programs that prepare them to be pilots or naval officers or electronics engineers. If he imagines that the call is also directed to him—he too is an Israeli youngster—it must be explained to him that the Israeli suit has different sizes, depending on who is wearing it. Said is an Israeli, but—apparently—not all *that* Israeli. . . . To educate young Arabs to be 'realistic' means to curtail the sweep of their imagination, to cut down their ambitions, to clip their wings, and with the motto 'be a realist' to distort their being. There's an education for you!"[81]

Without context, the Arab in Israel must imitate and falsify his own culture. Anton Shammas, an Arab poet and writer, speaks of this in terms of language. "At the age of eighteen," he says, "I chose what I had no choice but to choose: Namely, to regard Hebrew as my stepmother tongue. Sometimes I feel that this was an act of cultural trespass, and that the day may come when I shall have to account for it." And then he goes on:

Nowadays to write in Arabic in Israel is a very lonely undertaking, and a courageous one. It is lonely because the infrastructure is missing. The outline plan is blurred and the writers cannot come home again. The traditional house has given way to the modern villa, wherein everything is counterfeit. The walls are no longer built of stone—they are, at best, surfaced with it. . . . The system of Arab education in Israel, at least in my time, produced tongueless people, more at home with seventh century Arab poetry than with that of the twentieth century. These are people without a cultural past and without a future. There is only a makeshift present and an attenuated personality.[82]

Adrift in Israel, the Arab can hold fast to a few different pieces of flotsam. He can reach for his rights as a citizen, cling fiercely to his village and his land, or embrace political militance. As he is excluded from being fully Israeli, he may naturally become more Palestinian in his definition of himself, although many believe that he is growing more Israeli and more Palestinian at the same time, more insistent on his rights as a citizen and more sympathetic to the nationalist aspirations of his fellow Palestinians in the West Bank and beyond. Nevertheless, studies show how diverse the self-affixed labels can be. Of 1,185 Israeli Arabs questioned in 1980, 28.5 percent defined themselves as Israeli-Arab, 24.4 percent as Palestinian-Arab, 21.4 percent as Palestinian in Israel, 9.8 percent as Arab, 8.2 percent as Israeli-Palestinian, 4.2 percent as Israeli, and 3.6 percent as Palestinian. As expected, the formulas correlated closely with political views; all of those who said they agreed with the rightist Likud Bloc included "Israeli" somewhere in their label, and most of those on the political left did not.[83]

Nevertheless, Israeli Arabs are generally revealed in public-opinion surveys as more moderate than Jews think they are. In one study, 29.1 percent of the Arabs and 51.6 percent of the Jews questioned said they believed that large numbers of Arabs in Israel hated Jews. To the question "Have Israeli Arabs reconciled themselves to the existence of Israel?" an affirmative reply was given by 67.7 percent of the Arabs and only 29.2 percent of the Jews.[84] Another study, done in 1980, found that only 4 percent of the Israeli Arabs surveyed would move to a Palestinian state if one were created adjacent to Israel; 16 percent wanted such a state to include the Galilee, where most Israeli Arabs now live; another 16 percent advocated a secular democratic state in all of Palestine, which would mean the end of the Jewish state; and 64 percent said that they wished to live with equal rights in Israel.[85]

None of this complicated equation applies to the Druse, an Arab minority which regards itself as a separate people distinct from the Muslims and Christians. The Druse live largely in their own villages in the Galilee, where they maintain their own traditions, their own dress, and their own extended families. They marry within the Druse community, for the most part, and those who venture outside usually do so only to study, work, or do army or police service. The few who have intermarried with non-Druse often find themselves ostracized by both societies; one Druse-Muslim couple I knew had tried living in various places without success. In a Druse village, their son was derided by other children as a "dirty Muslim," and in their predominantly Muslim neighborhood of East Jerusalem he was rejected as "Druse." They were considering moving to a Jewish neighborhood of West Jerusalem.

Because the Druse are a small group—only about 67,000, or 9.5 percent of the non-Jews in Israel—they have felt quite vulnerable in Israel, Syria, and Lebanon. And except in Lebanon, where the disintegration of the society into civil war has driven all factions, Druse included, into battle against each other, the Druse have generally been able to weave a delicate pattern of submissiveness and cultural integrity. Jewish authorities have regarded Israeli Druse as mostly loyal to Israel, receiving them into the army and the border police and often giving them the nastiest jobs facing the Arabs, who in turn hate them.

True to the regional style of dealing in religious and ethnic stereotypes, the Israeli authorities in 1981 made the mistake of imagining that all Druse were equally pliable, and so the Druse on the Golan Heights were offered Israeli citizenship in conjunction with the annexation of the formerly Syrian territory to Israel. Overlooked were the strong family and political bonds that remained between Golan Druse and Syria; Druse in the Golan had relatives in the Syrian government and armed forces. And more persuasively, many expected Syria to return to control the Golan Heights someday, so they put their chips on the longer bet and rejected the Israeli citizenship and identity cards, ostracizing and excommunicating those few Druse who accepted. The response by the Israeli government, which had just withdrawn military rule and extended the country's laws and procedures to the Golan Heights, was to seal off the entire zone for weeks, barring any travel by Druse within the area and any movement into or out of the territory by Druse, foreigners, or Israelis, except for Jewish settlers. No journalists could get in either, so a blackout of news descended on the Druse villages there. Thus was the Golan welcomed into the bosom of Israeli democracy.

Israeli Druse have had mixed experiences as citizens who are regarded as quasi-Arabs. Rafik Halaby, who comes from a Druse village near Haifa, reported for several years on the West Bank for Israel Television, a responsible post that put him into frequent conflict with his Jewish superiors. Nazzi Dabbour, a Druse at Hebrew University, had some difficulties in the army, where he was a staff sergeant, although he also made friends with Jews. His unit, mostly Druse but also Jewish and Circassian, fought in Lebanon. "I don't look at whether he is Muslim or Jewish or Druse," he told me. "It depends on the person himself. If it is a good person, then I can speak with him, I can sit with him."

He did recall an officer and a sergeant he ran into during a training course. "They said that they hated us because we were Druse, not Jewish, and they didn't give us all the rights, and every time there was hard work they gave it to us, the Druse." One day, when he and a Druse friend were speaking to each other in Arabic, the officer scolded them, saying, "Don't speak in Arabic. You are in a Jewish community now, and don't listen to Arabic music." There were punishments for speaking Arabic. "One day they said to my friend, 'Go run around a hill and come back,' because he was speaking Arabic with me. If we wanted to listen to Arabic music, we had to go to a place where there wasn't anyone and listen there."

At the end of the course, the officer asked the troops whether they had any complaints. When the Druse kept silent, their Jewish friends spoke up and criticized the officer for denying the Druse their rights. Dabbour had heard of similar, though somewhat less blatant, experiences from other Druse. I asked why he thought this happened. "I don't know exactly," he said. "They only hate the Arabs, and they don't want to hear Arabic."

Being Druse can also have its positive side; Dabbour's identity once rescued him from an unpleasant encounter with the police. Walking one day in the Old City of Jerusalem, he noticed a pair of policemen, one Druse and the other Jewish, standing at Jaffa Gate with nothing to do but hassle passing Arabs. "They were bored," Dabbour observed. "Every Arab who came by, they called to him, 'Come here,' and checked his identity card and wrote it down." They stopped a boy of about ten who was wearing a shirt reading "I Love Palestine." They asked for his card, and when he said he didn't have one, they arrested him. "They wanted to make fun, something to do. The Druse one, I could see that he was new and didn't know anything."

The boy's family came crying, and Dabbour intervened, speaking Hebrew. The Jewish policeman pushed him. "I said to him, 'Don't push,' and he began to curse, and I also cursed him, and he said to the people to go away, with the gun. I said to him, 'They are human.' He said to me, 'They are not human for me. They are animals.' " Dabbour then broke into Arabic to say something to the relatives, and when the policeman heard the Arabic, he said to Dabbour, "You are arrested. Give me your particulars." Dabbour refused to show his identification, knowing that the policeman would release him as soon as he saw that he was a Druse who had served in the army. He wanted to be taken with the boy to make sure the boy was set free. Only at the police station did he show his identity card. When the duty officer saw that he was a Druse, he said, "Okay, go."

"No," Dabbour replied. "Look, the boy didn't do anything."

"Okay, go together."

"No. You must take us back to the place you took us from." And so the policemen drove them back to Jaffa Gate and dropped them off where the journey had begun.

The lines of discrimination are blurred. Hands reach out through the vacuum, and touch. A personal friendship, a partnership in business, a soccer team, a try at the other's language, an attempt at love—these are the wild flowers that always seem to bloom through cracks in the pavement.

I was sitting with Nakhle Shakar in his family's old stone house in Jaffa, listening to him tell me about the Jews' destruction of the Arab neighborhoods, about the authorities' efforts to drive Arabs out of Jaffa, about the Shin Beth's breaking up the league of Arabs that had been organized. Suddenly a friend burst in—a Jewish friend, a tall young man who had gone with Nakhle years ago to a private Catholic school in Tel Aviv. They embraced warmly and engulfed each other in a flow of rapid, laughing Hebrew. "You see," Nakhle explained, "this is our relationship. So you can't hate Jews. But you can hate the policy."

When the personal is cut loose from the communal, and Jews and Arabs can interact in two entirely separate dimensions, both sides often maintain friendship by avoiding politics in their conversations. They grope for common language. When Mouin Daoud, the Arab accountant, first began working years ago in the municipal offices of Maalot, he spoke no Hebrew at all. Taking a seat in a cafeteria table across from a Jewish worker, he found himself the object of a fumbling effort to make contact.

"Be'teavon," said the Jew, using the Hebrew expression for *bon appétit*. Daoud thought the Jew was asking his name, so he replied, last name first, "Daoud, Mouin." The next day at lunch the same thing happened.

"Be'teavon," said the Jew.

"Daoud, Mouin," the Arab replied.

Daoud decided he had better find out the exact meaning of *be'teavon*, and he felt somewhat sheepish when he learned that it was simply a wish that he enjoy his meal. The Jew, meanwhile, apparently thought that he had memorized the appropriate reply in Arabic, and so when they next shared the table, and Daoud began by uttering the Hebrew greeting, *"Be'teavon,"* the Jew answered proudly, *"Daoud Mouin."*

Actually, Daoud's story may have been apocryphal, so closely did it resemble a joke that a friend of mine had heard Jews tell in the thirties. A man named Goldberg is dining on a passenger ship when a Frenchman sits down across from him and says, *"Bon appétit."*

"Goldberg," says the man.

The next day, the same thing happens.

"Bon appétit."

"Goldberg."

A companion of Goldberg's asks him what the Frenchman's name is. *"Bon Appétit,"* says Goldberg, sending the companion into a burst of laughter. He tells Goldberg what the French words mean. Humiliated, Goldberg resolves to set things straight at the next meal. So when the Frenchman takes his seat, Goldberg says, *"Bon appétit."*

"Goldberg," the Frenchman replies.

Either this old joke had worked its way into Mouin Daoud's imagination, or, perhaps equally likely, life in Israel had begun to imitate comedy.

Here and there in the Galilee, the Arab-Jewish relationship has become considerably more intimate and fruitful than a few tentative words across a lunch table. Some on both sides have discovered the profitability of going into business together. I met one Arab who shared an electrical-contracting firm with a Jew, and although he could not be involved in work on military bases, his partner could, and both benefited. In Pardes Hanna, a Jewish town between Haifa and Tel Aviv, an Arab named Khalil Atamna and a Jew named Lucien Ben-Shoshan jointly owned a small enterprise manufacturing concrete building blocks. They believed that they were doing something special—not because they were Jew and

Arab, a fact they merely shrugged off, but because their blocks were of such fine quality that they were used from Haifa to Eilat. "He's a businessman, I'm a businessman—no problems," said Ben-Shoshan, a Moroccan-born Jew. Furthermore, he added, he preferred to hire Arabs over Jews because he found that the Arabs arrived on time and worked harder, a reverse discrimination hardly typical of the country as a whole. "I gain and he gains," said Atamna, who came from the neighboring Arab village of Kfar Qara. "With us, it all goes like halva."

But the canniest joint Arab-Jewish business I found was a used-car lot on an intersection near Pardes Hanna. I could just imagine the customer walking in and asking himself, Would you buy a used car from this man? Well, no, but I would from that guy over there. Sharif Atamna—no close relation of Khalil—and Moshe Gendler worked together cleverly. Jewish customers usually asked for Moshe, and Arabs asked for Sharif. "I don't think of him as a Jew or as an Arab," Sharif said of his partner. "I just get along with him. If you offered to exchange Moshe for fifty Arabs in terms of work, I wouldn't agree, and I believe it's mutual. I can leave a whole roomful of money and come back and find the money there. I can trust him."

In the ten years that the two had been selling cars together at the time I met them, they had formed a close friendship. Once, in the middle of the night when Moshe was away doing army reserve duty, his wife had to take their daughter to the hospital. "She didn't phone her father or her sister," Moshe said. He pointed to Sharif. "She phoned him at two o'clock in the morning, and he got up and took her."

Ben-Shoshan, convinced that Arab-Jewish business was the wave of the future, made a prediction: "I think in a few more years you'll find a lot more of this."

Rifat Turk, the Arab soccer star, was born in Jaffa twenty-eight years before I visited him there in his spacious old house, a cavernous and elegant place of high ceilings, Oriental rugs, and antique furniture. He was surprisingly short, a swarthy, balding man with a sinewy body, a full black beard, and a talent for directness as he told the story of his rise into the ranks of Israel's athletic elite. Here was a temptation to see the Israeli Arab-Jewish conflict through the prism of the American black-white conflict, with all the insights and inadequacies inherent in the parallel. Rifat Turk was a Jackie Robinson character who grew up in the sandlots of Israel's national sport, broke through the veil of discrimination into the big leagues, became the target of the society's mean-mindedness, and emerged as a hero of perseverance and tolerance. The rawest elements of his struggle were reminiscent of the battle of American blacks into professional athletics and into a wider acceptance by American society. Yet the historical setting of his fight was entirely different, of course, and in Jewish perceptions its overtones were heavy with the rumblings of nationalism, terrorism, warfare—dimensions of conflict that never played the same role in the resistance to blacks' efforts toward equality in America. On some level for many Jews, Rifat Turk's prowess seemed a symbol of Israeli vulnerability in the surrounding sea of Arab hostility.

"We were born here," he said. "My father and my father's father were born in Jaffa. We were here before them. This is our land." He gave no inch on his pride in being Arab, and if Jews found that threatening, then let them. But on a political spectrum, Turk was a very conciliatory man. "This state could be the number-one state in the world," he said expansively, "not America, not anyplace, in terms of life, in terms of everything." He added, "I never hated Jews. I look at a Jew and a Kurd and an American as the same thing—as people, as equal. He is a person, and I honor him and give him respect. The Jews—I have a lot of Jewish friends. I wish I had Arab friends like that. As in every place, there are good and there are bad. When I have a problem, I don't say that all Jews are bad like him."

Interestingly, even nationalist Palestinians on the West Bank and Gaza Strip seemed to appreciate his popularity as a soccer player on an Israeli team, and only a few fanatical Arab groups condemned him as having sold out to the Jews. "Most of the Arabs here in the country—even in Gaza and the West Bank—encouraged me," he said. "They think it's a good thing that I'm popular. I try to represent them. West Bank and Gaza teams call me and invite me there. Sometimes I go to clubs and they ask me how I got to where I am."

Turk began to play soccer in the streets and vacant lots of Jaffa, and he got good quickly. At the age of thirteen he made a team on which Jews and Arabs played together, and by the time he was sixteen and a half he got onto a farm team of Hapoel Tel Aviv, one of the top professional teams in the country. His debut in the youth league was tumultuous. "The first game, when I got onto the field, a player stuck to me, guarded me the whole time and shouted, 'Dirty Arab!' 'Terrorist!' 'You shouldn't play here! Your place is in Saudi Arabia!' I was really in shock because I had played in Jaffa with Jews and Arabs together, and I hadn't had any problems. In that game I played well, and I scored two goals, and it really amazed people there because it was something unusual." But the epithets there were "only an appetizer," he said, for the main course in the adult league, which he joined at age eighteen.

The fact that he was an Arab provided the substance of the jeers and heckling from his team's opposing fans. At every game, whether home or away, the stadium would roar in chants of "Dirty Arab!" and "Terrorist!" He was unable to shrug them off. And things weren't any better on the field. "A lot of players would kick me in the legs because I was an Arab," he said. "Sometimes in the middle of the game I would cry because I was sensitive to everything and I wasn't used to it. Sometimes I would sit and think alone and talk to myself and say, 'What do I need this for? Why are they cursing out my father and my mother? Because I'm dark-skinned?' "

An especially rough experience followed a terrorist attack on the Savoy Hotel in Tel Aviv by a squad of Palestinians who landed by boat from Lebanon. Turk's team was playing a few days later against Maccabee Netanya. "Suddenly the player who was guarding me the whole game said, 'Tell me, don't you think your place is in Lebanon? You were probably at the Savoy Hotel.' All the time he was saying, 'Terrorist, you should be in Lebanon,' the whole time we were facing each other. So at halftime I just couldn't stand it any longer. I started to cry, hysterical crying. So the coaches and all the players on my team said, 'What's happened? What's happened?' And I said this guy has made me crazy. I can't play. So they said, 'Don't mind; the only answer to that is to put the ball in the net.' I could not play. And after that game I decided I couldn't play any more soccer."

Turk loved the sea, had worked as a fisherman, and simply disappeared from his practices and games, spending a week on the water. His teammates thought at first that he was just sick, but when he failed to show up for a long time, they began looking and finally found him. "I said, 'I can't cope with this.' They said, 'You're a big player, you're a star. We'll do everything to help you.' They got it into my head that these people were primitive." And they began a campaign in the press and on radio and television to expose the racism. He went back to the field.

"It didn't really stop," he said. "Even today there is some, but not at the level it was." After Palestinians in the Ansar prison camp were exchanged for Israeli prisoners of war, opposing fans shouted, "You belong in Ansar!" But Turk learned to respond differently. "Today it doesn't bother me at all," he said. "I used to take it to heart, but today if someone curses me, I take revenge. If he calls me a dirty Arab, I try to play doubly well to show him that an Arab is better than him." His own teammates, all Jews, have always stuck by him closely.

Since Turk has played in the big leagues, he has brought other Arabs in behind him, partly to give kids a way up and out. "Jaffa is like Harlem in the States," he explained. "There are a lot of criminals, a lot of drugs. So I was a youth counselor in the club. There were a lot of kids who were really talented. It hurt me that they would degenerate like a lot of kids in Jaffa into drugs and crime." As he coached teams for Arab kids in Jaffa, he seethed over the poverty. "I'd go to the city government and ask for soccer balls. They'd give me two or three balls for fifty kids, and they're small kids on a concrete court, so in a week we'd finish them off. And we'd go and ask for more, and they'd say, 'That's all you get.' At the same time, we'd play against a Jewish club. I was at one club where the counselor took me into a storeroom and showed me: Closed up in plastic bags, sixty soccer balls, thirty to forty basketballs. So much equipment. I really went crazy. I'd go into a locker room in the club— there are four air conditioners. In our club there is a broken window, not even one air conditioner."

No Arab's struggle into Jewish society is painless. With defenses stripped clean and senses laid bare, he moves into a mood of quivering vulnerability where no wound ever quite heals. Hashem Mahameed, the mayor of Um el-Fahm, had not talked in years about this aspect of his youth before I went to sit in his living room and prompt him with questions. And then the memories came back like needles scratching at the old scars.

He was only three when Israel became independent in 1948, and his recollections are nothing more than sparse sketches. His family lived in an old house built of mud and stones and a little wood, with lots of mice running around. "I remember one day I could see from the roof some soldiers with their helmets. I heard the Jews were coming to Um el-Fahm. I remember my father picking me up in his hands and trying to get me near to him so I wouldn't be afraid. I was crying and shaking. I

remember they had some branches of olives covering their helmets."
Perhaps he was afraid of being killed, because Arab mothers, to stop
their sons from leaving the house, would fill them with stories that Jews
were waiting outside to kill them. These were the first memories.

When Hashem was fifteen, his father arranged for him to study in a
Jewish high school. "My mother is illiterate," he said. "She cannot read
or write. My father never could either. But for them, I was the spoiled
child. They gave me the choice of studying anywhere I wanted. They
were not rich. We were a poor family. I decided to study in the Afula
high school." Even for public schools there were nominal tuition charges,
nothing difficult for a middle-class family but an overwhelming sum for
those in poverty. They scraped together the money, but it didn't last.
"I remember the first semester I got very bad marks because it was hard
for me to understand the Bible lessons given in Hebrew," he said. "Most
of my books were lent by people. I walked from the main road to home
so I could save the twenty-five piasters in bus fare. After six months, I
decided to stop my lessons and go to work and get money to pay for my
lessons, the bus, and books." For a month or two he labored on construction sites and in factories, having to run and hide many times when
inspectors came by checking for children who were working illegally.
"One day, when I was standing and waiting for the bus to come, a man
suddenly called me from the window of the bus and said, 'Hashem, what
are you doing here?' He was Mr. Sariq, my English teacher at high school.
I said that my father doesn't have money and the government doesn't
help me. He said, 'Let your father come to school tomorrow.' Many
people said that Hashem had failed at school, that's why he isn't studying.
Many times my father came to my room and found me crying alone
because I wanted to continue my studies." When his father then went
to the school, the payments were somehow arranged. Hashem was never
quite sure how. "They said I didn't have to pay."

This generosity of the Jews Hashem encountered clashed with the
hardness and hostility of students who were steeped in their images of
Arabs. "When I came back to school, they had their stereotypes of Arabs
that they get married at fifteen, and they asked me if I had gotten married.
I said no, I was in the hospital. I didn't want to tell them I didn't have
money. This was the first time I really met Jews and talked to Jews. I
heard all these words: 'You are playing football like a dirty Arab,' and
then later some guy would come and say, 'Hashem, I'm sorry, it's just

the expression we use.' The teachers came and apologized. The principal was very kind. I'd love to see old Mr. Sariq."

But he was never a full participant. "I always knew my limits," Hashem recalled. Once, his fellow students went off to a paramilitary activity. "I didn't think of going," he said. And at one Jewish festival, the Jewish children sang a cruel verse in Arabic,

> Muhammad is dead,
> And he fathered only girls.

"Historically, it's true," Hashem remarked, but he was offended. "I remember one student said, 'This is not your place. You should go to Amman.' I said, 'I was born here, my parents were born here. You weren't born here. You were born in Europe.'

"I can remember nice things too, when we saw a beautiful girl, we'd all run together and look at her," and he laughed at the memory. "Only two or three times I visited Jewish homes. I expected my friend to ask me to eat, and ask again and again as we used to do. I remember him asking me if I wanted to drink milk, and because I was shy I said no. He said, okay, he'd give it to the dog. I felt maybe I didn't behave in the right way. I should have said yes. I really wanted milk. I just thought he should have asked again."

Even while in school he continued to find odd jobs. "Every holiday I used to go to work, any kind of work. I would take two blankets, one under me and one over me and just sleep anywhere. The most depressing thing I remember was sleeping on the roof of a factory and looking in at a window with electric lights and hearing a radio and seeing people sitting and laughing, and I felt so bad looking in there at the people laughing and listening to the radio." But he studied well. "I studied what the Jews studied—Talmud, Halakha. I remember in Talmud I was one of the best students. A rabbi came and examined us. The principal asked me to put a *kipa* [yarmulke] on my head. I said it's not nice; he'll know I'm Arab when I say my name is Hashem Mahameed. I took a paper and answered the question. I took another and answered it." The rabbi was so impressed and touched that he invited Hashem to his house in a religious neighborhood. "He was very proud of me. I went for one night."

Other recollections came bolting back at him as we sat and talked.

"My parents, I don't think they ever liked Jews. My mother, for example, still remembers the time she lived in Megiddo," before her family's land was confiscated. "She went with a jar on her head going to get water from wells. She remembers every fig tree and cactus." And Hashem has his sweet and bitter memories too.

"I had a Jewish girlfriend. We were eighteen, nineteen years old. We really loved each other, and we thought about getting married. She came to visit us many times at home. I remember asking my family if I could marry her, and my father's answer was, 'We can't live with the Jews. And you want to bring a Jew into the house?' Her parents weren't any better. They would put a cupboard in front of her [bedroom] door so she couldn't come out to see me. One day, the head of the teacher's college where we went called us for investigation, me and her separately. He said, 'How can you think of marrying Hashem and going to live in an Arab village? Don't you know the Arabs are primitive?' He talked about the caves where he said the Arabs lived. 'Don't you know they eat with their hands? Don't you know they're primitive?' Then he called me in and said he'd throw me out because 'You did something wrong on the grass with the girl. You kissed her, etc.' I said, 'I never did such a thing. I come from an Arab family.' I talked to some of the teachers. One said, 'If they make you leave this college, I'll leave with you.'

"We felt so powerless, we felt so weak. They let me stay. But we had to break these relations after two years. It was very painful for us, but we had to do it."

SEVENTEEN

The Sin of Love

Hatred stirreth up strifes: but love covereth all sins.
—Proverbs 10:12

HERE AND THERE, TUCKED OCCASIONALLY INTO THE HARD LAND-
scape of Arab-Jewish friction, lies a pocket of intimate tenderness so
fragile that it is cushioned in a hush of secrecy. Now and then, hidden
in the wind of bitterness, devotion huddles in a calm of honesty. An
Arab man and a Jewish woman fall in love, marry, and make a family
in a lonely wilderness the way a Bedouin makes a small fire of closeness
in the desert.

No one knows exactly how many mixed marriages have occurred among
the Arabs and the Jews who live between the Jordan River and the
Mediterranean Sea. Israeli government agencies and religious authorities

display a certain pride in not knowing: No such records are kept, they say defiantly, as if to banish the small problem with a declaration of ignorance. Marriages across religious lines are prohibited by law in Israel. Jews may not marry Christians; Muslims may not marry Jews; Christians may not marry Muslims. So an Arab and a Jew who wish to marry each other must either do so outside the country, in which case their marriage is not recorded by Israeli officials, or one of them must convert to the other's religion, in which case their marriage is registered as if it were simply between Muslim and Muslim, Christian and Christian, or Jew and Jew. There is raw information in the files, marriage by marriage, but according to the spokesman of the Interior Ministry, no one cares to pull it together.

In the absence of data, rumors flourish. Right-wing Jews spread scare stories picturing thousands of innocent Jewish women being carried off into lewd bondage among the cloistered villages of the West Bank. And those couples who have managed to reach quietly across the great divisions between their two peoples are usually determined to keep their lives private, lest they and their children become sideshow freaks and targets of hostility. In my years in Israel, I almost always found Arabs and Jews willing to speak for publication if the things they had to say were imbued with hatred. But I never found a happily married Arab-Jewish couple willing to see their names in print as they spoke about love. Some talked with me freely and replied readily to searching questions, but only on the condition that I promised to change or omit their full names. As Rafi, the racist of Upper Nazareth, observed, "Love is more dangerous than hate."

Practically everyone who enters into a mixed Arab-Jewish marriage faces some hardship, usually estrangement from society or family, sometimes a clash of styles and expectations in the home as the two cultures attempt to mesh. No middle ground exists in Israel between Arab and Jewish societies, and so the couple must choose to live on one side of the divide or the other. Never is the union allowed to have the simple, natural ease of loving; never can it soar, carefree. Always it must be an act of conviction, defiance, a statement of belief in the purity of the person above the society's neat grid of religious and ethnic definitions. In those homes you hear the finest faith articulated unequivocally: A human being is not an Arab or a Jew but a human being. It is a buoyant declaration, but the weight of the surrounding strife drags on it heavily.

The patterns here, supported by extensive impression but without statistics, indicate that practically all of the marriages occur between Jewish women and Arab men; rarely if ever does an Arab woman marry a Jewish man, although some premarital liaisons do take place. Quite a few Jewish women convert to Islam, and many then live in their husbands' Arab villages, which they find somewhat more tolerant of mixed couples than Israeli-Jewish society is. Most such marriages seem to involve Israeli Arabs rather than those from the West Bank, the Golan Heights, the Gaza Strip, or East Jerusalem, partly because opportunities for contact with Jews are greater in Israel, partly because a stronger propensity exists among some Israeli-Arab families to identify with Jewish society as the majority, dominant culture. The Jewish women appear to suffer more explicit, overt rejection from their parents than Arab men do from theirs, but this may be partly because those Arabs who would face a break with their families back away from intermarriage; the Jews may be more willing to resist family pressure where it exists.

I met a couple who were students at Hebrew University, for example— Nazzi Dabbour, the Druse from the Galilee village of Dalyat el-Carmel, and Judy Greenberg, a Canadian Jew just visiting for a year of study. They were dating seriously, but Nazzi had made clear immediately that marriage was out of the question. "He told me at the beginning, even on the second day, that no one can convert to become Druse," she said. "You can't marry a Druse. So we understood. It's a bit hard to face that I have to go home and we can't get married. But we can't, that's all." She shrugged cheerily.

His explanation of what would happen if he married her was grim and categorical. "First, I couldn't go back to my village, and I couldn't see all my family. We have a community; everyone knows about all the things that go on in the village and go on in the Druse community. If I marry a Jewish girl or a Muslim or a Christian, all the family and all the Druse will look at me in another way. They will look at me as if I'm outside the community and I will not belong to this community. It would be difficult for my parents. They could not speak with the people. They would be ashamed." As it was, Judy said, she had to be careful when visiting his village to conceal her relationship by going with a whole group of students. "Even then," she added, "I'm the one who comes the most, so I stand out. So they're suspicious. They warn him about Jewish girls."

"They say, 'Be careful, don't go with a Jewish girl,' " Nazzi explained. " 'You must keep your religion. You must come back here and marry a Druse girl.' I feel terrible about that, but I haven't any choice. I don't want to cause pain to my parents. And not only to my parents, all the family, the wide family. At the least I must go back to the village and live with the village. And then I can find a nice girl, a Druse girl. And," he said with a broad smile, "there are a lot of nice girls."

At the other extreme, a Muslim family seemed to want their son to marry Susan London, an Israeli Jew who had studied Arabic in high school and had met an Arab boy during a school trip to the village of Taibe. When she graduated and entered the army, officers asked her whether she had any contacts with Arabs; she mentioned the boy and was told that because she was a soldier she must no longer see him. "I was scared," she explained, "because I thought I might give away secrets without knowing. So I let it fade out. He'd write and I wouldn't answer. Then after two years when I got out of the army I picked it up again and went to his village." But there was nothing romantic in it, at least "not from my side," she said, "because I didn't want it. I was always on guard. He was trying, and when I went to the village, his family greeted me so warmly, as if I were the love of his life. His father always says, 'Why don't you marry him? You can live in the village; you speak Arabic; we can build you a house over there.' I have a feeling that they have been trying to assimilate into Jewish society since the beginning of the state. I wasn't that interested in him personally. I wasn't that overwhelmed by his charm and personality. I thought to myself: Being dedicated to liberal ideas, why should I be the one to sacrifice my future and complicate my life? I want to raise my kids Jewish, and I want a husband who at least knows the traditions, even if he's not observant. I don't want to be explaining things all the time."

Susan's family would have been accepting, if not overjoyed, but others confront severe conflict with parents. One Jewish woman was kicked out of her house by her father when she dated an Arab seriously; they never married but live together in Haifa with their three children. Another woman was so frightened of her parents' wrath that she mounted an elaborate deception to have them believe that she lived in England, although in fact she and her Arab husband had a home in Jerusalem. She sent letters to friends in England to be mailed from there to her parents in Tel Aviv.

In October 1983, Israel Radio broadcast a remarkable interview with a twenty-eight-year-old Arab woman who had lived with a right-wing Jew. Her love and misery came spilling out in a bitter torrent of grief and anger. She did not give her name as she spoke in Hebrew, but the agony in her voice, the fury of her words, sketched a sharp portrait of despair.

He was "an ardent Likudnik," a supporter of Begin's rightist Likud Bloc, who "talked about slaughtering the Arabs," she said. "I was for a Palestinian state; he was against." During competing demonstrations at Hebrew University, he dragged her from the lawn by the hair. "Later, he saw me a few times in the student lounge, and he started to get interested. . . . So, he started to run after me for political discussions, right? Not really romantic dates. And after that he started to come over, to drink coffee, coffee with cardamom—son of a Polish family—and he started to tell me what hurt him, why he hated Arabs, because he simply hated. Why did he hate? His brother was killed in a war. I said, 'I'm very sorry about that, but it wasn't I, it wasn't I who started the war. I, I am just I,' " and she laughed. "And fine, dates here, dates there. As in everything, nature did its work—we fell in love." She sighed. "He fell in love with the Palestinian whom he yelled against in demonstrations, and I with the ardent Likudnik who appropriates lands. And it developed and it was great. We lived together and got along wonderfully. We didn't discuss politics. We always tried to ignore it; that's why we didn't have a television in the house either, so as not to watch the news and start to fight.

"My fellow Palestinian students ostracized me. They called me a whore because I socialized with Jews and probably thought I was sleeping with most of them. One day his friends organized with a bunch of Arab students—first time they had the same opinions, for a change—and they simply decided to get tough with the boy. The blows came down on him, and they knocked out his teeth. And he suffered, there's no doubt. And I suffered. His parents, I would go visit them a lot; they really loved me; they accepted me even though they knew I was an Arab. And it hurt them, the picture of his brother sitting there in the room. I understand them, right? True, I wasn't the one who killed him, they know, but they didn't want their son to marry a Palestinian. After his parents kicked us out of the house, we decided to go to the other side, to return to the [occupied] territories. My parents went through the shock of their lives. They knew I had such a boyfriend. They had seen him a few times. He was very nice, they said; he was very nice but too bad he was Jewish. He came from a very rich family, enlightened, a great guy, the kind you don't see every day. He was also very handsome, blue eyes. And my parents, he came to them and said, 'Cards on the table. Listen, I want her.' My father got stubborn, my mother got stubborn: 'No way, no. Our daughter isn't marrying you.' So he started up with all kinds of ideas. We'll run away, we'll go. I had to be the realistic one. What will we live on? What will we do? Where will we go?" Again she sighed a long, deep sigh.

"We decided to end the story. We tried, it didn't work. We tried again, it didn't work. We both really tried to fight our feelings. My parents saw I was having a hard time. It hurt them a lot. But they simply told me, 'That's it. Leave him' "

She began to have such psychological problems that she went into a mental hospital for six months. "For half a year they didn't let me see him. He would come, but they wouldn't let me see him, and apparently it worked. It sounds cruel, but it worked. And he, he ended up nowhere else but a yeshiva in Jerusalem; he became a *baal teshuvah*," a secular Jew who finds extreme orthodoxy, like a born-again Christian. "I run into him once in a while in the city. He doesn't speak to me because he's religious and I'm a woman, and when he looks at me I see the tears in his eyes. And he says to me, 'You haven't forgotten?' And I say, 'No, it's impossible.' He hasn't married yet, and every time I see him I'm torn apart again for a week. It sounds a little like an Arab movie on Friday or a soap opera, but that's what was. It still hurts. It's impossible to forget two years like that. And even now it's hard to find a fitting husband. He was the man I would have liked to dedicate my whole life to. And I lost him. Why? I don't know. Whom to blame? I don't know. I'm one big question mark, and I think I'll be left with this question mark until the grave. There's nothing to do. It is the state of Israel, it is the Middle East, it is all the problems between the Jews and the Arabs. There's nothing to do about it. It begins in politics and ends there. When it reaches the personal level, there, too, it's impossible to disconnect the politics. He, the boy I loved, his brother was killed in the war, his picture is on the wall, and there's nothing to do about it. I remember that at one point I used to wash his reserve uniforms so that he could wear them to some Sabra and Shatila out there. If he had taken part in what was done there, I wouldn't have been able to live with it, I wouldn't have been able to look him in the face, I wouldn't have been able to bear his children and cook him food when he was hungry. I wouldn't have been able to live with it. Despite everything, I am Palestinian. Despite everything, he is a Jew.

"I don't know if it would have been good," she went on. "I don't know. But with an Arab boy it definitely won't work. Now I'm twenty-eight. I know that for an Arab boy, my stock has gone down. He can be crazy for me; his family won't go along with it. I understand why Jewish society acts as it does; I understand why the Arab mentality is as it is. I understand why my parents are as they are. I even understand why *I* am as I am. But where do I end up in all this story? I get lost."

Mordechai Bar-On, former chief education officer of the army, member of the Peace Now movement, and later to become a member of the Knesset, was a liberal. But when his daughter decided to marry the Arab with whom she had been living for three years, he and his wife were concerned. They liked the man, and their reservations had nothing to do with any distaste for Arabs as a group. "We were worried," he said. "We had no ideological or emotional objection. We were worried that they were going to undertake a difficult life—the difference in mentality and culture. The main worry is the children, differences in upbringing."

Nevertheless, they supported their daughter. She wanted to remain Jewish and not convert to Islam, and so she flew with the groom to Cyprus, a favorite spot for marriages among Israelis who wish to avoid the strictures of religious law. "We brought them home," Mordechai explained, "gave them a big party to surround them with people who cared about them, and they felt very good—[it] cushioned them. Her basic stand is 'I love this man, and he's worthy of being my husband. I will not yield to the problems. What I have to do is live and solve the problems as they come. I'm Jewish and I'm an Israeli and I don't give in to this.'" And then her father added, "To be sensitive to his needs and not to give up her identity is very complicated. I do the Friday meal, and he has to listen to the prayer 'He has chosen us among all the nations,' and there is always a smile around the table. I don't believe in it, but I wouldn't change it, because I want to be traditional."

Those who choose to live between the two cultures, trying to keep a foot in each, often seek the leftist Israeli-Jewish milieu as the most supportive. Such has been the choice of "Tami," a plain woman of twenty-five. Her placid face is framed by stringy bronze hair that falls straight to her shoulders. Her husband, "Daoud," is a bald, cheery fellow of twenty-nine whose ready smile breaks from behind a full, neat black beard. He runs a café not far from their old stone house on the main street of a Jewish neighborhood of Jerusalem. The living room is comfortably shabby with a pleasantly disheveled feeling that says a happy family lives there. The couple's blue-eyed daughter, four months old, has been given the neutral name Mai. "It sounds good in Hebrew," her mother explains.

Tami was born in Israel and knew no Arabs personally until she was seventeen. "I was brought up tolerant," she said, "but I had an image of Arabs as something like Bedouin—primitive, dirty in a very diffuse sense." Neither her parents nor his, from Nazareth, were ecstatic about the marriage, but they went along with it, maintaining ties and keeping the families whole. The personal prices they have paid have been hard to reckon. Once, neighborhood youngsters broke their mailbox. "We didn't know whether it was because they knew an Arab was living here or whether it was just because kids break boxes," Daoud remarked. "We decided it was because kids break boxes."

Tami found that marrying Daoud meant curtailing her involvement with Jewish society. She had once thought of working in the Knesset but had to give up the idea. "People said I couldn't because of security," she said, "so I just joined the Arab community in that sense." But she has not found the Arab community all that welcoming either, especially on the West Bank and in East Jerusalem, where she worked for a while as a translator for the Hebrew-language edition of the pro-PLO newspaper *Al-Fajr*. Relations with Arabs were enervating, for every social encounter began with a distasteful political ritual. "First you have to prove to an Arab on the West Bank that you're a nice Jew, and I find it very unpleasant. In the first ten to fifteen minutes you have to prove that you're anti-Zionist and you're for the PLO. And only then can you talk about cooking. And I'm not sure they want to know that there are nice Jews. It's easier to hate the collective."

For Daoud, an Israeli citizen, West Bank Arabs also seem somewhat aloof. "They give me the feeling that I'm different," he said, "and that I'm guilty because I'm Israeli and I have an identity card and I speak

Hebrew and I'm married to a Jew. So I'm finished from two sides. I'm not Israeli for the Israelis, I'm not Palestinian for the Palestinians."

Where do they fit, and where do they go, and where will their daughter find her place in this society of sharply drawn categories? It is a troubling question for them. Muslim and Jewish religious laws are complementary in their contradictions, for under the Sharia, the Muslim law, a child is considered Muslim if his father is, and under Halakha, the Jewish law, a child's Jewishness is transmitted by his mother. And so each religion recognizes the child of such a mixed marriage as one of its own. But that is no resolution in the long term. When Mai was born, Daoud registered her at the Interior Ministry as Muslim and Arab. Tami objected, feeling that the girl should be allowed to make her own choice when she becomes seventeen. So they went back to the ministry and got the entries erased; they will be left blank until her seventeenth birthday, in the year 2000.

And what will be her future? "If we stay in Jerusalem it will be difficult," Tami said. "If we go to Nazareth it will be okay. They will accept her as an Arab. No problem at all."

"She should learn karate," exclaimed Daoud. "I'm serious."

But Tami herself has mixed feelings about moving into Arab society, despite her affinities for certain elements of Arab culture. "I listen to Arab music," she said. "I watch Egyptian films on TV Friday afternoon, with Hebrew subtitles. But some stereotypes are true. Women, for example. Very few women in [Daoud's] family have any feminist view." And this would be a hard value for Tami to abandon. And so she finds little to attract her in Israel, while Daoud is more devoted to his enclave of identity. "I want to leave the country," Tami declared. "I think it's a horrible place. People are mad."

"I don't want to leave," Daoud countered. "If we have the possibility to leave for Nazareth, I would prefer to live in Nazareth."

"Celia" had decided to move completely into Arab society—into her husband's village, into his restrictive world. This she would do as soon as she finished her studies. But for the moment, she was frightened. Leaflets calling on Jewish men to form a defense brigade for action against mixed Arab-Jewish couples had appeared in the mailboxes of the Hebrew University dormitory where she was living as a graduate student. Put out by Meir Kahane's Kach movement, which is known for its violence, the fliers had attracted considerable attention, and Celia would have been a prime target, except that only a few close friends knew that she had converted to Islam and married an Arab. Her husband, "Ahmed," a doctor, was living in his home village of Taibe, near Haifa, while she completed her studies in Jerusalem.

She was thirty when I met her, a happy, smiling woman with big glasses who had emigrated from Argentina eight years earlier. Her move to Israel had been motivated less by Zionism than by political radicalism, for she had some brushes with the Argentine secret police after a youth group she had led went to fight with the guerrillas. "They arrested me for four days," she said. "My father spoke with somebody, and he said it's better for me if I'm not in Argentina." So, as a Jew, she came to Israel, where she met Ahmed at the university.

They lived together for years, and both their families seemed to welcome their marriage. "I was there in his parents' house once a month, twice a month," she said in her lilting Spanish accent. "In the beginning maybe they thought we were not going to marry, that we are friends, not serious. But then [Ahmed] explained to them, and they love me. His family is open—they have a lot of Jewish friends." She spoke Hebrew with everyone in the family except Ahmed's mother, with whom she used the Arabic she had studied in college. Then Celia finally took Ahmed to meet her family in Argentina. "My parents love him," she declared brightly. "My mother asked me only one question: 'What do you think about his being Arab?' "

Celia came to this from a sense of identity very different from that of many other young Jewish women, especially those who grew up in Israel. "I didn't lose anything," she said, "because I never thought of myself as Jewish. Inside me nothing changed." She left something unchanged outside as well, however. Although she converted to Islam, she explained, "I didn't change my ID. It still says Jewish and single."

The conversion was fraught with obstacles thrown up by Muslim and Jewish officials who apparently sought to discourage the marriage. "Everybody didn't want to do it." Celia remarked, "so everybody made difficulty for us." First, she was sent to an official in the Ministry of Religious Affairs whose job, obviously, was "to convince me not to convert," as she put it. He asked why she wanted to convert, took the names and telephone numbers of her relatives. "He had to make a paper to go to the qadi [Muslim religious judge] in Taibe, then to the lawyer, then to

Jerusalem, then back to Taibe, then back to Jerusalem. It was crazy. I don't know how many kilometers we did in the car. The qadi asked why I wanted to convert. I said because I intend to marry. He said, 'I don't like this,' " But the finale was all anticlimax. In the Muslim religious court, Celia merely had to repeat a phrase. " 'I believe in Muhammad,' and I don't know [what else]," she remarked laughingly. "He said the words and I had to say them back."

Celia was happily mobile emotionally, able to wear and shed whatever cloaks of identity got her through the categorical checkpoints of life in the Middle East. She was simply a human being, and therefore she was nothing, nothing that could be placed in any of the neat compartments that facilitate people's senses of themselves and hatreds of each other. And so when she finished writing her dissertation, she intended to go to Taibe to live as an Arab wife of an Arab man raising Arab children. Her trepidation had to do with culture, not identity. She would undoubtedly be the only woman with a Ph.D. in a village where women's lives are severly circumscribed.

But that would be better for her husband, she felt, than trying to live in Israeli-Jewish society. "In the village, it is possible for him to be the mayor," Celia said. "In Jerusalem, it is possible for him to be in jail. When he lived in Jerusalem, two or three times somebody waited for him in the stairwell, asked, 'Who are you? What are you doing here?' Asked for his ID. This decision is the result of seven years of thinking. He said, 'If you want to be my girlfriend, we can be friends and we can finish. But if we get married, you have to know I want to go back to the village. This you have to know.'

"I don't have anything to give him," Celia continued. "I have no roots. I can only take him from his place. I can take him from Arab society and put him in Israeli society, which doesn't love him. I have no family to give him, no friends, no status." The hardships in Jewish society would be too great. Jews don't want to rent to Arabs, she said, and even her acquaintances over the years scolded her for marrying him until, finally, she stopped telling people who her husband was. Also, she added, life in the village is cheaper—a common argument made by mixed couples. For the amount of money they had, they could rent only two rooms in Jerusalem. "In the village, with this money we can build a three-hundred-square-meter house with garden."

She felt that the children they planned to have would be better off in the village, where they would have one identity, than in Jewish society, where they would be torn between two. "They are going to be Arabs," she said firmly. "Maybe somebody will tell them, 'Your mother is Jewish,' but I don't think so." In her mixed anticipations about her own life, she noted that Ahmed was less conservative about women's roles than many Arab men, but only to a point. "He says, 'I don't mind if you go out and work, but food has to be in the house, children have to be okay.' I think it's going to be difficult, but if I have a job, and if I have a car . . ." and her voice trailed off on a tentative note. "Maybe I'll get half-time work, teaching." She expected the difficulties to include the boredom, the enveloping neighbors and relatives, the lack of solitude. "With the [Arab] boys I have friends and good conversations about politics and everything," she said. "But with the girls, nothing. We are going to speak about cakes and children, and to watch television together."

"They call me Leila," said Lilly Solomon. Since 1960 she had lived in the Arab village of Tamra in a brutal, unhappy union that she was afraid to leave, a wrenching illustration of how much the tensions in a bad relationship can be magnified by the surrounding conflict of politics and culture. Born in Burma of Iraqi-Jewish parents, she had grown up in India and London before going to an Israeli kibbutz for several months in 1958, when she was twenty. Unhappy with kibbutz life, she went to work in a restaurant in Haifa, where she met an Arab man from Tamra. "He used to come into the restaurant to have tea, to have coffee," she said. "He was married, didn't have any children." They fell in love, he divorced his wife, and Lilly moved in with him along the narrow alleys that twist up and down the hills and among the stone houses of the village. She gave birth to nine children. "Some have Jewish names, some Arabic names," she said. "I named some, he named some. Khalil, Walid, Ibrahim (I call him Abraham), Jamili, Aida, Samya, Sarah, Hamad, Kwaiti."

Lilly never really became an Israeli. She never learned Hebrew but spoke Arabic and English, using Arabic with her children. She did remain Jewish, however, which became a source of friction and a reason that she detested life in Tamra. "I don't mix with the people here," she said as she twisted the rings on her left hand and crumpled a small handkerchief, dabbing occasionally at her eyes. "His parents, brothers don't come to us, don't speak to me, because I'm Jewish." Her husband used to drink heavily, she reported, and beat the children. Although she did not say so explicitly, I had the impression that he also beat her. And since he refused to allow her to go visiting out of the house and exploded into a towering rage when she defied him, she had made only one friend. "There is a neighbor, she's really friendly with me. She comes to me every day to talk," Lilly said. She was able to get away for a couple of hours, to the house of some friends of mine in the village, only because she told her husband she was coming to show the women how to cook Indian food. "He doesn't like Indian food," she said.

Wringing her handkerchief, she talked about her efforts to maintain Jewish traditions in her house. Her children had a good feeling for the religion, she explained, despite her husband's antagonism. "He won't allow me to keep Sabbath," she said. "My parents told me to keep Sabbath, but I can't. On Yom Kippur, only I fast. My daughters do not, my sons don't."

Lilly wanted to leave her husband and the village but seemed somehow incapable of doing so. Without money of her own, surrounded by people she considered hostile, she was afraid that she would never be able to take her children with her. She had renewed connections with her own family some months earlier, when Israel Television had broadcast a report on her situation; her brother, living near Tel Aviv, had not even known that she was in Israel until he saw the broadcast. He contacted their parents in London, whom she had not seen in thirty years. "They came to Israel looking for me," she said, tears filling her eyes. "They didn't come to Tamra. They came to a restaurant, and we went there. Only my mother didn't want to meet him. Because she's religious she didn't want to. She asked me to return to my family. If I could, I would leave, but I can't. I might leave in the future. I have great hopes of leaving. My brother is willing to help. It is very difficult to leave because of my children. I hope to go to London. Israel, no."

Lilly was strangely oblivious to the hospitality with which Jewish-Arab marriages were greeted in other circles of Tamra, and she had never even met the other mixed couple I visited in town that day. They welcomed me into their stone house, where "Sarah" served small cups of strong coffee in the Arab style, and we talked while an unending flow of friends and neighbors came in and out of their sitting room, pausing to listen and then moving on. This was a mark of an accepted Arab household, and clearly this family was strongly connected to a broad community.

Sarah wore her light-brown hair fairly short, and her eyelids were decorated with thick blue-black shadow. Her garish lipstick had been freshly applied. She smiled and laughed a great deal, creating an opposite impression from the tearful, helpless Lilly. More somber elements lay beneath the surface of gaiety, however.

She had grown up in the Jewish town down the road, Kiryat Ata, where her mother and father, Jews from Turkey and Morocco respectively, still lived. She was eighteen and working in a factory when she met "Jalal," a slim, dark, good-looking bus driver five years her senior. In six weeks they were married, and in less than a year had the first of their three sons. They called him Amir, a name that could be either Hebrew or Arabic, she noted. Her younger boys were given the Arab names Bilal and Nibal. She worried now about their possibly being drafted into the army at eighteen, despite her conversion to Islam and their having been registered at birth as Muslims. "Under Jewish law they are Jews," she said. As I learned later, this commentary was apparently designed for the public consumption of the village neighbors who were sitting in on the conversation; there was a complexity here that she preferred not to have the villagers know.

The larger families surrounding Sarah and Jalal provided both acceptance and rejection. Jalal's parents accepted the marriage willingly, for his older brother had married a Jew more than a dozen years before and, in addition, had converted to Judaism, had taken his wife's maiden name as his own, and had moved with her into the Jewish town of Kiryat Ata. It was a departure from the normal pattern, and it had produced some bizarre scenes, including a visit by the older brother during the Lebanon war. He had been fighting in Lebanon and while on leave came home to the Arab village in his Israeli army uniform. Yet neighbors and relatives, hearing of his arrival, gathered to welcome him with a surprising display of warmth and affection.

This has eased Sarah's life in Tamra but not eliminated her sense of apartness. Her initiation into Arab culture was difficult. She learned Arabic on her own, "slowly, slowly," as she put it, and she watched the way villagers dealt with each other to pick up cues for her own behavior. "The main thing was that you had to go in the streets and say hello,

hello, hello to everyone whether you knew him or not," she explained, "and if you didn't, it was considered rude." Jalal remembered Sarah's hardest and most important lesson as learning "how to receive people in the house." Laughing, he gave an example of an incident when they had guests. "I said something to her, and she said, 'Kiss my ass!' I took her aside and said, 'Look, you can't say that in front of people.' "

Even in her own adaptation to Arab culture, Sarah remains at the outer edge. "I identify myself as a Muslim," she said, "but people in Tamra see me as a Jew and always will see me as a Jew. When I talk to people in the village, I have to think twice about what I say because it might hurt people." She gave the example of the massacre of Palestinians by Lebanese Christians in the Beirut refugee camps of Sabra and Shatila. "I heard people saying that the Jews did everything there. I could have said something. I could have spoken, and I could have hurt people, but I preferred to keep quiet." She recognized the anxiety the Arab villagers had about their relatives in the Lebanese camps. "Because I have lived in a Jewish neighborhood and an Arab neighborhood," she explained, "I now know that Jews and Arabs are both the same thing. For me, everybody's the same. Everyone goes through the nine-month process, a Jewish mother and an Arab mother—isn't it the same thing? If a mother loves a son or a husband, it's the same pain." She described herself as apolitical, never having voted at all except in one village election.

From her own family's side, she has found more explicit rejection. Sensing her parents' attitudes, she told them only that she was going with Jalal, revealing only after the fact that she had married him. They knew him because he used to work with her father, but they were furious. "They took it hard, and they even came to the village to try to take me back," she recalled. "I was the oldest one at home, and I had younger sisters, and you know how people in Kiryat Ata talk, and they pass rumors, and they thought this would bother my sisters. In school, the other kids talked about the girls, gossiped." She lost some friendships and strengthened others. Her three sisters, for example, did not invite her to their weddings. "There are people, and there are people," she said in resignation. "One of my friends from childhood comes here with her children." Once, her mother came to talk very nicely and try to convince Jalal to leave her. And although he and Sarah used to take the children to visit her parents, she stopped. "Every time I went," she said, "we had arguments." Jalal added, "I used to go and drink coffee with them, but when she stopped going to see them, I also stopped going to see them." Her father cut off all contact at one point, and her mother then came occasionally to visit secretly, without telling him.

Sarah came through as more toughened than pained by all of this. "It hurts because it's my mother, my father," she remarked. "But I'm not really angry. I cooked it, I have to eat it."

A couple of her American friends had a somewhat different picture from the one she was presenting to me in her semi-public sitting room, however. During a time of strains in the marriage, she had told them, she had left Jalal, returned to live with her parents, converted back to Judaism, and registered two of her sons as Jews. She had shown one of her friends the reconversion papers. My probing around in this area prompted only confused answers and looks of discomfort, probably because even if Jalal knew about her reconversion, the rest of the village did not.

He was rather taciturn, especially on the subject of relationships with Jews. "Relations were good" in Arad, a Jewish town where his job had taken him for a while after their first baby was born, he declared. Apparently there was nothing more to be said on the subject. His preference now for living in his hometown—instead of following his brother's path and moving to a Jewish area—was based on nothing beyond economics and convenience. "As you see," he said, "I have a house here. And the reason I live here is because I have a house. There isn't any special reason that I'm not going to live there."

The difficulties that preoccupied Sarah were not her own but those she anticipated for her children. The boys were basically all right at the moment, she contended. In school they got some heckling and teasing at first, until the other children grew used to them and to the idea of their Jewish mother. "According to the education I am giving them right now, I don't think they'll have problems," she said, "but they have to live with the fact that their mother is Jewish and their father is Arab. And that's their reality. They have to know it from now, and there is no escaping it." The oldest boy, six, asks, "Why in my grandfather's house in Kiryat Ata does everyone speak Hebrew and here everyone speaks Arabic?" Sarah answers, "Your grandfather in Kiryat Ata is Jewish, and your grandfather here is Arab." I asked her how she thought their lives would be in Kiryat Ata. "In the beginning there would be rumors," she said, "and things would have happened. But the environment would accept it. Society goes on learning."

So it has seemed to Jalal's brother. He appears a kindly man, his bronzed, creased face capped by a full head of curly hair. His pleasant, newly built house in the Jewish town of Kiryat Ata is swathed in an aura of relaxed contentment. His children come and go quietly, and there are no streams of neighbors to interrupt the sense of privacy in his living room. In his conversion to Judaism, he has yielded completely to the cultural artifacts of Israel, allowing the atmosphere and decor of his home to grow wholly un-Arab. Against one wall stands an elaborate aquarium containing tropical fish that swim among columns of rising bubbles. There are lampshades made of fish skins. Plastic flowers grace the tables, as do cheap china figurines of a Chinese couple and a ballet dancer. A mezuzah is nailed to the doorpost. And in the vacant lot across the street he parks the gleaming chrome and glass tour bus that he drives around Israel, taking foreign vacationers who rarely seem to suspect that he is not a Jew. Indeed, practically everything about his home, his life, and his family has become Israeli Jewish. His Hebrew is flawless, his accent perfect. His children all have Hebrew names. He even thinks politically like a tough-minded, moderate Israeli Jew, opposing any retreat from the Golan Heights, advocating only a modest withdrawal from the West Bank, doubting that real peace can come with the Palestinians. "Something of the hate remains," he said. "Where can we go? Only to the sea." His army service during the Lebanon war was performed in a highly secret intelligence unit, he bragged, proudly showing photographs of himself on Mount Barukh, where Israeli spy equipment was positioned.

When he met "Ofra" and dated her, she thought he was a Jew. But by the time he revealed that he "wasn't of the same origin," as he gently put it, she was already in love with him, and they decided to marry. When he converted, he changed his first name to Avraham and his last to her maiden name, as dramatic a shift as if he had changed it from Nasser to Cohen. "We're all the sons of Avraham the father," he reasoned, "so I am the son of Avraham." And his wife added with a laugh, "When he used to go out with [Jewish] girls he changed his name anyway."

Ofra, a trimly built dyed blonde, was an Egyptian Jew, the only daughter of a very religious family; her father served as a cantor in the synagogue. It is the Egyptian background that she cites as the reason for her and her parents' acceptance of the idea of her marrying an Arab. "I was ten when we came from Egypt," she explained. "We knew Arabs, we speak Arabic." And yet a tug of apprehension pulls at her, for she obviously prefers that outside the immediate community her husband be taken for a Jew, that his Arab background remain invisible. She doesn't want her real name published on the fear that someday a son might want to make a military career, only to be thwarted if he is known to be half Arab. This despite Avraham's sensitive army duty, which has placed her in much the same position as other Jewish wives who sit at home and wait and hope. Her walls are hung with framed works of needlepoint, one an elaborate country scene she stitched during the 1973 war when she had nothing else to do but worry about him in battle.

They have made careful efforts in their marriage to keep their extended families together. Most mixed couples marry, "leave the house, and never see the family again," Avraham said in only slight exaggeration. "Even if an Arab is so good, good to the state, good to the Jews—despite that, the Jew looks at an Arab as an Arab." His calculation, in converting and living in Kiryat Ata, held that he and Ofra could thereby maintain close ties with both sides of the family. He figured that if they moved to his home village of Tamra they would keep the contacts with the Arab relatives but not with the Jewish. The couple made it clear that they wanted family closeness to remain. "The first step we took after the wedding," he said, "was to let the families visit immediately."

Here was an easy flow of comfort, I felt, a relaxed air of accommodation with few of the tensions apparent in other mixed marriages. Even the conversion became a subject of hilarity. "It was pretty quick," Avraham recalled. "Moses had to run after them for forty years to give them the Torah. I accepted it in a week. It was so funny. It would be better if they didn't do this and just let people marry. I almost drowned in the *mikvah* [ritual bath]. They looked at me down below and they said, 'Circumcised? Who did this?' A doctor in the village. Seven times they put me under the water, and after that I was a Jew. They asked me questions, such as why do we celebrate Passover, etc., and that was all." He and Ofra practice no religion, for despite her upbringing, she is not observant.

Nor do they seem to find meshing cultures beyond their capacity to compromise, although disagreements occasionally flare. Avraham is so anxious to be modern Jewish that once during our conversation, when he caught himself sitting with his feet tucked under his legs folded on an easy chair, he apologized and explained with embarrassment, "That's from the village." But he has not gone far enough in shedding Arab norms to suit Ofra, who finds her life curtailed. "The women in my house used to be freer," she said. "With him I'm not so free. We fight over clothes every summer. My sisters-in-law walk around in shorts; when they see Avraham coming to visit, they change their clothes."

"I say this from the standpoint of honor," Avraham declared solemnly. "It is not so honorable that a woman is walking with her children and people see her bottom or her chest. I like a woman dressed nicely. Honor and respect. It's respectful. In the village now they're all pretty free too. I can see my niece wearing narrow, narrow pants where you can see everything. I have to tell her."

"It's the mentality," Ofra observed. "It's inside you."

"I haven't forgotten that Arab mentality," he conceded.

"Let's say there's a wedding. He's at work. There are a lot of people who would go without a husband. He says no."

"There is no reason a woman should go without her husband," he asserted. "Everyone is sitting with husbands, and she's all alone. It's not nice." Then he added, reflectively, "I can't deny and I can't forget that I'm from Arab origins. I also feel like an Arab. I feel a human of Arab origin who lives among Jews, and I'm no different from them. I like the Arabs and I like the Jews. I like any man who doesn't hurt me. I think of myself as a human—the same ears, the same eyes, the same hands as a Jew. I hate racism, the Arab and the Jewish racism. I hate it."

The children of mixed, Arab-Jewish parentage carry the crisis of the conflict in their deepest souls. Unless they escape outside the Middle East and allow their dual identities to dissolve, they must decide who they are, what they believe, where they belong, how to squeeze themselves into the boxes of definition imposed on them by the struggle between their two peoples. Some seek resolution in an extreme embrace, as did a young man recalled by Sari Nusseibeh, who remembered a schoolmate in Jerusalem and the son of a pre-1948 mixed marriage. "He was always drawing swastikas," Sari said. "He was later arrested for doing something for the PLO."

But others leave the question almost unresolved, trying to blend into one nation without denying the other, or trying to exist above both. Such a man is Juliano Mer, whose father is an Arab, whose mother is a Jew, and who hovers between and outside the two cultures, suffering the curses that each aims at the other. He is an actor by profession, playing roles onstage, in films, in life.

I watched him do a scene in a narrow Jaffa street for an Israeli film in which he was cast as a Jewish guerrilla in the Stern Gang of pre-state days. It seemed an odd part for a man with an Arab father, but he relished the subliminal theme of parallels between the Jews then and the Arabs now: "the struggle against occupation, against foreign rulers," as he put it. The Jewish director also liked the parallel, but because of the need for financing and the sensibilities of the Israeli audience, he barred his actors from pointing it out to Israeli reporters, and he made it too subtle in the film for Juliano's taste, subtle enough, in fact, that former Stern Gang members took pleasure in coming to the set and advising the filmmakers without ever seeing the message beneath the story. This was my introduction to Juliano, twenty-five years old with thick black hair, a strong jaw, and a dark gaze as hard as coal on camera, as soft as black water in the privacy of conversation about himself.

On the set, we exchanged a few words between takes and agreed to meet the following week at his house in Haifa. It was a crash pad, the apartment of a couple of young Jewish women where Juliano was apparently a welcome member of the collective. He also kept a place in Tel Aviv, where he had to go often to work, but Haifa, the lovely seacoast city that rises on steep hills above the Mediterranean, was his home.

He had been born there not as Juliano Mer but as Sputnik Hamis, named after the Soviet Union's first satellite by his father, Saliba Hamis, a prominent Arab in Israel's Communist Party. His mother, Arna Mer, the daughter of Russian Jews who had immigrated to Palestine, had fought in the Palmach and had then joined leftist causes, where she had met Hamis during a conference in Nazareth. They were now separated.

Juliano was the middle of three sons. The oldest, Spartak, had chosen a radical Arab identity, living now in London and working on a book about anarchism and communism. The youngest, Abir, had gone into the Israeli army, but where he would emerge Juliano wasn't sure. "We, three brothers, we always had to face this question," he said, "always, every minute everywhere. And all the energy was upon this thing, how to create something that does not exist." Perhaps he, Juliano, had reached a state of mind independent of ethnic, religious, national labels; he hoped so. "That can be the solution of wars," he said. "No religion, no identity, no nothing—a human being, that's all: My name is Juliano."

His name became Juliano out of a long childhood of discomfort. As a boy, his family took him to live in Prague, where his father was assigned as a representative of the Israeli Communist Party. He remembered the Soviet invasion in 1968 when, with his older brother, he joined the protesting Czechoslovak students and tossed a Molotov cocktail at a Soviet tank. (He noted wryly that the next time he threw one was in his film role as a Jewish guerrilla.) After the invasion, his family moved to Moscow for a few years, where he was confronted with a baffling epithet from Soviet Jews. Knowing that his Jewish mother was married to an Arab, they called Juliano "Jewish face" and other names, he said. But when he was fifteen and his family returned to Israel, he suddenly found himself vilified as an Arab. Sitting on a baggage cart at the airport, he was accosted by a porter who saw the name Hamis on a ticket or a tag. "Fuck off, you fucking Arab," the porter shouted. "That switch made me very confused," Juliano said. "I'm a Jewish face to Jews in Russia, a fucking Arab here."

It was not an easy reentry into his native land. They lived in Haifa. "I didn't know Arabic, I didn't know Hebrew. I knew half Russian, half Czechoslovakian. So I was half, half, half, half, half." At home they spoke, "half Arabic, a few words in Hebrew, a few words in Russian, a few words in Czechoslovakian," he said. "With my father I was talking a few words in English, a few words in Hebrew, a few words in Arabic. With my mother I was talking a few words in Russian, a few words in Hebrew. So we came here neutral, you could say."

"My father said it was better for us to go to an Arabic school because in a Jewish school they would tease us and there would be provocations because we were communists and Arabic. And he thought that in Arabic school we would feel freer because the Arabs don't care much about Jewish and Arabic; they're more open because they have the same problems; they suffer the way we suffer. But when I think about it today, I think he wanted us to be more Arabic than Jewish. I think so. 'Cause he's still stuck in his nationality. So we went to Arabic school, and it was like going from cars to horses. It was a very primitive way of teaching. They still were hitting with sticks. And no long hair. And we came from Czechoslovakia after the invasion, and it was jeans and hippies and long hair. And here they still had short hair. So we just were there for four months and it was impossible to stay, so my mother went to a Jewish school and talked to the principal and talked about this problem and he said okay. He was very nice and understanding, and we went to the Jewish school. And except for one teacher, I don't remember any problems about being Arab or Hamis or communist."

As the reality of life in Israel imposed itself on the boy, he moved quickly into a Jewish role. His Hebrew became better than his Arabic, which he now speaks adequately but cannot read or write. His neighbors were Jewish, and since he attended Jewish school, he observed, "naturally all my friends were Jews. So I said, Okay, I'll be with them, I'll be one of them."

Fairly early on, his parents changed his first name from Sputnik to Julio, and despite his Arab last name he managed to pass as a Jew in the eyes of many of his classmates. Some suspected that his father's father was non-Jewish. "At that age I was hiding my real identity," Juliano said. "I was saying that my father was the son of a Jewish mother and she changed her name, dah, da-dah, da-dah. I couldn't say the word Arab, because it was shocking at that time in Israel. So nobody knew really." The truth burst out one day in class. "It was one teacher. She was a history teacher, and every time there were arguments about the Palestinians and the Arab governments, I was talking as you can imagine. So once she said, 'Mr. Julio, would you please tell the class who your father is?' So I stood and said, 'My father is an Arab, and I don't give a shit. And I piss on you.' I was sixteen. The other kids were shocked. They had some suspicions. They thought my father was from a Jewish mother and he was half and half, mixed. But this was the first time they knew he was an Arab and a Communist."

The news did not ruin his friendships, however, because he suddenly became fascinating. "In most friendships, it was a plus because people were interested in being my friend. I was different. The same with girls. 'She's a friend of Julio, an Arab, communist.' But her parents felt differently and I was kicked out of some houses because of it. I remember I was in one house and there was an Arabic movie on television, and I was translating for my friend, and her father suddenly said, 'Tell me, where is your Arabic from?' 'Oh, you know, my father is an Arab.' 'Ohhhh. Well, child, come please to the kitchen. Ragh, ragh, ragh, ragh, I won't see this Arab in my house!' I walked out and never came back."

When Juliano turned eighteen and all his friends were going into the army, he came finally to the decision that he too wanted to join, and not just to belong but to volunteer for an elite paratroop unit. "You can't imagine what pressure the army thing makes here," he explained, "because anywhere you go, before they ask your name they ask what profile you have in the army. And it's such a brainwash here, you grow with it, you live it. The army is a thing you naturally have to pass through." But the army didn't send him a draft notice. "When I was born, on the papers you had to write the nationality of the father, the nationality of the mother, the nationality of the son. So I was Jewish-Arab. You see the paradox? It's funny. So I stayed, in the papers, Jewish-Arab. So I went to the army and I said, 'Listen, you forgot me. I am a Jew. I'm a good Jew. I want to fight for my country. I want to be like you.' "

His parents had contrasting reactions. "I think [my father] was very disappointed, very. My father is very radical. I once asked him, 'Tell me, why don't they send you to the Knesset? You are one of the leaders of the Communist Party here. What is happening? Instead of going up you are going down.' He said, 'Heh, if I can't impress my children, so how can I impress other people?' That's when I was going into the army. He said, 'You're going to be sorry for that; you're going into a fascist army.' I said, 'I know, I know, I know, but I must do it for myself. It's a step that I must pass. I must see with my eyes that they are really fascist. I must see with my eyes that what you are saying is true.' My mother understood. She said, 'It's good. Go, go, and you'll see yourself. It's better that you see it yourself than that we tell you and you think what we want. If it comes from you, it will be real and true.' "

Juliano figured that before going into the army he ought to have a Jewish family name, and so he dropped Hamis and took his mother's maiden name of Mer. He had had enough trouble with Hamis, in school, at the health clinic, at the airport. "When everybody heard Hamis, the atmosphere changed. Every time when I was leaving the country and coming in there was questioning and investigations for eight, five, six hours. So I decided if I'm going to the army, I'll change my name; it's going to be easier for me. But it was connected with many, many other problems that I had with myself, with my identity and who I am and who I will be. So it was one of the steps to try to be Jewish, completely, to identify with the Jewish people and to go to the army and to be the best in the army." He added the change from Julio to Juliano when he went to the government offices and "saw that it was so easy to change names—you pay twenty shekels and you change names. So I said I'll change my first name, I'll change my second name."

But the change did not alter what was inside him, and that ultimately had the telling effect on his abbreviated career in the army. As a paratrooper, Juliano was assigned to control Arab demonstrators on the West Bank, and he did so with alacrity. In Jenin in 1979, he beat Palestinian protesters who ignored an order to disperse. Why? I asked. "Because I wanted to be on one side. I wanted to be with somebody. Because I felt like nobody."

He failed. "It didn't work," he explained, "because inside of me, every time I faced a problem when I was standing at checkpoints on the West Bank or when I was watching demonstrations of Arabs in the West Bank and Gaza, it always came up, the Arabic thing, inside me. I felt that I'm not well with myself when I'm doing it. It's not like with my Jewish friends. They were happy, and it's power, and I saw in their eyes the satisfaction of searching somebody or stopping somebody or beating. I did it because I had to show them that I'm one of them. But I felt sick. Arresting Arabs and beating Arabs and stopping Arabs at checkpoints and searching. I felt sick." All this came to a head one day as he was standing at a checkpoint on the main road at Jenin. Cars were being stopped and searched. And suddenly a car came along full of Arabs he recognized, Arabs he knew. "They were relatives of my father." Something snapped. "There was some flash. I don't know what happened, it was BUK! and I said, 'That's it.' I threw the gun, and I said, 'I'm going home.' I said to the commander, 'I'm leaving.'

" 'No! Come back!'

" 'No, I'm leaving.' And I just walked home. I was home two weeks, and they found me and I went to jail for three months. Then they wanted to send me to tanks as a punishment. So I refused, so I went to jail for another month. And again and again and again." Finally, faking an attack of claustrophobia in his cell, he got himself transferred to a psychiatric hospital, and from there to duty entertaining wounded troops in a Haifa hospital, and then out of the army. He went to live for a while in England and West Germany, flirted with activity in the PLO, but in the end rejected terrorism as a way.

Every effort to assemble a fully Jewish or a fully Arab identity disintegrated for Juliano; to each side, he was always part of the enemy, and the hostility erupted even with friends. "I had a very good friend, Moshe," he said, "and one day we had a fight, and during the fight he was shouting, 'You fucking bloody dirty Arab!' I was shocked. He was a good friend for years." And on the Arab side the same thing happened. "My neighbor is an Arab, and he's my age. I wanted to make sure that I could be with anyone without noting that he was an Arab or a Jew, but I felt some distance because he's stuck with traditional ways of thinking. Once I was kissing my friend in front of him. He was very angry, he left my room. And once I said, '*Kus ukhtak.*' It's like 'Fuck your sister' to a friend, jokingly. It was a scandal. He said, 'What? You're cursing my sister? My honor? My respect? My sister?' He said, 'I'm an Arab and maybe one day you will become my enemy!' " Juliano paused. "It's not their fault. I don't blame them, as I don't blame myself. Roots. Roots."

Arab culture and traditions hold no attraction for him. Indeed, he finds many of them repulsive. His sharpest criticism of his father, mixed into personal tension, is of a man publicly devoted in the Communist Party to equality and progress and privately devoted to male supremacy at home. "I see my mother more than my father. I don't have any special relationships with my father. He's an Arab. I say to him, 'When you take off your suit you become an Arab, a real Arab. When you put on your suit you become a liberal Arab.' That's the reason, I think, that makes it harder for me to have relations with Arabs, because I was seeing my father when he was outside the family and when he was inside the family. He was talking outside about communism, equal rights, and so on. And he was coming home as a real primitive Arab, treating my mother, treating us. This is what I remember from when I was a child. I always saw the schizophrenic life of my father. And that's true. Most of the Arabs of Israel are still like that. Talk, talk, words, words, but when they have to do themselves what they are saying, they are still stuck on those traditions.

"I don't know how he feels," Juliano went on. "He is very much the father, very much. Father. Money, car, and don't smoke and don't go and don't do that and don't do this. I don't remember even one conversation about what I feel or what's hurting me with him—nothing. Even when they were together, his work always made him be out of the house, traveling, congresses, and jails. He saw me first in his life in jail. My mother took me to him when I was eight days old. It was in Nazareth and there was a big demonstration on the first of May and he was put in jail."

When Juliano returned from London, he went to acting school for a year and a half, where he learned that a certain satisfaction could come not only from belonging but from playing parts. In a Tel Aviv theater he was cast as Stanley in *A Streetcar Named Desire.* He has done Chekhov. He had a role as a Jewish Mossad agent in the film of John le Carré's *Little Drummer Girl* and has played Jews in Israeli-written productions— a member of the Stern Gang, a soldier in Lebanon. He got the Jewish roles down pat. And then, when he was asked to play an Arab, he was ecstatic to find that he could do it. "I said, Wow, it will change my head to be Arabic and my identity and to identify. And I made the audition and like that"—he snapped his fingers—"complete Arabic, talking Arabic, moving Arabic, behaving Arabic, looking Arabic. And suddenly I felt that I really lost—I wouldn't say I lost myself—maybe, but I lost the pillars of identity. As a human being I feel that I can move very easily between languages and behaviors, and it's made it easy."

Well, not so easy. "I feel outside. But you know, now that I think of it, everywhere I felt an outsider, everywhere. Czechoslovakia, London, Germany, here. Sometimes I feel sorry that I'm an outsider. It was funny, when Maccabee Tel Aviv took the European {basketball} title, everybody was in the streets dancing, and I was sitting in the balcony looking, and I said, Fuck it, I want something too—Maccabee, army, paratroopers, television, but something that I can say, 'Wow, it's mine.' " He took a long drag on his cigarette. "I felt very sad."

Would he ever leave Israel for good? "To leave Israel, you have to be ready to leave Israel," he answered carefully. "It's still the warmest place, the mother, father, friends, language. If you live in one country for years and you're used to the language and you feel at home and suddenly to leave for a new place, nobody cares and nobody knows. You should be ready for that. I tried it in England. It was terrible. One year. I didn't like it. So I came back. Now I'll try New York."

About six months later, after I had left Israel, a friend in Jerusalem who knew of my interest in Juliano noticed a small item in *The Jerusalem Post* and mailed it to me:

> Tel Aviv—Two young men broke into the apartment of a student here yesterday, cut his face with knives and threatened to kill him if he continued to live with a flatmate whose father is an Arab, he told police.
>
> The student is Yosef Saguy, 23. His flatmate is Juliano Mer, a movie actor whose mother is Jewish.
>
> Saguy was sent home after being treated in the hospital.
>
> Police are investigating.

EIGHTEEN

The Dream

If you will it, it is not a dream.
—Theodore Herzl

It is a thin, winter dawn that casts its pallor on the land. In this season of the year, the morning brings only lingering colors of unreality.

An hour before the Jewish youngsters come to the hilltop community of Neve Shalom, the Arab teenagers arrive. They step off the bus that has brought them from their village, put their backpacks and overnight bags in a heap outside, and tentatively, quietly walk among the scattering of little box-shaped concrete houses toward the edge of the slope that sweeps down into the lower hills and valley. As they grow comfortable, their paces quicken, their voices come in scraps of Arabic across the high meadow as they explore the hill and gaze at the land that stretches out and away toward the heart of Israel.

A cold January mist floats softly in the valley below, blurring the lines of terraced vineyards and moistening the silvery leaves of ancient olive trees. The mist lends a diffuse air of isolation and remoteness to the small community and to the endeavor here; the Arab and Jewish high-school students, most in eleventh and twelfth grades, will spend four days together in workshops and conversations in an effort to reach across the great divide.

Soon the Jews arrive. They and the Arabs are asked to assemble in a square, prefabricated building comprising only one large room with big windows on three sides and a blackboard on the fourth. Self-consciously they begin to form a circle. Both Arab and Jewish boys and girls are wearing the rough khaki Israeli army jackets that have become the style, so that a glance cannot tell the Arabs from the Jews.

It is the morning of the first day.

Neve Shalom was founded as a model of a dream. Conceived in 1970 as an interfaith community, it was designed to draw Muslims, Christians, and Jews to reside on the hilltop with each other as a demonstration of harmony across the barriers of distrust. By 1984, when I spent time there, it had failed to grow into a flourishing settlement, containing only thirty-five permanent residents. One of the six families was Arab, the others Jewish, and over the years most of the Arab participants had been single men who had stayed for a while and then returned to their villages to marry and raise their families in the extended support system of their own culture. The community grew only slightly, to four Arab and eight Jewish households in 1986. Those Arabs and Jews who did live and work the land together raised sheep, kept bees, grew almonds, and picked olives on a 100-acre tract that was about as neutral as a piece of earth could be in the Middle East. Situated right on the line between the West Bank and Israel, it had been a no-man's-land until Israel took the West Bank in the 1967 war. Even its ownership was divorced from the current politics of the conflict, for it was the property of the Latrun monastery, an imposing, walled compound in the valley where Trappist monks, enveloped in their vows of silence, distinguished themselves primarily by making a rather good red wine. Neve Shalom paid the monastery rent for the land.

More significant than Neve Shalom's minuscule contribution to the Arab-Jewish community was the role of its residents in conducting workshops for Arab and Jewish high-school students and in training young counselors to work with mixed Arab-Jewish groups. Here its meager facilities were in great demand, constantly in use throughout the academic year with many more Arab and Jewish schools pressing for the opportunity than the settlement had space or personnel to provide. Thus, the modest hilltop community became part of Israel's cleansing backlash against its own bigotry, a purifying reaction that spread during my years there into a variety of quiet activities. Their scope was not large. Certainly they did not touch even a noticeable minority of the Arab and Jewish populations. But even if these efforts were not likely to produce social change, at least they testified to the small sparks of decency that were alive in the gloom of conflict.

In the Galilee, Interns for Peace took Jews and Arabs in their twenties and had them live for two-year tours in Arab villages and Jewish towns, where they organized visits between Arab and Jewish schools, sports field days, joint playground-construction projects, hikes, summer camps, family picnics, and other activities to bring Arabs and Jews into personal contact. In Nazareth, a group placed Arabs in volunteer work on kibbutzim during the war in Lebanon. Partnership, an organization active mostly in northern Israel, conducted seminars for teachers, introduced a "peace studies" curriculum on coexistence in several Jewish junior high schools, and ran workshops for Arabs and Jews in Haifa. At Givat Haviva, in the Galilee, the Hashomer Hatzair kibbutz movement of the Mapam socialist party maintained an institute for Arab-Jewish studies to sensitize teachers and others to issues in promoting tolerance between the peoples. At Hebrew University's Beit Hillel in Jerusalem, Arabs and Jews met regularly for discussions of politics, cultural affairs, and life on campus. At the Martin Buber Center at Hebrew University, Arab adults from East Jerusalem and the West Bank studied Hebrew, and Jews studied Arabic. Between classes the students mixed in the lobby; the center organized joint outings and celebrations of Muslim and Jewish holidays. Here and there, some Jews and Arabs even joined encounter groups together, engaging in cathartic displays of shouting, crying, and innermost confession as a method of confronting their prejudices.

For the most part, such efforts proceeded without any support from any of the mainstream organizations of Israeli society. Neither the government nor the rabbinate nor the Muslim Council nor the Jewish Agency (which allocates millions in private donations annually from the Diaspora) spent a shekel on any of the most significant programs, except where the Education Ministry helped support an important effort to revise the school curriculum. While the government poured millions of dollars into the abrasive, nationalistic Jewish settlements on the West Bank, it provided nothing at all to the modest Neve Shalom settlement; residents had to build their own houses, live in extremely cramped rooms, conduct seminars on cold floors, and depend for years on a generator for electricity. Small, well-placed grants came from the New Israel Fund and other American-based foundations, contributions that could not create the amenities that might have come from all-out government support. The settlement was finally hooked up to the electricity grid, but its long, winding road up from the valley remained unpaved and barely passable in the wet winters. In its struggle against neglect, Neve Shalom stood as a monument to the finest qualities of individual Israelis and to the shame of the society's major institutions.

The dirt road up from the valley is mud, and the paths among the buildings are soaked with a reddish-brown earth that sticks to the soles of boots. The mud is tracked into buildings, streaking the floors with a slippery grime.

The Arab and Jewish youngsters are sitting in a circle, and Ariela, a Jewish woman in her twenties with a plain-spoken perceptiveness, is welcoming them, speaking to them in Hebrew, while Aziz, a young Arab man and co-leader, is translating into Arabic. There are twenty-six Arabs from the village of Taibe and nineteen Jews from the Tel Aviv suburb of Rishon Letsiyon; though most of the Arabs have studied Hebrew in school, not all of them have it fluently, and it is especially weak among the girls. None of the Jews speak Arabic at all, except for the phrases they have learned as part of their Hebrew slang.

Ariela believes that four days are essential for this. One-day workshops can be more destructive than none at all, since the teenagers often plunge immediately into political discussions that become vehicles of animosity. Stereotypes are confirmed, she notes. If you want to know that Jews are domineering, you will learn in a day that Jews are domineering. If you want to know that Arabs are passive, you will learn that Arabs are passive. An Arab girl remarked after one acrimonious session, "I always knew I hated Jews, but I didn't know why. Now I know why." And so Ariela and her colleagues here are devoted to stepping slowly toward politics. Only on the third day will political issues be joined. Until then, the process is devoted to establishing personal bonds on which sensitive discussions can be based.

Ariela, standing on a chair, is beginning by loosening up the mood, playing "recognition games" to break the uneasiness. She is asking each person in the circle to name a fruit, and then she chooses someone to stand in the middle and to announce all the kinds of fruit he would like to put into his fruit salad. When Ariela claps, everyone whose fruit has been mentioned must jump up and run to change seats with someone across the circle. She claps, and the Arab and Jewish youngsters run across the room, bump into each other, laugh, and drop into vacant spots.

Now she is telling the students to walk around the room and look into the eyes of people they don't know. "Just make eye contact and keep walking, without saying a word," she instructs. And they begin, most of them mustering up the courage to look at each other directly and quickly before moving on. A couple of the Arab girls look mostly at the floor. "Now," Ariela continues, "shake hands and say 'Marhaba' [Arabic for "hello"] or whatever. Make sure you go up to the people who look like they're embarrassed or shy."

They play a few more games, and then Ariela gives them a short lecture on the lack of funding, the primitive conditions, the need not to break things, the fact that the residents have built everything with their own hands, the rules about everyone participating in cleaning up. She explains that few people have the opportunity to spend time in a camp like this one, that the workshops are for their benefit and that they should take advantage of the four days. Pointing in the direction of the dormitory across a field, she says, "You can divide up in rooms as you like—boys and girls separately."

"Why?" ask a couple of Jewish girls, and they laugh.

"If we have common sleeping quarters," Ariela explains, "there won't be any Arab schools that will send their students here." Indeed, the Arab chaperon, a male teacher from the village, could persuade the parents of only seven of the class's twenty girls to allow them to come, and he has made such binding personal pledges to those reluctant fathers that he feels obliged to sit up nervously until three or four in the morning between the girls' and boys' sections of the hostel. Ariela suggests that the Jews and Arabs mix up together in rooms, and adds, "if you want to get the most out of it."

The Lebanon war, followed by the election of Rabbi Meir Kahane to the Knesset on a platform of hatred, had a complex impact on the willingness of Arabs and Jews to search for contact. Many of the programs gained impetus from the war even while some Arabs grew more skeptical about the prospects for reconciliation. The currents and counter-currents of attitude were enhanced by the peculiar nature of the battle in Lebanon.

When the Israeli army invaded Lebanon in 1982, young soldiers and older veterans of other, cleaner wars had to fight through refugee camps crowded with Palestinian families, had to shell the densely populated neighborhoods of West Beirut, had to look into the frightened eyes of Arab children. Their misgivings, which filtered into the larger society and accumulated gradually during that painful summer, came to a climax when the Phalangists, Israel's Lebanese Christian allies, massacred Palestinians in the Sabra and Shatila refugee camps of West Beirut in September 1982. A gathering storm of guilt and outrage burst from a large body of Israeli Jews. Enormous numbers—perhaps as many as 400,000, one out of every ten Israelis—demonstrated in Tel Aviv to press their demand that the government appoint a formal state commission of inquiry to define the scope of Israeli responsibility. In the complete absence of moral leadership from the country's governmental and religious hierarchies, the citizenry itself mobilized into an explosion of conscience unparalleled in the modern history of Western democracy. Nothing like it ever happened in the United States after American soldiers massacred Vietnamese at My Lai. And the exhilarating indignation of the Israeli people, springing from the deepest need for righteousness, created its own interaction with Jewish perceptions of Arabs. Suddenly the Palestinian had a human face behind the numbing label "terrorist." Suddenly Arab innocents stood close behind the facade of hostility. Suddenly Israelis doubted their own morality, a self-criticism in which some, such as Rabbi David Hartman, saw healthy signs. "Some things are happening here which are very important," he told me just a month after the massacre, "a shift toward an awareness that the internal quality of life in this society is really as important for security as a significant army is. The awareness that political and military decisions have to, in some way, take into account the moral purposes of our renewal. Israel demands that the voice of Isaiah be heard in the corridors of power, and if the voice of Isaiah is not heard in the corridors of power, then Israel has itself become a pagan nation."

The men who served as soldiers of Israel were as diverse as the society for which they fought, as callous, as stricken, as tough, as tortured as their compatriots at home. A few even admired their enemy, as Rami Givoni declared in a letter to the defense minister explaining why he had refused the army's order sending him to Lebanon a second time. He had fought house to house in the city of Sidon, encountering the old women who would ask after their sons, the Palestinians who suffered economically from the Lebanese, and he concluded, "I have no doubt that if I had grown up and had been educated in Sidon, in whose conquest I participated, I would have fought with full faith with the other side. In the atmosphere of a refugee camp I would surely have grown up a 'terrorist.' In the refugee camp of Ein Hilwe, youths fought, a few against the power of many, with bravery and self-dedication no less than the historic Jewish heroes on whose heroism I was educated. Young boys full of conviction fought unto death, carrying Russian [rocket] launchers. In groups, couples, and alone they stood against well-armed soldiers to stop the attack. I don't know if history makes comparisons, I don't know if the values of tradition and national honor allow parallels, but to me the fighters of the Palestinian underground in Ein Hilwe seemed to have no less courage than the fighters of Masada."

Others' humanism took more moderate forms. "Every kid who was running there, who was something between two and four years old, looked like my daughter," said Uri Maydan, a mechanical engineer and factory owner who went to Lebanon as a major in the supply corps. "When I looked at her, I thought about my daughter. And when I saw the fear in her eyes, I had a problem. It's one thing to fight against fighters, to kill them if it's necessary, to wound them, to do whatever is done in a war. And it's another thing to fight kids like this and to see them damaged. And there really were a lot of kids who were scared to death. That was something that was really hard to face." Then he used a curious turn of phrase. "The only Palestinians we have seen were women and children, and it's not working: You can't hate women and kids." It's not working. The old reflexes of rejection and hatred, the categorical imperatives of war—these were the mechanisms that were not working for Uri Maydan and some others.

Gidon Shamir, the book publisher who fought with an elite combat unit in the 1967 and 1973 wars as well as in Lebanon, remembered a Palestinian woman with a child, a girl of three who had been hit with three bullets in the chest. The father was a PLO guerrilla, and the Israeli commander was faced with a tough decision. Should he call in a rescue helicopter for the girl while the battle was raging? If he did not, she would surely die. If he did, the chopper might be shot down. He went ahead, and the helicopter flew in and evacuated the girl safely to a hospital in the Israeli city of Safed, where she survived.

After the massacre at Sabra and Shatila, Menachem Brinker happened to be lecturing at an army outpost in the mountains overlooking the Bekaa, the broad valley of eastern Lebanon. A teacher of philosophy and comparative literature at Tel Aviv University, Brinker was assigned duty as an education officer; he provided troops with some intellectual diversion during their monotonous duty. "Most of the soldiers I met were for a committee of investigation," he said. "The nearer you come to the front, the more dovish the soldiers. In the rear, more hawks. But you can find soldiers who are very chauvinist, very pro-Begin and -Sharon, in the combat units. One said, 'Now that the Phalangists have done their job, let them enter the West Bank.' So I asked him rhetorically, 'Why not after the West Bank have them enter Israel itself and deal with the opposition?' This stopped him. Arabs are one thing, Jews are another thing."

The Jews' moral debate over the war and the massacre—as over the later exposure of Jewish terrorism—focused not on the fate of the Arab victims but on the fate of the Jews themselves. It was an echo of Golda Meir's comment that she could forgive the Arabs for what they had done to Jews but could never forgive them for what they had made Jews do to Arabs. "I don't care if Arabs kill each other," said Uri Maydan. "I don't feel myself responsible for it. I feel very good about the war between Iraq and Iran—I'm not happy that there is a war anywhere in the world, but I don't care about the war between Iraq and Iran personally. The war between Iraq and Iran, in a way, is good for us. But I can't say the same thing about Sabra and Shatila, because in this case we were the responsible people there. Let Arabs kill themselves. I don't care if Arabs kill themselves in Jordan. But in Lebanon, we are responsible for the situation."

Indeed, if the Israelis' first few months in Lebanon gave the Palestinians a human face, the last year erased it. So vulnerable were Israeli troops, so jittery had they become from guerrilla attacks, that every Arab in Lebanon became a threat—every man, woman, and child, every man on his bicycle, every boy on his mule. Unable to distinguish between the friends and the enemies, many soldiers yearned to impose a grid of simplicity on the complexity, order on the ambiguity. One answer was found in Rabbi Meir Kahane's easy solution—expel all Arabs—an appeal that won the support of 42.1 percent of a sample of 600 young Jews, ages fifteen to eighteen, polled by the Van Leer Foundation in April 1985. By the end of their three years in Lebanon, many Israeli Jews had developed a contempt for the Arabs' display of viciousness. Blood was the only law in Lebanon. The suicide car-bombings, the slaughter along religious and ethnic lines, the disintegration of a state into the chaos of warring factions contributed strongly to the image of the Arab as a primitive who attached little value to human life. This seemed to generate two broad reactions among Israeli policy-makers. Some were inclined to stay pure by rejecting and withdrawing from the surrounding Arab world's sordid propensity for politics by violence; others were persuaded that Israel had to become more Middle Eastern to survive in the Middle East, more "Arab" to deal in the Arab world, more brutal and less honorable to make its way in the jungle.

The latter emotions, also felt among segments of the larger population, frightened some liberal-minded Jews. Some believed their dream for Israel was being lost; others were driven to action against the intolerance they felt was on the rise, an impression reinforced by the election in 1984 of Kahane as he preached the expulsion of the Arabs from Israel and the West Bank. The surge in his popularity provoked opposing moves in 1985 and 1986. The Knesset barred from future elections any political party preaching racism. Army Radio broadcast an eighteen-hour talkathon on which prominent Israelis denounced Kahane and his repugnant ideas. Several families of Jews slain by Arab terrorists rejected Kahane's bid to stage demonstrations of indignation and support outside their houses.

But the soul-searching had limited scope, in Meron Benvenisti's view. It embraced only a small fragment of Israeli Jews who remembered the dream. "I see my father, he is eighty-five. He is a broken man. He doesn't know what happened, what hit him. You see, he came here in 1911 from Greece. My mother came in 1921 from Lithuania. They say, 'What happened to my dream?' They are both socialists. They came here to build a new society, a just society. They believed it shouldn't be at the expense of the Arabs; they really believed that. And now when they see the turn, what is now the meaning of nationalism, and they can no longer reconcile it with humanistic values, they are broken."

Measuring the degree of backlash against intolerance is difficult. In Jewish high schools, some teachers were disturbed enough by youngsters' reactions to the Sabra and Shatila massacre to initiate programs to deal with the issue. One of them was Gideon Lehman, who teaches geography in a leading religious school in Jerusalem. "I was shocked in the beginning," he recalled, "when I heard a few students say, 'Oh, it's okay. They killed Arabs. Arabs are Arabs. You have to kill them.' I was shocked. And I said, 'We have to do some very deep educational work.' " He asked the principal to invite lecturers from the Hebrew University, and he himself spoke earnestly with his students. "I explained the Jewish way of looking at such a thing," he said. "At the time of Passover, we spill some drops of wine because you're not supposed to be very happy when your enemy is killed." His students responded variously to the lesson. "Some of them accepted it, some didn't. One said, 'But he's an enemy. In a couple of years I will go into the army, and that's one enemy less. I have more chance to live.' Someone said his grandfather was killed by Arabs in the '30s, and I said that they weren't the same Arabs. And he said, 'Yes, but it's revenge.' So I couldn't convince him."

Jews and Arabs working in programs of encounter and cooperation discerned an upsurge of interest among Jews in efforts to establish contact and understanding with Arabs. Many experienced Jewish teachers, alarmed by what they saw as a decidedly rightward drift in students over the years, grew more positive about joint Arab-Jewish projects. After the massacre, and again after Kahane's election, some Jews who had been lukewarm to the practice of visiting Arab schools, for example, began to see its virtues, and organizations such as Interns for Peace encountered somewhat less resistance to their attempts. Thus, the move to the right was softening the center and, to a point, activating the moderate left.

The Arab reactions to Lebanon and Kahane were somewhat more difficult to appraise. West Bank, Golan, and Gaza Arabs had never demonstrated much interest in formal contacts with Jews or in programs to foster mutual tolerance, and the Jews involved tended to concentrate on cooperation with Arabs in Israel proper, not those in the occupied territories. Among Israeli Arabs there seemed to be as many cross-currents as among Jews, with an increase in radical Palestinian nationalism on the one hand and a continued high degree of interest in contacts with the Jewish population on the other. The massacre persuaded many Israeli Arabs that their ugliest stereotypes of the Jews were valid, but the huge demonstration in Tel Aviv and the honest results of the investigatory commission also presented Arabs with a reassuring display of Jewish conscience, one that generated much comment by Arabs both in Israel and the West Bank. Some Israeli Arabs involved in joint programs insisted that Arab interest had not declined. Others felt a growth of bitterness.

A survey of attitudes among students in eleventh and twelfth grades showed a slow decline in Arab interest in contacts with Jews and conflicting trends in Jewish attitudes. Interviews done in schools in various towns and cities around the country in 1971, 1975, and 1984 and analyzed by John Hofman, of Haifa University's psychology department, found the proportions of Arab students wanting to cultivate relations with Jews declining from 88 percent in 1971 to 60 percent in 1975, then rising a statistically insignificant amount to 62 percent in 1984. Clearer drops were registered on the statement "I think contact is possible," which got agreement from 75 percent of the Arabs in 1971, 66 percent in 1975, and 55 percent in 1984, and on the statement "I think contact is desirable," which was endorsed by 86 percent of the Arabs in 1971, 73 percent in 1975, and 68 percent in 1984. Jews also registered a decline in these categories.

In 1971, 19 percent of the Jewish students favored cultivating relations with Arabs, a figure that rose to 25 percent in 1975 and 33 percent in 1984. On the other statements, however, the opposite trend was noted, with 78 percent of the Jews in 1971 agreeing that contact was possible, falling to 77 percent in 1975 and 71 percent in 1984. The proportions of Jews agreeing that contact was desirable began in 1971 at a high level of 97 percent, then dropped to 88 percent in 1975 and 85 percent in 1984.

The Arab and Jewish boys and girls are being divided into discussion groups of about ten each. As Ariela reads the names, two Jewish girls insist on staying together. Ariela resists, but the two are so determined that she finally relents. And the teenagers go off to their assigned places.

One group is led jointly by Hila, a plump Jewish woman with a British accent, and Taher, a slender, kindly faced Arab man who seems always to have a nice, slight smile. Both are obviously experienced in the finest techniques of group therapy, and as they assemble their teenagers they begin gently. The session is held in a small concrete room with whitewashed walls, two wooden benches, a battered foam-rubber mattress covered with a torn green cover, and a faded Oriental rug. One window is missing two of its four panes of glass, and the holes are covered with foggy plastic. There is no heat, and the raw cold penetrates.

The teenagers find places, some on the benches, others on the mattress and the floor. There are six Arabs, four boys and two girls, and four Jews, two girls and two boys. Hila begins by explaining in Hebrew, which Taher translates into Arabic, that she would like each person to name something quickly that he or she likes. "I like to sleep," *says Hila.*

"I like sports," *says Ronen, a Jewish boy.*

"Children," *says Ricky, a Jewish girl.*

"Music," *says Diab, an Arab boy with an impish grin.* "Rock music."

"Football," *says Nasser.*

"Football," *echoes Emad.*

"Children," *says Sefi, a Jewish boy with the dreamy look of a hippie.* "I like to love."

"Dance," *says Inbal, a pretty, dark-haired Jewish girl with a nose gone red in the cold.*

"Karate," *says Salman, a tall Arab of Bedouin background.*

"I like my name," *says Taher. And a Jewish boy explains that* taher *means "purity" in Hebrew.*

"Basketball," *says Faida, an Arab girl. The other Arab girl, Samira, sits looking shyly at the floor. She won't say anything.*

Now each one is taking a turn repeating another's name and trying to recall the thing that he or she likes. The Jews are pronouncing the Arabs' names with the French R's of Hebrew, and the Arabs are pronouncing the Jews' names with the rolling R's of Arabic. They are coaching each other, reminding each other, laughing and warming to each other.

Hila stands and holds a sheet of paper high, explaining that when she drops it and calls a person's name, he must try to catch the paper before it floats to the ground. She begins. The paper sinks slowly as one after another dives to intercept it amid the cheers of the others.

Taher then suggests a way of remembering names. Everyone will say his name and then explain its significance and meaning.

Ronen: As far as I know it has no connection to anything. It means "singer."

Ricky: It doesn't have any meaning. Ricky comes from Rivka—it's a name from the Bible.

Diab: It means "light." It's a rare name, the name of an Egyptian announcer my father listened to over the radio.

Nasser: They called me Nasser after the Egyptian president.

Taher explains to the Jews that if you were an Arab born in '67 or '68, Nasser was a hero, and when he spoke, the whole street would be quiet, with everyone inside listening to him on the radio.

Emad: Someone who is independent.

Sefi: I was born on the eleventh of Adar—that's memorial day—to the memory of dead Israeli fighters. It's an important day. My name was Yosef. They called me Yosef because of my grandfather, who died when my father was three. He drowned in the Sea of Galilee.

Inbal: It means a clapper on a bell. I was given it because my mother liked it. I laughed a lot.

Salman: Comes from the Arabic meaning someone who was saved and came out whole.

Faida: It is "sacrifice." I don't know where I got it from.

Samira is staring at the floor in silence again, too shy to speak. They wait for a while, hoping the heavy quiet will break her reluctance. But it does not, and finally Taher explains that her name means "friends." In embarrassed discomfort, Samira and Faida smile and giggle together.

Hila: My name means "halo."

The late 1970s and early 1980s saw some articulate Israeli Jews in a spasm of self-flagellation. As if the sins of intolerance and brutality toward Arabs could be expiated by screams of outrage, they attacked themselves in newspapers, poetry, theater, and film using the most sacred symbols, turning the most vitriolic anti-Semitic imagery against their own society. After the arrest of the Jewish settlers accused of terrorism against Arabs. Amos Kenan wrote in the Tel Aviv daily *Yediot Ahronot* that Israel had become Goliath. "You can murder only people. Arabs, in Israel 1984, are not people. They are drugged roaches," he said in a paraphrase of Raphael Eitan's metaphor. "You don't murder roaches. At best, you exterminate roaches. The exterminator is a nice guy, his name is Goliath, and he is the king of Israel. Once upon a time, a long time ago, Israel had a different king. He was a red-headed lad with beautiful eyes and pleasant songs. Israel 1984 is not the state of the Jews and therefore doesn't need a king with pleasant songs. Israel 1984 is the land of the Philistines and therefore has a king armed from head to toe."

Other indictments come in other forms. The poet Yitzhak Laor writes in one verse, "In our matzo is the blood of Palestinian children," a remarkable allusion to the blood libel to which Jews have been subjected through the ages. A film entitled *The Night the King Was Born* portrays two army officers and an Orthodox merchant forcing the Arab Abu-Isa to give up his lands. Settlers in skullcaps join the officers in raiding the Arab's house during the night; they hit and kick him and force him to sign a contract. The scene of the Arab kissing the officer's feet was cut by the censor.

The censorship board comprises civilians who rule on matters of taste, as distinct from the military censor, who looks for security breaches, and the Cabinet censorship committee, which excises small and large embarrassments from manuscripts by current or former government officials. As Jews have increasingly expressed their social radicalism through theater and film, the censorship committee has found itself in growing opposition to certain scenes and passages. In *The Patriot*, a satire by Hanoch Levin, the censor took out a few choice and painful lines in a series of zany skits portraying a scheming Jew, a kind of Mr. Ugly Israeli, who tortures Arabs by burning them with Sabbath candles and finally emigrates to America.

"Yes, pure children," he muses in a reflection on the warmth of tradition. "Modesty. Kashrut. Love of Eretz Israel. The splendor of God. Shabbat. Sabbath candles. Ah, Sabbath candles. That picture, that grabs the heart: the whole family around the table. Faces shining with splendor. On the table a white tablecloth, covered challas, lit Sabbath candles. In the yard, Ahmed. We call him. He comes in. 'Shabbat Shalom, Ahmed.' 'Gut Shabbes, sir.' 'Come, come, get closer, Ahmed. These are Sabbath candles.' " The censorship committee then deleted the following: " 'Have you ever seen Sabbath candles?' The years unwind backward. Someone pulls his hand forward, puts one finger over the candle flame. The smell of roasting meat. The finger blackens." The conclusion is left standing: "Ahmed sings Sabbath songs. All of us, the whole family, all the children, all the children of Israel, join him." And so, by the deletion of a few lines, the censors have rendered a searing, ugly scene into a pretty picture.

Enough remains elsewhere to convey the vicious self-indictment, however. When Lahav applies to the Lands Administration to buy some acreage in Israel, the bureaucrat questions his patriotism in view of his plans to go to America. Of course he is a patriot, Lahav insists. Then kick the Arab boy polishing your shoes, orders the bureaucrat. Lahav tries to get up the hostile feelings he needs to do it, but the boy is insufferably obsequious, refusing to be provoked even when Lahav says, "I'll fuck your sister, the whore."

"Welcome, thank you . . ." the boy replies.

"Your mother, the whore?" But Mahmoud will not express hostility. Lahav raises his foot to kick him, and the boy kisses his shoe and licks it.

"Mr. Administrator, I can't kick Mahmoud's face."

"I can't sell you a plot of our forefather's bequest," the bureaucrat replies.

"Mahmoud, they're not giving me land," Lahav declares. "We won't be neighbors. What will you do? How will you support yourself in this empty wilderness? Without me you won't have bread. You'll go out to rob, what else? Do you have a choice? I'll be doing my studies and you'll go and murder whoever remains here. And who remains? My mother! My old, beloved mother! Oh, Momma, they're slaughtering my mother, burying my mother, Oh, Momma, Momma, God will avenge your blood!" And he kicks Mahmoud.

"We're selling you the land you requested," says the administrator.

But Lahav, in a trance, continues in a passage and a song deleted by the censor:

We will avenge your blood and the blood of all our massacred family, like then, Momma, when your little brother, a boy, stood alone against the German, in the evening, in the field, and the German aimed a rifle at his face, and your little brother, trembling from fear said: (Lahav sings)

Don't shoot.
I have a mother.
She's waiting for me at home.
I haven't eaten
dinner yet.
Don't kill me,
I'm a boy.
I'm a person like you.
What have I done?
What would it matter to you
if I lived on?

The censorship committee was obviously offended by the parallel between the Israeli and the German, between the Arab boy and the Jewish boy. It allowed only Mahmoud to sing the song, after which Lahav shoots the boy, who falls and dies.

In this current genre of Israeli fiction and satire, the former patterns of Hebrew literature are reversed. The Arab is made to look better than the Jew—kinder, more tolerant, less hostile. Yehuda Litany, for example, an Israeli-born Jewish journalist who has covered the West Bank and other subjects for *Haaretz* and *The Jerusalem Post*, turned to writing short stories because he found fiction the only medium in which he seemed able to capture the true nuances of Arab-Jewish tensions, friendships, and fears. In one, "Stranded Among Olives," a Jew driving home from his son's house on a West Bank settlement suffers a mechanical breakdown on a deserted stretch of road. It is late at night and he is terrified, sure that Arabs will come and murder him. He sees figures in the shadows through his car window, knows that the end is near, and is then surprised when they invite him cordially to stay at their house overnight. Discovering that he is a lawyer, they insist that God has sent him to them, for they need a Jewish lawyer to take their case against a nearby settlement that is behind a move to confiscate their land. Their kindness and hospitality are generous, and they see him home safely the next morning. He is touched by their plight and by their warmth and is left in a reflective mood, pondering whether to help them.

In another Litany story, "Thy Love to Me Was Wonderful," an Arab, Hussein, encounters a Jewish friend from college days, visiting him and his wife in their comfortable house. For long years the Arab, a poet, has heard nothing from his friend and has been hurt by the silence. The Jew, to his own embarrassment, has taken over his father-in-law's construction business and is making money building Jewish settlements in the West Bank. He has sworn to stop it, but his wife—shrill, hateful of Arabs— nags him on. She resents his friendship with the Arab poet, who has canceled a reading in Nazareth to spend the evening with them. The reunion, touching and awkward, is ultimately soured by the wife, who carps at them both about a mutual Arab friend who is now with the PLO in Europe. "He deserves to be shot in the head, filthy murderer!" she shrieks. Her husband tries to calm her, explaining that their PLO acquaintance is not a murderer. But Hussein sees that the visit is doomed; he excuses himself and leaves in a whirl of sorry bitterness. He drives for a while, then stops at a café where two guys from his village are drinking coffee. They accuse him jokingly of looking pale, of spending his nights with Jewish girls. "It's all because of the Jewish girls, *ya Hussein*," one says. "They're pretty, the daughters of the devil."

"Daughters of the devil, by God," Hussein agrees.

Litany has condemned the Jew and exonerated the Arab. But he has also conveyed the texture of truth. Like other, more notable and skilled Israeli writers—A. B. Yehoshua and Amos Oz, for example—he etches sharp portraits of individuals caught and torn by larger forces. And he has betrayed a vision in these stories, a yearning for humaneness.

One can look in vain for comparable writing on the Arab side. What theater and literature exists among the Palestinians in Israel, the West Bank, and Gaza is rarely self-critical, usually polemical within the limits of Israeli censorship, and never—that I could find—touched with that fine sense of decency around which the dissenting Jews spin their works. Perhaps it is morally easier to be the oppressed than the oppressor. Perhaps because the Palestinians have no state of their own where they can feel secure enough for introspection, perhaps because they live dispersed, under occupation, or as citizens of the Jewish state, they cannot muster the outrage over their own failings that the Jews can over theirs. Perhaps a smugness of suffering comes from chafing under the yoke.

El-Hakawati, an Arab theater troupe in East Jerusalem, does some clever, wacky plays and skits as slapstick commentaries on the political conundrum. One, called *The 1001 Nights of a Stone Thrower*, makes fun of every character on the stage of conflict—the military governor, the Arab money changer, the Arab nationalist, the Israeli tour guide, who announces, "On the lefthand side of the bus you can see one of the Arab neighborhoods that still remains. The taking of photographs is permitted, but the Ministry of Tourism suggests that you not eat or drink anything unless it is properly packaged." An Arab informer appears with eyes pasted all over him, and an Israeli officer seems more bumbling than threatening. When the young Arab Nassour is arrested and the noose is placed around his neck, villagers argue over who is to blame, and their arguments sound like a broken record with phrases repeated, cut off, and repeated, as the Arab world at large bleats hypocritically about the plight of the Palestinians. Nassour is saved when someone cuts the rope. The play is loud and witty, running at a circus pace. But in the end, as after the last act of a spectacular, it contains no moral agony.

One of the major productions of the troupe, *Ali the Galilean*, does a cutting commentary on the state of Arabs who are citizens of Israel. Written and directed by François Abu-Salem, a soft-spoken East Jerusalemite and not an Israeli citizen, it is the story of an Israeli Arab who works at a Tel Aviv felafel stand, tries for a while to pass as a Jew, and ends up holding on to a bit of his Arab identity out of sheer stubbornness. The Jews are portrayed as too arrogant to be clever enough to humiliate him. Ed Grossman, writing in *The Jerusalem Post*, found messages both for Arabs and Jews, but they were far shallower than the search for ethics seen in Jewish theater. To Arabs, "Keep your chins up and hang onto your culture, you poor good-for-nothings," as Grossman put it. To Jews, "Here's what you look like to the people who clean your streets and bake your bread."

In the concrete room, the loosening-up games are finished, and it is time to move closer together. Hila and Taher, the co-leaders of the group, are asking that the teenagers now divide themselves into pairs or threes to spend four or five minutes finding things they have in common. The youngsters group themselves, mixing Jews and Arabs, and talk quietly.

Hila and Taher take these minutes to explain softly to me that a gap always exists at the beginning of these sessions between the Jewish and Arab styles. The Arabs are discouraged in schools from coming forward with their own opinions, and the Jews are urged in their classrooms to do so. The workshops obviously operate more in the style of the Jewish schools, except with an unflagging commitment to listening: Everyone's view is respected. Arab girls in particular have trouble with this, since they are severely circumscribed both at home and at school. Suddenly released from the restraints, some girls retreat into painful shyness, as the two in this group, and some practically run the discussions. Often, when they finally get up the courage to break out, they do so with expressions of extreme Palestinian nationalism.

The youngsters are coming back to sit together again, and the leaders are asking for reports on their small discussions. Taher begins with Diab, the dark Arab boy with dancing eyes. "What did Ricky tell you?" Ricky is a Jewish girl with a plain, pleasant face and hair to her shoulders, and she listens closely while Diab explains in Hebrew. "She's the oldest sister in her family," he says. "They live in apartments, not in houses like us. She likes to read books. She has a big dog. She used to play the piano—did it for five years but hasn't done it for four years."

Ricky then describes Diab. "He has five brothers, likes to play basketball. He doesn't like to lose." Taber asks her if she feels she now knows Diab better than she does any of the other Arabs from Taibe. "Yes," Ricky says. "We're unhappy that there's no contact between Jews and Arabs on a social plane."

The rest of the youngsters exchange information. Nasser reports that Ronen, a good-looking and neatly groomed Jewish boy with hair much shorter than his classmates', spends vacations scuba-diving at the Red Sea reefs near Eilat. He has one brother and one girlfriend, and he likes sports. Ronen's description of Nasser, a quiet and reserved boy, includes the fact that six people live in his house, and the real shocker: "They're not allowed to have girlfriends until the age of twenty-one!"

"No, absolutely not," offers Salman.

"What did you have in common?" Taber asks.

"I guess we didn't talk that much," says Ronen. "It's very hard to talk." Taber then turns to Samira, who practically disintegrates with shyness. She just sits looking at her knee in long silence.

The Arab boy Emad takes up the conversation, saying that he and Inbal, the pretty Jewish girl, have found that they have sports in common. "I like volleyball, football," Inbal volunteers. Taber tries again to get Samira to speak, but she sits silently, her head tucked into her shoulders as she slumps with a thin smile of nervous agony. Her small cluster included Inbal and Emad. "He has eight brothers and five sisters," Inbal says of Emad. "Neither of their mothers works. They're farmers. They grow strawberries. It's really wonderful. It was hard to find something in common with Samira because she didn't talk."

Faida, the Arab girl who wears a long black braid tied with a blue ribbon, is slightly less withdrawn, and she musters the courage to take her turn. She has been with Sefi, the long-haired Jewish boy, and Salman. While looking at the floor, she manages to get one sentence out about Sefi. "He studies math and sociology, with a high IQ," she says in Arabic. Taber translates.

Sefi then reports at some length on Salman, who feels like leaving Taibe so he can go to a better school and be free. On Faida: "She really likes Arabic poetry," says Sefi, searching for common ground, "and I really like Arabic poetry." Sefi and Salman are horsing around together already, joking and laughing and pushing each other like old buddies. Slowly, slowly, something is beginning to happen beneath the gauze of inhibition.

Something is also beginning to happen in Israeli society at large. Anti-Arab attitudes that have long been blended smoothly into conventional wisdom are now becoming visible to some Jews as stark stereotypes and epithets of injustice. The camouflage no longer works quite as well: A few people are starting to notice ugliness in the landscape of general acceptance. Much as American whites were slowly sensitized to the anti-black images that had become integral to American literature, film, and language, a small minority of Israeli Jews can now see the bigotry that rests embedded in Israeli culture. Danny Rubinstein, the journalist, has witnessed the evolution within himself.

"It was in '59," he recalled. "In my class at Hebrew University there were about three or four Arab students. Looking in retrospect, there was one episode that had quite an effect on me. One of those students was from an Arab village, Kfar Qara. He asked me to help him do some homework, and there was a place where you could make noise and smoke cigarettes, a study room. I started to help him. Next to us there was another group of students; they were doing the same homework. One of the students started to shout at the other, 'You are doing an Arab job, it's an Arab job.' An Arab job in our slang means not a good job. *Avoda Aravit.* Done badly. Not serious. So they said, 'It's an Arab job. You have to rewrite it, because if you give it to the professor, it's an Arab job.' I didn't notice it. For me it was something usual. This term 'Arab job' was normal.

"My Arab friend asked, 'Tell me, what does it mean, Arab job? It means that we Arabs can't do anything right? It's not good?' and I told him, well, yes, and he was really angry, and he turned to this guy and told him, 'Listen, why do you use this term, Arab job? You mean that Arabs can't do it well?' And this guy told him, 'It's none of your business.' And he said, 'I asked you,' and they started to argue. And this guy, the Jewish guy, started to shout, 'Well, listen, it's a Jewish state here, my father came from the Holocaust to build it, and I'll use any term that I want here and don't tell me.' I expected that this guy would apologize and say, 'I'm sorry, I didn't mean to insult you.' But he didn't; the opposite; he defended himself and said, 'You don't have any right to open your mouth here. If you want to learn, you can learn in Damascus or you can learn in Cairo.'

"I really don't know if it was because in this situation I was a friend of the Arab student, but I started to defend him," Danny continued. "I started to defend this guy only because I was studying with him. We started to push each other; somebody came to help." An anti-Arab slur that Danny had accepted as a natural part of language and perception suddenly leaped out at him as an item of bigotry. "I remember, it came to my mind that there is something wrong with this approach. It was really in my first days at the university. Afterwards, I became more and more liberal."

A Jew does not have to grow up in Israel to acquire anti-Arab biases. "Karen," a young woman from North Carolina whose parents were involved in the civil-rights movement, recalled that her family had taught her tolerance for blacks and, perhaps unconsciously, prejudice toward Arabs. During the '60s, her parents risked going to jail, and they supported boycotts of segregated stores. "I remember, every time we would go out to eat we would check the restaurants before going in to see if they had a sign up saying, 'We reserve the right to refuse service,' " she said.

But she confronted their anti-Arab attitudes, and her own fears, during a high-school summer seminar run by the National Science Foundation. The list of students sent beforehand contained the name of a girl who was to be Karen's roommate; she had an Arab name. "When my mother saw that there was a girl with an Arab last name, she was concerned," Karen recalled. "What I gathered from her was that she was afraid." She said, 'It is better that you're not in the same room with this person,' out of this fear of something—I don't know what it was. Anyway, it was a six-week program, and we became friendly during the time." The girl was Lebanese American. "I don't think we ever really had any discussion about Arabs and Jews, but I remember at one point she took me outside of the university town to a place where there was a Lebanese restaurant, and took me into it. I remember very distinctly that that was my first experience in that kind of a setting, in this whole world that she was part of." At first, Karen felt a discomfort that seems alien to her now. She has moved to Israel with her family, has become active on the political left, and has made many close Arab friends.

The experience prompted her to look back on the origins of her attitudes about Arabs. She traced them partly to the Hebrew school she attended once a week in the United States. "I think that mostly the way I absorbed information about Arabs was lack of information," she said. "That is, the whole story about Israel was told as if Arabs didn't exist at all. I vaguely remember what I was taught about Israel at that point. I was taught that the Arabs were our enemy. I don't remember whether I even knew there was such a thing as Palestinians at that point. So, a very liberal background on the one hand and a lot of misinformation and lack of information on the other hand."

Some Arabs have gone through similar shifts as individuals, but Palestinians engage in less criticism than Jews of their culturally sanctioned prejudices. The changes I discerned in specific Arabs I knew during my five years in Jerusalem were usually expressed in political terms as a softening of the line, a growing appreciation of the variety of personalities and attitudes among the Jews.

Raymonda Tawil, the writer and Palestinian nationalist from the West Bank town of Ramallah, could see the small eddies of sensitivity and tolerance against the great currents of conflict. In her effusive style of embellishment, she displayed her own evolution. She was always more open-minded and flexible than many other visible Palestinian figures, but when I first met her in 1979, her conversation was devoted mostly to articulating the cause of suffering by Arabs on the West Bank. By the time I said good-bye to her in 1984, she seemed most concerned with the possibilities for intellectual and emotional contact between Arabs and Jews. "You can't find a society where the young people are so open-minded," she said of Israel, in typical exaggeration. "I have been going around giving speeches to Israelis, and I find a lot of sympathy on a human level. I said to people in Tel Aviv, 'If you come not with a gun but to live among us, you will be welcome.' The audience applauded. It was amazing." I suppose I raised an eyebrow at all this rose-colored wishfulness, for Raymonda caught my skepticism and added, "I went to Catholic school. Maybe it's the influence of trying to find the angel and not the devil."

Muhammad Bakri's light-blue eyes have a penetrating drowsiness. He is an Israeli-Arab actor, and his craggy face and wild, curly hair give him the look of a prophet. Indeed, at the time we sat in a Jerusalem café together, he was shooting a film in which he played Jeremiah the Prophet. "I hate religion," he said. "I hate my religion [Islam], I hate the Jewish religion. But I find some good and right smells about the Jews in Jerusalem. I am not speaking about Gush Emunim," he said in reference to the extreme-right-wing group of nationalist settlers. "I'm speaking about the traditional Jerusalem man who was born here. Something about him is very healthy, very right. The real Sabras—because they love the place, they love it, they know the land, they know the smell. I prefer them to the left in Tel Aviv. There is a big difference between the Jewish and the Israeli mentality. I prefer the Jewish mentality. Israel is more American in tempo. Jewish is more serious-minded, asking the right questions and bothered by the right things."

Bakri was not brought up to think this way. He was born in a village near Akko, and his experience with Jews was as narrow as that of many other Arabs; the only Jews he saw as a boy were policemen and soldiers. "Whenever I was crying, my mother said, 'Shhh. Police outside.' It's a saying, like 'Good morning.' It was scary to see the army; we'd always look from a distance."

He studied at Tel Aviv University, began in the theater, got to know many different Jews, and reached a level of moderation, sophistication. "We accept the Jewish people," he said, "and they do not accept us. And one of the proofs is the language: I know their language and they don't know my language. If I like your language, I like you. I like to speak Hebrew. It's one of the ways I can accept you. A lot of Palestinians now want to live with the Israelis. Not to live in one house, but they think Israelis have the right to live here and not to go to the sea. I don't want to kill you, so why do you say I'm a murderer? I know your language."

In collaboration with a Jewish actor, Bakri was in the process of writing an allegorical play "about two brothers, one Arab and one Jewish," as he put it, somewhat cryptically. The characters were "trying to find a way to prove that we can live together, especially in this hell, even if we hate each other," he explained. This, in a sense, was also a theme of the film he had just finished, *Behind the Walls*, an Israeli production that became an item of intense discussion when it was released in 1984.

The plot centers on two cells in an Israeli prison, one of Jewish criminals, the other of Arab terrorists. Although in reality, Arab "security prisoners" are almost never mixed with Jewish inmates, the film allows them contact on the cell block, in the dining hall, even across the corridor of a wing devoted to solitary confinement. The prison becomes a metaphor. A Jew convicted of having connections with the PLO meets hostility and threats of homosexual rape from the other Jews, who nickname him "PLO" and tell him brutally that he belongs in the Arabs' cell. The Arabs' reaction to him is divided. "They're all the same," an Arab extremist says of the Jews; Bakri, playing a relatively moderate Palestinian leader named Issam, retorts that the real similarity is between extremist Arabs and right-wing Jews.

The friction in the prison flares into a fight while the inmates are watching a television report on a terrorist attack in which Jewish children have died. And in the melee an Arab urges that a Jew who has insulted him be killed. Back in their cell, the Arabs debate the question; Issam dissuades them, arguing that a murder would simply play into the hands of the jailers, who are fostering violence between the groups of prisoners as a method of control. But the warden has the Jew murdered, frames the Arabs, and thus provokes the Jews into attacking Arab inmates. As Issam and the Jewish leader, Uri, are in solitary, they speak across the corridor and look through the bars into each other's eyes. Some bond of understanding is formed. In the end, they stand together in the mess hall, drop their metal trays clattering to the floor, and bring their fellow Arab and Jewish inmates together in a hunger strike against their jailers. Imprisoned together, the Arabs and Jews realize that they share a common plight, a cause.

It is raining, and the drops roll down the outside of the big windows, blurring the green landscape beyond. The large, square meeting room is full of music from a tape recorder, music that moves from folk to rock to Arab tunes to classical. Most of the teenagers are paired, one Arab and one Jew to each big sheet of brown paper, and they are painting with watercolors, designing their shapes and hues according to what they feel about the music they are hearing. No words may pass between them. Expression comes only at the tip of a brush.

For the most part the Arabs and Jews are not really cooperating but are merely painting their own pictures on different parts of the same piece of paper. Always, Hila and Taher observe, the Jews paint more abstractly, the Arabs more concretely—a result of contrasts in training in school. The differences are accentuated here by the special, counter-cultural nature of these Jewish students, who are not typical of the Jews who usually come to these workshops—and certainly not of Israeli Jews as a whole. These teenagers are more radical politically, more individualistic, less conformist in their dress and manner. One boy has a shaved head and a single huge, round earring. A girl wears a skirt made of orange rags. Many of the youngsters smoke. The Arab kids seem so straight by contrast.

The Arabs are drawing houses, trees, suns, skies. The Jews are painting in a riot of colors and designs. Ricky and an Arab girl are paired, Ricky doing lovely patterns of blue and green and yellow, the Arab girl drawing, at another point on the same piece of paper, a beautiful brown bird with a long beak. Two Arabs working together are doing two flags—Israeli and Palestinian next to each other. Faida paints a red flower while a Jewish girl on her left does an assortment of bright, warm colors. Then Diab and a Jewish girl begin to cooperate—a yellow sun by Diab floats in the upper-right-hand corner, above mishmashes of color by the Jewish girl. Each paints in the other's picture until the colors below begin to suggest earth and grass, the sun above a brighter light and a soaring mood. At another table, an Arab girl who did a picture of a blonde is now working with a Jewish girl, painting an abstraction, clearly allowing herself to be influenced by the Jew. Beginning at opposite ends of the paper, they paint toward the middle, two explosions of reds and blues and oranges until they overlap in the center in a smear of dark browns and reds.

The two Arab boys have finished their flags. Beneath them, they have drawn the words, in Hebrew, "We Want Peace." Above them, they have painted a dove with an olive branch.

It is the morning of the second day.

If learning the other's language is a form of recognition, as Muhammad Bakri believes, Israeli Jews have not done very well in regard to the great sea of Arabs who surround the tiny Jewish state. The school system, which requires all Israeli Arabs to study Hebrew extensively, makes no such demand on Jews for Arabic. Campaigns launched from time to time for compulsory Arabic have fallen under the weight of a Jewish ethnocentrism still raw from the defensive and vulnerable sense of siege and rejection. The attainment of Jewish statehood is too new, the rebirth of Hebrew too fresh. Even an American who lives in Israel for a few years finds himself castigated, as I can attest, for not having learned Hebrew well. The criticism is often laced with a deeper hurt, a feeling that since learning language constitutes acceptance, not learning it represents denial. And so language carries the burden of existence and identity.

Just under 20 percent of all Jewish pupils were studying Arabic in 1984, a figure that was in a slight decline. About half the elementary schools required that Arabic be studied from the fourth grade, and in most of the others it was not offered at all. Junior-high-school students could take Arabic as an elective, and about 30 to 35 percent did so, according to Moshe Gargir, head of Arabic teaching in the school system. Few high-school students, concentrating on courses for the matriculation exams, bothered with Arabic. Only 5.1 percent of the seniors in secular, academic high schools and 1.9 percent in religious schools studied Arabic seriously in 1982–83, according to the Central Bureau of Statistics. The numbers had become symbols of a great vacuum, a profound void in educating young Jews about the people with whom they were destined to live.

Of all the scattered, fragmented efforts to revise Jewish and Arab thinking about each other, the greatest potential impact is carried by an ambitious program to reform the curriculum in Israel's schools. Conceived in 1981 out of alarm at the bigotry being bred in the country's classrooms, the project seeks to excise negative stereotypes from textbooks, expose Jewish pupils to Arab literature and culture, educate both Jews and Arabs in the democratic principles of civic equality, and fill the schools' great gap of silence on the pluralism that now characterizes relationships between the two groups. The Ministry of Education gave formal endorsement in 1983 to the program, which has been developed and organized primarily by Alouph Hareven of the Van Leer Foundation, a private institution and conference center in Jerusalem. But the obstacles posed by deeply ingrained attitudes and financial limitations have impeded progress and raised questions about how broad the reforms can ultimately be.

Since the founding of the state, the Israeli school system has simply ignored the complex multiplicity of relations between Jews and Arabs. "For thirty-five preceding years," said Hareven, "there has been no education at all. Pupils would go through twelve years without a single hour devoted to the question that every sixth Israeli is an Arab and that we live in a region where our historical destiny is to live with Arabs. A modern Israeli will have to develop a capacity to live in a multi-cultured society on the basis of equality. We believe we must educate young children not to categorize all Arabs instinctively as enemies." The problem, he explained, was symbolized by the title of a high-school textbook published after the peace treaty with Egypt, *The Arab-Israeli Conflict*. The new textbook, written under his guidance, is called *To Live Together*. "We are moving from a first generation of Israelis in which our relations with Arabs were contained mainly in terms of conflict," he said. "All our perceptions were channeled mainly by conflict." And in some sense his effort here has an autobiographical overtone, for Hareven himself spent most of his career as a military-intelligence officer and a strategic analyst. "For the first thirty years of my professional life I dealt with the conflict side of the relationship," he observed, "and now I've changed course."

But getting the school system to change course is something else. Hareven and other educational specialists are convinced that the curriculum has to be revised from kindergarten through the twelfth grade in many subject areas, including history, geography, literature, and civics. "The centerpiece is the recognition of Arab culture in its own terms, on the basis of equality," he declared. Two separate curricular projects have been conceived, one for the Jewish and the other for the Arab schools; the Jewish one, seen as the more urgent, advanced farther in the first years. By 1985, parts of the new curriculum for Jewish students had been tested in several hundred eleventh-grade classes around the country, teachers were being trained to deal with the sensitive material, new textbooks were being written, short stories on Arab-Jewish relations were being collected, and a series of prime-time television programs fostering tolerance was in preparation. Some new children's literature portraying Arabs in human terms was written for Jewish youngsters, most notably *Nadia*, by Galila Ronfeder, the story of a fourteen-year-old Arab girl who goes to a Jewish boarding school; it received praise from Arab as well as Jewish educators, became a best-seller, and was made into a film. A picture book for elementary pupils on an Arab family was also in the works, and a Hebrew reader was published with about twenty short stories by Arab writers.

The efforts drew support from key, high-ranking education officials and significant groups of teachers. But they were also undermined by serious resistance from some segments of the Jewish educational bureaucracy, especially teachers and principals of religious schools, where the most work was needed. In 1985 the head of the Education Ministry's religious schools barred joint Arab-Jewish activities. When the program's proponents pressed, he and the country's chief rabbis agreed to permit meetings between Arab and Jewish youngsters who were segregated by sex—no mixed groups, for fear of intermarriage.

This opposition came despite a firmly worded directive of February 1, 1984, from the Education Ministry's director general on the principles and advisability of the program. The need was described in the formulation of a simple truth: "Arab citizens will always live among us and within our society, and Arab nations will always be neighbors of Israel. Evading both these issues in education means raising the young generation on the basis of ignorance and alienation in regard to issues which will always be at the center of our existence." The official directive went on to lay out sweeping goals to be pursued from kindergarten through twelfth grade: "Pupils should acquire extensive knowledge about the history of the Arab nations, their language and literature, their past and present culture, Islam (and Christianity), and Arab-Islamic art. . . . Our pupils (Arab and Jewish) should acquire an openness toward other cultures, a readiness to become acquainted with them, to understand them, and to respect them, even though they are different from one's own national culture, and though they may at times seem strange. Our pupils should understand that a different and foreign culture is neither superior nor inferior to our own culture, and that all nations and communities have a right to develop their own culture, also within one state. Above all, our pupils must be brought up on the firm recognition that every man is created in God's image, and that every man must be respected as a human being, even though he may belong to another nation, and even though he may be politically our enemy. . . . We must educate our pupils to listen to others . . . to debate with tolerance and patience . . . and to develop a culture of discussion."

To rewrite textbooks, produce new volumes, develop curricula, conduct teacher-training programs, computerize the study of Arabic, and introduce other programs, a budget of about $3.73 million over three years, 1985–87, was drawn up by Hareven. But, amazingly, the major institutions that were in a position to finance the effort refused to do so. Only the Ford Foundation provided consistently generous funding—totaling more than $400,000 through 1986—supplemented by large grants from the Living Together Fund in Australia and the Buxenbaum Fund in Tel Aviv. The Israeli government, through the Education Ministry, provided only $50,000 a year. The Van Leer Foundation gave $75,000 annually. The Anti-Defamation League of B'nai B'rith sponsored a three-year effort in technical colleges to combat prejudices. But the United Jewish Appeal, which usually collects more than $300 million a year for Israel from American Jews, refused to contribute anything to the project.[86] "So far, Jewish organizations have been quite a disappointment," Hareven said. "They all pay lip service to fighting against prejudice," he noted, but "are reluctant to come to grips with the changing public climate in Israel" because that "may reflect on the image of Israel they prefer to retain." In other words, he seemed to be saying, they don't know what's going on, and they don't want to know. The United States Agency for International Development, which for years has funneled more than a billion dollars annually from American taxpayers into the Israeli treasury, also resisted funding the program to promote peaceful coexistence between the Arabs and Jews of Israel.[87] Only after considerable pressure did A.I.D. finally give three annual $40,000 grants for a teachers' training program, only a shadow of the contribution Hareven had sought.

To raise the alarm and bolster support for the project, the Van Leer Foundation commissioned a study of Jewish adolescents' attitudes toward democratic principles. Evidence had grown since the late 1970s that the central precepts of democracy were neither well understood nor widely endorsed by Jewish teenagers, a shortcoming with direct implications for their ideas about how Arabs in the society should be treated. Here was the confluence of two questions—attitudes toward democracy and toward Arabs. A major basis of the new curriculum was to be the equality of citizenship shared by both Jews and Arabs inside Israel. Their supposed civic equality formed the framework for much of the teaching of tolerance. And so the research effort on adolescents had the effect of highlighting the failure of the school system to impart democratic values to Israeli youth, a dangerous deficiency that worried a broader spectrum of educators than the narrower issue of youths' feelings about Arabs.

In August 1984, the Dahaf Research Institute conducted face-to-face interviews with 651 Jewish youngsters, ages fifteen through eighteen. Sixty percent said that they thought Israeli Arabs were not entitled to fully equal rights with Jews, 47 percent favored reducing Arabs' rights, and 42 percent favored restricting democracy to make it possible to deny civil rights to Arabs; 42 percent also supported a reduction in the rights of all non-Jewish citizens. Although "democracy" remained an attractive symbol, with relatively few endorsing statements explicitly opposing "democracy," fairly high numbers did endorse ideas anathema to democracy when the word itself wasn't used. Thus, for example, 44 percent favored a law prohibiting criticism of the government in the press regarding all matters that involved relations with the Arabs.

The researchers also found anti-democratic attitudes greater among the religious than among the secular; freedom to criticize the government was endorsed by 71.1 percent of the secular and only 59.9 percent of the religious youngsters, a variation visible in the degrees of resistance shown to the new curriculum. Aryeh Shoval, the Education Ministry's deputy director general in charge of pushing the program, could see the debate shaping up in meetings of district superintendents and ministry officials. "At the first meeting of Jerusalem inspectors [superintendents], a rabbi talked of coexistence based on Halakha," Shoval recalled. But then he added, "Many other people prefer the idea 'The Jews are a nation that lives isolated.' Many of the people I work with share this idea. They don't want to mix with non-Jews." He cited a religious woman who heads in-service teacher training; she resisted the program at first because she feared intermarriage, although she finally came around to supporting it with some enthusiasm. Many others held fast to their concerns about the implications of softening attitudes toward Arabs, and they worried especially about the joint meetings between Arab and Jewish classes.

Late in the rainy morning, when the small groups convene after the art exercise, Hila announces that Ronen, the nicely groomed Jewish boy, had threatened to go home. And so to keep him at the workshop, the leaders have let him switch to another group to be with his friends. A Jewish girl named Shelly will be joining this cluster, now sitting in the cold concrete room.

A good warmup game of Simon Says is begun. "Hila says all stand up! Hila says put your hands on your heads! Sit down!" And a few are caught sitting and laughing.

Taher explains that he has prepared some cards with subjects written on them—parent-child relations, holidays, and so on—which he is going to distribute to groups of twos and threes to form the basis of quiet discussion. "We go on the assumption that there are differences in culture, and we should talk about them," he says. The kids divide up, clustering in the corners of the room.

Three boys—Sefi, Salman, and Nasser—sit near the door and read from their card, headed "Questions in relations between people." The first item asks about the status of women. Sefi, the Jew, begins. "Not really equal. If a boy goes with lots of girls, fine. If a girl goes with lots of boys, she's considered a slut."

"That's not the question," says Salman, the tall Arab. "In the house, at work, what's her status, how does she relate to her husband?"

"In my house," Sefi replies, "my mother helps my father, but my father doesn't do much for her and the house. Now you should tell me, so I'm asking you, Nasser. What's the status of your mother?"

"It's a completely different tradition between the Jew and the Arab," Nasser answers in Arabic. "The woman is a 20 percent partner of the husband. She is the housewife, washes dishes. Some have started to go to work now, only a few. If the husband says, 'I want to do this thing,' he'll do it without consulting her." Sefi asks how Nasser will behave with his wife after he marries. Nasser replies, and Salman translates from Arabic to Hebrew: "The same method that his parents use he'll use. He won't let her go out alone in the street. He won't let her go out late with someone, like to see a movie. He wants to do it the way his parents do."

Sefi: Why?

Salman: He just does. He's very traditional, and he wants to keep the traditions.

Sefi: And you?

Salman: I have some rules that I've learned about the rights of women not in the Arab sector but in the Jewish sector. When I marry her, I want to really know her so I'll be able to let her go out to movies alone. I know I have to help in the house and wash dishes. I'm not imitating you. I just don't agree that a woman should be a slave.

Sefi: Another word about us. I would care if my wife betrayed me, but I would give her all possible freedom.

Salman: I am an Arab; if I give my wife all possible freedom, but if she were unfaithful, I would kill both her and myself.

Sefi: I wouldn't kill myself or her, but it would hurt me very much.

Salman: The next question: "What do you do when you go out together?" In the old days, when my grandfather loved a woman, he just loved her eyes or the way she dressed. He could go to her father.

Sefi: I can do anything I want to. We do everything.

Salman: If I love someone, I can't just sit and tell her I love her. I go to the parents and say I love her and want her hand. If they agree, they go to my parents.

Sefi: But what do you do before that?

Salman: I'm allowed to talk with her, but not to touch.

Sefi: At your age today, are you allowed to start up with a girl?

Salman: It's allowed. But to hold hands and kiss, it's allowed, but it has to be in secret. If anybody sees it, it will be a mess.

Sefi: They do it?

Salman: Yes, ninety percent do it.

Sefi: And really?

Salman: No, that's not allowed.

Sefi: How do you decide whether you love someone or not?

Nasser: If she treats me well, if she behaves well in school or in the street, if she doesn't go with anyone else.

Sefi: Is it important that she's pretty?

Nasser: Yes, it's important.

Salman: For me, it's not important whether she's pretty. The brain and the heart are important. I don't care if she's a beauty queen—but she shouldn't be so ugly that I have to suffer.

Sefi: Jews think being pretty is being very thin.

Salman: There are those who like thin, there are those in the middle. I prefer someone—to love and to marry—who is strongly built.

Sefi: Almost all Jews and Americans like really, really thin, but I'm not like that. I like sort of a full body. Wise eyes and a difference from you. A soft body, not a hard body. And a question for you two: Are you jealous of Jews because they are allowed to go with girls and so forth?

Salman: You have your traditions, I have my traditions. You have your culture, I have my culture. So because of that why should I be jealous of you? I think in a few years the Arabs will be more like the Jews.

Sefi: I thought Arabs might be jealous, want to do that.

Salman: They're not jealous of you, but they would like to do it.

Sefi: You don't think they're angry?

Salman: No, it's their tradition.

Sefi (to Nasser): If you see a Jew kissing, what do you feel?

Nasser: Yes, I'm jealous of him because I don't have what he has.

Sefi: Are you angry?

Nasser: Yes, a little.

Sefi: At the Jews or at the Arabs?

Nasser: I do get angry, but I don't get angry at the Jews but at the traditions of the Arab, which don't let me do that.

Sefi: Would you have a Jewish girlfriend?

Nasser: No. Because she wouldn't go only with me.

Sefi: Wouldn't you ever try to go out with a Jewish girl? Do you think Jewish girls won't like you because you're an Arab?

Salman: One time I went out with a Jewish girl and they didn't look at me badly. There were Jewish friends who said they were very happy. One Jewish girl I loved, and she said, "Salman, not because you're an Arab, but people will look at me badly."

Sefi: Weren't you insulted? Didn't you hate her?

Salman: Yes. I was insulted, and I hate her even today.

When the small clusters finish and the larger group reconvenes, a discussion begins about language. Inbal, the Jewish girl, observes that the Arabs give much longer answers when they speak Arabic than when they speak Hebrew, and Taher suggests that perhaps everyone should speak the language in which he is most comfortable. Sefi expresses guilt that he cannot speak Arabic and that Hebrew is virtually the common language, as if "we are the superior ones—you have to come to me."

"You can solve that problem if you learn Arabic," says Diab with a grin. Sefi agrees in a long dissertation on how Jews should be required to study Arabic from kindergarten. And Inbal adds a note of concern, fumbling for the right way to put it.

"They're always coming to us, all this business of yes, yes. It's sort of a self-cancellation. It's a feeling that I've had the whole time, that they speak Hebrew. I don't know how to explain it. The whole direction is to be like us, to look to me as something good and not as something opposing them."

"The Arabs," Diab cuts in, "are wise enough to take the good of the Jews and reject the bad."

Sefi tries some broken Arabic, disjointed words scattered into his Hebrew, saying that people seem to think that what is modern is automatically good, and what is modern gets identified with the Jews: "What should be done is Jewish education with Arab teachers and Arab education with Jewish teachers," he declares in fragmented language, and everybody applauds his little speech, his comical effort at Arabic.

The morning is gone; lunch is ready in the dining hall. Usually at this stage, the Jews say the Arabs don't want to sit with Jews, and the Arabs say the Jews don't want to sit with Arabs. And as the young people gather through the misty rain and seat themselves, they gravitate to their own, collecting around tables in separate groups of Jews and groups of Arabs, babbling in their own segregated languages.

The potential for Arab-Jewish closeness, politically and sexually, loomed as a source of apprehension among the thirty or so district school super-intendents who met one day at the Van Leer Institute to be introduced to the new curriculum. The program had been tested as an elective the previous year, 1983–84, on about 50 eleventh-grade classes. It was being offered during the current year to about 100 classes, and the following year would be expanded to about 250.

The superintendents, men and women of long experience, sat in a comfortable conference room as one of their supervisors opened by posing the nagging question: Did coexistence mean just living side by side, or did it imply giving up your identity? For Jews who had suffered because of their identity or had rejected their parents' denial of their identity in the Diaspora or had come to the Jewish state precisely to act firmly on the basis of their identity, this was a key issue, and it formed an important source of skepticism about the program.

A senior Education Ministry official warned against one-sided portrayals of the Israeli-Arab power relationship in which the Israelis are seen as oppressors, for this can cause identification by Jewish youngsters with the Arab side. Thus, he argued, the subject of coexistence must be taught only while emphases on two other subjects are strengthened—"Zionism and the deepening of their attachment to this land."

Another senior official followed with a partial rebuttal, noting that Israeli Jews had to learn to live with ambivalence; the goal would be to bring a boy or girl to know which Arab is hostile and which he must fight, and which he must respect and live with in peace and pride. Alouph Hareven then stood and said that there was no need to feel so defensive about students' losing their identity. So far, Jews who had taken the course seemed only to strengthen their sense of themselves. "You feel your identity much more strongly in confrontation or clarification with others," he declared.

A teacher who had conducted a class described the experience. And a high-school senior named Gil gave an enthusiastic account of his class's meeting with students from an Arab school. An elderly, white-haired superintendent, puffing skeptically on a pipe, asked the boy a question: "Next year, you will go to the army. If you are ordered to do some kind of attack, like a curfew [on a West Bank Arab village], what will you do?"

Gil paused for a moment. "Well," he said, "I guess I'd have to think about that."

"Thank you," said the elderly man. "You've answered my question."

Again and again, dubious adults inside and outside the school system have raised the specter of their youngsters' becoming like Udi Adiv, a young kibbutznik and former paratrooper who was convicted in 1973 of helping to lead an Arab-Jewish espionage ring that had passed unspecified secrets to Syria, where he also received some military training. He was sentenced to seventeen years in prison and was released in 1985, five years early. The attorneys who defended him and other members of the ring portrayed their activities as political, not military, arguing that the group had merely wished to establish a left-wing government under which Jews and Arabs in Israel could live together harmoniously. Much was made of Adiv's profile as a "good Israeli," raised on the liberal, humanistic education of the socialist Hashomer Hatzair kibbutz movement, joining an elite army unit, studying at Haifa University, believing in brotherhood. His lawyer, Shlomo Toussia-Cohen, argued that he and his organization posed no threat except that of unpopular political ideas. He had never collected secrets to pass them on, the attorney argued; he had conveyed only minor material known to every soldier—precisely what material remained obscure during the public trial. Adiv had no intention of damaging Israel's security, Toussia-Cohen maintained. "He wanted to improve the world, not to harm Israel," the lawyer declared.

Nevertheless, for many Israelis "Udi Adiv" has become a code word for what can go wrong when a nice Jewish boy becomes too soft on the Arabs. "We don't want to create more Udi Adivs," fellow teachers in one religious school said to "Leora," a social-studies teacher who decided to offer the new course during the first year it was tested. "Some of the teachers wanted to stop me," she recalled. "My good friends were very angry at me." And they tried to undermine her. "They talked with the class after I finished, during the next lesson; some of them said, 'Don't believe [Leora], don't take her seriously.' " Her district superintendent also opposed the course, which was being offered in no other religious high school in the country at the time. Leora persisted, and he gave in. But he never provided support and never reacted later, once it had scored an obvious success.

The course is to begin with a few exercises designed to expose the eleventh-graders to their own prejudices. The teacher is advised to pose questions and give students three minutes to write their answers on a piece of paper that will not be handed in:

1. The central problem among the Arabs of Israel is _____.
2. You place an ad in the paper to rent out your apartment. An Arab student responds to it. Your reaction is _____.

3. You are Education Minister. Will you approve the appointment of an Arab inspector of mathematics courses who will also be responsible for inspecting Jewish schools? Why?

4. You are the owner of a food preservatives factory. You need a mechanical engineer. A Jew and an Arab respond to your ad. The Arab has slightly more experience with the required work. Your reaction is _____. Why?

5. An Arab couple wants to buy your neighbor's apartment. Your neighbor asks you what to do. Your reaction is _____.

6. You are a Jewish judge in a labor court. You are judging a complaint by an Arab worker from Nazareth against his employer who fired him. The worker asks to make his case in Arabic. How do you act?

Students are asked to imagine that they have heard about a traffic accident involving fatalities. Then they learn that those who died are Arabs. Are they relieved that no Jews were killed? Almost everyone says yes.

Early testing of the program was done by Ori Geva, a jolly, thirty-year-old teacher at University High School in Jerusalem, which serves a mostly liberal, middle-class neighborhood. He began by asking his students to write down the words that came to mind when they thought of Arabs, assuring the class that they would not have to turn their papers in; this allowed them to record their associations with little inhibition. Then he invited them to talk about what they had written if they wished, and as they spoke their words aloud, he wrote them on the board:

PRIMITIVE

JEW HATER

FOOL

NAIVE

TERRORIST

I'M AFRAID

FIGHTS US

ANIMAL

"I wrote what they said on the blackboard, right in front of them," he explained. "They had to see it. I said, 'How do you feel about it?' They said, 'Terrible. We want to do something about it.' "

"We were amazed by what we ourselves had said," recalled Gili Tocatly, one of the students. "We related to Arabs all in stereotypes and not as people. All the Arabs were perceived as one body, not as people." Seeing the words on the board also disturbed Michal Simchen, a girl with sandy-blond hair and blue eye shadow. "I was very frightened," she said, "because you're not conscious of these things until you see them in front of your face." Where did she think the stereotypes came from? "Children's literature, parents, education. I think we live with the feeling that a bomb could go off any minute."

Ori's students, in jeans, sweatshirts, vests, and sweaters, were casual and boisterous as they ambled into the classroom, but they quickly settled down and listened intently as he talked to them about discrimination against Israeli Arabs. The youngsters spoke up, asked pointed questions, challenged some of his statements, but followed respectfully as he led them through discussions of the position in which the Arabs of Israel find themselves. "For the fifth time," he declared, "I want to tell you that your stereotypes of the Arabs are much worse than the Arabs' stereotypes of you. Very few Arabs want to screw the country."

Then he did a revealing exercise. He wrote three categories on the board: Jew, Israeli, and Zionist, and asked the students to choose the one that they felt best defined them. Four identified themselves as Jews, nine as Israelis, and two as Zionists. One boy said that he couldn't define himself at all. Although only four called themselves Jews, Ori said, "This is the most Jewish class I've had so far. Generally not a single student defines himself as Jewish. Most define themselves as Israeli. Now, who is an Israeli?"

"A person who lives in Israel," one boy answered.

"A citizen in Israel," said another boy. Ori wrote "Citizen in Israel" on the board.

"This definition," Ori said, "also includes those [extreme Orthodox] in Mea Shearim and all the Arabs in the state. Every citizen. That means that all the Arabs in the state you'd put in the category of Israeli."

The students took this in. But not all sixteen-year-olds are as introspective or as sensitive as this class, which was farther to the right politically than some of Ori's others. The more liberal youngsters are often more difficult to reach, he observed, because they spend a long time at the beginning of the course denying the prejudices they harbor. Group leaders at Neve Shalom have had similar difficulties with children from leftist kibbutzim: The stereotyping is there, but they don't want to admit it. Working with them is like spinning your wheels on a slick road. The harder-line, less sophisticated students who let their bigotry hang out boldly give the teachers and group workers some traction.

Such was the case for Rivka Ben Aharon, a young woman who taught the course in a religious school with students mostly from working-class, Sephardi families. As is customary in the religious sector of the public school system, boys and girls were placed in separate classes, enabling Rivka to make some generalizations about boy-girl differences in approaching the material. The girls were more malleable, the boys full of a tough-guy machismo. Initially, almost all the children displayed extreme hostility to the subject and to her for wanting to teach it. She came close to giving up. But once she had seen it through, she judged it fairly successful in provoking some rethinking among youngsters who were such poor students, with such low reading abilities, that for some she had to read from the textbook aloud and explain passages line by line.

"I felt very strongly [among the students] a hatred for every stranger," Rivka wrote in a report on the course, "also, hatred for any Jew of different community or different opinion, and hatred for the non-Jew. . . . I thought I would encounter difficulties, but I admit I never imagined . . . how much resistance the initial encounter would arouse. . . . About 80 percent of the class shouted that there was no need to learn about the Arabs, and 'we should learn about things that relate to us.' " As the students worked on the quiz designed to reveal prejudices, they seemed to have the opposite reaction of Ori's youngsters. "The raucous part of the class cried out that the Arabs should be taken and killed as fast as possible," Rivka reported. "The more 'sensitive' ones proposed the method of deportation from the country. . . . At this stage, there was no opposition to the dominant views in the class. Even if there were some who opposed them, they didn't dare open their mouths."

She devoted the last four months of the year exclusively to the course, and in the beginning she let the teenagers sound off as they wished, hoping to defuse the anger. She was unprepared for the anger that they turned on her personally; although she had never expressed any political views, and certainly no opposition to the government—then led by the right-wing Likud Bloc—the students labeled her anti-government and made her a target of their hatred. "All the trust I had gained in my classes up to that point went by the boards," she said. "I had to instill once again the lost trust and create the kind of atmosphere conducive to learning together." By the fourth lesson she managed to gain a modicum of cooperation, and some students gave a possible reason for their hating Arabs: "because actually we don't know so much about them." Then they added, "But even when we know more, our hatred won't stop for sure, because it's in the blood."

Slowly she regained their trust by convincing them that she was not out to impose her opinion on them. "I tried not to retort, although sometimes I had to bite my tongue to remain silent," she said.

"The dominant stereotype in the class about the Arab was that he was dirty, worked with garbage, was primitive and a dangerous enemy of the country," Rivka noted. "We tried to understand how stereotypes are formed. Part of the lesson consisted of a debate among the pupils as to whether their view of the Arab was a stereotype or he was actually like that. To explain the concept of a stereotype, I tried analyzing stereotypes about the Jews. The arguments against me were that I had no right to make that kind of comparison, the two cases were completely different." At the end of that lesson in the girls' class, one student got up the courage to say that her family's Arab cleaning woman was really a good person, that she didn't steal. The girl went on to condemn Arabs as a group, however, saying that they were enemies. The class's reaction was milder than it would have been at first, Rivka noted, although some students "shouted at her that she was being influenced by the teacher." But Rivka judged the lesson in stereotypes successful because both classes, and particularly the girls, "got the feeling that they had to study reality in all its complexity and that anyone who stuck to his prejudices somehow refused to learn because he was afraid that study would undermine his opinions." Some of the boys were determined to seem tough. They "reached the conclusion that we should actually treat the stranger in our midst harshly," she said, "since when all is said and done, we thus pay back only a small part of what was done to us as Jews; the time had come to stop being bleeding-hearts."

When Rivka reached the part of the course on Arab society, the students grew "so enthusiastic," she said, "that they came to my defense when other teachers spoke out against the study of this subject." But much of their interest was patronizing: "What else do they want? Look what we gave them; would they have given that to Jews in their lands?" When the rights of Arabs were discussed, most of the students were astonished and outraged to learn that Arabs in Israel were citizens, having envisioned all Arabs in the same status as those under military occupation on the West Bank—that is, without the right to vote, without civil liberties. "I was absolutely shocked," said Rivka. "The moment they had to apply in practice what they had learned about the democratic basis of Israel, it was as though they had learned nothing. They argued that it didn't matter what the Declaration of Independence said about the Arabs; it wasn't important; it could be amended or expunged. I had to work very hard in order to explain once again that the principle of civil equality is unassailable, and that in a democracy you couldn't choose just what was convenient for the majority."

The turning point, Rivka felt, came in a section of the course called "To Be an Arab in Israel," in which the students read touching essays by Israeli Arabs about their experiences under the Jews. One in particular, "Testimony," by the Arab writer Anton Shammas, cracked the wall of resistance for some of the girls, who "came to class in the morning and related that they had actually been unable to sleep after reading the texts." Rivka continued, "It was interesting that the girls who most identified with the personal accounts were the same ones from Tehiya youth who, at the start, had been really aggressive." The boys, less willing to have their minds changed, "insisted that the passages of personal testimony couldn't possibly be true." But for the first time, the boys began debating the question "Suppose you were in their place?" Rivka finally felt that she could ask whether they thought both Jews and Arabs should change their attitudes and behavior, and in what ways. The replies were gratifying. "I could hardly believe that the same pupils who had been so aggressive at the outset of the program were already having doubts, asking me what I thought in order to help them perhaps arrive at some sort of solution." The students had grasped the essential fact that Israel was not only Jewish but also a society with a non-Jewish minority, the Arabs, who also felt attachment to this land, who did not wish to go elsewhere, and who would inevitably continue living with the Jews.

The classes calmed down. The discussion proceeded intelligently on how Arab-Jewish relations should be conducted, both inside Israel and between Israel and neighboring Arab countries. "The answers were diversified," Rivka reported, "no longer so one-sided or unequivocal. Most of the pupils had undergone a significant shift, both emotionally and in terms of their knowledge. All of them said that the truth was that they had known practically nothing about the Arabs in Israel. Many said they had mixed up the Arabs of the [occupied] territories with the Arabs of Israel; they hadn't known the difference. All felt there was a problem here which couldn't be ignored."

Teachers have faced little interference from parents in this course, although a few told Rivka that they thought their youngsters shouldn't be wasting time on such nonsense. A few parents have barred their children from participating in class visits to Arab schools, which were conducted routinely as part of the course until funds became tight. "My parents were okay," said Tali Miron, a dark-eyed girl who took the course from Ori Geva. "But after we hosted the Arabs, a boy wrote a thank-you note, and I wrote back, and my father said, 'Don't get too personal.' We had terrible fights."

At lunch in the hilltop settlement of Neve Shalom, stereotypes are the subject. A slender Jewish woman named Nava Sonenshein, who lives here with her husband and children, is talking about the discussion that morning in the group of Arab and Jewish teenagers that she is leading. "Jews said Arabs were violent. One Arab girl said sometimes in her case all the anger and pain comes out in a violent way. Arabs said Jews ignore Arabs as if Arabs don't exist. One of the Jewish boys, Ronen, said, 'I know there is discrimination and I am against it. But when you are talking about Jews, don't include me in the things Jews do to Arabs. I am against it, and I am very insulted when you include me in that.' Jews said that Arabs follow their leaders like sheep. Arabs said Jews also sometimes go after their leaders like sheep." At the end, Nava explains, she asked everyone to think about somebody who is against what is being done here at Neve Shalom, for on this hilltop there is an acute awareness of the less congenial world outside. "There are Arabs who say you're succumbing to Zionist brainwashing and Jews who say we're a bunch of leftists."

Ariela adds, "This voice against what we are doing also exists inside each of us. This"—and she gestures around at the rudimentary community on the hill—"can seem like a dream."

On the wall of Ariela's small room, where she conducts her group workshop, hangs an embroidery of two little girls, one sitting and one sweeping. Above them, in English, are sewn the words "In spite of all the ideas and all the technology and atoms in the world . . ." And below, ". . . it all comes down to shaping one individual at a time."

Arabs and Jews involved in these programs debate their usefulness. If one individual is to be shaped at a time, then the efforts are truly nothing but drops in a bitter sea. And if the communal hostilities do run on an entirely separate plane from the personal attitudes, then, too, the work can bring little encouragement. Furthermore, although stereotypes certainly get erased in the courses and workshops, the durability of those changes in viewpoint is questionable.

A survey in one Jerusalem high school found moderate shifts among eleventh-graders during a course under the new curriculum. The percentage of students who saw themselves as nicer than Arabs dropped from 91 percent before to 84 percent after the course. Before, 97 percent regarded the Arabs as "dirty," 2 percent as "clean." Afterwards the figures changed to 87 percent "dirty" and 12 percent "clean," hardly a revolution of views. Even this small shift is susceptible to some backsliding after time has passed, once the youngsters move away from the experience of the curriculum or the workshop and more deeply into the society that breeds bigotry. There, it is hard to hold on to the fragile ideal of a tolerant mind.

The difficulties on the Arab side are no less daunting, but the new curriculum for the Arab schools has proceeded more slowly. Majid al-Haj, who headed the education department in the village of Shfar Am and served as a research fellow at Haifa University, described his work on a textbook for eleventh graders, a task taken over by others after he went on a sabbatical to the United States. His curriculum would contain four main elements, he explained. "First of all, I want the Arab pupil to feel that as a minority in Israel, he is not the only minority in the world. We have in the world many successful minorities, and many less successful minorities—Kurds in Iraq, minorities in Ireland, in the United States. I'll give him many different examples of more and less successful minorities."

Then, he continued, "I want the Arab pupil to learn about Jewish society from the objective point of view, that the Jewish majority is not unified against the Arab minority, that the Jewish majority has its problems, that it is divided into groups—Ashkenazi and Sephardi, religious and secular, and so forth. Thirdly, I want the Arab pupil to know about himself. I am convinced that if you want a person to trust somebody, he must trust himself first. I want the Arab pupil to learn about national identity, about many views of national identity and how to connect between Arab identity and Israeli identity."

The fourth element, al-Haj explained, would be the exploration of what Arabs and Jews can do together as members of the same society. "Many Arabs in Israel today feel more and more that they are an integral part of Israeli society," he said. "They want to do something for Israeli society, and they want to integrate into Israeli society. I think we must give a balanced picture to the Arab pupils. We must make them optimistic about the future so that they will seek to meet, to cooperate with the Jews. They will seek to be active citizens, to be integrated into Israeli society."

It is a brighter morning, and sunlight streams into the concrete room through the open doorway. The small group is together again playing games. This is the day that discussion gets more sensitive and more political.

The seven youngsters who have arrived on time are beginning by throwing an orange into the air, calling a person's name to catch it, throwing it again with another's name, and again and again as the whoops of laughter fill the room. Then they all crowd together, take each other's hands, and turn around until they are enmeshed in a tangle of arms. Intertwined with each other, they try to unravel themselves without letting go. They talk to each other, giving advice, crouching so another can step over an arm, stooping so others can swing arms over heads, spinning around, trying to turn the snarled mess of Arab and Jewish bodies into a clean circle. "This maze is like the Middle East," someone says.

Finally, after patient reasoning and cooperation that render the maze quite unlike the Middle East, the youngsters manage the untangling. Forming a circle of firmly held hands, they put Inbal in the center. "She has to get out," Hila says. "Don't let her." Inbal rushes toward the outstretched arms of the circle. She pushes. She shoves. At last she breaks through. "Now I have to get in," says Hila, who pushes hard. But every place she tries, they stop her. So she crawls inside beneath the arms of Taher and Inbal. Another interesting variation is played in other workshops: A person stands in the center of a tight circle of held hands, closes his eyes and falls backwards, relying on the others to catch him.

They stop his fall, boost him up, and he falls again in another direction. The idea is to develop and demonstrate complete trust.

The teenagers take their seats and get ready to tackle some serious questions. Emad is absent because he is sick. The two shy Arab girls, Faida and Samira, are also missing, so Hila goes off to look and returns with them a few minutes later. For the first time since they arrived at Neve Shalom forty-eight hours ago, the youngsters are asked to divide into an Arab and a Jewish group, with the two seated facing each other on opposite sides of the room. "This," says Hila, "is an activity called 'Questions and Answers.' "

Quietly, almost secretly, small numbers of Jewish and Arab adults have been gathering since the mid-1970s for intense encounter sessions in which their prejudices are purged in fits of shouting, screaming, and crying. These groups, whose methods have been used to treat bigotry in the United States, Northern Ireland, and other Western societies, have not been publicized because some of their organizers and participants are afraid of being branded with two onerous labels: the stigmas of radicalism and cultism. Neither is accurate, for many of the Jews involved are middle-class Sephardim whose politics never stray left of center, and the Arabs are mostly university-educated professionals in the mainstream of Palestinian life. But the apprehensions are such that one young Jewish woman asked that names and places of meetings be blurred to avoid problems for the groups.

The central purpose of the sessions is to deal with prejudice as a source of pain for the person holding the bigoted views. "It is no less painful on the emotional level to be the oppressor," she said. The assumption holds that the person with biases is not to blame, that he can recover from past hurt, that he can listen to the targets of his prejudice and feel secure in the emotional discharge that comes in some of the encounters. "Crying is recovery from grief," she explained, "shaking is recovery from fear." Jews meet separately at first, and they are urged to work out their racism. When they sit down with Arab group members, the importance of listening is stressed, listening without answering back, a very difficult task for Israeli Jews on this subject.

"Israelis don't want to listen," she observed. "They say, 'I don't want to hear about it, I don't want to hear about what you think about the Lebanon war, I don't want to hear about what you think about the West

Bank, I don't want to hear about what it was like in '48.' " Arab resistance moves in a different direction. "They say, 'You're trying to get us to feel differently so we won't feel we have legitimate [national] rights anymore.' "

But they do talk, they do listen, and they do change. In the fall of 1983, about forty Jews gathered for a weekend workshop under the direction of Ricky Sherover-Marcuse, a Hebrew-speaking American and the widow of the Marxist thinker Herbert Marcuse. She had conducted many such sessions with American whites, and seeing strong parallels between anti-black and anti-Arab attitudes, she used her American techniques to good effect in the Israeli setting. Of course, whites in the United States have never been in a life-threatening situation surrounded by hostile nations, she observed, nor have Israeli Arabs and Jews ever shared the anomaly of the American black-white intimacy, in which some white children were raised by black nannies. But the parallels, the universal attributes of stereotyping, allowed the use of familiar tools.

Much of the methodology involves straight talk, but some rests on euphemism and jargon. The minority victims of bigotry are called the "target group," for example, and the powerful majority is known as the "non-target group." Jews may be a target group in the United States, but in Israel they are the non-target group. And Sherover-Marcuse explained her objectives in those terms. "I want to show people in the non-target group that the oppression they carry out, either actively or passively, is a disaster for them. The socially oppressive role is painful, but socially normal."

Her approach was a blend of political radicalism and social therapy. She began by asking each member of the group to say his name and describe what gave him pride in being a Jew, this in the belief that "an attempt to assist somebody else's liberation struggle goes much better if it comes from a point of pride." Then she asked each to talk about "some action, no matter how small, they'd taken to assist in the struggle for Palestinian liberation." Many of the group members were not especially keen on the formulation of the question, but some mentioned that they had interrupted pejorative comments being made by other Jews about Palestinians. Others said they couldn't remember doing anything. So she asked them to make something up "because probably they had done something but couldn't remember." Her working assumptions, she explained, were that "nobody sets out voluntarily to acquire the role of oppressor," that those in the role are not to be blamed personally, that the "content of racism is misinformation—it's just socially recycled lies, no truth in it." In other words, "Israelis have been forced by the larger social system to take on the role of oppressor, and this is damaging for every Israeli."

In this frame of mind, when she asked, with false naiveté, "Is it true what they say about Palestinians?" she got people to repeat the racist phrases that have been so neatly spliced into the Israeli vocabulary. But when they did so, they began to laugh at the absurdity of their own words. "Through some process I don't understand, it loses its heaviness," she observed. "They're animals, you can't talk to them, they're not like us, the notion that they're subhuman. People changed their minds all over the place," she said. They came to understand that "first of all, you can work on it," she explained. "One woman said, 'I thought I knew what I thought, but now I'm quite confused.' She began to think that maybe she didn't really know about Arabs, maybe she had been told lies about them. Another woman said, 'I don't care what happens to them. They can just kill each other.' I showed her that she did care, she would like things to be different, she would like to have an Arab woman friend. 'Why do they have to be here? They can go anywhere.' I want you to ask yourself if they love the land as much as you do, and she said, 'Oh, of course they must love the land.' " One woman finally came to a breaking point. "She was crying, raging, screaming, pounding on me, saying, 'It's got to stop.' I said, 'Every Israeli needs to do this.' "

". . . it all comes down to shaping one individual at a time."

The Arabs are sitting on one side, the Jews across the concrete room. Each group is huddling to draw up questions it wants to ask the other. Then they face off, the Arabs on one bench, the Jews on another, and they begin.

Inbal asks the Arabs how their parents will react to their having come to this workshop.

Nasser: My parents agreed.

Inbal: What does it mean that they agreed? That they had no opposition, or that they thought it was good?

Nasser: My parents agreed because they thought I could learn from it. I would get to know Jews and learn about their customs.

Inbal: And your parents didn't oppose it?

Nasser: No.

Sefi: Are your parents angrier at the Jews than you? Did they want you to come less than you did? Is there a difference between the way you and your father relate to Jews?

These questions are more interesting than the answers. The Arabs evade the sensitive issue, and finally Hila gives the Arabs a turn to ask.

Salman: How did you see an Arab person before the meeting and after?

Inbal: Before the meeting I think I had more fear than opposition, and a lot of ignorance. It's hard for me to explain exactly what I expected, but what I saw here was very different, and I was surprised: your openness. Suddenly I came and saw a lot of openness, and you weren't so far from me, and it was good. And you came toward us. I've been very surprised, and it's been very good for me. It's been very good to see you up close, and things were very different from what I thought. I didn't see Arabs in a personal way. Arabs were a very abstract thing. I didn't see faces. Now everyone has a personality, and I can see a person, not an Arab without a face.

Sefi: It's not that what has happened here has changed what I thought. I always thought of Arabs as a mass together, not one by one, not person by person. I know Samira has a heart. I know Salman has a brain. I knew it, but I had never met it before.

The discussion gathers speed, becoming a blizzard of darting impressions, arguments, questions, retorts. Sefi asks if the Arabs don't feel anger when they see Jews drive through their village of Taibe. Diab replies that it depends. Sometimes Jews drive quickly through puddles, trying to splash Arabs walking on the side of the road. Salman says he has Jewish friends because he once attended a Jewish boarding school, but that he's angry if a Jew passes him by when he's hitchhiking. "Maybe he's afraid of you," Sefi suggests.

Diab suddenly plunges into the heart of the question. "Do you think that the PLO wants peace after Sabra and Shatila and the Lebanon war?" Sefi gives a clever answer. "I think that both the PLO and the government and the Israeli army take care of themselves and not their people," he says. "Arafat takes care of Arafat, Jabril of Jabril. Everyone worries about his own power. If Arafat were a man and also politically wise, then he would know that the person who wins is also the person who says, 'Both me and you, not only me.' "

This sets Diab off. "Okay, what do the Jews have in Lebanon? Is it their fathers' homeland? Is it their state? Why do they go there? What happened in Sabra and Shatila, isn't that enough?" Sefi speaks out against the war as well, and he holds his head in his hands. But Diab isn't through. The congenial boy *with the impish smile spouts his attacks as if they were slogans memorized from Arabic broadcasts: "Israel's political line is greater Israel and Syria and Sinai, and how do you explain that they took the Golan and asked Syria to remove the missiles from the confrontation line? It means an intention to advance even farther." Sefi tries to slow this down, describing each of the various views among the Jews, placing those few who aspire to a Greater Israel in perspective as a small fraction of the whole. And Inbal jumps in. "I want to ask Diab, how do you feel?" she says. "We're here together. Another year from now, we go to the army. How will you feel?"*

"That was my question," he replies.

Taher tries to explain the Arabs to the Jews. "Everybody's talking about feelings, and I'm very anxious for people to talk about feelings, but they're not used to expressing their feelings in words like you. So just understand that they're not trying to hide their feelings."

Diab struggles to find what he feels as he looks across the room at the row of Jewish boys and girls. "When I see them in the army, I'll know what I'll feel about it," he finally says. And then he adds, in Arabic, "The army is three years, and there are big chances that the army will influence you and that what happened here will be forgotten. I distinguish between two kinds of army—refusers who go to prison, and I believe that among you there will be people like that, who won't go out to unjust wars even if you pay a big price."

Inbal, with terribly sad eyes, asks, "You don't believe that we're forced to?"

"I think you can refuse."

"I'll go to the army," Sefi declares, "but not to the army that fights—to the army that thinks!" Laughter lightens the mood.

The Jews are now trying to slice Diab's feelings with thin precision. How does he define an unjust war? Are some wars just? Who is a real enemy? The boy replies with a dissertation on the Syrians' having abandoned the Palestinians in West Beirut, and then he says to the Jews, "I swear to you by my father that if the Syrians go to war against you, I will go to war against them with you." But he is clearly speaking as a Palestinian, not an Israeli; he is moved by the Palestinians', not the Israelis', grievances against the Syrians.

"Sabra and Shatila was done by Arabs," says Sefi the radical, his patriotism bristling. "Here there were 500,000 people in the streets. Does anyone in Syria care? No, only in Israel do we care. So, we're not good, but we're the best."

"I see that you're forced into the army," Nasser says. "There's no choice for a Jew in the state. You have to go into the army. The question is what does it do to you?"

Inbal is peeling an orange. She gives it to Diab, who breaks it into sections and offers her one. She declines, and so he passes them around to Sefi, Ricky, and Taher, and eats some himself.

Samira reads a written question. "Do you think Arabs in Israel get equal rights?" The whole group of Jews bursts into laughter at the absurdity of the idea. "No," says Ricky, "but there are some people who would say yes."

"How do you feel about that?" a voice from the Arab side inquires.

"Shit," says Shelly, a Jewish girl in an oversized sweater.

"But it's not us who did it," Ricky adds.

"We know in general that there's no justice," Inbal says. "There's something very unjust in the law and who administers it." The discussion winds along into details, more amicably than it would if the Jews were more representative and not so sympathetic to the Arab situation.

It is the Jews' turn to ask a question. Ricky directs it to Faida and Samira, the two shy girls. She asks why the two Arabs left the dormitory room when a few Jewish girls were talking among themselves. "It bothered me because I want you to be with us and to talk—not necessarily about serious things but just anything. And it bothered me and I wondered why."

Faida answers in her soft, purring Arabic; Taher translates. "There's a problem with the language. Sometimes they feel they don't understand when you speak, so it's tense."

"So what do you want to do about it?" Ricky asks. "I know language is a problem, but is that the solution, just to go outside?"

"It's not personal," Faida explains.

Diab, with that impish grin, is singing in Hebrew, "Come, come, sit next to me, / Come to me, little butterfly."

"They went outside as if it were Ricky's room and not theirs," says Shelly.

"The room that we sleep in is theirs as much as it's ours," says Ricky. "That's what bothers me, as if they don't feel that."

It is the morning of the third day.

Rabbi Bruce Cohen, who runs the project called Interns for Peace, believes that dialogue is less effective than activities are. And so since the late 1970s he has recruited a few young people each year, mostly American Jews in their twenties, put them through intensive Arabic and Hebrew courses, and assigned them to live for two years in Arab villages in the

Galilee with the aim of building up a network of joint Arab-Jewish construction, recreation, and educational projects.

The early years of this effort were difficult, with considerable suspicion and lack of interest on both sides. Radical Arabs spread accusations that the Jews were spies and foreign agents. Some Israeli Jews looked on them as naive, outside do-gooders without the sophistication to understand the ways of the Middle East. But gradually they gained the respect of the communities they worked with, and I found them to be among the most remarkable and impressive young people I have encountered anywhere. They were full of an idealism that never flew off into fantasies about saving the world, a conviction firmly rooted in reality that they might be able to stimulate a process that could do some limited good. Neither romantic nor cynical, they were perceptive about the obstacles but determined to try to mount them. They devoted themselves to taking the small steps that can make small differences, and they were guided skillfully by Farhat Agbaria, a warm, open-minded Arab who provided a healthy balance between the desirable and the possible.

At first, Bruce was able to recruit an occasional Israeli Arab to join the interns, but he had trouble attracting Israeli Jews. This seemed partly because the three years of mandatory army service, followed by college, put a Jew into his mid-twenties by the time he was available for such an enterprise, and at that age he wanted to get on with his life. But it was also the result of a broad lack of sensitivity in Israel to the need for an effort like this, a sensitivity that began to rise during the Lebanon war. In 1984, after a public-relations campaign helped by Arab and Jewish soccer stars, 170 Israelis applied, and three Jews were selected. The program went into four Arab and three Jewish towns. By 1985, with concern stimulated by the rising popularity of Kahane racism, the program expanded further, into a total of seven Arab and nine Jewish communities.

Like the Peace Corps, the experience was probably more beneficial for the interns than for the Arabs and Jews they were trying to bring together. But by the mid-1980s, the program was beginning to have some visible effects. After completing their two years, some of the interns used their newly gained expertise to foster and lead other projects promoting Arab-Jewish cooperation, thus forming a growing reservoir of talent for Israel in a vital area. And some of the joint efforts they launched as interns were being absorbed into the established routines of local institutions.

Some Jewish and Arab elementary schools made periodic visits between fifth-grade classes part of their normal calendar. A joint summer camp was operating for a couple of weeks each year. Community centers were running sports programs for Arabs and Jews, and playgrounds were being constructed and refurbished by Arab and Jewish youngsters working together.

Points of resistance were encountered constantly, however. A wealthy donor in the Jewish town of Pardes Hanna vehemently rejected plans for Arab youngsters from neighboring Kfar Qara to join Jews in making repairs and improvements to a playground he had financed. Arabs sometimes agreed to participate in a program and then just didn't show up. A fifth-grade teacher in a Jewish school rigidly refused to take her pupils on a visit to an Arab school. But one pair of schools, in Tamra and Kiryat Ata, slid into a regular exchange program of visits.

On Tubi-Shvat, a Jewish holiday devoted to tree-planting, Jewish fifth-graders came to see an Arab fifth-grade class in the village of Tamra, one of a schedule of visits instigated three years earlier by the interns. The hosts began with a few Arab songs as they sat around the edge of a classroom lit only by two bare bulbs hanging from the ceiling. The Jews responded with a small skit about a tree that narrowly avoids being cut down. The Arabs did the same skit in Arabic (a Jewish teacher had given the Arab teacher the script), and the Jewish kids then passed out cake to everyone. Generally, the Jews stayed on one side of the room, the Arabs on the other.

"Children are born without opinions," remarked the Jewish teacher, Shalom Vaknine, who arrived in Israel from Morocco in 1951. "An adult can turn his children into anything he wants." He did not have trouble getting his pupils interested in visiting an Arab school. "First of all, I speak Arabic, so I already have something to pass along. They see that I'm connected in some way to the Oriental framework, and I want to show them that abroad [in Morocco and elsewhere] Arabs and Jews lived together for hundreds of years without any problems. Neither Jews nor Arabs have tails and horns. An Arab boy likes to play football, and so does a Jewish boy. An Arab boy likes to eat, and so does a Jewish boy." When he introduced the idea of a visit, he asked his class, "What do you say about the Arabs?" A little girl answered, "I know the Arabs throw rocks." And the teacher asked, "Do you want to see the people we tell stories about?" They said yes. "I said, 'I have a surprise for you.

There's a school ready to accept us.' " And the messages that come through are invaluable, he believes. "When they see you also hug a boy and kiss him the way you do a Jew, they understand."

After their cake, the children were mixed up into groups, blindfolded, and asked to identify raw cabbages, tomatoes, lettuce, turnips, lemons, and other fruit and vegetables by smell. Joking, one boy said that parsley smelled like watermelon, and both classes exploded into giggles and laughter. Then the kids were mixed up at eight tables to cut the vegetables and make salads amid a din of screaming and yelling and fun. Finally they planted a little rubber tree together behind the school. No kids seemed to have formed any personal attachments, and at the end, when the Jews got into their bus to drive off, there were no individual good-byes but friendly waves, group to group.

When the bus had gone, I asked a few of the Arab children how they felt, whether they liked the Jews.

"Yes," said one boy with a smile. "They don't bother me; they're nice. I like them."

"Yes," said another. "I like them because they cooperated. They weren't bad, they were good."

"I like them," a little girl remarked, "because they're not violent with us. They play with us. They speak like us and play just like us."

"They're good," said another girl, "because they don't pinch us, and they're friendly."

A third girl explained, "I like them because there was one boy who let me sit. He got up and let me sit when there wasn't a place to sit."

"Here at this age," an Arab teacher said happily, "you can observe the simplicity and the purity of the children. All of them are small; they don't understand a lot about the world yet. Here you can see everyone's smiling. In high school they're all sour already."

"Is Zionism a racist movement?" Diab has asked as the Arab high-school students sit on the bench facing the Jews. The question falls like a stone in the concrete room.

Inbal: I don't know what racism is.

Sefi: I don't think anyone here knows exactly what Zionism is. The Arabs don't know, the Jews don't know. It's not relevant.

Shelly: We don't know exactly what they mean by Zionism.

The Arabs burst into argument in Arabic among themselves. Taher explains that they are debating the question, disagreeing whether Zionism is racism.

Diab: The Zionist movement doesn't want a single Arab person to be in its country.

Sefi: He's right, he's right. By definition it's racist.

Inbal: I don't know what the Palestinian movement is.

Shelly: Is every group that wants a home for its people racist?

Inbal: It's not fair that Sefi answered, because he's not a typical kid.

Diab: Shall we go to the Knesset and ask the [National Religious Party] and Rabbi Kahane?

Ricky: Rabbi Kahane is not Zionist.

Shelly: He's not me.

Sefi: Someone who doesn't know what it is can't be a Zionist.

Diab: I can't believe you don't know what Zionism is.

Ricky: Oh, in first grade you learn about the first aliya [immigration], the second aliya, but you don't know what Zionism is.

Shelly: Don't say what Zionism is. Say what racism is.

Inbal: I feel that Zionism today doesn't leave a place for the Arabs.

Sefi: I want to ask him a question. If the head of this state were Arab, and in Argentina they were killing Jews, would you agree that they all come to this country?

Diab: I'll explain why we have to bring Palestinians here—because we brought enough Jews already.

Sefi: His answer was that we have brought enough Jews and now we have to bring more Palestinians—and that's exactly the problem.

Hila: Let's come back to the question: Is Zionism racism? You got your answer. The answer was that it's very hard to answer. Ask something else and try to remain more inside the rules.

A long, frustrated silence hangs over the room. Finally Ricky speaks up. "What do you feel about the Arabs in the occupied territories? Do you feel together with them, a connection with them?

Diab: I'd like to talk about the Palestinian fighters.

Ricky: No, that's not what I asked. You have to answer the question that was asked, not another question.

Taher: First answer the question and then explain what you want to explain.

Diab: I don't want to talk about the other thing.

Taher: Okay, go ahead.

Diab: Is it important for me to know what my relation is to Arafat and the

Palestinian fighters? The Palestinian fighters, I'm with them both in my heart and body. My first obligation is to feel close to them, just as I understand about all the fighters in the world.

Sefi begins to probe and slice, his questions like a scalpel. If a Palestinian state emerged, would Diab want his home village in the Galilee to be part of it, or would he want it to remain under Israeli jurisdiction? Diab opts for Israel. Then how about the larger village of Sakhnin? The Arabs break into animated cross-talk. Where would the Israeli border be? On the pre-'48 lines, Diab says.

"If I were prime minister," Sefi asks, "would you agree to live in Israel?"

"You make me angry," Diab shoots back. "I want a Palestinian state. What do you want to do, change my mind?"

"No, you don't understand," Sefi replies. "I was just asking."

Salman: I think if a Palestinian state is established, I'm not going to leave my land to go and live in a Palestinian state. But I won't help the Israelis.

Hila: What do you mean you won't help them? You'll be a citizen.

Salman: I would believe in a Palestinian state and I wouldn't be active for Israel.

Sefi: Would you go to war?

Salman: No.

Sefi: What do you mean, no? You're a citizen.

Taher: Would you remain and go to the army? Either you serve and you're a real citizen—

Salman (biting his lip): But—

Taher: No. No buts.

Salman: One hundred years ago, my grandfather—

Taher: No, I want this to be hard for you. The Jews have their history too.

Salman: Then I'd prefer to go to the Palestinian state.

The discussion winds on and climbs, heading for some bursting point of futility. Diab asks Sefi if he would leave his land.

Sefi replies carefully, passionately. "There's one holy thing—a man. Not land, not a wall, not a house. A man. Because otherwise we'll kill each other."

"Don't you want to live in your place?" Diab asks with a touch of confusion that this Jew does not share so elemental a drive.

"The land belongs to God," Sefi says.

"If it is God's land," Diab retorts, "why does Israel want to cut it up?"

Sefi shouts, waves his arms, his voice a groan of despair: "Arafat's crazy! Begin's crazy! I'm not crazy!"

A moment of quiet embraces the concrete room in the hilltop settlement of Neve

Shalom. Sefi looks at the floor. Ricky holds her head. Shelly is sitting staring at the Arabs as if they were new people, not the friends she began to make three long days ago.

"What silence," says Salman uneasily.

"Why are you afraid of silence?" Taher asks gently. It is finally broken by Sefi.

"I'm not concerned with Palestinian rights, or even with my own rights," he says. "All I'm concerned about is happiness. Neve Shalom won't change anything."

The Arabs and Jews stand, form a circle, and join hands.

All these attempts to reach across the divide ignore the Arabs who live in East Jerusalem, the West Bank, and the Gaza Strip. Rarely does anybody try to work with them. Almost never does any skilled organization make an effort to bring Jews together with those Arabs under occupation. And this grave shortcoming goes largely unrecognized. The projects, the programs, the curricula, the exchanges, the workshops involve only Israeli Jews and Israeli Arabs. The other Arabs, who have lived under Israeli jurisdiction since 1967, simply do not exist in the notion of what is needed and what is possible.

When I questioned organizational leaders on this point, they had several reasons for steering clear of the West Bank. Some, who stand on the left politically and oppose the occupation, believed that conducting visits and workshops would be tantamount to recognizing Israeli sovereignty over the territories, a form of private annexation. They felt that West Bank schools and other institutions would refuse to cooperate in joint efforts for the same reason—that collaboration with Israeli Jews would be construed as a statement of sorts that the West Bank was rightfully and indefinitely attached to Israel. Furthermore, they explained, the Arabs in the territories didn't speak Hebrew. And, finally, since they lived under martial law, they would not come to meetings on an equal footing with the Jews; no common ground of equality under the law would exist as the basis for discussion.

"I am very afraid to try it," said Nava Sonenshein. "You can't work with them. They are not citizens. They don't have equal rights. People are dying in demonstrations. How can you change attitudes in a workshop? I don't think there is one class in the West Bank that would come to such a meeting even if we tried. I wouldn't feel honest doing this with them. They are not free to say what they want. They are not free from the military government, and they are not free from the PLO people.

"The Jewish kids," she continued, "what will happen if they sit in a workshop and hear for four days Arabs blaming them for what happens? People will come with all their anger and pain. Not every group is strong enough to hear awful things about themselves."

Yes, yes, I said, perhaps all that is correct. True, most West Bank classes would not come. But perhaps there would be one or two, not from the militant refugee camps but from a rural village or a private school. A few Jewish settlers have managed to arrange joint soccer games with adjacent villages. Discussions would admittedly be hard on the Jewish kids, who would have to be chosen carefully. Some ground rules, some preparation, would be required. Both sides would have to be taught what they already know, that all who are now sixteen were born into this; it is not of their making. And how is it annexation? Palestinian Arabs on the West Bank and Israeli Jews are going to live next to each other, with each other, locked into each other's worlds for a long, long time, even if the political formulations change. And this time of occupation is, strangely, a time of opportunity—not the ideal situation, to be sure, but a moment to seize—to help both sides look into each other's eyes.

Nava Sonenshein and the others listened to my questions politely, but they did not budge. I kept remembering the freckles of Amal, the pretty little girl in the Dheisheh refugee camp, who had never seen a Jew without a gun.

The group, hands joined in a circle, is in a somber mood, and it is their last meeting. This evening they will do some role-playing, with Arabs playing the part of the racist Rabbi Kahane, with Jews playing the role of Arab victims, a mind-bending exercise of extreme discomfort. They will eat their last dinner together, mixing Arabs and Jews as they have now begun to feel comfortable doing in the dining hall. And they will stay up late singing and talking. But now is the last moment for this small group that has moved from the most tentative recitations of their names into the most hurtful renditions of their politics.

"What we're going to do is called Ping-Pong," Hila explains. "There are a lot of things we've said, a lot of things we haven't said, and a lot of things we

won't say. I give this orange to you, and I tell you something I want to say to you, and you can't answer back. You can only say thank you and pass the orange on, saying something to the person you give it to."

Ricky to Salman: I really enjoyed myself.

Salman to Taher: I'm glad I got to know you.

Taher to Diab: You're a very enlightened man. I really feel inside what you feel and what you said, and I felt your pain. But I also want to tell you: Problems are not solved this way, and when you come to know reality more and see things with wider eyes, I hope you reach the conclusion that this is not the way to solve the problems.

Diab to Sefi: You're very smart, you're very wise. I'm glad we got to know you. It's hard for Arabs to understand that people can be like you. If you were in Arab society it would be very hard because nobody would support you.

Sefi, looking down, stands holding the orange in silence for a long time. "I can't talk," he says. "I'm too moved. I'm not happy or sad; I just can't talk. There's something a little artificial in talking. I can't even think." He looks over at Faida and speaks in slow Hebrew in the hope that she can understand. "I just think—I just think I love everyone pretty much. So everyone can take it." He holds the orange in the middle of the circle, and all the Arabs and the Jews come forward and put their hands on it. A frozen tableau, suspended on this hilltop, then dissolves as Inbal takes the orange and hands it to Hila.

"I'm very happy to get to know you."

Hila to Faida: I value your contribution because I know it was harder than for most, and I think you spoke very honestly. Thank you for that. I think the expectations of our group on you were very different from what people expect of you at home and at school. Maybe people don't expect you to talk, and here you tried totally, and I value that.

Faida to Taher: Thank you for pushing me to participate.

Taher to Samira: I give it to you as an attempt to break your block of closedness, and I do it in the belief that you have the potential to break it and be a part.

Samira to Salman: You helped me and supported me all the time.

Salman to Ricky: I'm glad I met you.

Ricky to everybody: I really had fun. My fears passed, and I really felt good. I can't say that everything was smooth, but it was fun. And I want to say to Samira and Faida not to take what I said as anger: I'm not angry at you.

Faida: I have to say something to everybody too, not just to one person: Thank everyone for letting me feel like a member, a part of this.

Salman to Sefi: I really felt your feelings. I agreed with a lot of what you said. Your face looked as if it were in mourning or something, and it really hurt me.

Sefi hands the orange to Samira and says something about loving the pictures she did. And Samira hands it wordlessly to Nasser.

Nasser to Inbal: You gave me a comfortable feeling, and I got the impression that you think about what you do before you do it.

Inbal to Salman: Because you're so human.

Salman to Shelly: I'm very happy to see you in the group. When someone asks you a question, you don't say your whole answer. You always end up saying you don't know.

Shelly says nothing; Inbal says that she feels close now to some of the Arabs in the group. Nasser says that he is surprised by how close and sensitive the atmosphere became. Diab ends it by holding the orange. "Thank you to everyone," he declares. "Thank you to everyone. Really."

The most intimate and extensive Arab-Jewish cooperation comes at a point of total vulnerability, in sickness. In Hadassah Hospital in Jerusalem, both at the facility on Mount Scopus and the one in the Ein Kerem section of the city, Arab doctors treat Jews, Jewish doctors treat Arabs. The boundaries of religion, ethnicity, and politics pretty much dissolve in the face of urgent need.

One of the best kept secrets in the Arab world is the extent to which prominent Arabs—including some from Saudi Arabia—journey to Jerusalem to be treated at Hadassah Hospital by Jewish doctors they are sworn to hate and are raised to respect. Relatives of PLO officials receive treatment there as well. "We have had children with interesting names— like Arafat," one doctor said. And a prominent West Bank Palestinian told me that he had gone to the original Hadassah years ago, before the founding of the state, to visit the newly born grandson of Jordan's King Abdullah. The infant, born in the Jewish hospital in Jerusalem, grew to succeed his grandfather; he is King Hussein, of Jordan.

The Israelis would love to boast about all of this, but they insist on keeping medical confidences. Their pride comes in having built an institution where the two peoples can merge and care together. Hadassah has a good name in the Arab world, and some Jordanians kept their

Hadassah cards from 1948 to 1967, returning to use the hospital after the end of the Six-Day War.

"People who are drowning aren't particular about whose hand is stretched out to help," said Dr. Shmuel Nissan, a surgeon at Mount Scopus. "When people are in trouble, everything else becomes unimportant." About 40 percent of the children admitted to the hospital's pediatric department are Arabs, and they tend to be more seriously ill than the Jews, since most of them are transferred to Hadassah from Arab hospitals on the West Bank after their condition worsens beyond what those more rudimentary facilities can cope with. Among the Jewish staff of Hadassah there runs an ugly rumor that "an Arab hospital, thinking a child is going to die, would rather have him die here so they can say the Jews killed him," in the words of one doctor.

Payment is a problem for many of the Arabs, since West Bank and Gaza residents are not entitled to carry Israeli medical insurance. The Israeli government ends up paying the bills of those who are poor. These amounted to a total of $1.5 million during the fiscal year ending March 30, 1984, for example.

Tensions do seep in to the hospital, although they are rarely severe. Some Jewish staff members imagine that the Arabs are callous toward pain and death, less caring about their children. And some Arabs are frightened. "They've heard stories about what the Jews are going to do to you," said Dr. Simon Godfrey, head of pediatrics. "But you can see an old Palestinian grandma sleeping right next to the elderly Jewish grandma. Occasionally we'll have a little feud about whether they watch Jordanian television or the Israeli program."

In such a situation, the anomalies abound. In 1980, a twelve-year-old Arab girl, described as outspokenly anti-Jewish, received a kidney transplanted from the body of a Jewish settler, Jesper Jehoshua Sloma, who had been slain in the Arab market of Hebron. The match was coincidental, a function of blood type and timing rather than religion or politics. But it ignited an outcry when a nurse in the dialysis unit of another hospital, Shaare Zedek, complained that the girl, Amira Aabi Bukassah, from a West Bank refugee camp, had made anti-Jewish remarks and had worn a pendant with a sword engraved with the word "Palestine," a symbol meaning that Palestinians should take over and drive the Jews into the sea. "She spoke all the time against Jews," declared Menachem Porush, a Knesset member from the extremely orthodox movement Agudat Israel. "In this case, a boy has been killed by Arabs. To transplant his kidney into an Arab girl who is hating Jews, this is too much." The Knesset later enacted a prohibition against transplants without a relative's permission.

In another strange circumstance, Dr. Haim Weinberg, an orthopedic surgeon, noted that the staff of Hadassah included a young Arab doctor from the family of the mufti of Jerusalem, Haj Amin el-Husseini, who was a pro-Nazi during World War II. Once, an Arab patient who needed an artificial joint to replace a degenerated hip refused to have a Jew do the surgery. He told the Arab doctor, "You must operate on me. I don't want any Jew to stand over me with a knife while I'm asleep." The Arab doctor came in and said, " 'You have to decide: Operate on him or throw him out,' " Dr. Weinberg recalled. "I brought it up with the staff, said what do we do? Here is a man who is sick, but he was brainwashed to hate us. The first reaction was throw him out. Then we decided to operate. I didn't mind." The Arab doctor did the surgery.

"We're not an oasis here," Dr. Nissan said. "I don't think peace is just around the corner. I don't think what we're doing here is for the promotion of peace; we're not going to make them Zionists. We may spend $50,000 on a baby from Hebron, and it may sound foolish. Even though I know that in eighteen or twenty years that baby may put a bomb and kill my grandson, for us at that time that little baby is 100 percent. This is absurd. Don't try to find any logic to it. We do it because of what we are and not because we think that by doing it we are going to bring peace. There is a tremendous gap culturally, emotionally, in mentality. I don't see how this gap is going to be bridged in a hundred years."

It is the morning of the fourth day. Ricky is wearing a keffiyah around her neck, a black and white checked scarf given to her by Salman in a gesture of tenderness. It is over now. They are filling time until the buses come to take them out of their dream and back into their worlds. The morning is clear, and she and a few other Jewish teenagers stand outside in the warming sun, reflecting on what they have learned.

What they knew about Arabs before, they explain, was very general and ill defined. "I was very surprised that the girls wore clothes like us," Ricky says—

jeans, sweatshirts, khaki army jackets. They were surprised how freely and openly most of them spoke, and they were surprised at themselves. "I thought I would be closed as well and would talk only from a distance," she explains. Of course she didn't say everything she felt. Her new Arab friends' affection for the PLO bothered her more than she was willing to tell them. "How can you talk about people who come to kill as being moderate?" she asks.

Another Jewish girl, Dikla, agrees that she has come to know some Arabs as individual human beings now, but she instinctively draws that line between the personal and the communal. "I still have my preconceptions in my head," she says. "Now, here, I behave with them as if they are human beings, like me. When I try to think of them more in depth, they're Arabs, and I know that when they go home they'll still have the flags of the PLO."

"Some of them," Ricky corrects.

"And some of the parents do hate the Jews," Dikla goes on, "and when I start to think of them in more depth, it's still frightening. And I don't think you can get rid of all this in four days." Around her neck she wears a metal peace sign on a leather thong.

The Arab youngsters have changed, at least on the surface. Their comments now are quite different from their answers to my questions before the Jews arrived the first day. Before, when I asked what came to mind when they thought of a Jew, the answers were stark and angry: "Different from us." "Murderer." "He hates Arabs." "Thinks himself better than Arabs." "Fire—meaning it's going to be hot."

Now I ask again, and the same Arab boys and girls have other things to say. "A human being, like us." "Something has changed in us." "They are human beings." "I came with the idea that Jews are murderers. Now, human beings, like others. We can give him his right to live." "I didn't feel as if he's an Arab and he's a Jew; I felt just as if he were any friend of mine. I felt the same about all of them, that they were friends of mine." "In my community it is forbidden to dress as they do, and wear as little as she can; in our community we were educated that it isn't nice." "After these four days, I think Arab and Jewish people can live in one country. Before, I didn't know." "I really don't want to go home; I want to stay here with my friends. I really think this is the beginning of Arab-Jewish life."

But this is not the beginning of a new Arab-Jewish life; it is just the end of a fleeting dream. And many of the youngsters feel the ending drawing them heavily back beneath the old burdens that lie outside. The moment is joyous and sorrowful, for what has happened here is beautiful and futile.

Salman says he has fallen in love with Ricky. A Jewish boy is looking lovestruck over an Arab girl. The teenagers are standing in the high meadow, talking quietly, exchanging addresses, promising to write, gazing down from the tranquility into the distant valley of vineyards and olive groves, and beyond to the smudge of the Tel Aviv area that lies out there, waiting to receive these young citizens.

Arab and Jewish girls are hugging, holding each other, weeping silently, the tears streaming down their faces. Some of the boys blink quickly and turn away to wipe their eyes.

Finally, cars begin to come to take the Jews down to the bus stop on the main road, and they go in threes and fours, saying, "Shalom" (Peace), the Arabs calling, "Ma Salaami" (Go in peace).

Soon, all the Jews have gone, and the Arab youngsters are left on the hill alone. And then, when their bus comes, they are gone as well. And Neve Shalom is enveloped in sunlight and sadness, having seen its seed sown in the brass earth.

N O T E S

1. Raija-Lena Punamaki, a Finnish psychologist, surveyed 185 Israeli Jewish and 128 West Bank Arab children in 1981. Initially published in Finland under the title *The Children of the Conflict: The Attitude and Emotional Response of Israeli and Palestinian Children*, the results were summarized in *Haaretz*, May 3, 1985.

2. First published in *The New York Times*, October 23, 1977, according to manuscript provided by the translator, Peretz Kidron, and confirmed by Rabin in an interview with the author.

3. Larry Collins and Dominique Lapierre, *O Jerusalem!* (New York: Simon and Schuster, 1972).

4. Benny Morris in *Monitin*, April 1984.

5. Benny Morris, letter to the author, January 13, 1985.

6. Jabotinsky archives, Tel Aviv, quoted by Eric Silver, *Begin: The Haunted Prophet* (New York: Random House, 1984), p. 88.

7. Menachem Begin, *The Revolt* (New York: Dell, 1951), pp. 226–227.

8. *Jerusalem Post*, March 27 and 29, 1957; April 1, 2, 4, 5, 9, 10, 11, 12, 25, 26, and 30, 1957; November 21 and 22, 1957; December 2, 13, and 15, 1957; October 13, 14, 19, and 21, 1958; November 13, 1959.

9. *Hadashot*, May 14, 1984.

10. *Jerusalem Post*, November 21, 1957.

11. Raja Shehadeh, *The Third Way: A Journal of Life in the West Bank* (London: Quartet Books, 1982), pp. 123–124. Published in the United States as *Samed: A Journal of Life in the West Bank* (New York: Adama Books).

12. Amos Oz, *In the Land of Israel* Translated by Maurie Goldberg-Bartura (New York: Harcourt Brace Jovanovich, 1983), p. 157.

13. The Manifesto of Bilu, issued in Constantinople in 1882 by a group of Biluim, a segment of the Lovers of Zion. Quoted in *The Israel-Arab Reader*, Walter Laqueur and Barry Rubin, eds. (New York: Penguin, 1984), p. 3.

14. Sammy Smooha and Don Peretz, "The Arabs in Israel," *Journal of Conflict Resolution*, September 1982.

15. Amos Oz, *In the Land of Israel*, p. 144.

16. Sammy Smooha and Don Peretz. "The Arabs in Israel," *Journal of Conflict Resolution*, September 1982.

17. The dates mark the interim period between the two Israeli invasions of southern Lebanon, the Litany Operation of 1978 and Operation Peace for Galilee in 1982. The Israelis withdrew from the second invasion in 1985. Fifteen of the twenty-nine who died in northern Israel were soldiers. The figures come from the Israel Defense Forces spokesman, the Israel National Police, and the Central Bureau of Statistics.

18. Sammy Smooha, "Minority Responses in a Plural Society: A Typology of the Arabs in Israel," *Sociology and Social Research*, Volume 67, No. 4.

19. See, for example, Sura XV, Hedjr, Verse 17: "And we guard them from every stoned Satan," and Verses 34–35: "He said, 'Begone then hence; thou art a stoned one, and the curse shall be on thee till the day of reckoning.' " (God speaking to Eblis.) According to the notes in the 1978 Everyman's Library edition of J. M. Rodwell's translation, "stoned" in this context means "accursed." In the valley of Mina, near Mecca, pilgrims throw stones at the spot where the apparition of Satan is believed to have appeared to Abraham.

20. *Davar*, August 19, 1983.

21. *Haaretz*, June 20, 1984.

22. Mina Tzemach and Ruth Tzin, *Attitudes of Adolescents with Regard to Democratic Values*, the Dahaf Research Institute and the Van Leer Jerusalem Foundation, September 1984.

23. *Hadashot*, May 18, 1984 (article by Naama Cohen).

24. S. D. Goitein, *Jews and Arabs: Their Contacts Through the Ages* (New York: Schocken Books, 1964), pp. 21–22.

25. Judah Halevi, *The Kuzari* (New York: Schocken Books, 1964), p. 49.

26. Ibid., p. 47.

27. Ibid., pp. 106–107, 142.

28. Yehoshafat Harkabi, *Arab Attitudes to Israel* (Jerusalem: Keter, 1972), p. 288.

29. Bernard Lewis, *The Arabs in History* (New York: Harper & Row, 1967), pp. 42, 44–45.

30. Bernard Lewis, lecture, Ben-Zvi Institute, Jerusalem, May 23, 1984.

31. Syrian and Jordanian Ministries of Education, *Teacher's Guidebook for the Instruction of Islamic Culture* (1977), p. 112.

32. Quoted in Harkabi, p. 129.

33. Yehoshafat Harkabi, *Arab Attitudes to Israel* (Jerusalem: Keter, 1972), p. 227.

34. Bernard Lewis, *The Jews of Islam* (Princeton, N.J.: Princeton University Press, 1984), p. 21.

35. Bernard Lewis, lecture, Ben-Zvi Institute, Jerusalem, May 23, 1984.

36. Yehoshafat Harkabi, *Arab Attitudes to Israel* (Jerusalem: Keter, 1972), pp. 134, 193.

37. Bat Ye'or, *Jewish Chronicle*, May 28, 1982.

38. Muhammad Ali Aluba, *Palestine and the Conscience of Mankind*, (Cairo: Dar al-Hilal, 1964), p. 65, cited in Harkabi, p. 248.

39. Yehoshafat Harkabi, *Arab Attitudes to Israel* (Jerusalem: Keter, 1972), p. 263.

40. Ibid., p. 237.

41. *Al-Jazira*, September 6, 1981.

42. Raphael Israeli, *Anti-Jewish Attitudes in the Arabic Media, 1975–1981* (London: Institute of Jewish Affairs, September 1983) p. 18.

43. Quoted passages drawn from Menachem Regev, " 'The Arab Problem' in Israel Children's Books," *Dispersion and Unity*, Journal on Zionism and the Jewish World, Jerusalem, No. 9, 1969, pp. 84–110.

44. Gershon Shaked, "The Arab in Israeli Fiction," *Ariel*, Jerusalem, No. 54, 1983.

45. Mina Tzemach, *Attitudes of the Jewish Majority Toward the Arab Minority*. (Jerusalem, Van Leer Jerusalem Foundation, 1980) Face-to-face interviewing, on the basis of a questionnaire with both open and closed questions, was done in January 1980 of a representative sample of Jewish adults from throughout Israel.

46. Sammy Smooha and Don Peretz, "The Arabs in Israel," *Journal of Conflict Resolution*, September 1982.

47. Tzemach, *Attitudes of the Jewish Majority Toward the Arab Minority*.

48. *Haaretz*, December 1, 1983.

49. Sammy Smooha, "Minority Responses in a Plural Society: A Typology of the Arabs in Israel," *Sociology and Social Research*, Vol. 67, No. 4.

50. Meron Benvenisti, *Conflicts and Contradictions* (New York: Villard Books, 1986), p. 100.

51. Gerald Caplan, *Arab and Jew in Jerusalem: Explorations in Community Mental Health* (Cambridge, Mass.: Harvard University Press, 1980), pp. 33–60.

52. Quoted in Gershon Shaked, "The Arab in Israeli Fiction," *Ariel*, Jerusalem, No. 54, 1983.

53. Quoted in Menachem Regev, " 'The Arab Problem' in Israel Children's Books," *Dispersion and Unity*, Jerusalem, Issue No. 9, 1969, pp. 84–110.

54. Regev, loc. cit.

55. Mina Tzemach, *Attitudes of the Jewish Majority Toward the Arab Minority*.

56. Hashem Mahameed and Yosef Gottman, "Autostereotypes and Heterostereotypes of Jews and Arabs Under Various Conditions of Contact," *Israeli Journal of Psychology and Counseling in Education* (Jerusalem: Ministry of Education and Culture), No. 16, September 1983.

57. Yehoshafat Harkabi, *Arab Attitudes to Israel* (Jerusalem: Keter, 1972), p. 97.

58. Hashem Mahameed and Yosef Gottman, "Autostereotypes and Heterostereotypes of Jews and Arabs Under Various Conditions of Contact," *Israeli Journal of Psychology and Counseling in Education* (Jerusalem: Ministry of Education and Culture), No. 16, September 1983.

59. Menachem Regev, " 'The Arab Problem' in Israel Children's Books," *Dispersion and Unity*, Jerusalem, No, 9, 1969, pp. 84–110.

60. Interviewers, Arabs and Jews who spoke Arabic, questioned 92 Jewish family heads and 63 Arab family heads.

61. A Puri Poll of 1,200 adults throughout Israel, published in *Haaretz*, January 30, 1984.

62. The Arab interviewees were categorized on the basis of their responses to eleven questions, including their support for or opposition to the Israeli-Egyptian peace treaty, self-identification as Israeli or Palestinian, attitudes on the creation of a Palestinian state and Israel's right to exist, endorsement or rejection of the formation of an independent Arab trade union and the use of general strikes to improve Arabs' positions in Israel, and ideas about the degree to which Palestinian nationalism should be part of Arab education.

63. For further discussion of the universality of sexual stereotypes, see Harold R. Isaacs, *Idols of the Tribe* (New York: Harper & Row, 1975), p. 49, and Gordon W. Allport, *The Nature of Prejudice*, (Garden City, N.Y.: Doubleday Anchor, 1958), pp. 349–355.

64. Quoted in Menachem Regev, " 'The Arab Problem' in Israel Children's Literature," *Dispersion and Unity*, Jerusalem, No. 9, 1969, pp. 84–110.

65. Gershon Shaked, "The Arab in Israeli Fiction," *Ariel*, Jerusalem, No. 54, 1983.

66. Raja Shehadeh, *The Third Way: A Journal of Life in the West Bank* (London: Quartet Books, 1982), pp. 88–89.

67. S. D. Goitein, *Jews and Arabs: Their Contacts Through the Ages* (New York: Schocken Books, 1964), pp. 20–21.

68. Yehoshafat Harkabi, *Arab Attitudes to Israel* (Jerusalem: Keter, 1972), p. 225.

69. Ibid., p. 235.

70. Ibid., pp. 271, 273–274.

71. This according to Joel Greenberg, an American-born Israeli who was jailed for twenty-eight days for refusing to accompany his reserve unit to Lebanon. I knew Joel as a careful, responsible young man who worked as a reporter for the Government Press Office, where he covered Knesset debates, speeches, and other official events and then wrote them up for distribution to foreign correspondents. His account here is entirely credible. At least one soldier wrote a letter to an Israeli newspaper about the vicious prank, but the military censor barred publication.

72. Recorded and translated by Clinton Bailey and first published in *The New York Times*, April 4, 1982. To appear in a forthcoming volume of Bedouin poetry.

73. Most of the historical material in this chapter is drawn from S. D. Goitein, *Jews and Arabs*; Bernard Lewis, *The Arabs in History*; and a lecture by Professor Lewis at the Ben-Zvi Institute in Jerusalem on May 23, 1984. See also Bernard Lewis, *The Jews of Islam* (Princeton, N.J.: Princeton University Press, 1984).

74. Gerald Caplan, *Arab and Jew in Jerusalem: Explorations in Community Mental Health* (Cambridge, Mass.: Harvard University Press, 1980), pp. 87, 94.

75. Raija-Lena Punamaki, *The Children of the Conflict*, reported in *Haaretz*, May 3, 1985.

76. *Haaretz*, February 10, 1984.

77. *Haaretz*, April 4, 1961. Lubrani, a Mossad official, served as Israel's secret liaison with several countries that did not maintain diplomatic ties, including Ethiopia under Haili Mariam Mengistu and Iran under the Shah. In 1983, following Israel's invasion of Lebanon the previous year, Lubrani became the head of Lebanese affairs for the Israeli Defense Ministry.

78. Sammy Smooha and Don Peretz, "The Arabs in Israel," *Journal of Conflict Resolution*, September 1982.

79. Central Bureau of Statistics, Jerusalem, *Statistical Abstract of Israel, 1985*.

80. Alouph Hareven, editor, *Every Sixth Israeli* (Jerusalem: Van Leer Jerusalem Foundation, 1983), pp. 4–5.

81. Hana Abu-Hana, "Testimony of an Educator from Haifa," in Hareven, *Every Sixth Israeli*.

82. Anton Shammas, "Diary," in Hareven, *Every Sixth Israeli*.

83. Sammy Smooha and Don Peretz, "The Arabs in Israel," *Journal of Conflict Resolution*, September 1982.

84. Alouph Hareven, editor, *Every Sixth Israeli* (Jerusalem: Van Leer Jerusalem Foundation, 1983), p. 10.

85. Sammy Smooha, "Existing and Alternative Policy Toward the Arabs in Israel," *Ethnic and Racial Studies*, Vol. 5, No. 1, January 1982.

86. Letter to Van Leer Institute from Irving Bernstein, executive vice-chairman of the United Jewish Appeal, August 5, 1983.

87. Letter to Van Leer Institute from W. Antoinette Ford, assistant administrator, Bureau for the Near East, Agency for International Development, October 4, 1982.

I N D E X

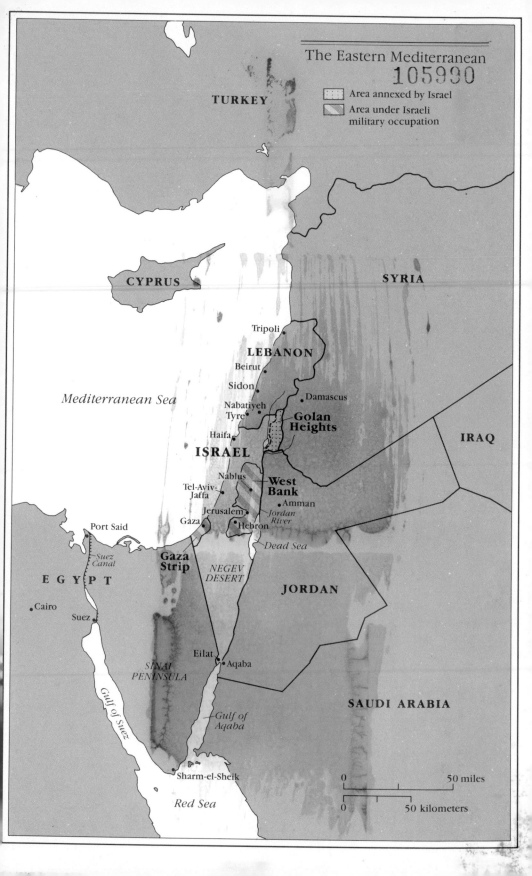

The Eastern Mediterranean

105990

Area annexed by Israel

Area under Israeli military occupation

TURKEY

CYPRUS

SYRIA

Mediterranean Sea

Tripoli

LEBANON

Beirut

Sidon

Damascus

Nabatiyeh
Tyre

Golan
Heights

Haifa

IRAQ

ISRAEL

Nablus

West
Bank

Tel-Aviv-
Jaffa

Amman

Jerusalem

Jordan
River

Gaza

Hebron

Dead Sea

Gaza
Strip

NEGEV
DESERT

JORDAN

Port Said

Suez
Canal

E G Y P T

Cairo

Suez

Eilat

Aqaba

SINAI
PENINSULA

SAUDI ARABIA

Gulf of Suez

Gulf of
Aqaba

Sharm-el-Sheik

Red Sea

0   50 miles

0   50 kilometers